MOON

CANCÚN &
COZUMEL

LIZA PRADO & GARY CHANDLER

CANCÚN & COZUMEL

GULF OF MEXICO

Dzilam
de Bravo

Telchac
Puerto

27

Progreso

172

176

Sisal

DZIBILCHALTÚN

Temax

Motúl

Hunucmà

281

176

281

Mérida

Celestún

180

Maxcanu

261

Chichén
Itzá

Pisté

Sagrado Azul

Grutas de
Balankanche

Estero
Yaltún

OXKINTOK

Muna

184

PARQUE
ECOARQUEOLÓGICO
IK KIL

Parque Natural
Petenes-
Ría Celestún

184

Bahía de
Ensenada

180

261

Ticul

Campeche

Tekax

Tzucacab

180D

188

293

109

**Riviera
Maya**

DOLPHIN DISCOVERY ★

Puerto
Aventuras

Cenote Azul
Cristalino
Jardín Del Eden

XPU-HÁ ★

307

*Laguna
Yal-Ku*

*Half Moon
Bay*

Akumal

Akumal Bay

AKTUN CHEN ★

Aventuras
Akumal

Dos Ojos
El Pit

Chemuyil

Playa X'cacel

Yax Kin

XEL-HÁ ★

Zazil Ha
Car Wash

Manatí

Soliman Bay

Gran Cenote
Calavera

Tankah Tres

Escondido
Cristal

Tulum

Encantado

★ Tulum's Southern Beaches

307

TULUM

KINICHNÁ

DZIBANCHÉ

30

CANAL DE
LOS PIRATAS

Bacalar

Cenote Azul

OXTANKAH

Calderitas

269

Morocoy

186

Francisco
Villa

186

Chetumal

XPUJIL

Nicolas
Bravo

KOHUNLICH

Corozal

BELIZI

*Calakmul Biosphere
Reserve'*

0   20 mi

0   20 km

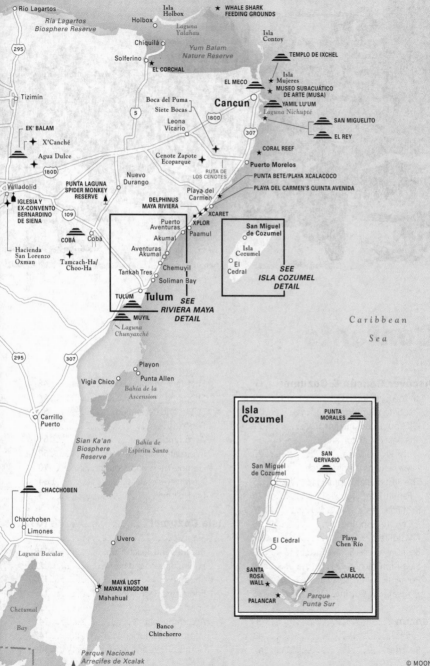

Río Lagartos

Ría Lagartos
Biosphere Reserve

295

Isla
Holbox
Holbox
Chiquilá

Laguna
Yalahau

★ WHALE SHARK
FEEDING GROUNDS

Isla
Contoy

TEMPLO DE IXCHEL

Solferino ★
EL CORCHAL

Yum Balam
Nature Reserve

Isla
Mujeres

Tizimín

5

Boca del Puma
Siete Bocas

EL MECO

MUSEO SUBACUÁTICO
DE ARTE (MUSA)

Cancun

YAMIL LU'UM

EK' BALAM
X'Canché
Agua Dulce

Leona
Vicario

180D

307

Laguna Nichupté

SAN MIGUELITO

EL REY

180D

Nuevo
Durango

Cenote Zapote
Ecoparque

RUTA DE
LOS CENOTES

CORAL REEF

Puerto Morelos

PUNTA BETE/PLAYA XCALACOCO

Valladolid

PUNTA LAGUNA
SPIDER MONKEY
RESERVE

Playa del
Carmen

PLAYA DEL CARMEN'S QUINTA AVENIDA

IGLESIA Y
EX-CONVENTO
BERNARDINO
DE SIENA

109

DELPHINUS
MAYA RIVIERA

San Miguel
de Cozumel

COBÁ
Cobá

Puerto
Aventuras

XPLOR

XCARET

Paamul

Isla
Cozumel

Hacienda
San Lorenzo
Oxman

Tamcach-Ha/
Choo-Ha

Akumal

Aventuras
Akumal

Chemuyil

El
Cedral

SEE
ISLA COZUMEL
DETAIL

Tankah Tres

Soliman Bay

TULUM
Tulum

Caribbean

MUYIL

SEE
RIVIERA MAYA
DETAIL

295

307

Laguna
Chunyaxché

Sea

Playon
Punta Allen

Vigia Chico

Bahía de la
Ascensión

Carrillo
Puerto

Sian Ka'an
Biosphere
Reserve

Bahía de
Espíritu Santo

CHACCHOBEN

Chacchoben
Limones

Laguna Bacalar

Uvero

MAYÁ LOST
MAYAN KINGDOM
Mahahual

Chetumal

Bay

Banco
Chinchorro

Parque Nacional
Arrecifes de Xcalak

Xcalak

Isla
Cozumel

PUNTA
MORALES

San Miguel
de Cozumel

SAN
GERVASIO

Playa
Chen Río

El Cedral

SANTA
ROSA
WALL

EL
CARACOL

PALANCAR

Parque
Punta Sur

Contents

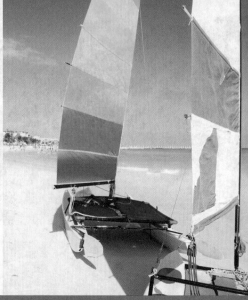

DISCOVER

Cancún & Cozumel

Cancún and Cozumel are places that deserve—and defy—the myriad descriptions given them. The name Cancún evokes images of white-sand beaches, turquoise seas, and raucous nightclubs. Isla Cozumel is no less mythic, at least among divers, with its pristine coral reef and abundant sealife. And the secret is out on the Riviera Maya, the long coastline south of Cancún, with resorts of all sizes and getaways like Tulum and Playa del Carmen. But farther south, the Costa Maya remains relatively undeveloped, while the inland archaeological sites, which range from packed to practically empty, never fail to impress.

Some people dismiss Cancún and Cozumel for being overcommercialized and "Americanized." True, there are places saturated with American stores and chain restaurants (and actual Americans), where you hear as much English as Spanish. But you may be surprised to learn how culturally rich those cities, and the whole region, really are. Just minutes from Cancún's hotel zone is a lively downtown where you can sip pinot grigio at a wine bar, listen to live music, or eat tacos in a park without another tourist in sight. Likewise, just a couple of

Clockwise from top left: coral reef with tropical fish; catamaran on Playa del Carmen; Maya mask at Museo Maya de Cancún; handmade tortillas; Cancún beaches and hotels; palm fronds are used for shade and roofing.

blocks from Cozumel's touristy main drag is a friendly island community where kids play soccer in the street. Large parts of Cozumel have no roads or power lines, just miles of deserted beach where you hear nothing but the birds and the surf.

Equally unexpected are the area's natural and ecological attractions. You can dive and snorkel in the longest underground river system in the world, kayak through mangrove forests and freshwater lagoons, and even go snorkeling with whale sharks. At Cobá, you can climb the second-highest Maya pyramid, *and* see parrots and toucans, *and* bike from temple to temple on wide forest paths, all in the same visit.

So what sort of trip will it be? Sunbathing by the pool, diving the coral reefs, snorkeling with whale sharks, or exploring the Maya ruins? With luck, you'll do a little of each, and more. In the process, you may discover that Cancún, Cozumel, and the Riviera Maya are much more than they seem.

Clockwise from top left: bikes can be a great way to get around Tulum; Isla de la Pasión; Tulum ruins; a fountain light show in Cozumel.

10 TOP
EXPERIENCES

1 Beaches: Bask in the sun on some of Cancún and Cozumel's most beautiful stretches of sand (page 27).

2 **Yucatecan Cuisine:** Enjoy some of the region's most delicious dishes featuring traditional Maya ingredients with dashes of Caribbean and Middle Eastern flavor (page 36).

>>>

3 **Cenotes:** The freshwater pools of shimmering water can be found all over region, with some of the best in the Rivera Maya (page 157) and Tulum (page 218 and page 240).

<<<

4 **Wildlife:** Get acquainted with some of the region's magnificent critters. Tour a **spider monkey** preserve, admire toothy **crocodiles,** and watch baby **sea turtles** hatch (page 30).

>>>

5 **Maya Ruins:** Mexico's Caribbean coast includes some of the most important ancient sites in North America. **Chichén Itzá** (page 284), **Cobá** (page 235), and **San Gervasio** (page 113) are a few of the best.

^
^
^

6 **Diving and snorkeling:** Get up close and personal with underwater treasures (page 57, page 94, and page 160).

7 **Cancún Nightlife:** You don't have to be on spring break to join in on the fun (page 50).

8 **Romance in Tulum:** Get away from it all in a cabana right on the beach or enjoy a couples massage at a beautiful wellness spa (page 35).

9 **Sportfishing:**
World-class
fishing attracts
ambitious anglers
from all over
(page 245).

>>>

10 **Ecoparks:**
These endlessly
entertaining parks
teem with wildlife and
outdoor activities
(page 135 and
page 172).

>>>

Planning Your Trip

Where to Go

Cancún

Cancún has two parts: The **Zona Hotelera** (Hotel Zone) has Cancún's top resorts and nightclubs, plus miles of beautiful beaches. But if you don't mind hopping a bus to the beach, **downtown** has cheaper food and lodging, plus some unexpectedly cool bars and cafés. Most travelers visit **Isla Mujeres,** a sliver of an island offshore from Cancún, as a day trip, but nice hotels and a mellow ambience make it a tempting place to stay. **Isla Holbox** is even smaller, with sand roads and virtually no cars. The beaches aren't glorious, but the tranquility is sublime.

Isla Cozumel

Cozumel's pristine **coral reefs** and crystalline water attract divers the world over; fewer people realize the island also has a scenic **national park,** numerous beach clubs, a tournament golf course, and an important **Maya ruin.** Beat the cruise ship crowds by heading to the east side's isolated beaches and dramatic surf. Most people arrive by ferry—it's just a half-hour ride from Playa del Carmen—but there's also an airport with international arrivals.

The Riviera Maya

Stretching 130 kilometers (81 miles) from Cancún to Tulum, the Riviera Maya has mega-resorts and boutique bed-and-breakfasts, busy cities and quiet towns, great reef diving and amazing cenotes (freshwater sinkholes). **Playa del Carmen** has the area's largest selection of hotels, food, nightlife, and services; try **Puerto Morelos** and **Akumal** for something a bit smaller, or isolated clusters of beachfront hotels

Boats are a part of life on Isla Cozumel, for locals and visitors alike.

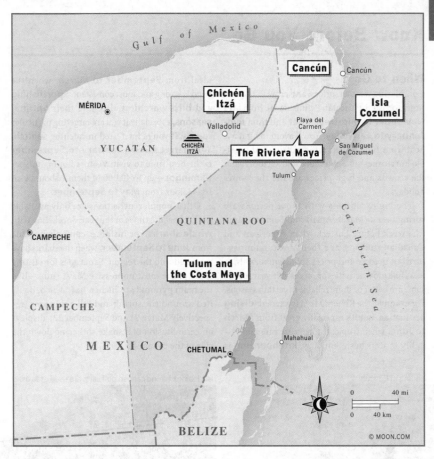

like **Tankah Tres** and **Soliman Bay** for even more R&R.

Tulum and the Costa Maya

Tulum is justly famous for its stunning beaches, boho-chic bungalows, and namesake **Maya ruin,** with a dramatic view of the Caribbean. An hour from Tulum, **Cobá** boasts the second-tallest Maya pyramid and a lovely forest setting teeming with birds. Directly south of Tulum is the pristine **Sian Ka'an Biosphere Reserve** and beyond that the isolated towns of the **Costa Maya.** There's a lovely freshwater lagoon, **Bacalar,** with a like-named town that is

growing in popularity with independent travelers. Just south is **Chetumal,** the busy state capital and gateway to Belize.

Chichén Itzá

Several fascinating Maya ruins are within easy reach of Cancún and the Riviera Maya. **Chichén Itzá** is one of the most impressive and recognizable of all Maya ruins, and just two hours from Cancún. Even closer, **Ek' Balam** is small but has a spectacular stucco frieze and relatively few visitors. Visit both with an overnight stay in **Valladolid,** a charming colonial town with several cenotes nearby.

Know Before You Go

When to Go

Considering weather, prices, and crowds, the best times to visit the Yucatán Peninsula are from **late November to mid-December** and from **mid-January to early May.** You'll avoid the intense heat from June to August, the rain (and possible hurricanes) in September and October, and the crowds and high prices around the winter holidays.

The big exceptions with those periods are spring break (March/April) and Semana Santa (the week before Easter), when American and Canadian students, and then Mexican tourists, turn out in force and prices spike temporarily.

While most activities are accessible year round, some are better or more reliable in certain seasons. For example, the Riviera Maya is a superb **diving** destination, but it's especially great from **March to June,** when tropical storms are rare and visibility is at its best. Similarly, **kiteboarding** is ideal from **September to March,** when the wind is strong and most consistent. **Sportfishing** and **bird-watching** also have their **optimal seasons,** especially if you are targeting particular species: If you're interested in catching **sailfish,** a top target species, **January to September** is the best time to visit; visitors hoping to spot **flamingos**—up to 40,000 of them—should visit Isla Holbox from **May to September.**

Other popular attractions are only available during specific times of the year. Snorkeling with **whale sharks,** for instance, can only be done from **June to September,** when the sharks have migrated into the region. Same goes for visiting some of the most impressive Maya ruins—like the main pyramid at Chichén Itzá, which, if visited around the spring and fall equinoxes (respectively March 21 and September 22), displays an eerie illusion of a snake slithering down the side of the pyramid.

landing in Cancún

Isla Holbox has no cars, so golf carts are used as taxis.

- **Diving and Snorkeling:** Go to Isla Cozumel, Puerto Morelos, Banco Chinchorro, or Tulum

- **Cenotes:** Go to Ruta de los Cenotes, Xpu-Há, Tulum, Cobá, Valladolid, or Ek' Balam

- **Nightlife:** Go to Cancún or Playa del Carmen

- **Mayan Ruins:** Go to Chichén Itzá, Cobá, Tulum, Ek' Balam, or Kohunlich

- **Romance:** Go to Tulum or Isla Holbox

- **Beaches:** Go to Tulum, Cancún, Isla Mujeres, or Playa X'Cacel

- **Beach Clubs:** Go to Tulum, Playa del Carmen, or Isla Cozumel

- **Wildlife:** Consider Sian Ka'an Biosphere Reserve, whale shark tours in Isla Holbox, snorkeling with turtles in Akumal, releasing baby turtles in Isla Cozumel, Punta Laguna Spider Monkey Reserve, and Isla Contoy

Tulum's beaches are truly picture perfect.

Day Trips:

- **From Cancún:** Head to Isla Mujeres, Chichén Itzá, Valladolid, and Ek' Balam

- **From Isla Mujeres:** Head to Isla Contoy

- **From Playa del Carmen:** Head to Isla Cozumel, Tulum, or Cobá

- **From Tulum:** Head to Sian Ka'an Biosphere Reserve, Cobá, or Punta Laguna Spider Monkey Reserve

- **From Mahahual:** Head to Chacchoben or Laguna Bacalar

- **From Chetumal:** Head to Laguna Bacalar, Kohunlich, and Dzibanché or Kinichná

- **Sportfishing:** Try Sian Ka'an Biosphere Reserve, Xcalak, or Isla Cozumel

- **Budget Travel:** Try Valladolid, Laguna Bacalar, or Chetumal

- **An Escape:** Try Isla Holbox or Xcalak

Passports and Visas

American and Canadian travelers must have a valid passport to travel to and from Mexico. **Tourist visas** are issued upon entry; you technically are allowed up to 180 days, but agents often issue just 30 or 60 days. If you want to stay longer, request the time when you present your passport. To extend your visa, visit the immigration office in Cancún.

Vaccinations

No special vaccines are required for travel to the Yucatán Peninsula, but it's a good idea to be up-to-date on the **standard travel immunizations,** including hepatitis A, MMR (measles-mumps-rubella), tetanus-diphtheria, and typhoid.

Transportation

Cancún International Airport (CUN) is far

kayaks awaiting kayakers

and away the most common and convenient entry point to the region. A handful of flights go directly to Cozumel or Chetumal, and there are plans (but nothing more) for a new airport outside Tulum; there also is an airport near Chichén Itzá, though at the time of research it was not in use. An excellent network of **buses, shuttles,** and **ferries** covers the entire region, though a rental car makes a world of difference in more remote areas.

What to Pack

Bring to Cancún and Cozumel what you would to any beach destination: light cotton clothing, hat, sunscreen, sunglasses, flip-flops, and so forth. Beach buffs should bring two or even three swimsuits, plus snorkel gear if you have it. Water shoes come in handy wherever the beach is rocky, while sneakers and bug repellent are musts for the Maya ruins. Finally, it's always smart to bring an extra pair of glasses or contacts, prescription medications, birth control, and a travel clock. If you do leave anything behind, no worries—there's a Walmart in all the major cities.

The Best of Cancún and the Riviera Maya

There's *a lot* to do in Cancún, Cozumel, and the Riviera Maya, so this itinerary packs a lot into a little time. You'll hit the beach, go diving and snorkeling, explore Maya ruins, take in a museum, discover out-of-the-way places, nosh on local food, go to a nightclub or two, and still be back in time to catch your flight home. Ready, set, go!

Day 1

Arrive in **Cancún.** If you're staying in the Zona Hotelera, head straight to the sand after you check in—the beautiful beach will be a welcome sight after hours on a plane. If you're staying downtown, you can either hop on a bus to the beach or stroll **around Parque Las Palapas.** In the evening, head to dinner at one of Cancún's fabulous open-air eateries.

Day 2

Spend the morning on the beach or by the pool. In the Zona Hotelera, you're just steps away from either. Those staying downtown can take a bus to one of the public beaches—**Playa Delfines** has a bus stop right in front, and **El Rey,** a Maya ruin, is across the boulevard for when you need a change of scenery. In the evening, head to one of Cancún's iconic nightclubs—**CocoBongo** and **Grand Mambo Café** are always hopping. For something mellower, join local hipsters at **Amarula Con Acento Tropical** for creative cocktails in a unique patio setting.

Day 3

Spend a day exploring the **Riviera Maya.** A rental car makes life easier, but it's certainly doable by bus or taxi. **Playa del Carmen's** Quinta Avenida is good for window-shopping and

Beautiful Playa Delfines is at the southern end of Cancún's Zona Hotelera.

Maya Ruins Within Reach

one of the impressive stone pyramids in Cobá

Besides its incredible beaches and world-class resorts, Mexico's Caribbean coast is also home to (or within easy reach of) numerous ancient Maya ruins, including some of the most important archaeological sites in the country and the continent. A visit to one or more is well worth a day off the sand, even for committed beach hounds. (And at least one site—Tulum—has historical value *and* a pretty little beach. Sweet!)

- **Chichén Itzá,** with its iconic pyramid and massive ball court, is one of the New Seven Wonders of the World. Scores of tours head there from Cancún, but getting to the site early—by bus or rental car—lets you beat the crowds and enjoy this fascinating site at your own pace.

- **Ek' Balam** boasts one of the best-preserved stucco friezes in the Maya world and an all-embracing view from atop its main pyramid. A nearby cenote is great for cooling off.

- **Cobá** has an even better view from its main pyramid—at 42 meters (138 feet) high, it's the second tallest in the Yucatán Peninsula. Nestled in a forest near several small lakes, it's also a good place to spot birds and butterflies.

- **Tulum** is the subject of innumerable postcards, perched on a bluff overlooking the turquoise Caribbean Sea. Like Chichén Itzá, it's far more rewarding to skip the tour and make your way to Tulum early to enjoy the site before the throngs arrive.

- **Kohunlich,** in southern Quintana Roo, is the most remote of the ruins listed here and is best known for a series of imposing stucco masks. Nearby is a unique all-inclusive luxury resort with guided trips into the surrounding forest and lagoons.

- **San Gervasio** is Isla Cozumel's main archaeological site, with several modest temples connected by forest paths. Dedicated to the goddess of fertility Ixchel, San Gervasio was an important pilgrimage site for ancient Maya women.

- **El Rey, San Miguelito,** and **Yamil Lu'um** are small ruins right in Cancún's Zona Hotelera. El Rey is the largest and best preserved of the group and is also home to hundreds of iguanas—a sure hit with the kids.

people-watching, while Xpu-Há and X'cacel's strands make for excellent beach days. If you like snorkeling, consider going to **Puerto Morelos or Laguna Yal-Ku.**

Day 4

Leave bright and early to get to the Maya ruins of **Chichén Itzá** before the crowds do. Spend the morning there, followed by lunch in the colonial city of **Valladolid.** From there, go swimming in nearby cenotes, or visit **Ek' Balam,** a much smaller ruin. Both Valladolid and Ek' Balam have good lodging options if you want to overnight.

Day 5

Spend this day on either **Isla Mujeres** or **Isla Cozumel,** both easy to reach by ferry. Divers can enjoy a tank or two, especially at Cozumel. If you prefer snorkeling, trips can be booked at dive shops or on the ferry pier of either island. Or just chill out on the beach—Playa Norte in Isla Mujeres is a sure bet, and the windswept eastern side of Cozumel is a great option for beachcombing. Either way, definitely think about renting a car or golf cart, which allow you time and flexibility to explore either island beyond their central areas.

Day 6

Back in **Cancún,** this is your last full day. If you're up for it, book a snorkeling tour or visit the **Museo Maya de Cancún,** an excellent archaeological museum at the southern end of the Zona Hotelera. Otherwise, sit back, relax, and enjoy the pool and beach—it's been a busy week!

The Best of Isla Cozumel

Isla Cozumel is Mexico's third-largest island, with much to offer the curious traveler, from Maya ruins to deserted beaches. Cozumel's claim to fame is its diving and snorkeling, and this tour allots plenty of bubble time. If you prefer to stay on dry land, there's still plenty to do and see in Cozumel, although you also could just take the ferry to Playa del Carmen to explore the mainland for a day or two.

Day 1

Fly straight to **Cozumel.** There are numerous daily flights, including a few nonstops from the United States. (This saves you the time and expense of taking a bus or taxi to Playa del Carmen, then a ferry across to Cozumel.) Your first order of business is to book a day or two of diving or snorkeling. If you don't have your own snorkeling equipment, arrange an extended rental at any of the dive shops in town. Spend the balance of your day on the **beach,** whether at your hotel or at one of the beach clubs on the west side of the island.

Day 2

Revel in Isla Cozumel's richest resource: its marine park and pristine coral reef. **Palancar Reef** is a good warm-up site, with a shallow profile and mild current. In the evening, enjoy dinner and a stroll around the **central plaza.**

Day 3

Rent a car and spend a day exploring the island. **San Gervasio archaeological zone,** in the middle of the island, is a good place to start. Continue on to Cozumel's barely developed **east side** for lunch on a deserted beach while watching the waves crash ashore. Plan on returning to town in time for a **night dive**—an incredible experience.

Day 4

Spend the day at one of Cozumel's ecoparks, either **Parque Punta Sur** or **Chankanaab,** if you feel like more creature comforts. Take your snorkeling gear and a towel—both are great places to get in the water.

Family Fun

Cancún and the Riviera Maya are excellent family destinations, with plenty to see and do for kids and parents, and good hotels and restaurants to help take the stress out of traveling en masse. Here are some recommended spots:

CANCÚN

Isla Mujeres: Super-calm water, a turtle farm, and an ecopark, plus a ferry ride there and back—what's not to love?

Isla Holbox: Snorkel with whale sharks, beautiful and gentle giants of the sea, which congregate here between June and September.

Isla Holbox: On dark spring and summer nights, visit the island's Punta Cocos where bioluminescent plankton create an otherworldly glow as you walk or paddle through them.

Parque Las Palapas: Downtown Cancún's main plaza, where kids can run around and munch on chocolate-filled churros.

El Rey Archaeological Zone: Hundreds of beefy iguanas make this a fun stop for kids, even if they're lukewarm about piles of old rocks. (Hint: The iguanas love bananas!)

ISLA COZUMEL

Playa Chen Río: This protected ocean beach on Cozumel's east side is deserted midweek and busy with local families on weekends.

Parque Punta Sur: A scenic natural reserve with a nice beach and fantastic snorkeling, plus a maritime museum and a lighthouse you can climb.

Planetario de Cozumel: Cozumel's state-of-the-art planetarium is a nice place to cool off and enjoy films about the universe, Maya cosmology, and more.

Butterfly Sanctuary: Stroll through a protected garden filled with butterflies, some with no qualms about landing on visitors!

THE RIVIERA MAYA

Ruta de los Cenotes: From the main highway, this 20-kilometer (12-mile) forest road winds past numerous cenotes—some busy and commercialized, others delightfully quiet and remote.

Xcaret: This huge ecopark is an all-day excursion, with snorkeling, tubing, an aquarium, and a fun evening show.

Croco Cun Zoo: At this charming little zoo near Puerto Morelos you can see, pet, and even hold animals (including babies).

fun at the beach

TULUM AND THE COSTA MAYA

Dos Ojos Cenote: Great cenote snorkeling for all ages, either with a guide or on your own.

Xel-Há: A family-friendly ecopark built around a natural inlet, with easy-to-access snorkeling, tubing, and other aquatic fun.

Cobá: Renting bikes or bicycle taxis makes visiting these ruins especially fun for kids, while the thick forest provides cool shade and a chance to spot birds and insects.

Punta Laguna Spider Monkey Reserve: A great family destination where you'll spot not only spider and howler monkeys, but a slew of birds, tropical vegetation, and more.

Maya Lost Mayan Kingdom: This Maya-themed water park in Mahahual has zip lines, a lazy river, and heart-stopping waterslides.

Laguna Bacalar: Explore lovely Laguna Bacalar by kayak, with its remote beaches, mangrove forests, and great birdwatching.

CHICHÉN ITZÁ

Chichén Itzá: Impressive ruins with several family-friendly hotels nearby. The Ik Kil cenote just east of town is a sure hit.

Valladolid: A charming midsize city with several impressive cenotes nearby for swimming.

Best Beaches

If you love beaches, you've come to the right place. Remember that beaches in Mexico are public; hotels can "claim" an area by setting out guest-only lounge chairs, but you are free to lay out your towel and umbrella wherever there's space.

Cancún

Cancún's beaches are in the Zona Hotelera and are famous for their deep, powdery white sand. Along the Zona Hotelera are numerous public access points, so people staying elsewhere don't have to pass through hotels to get to the beach. Be aware that the surf can be quite heavy at times.

- **Playa Gaviota Azul** is centrally located and has parasailing and other beach activities. The high-rise hotels behind it cast cooling shadows over the beach in the afternoon.
- **Playa Delfines** is at the southern end of the strip and the only beach not backed by hotels.

It has the largest waves of Cancún's beaches— you may even see a few surfers—and there's a Maya archaeological site just across the road.

- **Playa Marlín** is near Plaza Kukulcán mall, which has numerous restaurants and shops if you need a break from the sun (or each other).

Isla Mujeres

Isla Mujeres's best beaches are located at the northern tip of the island. Unlike Cancún, the beaches here have virtually no surf, making them ideal for families traveling with small children.

- **Playa Norte** has soft white sand and water so shallow and calm you have to wade out nearly 100 meters (328 feet) before it's deep enough to swim. Beach gear can be rented, and there are a handful of oceanfront restaurants.
- **Playa Centro** is around the corner from Playa Norte and is also quite beautiful. Larger and nearer to the ferry pier than Playa Norte, it can get crowded with day-trippers from Cancún.

Playa Gaviota Azul in Cancún

Isla Cozumel's Playa Palancar

Cenote Hopping

All along the coast and well inland are dozens of cenotes—pools of shimmering blue water fed by a vast underground freshwater river system. Some look like large ponds, others are deep sinkholes, others occupy gaping caverns or have dramatic rock formations. Many cenotes are open to the public, and their cool, clear water is perfect for swimming, snorkeling, and scuba diving. Facilities range from simple restrooms and snorkel rental to full-service "cenote parks" with guided tours. Some favorites include:

THE RIVIERA MAYA

Ruta de los Cenotes: Sure, some spots along the "Cenote Route" are tourist traps, but others are sublime, like Siete Bocas, a huge, eerie cavern filled with shimmering water, and Verde Lucero, a gorgeous open-air pool that's home to freshwater turtles and fish.

Jardín del Edén: The best and biggest of a cluster of cenotes near Playa Xpu-Há, with a large cavern that forms a dramatic overhang.

Cristalino: Next to Jardín del Edén, Cristalino also has an overhanging cliff but a smaller swimming area.

Azul: A set of three cenotes near Playa Xpu-Há with impossibly clear waters and a small cliff for jumping into one of them.

Manatí: Near Tankah Tres, this is actually a series of connected cenotes and lagoons that wind inland through a tangled scrub forest.

NEAR TULUM

Dos Ojos: A cenote park with rentals, guides, and spectacular caverns.

Gran Cenote: East of Tulum on the road to Cobá, this lovely cavern boasts natural arches and stalactite formations.

Car Wash: Just past Gran Cenote, this innocuous-

snorkeling in Cenote Azul

looking cenote has stunning rock formations below the surface.

INLAND AREAS

X'Canché: A pretty 12-meter-deep (39-foot) cenote, 1.5 kilometers (0.9 mile) down a forest path from Ek' Balam ruins.

Choo-Ha: One of four dramatic cenotes near Cobá, with a high domed ceiling and iridescent blue water.

Hacienda San Lorenzo Oxman: A beautiful and accessible cenote, with stairs, a rope swing, and even a restaurant and pool at the top.

Cenotes Agua Dulce: This collection of four lovely cenotes include two with deep turquoise water that's great for swimming.

Isla Cozumel

Cozumel is better known for its diving than its beaches, but there are a few spots where you can catch some rays. The island's west side has calm seas and several beach clubs, while the east side has scenic windswept beaches and heavy surf.

- **Playa Palancar** is the most low-key of the west-side beaches, with a well-maintained beach area and a restaurant serving tasty meals.

- **Playa San Francisco** is another fine west-side beach, with a string of large beach clubs. It's good if you want a bit more action than the scene at Playa Palancar.

- **Playa Chen Río** is one of several beaches on the east side, but is the only one protected from the waves so you can swim. It can get crowded on weekends, but it's wide, so a quiet spot always can be found. A lone restaurant serves pricey meals—do like the locals do and bring your own eats.

- **Isla de la Pasión** is a private island off Cozumel's north coast, and the only practical way to get there is by package tour. But the beach is gorgeous—Corona filmed one of its commercials there—and the open bar and open buffet make it a worthwhile splurge.

Isla Holbox

Isla Holbox's scenic main beach, Playa Norte, extends several miles and is backed by a low coastal forest that is dotted with small hotels and bungalows.

Playa Norte

The sand and water at **Playa Norte** aren't as classically idyllic as, say, Tulum, but are still lovely and striking in a Robinson Crusoe-type way. Plus, a long sandbar often emerges just offshore; covered in an inch or two of water, it's perfect for wading and cooling off.

The Riviera Maya

If you're staying at a resort in the Riviera Maya, there's likely a great patch of sand just steps away. But there are plenty of excellent ones accessible to all travelers.

- In Playa del Carmen, **Playa Tukán** is a long swath of blond sand with medium surf. Two beach clubs here rent chairs and umbrellas and offer meal service and swimming pools. There's also plenty of open sand, if you'd rather just lay out a towel.

- South of Playa del Carmen, **Xpu-Há** is easy to miss but rewards those who find it with a broad white-sand beach and mellow surf. There are fewer services here than elsewhere—and fewer people, too—but a couple of beach clubs make Xpu-Há a great place to spend the day.

- Farther south, Half Moon Bay in the town of

Wildlife

Whale sharks are often spotted near the ocean's surface, where they skim the warm water for plankton.

Cancún and the Caribbean coast may be best known for white-sand beaches and deluxe resorts, but they also have many excellent areas and opportunities to spot wildlife, especially birds. When you need a break from the sun and surf, here are some places to get back in touch with nature:

- **Sian Ka'an Biosphere Reserve:** This sprawling coastal reserve south of Tulum is home to an astounding array of wildlife, including dolphins, howler monkeys, crocodiles, sea turtles, and hundreds of bird species. Harder to spot, but still there, are manatees, tapirs, and even jaguars.

- **Isla Holbox:** Come here to snorkel with whale sharks, gentle giants that congregate just offshore between June and September. You can also book a kayak or motorboat tour to visit the island's bird-rich lagoons any time of the year.

- **Isla Cozumel:** Cozumel's protected coral reef system teems with sponges, sea turtles, rays, eels, and countless tropical fish. Divers can get up close and personal, but even snorkelers get an eyeful in these pristine waters. The island's ecology department also welcomes visitors on nighttime excursions to find and protect sea turtle nests (May-September) and to release hatchlings back to the sea (August-November).

- **Punta Laguna Spider Monkey Reserve:** This small reserve north of Cobá is home to several families of rambunctious *monos arañas* (spider monkeys). A small lagoon has canoes to go looking for crocodiles.

- **Akumal:** Yucatec Maya for "Place of the Turtle," Akumal is the center for turtle preservation along the Riviera Maya. Guides here lead snorkelers through turtle feeding grounds in Akumal Bay. A local organization also organizes monthlong volunteer opportunities to help with sea turtle and reef monitoring.

Mahahual's main beach

Akumal is a long, curving public beach with great snorkeling. Hotel guests can use beach chairs; others should bring a towel and stake out a spot under a palm tree for shade.

- For maximum isolation, **Playa X'cacel** has a small parking lot, simple restroom area, and over a mile of gorgeous white sand. (There's a small freshwater cenote, too.) Located between Xel-Há ecopark and Chemuyil community, X'cacel is a sea turtle nesting ground, so it's off-limits to construction. Good for turtles—and beach lovers, too!

Tulum and the Costa Maya

Many people consider Tulum's beaches to be the best of Mexico's Caribbean coast. It's hard to disagree with deep white sand, gentle azure surf, and a backing of palm trees and bungalow-style hotels. Costa Maya beaches are slightly less jaw-dropping (though Mahahual gets close) but make up for it with stellar fishing, kayaking, snorkeling, and diving.

- **Tulum's northern beaches** are easier to reach if you're not staying at one of the beach hotels, with several public access points, restaurants, and beach clubs.

- **Tulum's southern beaches** are truly stunning, plucked from a postcard. Hotel guests have easy access, though nonguests can park just south of Punta Piedra and walk down the shore. Bring your own supplies or plan to eat at one of the small hotel restaurants to reach the beach.

- **Mahahual** has a lovely stretch of beach right in town, with warm white sand and calm turquoise water. A pedestrian-only walkway hugs the shore, and there's great diving, snorkeling, paddleboarding, and kayaking.

Best Diving and Snorkeling

For many travelers, the Riviera Maya's underwater treasures are as compelling as its terrestrial ones. The region includes the world's second-longest coral reef, the longest known underground river system, and the Northern Hemisphere's largest coral atoll. Below are some of the region's top spots to get underwater.

Isla Holbox and Isla Mujeres

From June to September, large numbers of whale sharks congregate between **Isla Holbox** and **Isla Mujeres,** gorging themselves on krill. Guided **whale shark trips** from either island allow you to snorkel beside these gentle giants.

Isla Cozumel

Isla Cozumel's crystal-clear water, vibrant coral reef, and myriad first-rate dive operators make the island a premier underwater destination. It's especially suited for expert divers, with challenging wall, deep, wreck, and drift dives—too many to name. Snorkelers should check out **Parque Punta Sur and Chankanaab,** which also have nice beaches.

The Riviera Maya and Tulum

The **Riviera Maya** is dotted with hundreds of eerily beautiful **cenotes** (freshwater caverns and sinkholes) offering out-of-this-world snorkeling and diving for novices and experts alike. **Tulum**'s dive shops specialize in cenote dives and cave diving courses, while snorkelers can grab their gear and spend the day cenote hopping. Try **Siete Bocas** and **Verde Lucero** on the

Ruta de los Cenotes, just south of Puerto Morelos; **Jardín del Edén** and **Cenote Cristalino,** both on Highway 307 across from Xpu-Há; and the string of cenotes west of **Tulum** including **Car Wash** and **Gran Cenote. Dos Ojos,** near Tulum, also offers full-service guided tours for snorkelers and divers, visiting a gorgeous stalagmite-filled cavern.

Puerto Morelos is a low-key town between Cancún and Playa del Carmen that's famous for the exceptionally rich and well-preserved coral reef just offshore. A local cooperative takes travelers on rewarding snorkeling tours, while local dive shops offer excellent reef dives.

The appealing beach town of **Akumal** has two great snorkeling options. **Laguna Yal-Ku** is an estuary zone where fresh cenote water pours into the ocean and is brimming with fish and sea plants. Unique sculptures adorn the water's edge. **Akumal Bay,** meanwhile, has shallow protected water and is a known feeding ground for sea turtles.

The Costa Maya

Banco Chinchorro is the largest coral atoll on this side of the planet, and has spectacular diving and snorkeling. Getting there can be a bear—2-3 hours by boat each way—but the massive and pristine atoll is worth the time and expense. Dive shops in **Mahahual** or **Xcalak,** two small towns near the Belize border, offer Chinchorro trips. There's also fantastic snorkeling and diving right from the shore, including at night.

Clockwise from top left: a whole other world awaits you just beneath the surface; MUSA's statues were specially designed to become habitats for plants and sealife; spotted eagle rays swim in open ocean near Cozumel.

Side Trip: Chichén Itzá

Day 1

Get an early start in order to beat the crowds and tour groups. Visit the amazing **Chichén Itzá ruins.** The site is huge and impressive, so plan on being there for a few hours. Have lunch at **Los Faisanes Bistro** in the historic **Hacienda Chichén,** adjacent to the ruins. Check into your hotel; the **Zona Hotelera** hotels are a nice option, budget permitting, with their leafy grounds and refreshing pools, just steps from the ruins. If you've got time and energy, make an afternoon visit to **Cenote Sagrado Azul** or **Balankanché Caves.** Have dinner in Pisté—try **La Gran Chaya** for some local flavor—and, that night, attend the **Sound and Light Show,** which uses projections on the structures to tell Chichén Itzá's history and lore. (Remember you need to buy tickets online in advance.) Hit the sack—you've earned it!

Day 2

Make your way to **Valladolid,** a charming colonial town just east of Chichén Itzá. Spend the day poking around—there's terrific **folk art** in **Casa de los Venados,** fascinating history at the **Iglesia and Ex-Convento San Bernardino de Siena,** and several impressive **cenotes** in town and just beyond. When you need a lunch break, try **Yerbabuena del Sisal** for its tasty Mexican food and bright garden patio. That evening, learn more about Valladolid at the gorgeous and hi-tech **Sound and Light Show** at Iglesia San Bernardino, followed by drinks and Yucatecan food at **Casa Conato.**

Day 3

Start the day with a hearty breakfast at **Squimz,** where it's never too early for a milk shake, and then head to the Maya ruins of **Ek' Balam.**

El Castillo, as seen from the Group of a Thousand Columns

Valladolid's central plaza

The site is small but spectacular, with an intricate stone frieze atop a soaring pyramid. From there, spend time **cenote hopping—Cenote X'Canché** is a short walk from the ruins, while **Cenote Sak' Awa** and **Cenotes Agua Dulce** are easily reached by car. Plan on having lunch at the restaurant at Cenotes Agua Dulce. Afterward, head back to the coast.

Romantic Tulum Getaway

TOP EXPERIENCE

Although a number of places in and around Cancún have the makings of a romantic getaway—picturesque beaches, elegant restaurants, relaxing spas, and cozy accommodations—we picked our favorite for this itinerary: Tulum. The beaches are spectacular, and the *cabaña*-style hotels exude a quiet charm like nowhere else.

Day 1
Fly into Cancún, and head by bus or taxi to **Tulum.** Settle into your **beachside bungalow,** complete with a hanging bed, mosquito net, and candles. If you want something a little more upscale, consider a suite at one of the chic high-end hotels. Spend the rest of the day on the beach. In the evening, head to **Kitchen Table** for dinner, followed by drinks and live jazz at **El Batey.**

Day 2
Visit the **Tulum ruins** in the morning before the crowds arrive. Bring your swimsuits to enjoy the small beach there. Afterward, walk to gorgeous **Playa Mar Caribe,** just south of the ruins. Enjoy lunch at **Mezzanine.** If you're up for it, head down the road for a drop-in yoga class at **Yoga Shala Tulum** in the late afternoon.

Day 3
Choose between an organized **ecotour** in the **Sian Ka'an Biosphere Reserve** and

Yucatecan Cuisine

Like many regions of Mexico, the Yucatán Peninsula has a cuisine all its own. The base is recognizably Mexican, but the dishes here are strongly influenced by traditional Maya ingredients and techniques, with dashes of Caribbean and Middle Eastern flavors. Some popular menu items include:

- *Cochinita Pibil:* pork that has been marinated in achiote, Seville orange juice, peppercorn, garlic, cumin, salt, and pepper, wrapped in banana leaves, and baked. It's typically served on weekends.

- *Dzoto-bichay:* tamales made of *chaya* (a leafy vegetable similar to spinach) and eggs. It comes smothered in tomato sauce.

- *Empanizado:* slices of pork or chicken that has been breaded and fried, often served with salad, rice, and beans.

- *Panucho:* handmade tortilla stuffed with refried beans and covered with shredded turkey, pickled onion, and slices of avocado. Like a *salbute* plus!

- *Papadzules:* hard-boiled eggs chopped and rolled into a corn tortilla, smothered in a creamy pumpkinseed sauce.

- *Poc-Chuc:* slices of pork that have been marinated in Seville orange juice and coated with a tangy sauce. Pickled onions are added on the side.

- *Salbute:* handmade tortilla covered with shredded turkey, pickled onion, and slices of avocado.

Poc-chuc is a traditional Yucatecan dish.

- *Sopa de Lima:* turkey-stock soup prepared with shredded turkey or chicken, fried tortilla strips, and juice from *lima,* a lime-like citrus fruit.

You can find Yucatecan dishes just about anywhere, from hole-in-the-wall taco joints to gourmet restaurants—discovering them is half the fun! For a sure bet, check out La Habichuela (Downtown Cancún), Quesadillas Tierra del Sol (Downtown Cancún), Mercado Municipal (Isla Mujeres), La Candela (Isla Cozumel), La Gran Chaya (Pisté), and Taberna de los Frailes (Valladolid).

---

do-it-yourself **cenote hopping** (four cenotes on the road to Cobá are just minutes away). If you're at a high-end hotel, book a **beachside dinner for two** before starting your day. Consider reserving a **couples massage** at the **Yaan Wellness Energy Spa** for your final day.

Day 4

Have breakfast brought to your room. Spend your last full day beachcombing on **Tulum's southern beaches.** Take a private **paddleboarding** lesson together with **Pro Kite Tulum.** Afterward, relax on the beach—and don't forget to go to your massages!

Cancún

Highlights

★ **Playa Delfines:** Located at the far southern end of the Zona Hotelera, this is one of few spots with unobstructed views and a refreshing mix of foreign and local visitors (page 48).

★ **Cancún Nightlife:** You don't have to be on spring break to enjoy Cancún's nightclubs—but it helps! If the all-night-every-nightclub scene isn't for you, head downtown for wine bars and cocktail lounges (page 50).

★ **Museo Subacuático de Arte (MUSA):** This remarkable "museum" on the ocean floor has two sites featuring hundreds of statues made of material designed to promote coral growth, so they only get more interesting as time passes (pages 57 and 77).

★ **Isla Contoy:** Go island-hopping on this popular day trip from Isla Mujeres. A morning boat ride is followed by snorkeling on a rich coral reef, hiking and bird-watching, and digging into a fresh fish barbecue on the beach (page 78).

★ **Playa Norte:** Isla Mujeres's best beach has virtually no waves, just soft white sand lapped by glassy turquoise water (page 78).

★ **Whale Shark Feeding Grounds:** Get goggles-to-gills with the world's biggest fish (page 94).

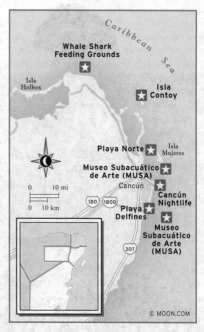
© MOON.COM

C ancún is a big, beautiful contradiction. For many people, it has all the makings of the ultimate vacation destination: five-star hotels, thick white sand, impossibly blue waters, and a nightlife that never stops.

Others chafe at Cancún for seeming more American than Mexican, a place where you need never speak a word of Spanish, never eat at a restaurant you couldn't find at a mall back home, and never convert your dollars into pesos.

Both perspectives are true, but one-sided. It's hard not to cringe at those loud tourists who don't bother to explore—or even care about—any part of Mexico beyond their beach chairs. Yet those who pooh-pooh Cancún are also selling the city short. Cancún is a working, breathing city that's vital to Mexico's economy and imbued with a fascinating history and plenty of "real" Mexican culture for those willing to seek it out. And contrary to impressions, Cancún has accommodations and services for visitors of all budgets and tastes.

Why not take advantage of both sides of Cancún? The resorts, beaches, and nightclubs will blow your mind—don't miss them!

But be sure not to overlook Cancún's more subtle side, too, from live music in a downtown wine bar to munching on *elote* (corn on the cob) sold from a cart in the city's pleasant central square.

And when you need to, just get away. A 15-minute ferry ride delivers you to the slow-paced Isla Mujeres, a sliver of sand surrounded by breathtaking blue waters. Farther north and even more laid-back is Isla Holbox, which has no cars, no banks, and no post office—it's a world away from Cancún yet reachable in a morning.

PLANNING YOUR TIME

A week will do just fine in Cancún, allowing time enough to get your tan on plus take a day trip or two, such as to Isla Mujeres or one of the nearby Maya ruins. Ten days gives you time to explore deeper and farther, turning a day trip to Isla Mujeres or the Maya ruins into an overnighter, or venturing north to

---

Previous: Playa Delfines; American flamingos on Isla Holbox. **Above:** Isla shopping.

Cancún

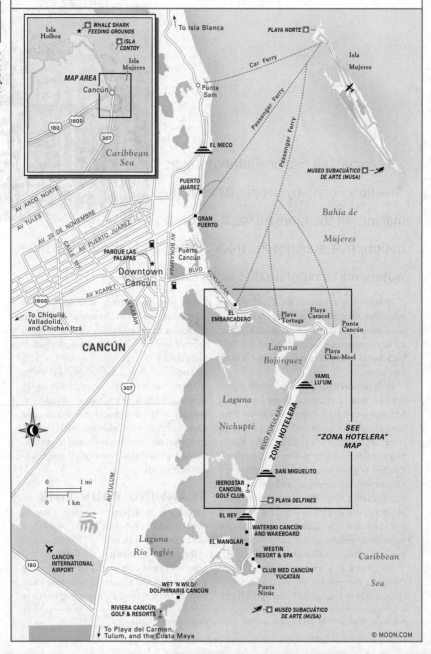

Isla Holbox

★ WHALE SHARK FEEDING GROUNDS

☩ ISLA CONTOY

Isla Mujeres

To Isla Blanca

PLAYA NORTE ☩ —

Isla Mujeres

MAP AREA

Cancún

180 180D

307

Caribbean Sea

Car Ferry

Punta Sam

Passenger Ferry

Passenger Ferry

▰ EL MECO

MUSEO SUBACUÁTICO ☩ — ✈ DE ARTE (MUSA)

Bahía de Mujeres

AV ARCO NORTE

AV TULES

AV 20 DE NOVIEMBRE

CALLE 107

AV PUERTO JUÁREZ

AV BONAMPAK

PUERTO JUÁREZ

GRAN PUERTO

PARQUE LAS PALAPAS

Downtown Cancún

Puerto Cancún

BLVD KUKULCÁN

AV XCARET

180D

AV KABAH

AV BONAMPAK

EL EMBARCADERO

Playa Tortuga

Playa Caracol

Punta Cancún

CANCÚN

To Chiquila, Valladolid, and Chichén Itzá

307

Laguna Nichupté

Laguna Bojórquez

Playa Chac-Mool

YAMIL LU'UM

BLVD KUKULCÁN

ZONA HOTELERA

SEE "ZONA HOTELERA" MAP

0   1 mi
0   1 km

AV TULUM

SAN MIGUELITO

IBEROSTAR CANCÚN GOLF CLUB

☩ PLAYA DELFINES

EL REY

WATERSKI CANCÚN AND WAKEBOARD

EL MANGLAR

WESTIN RESORT & SPA

Laguna Río Inglés

✈ CANCÚN INTERNATIONAL AIRPORT

180

CLUB MED CANCÚN YUCATÁN

Caribbean

Sea

Punta Nizúc

WET 'N WILD/ DOLPHINARIS CANCÚN

RIVIERA CANCÚN GOLF & RESORTS

✈ ☩ MUSEO SUBACUÁTICO DE ARTE (MUSA)

↓ To Playa del Carmen, Tulum, and the Costa Maya

© MOON.COM

Escape the Crowds

Valladolid street scene

So you booked a trip to Cancún because the flights were cheap, the lodging was easy to arrange, and the beaches sounded great. But you are still the sort of traveler who likes to go where the masses generally don't. We hear you. Here are some places within striking distance of Cancún for the traveler who wants something a little different.

- **Isla Blanca:** The beaches and resorts on Cancun's hotel zone are so famous that no one thinks to looks elsewhere. Too bad for them—Isla Blanca, just north of Cancun, is another long strip of lovely white sand beaches, and there's hardly a soul (or condo) in sight (page 48).

- **El Meco Ruins:** Most visitors to Cancún aren't looking for archaeological sites, so the area's Maya ruins are rarely busy. El Meco is the least visited of the bunch, yet it boasts the tallest pyramid and loads of iguanas. It's located just north of town so city buses can get you there in minutes (page 43).

- **Ruta de los Cenotes:** Travelers often forget that just beyond Cancún's manicured resorts is dense jungle and amazing natural sights. South of town, this well-marked jungle road winds past numerous cenotes—freshwater sinkholes found in stalactite-filled caverns or shimmering pools encircled by lush vegetation (page 157).

- **El Corchal:** The entire Yucatan Peninsula is a haven for birds, and Cancún is no different. At this little-known wetlands reserve, local guides takes visitors on canoeing trips to see flamingos, toucans and more (page 96).

- **Valladolid:** Mexico is filled with charming colonial cities. Valladolid is a perfect example, with quiet streets, colorful facades and centuries-old churches. It's a great escape from the hustle and bustle of Cancún, and just two-hours away by bus (page 295).

the remote Isla Holbox. Isla Mujeres and Isla Holbox are small but wonderfully relaxing; if either is your main destination, budget three or four days to experience them fully, but don't be surprised if you end up staying longer.

You don't *need* to rent a car to enjoy Cancún, Isla Mujeres, and Isla Holbox, especially if you don't plan on moving around much; all can be navigated easily by bus, ferry, taxi, and foot. That said, having a car makes many excursions easier, quicker, and more fun, especially if you've got kids in tow. Rather than booking a crowded and expensive tour to, say, Chichén Itzá, you can drive there yourself, arriving before the big groups and then hitting a second ruin or an out-of-the way cenote on the way home. With the relatively low price of rental cars, and the region's well-maintained roads and highways, it's certainly worth considering.

ORIENTATION

Cancún's Zona Hotelera lies on a narrow white-sand island in the shape of a number 7. The 7's short upper arm leads directly into downtown Cancún, while the longer one (13 kilometers/8 miles) connects to the mainland near the airport. The elbow of the 7 is Punta Cancún—this is the fast-beating heart of the Zona Hotelera's nightlife, including all the major nightclubs, plus several resorts, hotels, restaurants, and shopping malls. The rest of the resorts and several more malls, restaurants, and water sports agencies are spread along the two arms, especially the

southern one. The far southern tip of the 7 is called Punta Nizuc and has a few hotels, plus Cancún's largest archaeological site (El Rey). Busy Boulevard Kukulcán runs the entire length of the 7, and most addresses in the Zona Hotelera are simply a kilometer marker. Finally, the huge lagoon that's enclosed by the mainland and the Zona Hotelera is called Laguna Nichupté, and is a popular spot for fishing, waterskiing, and boating.

Downtown Cancún is on the mainland and is divided into numbered *super manzanas* (square blocks, or SM for short). Avenida Tulum is downtown's main thoroughfare; west of Avenida Tulum is Parque Las Palapas (downtown's central plaza), and beyond that Avenida Yaxchilán. East of Avenida Tulum is Avenida Nader. Most of downtown Cancún's hotels, restaurants, and music venues are on or around Parque Las Palapas, Avenida Yaxchilán, and Avenida Nader, primarily in SMs 22-25.

Isla Blanca is a thin peninsula just north of downtown Cancún. It's bordered by the white-sand beaches of the Caribbean on one side, and the huge saltwater Chacmochuch Lagoon on the other. It's virtually uninhabited, limited to a handful of private homes—both Maya huts and modern behemoths—plus a kiteboarding school and a rustic beach club. There's only one road on the peninsula; it begins as a paved street just north of the Isla Mujeres ferry terminals and quickly becomes a rutted sand road that leads almost to the very tip of the peninsula.

Sights

ARCHAEOLOGICAL ZONES

Cancún has three notable archaeological sites, two in the Zona Hotelera and a third north of town on Isla Blanca, near the Isla Mujeres ferry. None compare in size or wow factor to the Yucatán Peninsula's major sites, but they are still worth visiting, and the Zona Hotelera ones can be easily combined with a day at the beach.

El Rey Archaeological Zone

At the southern end of the Zona Hotelera, across from Playa Delfines, **Ruínas El Rey** (Blvd. Kukulcán Km 17.5, 8am-5pm daily, US$2.75) consists of several platforms, two plazas, and a small temple and pyramid, all arranged along an ancient 500-meter (1,640-foot) roadway. The ruins get their name (Ruins of the King) from a skeleton found during excavation and believed to be that of, well, a king. The ruins date from the late Postclassic period (AD 1200-1400); there's limited signage, though it is available in English and Spanish. El Rey also is home to hundreds of iguanas, some quite beefy, which makes a visit here all the more interesting. Last visitors are admitted at 4:30pm.

Yamil Lu'um Archaeological Zone

Lodged between the Park Royal Cancún and the Westin Lagunamar Ocean Resort, **Yamil Lu'um** (Blvd. Kukulcán Km 12.5, 8am-5pm daily, free) consists of two small temples built between AD 1200 and 1550: **Templo del Alacrán** (Temple of the Scorpion) and **Templo de la Huella** (Temple of the Handprint); unfortunately, neither the scorpion nor the handprint that gave the temples their names is visible anymore. The temples were built on Cancún's highest point, suggesting they were used as watchtowers or navigational aids. The ruins can be reached through the Park Royal (nonguests may need to ask permission) and are visible from the beach at Playa Marlin.

El Meco Archaeological Zone

Archaeologists think **El Meco** (Av. López Portillo s/n, 8am-5pm daily, US$2.75) was a major gateway to and from Isla Mujeres—fitting considering it's located just north of the modern-day ferry terminal at Puerto Juárez. The ancient city started out as a fishing village in AD 300 but grew to be a thriving port town, building the tallest pyramid along this part of the coast before collapsing abruptly around AD 600. It was reoccupied four or five centuries later, probably as an outpost for the powerful Chichén Itzá kingdom, before being abandoned in the 16th century. The site is smaller than El Rey but the structures are more substantial.

San Miguelito Archaeological Zone

Located on the grounds of the Museo Maya de Cancún, **San Miguelito** (Blvd. Kukulcán Km 16.5, tel. 998/885-3842, 9am-6pm Tues.-Sun., free with museum admission fee) was one of several Maya communities that occupied the present-day Zona Hotelera during the late Postclassic period around AD 1200 until the arrival of European explorers in the late 1500s. San Miguelito was apparently quite populous, though relatively few structures remain today—most were built of wood and palm and have long since disappeared. Most coastal Maya cities depended on fishing and maritime trade, and domination of the region likely shifted among them over the centuries. At that time, the long coastal island was covered in high sand dunes and dense mangrove forests, which served as a barrier against hurricanes and erosion. That natural protection has been mostly destroyed with the construction of Cancún's hotel

El Rey Archaeological Zone

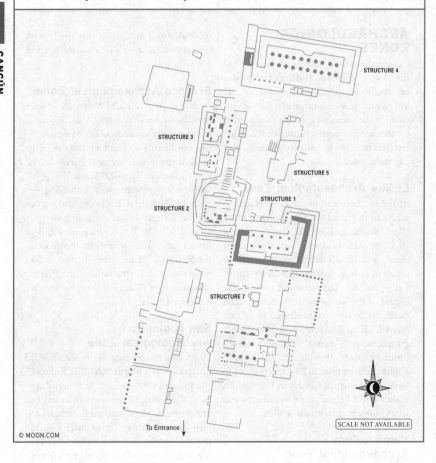

STRUCTURE 4

STRUCTURE 3

STRUCTURE 5

STRUCTURE 1

STRUCTURE 2

STRUCTURE 7

To Entrance ↓

SCALE NOT AVAILABLE

© MOON.COM

"strip," the effects of which are only now becoming clear.

MUSEUMS
Museo Maya de Cancún

Housed in a stark white modern building, **Museo Maya de Cancún** (Blvd. Kukulcán Km 16.5, tel. 998/885-3843, www.inah.gob. mx, 9am-6pm Tues.-Sun., US$3.50 including museum and archaeological site) has hundreds of Maya artifacts in bright, airy display rooms; vases, bowls, and masks figure prominently. Two permanent exhibition rooms are dedicated to finds from Quintana Roo and the greater Maya world, respectively, while a third room hosts temporary exhibits. Introductory signage is in Spanish and English, though many individual displays lack English translations. The San Miguelito archaeological site is also on the grounds. The entrance fee includes admission to the ruins, though the site itself closes at 4:30pm daily.

PARQUE LAS PALAPAS

Parque Las Palapas is a typical Mexican plaza, where locals congregate most nights

Beach Access

Look for these signs in the Zona Hotelera for public access to the beach.

There's a notion that high-rise hotels have monopolized Cancún's best beaches, but this is only partly true. While most hotels *do* front prime real estate, all beach areas in Mexico are public (except for military zones). Hotels cannot, by law, prohibit you or anyone else from lying on a towel and enjoying the sun and water. Many high-end hotels subvert this by making it difficult or uncomfortable for nonguests to use "their" beaches: Very few maintain exterior paths, and others spread guest-only beach chairs over the best parts. (In the hotels' defense, they also typically do a good job of keeping their areas clear of trash and seaweed, which can mar otherwise beautiful beaches.) If your hotel has a nice beach area, you're all set. If not, typically you can just walk through a hotel lobby to the beach—as a foreigner, you are very unlikely to be stopped. (Sadly, locals are likely to be nabbed if they do the same thing.) But even that is unnecessary: Cancún maintains several public access points marked with prominent blue and white signs along Boulevard Kukulcán. The area right around the access point is often crowded, but you can walk a couple hundred meters in either direction to have more breathing room. One public access point—Playa Delfines, at the southern end of the hotel zone—has no nearby hotels and is used by a refreshing mix of Mexican and foreign beachgoers.

and tourists have a chance to enjoy Cancún's quotidian side. The plaza doesn't have the grand cathedral and government buildings found in Mexico's older colonial cities—remember, Cancún isn't even 50 years old—but it's still a place for adults to chat with friends, for teenagers and couples to circle about, and for youngsters to chase balls and ride electric cars in the spacious central square. Dozens of stands and street carts sell *helado* (ice cream), *churros* (strips of fried dough sprinkled with sugar), *elote* (corn on the cob served with chile and mayo), and knickknacks of all sorts. The music and neon lights can be a bit much for some, but just as often there's an interesting performance in the plaza's huge *palapa*-roofed stage, whether live music or traditional dance. Along the edges of the main park are smaller squares, some used for art expositions, others favored by young bohos for plucking guitars and engaging in the occasional drum circle.

Zona Hotelera

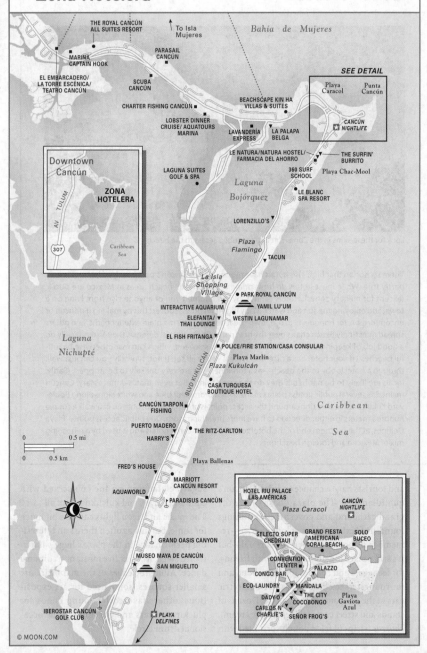

THE ROYAL CANCÚN
ALL SUITES RESORT

↑ To Isla
Mujeres

Bahía de Mujeres

MARINA
CAPTAIN HOOK

PARASAIL
CANCÚN

SEE DETAIL

EL EMBARCADERO/
LA TORRE ESCÉNICA/
TEATRO CANCÚN

SCUBA
CANCÚN

Playa
Caracol

Punta
Cancún

CHARTER FISHING CANCÚN

BEACHSCAPE KIN HA
VILLAS & SUITES

CANCÚN
NIGHTLIFE

LOBSTER DINNER
CRUISE/ AQUATOURS
MARINA

LAVANDERÍA
EXPRESS

LA PALAPA
BELGA

LE NATURA/NATURA HOSTEL/
FARMACIA DEL AHORRO

THE SURFIN'
BURRITO

Downtown
Cancún

ZONA
HOTELERA

LAGUNA SUITES
GOLF & SPA

360 SURF
SCHOOL

Playa Chac-Mool

*Laguna
Bojórquez*

LE BLANC
SPA RESORT

AV TULUM

307

*Caribbean
Sea*

LORENZILLO'S

*Plaza
Flamingo*

TACUN

*Le Isla
Shopping
Village*

PARK ROYAL CANCÚN

INTERACTIVE AQUARIUM

YAMIL LU'UM

ELEFANTA/
THAI LOUNGE

WESTIN LAGUNAMAR

EL FISH FRITANGA

*Laguna
Nichupté*

POLICE/FIRE STATION/CASA CONSULAR

Playa Marlín

Plaza Kukulcán

BLVD KUKULCÁN

CASA TURQUESA
BOUTIQUE HOTEL

Caribbean

CANCÚN TARPON
FISHING

Sea

PUERTO MADERO

HARRY'S

THE RITZ-CARLTON

0   0.5 mi

0   0.5 km

FRED'S HOUSE

Playa Ballenas

MARRIOTT
CANCUN RESORT

AQUAWORLD

PARADISUS CANCÚN

HOTEL RIU PALACE
LAS AMÉRICAS

Plaza Caracol

CANCÚN
NIGHTLIFE

GRAND OASIS CANYON

SELECTO SÚPER
CHEDRAUI

GRAND FIESTA
AMERICANA
CORAL BEACH

SOLO
BUCEO

MUSEO MAYA DE CANCÚN

SAN MIGUELITO

CONVENTION
CENTER

PALAZZO

CONGO BAR

ECO-LAUNDRY

MANDALA

DADY O

THE CITY
COCOBONGO

*Playa
Gaviota
Azul*

IBEROSTAR CANCÚN
GOLF CLUB

PLAYA
DELFINES

CARLOS N'
CHARLIE'S

SEÑOR FROG'S

© MOON.COM

Beaches

ZONA HOTELERA

The beaches in Cancún are among the most spectacular in the world. Looking at online images, it's easy to think they're digitally enhanced—the sand couldn't be *so* white, or the sea *so* turquoise blue. But a combination of clear Caribbean water, a shallow, sandy seafloor, and a high bright sun makes for a gorgeous sight. At high noon, even picture-perfect webpages don't compare to the living picture show that is Cancún's coastline.

Be aware that the surf along the Zona Hotelera's long, east-facing arm, though beautiful, can be heavy, and drownings and near-drownings do occur. There are lifeguards near all public access points, and colored flags (Green is Safe, Yellow is Caution, Red is Closed) for reference. But nothing is more important than common sense: Don't swim if the conditions (or your own condition) aren't suitable. The beaches along the short, north-facing leg are much calmer. For really calm waters head to Isla Mujeres, where there are no waves and the water in places is only waist deep more than 75 meters (250 feet)

from shore. The Laguna Nichupté is not recommended for swimming because of pollution and crocodiles.

Playa Caracol

Playa Caracol (Blvd. Kukulcán Km 8.5) has a small stretch of beach right at the public access point, but it's not too pleasant and often very crowded. The beach is much better just east of there, in front of the Fiesta Americana Coral Beach, but you have to cut through the hotel to get there, and the hotel lounge chairs take up most of the beach.

Playa Gaviota Azul

The pathway to **Playa Gaviota Azul** (Blvd. Kukulcán Km 10), a huge, beautiful beach, is between the City nightclub and Forum by the Sea mall, and it extends well north and south of there (merging with Playa Chac Mool just to the south) with plenty of room to set up a towel and umbrella. Parking can be tricky here—better to arrive by bus or taxi—but you've got plenty of eating and shopping options, if you need a break from

Playa Delfines

the sun. If you're interested in a beach club, **Mandala Beach** (Blvd. Kukulcán Km 8.5, tel. 998/883-3333, www.mandalabeach.com, 10am-6pm daily, US$40 pp) is open to the public and has beach beds, a swimming pool, full bar and restaurant service, and a DJ. It can be a scene, but that's pretty much the point. Adults only.

Playa Marlín

Playa Marlín (Blvd. Kukulcán Km 12.5) is a clean, attractive beach with an access point between Plaza Kukulcán mall and the police and fire station. There's plenty of parking on the road parallel to the beach, and the mall has restaurants just a few steps away.

Playa Ballenas

Playa Ballenas (Blvd. Kukulcán Km 14.5) is a long, pretty beach, with an access path between the Hard Rock and Secrets The Vine resorts. There is no food or drink service on the beach, but look for a few small shops selling water and snacks on the frontage road rear the public access point.

★ Playa Delfines

Located at the far southern end of the Zona Hotelera, **Playa Delfines** (Blvd. Kukulcán Km 17.5) is at the bottom of a bluff, so you can't see it from the road. But once parked, or off the bus (there is a stop directly in front), you're treated to a panoramic view of the beach and ocean, unobstructed by hotels. There are rows of fixed *palapa* umbrellas and plenty of open sand if you brought your own.

Perhaps best of all is the mix of people you'll find here: independent travelers, local families, even some surfers if the swell is high. (Take care swimming here, as the waves and tide can be strong.) The beach is across the road from the El Rey ruins, which makes a nice side trip. There is no food or drink service, but there are restrooms and outdoor showers on-site.

ISLA BLANCA BEACHES

Isla Blanca's white-sand beaches are wild and mostly untouched—all to say, perfect! Accessing them, though, can be a bit tricky. Though the land between the road and the beach is virtually undeveloped, it is almost entirely privately owned and fenced off. There are occasional breaks between fences, but fortunately a great beach club makes hunting down those openings unnecessary.

Isla Blanca Cabañas (formerly Pirata Morgan, Carr. Cancún-Isla Blanca Km 9, tel. 998/112-1227, dariorock2004@gmail. com, 9am-5pm daily, US$2) is an old-school beach club with a handful of small *palapas* on the beach, a rustic restaurant serving up fresh fish and cold beers, and miles and miles of beach. If you can't tear yourself away from the beach at the end of the day, there are basic *cabañas* (US$50 s/d) where you can spend the night. Each has screen walls to let in the sea breeze at night, cement floors, and private bathrooms; electricity is available 6pm-11pm only. A cab ride from downtown Cancún runs around US$14 each way.

Entertainment and Events

Cancún is justly famous for its raucous nightclubs, pulsing with lights and music and packed with revelers of all ages every night of the week. The club scene is especially manic during spring break, July, August, Christmas, and New Year's, but you can count on finding a party no matter when you visit. And those with quieter tastes will be happy to learn there's more to Cancún's nightlife than clubs, including a nice mix of lounge bars, theaters, and cinemas.

Authentic Cancún

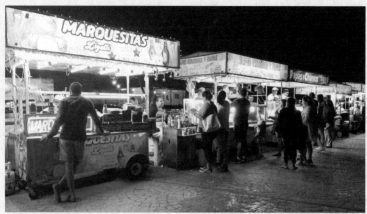

Food carts are perfect for a late-night snack in Parque Las Palapas.

It's easy to assume that Cancún, with its high-rise resorts and spring break ethos, has little to offer in the way of "authentic" culture. In fact, it's a rich and bustling Mexican city like any other, with plenty of culturally rich outings for those interested in finding them. Here are a few leads for having a locals' experience in Cancún:

- Spend an evening at **Parque Las Palapas,** Cancún's central plaza, where locals go for live music, a place for kids to romp around, and food carts galore. Try *elote*—a corn cob on a stick, slathered with butter or mayo, parmesan cheese, and chili powder (page 44).

- **Plaza de Toros,** Cancún's bullring, does have occasional bullfights—but it's better known as a nightspot. Grab some beers and snacks while taking in the scene in the many surrounding watering holes (page 52).

- Every city has an area that suddenly "pops"; in Cancún, that's **Avenida Nader,** with a crop of new bars and restaurants serving up creative drinks, high-end meals, and a hipster vibe (page 61).

- Nothing is more Mexican than shopping for produce at a local market. Head to **Mercado 23** to be wowed by the array of tropical fruits and vegetables, and to enjoy the sounds, smells, and bustle of a working market (page 64).

- Movies are a favorite outing for many Mexicans, including midweek. Treat yourself to a cushy reclining chair, waiter service, even a glass of wine at one of Cancún's **Cinépolis VIP theater** (by the way, popcorn in Spanish is *palomitas*) (page 53).

- Catch a show at **Teatro Cancún,** which brings live acts from around the country, from music and dance to comedy and theater (page 53).

★ NIGHTLIFE

Cancún's most popular nightclubs are within walking distance of each other in the **Zona Hotelera,** at Punta Cancún. Downtown, meanwhile, has some great cocktail bars and nightclubs specializing in Latin music.

Cuncrawl (Mex. cell tel. 984/165-0699, toll-free U.S. tel. 800/975-4349, www.cuncrawl.com, US$80 pp) does fun guided bar/club crawls in the heart of Cancún's Zona Hotelera, hitting three different clubs (they vary by night) with VIP entrance and seating, unlimited drinks, and bottle service, over the course of five hours.

Nightclubs
ZONA HOTELERA

Nightclubs in the Zona Hotelera charge US$60-80 admission with open bar included. Most clubs are open every day, from around 10pm until 4am or later. Special events, like ladies night or bikini parties, vary by the day, club, and season; check the clubs' websites or Facebook pages for the latest info and deals. Discounted tickets also are occasionally sold at concierge desks.

CocoBongo (Blvd. Kukulcán Km 9.5, tel. 998/883-2373, toll-free Mex. tel. 800/841-4636, www.cocobongo.com) is a spectacular club featuring live rock and salsa bands, flying acrobats, and impersonators ranging from Beetlejuice to Freddy Mercury. For dancing, hit the main floor; for free-flowing drinks, reserve a seat in the VIP section.

The City (Blvd. Kukulcán Km 9, tel. 998/883-3313, www.mandalatickets.com) is a megaclub with three levels and a total capacity of 6,000 (and allegedly the world's biggest disco ball). Be sure to take a whirl on the movable dance floor, which descends from the 3rd floor to the center of the club below. Open Friday only.

Palazzo (Blvd. Kukulcán Km 9, tel. 998/848-8380, www.mandalatickets.com) books big-name DJs and draws raucous crowds. The interior has a sleek Vegas-like look, huge chandeliers, and a VIP section. Open Wednesday and Saturday only.

Mandala (Blvd. Kukulcán Km 9, tel. 998/883-3333, www.mandalanightclub.com) is an upscale club with indoor and outdoor areas for partying. There's plenty of VIP seating in case you want to splurge on a private table (and better service).

Dady-O (Blvd. Kukulcán Km 9.5, tel. 998/883-3333, http://dadyocancun.com) is,

For clubs and nightlife, you've come to the right place.

Downtown Cancún

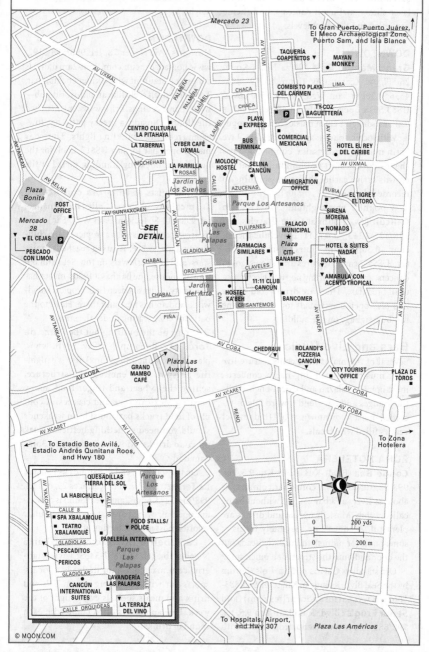

© MOON.COM

well, the daddy of Cancún's nightclubs, with seven different "environments," including laser shows, swimsuit contests, and theme parties on five different levels.

DOWNTOWN

Grand Mambo Café (Plaza Hong Kong, 2nd Fl., Av. Xcaret at Av. Tulum, tel. 998/884-4536, 9:30pm-3am Wed.-Sat., US$10 cover, US$3.50-8 open bar, free before 11pm) is Cancún's biggest Latin music club, and popular with locals, tourists, and expats alike. Live Latin music—mostly salsa, cumbia, and bachata—doesn't start until midnight, but the crowds arrive earlier than that, spinning to recorded rhythms.

A popular gay nightclub, **11:11 Club Cancún** (Av. Tulum at Calle Claveles, tel. 998/135-2243, www.1111gayclubcancun.com, 10:30pm-6am Thurs., 9pm-6am Fri.-Sat., US$5-7 cover) features drag shows, go-go dancers, and DJs spinning pop and electronica until breakfast. There are drinks sold by the liter plus open bar specials too. Look for the rainbow signage on the building.

Bars and Live Music

Several of the major nightclubs feature live rock music and even big-name concerts, most notably Palazzo and CocoBongo, while the lounges and bars tend toward DJs or recorded music. Downtown, you'll find smaller venues filled with locals.

ZONA HOTELERA

Congo Bar (Blvd. Kukulcán Km 9.5, tel. 998/883-0563, www.congobar.com.mx) is about as lively as a bar can get without being called a club. Music is upbeat and drinks are plentiful. A conga line inevitably forms at some point (or points) and usually heads out the door and onto the street for a quick spin.

Old standbys **Carlos n' Charlie's** (Forum by the Sea, Blvd. Kukulcán Km 9, tel. 998/883-1862, www.carlosandcharlies.com) and **Señor Frog's** (Blvd. Kukulcán Km 9.5, tel. 998/883-5644, www.senorfrogs.com) both

open at noon for meals and stay open until 3am for drinking, dancing, and general mayhem.

DOWNTOWN

Nomads (Av. Nader 78, tel. 998/898-3192, www.nomadscancun.com, 3pm-2am daily) is a hipster restaurant with a killer cocktail bar. The place itself feels like an old-world pub—wood-panel ceilings, brick walls, mismatched tile floors. Outside, a breezy patio has towering trees and twinkling lights. Thursday means open bar for just US$17. Look for the huge black duckling standing guard at the entrance.

Mixologists at **Amarula con Acento Tropical** (Av. Nader at Calle Huachinango, tel. 998/884-8046, 9pm-3am Wed.-Sat.) serve up strong cocktails with a tropical flair: chili-rimmed glassware, floating seashells, anise stars, and bright flowers on top. Set in an old Cancún house, the bar has a 1920s-meets-hacienda style with art deco flair, tropical woodwork, and arches here and there. Head to the patio for cozy seating under the stars.

It may be the bullring but the **Plaza de Toros** (Av. Bonampak at Av. Sayil, www.plazadetoroscancun.com.mx) also is a nightlife hotspot. Bars encircle the structure, selling cheap beer and finger food, many blasting Mexican rock and classics. A couple of food trucks park outside on weekends should you need something heftier to soak up your drinks. Most bars are open 3pm-3am daily.

On the southern end of Parque Las Palapas, **La Terraza del Vino** (Alcatraces 29, cell tel. 998/166-7273, 6pm-2am Tues.-Sun.) is a pleasant open-air wine bar that books live guitar soloists most nights starting at 9pm.

La Taberna (Av. Yaxchilán at Punta Nicchehabi, tel. 998/887-5433, www.lataberna.com.mx, 2pm-4am daily) is a locals' sports bar with lots of big-screen TVs and drink and meals specials every night of the week. Free appetizers often come with each round of drinks.

portrait artist at the artisanal market Manos Mágicas

THE ARTS
Theater

Teatro Cancún (El Embarcadero, Blvd. Kukulcán Km 4, tel. 998/849-5580, www.teatrodecancun.com.mx, ticket office on ground level 9am-9pm Mon.-Sat.) stages shows of all sorts, from music and dance to comedy and theater, both amateur and professional, mostly in Spanish. Ticket prices vary, but typically run US$5-30.

Teatro Xbalamqué (Hotel Xbalamqué, Av. Yaxchilán 31, www.teatroxbalamque.com, tel. 998/204-1028) stages experimental and one-act theater performances in a small space inside the hotel of the same name. Most shows are in Spanish; check the theater's website for showtimes. Tickets are typically US$5-10.

Cinema

Cancún has three convenient movieplexes, two in the Zona Hotelera and one downtown, both offering the latest American and Mexican releases. Most Hollywood movies are subtitled, but be aware that those made for kids, and even teenagers, are likely to be dubbed. Look for "DOB" (for *doblado,* or "dubbed") or "SUB" for (*subtitulada,* or "subtitled") to be sure. Ticket prices average around US$3.50, and US$5 for IMAX screenings; early shows may be discounted, and there's two-for-one Tuesday at the Cinemex.

In the Zona Hotelera, look for **Cinemex** at La Isla Shopping Village (Blvd. Kukulcán Km 12.5, 999/242-2126, www.cinemex.com), as well as **Cinépolis IMAX** at Puerto Cancún (Blvd. Kukulcán Km 1, 552/122-6060, www.cinepolis.com), the latter the only movie theater with IMAX screenings.

Downtown, there's a **Cinépolis** at Plaza Las Américas (Av. Tulum at Av. Sayil, tel. 998/884-0403, www.cinepolis.com). At the same location, there's also a **Cinépolis VIP**—a real treat—with reclining leather seats and wait service, plus a menu including sushi, baguette sandwiches, cappuccinos, and cocktails. Tickets are sold at a separate window, and cost around US$7.

FESTIVALS AND EVENTS

Taking place the last Saturday and Sunday of each month, **Manos Mágicas** (literally, magic hands) is an artisanal market held in the Jardín del Arte (across from Oasis Palm Hotel, Blvd. Kukulcán Km 4.5, 4pm-10pm). Dozens of local artisans showcase their textiles, paintings, jewelry, and more alongside organic foods and treats. At 6pm, live music and ballet *folklórico* (traditional Mexican folk dancing) are featured on a stage set up at the far end of the park.

Puerto Vallarta and Acapulco have long been Mexico's top destinations for gay travelers, but organizers of the **Cancún International Gay Festival** are working to put Cancún on the list. Inaugurated in 1995 and typically held in May, the festival includes beach parties, sunset cruises, city tours, and more.

The **Concurso Municipal de**

Artesanías, a citywide handicraft competition, is held every August in Cancún's Palacio Municipal. In addition to showcasing the city's best artisans, participants also sell their work. Look for the large white tents—and the crowds—on Avenida Tulum.

Shopping

Cancún has six major malls, a handful of open-air markets, and hundreds of independent shops, so you can buy just about anything. Most mall and independent shops accept credit cards, but plan on paying cash at the markets.

OPEN-AIR MARKETS

Mercado 28 (Av. Sunyaxchen at Av. Xel-Há, 8am-8pm daily) is a large open-air market featuring a wide variety of Mexican handicrafts: ceramics from Tonalá, silver from Taxco, hammocks from Mérida, *alebrijes* (wooden creatures) from Oaxaca, and handwoven shirts from Chiapas. You'll also find a fair share of T-shirts, key chains, coconut monkeys, and the like. A handful of restaurants in the center of the market offer traditional Mexican fare.

Adjacent to Mercado 28, Plaza Bonita (Av. Sunyaxchen at Av. Xel-Há, 9am-8pm daily) is a multilevel shopping center built to look like a colonial village—bright courtyards, fountains, greenery, and all. Folk art here is a bit more expensive than that in the market next door, but the quality is usually better.

On weekend evenings, stroll through Parque Las Palapas and Parque Los Artesanos, both great spots to pick up local handicrafts, Chiapanecan clothing, bohemian jewelry, and art.

MALLS

The Puerto Cancún Marina Town Center (Blvd. Kukulcán Km 1, 10am-10pm daily) is the newest and swankiest of the area malls. Modern and sleek, the open-air facility is home to high-end boutiques, international chain stores, and Cancun's only IMAX theater. Though it's just a two-minute walk along a landscaped walkway, a shuttle takes mall-goers to and from the main drag.

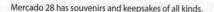
Mercado 28 has souvenirs and keepsakes of all kinds.

Black Coral: A Disappearing Treasure

Despite its name, living black coral is not black at all, but a rich blue-green. It's only when the shell is stripped and the skeleton polished that the namesake color emerges. Black coral belongs to a family of coral whose shells are semiflexible, and colonies grow into beautiful tree-like formations that bend and sway in ocean currents. It's the world's slowest-growing coral, adding just 1-2 *hundredths of a millimeter* per year. (That's 200 times slower than human fingernails.) Black coral is among a handful of coral species discovered at extreme depths—300 meters (984 feet) down, and more—far deeper than previously thought possible for coral. And perhaps most remarkable of all was the finding, in 2009, that a colony of black coral near Hawaii is over 4,000 years old, making it the oldest known marine organism. Vast colonies of black coral once populated Cozumel's waters, and the island was for many years the center of black coral collection and trade. That's less true today, thanks partly to stricter regulation but also to the fact that the island's black coral is so diminished that the species is becoming endangered. Still, black coral retains a certain cachet, and its collection continues. Buying jewelry, souvenirs, and other items made with it only supports its demise—please resist!

Plaza Caracol (Blvd. Kukulcán Km 8.5, 8am-9pm daily) is the best place in the Zona Hotelera to get beach essentials, with good brands and decent prices on bathing suits, flip-flops, sunglasses, sunscreen, and more. You can also grab a cup of Starbucks and good cheap grub at several small eateries.

Forum by the Sea (Blvd. Kukulcán Km 9, 10am-11:30pm daily) is a horseshoe-shaped mall with three floors opening onto the airy main lobby. It's home to Hard Rock Cafe—you can't miss the huge guitar out front—a good steak house, and various kitschy shops selling all manner of tourist souvenirs. The 3rd floor was under renovation when we passed through but has a balcony with a spectacular view of the beach and ocean, which is great for photo ops.

An open-air mall, **La Isla Shopping Village** (Blvd. Kukulcán Km 12.5, www. laislacancun.com.mx, 10am-10pm daily) is set around an artificial river, with wide shady passageways, a variety of international chain stores, and a food court featuring crepes, tacos, Italian, and more. The mall opens onto the lagoon, where there's a small marina and a nice boardwalk with half a dozen sit-down restaurants and a couple of water sports kiosks. A newer section called Fashion Harbour houses various luxury shops. La Isla is also home to the popular Interactive Aquarium and has a five-screen movie theater.

Plaza Kukulcán (Blvd. Kukulcán Km 13, 10am-10pm daily) is an everyday mall with knickknack shops and teen clothing stores, though it boasts a swanky section called Luxury Avenue selling fine watches, jewelry, and couture clothing. There's also a full-on grocery store on the 2nd floor, which is especially convenient to visitors staying on the south end of the Zona Hotelera.

You don't have to go to the Zona Hotelera for your mall fix. **Plaza Las Américas** (Av. Tulum at Av. Sayil, 9am-10pm daily) stretches almost a block and includes dozens of mid- to upscale shops, an arcade, and two movie theaters.

Sports and Recreation

While relaxing by the pool or on the beach is more than enough sports and recreation for many of Cancún's visitors—and who can blame them?—there *are* a number of options for those looking for a bit more action. From golf and fishing to scuba diving and kiteboarding (and a whole bunch of things in between), Cancún has something for everyone.

BEACH ACTIVITIES

Parasailing (*paracaídas* in Spanish) can be booked as a traditional one-person ride (with takeoff from the shore) or a two-person ride, in which you can take off from the boat or the water. Prices and duration are fairly uniform: US$55-60 per person for a 10-12-minute ride. Look for independent operators on the beach, especially on Playa Tortugas (Blvd. Kukulcán Km 6.5), Playa Chac-Mool (Blvd. Kukulcán Km 10), Playa Ballenas (Blvd. Kukulcán Km 14.5), and Playa Delfines (Blvd. Kukulcán Km 17.5). Or sign up at **Parasail Cancún** (Playa Tortugas, Blvd. Kukulcán Km 6.5, toll-free Mex. tel. 800/220-5681, toll-free U.S./Can. tel. 800/247-1641, www.parasailcancun.com,

8am-8pm Mon.-Fri., 8am-4pm Sat.-Sun.) or **Aquaworld** (Blvd. Kukulcán Km 15.2, tel. 998/689-1013, www.aquaworld.com.mx, 7am-8pm daily).

WaveRunners are rented on the same beaches where parasailing is pitched. Prices average US$45-55 for 30 minutes; one or two people can ride at a time.

SNORKELING AND SCUBA DIVING

Cancún doesn't compare to Cozumel, Isla Mujeres, or really anywhere along the Riviera Maya for snorkeling and diving. Its coral and other sealife are less plentiful and far less healthy. That said, if you enjoy modern art, an underwater sculpture museum provides a special treat. Or consider arranging a snorkeling or diving trip in a cenote, the otherworldly freshwater caves that dot the coast south of Cancún. If you're really hankering for some bubbly, we recommend booking a trip with a shop in Isla Mujeres or Puerto Morelos, both easy to reach from Cancún. (Cozumel is harder to do as a day

Small kiosks along the beach offer parasailing and other activities.

trip, requiring a trip to Playa del Carmen and a ferry ride to Cozumel from there…and back again.)

Snorkeling

For the best open-water and cenote snorkeling, book a trip with one of the dive shops listed below. All offer guided snorkeling trips in addition to diving, and are invariably better than the "jungle trips" hawked around Cancún, even for beginners.

TOP EXPERIENCE

★ MUSEO SUBACUÁTICO DE ARTE (MUSA)

Two popular snorkeling sites are Cancún's Nizuc and Punta Sam reefs, where installations of the **Subaquatic Museum of Art** (MUSA, 998/206-0182, www.musacancun. org) are located. Created by six artists, the sites contain more than 500 life-sized statues of everyday people, from nuns to tribal leaders. Breathtaking exhibits in and of themselves, the works were created from a special cement that promotes coral and sealife formation. A third MUSA installation is located near Isla Mujeres, at Manchones reef, which is best for divers.

Scuba Diving

A number of shops offer fun dives as well as certification courses at all levels. Hotels with their own dive shop may offer special rates to guests, but not necessarily.

Solo Buceo (Hyatt Ziva Cancún Hotel, Blvd. Kukulcán s/n, tel. 998/260-4995, toll-free U.S./Can. tel. 800/348-3639, www.solobuceo.com, 9am-4:30pm daily) is a friendly shop with a strong reputation for service. Two-tank reef dives run US$90, while two-tank cenote trips cost US$195, including lunch; prices include all gear including wetsuit. Open-water certification classes (US$420, 3-4 days) can also be arranged.

Scuba Cancún (Blvd. Kukulcán Km 5, tel. 998/849-7508, www.scubacancun.com. mx, 7am-8pm daily) was founded in 1980 and is still run by the same family. It offers the standard selection of dives, including one-tank (US$62), two-tank (US$77), and two-tank cavern and Cozumel dives (US$165 and US$180, respectively); all prices include equipment except wetsuit (US$10, recommended for cavern trips). Snorkel trips are offered in Cancún (US$39), Cozumel (US$125), and nearby cenotes (US$92). Trips can sometimes get crowded—ask about the size of your group before you book.

parasailing off the beach

Aquaworld (Blvd. Kukulcán Km 15.2, tel. 998/689-1013, www.aquaworld.com.mx, 7am-8pm daily) is Cancún's biggest, most commercialized water sports outfit, of which scuba diving is only a small part. Come here if you're looking for activities for the whole family, divers and nondivers alike, all in one spot. Otherwise, head to smaller shops for more personalized attention.

KITEBOARDING

Ikarus (tel. 998/874-4246, www.kiteboard-mexico.com) is a full-service kiteboarding school on the lagoon side of Isla Blanca, just north of Cancún. Conditions for learning to kiteboard don't get much better than this: steady wind, kilometers of flat water with few boats or other obstacles, and water never more than waist deep. Private classes are US$80-95 per hour, while groups are US$65 per hour per person (3 hours, maximum 3 people). Equipment is included for students or can be rented separately (US$50-75 for two hours). Classes are held November-May, when the conditions are best. Simple lodging also is offered (US$7-8 pp hammock, US$7-15 pp tent, $25 pp tent with bed, US$75 s/d). There's a restaurant and free Wi-Fi too.

WATERSKIING, WAKEBOARDING, SURFING, AND SUP

Waterski Cancún and Wakeboard (Marina Manglar, Blvd. Kukulcán Km 19.8, cell tel. 998/874-4816, www.waterskicancun.com, by appointment only) has three slalom courses and a number of ski sites at the southern end of Laguna Nichupté. Free-skiing and wakeboarding costs US$200 per hour, while the slalom courses are US$60 for 15 minutes. All equipment is included, except carbon skis.

360 Surf School (Blvd. Kukulcán Km 9.8, cell tel. 998/241-6443, www.360surfschoolcancun.com, by appointment only) offers popular surfboarding classes on Playa Chac-Mool. Classes are geared toward beginners but can be tailored to any level. One-on-one classes run US$140 for 90 minutes; group lessons cost US$100 per person for 120 minutes (3 people maximum). Family packages and multiday packages also are offered. Surfing classes include surf equipment, Lycra tops, drinking water, and use of surfboard after the lesson. Private stand-up paddleboard (SUP) classes also are offered for US$140 or US$75-100 per person (2-8 students); each class is about two hours. Equipment rentals—bodyboards, short boards, longboards, fun boards, and paddleboards—also are available (US$15-65 per 24 hours). Look for the informational kiosk on the main drag, next to the Surfin' Burrito.

FISHING

More than a dozen species of sport fish ply the waters off Cancún, including blue and white marlin, blackfin tuna, barracuda, dolphin dorado, wahoo, grouper, and more. For those more interested in fly-fishing and light-tackle tours, there's no need to look past the Zona Hotelera's lagoon, which is home to tarpon, snook, snapper, barracuda, and jack.

Charter Fishing Cancún (Blvd. Kukulcán Km 6.5, cell tel. 998/200-3240, www.charterfishingcancun.com, by appointment only) offers excellent customer service on its small fleet of boats. Private charters range US$530-950 (4-8 hours); "shared" trips cost US$135-155 per person (4-6 hours). All trips include bait, tackle, ice, drinks (beer, soda, and water), and fishing licenses. Round-trip transportation to/from your hotel—anywhere between Cancún and Playa del Carmen—is included for private charters only.

Cancún Tarpon Fishing (Blvd. Kukulcán Km 13.5, cell tel. 998/126-6640, toll-free U.S./Can. tel. 866/607-2246, www.cancuntarponfishing.com, by appointment only) specializes in fly-fishing and light-tackle tours, all in the Zona Hotelera's lagoon, Laguna Nichupté, and just north near Isla Blanca. Trips are geared for one to two people and last anywhere from four to six hours. They include an experienced guide, equipment, box lunch, and soft drinks. Service is top-notch.

SWIMMING WITH DOLPHINS

Located within Ventura Park, **Dolphinaris Cancún** (Blvd. Kukulcán Km 25, tel. 998/881-3030, toll-free U.S. tel. 855/203-9863, www. dolphinaris.com) offers dolphin interaction programs that include "fin shaking" and receiving a "kiss" (US$99, 1 hour), as well as swimming with and getting a foot push from them (US$149, 1 hour). For those toying with the idea of working with dolphins, visitors also can help out as Trainers for the Day (US$199, 8 hours). Free shuttle transportation is provided within the Zona Hotelera.

Interactive Aquarium (La Isla Shopping Village, Blvd. Kukulcán Km 12.5, tel. 998/206-3311, www.interactiveaquariumcancun.com, 9am-8pm daily, US$15) has a modest number of tanks, including touch tanks where visitors can handle rays, starfish, and sea cucumbers. Its raison d'être, however, is the interactive dolphin program where activities range from receiving a "kiss" and getting a "foot push" (US$109-159, 45-60 minutes) to a couples-only program (US$199, 75 minutes) that includes a review of the anatomy and physiology of dolphins.

ECOPARKS AND WATER PARKS

Ecoparks

Despite the deluge of advertising you'll see for ecoparks like Xcaret, Xel-Há, Xplor, and Garrafón, none are actually in Cancún. Garrafón is the closest, situated on the southern end of Isla Mujeres. The others are 60-90 minutes south of Cancún, nearer to Playa del Carmen and Tulum. You can buy tickets at the gates, though most people buy them online or at their hotels so bus transportation is included in the cost; discounted park tickets also are popular giveaways for taking part in a time-share presentation.

Water Parks

In Ventura Park, on the southern end of the Zona Hotelera, **Wet n' Wild** (Blvd. Kukulcán Km 25, tel. 998/881-3030, toll-free U.S. tel. 855/203-9863, www.wetnwildcancun.com, 9:30am-5pm daily, US$48 adult, US$42 child) is a small but classic water park with a handful of twisting, slippery slides, high-speed water toboggans, and family-size inner tubing. It's a great way to cool off, especially if you're traveling with kids (or want to channel your own inner five-year-old). The all-inclusive plan includes all slides, meals, and drinks, though, oddly enough, not the inner tubes. BYO towel too. Check for online specials.

GOLF

Iberostar Cancún Golf Club (Blvd. Kukulcán Km 17, tel. 998/881-8016, http://golf.iberostar.com, US$199/99 public/hotel guests, US$149/49 public/guests after 2pm) is considered one of the finer courses in the region. This 18-hole par 72 course hugs Laguna Nichupté and boasts a great view of the Maya ruins of El Rey from the 16th hole. Alligators also are rumored to be in one of the water hazards, so consider leaving those water-bound balls behind. Food and drinks (including tequila shots and beer) are included.

Riviera Cancún Golf & Resorts (Blvd. Kukulcán Km 26, tel. 998/848-7777) is a challenging 18-hole par 72 golf course designed by Jack Nicklaus. Located on the southern end of the Zona Hotelera, it's a narrow course winding its way through low jungle and mangroves, with a distant view of the Caribbean. Greens fees are US$180 and drop to US$149 after 2:30pm. Rates include a golf cart, snacks, and drinks. There's also a driving range on-site.

If you feel like a short, easy (and cheap) round of golf, there are two par-3 courses in the Zona Hotelera: **Paradisus Cancún** (Blvd. Kukulcán Km 16.5, tel. 998/881-1100, www.melia.com, 7am-1pm last tee-off, US$45 greens fees, US$10 club rentals) and **Grand Oasis Cancún** (Blvd. Kukulcán Km 16, tel. 998/885-0867, www.grandoasiscancunresort.com, 8am-2:30pm last tee-off, US$35 greens fees including clubs).

SPECTATOR SPORTS
Bullfights

Though more often used as a concert venue, the **Plaza de Toros** (Av. Bonampak at Av. Sayil, tel. 998/884-8372, www.plazadetoroscancun.com.mx) still hosts bullfights throughout the year. Admission prices depend upon the headliner but typically run US$8-20. Tickets can be purchased online (www.superboletos.com) or at the box office.

Baseball

Baseball (*béisbol* in Spanish) is huge in Mexico, particularly in the north, where there are as many baseball diamonds as soccer fields. While still not having the pull in the Yucatán as it does elsewhere, it is a sport on the rise. The local team, **Tigres de Quintana Roo** (Quintana Roo Tigers), is one of the 16 teams that make up Mexico's professional baseball league, the Liga Mexicana de Béisbol (www.lmb.com.mx). You can catch a game March-September at the **Estadio Beto Avilá** (Av. Xcaret s/n, behind Walmart, tel. 998/887-3113, US$2-10).

Soccer

Arriving in Cancún from Mexico City in 2007, **Atlante** (www.atlantefc.mx) is the city's first professional *fútbol* team. And arrive they did: Atlante won both the Mexican League's championship and the Apertura Championship in its first year in residence. The following season Atlante won the CONCACAF Champions League, earning it a spot in the 2009 FIFA Club World Cup, where the team placed fourth. The team plays at the **Estadio Andrés Quintana Roo** (Av. Mayapán s/n, US$10-40), west of the baseball stadium, August-May.

SPAS AND GYMS

Many hotels and resorts have spas, but the following are some of the best that are open to the public. Reservations are strongly encouraged.

Spas don't get much better, or bigger, than the 40,000-square-foot **Gem Spa** (Gran Fiesta Americana Coral Beach, Blvd. Kukulcán Km 9.5, tel. 998/881-3200, www.coralbeachcancunhotel.com, 10am-10pm daily). There are dozens of available treatments, many using precious stones of the Maya, Asian/South Pacific, and Baltic regions. Obsidian, amber, amethyst, and even diamond dust are used to soothe and smooth your body and mind.

Bamboo (Plaza Teramar, Blvd. Kukulcán Km 8.5, tel. 998/883-0106, www.cancun-spa-relax.com, 9am-9pm daily) is a simple day spa offering everything from facials and massages to mani-pedis and haircuts. Service is excellent and prices are reasonable, making it a popular spot.

Downtown, **Spa Xbalamqué** (Hotel Xbalamqué, Av. Yaxchilán 31, tel. 998/887-7853, 10am-8pm Mon.-Sat.) offers a full line of massages, facials, and body wraps, plus Reiki, crystal therapy, and *temascal* treatments. The spa's entrance is on Calle Jazmines, around the corner from the main hotel entrance. Prices are very reasonable, most ranging US$30-50.

TOURS
Aerial Tours and Views

AeroSaab (Playa Del Carmen Airport, 20 Av. Sur near Calle 1, tel. 998/865-4225, www.aerosaab.com, 7am-7:30pm daily) offers scenic full-day tours from Cancún, running to Cozumel, Chichén Itzá, Isla Holbox, Chetumal, Mérida, and as far as Palenque, with time to visit the area. Trips are in five-seat or six-seat Cessna airplanes and run US$93-796 per person, plus airport fees. Most trips require a minimum of 2-4 people.

If you prefer to stay *somewhat* grounded, board **La Torre Escénica** (Scenic Tower, El Embarcadero, Blvd. Kukulcán Km 4.2, tel. 998/849-5582, 9am-9pm daily, US$15 during the day, US$18 at night), an 80-meter (262.5-foot) tower with a rotating passenger cabin, affording a beautiful 10-minute view of this part of the coastline. A brief history of the region is played over the audio system. **Note:** Admission to this site is included in the Xcaret ticket; show your Xcaret wristband—it must still be on your wrist!—for free entry.

Food

Cancún has dozens of excellent restaurants—the finest are in the Zona Hotelera, mostly in the high-end resorts and along the west (lagoon) side of Boulevard Kukulcán. Be aware that eating out in the Zona Hotelera can be shockingly expensive, similar to prices at top restaurants in major U.S. cities. There are a handful of Zona Hotelera gems, with great food at reasonable prices, and, of course, there are plenty of fast-food restaurants too. For something more authentic but still affordable, downtown Cancún is the place to go. The streets surrounding Parque Las Palapas and Avenida Nader have restaurants for all tastes and budgets, from fine dining to tasty street food, plus a number of great little cafés and sandwich shops.

ZONA HOTELERA
Mexican
The Surfin' Burrito (Blvd. Kukulcán Km 9.8, tel. 998/883-0083, 24 hours daily, US$5-8) is a hole-in-the-wall serving up a huge variety of burritos—pick your tortilla, protein (beef, chicken, or seafood), choice of salsas, and toppings. Rice and beans are a given. Wash it down with a mammoth one-liter margarita (US$7) or fruit smoothie (US$4). Delivery is available.

Easy to miss, ★ **Tacun** (Blvd. Kukulcán Km 11.5, tel. 998/593-3638, 8am-10pm daily, US$6-10) is a roadside taco joint at heart, and one of the few places in the Zona Hotelera to get good, genuine Mexican food at reasonable prices. Try a taco sampler platter with shrimp, beef, chicken, and *al pastor* tacos, served piping hot with a variety of fresh salsas. The staff and ambience are friendly. Look for it across from the Flamingo Mall. Cash only.

Seafood
A hidden gem, **El Fish Fritanga** (aka Pescadillas, Blvd. Kukulcán Km 12.6, tel. 998/840-6216, 11am-10:30pm daily, US$5-15) offers tasty home-style seafood at great prices. If you can't choose a dish, try the *pescadillas* or grilled nurse shark tacos, both house classics. The restaurant faces the lagoon and is

Ceviche is a popular seafood dish on beaches in Mexico.

below street level, making it easy to miss—look for the blue awning next to a Domino's Pizza sign.

★ **Fred's House** (Blvd. Kukulcán Km 14.7, tel. 998/840 6466, www.fredshouserestaurant.com, 1pm-midnight daily, US$22-45) is a lovely lagoon-side restaurant specializing in seafood dishes. Share an impressive iced shellfish tower featuring six varieties of crustaceans and then move on to any number of tartares, carpaccios, or sashimi. If you prefer your seafood hot, try one of the pasta dishes or wood-grilled entrees. For a memorable dinner, reserve a patio bungalow at sunset. Fred's is located across from the JW Marriott.

The nautical-themed **Lorenzillo's** (Blvd. Kukulcán Km 10.5, tel. 998/883-1254, www.lorenzillos.com.mx, 1pm-midnight daily, US$18-48) is known as one of the best lobster houses in town. Live lobster is kept in an adapted rowboat tank at the entrance—select the one you want, weigh it on an old-time scale, and before you know it, dinner is on. (All of the lobster comes from the restaurant's lobster farm off Isla Blanca, just north of the Zona Hotelera.) Ask for a table on the lagoon-side patio for a chance to see crocs.

Steak Houses

Puerto Madero (Blvd. Kukulcán Km 14.1, tel. 998/885-2829, www.puertomaderorestaurantes.com, 1pm-1am daily, US$20-55) is a longtime favorite serving carefully prepared meats in huge Argentinean portions. Choose a table in the warehouse-style dining room (a nod to the Puerto Madero shipyard in Argentina) or on the open-air patio with views of the lagoon. The menu includes salads, pastas, and excellent seafood, in addition to the many cuts of beef, some of which serve two. Prices are high, but you're sure to leave full.

Harry's (Blvd. Kukulcán Km 14.2, tel. 998/840-6550, www.harrys.com.mx, 1pm-1am daily, US$24-75) specializes in best-of-the-best beef, expertly prepared (some cuts are dry-aged for up to four weeks) and cooked in blazing hot broilers. There's also a long menu of sashimi, oysters, ceviche, tartare, and other seafood dishes, plus excellent wine and cocktails. The bill comes with a cotton candy fluff. It's a memorable and worthwhile splurge for steak lovers.

Other Specialties

Hidden in a small hotel, **La Palapa Belga** (Royal Cancún, Calle Quetzal 13, tel. 998/883-5454, www.lapalapabelga.com, 3pm-10:30pm Mon.-Sat., US$12-20) has been serving fine French-Belgian cuisine for two decades. It's worth searching out both for its views across the lagoon to the Zona Hotelera and its delicious food like beef tartare and escargot de Bourgogne. Reservations are recommended on weekends.

Le Natura (Blvd. Kukulcán Km 9.8, tel. 998/252-6799, 8am-11pm daily, US$5-9) is a casual bistro serving an amazing variety of whole foods and juices. The juice and smoothie menu alone is 33 items long (who knew a juice combo of carrots, beets, spinach, and celery could taste so good?); the breakfast menu has a number of fruit and yogurt plates, egg dishes, and comfort food like waffles and pancakes; and lunch and dinner is just as varied with salads, bagel sandwiches, pastas, seafood, and Mexican classics. There are lots of vegetarian-only options too.

For a change of pace, **Elefanta** and **Thai Lounge** (La Isla Shopping Village, Blvd. Kukulcán Km 12.5, tel. 998/176-8070, www.elefanta.com.mx, 6:30pm-1am daily, US$12-34) are sister restaurants serving quality Indian and Thai food, respectively. The ambience at both is quite chic, despite being in a mall; the Thai Lounge has private cabañas on stilts overlooking the lagoon and stays open late as a bar-lounge.

Groceries

Numerous mini-marts along Boulevard Kukulcán sell chips, water, sunscreen, and other beach basics. Most are open from 7am to midnight.

For a more complete grocery experience,

head to the upscale **Selecto Súper Chedraui** (Blvd. Kukulcán Km 9, tel. 998/830-0866, 7am-11pm daily), a three-story supermarket featuring organic foods, gourmet wines and cheeses, a sushi bar, and a popular prepared food section. Not as fancy but still well stocked is Soriana Super (Blvd. Kukulcán Km 13, 7am-11pm daily) on the 2nd floor of Plaza Kukulcán shopping mall.

DOWNTOWN
Mexican

★ **Quesadillas Tierra del Sol** (Margaritas near Tulipanes, tel. 998/271-0111, 8am-midnight daily, US$2-4) serves up hefty quesadillas (and *sopes, panuchos,* and *salbutes*) made with Oaxacan cheese and your choice of dozens of stuffings, from chorizo to *nopales* (cactus). Two will satisfy a decent appetite, four could push you over the edge. Fresh, fruity *aguas* help wash it down. Order at the register and they'll call your number.

Just a couple of blocks from the bus station, **Taquería Coapeñitos** (Av. Nadar 25, tel. 998/253-0360, 2pm-2am Mon.-Wed., 2pm-3am Thurs.-Sat., noon-midnight Sun., US$2-4) sells some mean street tacos. The kitchen is open, so you can watch your tacos being prepped while you wait. Be sure to hit up the fixins' bar for a variety of salsas, pickled onions, and lime. Beers are cheap too.

La Habichuela (Parque Las Palapas, Calle Margaritas 25, tel. 998/884-3158, www.lahabichuela.com, 1pm-midnight daily, US$10-26) is a longtime favorite for Yucatecan cuisine. The seafood is especially tasty—try the giant shrimp in tamarind sauce or *cocobichuela*, the house specialty, with big chunks of lobster and shrimp in a sweet curry sauce. For dessert, ask for a Maya coffee flambé: Chiapanecan coffee made with cinnamon, brandy, and *Xtabentún* (a regional liqueur made with anise, rum, and fermented honey).

Combine Disneyland and the Mexican Revolution and you might get **Pericos** (Av. Yaxchilán 61, tel. 998/884-0821, noon-1am daily, US$7-15), a classic Cancún family restaurant. *Bandito* waiters sport bandoliers, the bar has saddles instead of stools, and kids may get a rubber chicken on their plates instead of taquitos. Low-key it is not, but Pericos has a solid reputation for serving good grilled meats and seafood in a fun, boisterous atmosphere. Live marimba and mariachi starts at 8pm most nights.

On the north end of Parque Las Palapas is a set of **food stalls** (7am-midnight daily, US$1.50-4) selling cheap Mexican and Yucatecan eats—tacos, quesadillas, tostadas, and *salbutes*. It's perfect if you're looking for some good street food or are on a tight budget.

Seafood

Pescaditos (Av. Yaxchilán 69, 11am-midnight daily, US$5-9) is the sort of restaurant you'd expect to see on the beach, complete with reggae music, a handful of tables, and a sign made from an old surfboard. And like the best beach shacks, this place will wow you with simple, tasty seafood dishes. The ceviche, beer-battered shrimp, and fish tacos are all outstanding, and very well priced. Wash it down with a frosty beer or homemade *limonada.*

Sitting among several open-air eateries, **El Cejas** (Mercado 28, Av. Sunyaxchen at Av. Xel-Há, tel. 998/887-1080, 8am-8pm daily, US$3-6) is bustling most days for good reason—fresh seafood and ambience. Live marimba music is in the air, colorful *papel picado* (decorative paper) sways overhead, and a combo of tourists and locals fill the seats. Service can be painfully slow but the dishes—freshly fried fish, grilled shrimp, ceviche of all sorts—is worth the wait.

Pescado Con Limón (Mercado 28, Av. Sunyaxchen at Av. Xel-Há, tel. 998/887-2436, 11am-7pm daily, US$5-11) may be a little short on ambience—its plastic tables and chairs face the Mercado 28 parking lot—but the seafood is as fresh and good as it comes, an open secret among locals and expats. For a sure thing, try a shrimp dish or one of the fried-fish platters. The tip is typically included (and somewhat hidden) in the bill.

Other Specialties

★ **Sirena Morena** (Av. Nader 66, tel. 998/ 887-9774, 8am-10pm Mon.-Sat., US$4-6) is where it's at for veggie fans. The menu is all organic and all vegetarian and includes sandwiches and salads, egg dishes, even mushroom risotto and *pozole* (spicy soup made with hominy). There are lots of gluten-free and vegan options too. Tables are in a garden setting with shabby-chic flair. Look for the entrance down a small alley next to a natural food shop.

El Tigre y El Toro (Av. Nader between Calles Mero and Rubia, tel. 998/898-0041, 6pm-12:30am Mon.-Sat., 6pm-11:30pm Sun., US$8-15) is a trendy outdoor restaurant specializing in wood-fired pizza. The thin-crust pies are topped with items like prosciutto and burrata, lobster, and Argentinean sausage. Gourmet salads and homemade pastas round out the menu. This is a casual spot that doubles as a special (pizza) night out.

Rolandi's Pizzeria Cancún (Av. Cobá 12, tel. 998/884-4047, 1:30pm-12:30am daily, US$9-22) is an institution, with sister restaurants in Isla Mujeres, Playa del Carmen, and Cozumel. The food here—and at all of them— is consistently good; choose among thin-crust pizzas, calzones, and great homemade pastas. Pocket bread, warm and inflated, and a dish of olive oil come with every order. Sit on the veranda, which is draped in ivy that blocks out street noise.

La Parrilla (Av. Yaxchilán 51, tel. 998/287-8118, www.laparrilla.com.mx, noon-2am daily, US$7-28) is one of the most popular of the restaurant-bars on this busy street, grilling a variety of delicious beef fillets, plus shrimp and lobster brochettes, chicken, fajitas, and tacos—the fiery spit in front is for *taquitos al pastor*, a Mexican classic. The breezy street-side eating area is comfortable and casual and good for families. There's also live mariachi music every night starting at 8pm.

Light Fare

Get a tasty baguette sandwich at ★ **Ty-Coz Baguettería** (Av. Tulum at Av. Uxmal, tel. 998/884-6060, 8am-10pm Mon.-Sat., 8am-8pm Sun, US$2-5), a cozy eatery tucked behind the Comercial Mexicana supermarket opposite the bus terminal. The menu includes French- and German-inspired baguette sandwiches and *cuernos* (croissants). Most run around US$3, but you can always order the *económica* baguette with ham, salami, and cheese for just US$1.25. If you don't want to head downtown for a sandwich, visit its **Zona Hotelera branch** (Blvd. Kukulcán Km 9, 6am-9pm daily).

Rooster (Av. Nader 114, tel. 998/884-4252, 8am-10pm daily, US$2.50-6) is a cool-cat café serving up good breakfast dishes, fresh deli sandwiches, and a variety of coffee drinks and smoothies. Seating is either in a cozy corner or a leafy terrace. Tables fill up fast, so arrive early or take your eats to go.

Groceries

Chedraui (Blvd. Kukulcán at Av. Tulum) and **Comercial Mexicana** (Av. Tulum at Av. Uxmal) are huge supermarkets with everything from produce and in-house bakeries to pharmacies and beach supplies. Both are open 7am-11pm daily and have ATMs just inside their doors.

Just a couple of blocks from the bus station, **Mercado 23** (Calles Ciricote and Cedro, three blocks north of Av. Uxmal via Calle Palmeras, 6am-6pm daily) has stands of fresh fruits and vegetables. The selection is somewhat limited, but the produce is the freshest around.

DINNER CRUISES

For couples, the Columbus **Lobster Dinner Cruise** (Aquatours Marina, Blvd. Kukulcán Km 6.5, toll-free Mex. tel. 800/727-5391, toll-free U.S. tel. 866/393-5158, www.thelobsterdinner.com, US$89-109 dinner with open bar, no children under 14, departs at 5:30pm and 8:30pm nightly) offers a change of pace, serving three-course dinners aboard a Spanish-style galleon. The ship cruises the Laguna Nichupté for 2.5 hours, accompanied by live jazz.

If you're traveling with kids, the **Galleon**

of **Captain Hook** (Marina Captain Hook, Blvd. Kukulcán Km 5, tel. 998/849-4931, www.capitanhook.com, US$70-95 adult with open bar, US$35-51 child, departs at 7pm nightly, 3.5 hours) offers dinner plus a costumed crew and tales of pirate conquest while cruising the open sea. Be aware that a "surcharge"—US$14 adult, US$5 kids—is added to the bill. It covers travel insurance, security and, of all things, diesel fuel.

Accommodations

Cancún has scores of hotels, varying from backpacker hostels to ultra-high-end resorts. They're also divided by their location: the Zona Hotelera and downtown. The Zona Hotelera has spectacular views, easy access to the beaches, swimming pools, and excellent restaurants, but prices are higher and you won't get much "authentic" interaction with local people. Downtown Cancún has a variety of food, shopping, and services (from Walmart to laundries) at generally lower prices, but staying downtown also means driving or taking a bus to the beach and foregoing ocean-view rooms.

ZONA HOTELERA
Under US$100

Just steps from both the nightclubs and the beach, **Natura Hostel** (Blvd. Kukulcán Km 9.5, tel. 998/883-0585, cancunhostelnatura@gmail.com, US$30 pp dorm with a/c, US$65 s/d with a/c and shared bath, US$75 s/d with a/c) is as good as it gets in Cancún, location-wise. The rooms themselves are tiny but clean, many with colorful murals. Mattresses are on the thin side but bunks have privacy curtains, personal fans, and lights. There's also a rooftop lounge with a common kitchen, pool table, and enviable views of the lagoon. The hostel is located above the like-named restaurant.

Set on Laguna Nichupté, **El Manglar** (Blvd. Kukulcán Km 19.8, tel. 998/885-1808, www.villasmanglar.com, US$90-100 s/d with a/c) has simple and spacious rooms, each with cable TV, air-conditioning, a king-size bed, and two couches that double as twin beds. There's a well-maintained pool on-site and beach access nearby at Playa Delfines. With the marina next door, it's especially popular with people who enjoy fishing, waterskiing, and wakeboarding.

US$100-200

With just 30 suites, **Casa Turquesa Boutique Hotel** (Blvd. Kukulcán Km 13.5, tel. 998/193-2260, www.casaturquesa.com, US$143-210 with a/c, US$420 suite with a/c) is a welcome change of pace from the massive resorts lining Boulevard Kukulcán. Units are spacious and spotless, if somewhat dated in style (at the time of research, they were being updated); ocean views and whirlpool tubs more than make up for the old-school prints. Works of art also are featured throughout the property—paintings and sculptures from notable artists, mostly from Mexico. The hotel itself is perched above the beach, making for spectacular views from the pool. Service is warm and personalized.

An excellent value, **Beachscape Kin Ha Villas & Suites** (Blvd. Kukulcán Km 8.5, tel. 998/891-5400, www.beachscape.com.mx, US$144 s/d with a/c, US$230-413 suite with a/c) is a comfortable, low-key resort on a beautiful beach on the upper arm of the Zona Hotelera. The resort's one-, two-, and three-bedroom suites have fully equipped kitchens, living and dining areas, and ocean-view terraces; there also are a handful of standard hotel rooms. In addition to that huge beach, the property has a large (and rather plain) pool, restaurant-bar, and children's play area. Though lacking the style and ambience of Cancún's top resorts, Beachscape Kin Ha can hardly be beat for location and value. Coin-op laundry, an exercise room, and Wi-Fi (reception area only) are available.

US$200-400

★ **Grand Fiesta Americana Coral Beach** (Blvd. Kukulcán Km 9.5, tel. 998/881-3200, www.coralbeachcancunhotel.com, US$329-349 junior suite with a/c, US$649-849 master suite with a/c) is an elegant hotel offering spacious and comfortable suites, all with spectacular ocean-view balconies. It features a series of infinity pools, lush and manicured gardens, and one of the calmest beaches of the Zona Hotelera. The hotel has five restaurants and cafés, a luxurious spa, a kids club, and activities ranging from yoga to Jet Skis.

Marriott Cancún Resort (Blvd. Kukulcán Km 14.8, tel. 998/881-2000, toll-free U.S./Can. tel. 888/236-2427, www.marriott.com, US$219-282 s/d with a/c, US$302-402 suite with a/c) has over 400 rooms, all with private terraces and amenities like flat-screen TVs and wireless Internet. Guests can choose from eight eateries including an Argentinean steak house, a sushi restaurant, and a Thai restaurant. There's also a full-service spa, illuminated outdoor tennis courts, and a gym with separate men's and women's saunas. The hotel's main drawback is the pool, which is well maintained but small for the size and caliber of the resort; fortunately, it's just steps from the Caribbean.

Located alongside the Pok-ta-Pok golf course, **Laguna Suites Golf + Spa** (Paseo Pok-ta-Pok No. 3, tel. 998/891-5252, toll-free U.S./Can. tel. 866/760-1843, www.laguna-suites.com.mx, US$152 s/d with a/c, US$168-188 pp all-inclusive, children under 16 stay free) has just 47 rooms, allowing for genuinely personalized service with none of the hubbub of a large beachfront resort. There's a small pool and a chic *palapa* lounge, plus free hourly shuttles to three nearby sister resorts—the Sunset Royal, Sunset Marina, and Ocean Spa—where you can enjoy the pool, beach, restaurants, and amenities like any other

Cancún has miles of inviting resorts.

guest. It's a great option if you don't mind a little resort hopping.

Over US$400

The Ritz-Carlton (Blvd. Kukulcán Km 13.9, tel. 998/881-0808, toll-free U.S/Can. tel. 800/542-8680, www.ritzcarlton.com, US$707-837 s/d with a/c, US$927-987 suite with a/c) is unparalleled in its elegance. Fine art, chandeliers, and marble floors greet you the moment the white-gloved porter opens the door. All rooms have stunning ocean views and boast features like feather beds, downpour showerheads, and twice-daily housekeeping. Other high-end features of the resort include a full-service spa and gym, tennis courts, the Culinary Center (a gorgeous kitchen where guests can take cooking classes), and, of course, a well-maintained beach. The only hiccups are the unremarkable pools—nice enough but nothing special—an odd oversight given the luxuriousness of the rest of the hotel.

All-Inclusive Resorts

The Royal Cancún All Suites Resort (Blvd. Kukulcán Km 4.5, toll-free Mex. tel. 800/020-1761, toll-free U.S./Can. tel. 888/721-4431, US$155-173 pp all-inclusive) is a quiet resort that's especially well suited for families. It's located on the short, north-facing part of the Zona Hotelera, so the beach has virtually no waves—a big difference from the east-facing beaches, and a relief for parents with young children. There's also a popular kids club and lots of free sports gear, such as snorkeling equipment, sailboats, golf clubs, and bikes. The units themselves are spacious and have been recently updated (all have two bedrooms and a full kitchen). Guests also enjoy access to the property's all-inclusive sister resorts, the Royal Sands in Cancún and the Royal Haciendas in Playa del Carmen.

Located at the southernmost tip of the Zona Hotelera, **Club Med Cancún Yucatán** (Blvd. Kukulcán Km 20.6, tel. 998/881-8200, toll-free U.S. tel. 888/932-2582, www.clubmed. com, US$270 pp all-inclusive) is a secluded resort with a huge offering of activities—from paddleboarding and waterskiing to flying trapeze and golfing. If you have kids, the Mini Club keeps the little ones happy and busy all day long with activities like tennis and cooking lessons. There also are three good restaurants and a handful of bars—enough variety to keep most guests happy.

Hotel Riu Palace Las Américas (Blvd. Kukulcán Km 8.5, tel. 998/881-4300, www. riu.com, US$199-302 pp all-inclusive) is an adults-only hotel with 350-plus suites that, while not as elegant as the Victorian-style common areas indicate, are quite nice nonetheless. Each has a separate sitting area, a minibar that's restocked daily, and standard amenities like satellite TV and in-room safes; most rooms also have ocean views. Beds are ultra-firm—ask for a foam topper if that's an issue. Outside of the rooms, the beach is narrow but well maintained; there are also three infinity pools, endless water activities, five restaurants, and several bars.

A luxurious adults-only resort, ★ **Le Blanc Spa Resort** (Blvd. Kukulcán Km 10, tel. 998/881-4740, toll-free Mex. tel. 800/681-5338, toll-free U.S. tel. 888/702-0913, www. leblancsparesort.com, US$380-466 pp all-inclusive) offers all the amenities a vacationing couple could want: infinity pools, à la carte gourmet restaurants, a fully equipped gym and spa, Pilates and spinning classes, unlimited golf, bars and lounges, and yards and yards of white-sand beach. There's even butler service. The guest rooms are minimalist chic with whirlpool tubs. All have views of the Caribbean or the lagoon.

DOWNTOWN
Under US$50

★ **Mayan Monkey** (Av. Nader 3, tel. 998/217-5332, www.mayanmonkey.com, US$11-15 pp dorm with a/c, US$80 s/d with a/c) is a mid-century modern affair standing four stories high. Dorms are airy and bright, with custom wood bunks that have individual lights, two outlets, privacy curtains, thick mattresses, and big built-in lockers; all have en suite bathrooms. There are cozy common areas on every level but the rooftop is where's it at, with a pool with great city views, a bar, and an open-air restaurant. Best of all? The rate includes breakfast and dinner.

Moloch Hostel (Margaritas 54, tel. 998/884-6918, www.moloch.com.mx, US$11 dorm with a/c, US$29/34 s/d with a/c) a/c) is a low-key hostel with mini-split air conditioners in all the rooms, including the dorms (8am-8pm only), and an inviting kidney-shaped pool in back. Dorms are a bit cramped, but the beds are good; private rooms are larger and would even work for families. There's a fully equipped communal kitchen, as well as continental breakfast, a TV lounge, Wi-Fi, and a computer station. It's located a block from both the bus station and Parque Las Palapas.

A social place, **Hostel Ka'beh** (Calle Alcatraces at Calle Claveles, tel. 998/892-7902, www.hostelkabeh.com, US$19 dorm with a/c, US$44 s/d with a/c) has welcoming lounge areas and daily activities like clubbing trips, movie nights, and barbecue nights. Breakfast—oatmeal, pancakes, eggs, waffles, PB&J—is self-service and available 24-7. There's also a common kitchen and a huge lending library of travel guides. Dorms are mixed and comfortable enough; ask for a bed in the new section—they're away from the hubbub so you can actually get some shut-eye. Private rooms are located across the street and are even quieter. There's a two-night minimum during the high season.

US$50-100

Half a block from the bus station, ★ **Selina Cancún** (Av. Tulum 75, toll-free Mex. tel. 800/ 953-0822, www.selina.com, US$18-20 pp dorm with a/c, US$34 s/d with shared bath and a/c, US$60 s/d with a/c, US$75 suite with a/c) is an artful hotel-hostel with boho-hipster style. Murals, Talavera tiles, and tropical woods accent most rooms and common areas, including a fully equipped kitchen, movie screening room, and library. Outdoors, there's an expansive garden with a pool, lounge, and bar/restaurant; many nights a DJ is working the tunes. There's a gorgeous co-working space too.

Cancún International Suites (Calle Gladiolas at Av. Alcatraces, tel. 998/884-1771, cancuninternationalsuites@gmail.com, US$65 s/d with a/c) has large, comfortable rooms with a hacienda-like feel. Rooms combine warm colors, wood furniture, and

high ceilings with modern amenities like glass showers, flat-screen TVs, and Wi-Fi. The downtown location, just a half block from Parque Las Palapas, could not be more perfect. A rooftop lounge has superb views.

Located on a quiet stretch of Avenida Nader, **Hotel & Suites Nader** (Av. Nader near Av. Cobá, tel. 998/884-1584, www.suitesnadercancun.com, US$54 s/d with a/c, US$63-75 suite with a/c and kitchenette) is a comfortable and modern hotel. Rooms are somewhat sparse but have updated amenities like flat-screen TVs, silent air-conditioning, and free Wi-Fi. The owners are often on-site, which makes for warm, personalized service. Discounts are often offered if you reserve by phone.

Over US$100

Bougainvillea and a gurgling fountain welcome you to **Hotel El Rey del Caribe** (Av. Uxmal at Nader, tel. 998/884-2028, www.elreydelcaribe.com, US$170 s/d with a/c and kitchenette), an eco-friendly hotel two blocks east of the bus terminal. Rooms are clean and comfortable (those in the newer section are more spacious, with lovely wood floors), but it's the verdant tropical garden with hammocks, a pool, and an outdoor dining area that really sets El Rey apart—you might even forget for a moment you're in the city. The hotel employs solar heating, rainwater recovery, and organic waste composting. Breakfast is included in the rate.

Information and Services

TOURIST INFORMATION

Downtown, the **City Tourist Office** (Av. Nader at Av. Cobá, tel. 998/887-3379, www.fonatur.gob.mx, 9am-4pm Mon.-Fri.) is a bustling office with staffers who happily provide information on city and regional sights. English is spoken.

Note: Be aware that booths with "Tourist Information" signs along Avenida Tulum and

Boulevard Kukulcán are in fact operated by **time-share companies,** offering free tours and other goodies in exchange for attending a sales presentation.

Casa Consular (Blvd. Kukulcán Km 13, tel. 998/840-6082, www.casaconsular.org, 9am-3pm Mon.-Fri) has helpful staffers who act as liaisons between international travelers and their consular representatives. The office also offers advice to those travelers needing to contact Mexican authorities with everything from immigration issues to theft. English is spoken. Look for it next to the fire station in the Zona Hotelera.

There are also a few publications that are worth picking up: *Cancún Tips* (www.cancuntips.com.mx) is a free tourist magazine with general information about Cancún and nearby sights; both *Restaurante Menu Mapa* and *Map@migo* have maps, restaurant menus, reviews, and discount coupons; and *Agenda Cultural* has listings of Cancún's upcoming cultural events, exhibitions, and workshops. This last one can be hard to find—ask at the tourist office.

EMERGENCY SERVICES

There are several recommended private hospitals within a few blocks of each other in downtown Cancún. All have emergency rooms and English-speaking doctors and are open 24 hours daily: **Hospitén Cancún** (Av. Bonampak s/n, south of Av. Nichupté, tel. 998/881-3700, www.hospiten.com), **AmeriMed Hospital** (Av. Tulum at Av. Nichupté, behind Las Américas mall, tel. 998/881-3400, www.amerimedcancun.com), and **Hospital Galenia** (Av. Tulum at Av. Nizuc, tel. 998/891-5200, www.hospitalgalenia.com).

For meds in the Zona Hotelera, try any of the malls or head to **Farmacia del Ahorro** (Blvd. Kukulcán Km 9.5, tel. 998/892-7291, 24 hours). Downtown, **Farmacias Similares** (Av. Tulum near Calle Crisantemos, tel. 998/898-0190, 24 hours) is a reliable national chain.

The **police department, fire station,** and **ambulance** all can be reached by dialing toll-free 060 or 066 anytime. In the Zona Hotelera, all three are located in the same building next to Plaza Kukulcán (Blvd. Kukulcán Km 12.5). Downtown, the main police station (Av. Xcaret at Av. Kabah, tel. 998/884-1913, 24 hours) faces the Carrefour supermarket, and there's a small office on Parque Las Palapas, near the food stalls, which is usually open 24 hours.

MONEY

You'll have no problem accessing or exchanging your money in Cancún. ATMs are ubiquitous, including at all the shopping malls, and give the best exchange rate. Many resorts will exchange dollars and euros, or simply accept them directly as payment. Ditto for many tour operators and even restaurants, especially in the Zona Hotelera. The exchange rate may be awful, however.

If you need an actual bank, head to **Plaza Caracol** (Blvd. Kukulcán Km 8.5), where you'll find Bancomer, HSBC, and Banamex. All have ATMs that accept foreign cards and are open roughly 9am-4pm Monday-Friday.

Downtown, the most conveniently located banks are on Avenida Tulum between Avenida Cobá and Avenida Uxmal: **Bancomer** (Av. Tulum 20, 8:30am-4pm Mon.-Fri.) and **Citi-Banamex** (Av. Tulum 19, 9am-4pm Mon.-Fri., 10am-2pm Sat.).

MEDIA AND COMMUNICATIONS
Post Office

The **post office** (Av. Sunyaxchen at Av. Xel-Há, tel. 998/834-1418, 8am-4pm Mon.-Fri., 9am-12:30pm Sat.) is located in front of Mercado 28. There is no post office in the Zona Hotelera, though your hotel may mail postcards for you.

Internet and Telephone

Wi-Fi is offered by most hostels, hotels, and resorts, whether for free or at a small cost, and some have computers available for those without a laptop or mobile device of their own. Malls, restaurants, and even the Mexican government is following suit: Most Mexican cities, Cancún among them, have public Wi-Fi in their main plazas. If all else fails, you can get online at a few *cibercafes*, which are located downtown. Most have Skype-enabled computers too.

Recommended Internet cafes include **Cyber Café Uxmal** (Av. Uxmal near Margaritas, no phone, 24 hours daily, US$0.75 per hour) near the bus station, and **Papelería**

Internet (Margaritas near Gladiolas, 8am-10pm daily, US$0.60 per hour), facing Parque Las Palapas.

Newspapers

There are a handful of newspapers for local and regional news: In Spanish, *Novedades Quintana Roo* (www.sipse.com/novedades) is the state's oldest newspaper, centrist in coverage; *¡Por Esto!* (www.poresto.net) is a left-of-center paper with Quintana Roo and Yucatán versions; and *Diario de Yucatán* (www.yucatan.com.mx) is more conservative and covers the entire region. The Cancún version of the *Miami Herald Tribune* is a good English-language alternative.

LAUNDRY AND STORAGE

Downtown, **Lavandería Las Palapas** (Parque Las Palapas, Alcatraces near Gladiolas, 7am-9pm Mon.-Fri., 7am-8pm Sat.) will do your laundry for US$3.50 per three kilos (6.6 pounds); same-day service is available if you drop off before 9am.

In the Zona Hotelera, **Eco-Laundry** (Kukulcán Km 9.5, tel. 998/883-4315, 9am-8pm Mon.-Sat., 9am-2pm Sun.) offers same-day laundry service for US$2.50 per kilo (2.2 pounds). With similar prices, **Lavandería Lumi Express** (Blvd. Kukulcán Km 8, tel. 998/883-3874, www.lumiexpress. com.mx, 8am-8pm Mon.-Sat., 9am-5pm Sun.) also offers self-service machines. Pickup and drop-off is available.

At the bus station, near the second-class departure area, **Guarda Equipaje** (tel. 998/884-4352, ext. 2851, 6:30am-10pm daily) will store luggage for US$0.50-1 per hour, depending on the size.

Storage lockers (US$6 per 24 hours) also can be rented in Terminal 3 at Cancún International Airport; they are big enough to hold carry-on bags only. Look for the lockers as you exit customs.

INSTRUCTION

The welcoming **Centro Cultural La Pitahaya** (Av. Yaxchilán near Av. Uxmal, cell tel. 998/118-0099, 4pm-11pm Mon.-Fri., prices vary) offers a wide range of workshops in theater, music, art, and even jewelry design. If you're going to be in town for a month or longer, consider checking out the offerings.

Getting There and Around

GETTING THERE
Air

The **Cancún International Airport** (CUN, Hwy. 307 Km 22, tel. 998/848-7200, www.cancun-airport.com) is 20 kilometers (12.4 miles) south of Cancún. Most international flights arrive and depart from Terminals 3 and 4, which have taxi, bus, and car rental desks. All have ATMs or money exchange kiosks. In general, Terminal 2 is used for domestic flights; Terminal 1 is reserved for charter flights. A free shuttle ferries travelers between the terminals.

The following airlines serve Cancún International Airport:

- **Aeromar** (toll-free Mex. tel. 800/237-6627, www.aeromar.com.mx)
- **Aeroméxico** (Av. Cobá at Av. Bonampak, tel. 998/884-1186, toll-free U.S. tel. 800/237-6639, www.aeromexico.com)
- **AeroTucán** (toll-free Mex. tel. 800/640-4148, www.aerotucan.com)
- **Air Canada** (toll-free Mex. tel. 800/719-2827, toll-free U.S./Can. tel. 888/247-2262, www.aircanada.com)
- **Alaska Airlines** (toll-free Mex. tel. 800/654-5669, toll-free U.S./Can. tel. 800/252-7522, www.alaskaair.com)
- **American Airlines** (toll-free Mex. tel.

800/904-6000, toll-free U.S./Can. tel. 800/433-7300, www.aa.com)

- **Cubana de Aviación** (Av. Tulum 232, tel. 998/887-7210, airport tel. 998/886-0355, www.cubana.cu)

- **Delta** (toll-free Mex. tel. 800/266-0046, toll-free U.S. tel. 800/241-4141, www.delta.com)

- **Frontier Airlines** (toll-free U.S. tel. 801/401-9000, www.frontierairlines.com)

- **InterJet** (toll-free Mex. tel. 800/011-2345, toll-free U.S. tel. 866/285-9525, www.interjet.com.mx)

- **JetBlue** (toll-free Mex. tel. 800/861-3372, toll-free U.S. tel. 800/538-2583, www.jetblue.com)

- **MAYAir** (airport tel. 998/881-9413, toll-free Mex. tel. 800/962-9247, toll-free U.S./Can. tel. 844/622-0800, www.mayair.com.mx)

- **Southwest Airlines** (toll-free Mex. tel. 800/083-1179, toll-free U.S. tel. 800/435-9792, www.southwest.com)

- **Spirit Airlines** (toll-free Mex./U.S./Can. tel. 801/401-2222, www.spiritair.com)

- **United Airlines** (toll-free Mex. tel. 800/900-5000, toll-free U.S./Can. tel. 800/864-8331, www.united.com)

- **VivaAerobus** (toll-free Mex. tel. 818/215-0150, toll-free U.S. tel. 888/935-9848, www.vivaaerobus.com)

- **Volaris** (tel. 551/102-8000, toll-free U.S. tel. 855/865-2747, www.volaris.com)

Bus

Buses leave Cancún's clean and modern **bus terminal** (Av. Tulum at Av. Uxmal) for destinations in the Yucatán Peninsula and throughout the interior of Mexico.

*Schedules are subject to change.

Combi

Combis, public shuttle vans, run between Cancún and Playa del Carmen. They queue up directly across Avenida Tulum from the bus terminal, near the Comercial Mexicana,

and depart every 10-15 minutes 24 hours a day (US$2, 1 hour). For slightly more, **Playa Express** has larger, air-conditioned shuttles, departing on roughly the same schedule from the parking lot in front of the bus terminal (US$2.25, 50 minutes). Both services make stops along the way, including Puerto Morelos (US$1.25, 30 minutes).

GETTING AROUND
To and from the Airport

Cancún's airport is served by taxi, shuttle, and bus. The authorized airport taxi service, **Yellow Transfers** (toll-free Mex. tel. 844/373-6983, www.yellowtransfers.com), has booths inside the airport terminals. It offers taxi and shuttle service, including luxury class and for the disabled, anywhere on the coast. Fares are fixed and prominently displayed at the airport and online (where rates are sometimes discounted). Rates to the Zona Hotelera or downtown are the same; private taxis and shuttles run US$44-66 (4-8 people), while shared shuttles are US$18 per person. Yellow Transfers offers round-trip service at a discount, or you can hire an ordinary taxi; you'll end up paying roughly the same. Service along the coast includes Playa del Carmen (US$90-171) and Tulum (US$152-375).

ADO provides bus service from stops just outside each Terminal. Tickets can be purchased at ADO booths inside the airport or at kiosks located at each bus stop. Comfortable, air-conditioned buses leave every half hour for downtown Cancún (8:15am-12:30am daily, US$4, 25 minutes) and every 30 minutes for Playa del Carmen (12:30am-11:59pm daily, US$9.50, 1 hour); the latter stops in Puerto Morelos (US$6, 25 minutes) along the way. There also are eight daily departures for Mérida (2:05-9:15pm, US$19-34, 3.5-4.5 hours). For other destinations, take any bus to Cancún or Playa del Carmen and transfer. ADO's airport buses do not enter Cancún's Zona Hotelera, however.

Bus

Frequent buses (US$0.75) run between

Cancún Bus Schedule

Cancún's **bus station** (tel. 800/702-8000) is located downtown at Avenidas Tulum and Uxmal. Departures listed below include both first- and second-class service; in many cases, second-class buses take significantly longer for only marginal savings.

DESTINATION	PRICE	DURATION	SCHEDULE*
Cancún Int'l Airport	US$4	25 mins	every 30 mins 4:30am-11pm
Chetumal	US$21-27	5-6 hrs	every 30-90 mins 12:30am-11:59pm
Chichén Itzá	US$15	4 hrs	8:45am or take any Pisté bus
Chiquilá (Isla Holbox)	US$6.75	3-3.5 hrs	five departures 7:40am-2pm
Mahahual	US$12-23	4.5 hrs	6:50am and 4:45pm
Mérida	US$14-32	4-4.5 hrs	every 30-60 mins 1am-11:59pm
Pisté	US$7.50-15	3.5-4.5 hrs	8:45am and every 30-60 mins 12:30pm-11:30pm
Playa del Carmen	US$2-4	1 hr	every 15-30 mins 12:30am-10:30pm
Puerto Morelos	US$1.75	45 mins	every 15-30 mins 6am-10pm
Tulum	US$4.50-11	2.5 hrs	every 45-90 mins 5:30am-11:15pm
Valladolid	US$8-11	2-3.5 hrs	every 60-90 mins 4am-8pm

downtown Cancún and the Zona Hotelera—you'll rarely have to wait more than five minutes for one to pass. The buses are red and have "R-1," "Hoteles," or "Zona Hotelera" painted on the front, and stop along Avenida Tulum, at the bus station, and near most major hotels, beaches, and ferry ports.

Taxi

You'll have no trouble finding a taxi around town or in the Zona Hotelera—they're everywhere tourists are. Before getting into one, however, make sure to agree upon a price—meters aren't used, and drivers sometimes overcharge. As of this writing, the rate around downtown is US$2.50, from downtown to the Isla Mujeres ferries US$3.50, and from downtown to the Zona Hotelera US$10-20, depending on the destination. Rates within the Zona Hotelera jump dramatically and depend on how far you're going. Ask your concierge for specific rates, but expect to pay US$8-20.

Car

Although you won't need a car to visit Cancún proper, renting one is a great way to visit the nearest archaeological sites (i.e., Tulum, Cobá, Ek' Balam, and Chichén Itzá) without being part of a huge tour group. A rental also makes exploring the Riviera Maya a little easier, though buses cover that route fairly well. Driving in the Cancún area is relatively pain-free—unexpected speed bumps and impatient bus drivers are the biggest concerns.

Driving Distances from Cancún

LOCATION	DISTANCE	LOCATION	DISTANCE
Airport	20 km (12.4 mi)	Puerto Aventuras	87 km (54 mi)
Akumal	105 km (65 mi)	Puerto Morelos	36 km (22.5 mi)
Bacalar	320 km (199 mi)	Punta Allen	182 km (109 mi)
Chetumal	382 km (237.5 mi)	Tulum	130 km (81 mi)
Chichén Itzá	178 km (110.5 mi)	Valladolid	158 km (98 mi)
Cobá	173 km (107.5 mi)	Xcalak	411 km (255.5 mi)
Mahahual	351 km (218 mi)	Xcaret	74 km (46 mi)
Mérida	320 km (199 mi)	Xel-Há	122 km (76 mi)
Paamul	82 km (51 mi)	Xpu-Há	101 km (63 mi)
Playa del Carmen	68 km (42.5 mi)		

Most international car rental companies, and a few local ones, have offices at the airport (some are right at the terminal, others in a purpose-built rental center few miles away) as well as in select resorts and at offices downtown and in the Zona Hotelera. Various sizes and types of vehicles are available, from SUVs to Volkswagen Bugs (optimistically dubbed VW sedans); prices with insurance and taxes start at around US$32 a day. The best rates are online; you also can sometimes get discounted rates by spending half a day in a time-share presentation. Commonly used companies include:

- **America Car Rental** (Cancún Airport, tel. 998/253-6100; Flamingo Plaza, Blvd. Kukulcán Km 11.5, tel. 998/883-0160, www. america-carrental.com)

- **Avis** (Cancún Airport, tel. 998/886-0221; La Isla Shopping Village, Blvd. Kukulcán Km 12.5, tel. 998/883-1436, www.avis.com)

- **Easy Way** (Cancún Airport, toll-free Mex. tel. 800/327-9929, toll-free U.S./Can. tel. 877/640-3279, www.easywayrentacar.com)

- **Hertz** (Cancún Airport, tel. 999/999-8040; La Isla Shopping Village, Blvd. Kukulcán Km 12.5, tel. 999/118-040, www.hertz.com)

- **National** (Cancún Airport, tel. 998/277-2796; La Isla Shopping Village, Blvd. Kukulcán Km 12.5, tel. 998/176-8117, www. nationalcar.com)

- **Thrifty** (Cancún Airport, tel. 998/886-0333; Westin Resort & Spa, Blvd. Kukulcán Km 20, tel. 998/885-0086, www.thrifty. com)

Parking lots in the Zona Hotelera are in the shopping centers: La Isla Shopping Village, Forum by the Sea, Plaza Kukulcán, Plaza Caracol, and Puerto Cancún Marina Town Center. Rates are typically US$1 for the first hour and US$0.50 for each additional hour. Downtown, it's easiest—and relatively safe—to park on the street or in the public lots around Parque Las Palapas.

Travel Agencies

Most travelers handle their travel and hotel bookings online, but there are still a handful of travel agencies in Cancún for anyone who finds a need for their service—look especially on Avenidas Tulum and Uxmal. Worth noting is **American Express** (Plaza Las Americas, Av. Tulum at Av. Sayil, tel. 998/881-4000, 9am-5pm Mon.-Fri., 9am-1pm Sat.), which has special services for cardholders.

Isla Mujeres

Just eight kilometers (5 miles) long and no more than a quarter mile wide, Isla Mujeres is a sliver of land fringed by white-sand beaches amid the wide turquoise sea. It actually was one of the first places in the Mexican Caribbean to have hotels and other tourist developments, but attention quickly shifted to Isla Cozumel and then Cancún proper. It may have been a blessing in disguise: As those areas exploded, rushing to build high-rise hotels and ports for cruise ships, Isla Mujeres developed more slowly, attracting backpackers and bohemians while remaining pretty much what it always was—a quiet, picturesque fishing community.

Of course, even slow change adds up, and today Isla Mujeres is a well-established tourist destination. Thousands of day-trippers come from Cancún to shop, eat, and relax on the island's calm beaches. While still popular with backpackers, Isla Mujeres now also attracts midrange and upscale travelers with a solid selection of boutique hotels and bed-and-breakfasts.

Despite higher hotel prices and T-shirt shops, golf carts, and sometimes pushy tour operators, Isla Mujeres remains at its core a mellow tropical island with a friendly and laid-back population. Passersby greet one another, people stroll in the middle of the street, and many businesses close for long lunches. Add to that beautiful beaches and numerous options for snorkeling, biking, and other outdoor excursions, and it's no wonder so many visitors find themselves extending (and re-extending) their time here.

The precise origin of the name Isla Mujeres (Island of Women) is unknown, though not for lack of theories. Some say the name comes from the days of pirates trolling the Caribbean; they allegedly kept their female captives on Isla Mujeres while they ransacked boats sailing along the coast. Another more likely story is that the island served as a stopover (or secondary site) for Maya pilgrims on their way to Isla Cozumel to worship Ixchel, the female goddess of fertility. When Spanish explorers landed here, they reportedly found a large number of female-shaped clay idols and named the island after them.

ORIENTATION

The town of Isla Mujeres (known as the *centro,* or center) is at the far northwestern tip of the island; at just eight blocks long and five blocks deep, it is very walkable. This is where most of the hotels, restaurants, shops, and services are. There is no main street per se, although Avenida Hidalgo intersects with the town *zócalo* (central plaza) and has a bustling pedestrian-only section. Avenida Rueda Medina is the busy street that runs along the south side of the *centro* past the ferry piers and continues all the way to the island's other end, becoming Carretera Punta Sur at Parque Garrafón (and therefore also known as Carretera Garrafón). The road that runs along the north side of the island is Avenida Martínez Ross as it leaves the downtown area, becoming Carretera Perimetral partway down the island.

SIGHTS
Hacienda Mundaca

A dilapidated estate, **Hacienda Mundaca** (Av. Rueda Medina at Carr. Garrafón Km 3.5, no phone, 9am-4pm daily, US$1) is not interesting enough to visit, but is just historical enough that tourism folks (including guidebook authors) can't just ignore it. It was built by a 19th-century retired slave trader, Antonio Mundaca, to woo a local woman. Legend has it that when she rejected his advances, Mundaca went crazy, holing up in the estate while it crumbled around him . . . and that's pretty much where things stand today: You'll find a small home, the platforms of a Maya ruin, two caged crocs, a lagoon, and lots and lots of mosquitoes.

Isla Mujeres

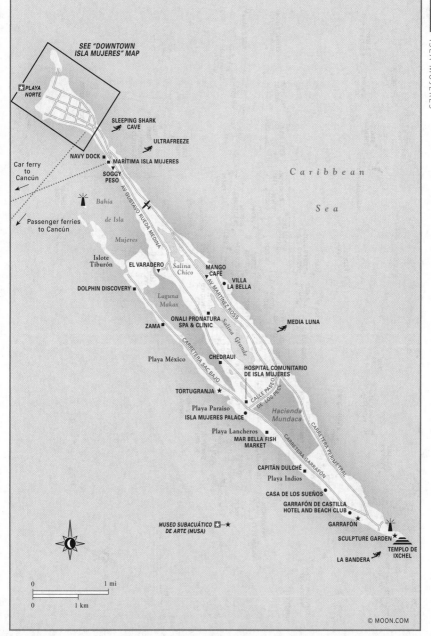

SEE "DOWNTOWN ISLA MUJERES" MAP

PLAYA NORTE

SLEEPING SHARK CAVE

ULTRAFREEZE

NAVY DOCK

MARÍTIMA ISLA MUJERES

Car ferry to Cancún

SOGGY PESO

Bahía

Passenger ferries to Cancún

de Isla

Mujeres

AV GUSTAVO RUEDA MEDINA

Islote Tiburón

EL VARADERO

Salina Chico

MANGO CAFÉ

VILLA LA BELLA

DOLPHIN DISCOVERY

Laguna Makax

AV MARTINEZ ROSS

MEDIA LUNA

ONALI PRONATURA SPA & CLINIC

ZAMA

Salina Grande

Playa México

CARRETERA SAC BAJO

CHEDRAUI

HOSPITAL COMUNITARIO DE ISLA MUJERES

TORTUGRANJA

CALLE PASEO DE LOS PECES

Playa Paraíso

ISLA MUJERES PALACE

Hacienda Mundaca

Playa Lancheros

MAR BELLA FISH MARKET

CARRETERA GARRAFÓN

CARRETERA PERIMETRAL

CAPITÁN DULCHÉ

Playa Indios

CASA DE LOS SUEÑOS

GARRAFÓN DE CASTILLA HOTEL AND BEACH CLUB

GARRAFÓN

MUSEO SUBACUÁTICO DE ARTE (MUSA)

SCULPTURE GARDEN

TEMPLO DE IXCHEL

LA BANDERA

Caribbean

Sea

0   1 mi

0   1 km

© MOON.COM

Downtown Isla Mujeres

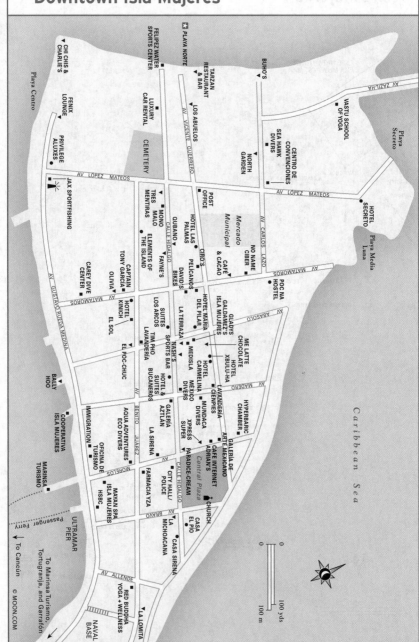

★ PLAYA NORTE

CHI CHI'S & CHARLIE'S ▲

FELIPE'Z WATER SPORTS CENTER ▲

FENIX LOUNGE ▲

PRIVILEGE ALUXES ●

Playa Centro

JAX SPORTFISHING

LUXURY CAR RENTAL

CEMETERY

AV. VICENTE GUERRERO

LOS ABUELOS

TARZAN RESTAURANT & BAR

BUHO'S ▲

SEA HAWK DIVERS

CENTRO DE CONVENCIONES

NORTH GARDEN

AV. ZAZIL-HA

VASTU SCHOOL OF YOGA

Playa Secreto

AV. LÓPEZ MATEOS

AV. LÓPEZ MATEOS

AV. CARLOS LAZO

HOTEL SECRETO

Playa Media Luna

POST OFFICE

Mercado Municipal

TRES MENTIRAS

MONO MALO

CALLE HIDALGO

QUBANO ▼

ELEMENTS OF THE ISLAND

HOTEL LAS PALMAS

CIRO'S ▼

NO NAME CIBER

CAFÉ & CACAO

AV. MATAMOROS

CAPTAIN TONY GARCIA ▼

CAREY DIVE CENTER

OLIVIA ▼

FAYNE'S

DAVID'S BIKES

PELICANOS

POC NA HOSTEL

AV. GUSTAVO RUEDA MEDINA

HOTEL KINICH ▼

EL SOL

AV. MATAMOROS

SUITES LOS ARCOS

HOTEL MARIA DEL PILAR

LA TERRAZA ▼

NASH'S SPORTS BAR

GALDAMEZ'S

GLADYS ▼

HOTEL XBULU-HA

AV. ABASOLO

EL POC-CHUC

TIM PHO LAVANDERIA

HOTEL & SUITES BUCANEROS

MEDISLA

HOTEL CARMELINA

LAVANDERIA

AV. MADERO

ME LATTE CHOCOLATE

CIENPIES

MÉXICO DIVERS

MUNDACA DIVERS

HYPERBARIC CHAMBER

BALLY HOO ▲

COOPERATIVA ISLA MUJERES

IMMIGRATION

AGUA ADVENTURES ECO DIVERS

GALERIA AZTLAN

AV. BENITO JUAREZ

LA SIRENA

XPRESS SUPER

PARADICE-CREAM

CAFÉ INTERNET

ADRIAN'S

GALERÍA DE ARTE MEXICANO

CALLE HIDALGO

Central Plaza

Caribbean Sea

MARINSA TURISMO

OFICINA DE TURISMO

MAYAN SPA ISLA MUJERES

HSBC

AV. MORELOS

FARMACIA YZA

CITY HALL POLICE

FARMACIA CRUZ

✝ CHURCH

CASA EL PÍO

ULTRAMAR PIER

Passenger Ferry

To Cancún

LA MICHOACANA

AV. BRAVO

CASA SIRENA

AV. ALLENDE

© MOON.COM

To Marinsa Turismo, Tortugranja, and Garrafón

RED BUDDHA YOGA + WELLNESS

LA LOMITA ▲

NAVAL BASE

0
0

100 yds

100 m

Tortugranja

A modest sea turtle sanctuary on the island's southwestern shore, **Tortugranja** (Carr. Sac Bajo 5, tel. 998/877-0595, 9am-5pm daily, US$3) makes for an interesting stop on your golf-cart tour of the island. The one-room cement structure contains several enclosures with sea turtles of different ages and species. The tank of just-hatched *tortuguitas* is always a hit; please respect the rules (and huge signs) and refrain from touching or picking them up. Small aquariums along the walls also contain sea anemones, sea horses, lionfish, and the deadly rockfish, among others. Outside there are three tanks with more turtles as well as a large fenced-in area of the ocean that is home to a nurse shark. During the nesting season (May-October), one section of sand is fenced off, and eggs collected from nests are transplanted here for protection.

Between July and November, travelers may be able to accompany the center's workers to look for fresh sea turtle nests on the island's eastern shore and relocate eggs to protected areas, and, until October and November, help release hatchlings into the sea. Both activities take place in the evening several nights a week, typically starting around 9pm, but are not formal tours. Those interested should inquire at the center; having basic Spanish skills (and possibly your own vehicle) will make participating much easier. There's no charge, but a tip is customary.

★ Museo Subacuático de Arte (MUSA)

Underwater sculpture is nothing new, but there's never been a project as ambitious—or as gorgeous, frankly—as the **Subaquatic Museum of Art** (www.musacancun.org). British sculptor Jason de Caires Taylor, along with four Mexican sculptors (Karen Salinas Martínez, Roberto Díaz Abraham, Rodrigo Quiñones Reyes, and Salvador Quiroz Ennis) and one Cuban artist (Elier Amado Gil), created hundreds of life-size statues of everyday people—garbagemen, pregnant women, wizened tribal leaders, and more—and sank them in two separate sites; one is near Cancún's Nizuc reef (approximately 12 feet deep), the other near Isla Mujeres's Manchones reef (approximately 24 feet deep). Striking for their lifelike quality, the figures were made from a special cement that will promote coral and other sealife, eventually forming an artificial reef system. Most dive shops offer dive and snorkeling trips to both sites.

Each MUSA statue depicts a different person and emotion.

Templo de Ixchel and Sculpture Garden

At the far southern tip of the island, a crumbling Maya temple stands on a cliff overlooking the sea. Its original function is unknown: The location suggests it was an observation post or even an astronomical observatory, but most experts believe it was related to Ixchel, the Maya goddess of the moon, fertility, weaving, and childbirth, possibly as a secondary pilgrimage site after Isla Cozumel. Whatever its history, the temple was abandoned long before Francisco Hernández de Córdoba first reported its existence in 1517.

The temple alone isn't too exciting, as time and weather have all but destroyed it. But a visit here also includes pondering a dozen or so multicolored modern sculptures lining the path to the ruins as well as enjoying an oceanside trail past the ruins that continues to the very tip of the island—the easternmost point of Mexico, in fact—before looping back along the craggy waterfront to the entrance. It's a decent side trip, with some fine photo ops along the way.

Admission to the Ixchel ruins is included in the ticket price to Garrafón park; all others must pay US$1.50 (9am-5pm daily).

★ Isla Contoy

Peeking out of a crystal-clear sea and dotted with saltwater lagoons, mangroves, and coconut palms, Isla Contoy is home to over 150 species of birds, including herons, brown pelicans, frigates, and cormorants, and is a preferred nesting ground for three different species of endangered sea turtles. The island was decreed a national park in 1998, and its only structures are a three-story viewing tower, a visitors center, and a small museum; a few trails allow for appreciating the otherwise pristine island environment. Just 24 kilometers (14 miles) north of Isla Mujeres, Isla Contoy is a popular and rewarding outing for nature buffs and average day-trippers alike.

Various tour operators on Isla Mujeres offer the same basic trip for a standard price (US$75-100, including the park entrance fee):

Isla Contoy is home to brown pelicans and numerous other bird species.

Depart around 9am with a 30-45-minute stop for snorkeling along the way, then three hours to explore the island or just relax, including lunch on the beach (typically freshly grilled fish or chicken). Boats head back around 3pm, reaching Isla Mujeres at 4pm.

Recommended operators include **Captain Tony García** (Av. Matamoros near Av. Benito Juárez, tel. 998/877-0229, captaintonys@hotmail.com), a friendly English-speaking guide with over 25 years' experience whose house doubles as his office, and **Cooperativa Isla Mujeres** (end of Av. Madero at Pier 7, cell. tel. 998/198-0893, www.islamujerestours.com.mx, 7am-7pm daily).

BEACHES
★ Playa Norte

Playa Norte (North Beach) is a long, undulating strip of sand on the northern edge of Isla Mujeres. Its fine white sands descend ever so slowly into a gorgeous turquoise sea—you can wade almost a hundred yards out and still be only waist deep. The long, shallow shelf means

Playa Norte has virtually no waves, adding to the beach's tranquility. It's a favorite spot for visitors of all ages: couples sunning themselves and sipping margaritas, backpackers on colorful beach towels, kids frolicking in the calm water, and older travelers relaxing under huge umbrellas.

You can rent beach chairs and umbrellas at a number of spots along Playa Norte, including **Buho's** (end of Av. Carlos Lazo, no phone, US$4.50 chair, US$4.50 umbrella); **Chi Chis & Charlie's** (southwestern end of Playa Norte, no phone, US$12.00 chair and umbrella); **Tarzan Restaurant & Bar** (end of Av. Guerrero at Playa Norte, tel. 998/877-0679, US$11.50 chair and umbrella); and **Fenix Lounge** (end of Av. Rueda Medina, tel. 998/274-0073, www.fenixisla.com, US$12 chair and umbrella, US$25 beach bed).

Tarzan Restaurant & Bar (end of Av. Guerrero at Playa Norte, tel. 998/877-0679) also rents snorkel gear (US$10/day), single and double kayaks (US$15-20/hour), Hobie Cats (US$45/hour), and stand-up paddleboards (US$12.50/hour) and can arrange snorkel tours (US$30 pp, 2 hours). **FeliPez Water Sports Center** (end of Av. Hidalgo at Playa Norte, tel. 998/593-3403) rents the same gear at similar prices.

Playa Centro

Around the corner, Playa Centro (aka Playa Sol) is also lovely, with deeper water and a wider beach than Playa Norte's. One end of the beach is packed with fishing boats, while the other is cordoned off for use by guests at a nearby resort and day-trippers from Cancún. That said, there's still a large section in the middle where you can stretch out a towel. Lounge chairs and umbrellas also can be rented here for US$10-15 for the day.

Playa Secreto

East of Playa Norte (around the *other* corner), Playa Secreto sits on a wide lagoon facing a resort hotel. The water is calm, shallow, and clear, making it a perfect spot for children. This is a popular place for locals, especially on weekends, when extended families come with coolers filled with food and drinks to enjoy a day off.

Other Beaches

Zama (Carr. Sac Bajo s/n, tel. 998/877-0739, www.zamaislamujeres.com, 10am-6pm daily) is a small beach club on the island's calm southwest shore that's a popular wedding spot, if that gives you an idea of how pretty it is. You can relax in a comfy beach bed on

Few spots are more laid-back than Playa Norte on Isla Mujeres.

Island Murals

Mercado Municipal on Isla Mujeres

It's impossible to miss the massive ocean-themed murals dotting Isla Mujeres, their vibrant, colorful designs adorning seawalls, hotel exteriors, even city hall. They extend up to a half block long or several stories high, and range from highly realistic to psychedelic to abstract modern to urban street art. The murals are the work of various artists belonging to **PangeaSeed** (www. pangeaseed.org), a nonprofit organization that uses education and "artivism" to promote marine conservation worldwide. In 2014, Isla Mujeres became one of several communities selected for the group's "Sea Walls for Oceans" mural project; others are in Florida, New Zealand, Vietnam, Sri Lanka, and elsewhere. Of course, Mexico was once a muralist's mecca, the birthplace and inspiration of world-famous painters like Diego Rivera, José Orozco, and David Siqueiros. The murals in Isla Mujeres are not only gorgeous and impactful, but are a refreshing revival of the art form, connecting the greats of the early 20th century to contemporary street artists like Banksy and Shepard Fairey.

the well-tended beach or in a hammock in the shady garden. The sand is a bit thin and there's seagrass in the shallows, but you can swim comfortably from the long pier or in one of the two appealing mosaic-tiled pools. The classy open-air restaurant is reasonably priced and has everything from burritos to shrimp dishes, plus a kids menu (US$5-20). There's no admission or minimum consumption, but they charge US$10 for use of the lounge chairs, US$25 for the beach beds.

Capitán Dulché (Carr. Sac Bajo s/n, tel. 998/355-0012, www.capitandulche.com, 10am-6pm Mon.-Wed., 10am-8pm Thurs.-Sun.,

US$15) is a beach club with a relaxed marina feel. It's divided into three sections—a well-tended beach with calm waters and *palapa* shade, a wide grassy area with antique anchors and thick tow chains, and a modern beachfront restaurant (US$8-17) with a solid menu of international dishes. Be sure to check out the bar that also happens to be housed in a repurposed sailboat. There's a small nautical museum onsite, too—good if you're interested in model sailboats. Admission is applied as credit towards food and drinks. Poolside cabanas and oceanfront *palapas* also can be rented (US$17-23, including towels and two drinks).

ENTERTAINMENT AND EVENTS

Isla Mujeres's nightlife ranges from beach bars to sports bars. Fortunately, the town is small enough that you can wander about until you find the scene that suits you best.

Bars

On the pedestrian walkway, **Tres Mentiras** (Av. Hidalgo s/n, no tel., 5pm-1am daily) is a colorful little restaurant-cantina serving up creative cocktails, many made with mezcal. Combos like kiwi with ginger beer, pineapple with coriander and jalapeño, even popcorn are commonplace. (You also can get a pint of locally made craft beer.) It's popular with just about everyone, so get here on the early side if you want a seat. There's live music on weekends.

Sitting pretty on Playa Norte, **Fenix Lounge** (end of Av. Rueda Medina, tel. 998/274-0073, www.fenixisla.com, 11am-11pm Mon.-Sat., 11am-8pm Sun) is a classic beach club that transforms into a lively bar scene around sunset. A changing lineup of DJs typically keeps the crowd happy, either on the dance floor or at their seats. Sundays brings salsa dancing and occasional live music.

Nash's Sports Bar (Av. Hidalgo s/n, tel. 998/705-9005, 9am-midnight daily) is a dive bar with at least eight TVs tuned to the big game of the day pretty much every day. A favorite of American expats, you'll find cheap buckets of beer, wings, and a friendly crowd. Nash himself is often on-site, checking in on guests.

Soggy Peso (Av. Gustavo Rueda Medina, tel. 998/274-0050, www.soggypeso.net, 9am-8pm daily) is a favorite for daytime drinkin' Americans, open early and closed not long after sunset (the view, by the way, is terrific here). The vibe is casual and jocular, and every day there's a different special from the kitchen: Hot Wings Wednesdays, BBQ Sundays, and so forth. It's located south of the center, on the waterfront.

Live Music

La Terraza (Av. Hidalgo at Av. Abasolo, tel. 998/236-3879, 11am-midnight daily, no cover) has great live salsa, cumbia, and other Latin dance music most nights after 10pm. Drinks here are excellent—try the watermelon and jalapeño margarita for something with a kick—and the food isn't bad, but it's the music and lively atmosphere that draw folks in, night after night.

Fayne's (Av. Hidalgo 12, tel. 998/877-0525, 5pm-midnight daily, no cover) features live nightly music, mostly Caribbean but with a smattering of rock and reggae acts as well. The high *palapa* roof and spacious bar area make it equally suited for dancing or just chilling out. Thursday-Sunday are the busiest nights, often with two bands starting as early as 6pm; otherwise, things get hopping around 10:30pm.

SHOPPING

It's easy to be put off by the onslaught of kitschy souvenirs shops that greet you as soon as you step off the ferry. But fear not: Isla Mujeres has a number of genuinely good specialty stores, especially for Mexican *artesanía*, if you keep your eyes open.

Located in a Caribbean clapboard house, **Galería Aztlán** (Av. Hidalgo at Av. Madero, cell. tel. 998/110-3782, 9am-9pm Mon.-Sat.) sells gorgeous Mexican masks from every corner of the country. The owners, transplants from Mexico City, also design specialty T-shirts and religious art.

Mono Malo (Av. Hidalgo between Avs. Lopez Mateos and Matamoros, no phone, www.monomalo.com.mx, 2pm-10pm daily) specializes in original high-end T-shirts, most inspired by Mexican skeleton art, Revolution heroes, and *lucha libre* (wrestling) stars. Check out the website to shop the store's entire line.

Galería de Arte Mexicano (Parque Central, Av. Guerrero 3, tel. 998/877-1272, 10am-8pm daily) has fine talavera pottery as well as an extensive selection of silver jewelry.

The prices are somewhat higher here than elsewhere, but so is the quality.

Specializing in beachwear, **Gladys Galdamez's Isla Mujeres** (Abasolo 40, cell. tel. 998/147-1115, ggaldamez59@hotmail.com, 9am-6pm Mon-Fri., noon-6pm Sat.) sells everything from swimsuits and cover-ups to flip-flops and seashell jewelry. The shop makes custom bathing suits for women—choose from a huge variety of patterns or bring your own.

La Sirena (Av. Morelos near Av. Hidalgo, tel. 998/877-0223, 10am-6pm Mon.-Sat.) is a tiny shop that's jam-packed with high-quality folk art from all over Mexico: textiles from Chiapas, masks from Guerrero, skeleton art from Mexico City, and *alebrijes* (wooden creatures) from Oaxaca.

SPORTS AND RECREATION
Scuba Diving

Beginner divers will appreciate the calm waters and vibrant sealife on Isla Mujeres's western side, while the east side presents more challenging options for advanced divers, with deeper water (up to 40 meters/131 feet), more varied terrain, and even a couple of shipwrecks. Favorite sites include La Bandera (a reef dive), Media Luna (a drift dive), Ultrafreeze (a shipwreck, in notoriously chilly water), and the famous Sleeping Shark Cave—a deep cave known to attract sharks, where they fall into a strangely lethargic and nonaggressive state. Explanations for this last phenomenon vary: Salinity of the water, low carbon dioxide, and underwater currents are some theories. Unfortunately, overfishing (and overdiving) has disrupted the slumber party, and there's only a 50-50 chance, at best, of seeing sharks on any given day. When sharks are seen, they're typically nurse sharks these days. September seems to be the best month to spot them, but you just never know.

Isla Mujeres's dive shops charge fairly uniform rates: US$65-70 one tank, US$80-90 two tanks. Gear and marine park admission is sometimes included; otherwise, an additional US$10-20 per day is tacked on. The Sleeping Shark Cave and deep dives run a little higher, and most shops offer multi-dive specials. Open-water certification courses cost around US$395, including equipment and materials.

Aqua Adventures Eco Divers (Av. Juárez at Calle Morelos, cell tel. 998/322-8109, www.diveislamujeres.com, 9am-7pm Mon.-Sat., 10am-6pm Sun.) goes the extra mile to provide friendly, professional service.

Carey Dive Center (Av. Matamoros near Av. Rueda Medina, tel. 998/877-0763, www.careydivecenter.com, 8am-8pm daily) is a recommended dive shop that enjoys lots of repeat customers.

México Divers (Av. Madero at Av. Hidalgo, tel. 998/877-1117, www.mexicodivers.com, 8am-8pm daily) is a popular dive shop with a youthful vibe.

Mundaca Divers (Av. Madero 10, tel. 998/877-0607, www.mundacadiversislamujeres.com, 8am-8pm daily) has been in business for more than 35 years, making it one of the longest standing and well-respected operations in the region.

Sea Hawk Divers (Av. Carlos Lazo at Av. López Mateos, tel. 998/877-1233, www.seahawkislamujeres.com, 9am-8pm daily) is a recommended dive shop owned and run by island locals Ariel and Bonnie Barandica. Sea Hawk has a half-dozen comfortable rooms and studios attached to the dive shop, which are often included as part of dive packages.

Snorkeling

Isla Mujeres's western side has calm water and extensive coral reefs that make for excellent snorkeling, though relatively few spots are accessible from the shore. Snorkeling tours can be booked at **dive shops** or with the **Cooperativa Isla Mujeres** (end of Av. Madero at Pier 7, cell. tel. 998/198-0893, www.islamujerestours.com.mx, 7am-7pm daily). Most operators take snorkelers to El Farito (The Lighthouse) and other spots near the northern end of the island, where the coral is decent but somewhat trafficked; tours run around US$25-35 per person. Dive shops are more likely to take you to less-visited spots.

You can also arrange to snorkel at **Museo Subacuático de Arte** (MUSA), the remarkable underwater sculpture park near Manchones reef, at the southern end of the island. Dive shops and other operators charge around US$40-45 per person for a trip combining MUSA and one other spot.

Yet another option is to take a trip to **Isla Contoy** (US$75-100 pp), which includes snorkeling on Ixlanche reef in addition to exploring the island. Boats depart Isla Mujeres around 9am and return at 4pm.

Snorkel on your own at **Garrafón de Castilla Hotel and Beach Club** (Carr. Punta Sur Km 6, tel. 998/877-0107, 10am-5pm daily, US$3.50), at the southern tip of the island. The club itself is pretty desultory, but you can explore over 300 meters (894 feet) of coral reef, including the part used by its much-hyped neighbor, Parque Garrafón. Snorkel gear rents for US$5, and lockers and towels can be rented for around US$1.50 each.

Whale Shark Tours

Snorkeling with whale sharks, the world's largest fish, is an experience you won't soon forget. These gentle giants congregate along the northeastern tip of the Yucatán Peninsula mid-May-mid-September and typically measure 6-7.5 meters (20-25 feet) and weigh more than 10 tons. (They're known to grow upwards of 18 meters, or nearly 60 feet, though such behemoths are rare here.) From Isla Mujeres, whale shark tours leave around 8am for a 60-90-minute boat ride northwest past Isla Contoy toward Isla Holbox (where such tours first became popular). Once in the feeding grounds, you'll see the huge sharks trolling along the surface, feeding on krill. The boat is maneuvered nearby the shark, and a guide plus two guests slip overboard and swim alongside. The sharks are surprisingly fast, despite their languid appearance, and you have to kick hard to keep up and get a good look at their sleek spotted bodies and massive gaping mouths. The smaller your group,

the more chances you'll have to get into the water, though most people welcome the short breathers between turns. Rules also require that boats not linger with any one shark more than 30 minutes; in all, each guest can expect to have 2-4 chances to jump in. Lunch and beverages are included. Boats typically return to Isla Mujeres by 3pm.

Cooperativa Isla Mujeres (end of Av. Madero at Pier 7, cell. tel. 998/198-0893, www. islamujerestours.com.mx, 7am-7pm daily) handles most whale shark tours, charging around US$125 per person. Most **dive shops** in Isla Mujeres also offer whale shark tours, charging around US$150 per person. Always confirm the departure times, how long the tour will last, and whether lunch and water are provided.

Swimming with Dolphins

Dolphin Discovery (end of Carr. Sac Bajo, toll-free Mex. tel. 800/727-5391, toll-free U.S. tel. 866/393-5158, www.dolphindiscovery. com, US$109-199 adult, US$89-119 child) offers various dolphin interaction programs on the island's calm western shore, as well as ones with manatees and sea lions. Garrafón, a nearby sister park with snorkeling, zip lines, and more, has packages combining Dolphin Discovery programs with admission to Garrafón, a good option if you'd like to make a day of it. Most visitors come from Cancún on Dolphin Discovery's private ferry (included in the price), though no transport is provided for guests staying on Isla Mujeres. Reservations required.

Ecoparks

Built on a bluff at the southern end of Isla Mujeres, **Garrafón** (Carr. Garrafón Km 6, tel. 998/849-4748, toll-free U.S. tel. 866/393-5158, www.garrafon.com, 10am-6pm daily, US$89-189 adult, US$59-99 child) is a combo ecopark and water park. There's snorkeling, kayaking, zip-lining, an interactive dolphin program (conducted at Dolphin Discovery, a nearby sister park), and, of course, just relaxing on the beach or by the pool. Ferry service to and from Cancún is included, as well as admission to Templo de Ixchel, a tiny Maya ruin.

Sportfishing

Cooperativa Isla Mujeres (end of Av. Madero at Pier 7, cell. tel. 998/198-0893, www. islamujerestours.com.mx, 7am-7pm daily) offers *pesca deportiva* (sportfishing) at reasonable prices. Boats typically carry up to six people for the same price, and prices include nonalcoholic drinks, sandwiches, and bait. Two trips are usually available, depending on the season: Pesca Mediana (US$330, 4 hours) focuses on midsize fish, including snapper, grouper, and barracuda; and Pesca Mayor (US$500, 6 hours) goes after large catch such as marlin and sailfish. Reserve directly at the pier. **Sea Hawk Divers** (Av. Carlos Lazo at Av. López Mateos, tel. 998/877-1233, www.se-ahawkislamujeres.com, 9am-8pm daily) offers comparable services and prices.

JAX Sportfishing (JAX Bar and Grill, Av. López Mateos at Av. Rueda Medina, tel. 998/877-1254, www.jaxsportfishing.com, US$950) has an experienced English-speaking captain and offers all-day charters for a maximum of four anglers, ensuring highly personalized service.

Spas

Just one block from the ferry terminal, **Mayan Spa Isla Mujeres** (Av. Morelos near Av. Rueda Medina, tel. 998/257-4614, www. themayanspaislamujeres.com.mx, 10am-8pm Mon.-Sat.) is a small family-owned spa offering top-rated massages and body treatments. It's nothing fancy, but it's welcoming and professional.

Onali Pronatura Spa & Clinic (Calle Cayo Ratón s/n, tel. 998/240-5524, 10am-6pm Mon.-Sat.) is a full-service spa offering a wide range of massages, body treatments, and facials in a serene setting near the Salina Grande lagoon.

Yoga

Red Buddha Yoga + Wellness (Av. Juárez 22, tel. 984/159-5508, www.redbuddhayoga. com, US$7.50 class) is an upscale yoga studio and spa offering a cozy indoor studio and breezy thatch-roofed studio for instruction. Vinyasa, hatha, power, yin, and slow flow are among the classes offered. Body treatments like massages, reiki, and acupuncture are also available.

Vastu School of Yoga (Calle Zazil-Ha 118, tel. 866/719-2138, www.vastuyoga. com, US$15 class) offers yoga instruction in

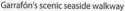

Garrafón's scenic seaside walkway

a breezy *palapa* studio at Na Balam Hotel. Classes are held daily at 9am, 11am, and 6pm; Monday and Thursday, there's also a class at 7:15pm. Workshops and private sessions also are available.

Yoga classes at **Poc Na Hostel** (Av. Matamoros near Av. Lazo, tel. 998/877-0090) are open to the public every morning at 9am. The price—US$5—can't be beat.

FOOD

Seafood is the specialty in Isla Mujeres, even more so than in Cancún. In fact, much of the lobster and fish served on the Riviera Maya is caught near Isla Mujeres, so it stands to reason that it's freshest here.

Mexican

Don't be put off by its garish mural with fluorescent fish: **El Poc-Chuc** (Calle Abasolo at Av. Juárez, tel. 998/152-2613, 7:30am-10:30pm Tues.-Sun., US$3-8) actually serves up delicious Mexican food, especially for breakfast. The setting is old-school: plastic tables and chairs crammed into a tiny dining room. Service is fast, though, which makes rubbing elbow (literally) with your neighbor no big deal.

La Lomita (Av. Juárez near Av. Allende, tel. 998/826-6335, 9:30am-10:30pm daily, US$5-9), a brightly painted restaurant frequented by locals, offers tasty Mexican fare. *Comida corrida*—a two-course lunch special with drink—is offered daily and often includes chiles rellenos, tacos, and stews. Ceviche, grilled whole fish, and other seafood meals also are featured at reasonable prices.

Though somewhat sterile in decor, the verdant outdoor café **North Garden** (Av. Carlos Lazo 14, tel. 998/151-6130, 7am-5pm daily, US$5-8) serves excellent Mexican dishes with flair: tostadas topped with ahi tuna, chicken tacos with pineapple and guacamole, sizzling chicken fajitas. There's also a good variety of salads, if you're hankering for something lighter. Drinks—both alcoholic on nonalcoholic—are not to be missed. The basil mint lemonade is a fan favorite.

Mercado Municipal (Av. Guerrero at Av. Matamoros, 6am-4pm daily, US$2-4) has a handful of simple eateries that serve good cheap meals. On Sunday, *cochinita pibil* (slow-roasted pork marinated in achiote sauce and wrapped in banana leaves) is offered at a handful of stands. Get there by 9am to enjoy some before it sells out.

Seafood

Bally Hoo (Av. Rueda Medina near Av. Abasolo, cell tel. 998/214-5805, 6am-10pm daily, US$5-11) may be stuck behind a gas station, but the Baja-style breaded fish tacos are to die for, and well worth any necessary searching. The fish-and-chips are great, too, and if you've got an appetite, the fish fillet or shrimp dishes are filling. Cold beers and margaritas are the perfect accompaniment.

★ **Mar Bella Fish Market** (Perímetral Poniente 80, cell tel. 998/577-8318, noon-8pm daily, US$12-40) is a swanky seafood restaurant, set on a gorgeous beach halfway down the island, that sells everything by the kilo. There's no menu. Instead, diners peruse the fresh fish and seafood on offer (all beautifully displayed on ice or in tanks) and are given suggestions of possible made-to-order dishes. Service is tops.

Los Abuelos (Av. Guerrero s/n, tel. 998/156-5689, 1pm-10pm Mon.-Sat., US$5-9) is a family-run restaurant serving up all manner of seafood dishes. The specialties are coconut shrimp and grilled lobster tail but the menu features everything from ceviche to fried fish. Takeout is available and a popular option for picnicking, especially because Playa Norte is just a half block away.

Other Specialties

Upscale but homey, ★ **Olivia** (Av. Matamoros between Calle Juárez and Av. Rueda Medina, tel. 998/877-1765, www.olivia-isla-mujeres.com, 5pm-9:45pm Mon.-Sat., US$7-18) serves up the best Mediterranean cuisine on the island. Owned by an Israeli couple who pooled their families' recipes and opened shop, the menu is a phenomenal amalgam of specialties from Morocco, Greece, Bulgaria, and Turkey. Seating is either in the *palapa*-roofed dining room or in the lush garden courtyard. Reservations are recommended. Cash only.

A farm-to-table eatery, ★ **Café & Cacao** (Av. Matamoros s/n, tel. 503/475-5596, 9am-1pm and 6pm-9:30pm daily, US$6-11) serves gorgeous and creative meals, many of which are vegan and gluten-free. The menu is seasonal and almost entirely organic. Breakfasts range from granola bowls to free-range egg dishes, while dinner often features lionfish and edible flowers. Freshly made baked goods (the quinoa bread is to die for), homemade cheeses, and a variety of coffee, teas and freshly pressed juices are a must.

Qubano (Av. Hidalgo between Avs. Matamoros and Mateos, cell tel. 998/214-2118, noon-10pm Mon.-Sat., US$10-15) is a colorful place with a tasty selection of Cuban sandwiches, burgers, and salads. Favorites include the Tostón (plantain slices stuffed with chicken, pork, or *picadillo*), the Cuban (grilled ham, pork, and cheese), and the goat-cheese-stuffed burger. Snag a table and enjoy a Cuban coffee while you wait, or take your eats to go.

In a clapboard house facing the lagoon, with fishing boats crowded up next to it, **El Varadero** (Calle de Septiembre s/n, tel. 998/877-1600, 1pm-8pm Tues.-Sun., US$10-19) doesn't really evoke the famous white-sand beach east of Havana that it's named for, but good food—and even better mojitos—have a way of trumping geography. Dig into classic Cuban fare while sitting at aluminum tables on an outdoor patio decorated with shipping buoys. Find it at the mouth of Laguna Makax, near Puerto Isla Mujeres.

Cafés

Located partway down the island, ★ **Mango Café** (Carr. Perimentral at Calle Payo Obispo, tel. 998/274-0118, 7am-3pm Tues.-Wed., 7am-9pm Thurs.-Mon., US$6-14) has a cheerful bohemian exterior that practically begs a closer look. You'll be glad you did: Dishes like coconut French toast and eggs Benedict with chaya and portabella mushrooms, plus drinks like ginger lemonade and bottomless organic coffee, make this small eatery an island favorite—and that's just breakfast!

Serving up organic products, **Elements of the Island Café** (Av. Juárez between López Mateos and Matamoros, cell. tel. 998/117-8651, www.elementsoftheisland.com, 7:30am-1pm Thurs.-Tues., US$4-6) serves up hearty and healthy meals. Breakfasts are especially popular, with homemade bread and marmalade, and cappuccinos to die for.

Me Latte Chocolate (Av. Guerrero 8, tel. 998/236-3879, 7am-6pm Mon.-Sat., US$2.50-6) sells a mouthwatering array of freshly made baked goods, fruit cups, sandwiches, and salads—all to go. There are also loads of smoothies and coffee drinks on offer. It's perfect when you're running to catch the ferry or for a picnic lunch on the beach.

Sweets

La Michoacana (Av. Bravo at Av. Hidalgo, 9am-11pm daily, US$1-2.50) offers homemade *aguas, paletas,* and *helados* (juices, Popsicles, and ice cream). Choose from seasonal fruits including passion fruit, watermelon, pineapple, and mamey. Of course, chocolate- and vanilla-flavored treats are available, too.

Try **ParadICE-CREAM** (Av. Hidalgo at Av. Morelos, 10am-10pm daily, US$2-6) for terrific handmade gelato.

Groceries

For a big supermarket, head to **Chedraui** (www.chedraui.com.mx, 7am-8pm daily), about halfway down the island, across from the baseball diamond. To get there, simply follow Avenida Gustavo Rueda Medina; the supermarket will be on your right, just before a sharp bend known as "devil's curve."

Xpress Super (Av. Morelos 5, www.sanfranciscodeasis.com.mx, 7am-10pm Mon.-Sat., 7am-9pm Sun.) is the island's longtime local grocery store, facing the central plaza.

Mercado Municipal (Av. Guerrero at Av. Matamoros, 6am-4pm daily) has a good selection of fruits, vegetables, and meats, a *tortillería,* plus fresh-squeezed juices sold by the liter.

ACCOMMODATIONS

Isla Mujeres has a wide variety of lodging options, from youth hostels to upscale boutique hotels. Most budget and midrange places are in the *centro,* while higher-end resorts occupy secluded areas farther down the island (which may mean you'll need to rent a golf cart to get around).

Under US$50

Isla Mujeres's longtime backpacker haven, ★ **Poc Na Hostel** (Av. Matamoros near Av. Lazo, tel. 998/877-0090, www.pocna. com, US$6.50 pp camping, US$10 pp dorm, US$11 pp dorm with a/c, US$23 s/d with shared bath, US$27 s/d with a/c) is a labyrinth of rooms, courtyards, and common areas, just steps from the island's best beach. Dorms have 4-9 bunks each and, like the private rooms, have cement floors and whitewashed walls. There's foosball, table tennis, and TV in the various common areas, plus a dining room with basic food service. The hostel hosts live music most nights starting at 9:30pm. The drawbacks are no kitchen access and a serious risk of never leaving.

Hotel Maria del Pilar (aka Posada Mary Pili, Calle Abasolo 15, tel. 998/877-0071, US$45 s/d) is a small, well-located hotel with tidy rooms, most with TVs, air-conditioning, and mini fridges, plus Wi-Fi and a shared outdoor kitchen. Bikes and snorkel gear are available for rent. It's a fine choice for budget travelers who want some of the conveniences of a hostel without the scene.

Hotel Carmelina (Av. Guerrero 4, tel. 998/877-0006, US$25-40 s/d with a/c) is a reliable budget choice. It has a slightly residential-motel feel (the family who runs it lives on the ground floor, and another room houses a manicure shop), but the rooms are clean, albeit small. Each also has a mini fridge, TV, and Wi-Fi.

US$50-100

The charming ★ **Casa El Pío** (Av. Hidalgo near Av. Bravo, tel. 998/229-2799, www.casaelpio.com, US$85-100 s/d with a/c) is a five-room boutique-ish hotel with minimalist decor accented with artful touches and splashes of color. Rooms are spacious and comfortably equipped with good beds, separate seating areas, balconies (two with ocean view), and Wi-Fi; each also has a mini fridge and a coffeemaker. There's a small mosaic-tile

Pick your pleasure at a local gelato shop.

plunge pool for cooling off after a day at the beach. Adults only; reservations are highly recommended.

Hotel Kinich (Av. Juárez near Av. Matamoros, tel. 998/888-0909, US$75-90 s/d, US$130 suite) is a great find: Rooms are simple but elegant with warm wood furnishings, muted colors, and Mexican wall art from Guadalajara. All rooms have quiet air-conditioning, cable TV, and Wi-Fi, and more than half of them have king-size beds. Two gorgeous suites occupy the top floor—modern one-bedroom apartments with state-of-the-art kitchens, outdoor whirlpool tubs, and views of town. Continental breakfast is provided. The only downer: The hotel is in a four-story building with no elevator.

Hotel Xbulu-Ha (Av. Guerrero between Avs. Abasolo and Madero, tel. 998/877-1783, www.islamujeres.biz, US$50-60 s/d with a/c, US$70-80 suite with kitchenette and a/c) offers bright and airy rooms with modern amenities like cable TV, mini-split air conditioners, and safety deposit boxes. The beds are double sized—something to consider if you plan on sharing. Suites are larger versions of the standard rooms, with fully equipped kitchenettes and king-size beds. Wi-Fi and beach towels and chairs are included in the rate. The hotel is just one block from the Caribbean.

Hotel & Suites Bucaneros (Av. Hidalgo near Av. Madero, tel. 998/877-1228, www.bucaneros.com, US$85-94 s/d with a/c, US$94 d/t with a/c and kitchenette) has 20 comfortable rooms, all with modern bathrooms, air-conditioning, and Wi-Fi, plus continental breakfast. The budget rooms are quite small, though not uncomfortable, while larger ones have small equipped kitchens (hot plate or gas stove, minifridge, and toaster) and in some cases a sofa bed, balcony, and separate dining area. The location couldn't be more central, but that also means it can be noisy at night.

US$100-200

Elements of the Island (Av. Juárez between Avs. López Mateos and Matamoros, cell tel. 998/117-8651, www.elementsoftheisland.com, US$114 s/d with a/c) has three lovely studio apartments, each with fine wood furnishings, flowing white curtains, and bursts of color. All rooms have king-size beds and basic kitchenettes, plus Wi-Fi and TVs with DVD players. Guests pass through a leafy courtyard with a gurgling fountain to access the rooms, which are behind the hotel's recommended restaurant. Common spaces include a sundeck with a hot tub, lounge chairs, and hammocks. Kind and attentive owners provide excellent service.

Simple and well located, **Suites Los Arcos** (Av. Hidalgo near Av. Abasolo, tel. 998/877-1343, US$104-126 s/d with a/c) has large, colorful rooms with gleaming bathrooms and heavy wood furnishings. All have a small fridge, microwave, and coffeemaker, plus TV, air conditioner, and Wi-Fi. Four of the 12 rooms have balconies—two overlook the pedestrian walkway and are great for people-watching (but can be noisy), while the others face the opposite direction and are huge and sunny.

A colonial-style home turned boutique inn, ★ **Casa Sirena** (Av. Hidalgo near Av. Bravo, no phone, www.casasirenamexico.com, US$139-159 s/d with a/c) has just six rooms, all sumptuously appointed with teak furnishings, Tiffany lamps, stone-tiled bathrooms, and extras like iPod docks and laptop-size safes; some rooms also boast beautiful Talavera tile floors. A full Mexican breakfast—*huevos divorciados, enfrijoladas,* chicken enchiladas—is served daily (except Sunday) on the small, leafy patio. Every evening (Monday-Saturday), guests also enjoy a happy hour with the gregarious owner, who serves up potent cocktails on the rooftop terrace. Other features include two plunge pools (one with Venetian glass tiles), a sundeck with almost 360-degree views of the Caribbean, and Wi-Fi. Online reservations are required; adults only.

The adults-only **Villa La Bella** (Carr. Perimetral s/n, tel. 998/888-0342, www.villalabella.com, US$175 s/d with a/c, US$185 suite, US$240 honeymoon suite with a/c) is run by an amiable American couple who give warm, personalized service to all their guests. There are just six units: three bright pool-front rooms with whimsical decor, two 2nd-floor *palapa*-roofed units with hanging beds (but no air-conditioning), and a colorful honeymoon suite with fantastic ocean views from its two terraces. There also is a well-maintained pool on-site. A gourmet breakfast is included (except Monday) and served in the eclectic open-air lounge, where you can also score cocktails and ice-cold beer.

Hotel Las Palmas (Av. Guerrero near Av. López Mateos, cell tel. 998/877-0043, www. laspalmasonisla.com, US$60-130 s/d with a/c, US$140-170 penthouse) is a homey hotel run by a friendly mother-daughter team from Canada. Rooms are small but tastefully decorated, with creature comforts like good water pressure, pillow-top beds, and full-length mirrors. There's lots of common space for relaxing and socializing, including a rooftop lounge with hammocks, shared kitchen, and a plunge pool. Most guests enjoy the camaraderie, but those seeking seclusion may find it overly hostel-like. Complimentary use of snorkel gear and coolers also available (first come, first served). There's a five-night minimum in high season.

Over US$200

Hotel Secreto (Sección Rocas 11, tel. 998/877-1039, www.hotelsecreto.com, US$231-281 suite with a/c) is a classy glass and stucco hotel that's good for couples who want a quiet getaway without having to go down island. The beach here isn't swimmable (Playa Norte is a short walk away), but there are gorgeous views from the rooms and the hotel's long, narrow infinity pool. Rooms have native stone floors, plasma TVs, pillow-top mattresses, and huge private balconies. Upkeep can be lacking, but not egregiously. Continental breakfast is included, and there's a small gym.

★ **Casa de los Sueños** (Carr. Garrafón s/n, tel. 998/888-0370, toll-free U.S. tel. 877/372-3993, www.casasuenos.com,

US$217-399 s/d with a/c, US$599 presidential suite) is a boutique hotel with 10 immaculate rooms. Located on a bluff at the southern end of the island, the hotel has gorgeous views, including from the large infinity pool. There's no beach, unfortunately, but a large pier does well for swimming, sunbathing, and spa treatments, while the hotel's excellent restaurant-bar is on the water's edge. Bikes, kayaks, and snorkel gear are available for exploring. Full breakfast is included (and served until noon!).

All-Inclusive

Privilege Aluxes (Av. Lopez Mateos at Gustavo Rueda Medina, tel. 998/848-8470, toll-free U.S. tel. 877/635-5293, www.privilegehotels.com, US$243-347 s/d with a/c, US$157-189 pp all-inclusive) is a resort offering both all-inclusive and B&B options. The beach club is lovely and a highlight for most travelers, despite having to walk across the street to get there. The hotel's pool is sleek and clean (though oddly chilly), and rooms, though somewhat sterile in decor, are large and comfortable. All in all, it's a good option if you're looking for a resort experience in downtown Isla. Adults only.

Isla Mujeres Palace (Carr. Sac Bajo s/n, tel. 984/873-4960, toll-free U.S. tel. 800/986-5632, www.palaceresorts.com, US$240-278 pp all-inclusive) is an upscale, couples-only all-inclusive resort with just 62 rooms and an exclusive getaway vibe. Suites have king-size beds and muted modern decor. There are only two restaurants, but they are good ones, with international cuisine, including a full offering of ceviches. The beach and pool areas are lovely, though noise from neighboring beach clubs can be irritating.

Apartments and Private Homes

If you feel like lingering for a while in Isla Mujeres—and who doesn't?—consider booking an apartment or private home. There are a surprising number available, both in town and down island, running the gamut in size and price, and available by the week or month.

Check out the options at agencies like Lost Oasis (www.lostoasis.net) and Isla Beckons (www.islabeckons.com), which specialize in Isla Mujeres. Or, of course, there's always Vacation Rentals by Owner (www.vrbo.com) and Airbnb (www.airbnb.com).

INFORMATION AND SERVICES
Tourist Information
The **Oficina de Turismo** (Av. Rueda Medina 130, tel. 998/877-0307, www.islamujeres.gob. mx, 9am-4pm Mon.-Fri.) sometimes has maps and useful information.

The English-language website **www. islamujeres.info** has concise and accessible descriptions of various aspects of Isla Mujeres, including activities, tours, taxis, ferry schedules, and history, plus a Q&A section frequented by longtime expats.

Soul de Isla Mujeres (www.souldeisla. com) also has information and recommendations about Isla Mujeres, from restaurants to wedding planners. Also try **www.isla-mujeres.net** for information about visiting Isla.

MapChick Isla Mujeres (www.cancunmap.com, US$15) is a fantastic professional-quality color map of Isla Mujeres. It is extremely detailed, including annotated listings of almost every restaurant, hotel, and point of interest on the island. It is available at a handful of Isla's restaurants and hotels, and also can be ordered online.

Emergency Services
MEDISLA (Av. Abasolo 40, tel. 998/688-4364, 24-hour tel. 998/845-2370, dr.asalas@hotmail. com, 9am-3pm and 4pm-9pm Mon.-Sat.) is the office of Dr. Antonio Salas, who is highly recommended by islanders for non-urgent medical needs. English and basic German are spoken.

The **Hospital Comunitario de Isla Mujeres** (Av. Rueda Medina at Calle Paseo de los Peces, tel. 998/877-0117, 24 hours) is a small but modern hospital equipped to handle walk-in consultations, emergencies, and surgeries. It also has a hyperbaric chamber for diving-related injuries.

Isla Mujeres's primary **hyperbaric chamber** (tel. 998/877-0819, 9am-4pm daily), or *cámera hiberbárica* in Spanish, is on the pedestrian-only extension of Avenida Morelos, just north of the *zócalo*.

Farmacia YZA (Av. Benito Juárez at Calle Morelos, tel. 998/999-0234, 24 hours) has sunscreen, bug repellent, and toiletries in addition to medications.

The **police station** (tel. 998/999-0051, 24 hours) is on the central plaza.

Money
HSBC has a bank and ATMs across from the UltraMar pier (Av. Rueda Medina between Avs. Madero and Morelos, tel. 998/877-0005, 9am-5pm Mon.-Fri.) and an ATM only at Xpress Super grocery store on the central plaza.

Media and Communications
Like many cities in Mexico, Isla Mujeres has **free public Wi-Fi** in the central plaza, available to anyone with a computer or mobile device. Most hotels offer Wi-Fi to guests, too.

There are two Internet cafés in town: **Café Internet Adrian's** (An. Morelos s/n, no tel., 8am-10pm daily, US$1 per hour), facing the central plaza; and **No Name Ciber** (Av. Matamoros near Av. Carlos Lazo, no tel., 9am-9pm, US$0.75 per hour) near Poc Na Hostel.

The **post office** (Av. Guerrero at Av. López Mateos, tel. 998/877-0085) is open 9am-5pm Monday-Friday, and 9am-12:30pm Saturday.

Laundry and Storage
Lavandería Cienpies (Av. Vicente Guerrero at Av. Madero, no phone, 7am-9pm Mon.-Sat., 7am-2pm Sun.) will wash, dry, and fold for US$4 per four kilos (8.8 pounds).

Tim Pho Lavandería (Av. Juárez at Abasolo, no phone, 8am-8pm Mon.-Sat., 8am-2pm Sun.) offers same-day service with a two-hour wait. Loads cost US$4.50 per four kilos (8.8 pounds).

Storage lockers (US$5 per 24 hours) are available at the Ultramar ferry pier; they are

Ferries to Isla Mujeres

Various passenger ferries (and also a car ferry) leave for Isla Mujeres from Cancún every day. Those leaving from the Zona Hotelera are more expensive and take longer but may be more convenient. There's also a vehicle ferry. **Note:** During the high season, additional departures are occasionally offered.

ZONA HOTELERA

El Embarcadero
UltraMar (Blvd. Kukulcán Km 4, tel. 998/881-5890, www.ultramarferry.com, US$14/19 one-way/round-trip, 30 minutes). **Departure:** 9:15am, 10:30am, 11:45am, 1pm, 2:15pm, 4:30pm, 6:15pm, and 8:45pm. **Return:** 9:45am, 11am, 12:15pm, 1:30pm, 4pm, 5:15pm, 6:45pm, 8pm, and 9:15pm.

Playa Tortugas
UltraMar (Blvd. Kukulcán Km 7, tel. 998/881-5890, www.ultramarferry.com, US$14/19 one-way/round-trip, 30 minutes). **Departure:** hourly 9am-6pm, 7:15pm, and 8:30pm. **Return:** hourly 9:30am-5:30pm, 6:45pm, 8pm, and 9:15pm.

Playa Caracol
UltraMar (Blvd. Kukulcán Km 9.5, tel. 998/881-5890, www.ultramarferry.com, US$14/19 one-way/round-trip, 30 minutes). **Departure:** 9am, 10:15am, 11:30am, 12:45pm, 2pm, and 4:45pm. **Return:** 9:45am, 11am, 12:15pm, 1:30pm, 4pm, 5:15pm.

DOWNTOWN

To get to either of the passenger ferries in downtown Cancún, take the red R-1 bus (US$0.75) on Boulevard Kukulcán or Avenida Tulum; continue past the downtown bus terminal and north out of the city. **Gran Puerto** is easily located by its tall observation tower. (Be aware that you may be approached by people dressed in UltraMar uniforms who are in fact selling time-shares here.) **Puerto Juárez** is two blocks past Gran Puerto. It's the original Isla Mujeres ferry pier, but the boats and waiting area are older. The vehicle ferry at **Punta Sam** is located on Avenida López Portillo, about five kilometers (3 miles) north of Gran Puerto. On Isla Mujeres, the car ferry pier is a few hundred meters south of the passenger piers, past the naval dock.

Gran Puerto
UltraMar (Av. López Portillo s/n, tel. 998/881-5890, www.ultramarferry.com, US$8/15 one-way/round-trip, 15 minutes) boats feature comfy seats in an air-conditioned cabin and an open-air deck, with televisions playing a short promotional program on Isla Mujeres. There's often live music on the open deck. **Departure:** every 30 minutes 5am-9:30pm, then hourly until 11:30pm. **Return:** every 30 minutes 5:30am-9pm, then hourly 10pm-midnight.

Puerto Juárez
Marinsa Turismo (Av. López Portillo s/n, tel. 998/478-0011, www.marinsaturismo.com, US$8/15 one-way/round-trip, 45 minutes) utilizes traditional vehicle ferryboats to transport people; the trip takes longer than its competitors but, if you're not in a rush, it's a beautiful ride. **Departure:** every hour 6:15am-9:15pm. **Return:** every hour 7:15am-10:15pm.

Punta Sam (vehicle ferry)
The lumbering vehicle ferry to Isla Mujeres is run by **Marítima Isla Mujeres** (Av. López Portillo s/n, tel. 998/878-4171, www.maritimaislamujeres.com, 45-60 minutes). Rates are according to vehicle: US$15 for cars, US$26 for SUVs and vans, US$5 for motorcycles or mopeds, and US$4.75 for bicycles. Rates include the driver only—each additional passenger costs US$2. Arrive about an hour early to get in line; tickets go on sale 30 minutes prior to departure. **Departure:** 7:15am, 9am, 11am, 1pm, 5:30pm, and 8:15pm Mon., 7:15am, 9am, 11am, 1pm, 3pm, 5:30pm, and 8:15pm Tues.-Sat., and 11am, 3pm, and 8pm Sun. **Return:** 6am, 8am, 10am, noon, 4:15pm, and 7:15pm Mon., 6am, 8am, 10am, noon, 2pm, 4:15pm, and 7:15pm Tues.-Sat., and 10am, 2pm, and 7pm Sun.

big enough to hold carry-on bags only. If it's really early or late in the day and there's no staffer around, ask for help from the parking lot attendant, just east of the pier.

GETTING THERE

A number of ferries ply the turquoise waters of the Bahía de Mujeres (Bay of Women) between Isla Mujeres and various mainland ports in and around Cancún. There is no direct ferry service from Isla Cozumel, however, and despite having an airstrip, no regular air service either.

Passenger Ferries

Passenger-only ferries leave for Isla Mujeres from Cancún in the Zona Hotelera and from Puerto Juárez, about three kilometers (1.9 miles) north of downtown Cancún. If you are just visiting for the day, reconfirm the return times and remember that service to the Zona Hotelera ends earlier than service to Puerto Juárez.

Car Ferries

A vehicle ferry operates from Punta Sam, about eight kilometers (5 miles) north of Cancún past Puerto Juárez.

GETTING AROUND

Isla Mujeres is a small and mostly flat island. In town you can easily walk everywhere. Buses and taxis are available for exploring farther afield, but definitely consider renting a golf cart, moped, or bike for more flexibility and independence.

Taxi

Isla Mujeres has many more taxis than seem necessary—in town, it feels more likely that you'd be hit by a taxi than have trouble finding one. Out of town, you shouldn't have to wait too long for a taxi to pass, either, and Garrafón, Dolphin Discovery, and Playa Lancheros all have fixed taxi stands. From downtown, rates are US$2.50 around town (including the beaches) and US$4-6 elsewhere on the island. Official rates are posted wherever taxis line up, including the ferry terminal and Punta Sur. Taxis are per trip, not per person, and drivers may pick up other passengers headed the same direction. You can also hire a taxi to give you a private driving tour of the island for US$15 per hour. **Note:** Taxi fares double after dark until 6am.

Golf Cart, Moped, and Bicycle Rental

Most rental operations on the island share the same fixed rates: golf carts US$12-15 per hour, US$35-40 per day (store hours), and US$45-60 for 24 hours; mopeds US$6 per hour, US$15 per day, US$20 for 24 hours; and bicycles (including lock but often not helmet) US$7-10 per day, US$10-13 for 24 hours.

Note: Isla Mujeres has a regular occurrence of serious accidents involving tourists driving mopeds. Riding double is a major culprit: Mopeds are much harder to control with two people riding instead of one. Poor roads and wet and windy conditions also are dangerous, not to mention unpredictable. Better to rent a bike or golf cart, or at least separate mopeds.

Agencies right at the ferry pier sometimes charge slightly more than those a few blocks away. Solid choices include **Ciro's** (Av. Guerrero near Av. Matamoros, tel. 998/877-0568, 9am-5pm daily), **El Sol** (Av. Juárez between Avs. Abasolo and Matamoros, tel. 998/877-0791, 9am-5pm daily), **Luxury Car Rental** (Av. Hidalgo near Playa Norte, tel. 998/877-0392, 8am-6pm daily), **Pelícanos** (Av. Matamoros near Av. Guerrero, no phone, 8am-5pm daily), and **David's Bikes** (Av. Matamoros near Av. Guerrero, no tel., 8am-8pm Mon.-Sat., 8am-5pm Sun.).

Isla Mujeres Golf Cart Rentals (cell tel. 998/857-5266, www.islamujeresgolfcartrentals.com) is a convenient service that makes renting a golf cart easy. Rates are slightly higher than you'd pay normally, but you can reserve and pay online, the cart can be delivered to your hotel, and someone even comes by every day or two to fill the gas tank. Four- and six-seat carts are available; there are discounts for longer rentals.

Isla Holbox

At the northeastern tip of Quintana Roo, where the Caribbean Sea mingles with the Gulf of Mexico, and completely within the Yum Balam Reserve, sits Isla Holbox (hole-BOASH). Once reasonably obscure, Holbox is hitting the radar of independent travelers, which may spell big changes in the future. For now, the town of Holbox is tropical and—a fishing village with sand roads, golf carts instead of cars, no hospital, and no post office. (There *are* three ATMs on the island, though they're often empty.) You'll find brightly painted homes, *palapa*-roofed hotels, and Italian and Argentinean expats who have opened bed-and-breakfasts and small restaurants. The water here is

Isla Holbox

Playa Norte

HOTEL CASA LAS TORTUGAS
HOTEL MAWIMBI
CASASANDRA
CALLE CHAC-CHI

HOLBOX DREAM HOTEL
TACO QUETA
STRING OF BOUTIQUES

EL CAFÉCITO
FARMACIA JESSY
COOPERATIVA TURÍSTICA PULPEROS DEL CARIBE

To Los Potrillos de Holbox, Casa Takywara, Casa Blat-Ha, and Punta Cocos
AVENIDA PEDRO JOAQUÍN COLDWELL
RENTADORA EL BROTHER
CHAPULIM
HOLBOX KITEBOARDING SCHOOL

BIKES HOLBOX
VIVA ZAPATA
CHEFO'S
PORQUÉ NO
VIP HOLBOX EXPERIENCE

TRIBU HOSTEL
LALO.COM
LOS PELEONES/ LA TORTILLERIA DE HOLBOX
Central Plaza
ROOTS

LE JARDIN
CEVICHES LA CHINGADA
ATM
El Pueblito Plaza
NÁAY

AVENIDA IGUALDAD
CALLE SAN PEDRO
CALLE YUUKAY
CALLE MAKUN
CALLE JUREL

RENTADORA GLENDY
LAVAMAR
To Ida y Vuelta Camping and Hotel Villa Flamingos

PORFIRIO DÍAZ
VILLAS EL JARDÍN
SUPER MONKEY'S
FRUTERÍA LA CONCEPCIÓN

Soccer Field
POSADA LAURY

CALLE ESCOBEDO
CALLE TIBURÓN BALLENA
CALLE ESMEDREGA
CALLE CANANE
MARIA CARLOTA HOTEL BOUTIQUE
CALLE HERNÁN CORTÉS

PASEO KUKA
CENTRO MÉDICO UTSTAL

CALLE TINTORERA
CALLE LISA
CALLE GONZALO GUERRERO
XPIL
AVENIDA PALOMINO
AVENIDA BRAVO
CALLE SIERRA
XOHITO
PEZ VOLADOR
AHKANHOC

KAN-KAI
RONCO
CANTO
CHEN-HA

Baseball Field
CALETA

AVE CALETA

Isla Holbox
WHALE SHARK FEEDING GROUNDS
MAP AREA
Isla Contoy

Chiquilá
El Corchal
Isla Mujeres

Cancún

0   15 mi
0   15 km
180
307

FERRY TICKET BOOTH

PASSENGER FERRY PIER

Laguna Yalahau

To Chiquilá

0   200 yds
0   200 m

© MOON.COM

emerald—not the clear turquoise of Cancún and Tulum—and while the sand is coarser, the beach is loaded with seashells and is no less scenic. Holbox is well known as a place to snorkel with behemoth but harmless whale sharks—present June-September—and also has great opportunities for bird-watching, kayaking, and sportfishing. Above all, Holbox offers a sense of peace and tranquility hard to find on Mexico's Caribbean coast. The island's growing popularity, though, means its vibe is changing. What direction it goes—bohemian chic, big eco-business, or something altogether different—remains to be seen.

Indigenous Maya inhabited Holbox for centuries but abandoned the island more than 300 years before the first Europeans arrived. The name of the island and town is a matter of some dispute. Some say *holbox* is derived from a Maya term meaning "black water" and is a reference to the island's natural springs, whose dark depths make the water appear black. A more popular, albeit fantastical, story is that the pirate Francisco de Molas buried a treasure on the island and cut off the head of his African bodyguard so that his ghost would watch over the spot for eternity. De Molas was promptly killed by a snakebite, but the disembodied head of his bodyguard has appeared occasionally to islanders, trying to divulge the treasure's location but succeeding only in scaring everyone away. By this latter account, the island originally would have been called *poolbox* (black head), and was altered later by European settlers.

Storms are serious business on this low, flat island, which is regularly buffeted by tropical conflagrations. In fact, the town was originally located farther west but was destroyed by a hurricane and rebuilt in its current location about 150 years ago. *Nortes* are fall and winter storms that sweep down the Gulf coast bringing rain and turbid seas. *Maja' che* is the Maya name for sudden winds that can knock over trees; they are most common in April and May. During major storms, the entire island is evacuated.

SIGHTS

TOP EXPERIENCE

★ Whale Shark Feeding Grounds

From June to September, large numbers of whale sharks—the world's largest fish, typically measuring 6-7.5 meters (20-25 feet) and weighing more than 10 tons—congregate in

Whale sharks are gentle giants of the sea—and the world's largest fish.

shallow waters about 16 kilometers (10 miles) east of Holbox village. Despite their size, the sharks are completely harmless, eating plankton, krill, and other tiny organisms, much like baleen whales. Snorkeling with whale sharks is a unique and (to some) nerve-wracking experience. The captain pulls the boat alongside a shark—at Holbox they tend to feed on the surface—and two guests and a guide slip into the water with life jackets, masks, snorkels, and fins. The water tends to be murky (it's all the sealife in the water that attracts the sharks in the first place), and the sharks are surprisingly fast. Still, you get a good view of these enormous, gentle animals, with their tiny eyes, bizarre shovel mouths, and dark spotted skin. It's best to be on a small tour—since you go in two by two, you'll get more time in the water. Tours cost around US$130 per person, last 4-6 hours, and typically include snorkel gear, a life preserver, a box lunch, and nonalcoholic beverages. Some trips also include a stop on the way back for snorkeling or to visit the island's inland lagoons and mangrove forest.

Playa Norte

Playa Norte is Holbox's scenic main beach, extending eastward along the island's long, north-facing shore; it is broad and flat, with white sand, and dotted with stands of tangled dune grass. The number of homes and hotels along the beach grows every year, and most have lounge chairs available to guests. There also are a handful of beach clubs (10am-6pm)—mostly restaurants with lounge chairs, umbrellas, and hammocks—open to the general public at no cost as long as you eat something (meals US$8-15). Whether you bring your own towel or set up at an establishment, Playa Norte is great for beachcombing, shell collecting, and sunbathing the farther you walk from town.

Bioluminescent Waters

During the summer months, the waters around Holbox are filled with plankton—tiny, harmless organisms that are a major food source for whale sharks and other animals. Around Punta Cocos, a particular variety of plankton light up when touched, forming a blue-green fluorescent glow around anything passing through the water—a fish, a hand, a paddle. It's otherworldly, to say the least. Mid-May through mid-August is the best time of year to check it out; try to go on a night with little or no moon for the best viewing. It's easy enough to see it on your own:

Head to Isla Holbox for long walks on the beach and plenty of peace and quiet.

Punta Cocos is located at the western end of Avenida Coldwell, about a 20-30-minute walk from the central park, along the beach. Tour operators also offer excursions (1 hour, US$15-20 per person), which include transportation and a guide.

El Corchal

Near Solferino, a village along the road to the Chiquilá, sits **El Corchal**, a 2,000-hectare (4,942 acres) swath of mangroves and protected wetlands. A local ecotourism initiative leads canoe tours through the area (cell. tel. 998/165-7105, pepecorcho05@gmail.com, US$35 per person)—ask for Pepe Quintal Olivar, the founder and experienced guide. Visitors glide past *corcho* trees, their thick roots curiously growing above the waterline, and see and learn about the myriad birds that inhabit the area, including flamingos, toucans, woodpeckers, and quails. If you're lucky, you might even see turtles and small crocs too. Tours last about 3-4 hours. Lunch can be arranged for an additional US$10 per person.

Isla Pájaros

Located in Yalahau Lagoon, Isla Pájaros (Bird Island) is a wildlife sanctuary and the permanent home to some 150 species of birds, including frigate birds, white ibis, double-crested cormorants, roseate spoonbills, and boat-billed herons. In addition, between May and September up to 40,000 flamingos nest on Holbox before their long winter migration to South America. Environmental restrictions mean you can't simply wander on Isla Pájaros, but two observation towers and walkways make spotting birds easy. Most tour operators offer bird-watching trips here (US$17-30 pp), usually by *lancha* (motorboat), though kayak tours also can be arranged.

Yalahau Spring

Said to have been used by pirates to fill their water barrels, Yalahau Spring is an *ojo de agua* (natural spring) on the edge of the mainland. Today, it is a picturesque swimming hole complete with a large *palapa*, picnic area, and pier.

A trip here typically is combined with a stop at Isla Pájaros.

Isla de la Pasión

Just 15 minutes from town by boat, Isla de la Pasión is a tiny deserted island just 50 meters (164 feet) wide. It's known for its white-sand beach and beautiful emerald waters that are perfect for a relaxing day. There are trees and a large *palapa* for shade. Be sure to bring plenty of water and snacks—there are no services on the island.

Street Art: Murals

Walking around Holbox, it's impossible to miss the gorgeous and dramatic murals around the island. They're the product of two projects: *Soñando por Holbox* (Dreaming for Holbox) and the *Festival Internacional de Arte Público* (International Festival of Public Art). The prior was a Kickstarter project that funded two of the murals; the latter funded the rest. Both projects involved artists from Mexico and beyond who met with islanders and explored the island for inspiration. Ask at your hotel for a map of the murals.

ENTERTAINMENT AND EVENTS
Festivals and Events
FESTIVAL DE SAN TELMO

Most of Holbox's residents live by fishing, and the island has over 400 fishing boats and numerous fishing cooperatives. It's no surprise, then, that San Telmo, the patron saint of fishermen, is celebrated here with fervor. The party lasts for two weeks in mid-April, with food stands, live performances, and special events, including a popular sportfishing tournament. The festival ends on April 19 when fishermen and their families participate in a huge boat procession followed by general revelry in the decked-out main square.

FESTIVAL DE LA VIRGEN DE FATIMA

In mid-May, Holbox celebrates the Virgin of Fatima, the community's official patron saint.

Bug Patrol

Isla Holbox's famous whale sharks may weigh 10 tons and have mouths that measure five feet across, but it's the island's itty-bitty residents that pack the meanest bite. Mosquitoes, sand flies, and *tábanos* (horseflies) can be fierce, particularly in the summer and after heavy rains. Bring bug repellent and use it liberally, day and night. Another tip: Always dry off and reapply repellent immediately after swimming—horseflies love skin that's moist, especially with seawater.

Held just a month after the San Telmo blowout, this festival is more austere, with religious processions and more folksy music and other performances. That said, it's still a party.

SHOPPING

Holbox isn't exactly a shopper's paradise, but there is a **string of boutiques** along Avenida Igualdad (just east of the central plaza) selling everything from handcrafted jewelry to whale shark magnets. Most are open 9am-8pm every day.

If you're into shells, **Lalo.com** (Calle Canane near Av. Pedro Joaquín Coldwell, tel. 984/875-2118) is jam-packed with beautifully polished *conchas* from around the world (plus a coconut monkey or two). The owner, *maestro* Lalo, lives below the shop—just ring his bell, and he'll open up the shop.

El Pueblito Plaza (Calle Tiburón Ballena near Porfirio Díaz) is as close as you'll get to a mall in these parts. Located just off the central plaza, it has a handful of boutiques, eateries, and even an ATM.

SPORTS AND RECREATION

There is a lot to do on Holbox, and various excursions can be arranged through your hotel, local tour operators, or done on your own. Most of Holbox's tour operators offer the full gamut of excursions, at comparable prices.

Recommended outfits include **Cooperativa Turística Pulperos del Caribe** (Av. Igualdad near Calle Sierra, tel. 984/875-2021), **Turística Moguel** (tel. 984/875-2028, www.holboxislandtours.com), and VIP Holbox Experience (Av. Igualdad near Av. Bravo, tel. 984/875-2107, http://vipholbox.com).

Snorkeling

Besides swimming with whale sharks, the best place to snorkel on Isla Holbox is **Cabo Catoche,** a coral reef in about 2-4 meters (6.5-13 feet) of water at the far eastern end of the island. The water isn't as clear as in the Riviera Maya, but the reef here is pristine and the animal life abundant, including stingrays, moray eels, nurse sharks, sea stars, and conch. Because it is so far from town, tours cost around US$75 per person (minimum 4 people). Alternatively, a stop at Cabo Catoche can be combined with another outing, such as an island tour or a whale shark excursion.

Wind Sports

Holbox's steady winds and shallow, nearly waveless coastal waters make it ideal for wind sports, particularly kiteboarding and windsurfing. The strongest winds are September-March, while July and August tend to have lighter, novice-friendly breezes. **Holbox Kiteboarding School** (Av. Igualdad s/n, tel. 984/875-2129, www.holboxkiteboarding.com, 8am-1:30pm and 5:30-8pm daily) offers all-level courses in several languages. Instruction prices, including gear, range US$57 per hour per person (group lessons, 3 students maximum) to US$72 per hour (private lessons). Rentals also are available. Lessons are offered November to May only.

Kayaking and Paddleboarding

Paddling is a great way to see the interior lagoons of the island, and especially for spotting birds. A fun and challenging option is to hire a golf-cart taxi to drive you and your kayak or paddleboard—balanced on the back—to the main inlet where you can put in. From there it's possible to wend through the lagoons to the other side of the island, then paddle along the shore to the main ferry dock, passing Isla Pájaros along the way. Several shops and hotels rent kayaks (US$10-15/hour), while Explora Holbox (tel. 998/304-6005) offers recommended group tours starting at US$35 per person. For customized trips, contact **Andrés Limón** (tel. 984/875-2220, kayak_holbox@hotmail.com), a popular local guide. Paddleboards can be rented through **Holbox Kiteboarding School** (Av. Igualdad s/n, tel. 984/875-2129, www.holboxkiteboarding.com, 8am-1:30pm and 5:30pm-8pm daily) for US$20 per hour.

Bird-Watching

Holbox has more than 30 species of birds, including herons, white and brown pelicans, double-crested cormorants, roseate spoonbills, and American flamingos (the brightest pink of the five flamingo species). Most hotels can arrange a standard bird-watching excursion (US$17-30 pp, 4 hours, minimum 4 people), which generally includes taking a motorboat or kayaks through the mangroves to Isla Pájaros and the flamingo nesting grounds at Punta Mosquita. More specialized bird-watchers may want to contact **Juan Rico Santana** (aka El Karateca, tel. 984/875-2347 or cell tel. 984/100-9132), a certified birder who leads many of the hotel trips, but also often arranges separate, more focused trips that are tailored to your interests.

Fishing

Holbox is an excellent spot for **sportfishing**, yet it's still relatively unknown. A deep-sea fishing excursion costs US$375-450, depending on duration. It typically includes gear, bait, drinks, and lunch. A coastal fishing tour with a local fisherman, going after smaller and more plentiful catch, lasts 4-5 hours and costs around US$140-190. Local tour operators, and most hotels, can help you organize either trip.

Holbox also has great **fly-fishing**, with 100-plus-pound giant tarpons cruising the coastal waters, and smaller juveniles plying the interior lagoons, along with snook and jack. **Holbox Tarpon Club** (tel. 984/875-2144) offers personalized tours, running US$420 per boat (8 hours, lunch included, maximum 2 anglers per boat).

Horseback Riding

Los Potrillos Holbox (across from airport, Av. Pedro Joaquin Coldwell s/n, tel. 984/129-9995) offers horseback riding tours into the interior of the island, along the beach, or both.

Isla Holbox has great conditions for kiteboarding.

Pirates of the Caribbean

For most of the colonial era, pirates were a major and constant threat to ships and port towns throughout the Yucatán Peninsula. They launched attacks throughout the region, creating virtual pirate colonies. Some of the region's more notorious and colorful nemeses include:

- **Francisco de Molas:** Said to have lived on present-day Isla Holbox for nearly four decades, attacking ships that approached looking for drinking water. The story goes that Molas had an African slave help him bury his treasure, then killed him so that his ghost would watch over the spot. Islanders say a wailing disembodied head haunts the island, and that the name Holbox is an alteration of the Maya term "pool box," or Black Head.

- **Henry Morgan and Jean Lafitte:** Pirates who used Isla Cozumel as a refuge and a base to launch attacks on the Yucatecan mainland and various Caribbean islands. Lafitte is said to have often used the island's safe northern harbors to hide from pursuers.

- **Pierre de Sanfroy:** A French corsair who occupied Cozumel's small village for several weeks in 1579, making the church his home, including sleeping on the altar, and harassing the local townspeople.

- **Lorencillo:** Born Laurent de Graff, the French buccaneer is best known for attacking Campeche City in 1685 with a pirate army of 700 men and holding the city ransom for two months. According to legend, he was captured in Valladolid after being lured there by a woman he captured on a ship. Held in the Ex-Convento San Bernardino, he was rescued by his crew before authorities could jail or execute him.

- **Peg Leg:** Cornelius Jol was one of the first privateers known to use a wooden prosthetic—and to go by the now-iconic pirate name. Technically an admiral in the Dutch navy, Peg Leg terrorized Spanish and Portuguese ships and ports, including a 10-ship assault on Campeche City in 1663.

Other notable pirates who sailed Yucatán's waters and who figure in the region's lore include Sir Francis Drake, John Hawkins, Michel de Grammond, and Jacobo Jackson.

Most tours last approximately 1.5 hours and cost US$25 per person.

Yoga

Hotel Casa Las Tortugas (Av. Igualdad s/n, cell tel. 984/252-2565, www.holboxcasalastortugas.com, US$10) offers hatha yoga sessions at 8am Monday-Friday in its gorgeous beachfront yoga studio; all classes are led by certified instructors. English is spoken.

Just a block from the central plaza, **Amaité Hotel & Spa** (end of Calle Tiburón Ballena s/n, tel. 984/875-2217, www.amaitehotelholbox.com, US$10) offers oceanfront yoga at 9am every day in its breezy palapa-roof studio.

FOOD

There are only a handful of restaurants on Isla Holbox, so anyone staying more than two days could easily sample them all. It wouldn't even take much effort either, as virtually all face the central plaza or are less than a couple blocks off it. A quick stroll around the plaza lets you whet your appetite while sizing up the options.

Mexican and Seafood

★ **Taco Queto** (Av. Pedro Joaquín Coldwell near Av. Palomino, 6pm-midnight daily, US$3-8) is a classic Mexican restaurant, down to the plastic chairs and tables, the tarp, and the spit of *al pastor* meat prominently placed at the front of the joint. As the name suggests, the specialty is street tacos, but the burritos are huge and delicious, too—jam-packed with meat, chicken, or beans, and doused in *crema*. Come hungry—the portions are hearty.

Chapulim (Calle Tiburón Ballena near

Av. Coldwell, cell tel. 984/137-6069, 6pm-10pm Mon.-Sat., US$15-30) serves gourmet meals, mostly seafood-based, in an artful locale. There is no menu. Instead, there are four main entrees and a signature cocktail offered each night, using fresh, seasonal ingredients found on the island. Almost best of all is the personalized service—the chef himself, Erik Winckelmann, visits with each table to describe the entrees and answer questions.

Viva Zapata (Av. Igualdad between Calle Tiburón Ballena and Calle Esmedregal, tel. 984/875-2362, www.vivazapataholbox.com, 10am-11:30pm daily, US$7-22) is a sand-floored *palapa* restaurant near the central plaza. It's all about seafood here, with dishes made from locally caught fish, shrimp, octopus, and other seafood. There's a kids menu, too, with tasty treats for the little ones like fish burgers and quesadillas. Come early to beat the crowd, or order a beer and kick back at the swing bar while you wait for a table.

A locals fave, **Las Panchas** (Calle Esmedregal near Av. Coldwell, tel. 984/120-8354, 8am-11am and 1pm-7pm daily, US$6-15) is a simple, open-air restaurant serving fresh seafood. The menu is classic: ceviche, cocktails, tacos, fish prepared seven different ways. The cost, given the high quality and big portions, is tough to beat. Come early for a seat—a line often forms during the dinner rush.

Ceviches La Chingada (Calle Esmedregal near Av. Porfirio Díaz, tel. 984/876-4439, 9am-6pm daily, US$2-7) is little more than a food stand on a side street: a handful of plastic tables on a dirt lot, the chef working furiously in the open kitchen, the waiter running to and fro. But the ceviche is so fresh, so perfectly tangy, and the stream of customers so steady, you'll find yourself waiting for a seat. But it goes fast. And whatever the wait, you'll find it was worth it.

International
La Tortilleria de Holbox (central plaza, tel. 984/875-2443, 8am-4pm daily, US$5-8) is a breakfast favorite with great fresh-brewed coffee to go along with omelets, yogurt and fresh fruit, and more—all with friendly service. For lunch, the Spanish tortilla is definitely the way to go, plus it feeds two.

Decked out with kitschy Mexican wrestling memorabilia, **Los Peleones** (central plaza, Calle Tiburón Ballena between Avs. Porfirio Díaz and Igualdad, no phone, 6:30pm-11pm daily, US$10-25) is a small 2nd-floor restaurant overlooking the central plaza. It specializes in classic Italian dishes, including great handmade pasta and seafood. Grab a table on the balcony for the best view and sea breeze.

Often bustling, ★ **Roots** (Av. Porfirio Díaz near Av. Bravo, tel. 984/241-5953, 4pm-11:30pm daily, US$7-10) specializes in thin-crust pizza with loads of Mexican-style toppings, all prepped in a wood-fired oven. Try the Poblana with chicken mole or the Oaxaqueña with grasshoppers and mushrooms. And the lobster tail pizza? An absolute treat. The restaurant itself is on a big open-air lot, the tables made of repurposed cable spools and the chairs upholstered barrels. If there's a wait, check out the trampoline or slackline. Even better, give the hula hoops a whirl. There's live music on weekends too.

Light Fare and Sweets
It's all about huge salad bowls at ★ **Náay** (Calle Porfirio Díaz near Av. Bravo, tel. 984/157-9220, www.naayholbox.com, 1pm-8pm daily, US$6-8), where customers can either create their own (including one protein, one grain, one topping, and dressing) or choose a house specialty like curry chicken or falafel mint on a bed of spinach. All meals include freshly made ice tea or an *agua fresca* (fruit-based drink). Enjoy your salad at a communal table or take it to go in a rentable glass container.

El Cafécito (Av. Pedro Joaquín Coldwell near Av. Palomino, tel. 984/136-0232, 8:30am-3pm daily, US$4-8) is a cozy café just steps from the central plaza. Diners enjoy croissant and focaccia sandwiches, hummus platters, lasagna, and—the pièce de résistance—giant crepes with fillings like Nutella, caramel and nuts, and fruit.

An artisanal French bakery, **Le Jardin** (Calle Lisa near Av. Pedro Joaquín Coldwell, 8am-12:30pm daily, US$2-5) specializes in simple breakfasts made with homemade breads like croissants, brioche, and baguettes. Diners order at the register and take a seat under the *palapa*-roofed dining room. Come early to be sure to get a meal—once the bread runs out (and it does), the place closes for the day.

Porqué No (Av. Igualdad near Av. Bravo, cell tel. 984/130-9133, noon-11:30pm daily, US$2-5) specializes in artisanal gelato. Flavors change periodically but include varieties like Oreo, pomegranate, coconut, and pistachio.

Groceries

Supplies ebb and flow in Isla Holbox, so you might have to go to more than one store to find everything you're looking for.

The souped-up **Super Monkey's** (Calle Tiburón Ballena near Calle Escobedo, 6am-midnight daily) has a decent selection of canned and packaged food, bug repellent, sunscreen, and toiletries.

For late-night munchies, check out **Chefo's** (central plaza, 24 hours daily).

The best selection of fruits and vegetables on the island is at **Frutería La Concepción** (Calle Escobedo near Av. Palomino, cell tel. 984/129-1240, 7am-10pm daily). You'll also find eggs, honey, and spices. Delivery is available.

ACCOMMODATIONS

For most travelers, Holbox's most appealing accommodations are its beachfront bungalows; they vary in style, amenities, and price, but all offer simple rest and relaxation in a peaceful seaside setting. Alternatively, hotels in town offer comfortable rooms at more accessible rates, and you're still just a short distance from the beach. Be aware that rates typically rise during whale shark season (mid-May-mid-September).

Under US$50

Though the mosquitos can be a problem (bring bug repellent), **Ida y Vuelta Camping** (Calle Plutarco Elias Calles between Róbalo and Chacchi, tel. 984/875-2358, www.holboxhostel.com, US$10 pp hammock, US$10 pp camping, US$13 pp dorm, US$39 s/d bungalow with shared bath, US$44 s/d *cabaña*, US$52 s/d suite with shared kitchen, US$60 house) has a good range of options, from hammock and tent sites to a fully equipped house. The most popular choices are the garden bungalows, which have sand floors, screened windows, and shared bathrooms, and the *cabañas*—wood-plank cabins on stilts, each with two basic rooms with private bathrooms. Breakfast included at the on-site restaurant. Free Wi-Fi too.

Located on a quiet residential street, **Posada Laury** (Paseo Kuka near Av. Palomino, tel. 984/875-2133, US$44 s/d with a/c) offers stark rooms with unexpected creature comforts: air-conditioning, cable TV, and mini fridges, plus hot water and decent beds, too. It's a great deal, especially considering it's just two blocks from the central plaza. If you want to check in and there's no staff onsite, go around the corner to the nearest house on Avenida Palomino, where the owner lives (look for the "Posada Laury" sign above the doorbell).

US$50-100

Located about half a mile west of the central plaza, **Casa Blat-Ha** (Calle Caguama at Calle Charral, tel. 984/807-8490, cell tel. 984/137-6721, www.casablatha.com, US$69 s/d) is a small B&B with a welcoming off-the-grid boho feel. It has 12 simple and clean rooms that are set in two buildings: the main one, where the rooms have ocean views and private balconies, and a building across the sand road, which has smaller, dark rooms with air-conditioning and king-size beds. The main building also has a cozy lounging area, a rooftop meditation and yoga center, an organic garden, and a vegetarian kitchen where continental breakfast is served. The beach is just a block away.

One of the best deals on the island, **Villas El Jardín** (Calle Esmedregal near Calle Escobedo, tel. 984/875-2326, reservaciones@villaseljardin.com, US$85 1-bedroom apartment with a/c) is a three-story bungalow hotel offering modern one-bedroom apartments. All have thick beds, downpour shower heads, well-equipped kitchenettes, and terraces or balconies. Details like hand-painted throw pillows and tropical wood accents make units homey. Daily maid service keeps them gleaming. The only bummer? Wi-Fi is accessible in common areas only.

Maria Carlota Hotel Boutique (Paseo Kuka near Calle Tiburón Ballena, cell tel. 983/111-5483, maria.carlota.hotelboutique@gmail.com, US$83-105 s/d with a/c) offers 18 sleek windowless rooms (read: dark and quiet) with low-lying beds that "float" above the polished cement floors (read: creative bed stands). Tropical wood and beautiful lighting add lots of personality. Rooms open onto a narrow interior garden that leads to a small reception area. The hotel is located on a quiet neighborhood street.

US$100-250

★ **Hotel Mawimbi** (Av. Igualdad s/n, tel. 984/875-2003, www.mawimbi.net, US$180-220 s/d with a/c, US$260 s/d with a/c and kitchenette, US$300 suite with a/c) offers modern rooms and comfortable bungalows with a touch of boho flair. Guatemalan bedspreads, colorful tiles, and shell accents all lend an artistic touch, while quiet air-conditioning and free Wi-Fi keep you cool and connected. The shady garden has plenty of lounge chairs and hammocks, and is just steps from one of the island's best-kept stretches of beach. The low-key Italian owners maintain a friendly, welcoming atmosphere and offer recommended island excursions. There also is a good restaurant on-site, El Barquito, where a complimentary continental breakfast is served.

About a 10-minute walk from town, **Casa Takywara** (Av. Pedro Joaquín Coldwell s/n, cell tel. 984/141-3381, www.casatakywara.com, US$144-155 s/d with a/c and kitchenette) offers six spacious and lovely units in a circular three-story building. All have fully equipped kitchenettes (down to blenders and lime presses) and share wood-floored porches. The oceanfront, just steps away, has plenty of lounge chairs, hammocks, and other places to relax. Continental breakfast is delivered to rooms daily. Service is friendly and efficient.

Hotel Mawimbi is a beachfront oasis.

Holbox Dream Hotel (Av. Pedro Joaquín Coldwell s/n, tel. 984/875-2433, www.holbox-dream.com, US$90-124 s/d with a/c, US$134-142 deluxe s/d with a/c) is a refreshing alternative to the deserted-isle getaways that make up most of Holbox's hotels. Standard rooms are comfortable and modern, with air-conditioning, good mattresses, stone basin sinks, and balconies with partial ocean views; deluxe rooms are bigger, with mini fridges, security boxes, and better balcony views, plus some even have whirlpool tubs. There's Wi-Fi in all the rooms. The hotel also has a well-maintained stretch of beach, two small and inviting pools, and a restaurant that is perfect for leisurely meals.

Over US$250

★ **CasaSandra** (Calle Igualdad s/n, tel. 984/875-2171, www.casasandra.com, US$260-298 s/d with a/c, US$337-469 suite with a/c) is one of Holbox's most exclusive boutique hotels, though it still maintains the welcoming feel of a home. The main building looks like a Swiss ski lodge (it houses ocean-view rooms, the library, and a restaurant), but it also has a handful of smaller *palapa*-roofed buildings, more in style with their island neighbors. Rooms are shabby-chic in decor and have features like claw-foot tubs and original art. Outside, guests can relax on the well-tended beach or by the large pool. A full breakfast is included in the rate.

Hotel Villas Flamingos (Paseo Kuka s/n, tel. 984/875-2167, www.villasflamingos.com, US$240-280 s/d with a/c, US$350-490 suite with a/c) is one of the nicest places to stay on the beach. Units are modern with boho flair: conch shell showerheads, coconut lamps, bamboo accents, and gorgeous mosaic tile bathrooms. All rooms have air-conditioning, private balconies, and ocean views (some partial, some dramatically expansive), and some even have private plunge pools and whirlpool tubs. There is a well-tended pool just feet from the ocean, as well as a high-end

restaurant/bar. Full breakfast is included in the rate.

INFORMATION AND SERVICES

While Holbox is making it onto more travelers' radars, there still is no bank (though there is one bank-affiliated ATM) and no post office. Also, note that hours of operation on the island are decidedly flexible—"open all day" usually means "closed for a couple of hours in the middle of the day for lunch."

Tourist Information

There is no tourist information office in Holbox, but https://the.holboxeno.com and **www.holboxisland.com** are good sources of information and listings.

Emergency Services

Centro Médico Utstal (Av. Tiburón Ballena s/n, tel. 984/875-2158, cell tel. 984/121-2332, 9am-9pm daily) offers basic health services, including x-rays and routine lab work. For more advanced medical attention, head to Cancún or Mérida; in emergencies, consider taking an air taxi.

Farmacia Jessy (Av. Igualdad near Av. Bravo, no phone, 9am-3pm and 5pm-10pm Mon.-Fri., 9am-3pm Sat.-Sun.) usually has a moderate selection of medications and basic toiletries.

Money

There is **no bank** on Isla Holbox, but there is one **Bancomer ATM** on the 2nd floor of the city hall (central plaza, Av. Porfirio Díaz s/n). There also are two **unaffiliated ATMs** in El Pueblito Plaza (Calle Tiburón Ballena near Porfirio Díaz) that charge an arm and a leg in fees. **Note:** The ATMs on the island often run out of money, so plan accordingly.

Though more hotels, restaurants, and tour operators are accepting credit cards, don't count on using plastic; be sure to **bring enough cash** for the length of your stay (plus an extra day or two, in case you decide to extend your visit).

Media and Communications

The days of Internet cafes are long gone on this little island. Instead, you'll find free Wi-Fi in your hotel—often in common areas only—and in a handful of restaurants and cafés.

Laundry

Just half a block from the central plaza, **Lavamar** (Av. Porfirio Díaz near Calle Esmedregal, 9am-6pm Mon.-Sat.) does a good job of washing, drying, and folding clothes; it charges US$0.80 per kilo, with a 3 kilo (6.5 pounds) minimum. Same-day service is available for a small additional charge.

GETTING THERE
Car, Ferry, Bus, Taxi, and Shuttle

To get to Holbox, you first need to get to the small coastal village of Chiquilá. There are buses from Cancún, Playa del Carmen, Valladolid, and Mérida. If you're driving, take old Highway 180 (not the *autopista*) to El Ideal, about 100 kilometers (62 miles) west of Cancún. Turn north onto Highway 5 and follow that about 140 kilometers (87 miles) to Chiquilá, passing though the town of Kantunilkín. (There are shortcuts from both Mérida and Cancún, but they follow smaller, less-maintained roads.) You'll have to leave your car in Chiquilá. Several families run small overnight parking operations, charging around US$5 per 24 hours; ask about weekly rates.

Ferries are operated by two companies: **9 Hermanos** (cell tel. 984/120-8655) and **Holbox Express** (tel. 984/875-2029). Holbox Express has a newer fleet with cushy seats, TVs, and floor-to-ceiling windows, while 9 Hermanos's boats are well maintained but no-frills. That said, the ride is so short that it doesn't really matter much which one you take. Between the two, boats leave Chiquilá for Isla Holbox (US$7 adult, $4.50 child, 25

Catch a ferry between Holbox and the mainland.

minutes) starting at 6am are run every 30 minutes from 7:30am until 8:30pm with the last boat leaving at 9:30pm. Returning boats leave Holbox at 5am and run every 30 minutes from 6:30am to 8:30pm. Going to Holbox, it's a good idea to get to the dock a half hour early, as boats occasionally leave ahead of schedule. Private boatmen also make the trip in either direction for approximately US$60-65 for up to six people; ask at the dock. **Note:** Private boats are prohibited from ferrying passengers to/from Holbox after dark.

From Chiquilá, **second-class buses** to Cancún (US$6.75, 3.5 hours) leave the dock parking area at 5:45am, 7:45am, 1:45pm, 2:15pm, and 3:15pm; the 1:45pm departure continues to Cancún International Airport (US$12.50, 4.5 hours). Two daily buses head straight to Playa del Carmen at 2:45pm and 4:15pm (US$11, 2.5 hours). To Mérida, there are two departures at 5:30am and 4:45pm (US$11, 7 hours); this bus also stops in

Valladolid (US$5, 2.5 hours). All buses wait for the ferry arriving from Holbox. **Note:** For other destinations on the Riviera Maya, take a bus to Cancún or Playa del Carmen and transfer from there.

Taxis also often are available at the dock to take travelers door-to-door to Cancún (US$70), Cancún International Airport (US$100), Playa del Carmen (US$120), and Valladolid (US$75); fares are often negotiable so be sure to agree on a price before you step into the car.

Chiquilá Shuttle (cell tel. 984/135-6451, www.chiquilashuttle.com) also provides private van service to/from Chiquilá and Cancún International Airport for US$115 (max 6 people) to US$125 (max 9 people). Shared van service is also available for US$17 per person with four daily departures. Advance reservations are required.

If you'd prefer someone else deal with transportation logistics (you are on vacay, after all), consider using **Balleneros Tour & Travel** (cell tel. 999/236-1524, ballenerosholboxgmail.com). It provides door-to-door service to/from Holbox and Cancún (US$34 per person), Cancún International Airport (US$34 per person), and Playa del Carmen (US$37 per person). The cost includes a taxi to/from your hotel in Holbox, ferry tickets, and pickup/drop-off on the mainland.

Air

If you've got the money and the stomach for itty-bitty planes, **AeroSaab** (tel. 998/873-0501, www.aerosaab.com) offers a full-day tour to Isla Holbox departing from several regional cities, including Cancún, Playa del Carmen, or Cozumel. Using Cessna airplanes, the trip begins with a scenic flight up the coast to Holbox, followed by a tour of Isla Pájaros and Yalahau Spring, lunch, and a chance to explore the village and beach (US$178-202 pp, minimum 4 people). Overnight trips and/or whale shark excursions also can be arranged.

For air taxi service, try **Flights Holbox** (cell tel. 984/136-8852, www.flights-holbox.com). The cost depends on the size of the plane and the destination. To Cancún International Airport, rates run US$470 (max 5 passengers) to US$1,090 (max 13 passengers). Check the website for last-minute deals, sometimes running as low as US$50 per person.

GETTING AROUND

Holbox is very easy to get around on foot. Even the farthest hotels are no more than a

Golf carts are an easy way to get around Isla Holbox.

half hour's walk from town, and it's very safe day or night. The only time you may really need a lift is when you're lugging your bags between the pier and your hotel.

Taxi

Golf carts serve as the island's taxis (some are even painted in yellow-and-black checkers). A ride from the pier into town is US$1.50-3 per person or US$3-5 per person to the hotels farther down the beach. They are almost always parked on the plaza, or your hotel can call one.

Golf Cart

Though you really don't need a golf cart to get around Holbox, you may enjoy the convenience of one. Rates, though not cheap, are

relatively uniform: US$15 per hour, US$30 for 4 hours, US$50 for 12 hours, and US$75 for 24 hours.

Recommended outfits include **Rentadora Glendy** (Av. Porfirio Díaz at Av. Morelos, tel. 984/875-2093, www.holboxglendytours.com, 7am-11pm daily) and **Rentadora El Brother** (Calle Tiburón Ballena at Av. Igualdad, tel. 998/875-2018, 8am-10pm daily).

Bicycle

Other than walking, the easiest—and most affordable—way of getting around town is by bike. **Bikes Holbox** (Av. Coldwell near Calle Esmedregal, tel. 984/212-5941, 8am-6:30pm Mon.-Sat.) rents bikes (no helmets, no locks) for US$1.50 per hour or US$10 per 24 hours. Delivery is available.

Isla Cozumel

Look for ★ to find recommended
sights, activities, dining, and lodging.

Highlights

★ **San Gervasio:** Smack-dab in the middle of the island is Cozumel's best and biggest Maya ruin, thought to be dedicated to Ixchel, the goddess of fertility (page 113).

★ **Playa Chen Río:** A rocky arm on Cozumel's east side forms a calm natural pool (page 120).

★ **Santa Rosa Wall:** Sit back and enjoy the ride at one of Cozumel's marquee dive sites, where a strong current whisks you past a long wall, home to various sea life (page 130).

★ **Palancar:** This massive dive site has something for everyone: shallows, winding ravines, and natural arches (page 131).

★ **Parque Punta Sur:** Snorkel the colorful ocean reef, or stay above water on the long curving beaches of this scenic nature reserve. There's also a small maritime museum, a Maya ruin, and a lighthouse (page 135).

All around Isla Cozumel, the Caribbean Sea glitters a hundred shades of blue. Beneath the waves, pristine coral reefs make for spectacular diving and snorkeling, the island's number one draw.

San Miguel de Cozumel—usually just called Cozumel, since it's the only city on the island—is where the ferries from Playa del Carmen arrive. It's also where cruise ships, as many as 30 per week in the high season, arrive; it's then that the waterfront promenade becomes a human river, flowing slowly down a channel of jewelry stores, souvenir shops, and open-air restaurants.

Just a few blocks from the promenade, another Cozumel emerges—a small, friendly community where old folks sit at their windows and dogs sleep in the streets. In spring, masses of orange *framboyán* (poinciana) flowers bloom on shade trees in the plaza, and festivals and religious celebrations are widely attended.

Cozumel's interior—including an important Maya ruin—and its eastern shore are yet another world, lacking even power lines and telephone cables. Heavy surf makes much of the eastern shore too dangerous for swimming, but you easily can spend a day beachcombing or relaxing on the unmanicured beaches and lunching at small restaurants overlooking the sea.

As Mexico's third-largest island, it shouldn't be surprising to discover that Cozumel is so multifaceted. But it's hard not to marvel at how stark the differences are. Come for the diving and snorkeling, but leave time to experience a side of Cozumel you may not have expected.

HISTORY

Cozumel has been inhabited since 300 BC and was one of three major Maya pilgrimage sites in the region (the others were Chichén Itzá and Izamal in Yucatán state). The name is derived from the island's Maya name, *Cuzamil* (Land of Swallows). The height of its pre-Hispanic occupation was AD 1250-1500, when Putún people (also known as the Chontol or Itzás, the same group who built Chichén

---

Previous: San Gervasio; the beach club at Chankanaab. **Above:** snorkeling tour along the reef.

Isla Cozumel

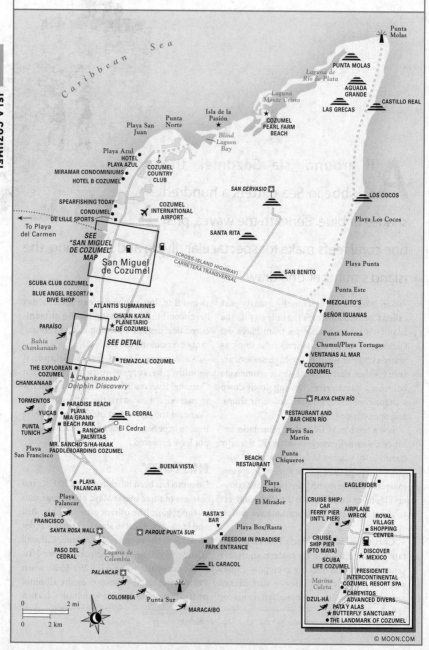

Caribbean Sea

Punta Molas

PUNTA MOLAS

Laguna de
Río de Plata

AGUADA
GRANDE

Laguna
Monte Cristo

LAS GRECAS

CASTILLO REAL

Playa San
Juan

Punta
Norte

Isla de la
Pasión

COZUMEL
PEARL FARM
BEACH

Blind
Lagoon
Bay

Playa Azul
HOTEL
PLAYA AZUL

MIRAMAR CONDOMINIUMS

HOTEL B COZUMEL

COZUMEL
COUNTRY
CLUB

SAN GERVASIO

LOS COCOS

Playa Los Cocos

SPEARFISHING TODAY

CONDUMEL

DE LILLE SPORTS

COZUMEL
INTERNATIONAL
AIRPORT

SANTA RITA

To Playa
del Carmen

SEE
"SAN MIGUEL
DE COZUMEL"
MAP

San Miguel
de Cozumel

(CROSS-ISLAND HIGHWAY)
CARRETERA TRANSVERSAL

SAN BENITO

Playa Punta

Punta Este

SCUBA CLUB COZUMEL

BLUE ANGEL RESORT/
DIVE SHOP

ATLANTIS SUBMARINES

CHA'AN KA'AN
PLANETARIO
DE COZUMEL

SEE DETAIL

PARAÍSO

Bahía
Chankanaab

TEMAZCAL COZUMEL

MEZCALITO'S

SEÑOR IGUANAS

Punta Morena

Chumul/Playa Tortugas

VENTANAS AL MAR

COCONUTS
COZUMEL

THE EXPLOREAN
COZUMEL

CHANKANAAB

Chankanaab/
Dolphin Discovery

PLAYA CHEN RÍO

TORMENTOS

YUCAB

PUNTA
TUNICH

Playa
San Francisco

PARADISE BEACH

PLAYA
MIA GRAND
BEACH PARK

RANCHO
PALMITAS

MR. SANCHO'S/HA-HAAK
PADDLEBOARDING COZUMEL

EL CEDRAL

El Cedral

BUENA VISTA

RESTAURANT AND
BAR CHEN RÍO

Playa San
Martín

Punta
Chiqueros

PLAYA
PALANCAR

Playa
Palancar

SAN
FRANCISCO

SANTA ROSA WALL

PASO DEL
CEDRAL

Laguna de
Colombia

PARQUE PUNTA SUR

PALANCAR

COLOMBIA

Punta Sur

MARACAIBO

BEACH
RESTAURANT

Playa
Bonita

El Mirador

RASTA'S
BAR

Playa Box/Rasta

FREEDOM IN PARADISE

PARK ENTRANCE

EL CARACOL

0   2 mi

0   2 km

EAGLERIDER

CRUISE SHIP/
CAR
FERRY PIER
(INT'L PIER)

AIRPLANE
WRECK

ROYAL
VILLAGE
SHOPPING
CENTER

CRUISE
SHIP PIER
(PTO MAYA)

DISCOVER
MEXICO

SCUBA
LIFE COZUMEL

PRESIDENTE
INTERCONTINENTAL
COZUMEL RESORT SPA

Marina
Caleta

CAREYITOS
ADVANCED DIVERS

DZUL-HÁ

PATA Y ALAS

BUTTERFLY SANCTUARY

THE LANDMARK OF COZUMEL

© MOON.COM

Itzá's most famous structures) dominated the region as seafaring merchants. Capitan Don Juan de Grijalva arrived on the island in 1518 and dubbed it Isla de Santa Cruz, marking the beginning of the brutal dislocation of the native people by Spanish explorers and conquistadors. It eventually was overrun by British and Dutch pirates who used it as a base of operations. By the mid-1800s, however, the island was virtually uninhabited. The henequen, chicle, and coconut-oil booms attracted a new wave of people to the Quintana Roo territory (it didn't become a state until 1974), and Cozumel slowly rebounded, this time with a mostly Mexican mestizo population.

Cozumel benefitted mightily from the worldwide popularity of Jacques Cousteau's early underwater films (which were not filmed there, contrary to legend, but inspired others that were) and later, of course, the establishment of Cancún in the 1970s.

PLANNING YOUR TIME

Don't let the cruise ship hubbub on Avenida Rafael Melgar turn you off from the town altogether. Besides the fact that most of the hotels, dive shops, banks, and other services are here, the town itself has much to offer, including a

pleasant central plaza and a great museum. Budget a day or two to rent a car and explore the rest of the island, including the beach clubs, Maya ruins, family-friendly ecoparks, and the wild beaches and deserted coastline of Cozumel's eastern side.

ORIENTATION

The town of San Miguel de Cozumel (aka "downtown Cozumel") is located on the west side of the island. The main passenger ferry arrives here, across from the central plaza.

Avenida Benito Juárez is one of the main streets in downtown Cozumel, beginning at the central plaza, crossing town, and becoming the Carretera Transversal (Cross-Island Highway). The highway passes the turnoff to the San Gervasio ruins before intersecting with the coastal road. The coastal road follows Cozumel's eastern shore, which is dotted with a few beach clubs and restaurants. Rounding the southern tip, the road heads north along the west shore before becoming Avenida Rafael Melgar and returning to the central plaza. Continuing north, the road passes turnoffs to the airport and a country club before turning to dirt and eventually dead-ending.

Sights

PARQUE BENITO JUÁREZ

Downtown Cozumel's central plaza has long maintained a surprisingly peaceful atmosphere, despite the mass of humanity that disembarks at the nearby ferry pier and cruise ship ports. It's been a place where locals and tourists come to stroll about, enjoy live music and dancing on weekends, and snack at small-time food vendors. The city municipal building, which occupies most of the plaza's east side, houses an airy commercial center on the ground floor and civic offices above. A recent M$95 million renovation to the plaza removed the central kiosk—an upset to many

locals—and replaced it with a ground-level water fountain that children often play in during the day. In the evenings, the fountain is roped off for a "Luz y Sonido" show, where the water "dances" in time to classical music and is lit by a colorful lights. Shows typically start at 8pm and make for great photo ops.

MUSEO DE LA ISLA DE COZUMEL

The town's small but excellent museum, **Museo de la Isla de Cozumel** (Av. Rafael Melgar at Calle 6, tel. 987/872-1434, 8am-4pm daily, US$4), is on the waterfront in a turn-of-the-20th-century hotel building.

San Miguel de Cozumel

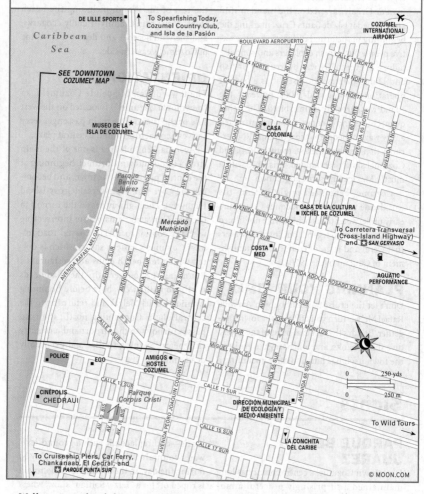

Well-composed exhibits in English and Spanish describe the island's wildlife, coral reefs, and the fascinating, sometimes tortured, history of human presence here, from the Maya pilgrims who came to worship Ixchel, the fertility goddess, to present-day survivors of devastating hurricanes. The museum also has a small bookstore and a library. For a good photo op head to the terrace, which has a great view of the main drag, ferry pier, and—on a clear day—Playa del Carmen. It's

also home to a popular restaurant (7am-11pm Mon.-Sat., 7am-3pm Sun., US$7-18) serving mostly Mexican fare.

COZUMEL PEARL FARM BEACH

Located on a remote private island on Cozumel's northern shore, the **Cozumel Pearl Farm Beach** (cell tel. 987/564-8698, www.cozumelpearlfarm.mx, US$110 adult, US$85 child ages 6-12, free age 5 and under) is a fun place to spend a day and learn about these unique nature-made jewels. The six-hour trip includes touring the farm's facilities to learn how pearls form and how they are farmed and harvested, followed by snorkeling around the underwater installations. Lunch on the beach is included (burgers, chips, and drinks), plus time for relaxing in hammocks and "speed snorkeling"—snorkeling while being tugged by a boat. Camping overnight is possible too, including gear and meals (US$225 adult, US$175 child ages 6-12, free age 5 and under). Boat transportation is provided from the Aqua Safari Pier (Av. Rafael Melgar near Calle 5).

PATAS Y ALAS BUTTERFLY SANCTUARY

Pata y Alas Butterfly Sanctuary (Carr. Costera Sur Km 6.8, tel. 987/ 869-0504, toll-free US tel. 866/732-8375, 9:30am-4pm Mon.-Sat., US$4) is a small site inside the Palmar Snorkel Beach Club dedicated to the protection and documentation of the butterflies in Cozumel. Visitors stroll through a protected garden while a variety of colorful butterflies flits about here and there, landing on tropical flowers and sometimes on guests. Keep your eyes peeled for caterpillars munching on foliage. Staffers are on hand to answer questions.

PLANETARIO DE COZUMEL

The Cha'an Ka'an Planetario de Cozumel (Av. Claudio Canto between Avs. Rafael Melgar and 65, tel. 987/857-0867, www.planetariodecozumel.org, 9:30am-6:30pm Mon.-Fri., 11:30am-7pm Sat., free) is a state-of-the-art planetarium with an observatory for viewing the skies (US$3/2 adult/child) and a domed planetarium with 3-D shows ranging from Maya astrology to the coral reefs (Fri.-Sat. only, US$8/7 adult/child); screenings are in English and Spanish. There are also educational exhibits on subjects like the biodiversity of Cozumel and water conservancy. It's a good stop for families traveling with children.

DISCOVER MEXICO

Discover Mexico (Carr. Costera Sur Km 5.5, tel. 987/857-2820, www.discovermexico.org, 8am-4pm Mon.-Sat., US$26 adult, US$19 child) boasts hundreds of enthusiastic reviews from visitors, but we're hard-pressed to understand the appeal. Exhibits include a video on Mexican history, scale models of various iconic Mexican structures (the cathedral in Mexico City, the pyramid at Chichén Itzá, etc.), a gallery of Mexican folk art, tequila tasting, and, of course, plenty of opportunities for eating, drinking, and shopping. The center's tour guides are peppy and well informed, and Mexican art never fails to impress, but the overall experience is too gimmicky to be truly satisfying.

ARCHAEOLOGICAL ZONES

Isla Cozumel played a deeply significant role in the Maya world as a vital port of trade and, more importantly, as one of three major destinations of religious pilgrimages (the others were Izamal and Chichén Itzá, both in Yucatán state). The island's primary site—known as San Gervasio today—was dedicated to Ixchel, the Maya goddess of fertility as well as of the moon, childbirth, medicine, and weaving. Archaeologists believe that every Maya woman was expected, at least once in her lifetime, to journey to Cozumel to make offerings to Ixchel for fertility—her own, and that of her family's fields. Cozumel's draw was powerful, as inscriptions there refer to places and events hundreds of miles away.

Over 30 archaeological sites have been discovered on the island, though only four are easily accessible, and only San Gervasio can properly be called a tourist attraction. San Gervasio is certainly not as glorious as ruins found on the mainland, but it's worth a visit all the same.

TOP EXPERIENCE

★ San Gervasio

The area around **San Gervasio** (Cross-Island

Downtown Cozumel

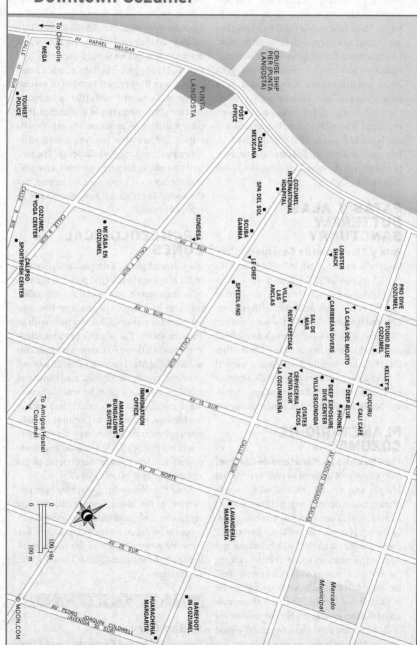

To Cinépolis ←

AV RAFAEL MELGAR

CALLE 11 SUR

■ MEGA

■ TOURIST
POLICE

CRUISE SHIP
PIER (PUNTA
LANGOSTA)

PUNTA
LANGOSTA

POST
OFFICE

CASA
MEXICANA

COZUMEL
INTERNATIONAL
HOSPITAL

SPA DEL SOL

CALLE 9 BIS

■ COZUMEL
YOGA CENTER

■ CALIPSO
SPORTSFISH CENTER

● MI CASA EN
COZUMEL

CALLE 3 SUR

KONDESA

SCUBA
GAMMA

AV 5 SUR

CALLE 7 SUR

LE CHEF

LOBSTER
SHACK

PRO DIVE
COZUMEL

AV 10 SUR

VILLA
LAS
ANCLAS

NEW ESPEGIAS

SPEEDL●MD

SAL DE
MAR

CARIBBEAN DIVERS

LA CASA DEL MOJITO

STUDIO BLUE
COZUMEL

KELLEY'S

CALLE 5 SUR

LA COZUMELEÑA

CERVECERIA
PUNTA SUR

OTATES
TACOS

VILLA
ESCONDIDA

DEEP EXPOSURE
DIVE CENTER

PHONET

DEEP BLUE

CUCURU

CALI CAFÉ

To Amigos Hostel
Cozumel ←

AV 15 SUR

■ IMMIGRATION
OFFICE

AMARANTO ●
BUNGALOWS
& SUITES

AV 20 NORTE

AV ADOLFO ROSADO SALAS

AV 25 SUR

0   0
100 m   100 yds

■ LAVANDERIA
MARGARITA

CALLE 3 SUR

Mercado
Municipal

■ BAREFOOT
IN COZUMEL

■ HUARACHERIA
MARGARITA

AV PEDRO JOAQUÍN COLDWELL
(AVENIDA 30 SUR)

© MOON.COM

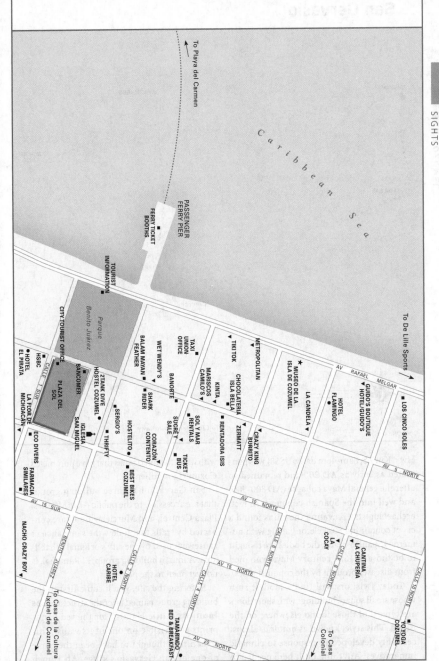

San Gervasio

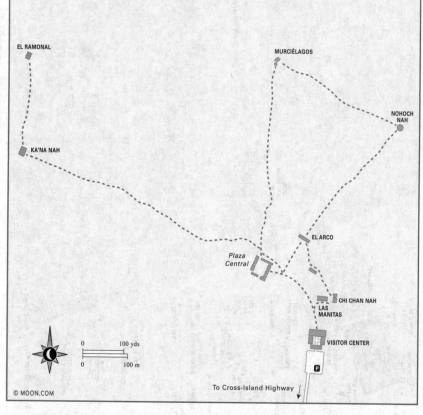

© MOON.COM

EL RAMONAL

KA'NA NAH

MURCIÉLAGOS

NOHOCH NAH

EL ARCO

Plaza Central

CHI CHAN NAH

LAS MANITAS

VISITOR CENTER

0   100 yds
0   100 m

To Cross-Island Highway

Hwy. Km 7.5, 8am-4pm daily, US$8) was populated as early as AD 200 and remained so after the general Maya collapse (AD 800-900) and well into the Spanish conquest. In fact, archaeologists excavating the ruins found a crypt containing 50 skeletons along with numerous Spanish beads; the bodies are thought to be those of 16th-century Maya who died from diseases brought by the conquistadors.

Today's visitors will find a modest ruin whose small square buildings with short doors are typical of those found elsewhere on the island. This style, known as *oratorio,* almost certainly developed in response to climatic imperatives: Anything built here needed to withstand the hurricanes that have pummeled Cozumel for millennia.

San Gervasio has three building groups that are accessible to the public—Las Manitas, Plaza Central, and Murciélagos; all are connected by trails that follow the same ancient causeways used by the city's original inhabitants. A fourth building group, El Ramonal, is not yet open to the public.

Entering the site, you'll come first to the building group named after the structure **Las Manitas** (Little Hands), for the red handprints still visible on one of its walls. This structure is thought to have been the home of one of San Gervasio's kings, Ah Huneb

Itza, and the inner temple was likely a personal sanctuary. Just east of the Las Manitas building is **Chi Chan Nah;** consisting of two rooms, it is the smallest structure in San Gervasio. The exact purpose of this building is unknown, though it is theorized that it was used for rituals.

Bearing left, the trail leads to the **Plaza Central,** a large courtyard surrounded by nine low structures in various states of decay; it is believed that the structures were made taller with wood extensions. The Plaza Central served as the seat of power in San Gervasio's latest era, from AD 1200 onward. At the northwest side of the Plaza Central is the somewhat precarious-looking **El Arco** (The Arch), which served as an entrance to this section of the city.

At 0.5 kilometer (0.3 mile) from the Plaza Central is the **Murciélagos** (Bats) building group, containing the site's largest and most important structure: **Ka'na Nah** (Tall House). Also dating to San Gervasio's later era, this was the temple of the goddess Ixchel, and in its heyday would have been covered in stucco and painted red, blue, green, and black.

Finally, on the northeastern edge of San Gervasio rests **Nohoch Nah** (Big House), a boxy but serene temple. With an interior altar, the temple might have been used by religious pilgrims to make an offering upon entering or leaving San Gervasio. It was originally covered in stucco and painted a multitude of colors.

Guides can be hired at the visitors center for a fixed rate: US$25 for a one-hour tour in Spanish, English, French, or German. Prices are per group, which can include up to four people. Tips are customary and are not included in the price.

El Cedral

El Cedral is the "other town" on Cozumel, a sleepy village south of San Miguel that's home to a small historic church and a modest Maya structure of the same name. It has a pleasant central plaza, and tour operators, including horseback riding guides, often bring visitors here to visit the church and temple, and to peruse the souvenir stands normally set up here. Once a year, El Cedral hosts one of Cozumel's largest festivals, a 10-day blowout celebration of the Catholic holy cross.

Although overshadowed by San Miguel today, El Cedral is actually the older settlement. It was here that a group of 18 families of indigenous Christian converts fled in 1847 to escape persecution by fellow Maya during the War of the Castes. They came bearing a small

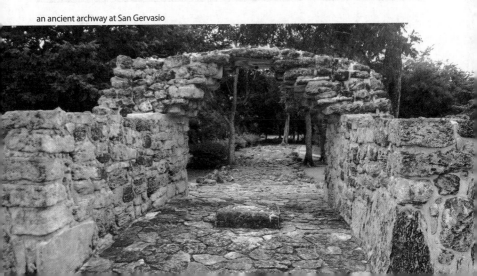

an ancient archway at San Gervasio

wooden cross known as *Santa Cruz de Sabán* (Holy Cross of Sabán) and founded their church and village alongside a Maya temple that they discovered just inland from their landing site. The group was led by Casimiro Cárdenas, whose descendants still serve as caretakers, or *mayordomos,* of the temple and church; there's a statue of Don Casimiro in the central plaza.

El Cedral is famous for its **Fiesta de la Santa Cruz** (Festival of the Holy Cross), which begins in late April and culminates on May 3. The celebration includes food, music, dance, performances, rodeos, and fireworks aplenty, and even some traditions of distant Maya origin. The party is open to everyone, including tourists, and makes for a fun and fascinating outing if your visit happens to coincide with it.

A well-marked turnoff just south of Playa San Francisco leads 5 kilometers (3.1 miles) to the village. El Cedral's **Maya ruin** (8am-5pm daily, free) is tiny and underwhelming, though it still bears a few traces of the original paint and stucco. The church is directly adjacent and contains the original wooden cross borne by El Cedral's founders.

El Caracol

Located inside **Parque Punta Sur** (Carr. Costera Sur Km 27, tel. 987/872-0914, www. cozumelparks.com, 9am-4pm Mon.-Sat., US$14 adult, US$8 child under 12), El Caracol is a small, conch-shaped structure that dates to AD 1200. It's believed to have been a light-house where Maya used smoke and flames to lead boats to safety. Small openings at the top of the structure also acted as whistles to alert Maya to approaching tropical storms and hurricanes. Admission to the reserve includes access to this small site.

Castillo Real

Castillo Real is a partially excavated site with a temple, two chambers, and a lookout tower. It is believed to have been a Maya watchtower to protect against approaching enemies. It's located on the remote northeastern corner of the island, along the sand road leading to Punta Molas. The road is quite treacherous, such that even ATVs and motorcycles can have trouble making it. Ask at the tourist office for the latest before making any plans to head up there.

Beaches and Beach Clubs

Cozumel isn't famous for its beaches, but it is not without a few beautiful stretches of sand. The best swimming beaches are on the protected southwestern coast, with soft white sand and calm azure waters. The finest stretches are occupied by large beach clubs, which have conveniences like lounge chairs, umbrellas, restrooms, restaurants, and water sports; a few even have swimming pools. Most beach clubs charge either a cover or a minimum consumption, but neither is exorbitant. The clubs cater to cruise shippers and range from peaceful and low-key to boisterous and loud. Independent travelers are perfectly welcome too, of course.

Beaches on Cozumel's east side are wild and picturesque, with virtually no development

beyond a few small restaurants. The surf can be fierce here, though a few sheltered areas have good swimming and are popular with locals. The municipal government has been steadily improving the road on the east side, including adding signs, stairways, and parking, but it remains a far different experience from the west-side beach clubs.

NORTHWESTERN COZUMEL
Isla de la Pasión

One of Cozumel's loveliest beaches is **Isla de la Pasión** (tel. 987/872-6941, www.islapasion. com.mx, US$70 pp via catamaran, US$90 pp via speedboat), a privately owned island and beach club just off Cozumel's north shore.

Although aimed squarely at cruise ship passengers, anyone can sign up for a package tour, which includes a buffet, open bar, and free beach activities. The beach is gorgeous—one of Corona's commercials was filmed here—and the island is covered, oddly, with wispy pine trees. (Scientists believe their seeds were washed or blown from the Atlantic coast of the United States.) The price is a bit steep, but the main bummer is you only get four hours at the beach. Tours leave from the Puerta Maya pier by catamaran or speedboat.

It's possible, though not easy, to visit Isla de la Pasión on your own; the beach itself is public, after all, and you can stay as long as you like. From the northern end of Avenida Rafael Melgar, a dirt road continues 5 kilometers (3.1 miles) past a water treatment plant to the port at Bahia Ciega. (The road isn't bad, but drive carefully, as your vehicle's insurance is probably void here.) At the port, ask around for a fisherman to take you across (around US$15, 20 minutes). Be sure to arrange a time for him to return, and cross your fingers he's got a good memory; otherwise, you'll be left begging a ride with a tour group. Bring food, water, and an umbrella—you won't be allowed to use the beach club facilities, but there's plenty of beach on which to lay out a towel.

SOUTHWESTERN COZUMEL

The majority of beach clubs are clustered on Playa San Francisco, a three-kilometer (1.9-mile) stretch of white-sand beach that begins just south of Secrets Aura Cozumel resort. Another beach, Playa Palancar, is farther south, near the tip of the island, and has a beach club of the same name.

Paradise Beach

Paradise Beach (Carr. Costera Sur Km 14.5, tel. 987/689-0000, www.paradise-beach-cozumel.com, 9am-sunset daily, US$10 minimum consumption) has a gorgeous pool and a spacious, picture-perfect beach that's dotted with palm trees. Oddly, they charge US$3 for beach chairs and US$18 for use of the water sports gear, such as kayaks, trampoline floats, paddleboards, and snorkel gear. Nevertheless, it's a lovely and not-too-raucous place to spend a day at the beach.

Playa Mia

Playa Mia Grand Beach Park (Carr. Costera Sur Km 14.25, tel. 987/872-9040, www.playamia.com, 9am-6pm daily, US$30/25 adult/child, US$45/35 adult/child with buffet, US$60/50 adult/child with buffet and drinks) is big and busy without being obnoxious. The beach is decent, though often very crowded, and there's an excellent beachside pool. There's also a small water park with two additional pools with features like water cannons and sprays as well as a pair of 61-meter-long (200-foot) waterslides. The restaurant-buffet area is cool and pleasant, thanks to a high-peaked, circus-like tent. And there's certainly no shortage of activities: volleyball, table tennis, a kids' play structure, floating obstacle course, an underwater sculpture park, snorkeling, and more.

Mr. Sancho's

Though you can pay as you go at **Mr. Sancho's** (Carr. Costera Sur Km 15, tel. 987/120-2220, www.mrsanchos.com, 8am-5pm Mon.-Sat., US$55 adult, US$40 teens, US$35 child), it's known best for its all-inclusive packages. It has a decent Mexican restaurant, fairly mellow ambience, and plenty of extras, from snorkeling to massage. There's also a floating aquatic park with trampolines, water tubes, climbing walls, and more (US$12 pp extra). The beach is a bit narrow, meaning the lounge chairs are squeezed pretty tight, but it's a lovely spot all the same, and a great option for a no-brainer beach day with kids.

Playa Palancar

With a calm atmosphere to match the tranquil turquoise waters, **Playa Palancar** (Km 19.5, cell tel. 987/118-5154, www.buceopalancar.com.mx, 8am-5pm daily, no cover or minimum consumption) is just the place to relax in a hammock or hunker down with a book while digging your toes into the thick white sand. Playa Palancar has gotten busier over the years, now with music and even parasailing, but it's still the mellowest of Cozumel's main beach clubs. And there happens to be great diving and snorkeling at nearby Palancar and Columbia reefs; an on-site dive shop offers fun dives (US$65/90 one/two tanks) and guided snorkeling trips (US$35-45, 60-90 minutes), with daily departures at 9am, noon, and 2pm. Snorkel gear can be rented separately (US$10), but there's not much to see close to shore. A *palapa*-roofed restaurant serves classic Mexican seafood and a wide range of drinks (US$8-20). The club is 750 meters (0.5 mile) off the main road.

SOUTHEASTERN COZUMEL

On the east side of the island, you'll find a wild and windswept coastline dotted with beaches facing the open ocean. The surf here can be quite rough, and only a few beaches are safe for swimming.

Parque Punta Sur

As the name suggests, **Parque Punta Sur** (Carr. Costera Sur Km 27, tel. 987/872-0914, www.cozumelparks.com, 9am-4pm Mon.-Sat., US$14 adult, US$8 child under 12) covers Cozumel's southern point, but the entrance is on the east side, and the ambience and appeal is certainly akin to that of the eastern beaches. It is an important natural reserve that happens to have a fine beach and outstanding snorkeling. Because it faces south, the surf tends to be light. There's a small eatery, plus restrooms, a changing area, and a kiosk renting snorkel gear.

Playa Box (Playa Rasta)

Playa Box (pronounced *boash*, Yucatec Maya for head) is also known as Playa Rasta for the two reggae-themed bars that share a kitchen—**Freedom in Paradise** (no phone, www.bobmarleybar.com, 9am-sunset daily, US$7-13) and **Rasta's Bar** (same hours and menu)—that occupy it. It's just past Punta Sur, where the road turns north along Cozumel's eastern

shore. It's a rocky stretch of coastline with only a few sandy inlets and the two restaurant/bars blasting reggae at each other. It's not really the best place to spend the day—unless you like rambling on rocks and have a serious craving for jerk chicken.

El Mirador

Spanish for "the Lookout," this is the best place to appreciate Isla Cozumel's dramatic ironshore formations, including a natural arch and exposed huge bulges of the black jagged stone. Ironshore is formed when waves, wind, and especially microscopic organisms erode the ancient limestone cap that underlies much of the island. Be very careful walking on the ironshore—it can be sharp and slippery. Wear water shoes or Teva-style sports sandals to help you stay standing!

Playa Bonita and Punta Chiqueros

Playa Bonita is another picturesque curve of sand with plenty of room to lay out a towel and soak in the sun. Heavy surf usually makes swimming here inadvisable, but it's beautifully dramatic. The northern end of the beach is Punta Chiqueros, where a small **beach restaurant** (no phone, 10am-5pm daily, US$7-18) serves hamburgers, fresh fish, and other standards. It's also the home of tacky tropical drinks—rum punch served in pineapples with mini-umbrella décor or massive margaritas served in half-gallon-size martini glasses.

Playa San Martín

A wooden stairway leads from the road down to the beach at this long, scenic, windswept beach. There are a handful of permanent *palapa* umbrellas near the stairway that are popular with couples and families, but otherwise you're likely to have the beach virtually to yourself.

★ Playa Chen Río

The best place to swim on the east side of the island is **Playa Chen Río** (1 kilometer/0.6

mile south of Coconuts Bar), where a rocky spit blocks the waves, forming a huge natural pool, and lifeguards are on duty on weekends. Quiet during the week, it's lively and bustling most Sundays, when local families turn out in force. **Restaurant and Bar Chen Río** (no phone, 11am-6pm daily, US$8-20) is located here, but it's a bit pricey for the quality so it's not uncommon to see families picnicking with coolers and even small grills.

Chumul (Playa Tortugas)

About six kilometers (3.7 miles) south of the Carretera Transversal intersection is Chumul, also known as Playa Tortugas, a broad beautiful beach on the north side of the Ventanas al Mar hotel. The scenic, windswept beach is good for surfing—and has nesting turtles May-November—but it is often too rough for swimming or snorkeling. Still, it makes a good place to watch the wild and crashing waves.

A few steps away is **Coconuts Cozumel** (tel. 987/107-7110, www.coconutscozumel. com, 9:30am-sunset daily, US$7-18). Set on a dramatic palm-studded bluff—the only piece of elevated land on the island, in fact—the tables are arranged for diners to enjoy the fabulous views of the beach below and the Caribbean beyond. Classic beach fare is served—ceviche, tacos, nachos—along with plenty of cold beer. Live music starts at 2pm.

Punta Morena

This scenic and little-used stretch of beach has a small restaurant with restrooms. Like elsewhere on the eastern shore, swimming here can be hazardous because of heavy surf and rocky outcrops, but it's still a nice place to relax or search for shells on the beach.

Mezcalitos and Señor Iguanas

These two low-key restaurants—**Mezcalito's** (tel. 987/876-0914, www.mezcalitos.com, 9am-6:30pm daily) and **Señor Iguanas** (no phone, 8am-6pm Mon.-Sat., 9am-6pm Sun.)—are located side by side, right where the Carretera Transversal hits the coast. Longtime Cozumel institutions, they have similar menus (ceviche, fried fish, hamburgers, US$8-15), drinks (beer, margaritas, and tequila shots, US$2.50-6), and services (beachside chairs, hammocks, and *pàlapas*, free if you buy something from the restaurant). Boogie boards also are available for rent at Señor Iguanas (US$6 for 2 hours)—a lot of fun if you can handle the rough surf.

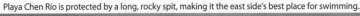

Playa Chen Río is protected by a long, rocky spit, making it the east side's best place for swimming.

NORTHEASTERN COZUMEL

Cozumel's northeastern shoulder is its long-lost coast, the wildest and least visited part of the island. The 25-kilometer (15.5-mile) stretch from the Carretera Transversal north to Punta Molas includes coastal dunes, scrub forest, and deserted beaches, plus the ancient Maya site of **Castillo Real** at around the 22-kilometer (14-mile) mark. This untended coast also is the final resting spot of a shockingly large amount of trash and jetsam, an ugly reminder of civilization in the one place on the island it ought to be easy to forget.

The road itself is a challenge—four-wheel drive is essential to avoid becoming mired in deep sand—and hurricanes and other storms can render it impassable. The area also is at the center of a bitter, on-again off-again land dispute and is occasionally closed without warning. Naval police patrol the area, too, on the lookout for both drug traffickers and turtle poachers.

If you do go, be aware that there are no facilities whatsoever, or any other people most of the time. If you plan to camp, take plenty of water and food, a flashlight, extra batteries, bug repellent, and a mosquito net. Remember, too, that most car insurance policies (including all policies sold by rental agencies on the island, regardless of the vehicle) specifically exclude this and other dirt roads from coverage.

Entertainment and Events

NIGHTLIFE

Most of the partying on Cozumel happens during daylight hours, when cruise ships disgorge thousands of tourists eager to stretch their legs and see some new faces. Beach clubs can get raucous, and many bars in town are open before lunch. Still, there are enough locals, expats, and overnight visitors to support a cadre of lounges and nightclubs. Most places don't charge a cover; if they do, it's on select nights, such as when there's a live band.

Bars and Breweries

At long last, Cozumel's first craft brewery! **Cerveceria Punta Sur** (Av. 10 between Av. Rosado Salas and Calle 3, tel. 987/119-2879, www.cerveceriapuntasur.com, 2pm-11pm Tues.-Sun.) serves up a changing variety of homemade brews, though the IPA is a local fave. Pints and flights run US$3-5. The tasting room has a mid-century modern-meets-Mexico look, and a kitchen serves wood-fired pizza, empanadas, and salad.

Pitched as a "Husband Day Care Center," **Kelley's** (Av. 10 between Calles 1 and Rosado Salas, tel. 987/878-4738, 9am-midnight daily) is an outdoor sports bar with nine HDTVs and a monster projection screen airing major sporting events, including pay-per-view. There's Guinness on tap plus weekly food specials like all-you-can-eat barbecue, twelve-for-six wings, and dollar taco day.

Set in a 102-year-old clapboard house, **Cantina La Chupería** (Av. 10 at Calle 8, cell tel. 984/132-6224, 1pm-2am daily) has a classic Mexican dive bar feel—dim lighting, traditional Talavera tiles, long family-style wood tables. It's no-frills except for the drinks—a full line of craft beer, domestic and foreign, is the poison of choice here. Mezcal cocktails give the taps a run for their money. Open late, this is an after-hours hot spot.

La Casa del Mojito (Av. 5 near Calle 3, tel. 987/111-4124, 4pm-midnight Mon.-Sat.) is a Cuban restaurant-bar that—surprise!—serves some of the best mojitos on the island. Fresh mint. Crushed ice. Lots of rum. Mojitos come in a variety of flavors but the classic—fresh mint, crushed ice, lots of rum—packs a punch. Sit at the bar or grab a table and order tostones to go with your drinks.

Sea Turtles of the Yucatán

sea turtle hatchlings waiting to be released into the sea

All eight of the world's sea turtle species are endangered due to a combination of antiquated fishing practices, habitat destruction, and a taste for turtle products. Four turtle species—hawksbill, Kemp's ridley, green, and loggerhead—nest on the shores of the Yucatán Peninsula, and until fairly recently, were a common supplement to the regional diet. Turtles make easy prey, especially females clambering on shore to lay eggs. They are killed for their meat, fat, and eggs, which are eaten or saved for medicinal purposes, as well as for their shells, which are used to make jewelry, combs, and other crafts.

Various environmental organizations collaborate with the Mexican government to protect sea turtles and their habitats; they maintain strict surveillance of known nesting beaches to stop poaching and have developed breeding programs, too. This, in combination with laws that prohibit the capture and trade of sea turtles or their products, has tremendously increased awareness about their protection.

On Isla Cozumel, travelers can volunteer to monitor nests (US$25-40, 3 hrs) and to release hatchlings into the sea (US$20, 1 hr). Nesting season runs May-September, and during that period volunteers join biologists on nighttime walks of Cozumel's beaches, locating and marking new nests, and helping to "search and rescue" baby turtles who are stuck in nests and need help reaching the water. From August to November, volunteers release hatchings, typically at sundown, by encouraging the tiny turtles to move toward the water (without touching them) and scaring off birds in search of an easy meal. Reservations are required; ages 10 and over are preferred.

The island's Ecology Department, **Dirección Municipal de Ecología y Medio Ambiente,** (Calle 11 at Av. 65, tel. 987/872-5795, ecologia@islacozumel.gob.mx) monitors Cozumel's sea turtles and manages volunteer opportunities. It maintains a **visitors center** (9:30am-2pm and 3:30pm-5:30pm daily May-Nov. only) in a small trailer, usually parked on the roadside near Playa San Martín on the eastern side of the island. Inside are a handful of aquariums, Plexiglas-enclosed nests, and more. Call for more information or to reserve a spot on upcoming beach walks and hatchling releases. Donations are appreciated. Spanish is useful but not required.

Similar volunteer opportunities also are available in Akumal at the **Centro Ecológico Akumal** (CEA, tel. 984/875-9095, www.ceakumal.org) as well as on Isla Mujeres at **Tortugranja** (Carr. Sac Bajo 5, tel. 998/877-0595).

Nightclubs and Live Music

Tiki Tok (Av. Rafael Melgar between Calles 2 and 4, tel. 987/872-5704, 11am-3am Mon.-Sat., no cover) sports a hodgepodge of beach-isle decor, from Polynesian lamps to Jamaican carved masks and figures. There's a dance floor, plenty of tables, and nice sea views. A live band gets the crowd moving to salsa and bachata Friday and Saturday nights, starting around 9:30pm. The bar is popular during the day with cruise shippers, and at night with locals.

Wet Wendy's (Av. 5 Norte between Av. Benito Juárez and Calle 2, tel. 987/872-4970, www.wetwendys.com, 10am-midnight Mon.-Sat., noon-10:30pm) is a classic expat island bar, with Monday Night Football, bacon burgers, and a jocular atmosphere. There's live music most nights too. But more than anything, Wet Wendy's is famous for its huge handcrafted margaritas: potent creations that look more like sundaes than cocktails and range from mango and ginger to peanut butter chocolate and cucumber jalapeño.

Metropolitan (Av. Rafael Melgar between Calles 2 and 4, cell tel. 987/119-6823, 7pm-4am Wed.-Sun.) is a bouncing 2nd-floor club with long, high tables and music and dancing most nights. Thursdays and Fridays often bring specials like US$5 open bar and US$1.50 beers.

THE ARTS
Cultural and Music Performances

Every Sunday evening, the city hosts an **open-air concert** in the central plaza. Locals and expats come out to enjoy the show—put on a clean T-shirt and your nicest flip-flops, and you'll fit right in. Concerts typically last two hours, beginning at 7pm in the summer, 8pm in the winter. Simple food stands selling homemade flan, churros, and other local goodies set up around the park on these nights.

Casa de la Cultura Ixchel de Cozumel (Av. 50 between Av. Benito Juárez and Calle 2, tel. 987/872-1471, 9am-5pm Mon.-Fri.) hosts free concerts, movies, and art exhibits year-round. If you'll be on the island for an extended stay, a variety of classes—dance, art, music, drama, creative writing—also are offered, with a wide selection for children.

Cinema

You can catch relatively recent releases at **Cinépolis** (Av. Rafael Melgar between Calles 15 and 17, tel. 987/869-0799, www.cinepolis.com.mx, US$3.75 adult, US$2.25 child, US$2.25 adult before 3pm), which is located in the Chedraui shopping center. All day Wednesday, tickets are US$2.25.

FESTIVALS AND EVENTS
Carnaval

Cozumel is one of the few places in Mexico where Carnaval is celebrated with vigor. Held in February, the one-night celebration centers on a parade of floats and dance troupes, all decked out in colorful dress, masks, and glitter. Entire families come to participate and watch. Spectators dance and cheer in the streets as the floats go by, and many join the moving dance party that follows the floats with the largest speakers. Eventually the parade ends up in the center of town, where more music, dancing, and partying continue late into the night. Typically, the weekends leading up to the party are filled with musical performances and events—such as the crowing of the king and queen of Carnaval—in the central plaza.

Festival de El Cedral

Residents of the village of El Cedral celebrate their namesake festival beginning in late April and culminating on May 3, the Day of the Holy Cross. Traditionally, the festival entails daily prayer sessions and ends with a dance called the *Baile de las Cabezas de Cochino* (Dance of the Pigs' Heads). The festival, started by a survivor of the Caste War to honor the power of the cross, has morphed over the years into a somewhat more secular affair, with rodeos, dancing, music, and general revelry.

Rodeo de Lanchas Mexicanas

Every May, Cozumel hosts a popular sport-fishing tournament known affectionately as the Mexican Boat Rodeo (tel. 987/564-0405, www.rodeodelanchasmexicanas.com). Prizes range from cash to luxury cars. Anglers from all over Mexico participate—including nearly 200 boats—and international anglers are welcome as long as they register their boats in Mexico. The tournament is timed to coincide with the arrival of big game to Cozumel's waters; tuna, dorado, marlin, and sailfish are often among the fish caught.

Fiesta de San Miguel Arcángel

You'd be forgiven for not knowing that the main town on Cozumel is officially called San Miguel. Hardly anyone, local or tourist, calls it that, preferring just Cozumel instead. One story, among many, is that the city got its name when construction workers unearthed a centuries-old statue of the winged saint on September 29, the very day Saint Michael the Archangel is traditionally celebrated. San Miguel was designated the town's patron saint, and every year September 29 is marked with a citywide celebration, including special masses and religious processions, a rodeo, food stands, music, and general revelry, mostly in and around the central square and San Miguel church.

Festival de Aves

Held in late October or early November, the **Festival de Aves** (Festival of Birds, tel. 987/872-4689, cozumelbirdingclub@gmail.com) is a three-day event that brings birders to the island to sneak a peek or learn more about the almost 350 species of birds found in Cozumel. Bird-watching outings are the highlight of the event, but bird-related conferences, workshops, and exhibits also are quite interesting.

Gran Fondo Cozumel

The Italian-born international bicycle racing craze that is *Il Gran Fondo* made its Cozumel debut in 2014, with over 400 riders participating in the inaugural event. By 2017, it had grown to over 2,500 riders. Like all Gran Fondo races, Cozumel's features a mass start, individual chip timing, and an atmosphere that's both jocular and competitive. The main 100-mile Gran Fondo takes riders twice clockwise around the island; a "Medio Fondo" option is 50 miles and just one lap. A "King of the Wind" medal is given to the racer with the fastest intermediate time along the 19-kilometer section from Punta Sur to Mezcalitos, infamous for punishing "Maya winds." Gran Fondo New York (www.gfny-cozumel.com) has good information about the race.

Ironman Cozumel

Ironman Cozumel (www.ironman.com) is one of two qualifying events in the Ironman series to be held in Mexico (the other is in Los Cabos). It features a course that's as beautiful as it is grueling. The swim (3.8 kilometers/2.4 miles) is certainly the most distinctly *cozumeleño* part, starting and ending at Chankanaab, with gorgeous underwater vistas, and scuba divers and sea creatures observing from below. The bike ride (180 kilometers/112 miles) entails three laps around the island, with lovely sea views but crosswinds strong enough to topple unwitting racers. The run is oddly uninspired—three laps between downtown and the airport—although the sunsets there are spectacular (and you've got until midnight to finish). Ironman Cozumel is usually held in late November and typically attracts around 2,800 triathletes from around the world.

Cozumel Scuba Fest

Every June, hundreds of divers from around the world converge on Cozumel for the annual **Cozumel Scuba Fest** (www.cozumelfest.com), a six-day celebration of the island's unique underwater wonderland. The marquee event typically is the "Jean Michel Cousteau Route," a four-day, nine-dive circuit that retraces signature dives made by Jean Michel's famous father. The festival also includes dive competitions, lectures, film screenings, equipment demos and sales, gala events, and plenty of impromptu carousing in venues throughout the island. Many hotels and dive shops offer special packages for what is arguably the premier diving festival in the Americas.

Shopping

Shopping in Cozumel is aimed straight at cruise ship passengers—and it's no wonder, since they tend to spend a lot of money quickly. Avenida Rafael Melgar is where most of the action is, with a succession of marble-floored shops blasting air-conditioning to entice sweaty passersby in for a refreshing look around. For better prices and more variety, head inland a block or two.

AVENIDA MELGAR

Populated with a mix of high-end jewelry shops and souvenir chain stores, Avenida Melgar has the highest prices in town for items that, on the whole, can be found back home. None of the shops are open to bargaining—at least when there is a cruise ship in port—so if you're looking for a deal, head inland a couple of blocks. In fact, unless you find something you absolutely can't live without, you're uniformly better off shopping elsewhere on the island.

The one exception to this rule is **Los Cinco Soles** (Av. Rafael Melgar at Calle 8, tel. 987/872-9004, www.loscincosoles.com, 8am-8pm daily). A labyrinth of rooms at the northern end of Avenida Melgar, it's filled with high-end Mexican folk art from every state in the country: pre-Columbian replicas, *barro negro* pottery, colorful *rebozos* (shawls), hand-carved furniture, silver jewelry, handmade wood toys, alabaster sculptures, wool rugs, and more. The prices are higher than others in town, but it's reflected in the quality. It's definitely worth a stop, if only to admire the artisanship.

CENTRAL PLAZA AND BEYOND

Acquatic Performance (Calle 1 between Avs. 85 and 90, tel. 987/869-8116, www.

Artists can be found demonstrating their skills and plying their wares in Cozumel's central plaza.

cozumelscubarepair.com, 8:30am-5pm Mon.-Fri., 8:30am-1pm Sat.) is a highly recommended shop selling and renting snorkel and dive equipment. It also repairs dive equipment, often with 24-hour turnaround times, and provides loaners if needed. If you plan to return to Cozumel to dive, long-term storage of equipment is available for US$120 per year and includes a complete regulator servicing.

Though pricey, **Pro Dive Cozumel** (Calle Rosado Salas at Av. 5, tel. 987/872-2420, 9am-9pm daily) is centrally located and has a great selection of snorkel and dive equipment—perfect if you've forgotten your mask or lost a fin.

Sergio's (Av. Benito Juárez between Avs. 5 and 10, tel. 987/872-7632, 10am-8pm daily) is a longtime mom-and-pop shop that specializes in high-end jewelry made from silver from Taxco, Mexico's silver mining capital. Most of the items are made by local artisans, which means you'll find unique and beautiful pieces of jewelry. Unlike other shops, there's no pressure to buy, though prices are nonnegotiable. If you don't find what you're looking for here, head to its second location one block east on Avenida Juárez between Avenidas 10 and 15 (same phone and hours).

Cucuru (Av. 10 near Av. Rosado Salas, no tel., 1pm-9pm Tues.-Sun.) is a lovely little shop selling gorgeous and wearable Mexican *artesanía*—shawls, dresses, purses—much of it from Chiapas and Oaxaca. There's also handmade jewelry for sale, made by local artisans. The staff is friendly and helpful and the items well priced. The name of the shop is a nod to a traditional Mexican lullaby.

If you're in the market for a pair of traditional leather sandals, check out **Huaracheria Margarita** (Av. 30 at Calle 3, no phone, 10am-8pm Mon.-Sat., 10am-2pm Sun.). Among the colorful jellies and flip-flops, you'll find rows and rows of handmade huaraches, many brought from the mainland. The leather inventory is well priced, especially considering the craftsmanship that goes into making each sandal.

Calipso Sportsfish Center (Calle 9 Bis. s/n, tel. 987/872-4105, 9am-2pm and 4pm-7pm Mon.-Fri., 10am-5pm Sat.) is a small shop specializing in fishing gear—everything from bait and tackle to clothing and flags to high-end fishing poles. There are no rentals, unfortunately.

Balam Mayan Feather (Av. 5 at Calle 2, tel. 987/869-0548, 10am-10pm daily) trades in a unique and dying art, selling oil paintings created on the feathers of regional birds. Most

ISLA COZUMEL
SHOPPING

Plaza del Sol has souvenirs and keepsakes of all kinds.

feathers depict scenes of traditional villages or ancient Maya people, but there is a decent variety beyond that, including tropical flowers and sealife. If you're lucky, an artist will be working on a new feather painting while you're browsing—feel free to watch. Prices range US$30-150.

SHOPPING CENTERS

Located in a yellow building on the east side of the main plaza, **Plaza del Sol** (Av. 5 Norte between Av. Benito Juárez and Calle 1, 9am-8pm Mon.-Sat., 11am-5pm Sun.) houses a labyrinth of small souvenir shops selling everything from T-shirts to silver jewelry. You'll have to poke around a bit to find items worth buying, but a little perseverance will go a long way, especially if you're on a tight budget.

Punta Langosta (Av. Rafael Melgar between Calles 7 and 11, 9am-8pm daily) is downtown Cozumel's biggest shopping center. The modern open-air building is home to air-conditioned jewelry stores, knickknack shops, and fancy ice cream stands. It's a decent place to window-shop, especially if you want to buy a memento but aren't sure exactly what you'd like.

Located across from the Puerto Maya and TMM International piers, **Royal Village Shopping Center** (Carr. Sur Km 4.5, tel. 987/857-0457, 9am-6pm Mon.-Sat.) is squarely aimed at cruise ship travelers. Shops are higher end and international—think Swarovski, Zingara, Harley-Davidson. There's also a Hard Rock Café.

Every weekend, a *mercado artesanal* (crafts market, Av. 10 between Av. Benito Juárez and Calle 1, 5pm-9pm Fri.-Sun.) is held behind Plaza del Sol. Handcrafted items, all locally made, are sold: jewelry, candles, clothing, soaps and lotions, decorative knickknacks. Live music plays and food stands pop up, making it a festive place to shop or just take in the scene.

Sports and Recreation

SCUBA DIVING

Cozumel is one the world's best (and best known) places to scuba dive and snorkel, so it's no surprise that the island is home to dozens of dive shops—more than 100 at last count. Virtually all offer diving, snorkeling, and all levels of certification courses; there are a handful of dive "resorts," too, which offer packages that include lodging, diving, gear, and sometimes food.

Rates can vary considerably from shop to shop, and season to season, so be sure to clarify all the details up front. For most of the year, a two-tank fun dive costs US$80-95, plus US$18-30 per day if you need gear. Low-season rates can be significantly lower, and often include gear rental. PADI open-water certification courses (3-4 days) generally cost US$420-500, including all equipment and materials. Most shops also offer advanced courses, Nitrox and night diving, and multi-dive packages. All divers also must pay US$2 per day for marine park admission and to support Cozumel's hyperbaric chambers and marine ambulance; ask if the fees are included in a shop's rates or charged separately.

Dive Sites

Cozumel's coral reef—and the world-class diving and snorkeling it provides—is the main reason people come to the island. The reef was designated a national marine reserve more than two decades ago, and the waters have thrived under the park's rigorous protection and cleanup programs. Dozens of dive and snorkeling sites encircle the island, and the 1,000-meter-deep (3,281-foot) channel between Cozumel and the mainland provides spectacular drift and wall dives. Here is a list of some of the most popular dives, though by no means all the worthwhile ones.

feet). Snorkeling is decent near the shore, but be very careful of boat traffic.

DZUL-HÁ (AKA THE MONEY BAR)

Located off the old coastal road (Km 6.5), Dzul-Há is a good spot for DIY snorkeling, with small coral heads and sea fans that support blue tangs, parrot fish, and queen angels. Steps lead into the ocean, where depths range 3-10 meters (10-33 feet), with boundary ropes for added safety. You can rent snorkel gear onsite for US$15. Plan to have lunch here; the restaurant has huge portions and a full bar fronting a small beach.

TORMENTOS

At this site divers can see about 60 coral heads, each decorated with an assortment of sea fans, brain and whip corals, and sponges. The site is known for its many crevices and overhangs; keep your eyes peeled for hidden-away invertebrates like flamingo tongue shells, arrow crabs, black crinoids, and, of course, lobster (especially at the north end of the site). Definitely bring your camera to this one. Depth ranges 5-15 meters (16-49 feet).

YUCAB

A perfect drift dive, Yucab has archways, overhangs, and large coral heads—some as tall as three meters (10 feet)—that are alive with an incredible array of creatures: Lobsters, octopus, scorpionfish, banded coral shrimp, and butterfly fish can almost always be found; photographers have a field day here. Try maneuvering behind some of the large formations—they block the current, giving you a chance to really enjoy the scenery. Depth ranges 5-15 meters (16-49 feet).

PUNTA TUNICH

Punta Tunich usually has a strong 1.5-knot current, which makes it a challenging but rewarding drift dive. The site itself has a white-sand bottom with a gentle downward slope that ends in a drop-off. Along the way, the reef is dotted with finger coral and elephant ear sponges. Divers regularly encounter eagle

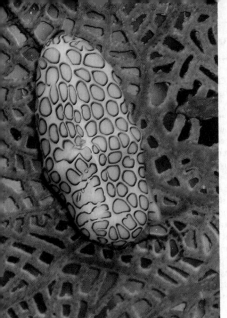
Flamingo tongues are a type of sea snail, with brightly colored skin (or mantle) covering its shell.

AIRPLANE WRECK

A 40-passenger Convair airliner lies on Cozumel's seabed, about 65 meters (213 feet) from the shore near El Cid hotel. Sunk in 1977 for the Mexican movie production of *Survive II*, the plane has been broken into pieces and strewn about the site by years of storms. The site itself is relatively flat, though with parrot fish, damselfish, and a host of sea fans and small coral heads, there's plenty to see. With depth ranges of 3-15 meters (10-49 feet), this is a good site for snorkelers.

PARAÍSO

Just south of the international pier, and about 200 meters (656 feet) from shore, lies Paraíso, an impressive three-lane coral ridge. Medium-size coral—mostly brain and star—attract sergeants major, angelfish, grunts, squirrel fish, and snappers; ask your guide about the endemic splendid toadfish. This also is a good site for night dives because of its proximity to hotels, which means less time on the boat in the dark. Depth ranges 5-13 meters (16-43

How to Choose a Dive Shop

There are more than 100 dive shops on Isla Cozumel, and scores more at Isla Mujeres, Playa del Carmen, Cancún, Tulum, and elsewhere. Choosing just one—and then placing all your underwater faith into its hands—can be daunting.

Safety should be your number one concern in choosing a shop. Fortunately, the standards in Cozumel and the Riviera Maya are almost universally first-rate, and accidents are rare. Still, don't dive with a shop that doesn't ask to see your certification card or logbook. Also ask how long the shop has been in business, how much experience the dive guides have, how long the captain and crew have been with the shop, and how many divers per guide will be on the tour. "Cattle boats" are a sign of shops trying to maximize profits; even if they're not unsafe, they often make for a less enjoyable experience due to the sheer number of people around you in the water.

Equipment is another crucial issue. You should ask to inspect the shop's equipment, and the dive shop should be quick to comply. Although few casual divers are trained to evaluate gear, a good dive shop will appreciate your concern and be happy to put you at ease.

The most important equipment is not what's on the rack but what you actually use. On the day of your dive, get to the shop early so you can **double-check your gear.** Old equipment is not necessarily bad, but you should ask for a different BCD, wetsuit, or regulator if the condition of the one assigned to you makes you uneasy. Learn how to check the O-ring (the small rubber ring that forms the seal between the tank and the regulator), and do so before every dive. You also should attach your regulator and open the valve, to listen for any hissing between the regulator and the tank, or in the primary and backup mouthpieces. If you hear any, ask the dive master to check it and, if need be, change the regulator. Arriving early lets you do all this before getting on the boat—ideally before leaving the shop—so you can swap gear if necessary.

There are some specific questions you should ask about a shop's practices. Has their air been tested and certified? Do they carry radios and oxygen? Does the captain always stay with the boat? Above all, be vocal and proactive about your safety, and remember, *there are no stupid questions.*

Finally, logistics can be a determining factor between two equally good dive shops. Items like: How is bottom time determined? How advanced are the other divers on your trip? (Some dive shops let you dive your own tank—as long as your computer safely allows—while others make

rays, barracuda, sea horses, bar jacks, and parrot fish. The depth ranges 5-18 meters (16-59 feet). Punta Tunich tends to be less crowded than other areas.

★ SANTA ROSA WALL

Santa Rosa Wall is a spectacular and iconic Cozumel dive—a must-see for intermediate and expert divers. With a sensational drop-off that begins at 22 meters (72 feet), Santa Rosa is famous for its tunnels, caves, and stony overhangs. Ask to start your dive on the northern end, where there are a series of swimthroughs that lead to the shallows. You're sure to see loads of sealife along the way: translucent

sponges, mammoth sea fans, file clams, horse-eyed jacks, fairy basslets, gray angelfish, black groupers. The site has strong currents and depths ranging 5-27 meters (16-89 feet).

PASO DEL CEDRAL

A strip reef lined with small corals such as disk and cactus, this site attracts large schools of fish that include blue-striped grunts and snapper, and also is a good spot to see nurse and reef sharks, southern stingrays, and turtles. The current is strong but the visibility is good. Experienced divers should check out the adjacent wall. Depths range 10-20 meters (33-66 feet).

Dive sites, here we come!

everyone surface as soon as the first diver's tank hits 700 psi.) Also does the shop provide pickup/drop-off at your hotel? Is it a one- or two-tank excursion? And, if you're short of time or get seasick easily, how far are the dive sites from the dock?

Feeling free to ask questions or raise concerns (of any sort at any time) is a crucial factor in safe diving. That's where a dive shop's **personality** comes in. Every dive shop has its own culture or style, and different divers will feel more comfortable in different shops. Spend some time talking to people at a couple of different dive shops before signing up. Try to meet the person who will be leading your particular dive—you may have to come in the afternoon when that day's trip returns. Chances are one of the shops or dive masters will click with you.

★ PALANCAR

This breathtaking five-kilometer-long (3.1-mile) dive spot is actually made up of five different sites—Shallows, Garden, Horseshoe, Caves, and Bricks. It's known for its series of enormous coral buttresses. Some drop off dramatically into winding ravines, deep canyons, and passageways; others have become archways and tunnels with formations 15 meters (49 feet) tall. The most popular site here is Palancar Horseshoe, which is made up of a horseshoe-shaped series of coral heads at the top of a drop-off. All sites are teeming with reef life but can also get packed with divers and snorkelers—book an early-morning trip to avoid the crowds. Depths range 5-40 meters (16-131 feet).

COLOMBIA

Colombia is another dive that is really two sites in one. Head to Colombia Shallows for gorgeous coral, abundant marinelife, and longer bottom time, or test your maneuvering skills at Colombia Deep, full of tall pillars separated by passageways, channels, and swimthroughs. Larger creatures—sea turtles, groupers, nurse sharks, and southern stingrays—are commonly seen here. The site is recommended for experienced divers. Depths range 5-40 meters (16-131 feet).

MARACAIBO

At the island's southern tip, Maracaibo is a deep buttress reef interspersed with tunnels, caves, and vertical walls. It's known for its immense coral formations as well as for the possibility of spotting large animals—sharks (blacktip and nurse) as well as turtles and eagle rays. Maracaibo is a deep-drift dive with strong currents, occasional up- and downdrafts, and rough surface conditions; it is recommended for advanced divers only. Descend slowly to maintain control. Depths range 30-40 meters (98-131 feet).

Dive Shops

Cozumel's diver safety record is good, and there are many competent outfits in addition to those listed here. Consider this list a starting point, to be augmented by the recommendations of trusted fellow divers, travelers, locals, and expats. Most important, go with a shop you feel comfortable with, not just the cheapest, the cheeriest, or the most convenient. Dive shops are generally open 8am-8pm daily, closing during those business hours only if no one's around to run the shop during a dive trip.

- **Blue Angel Dive Shop** (Carr. Costera Sur Km 2.2, tel. 987/872-0188, www.blueangel-resort.com)
- **Careyitos Advanced Divers** (Marina Caleta, cell tel. 987/117-6187, www.careyitosadvanceddivers.com)
- **Caribbean Divers** (Calle 3 between Avs. Rafael Melgar and 5, tel. 987/872-1145, cdivers@prodigy.net.mx)
- **Deep Blue** (Calle Rosado Salas at Av. 10 Sur, tel. 987/872-5653, www.deepbluecozumel.com)
- **Deep Exposure Dive Center** (Av. 10 Sur between Calles 3 Sur and Rosado Salas, tel. 987/872-3621, toll-free U.S. tel. 866/670-2736, www.deepexposuredivecenter.com)
- **Eco Divers** (Av. 10 at Calle 1 Sur, tel. 987/872-5628, www.ecodiverscozumel.com)
- **Scuba Gamma** (Calle 5 near Av. 5 Sur, tel. 987/878-4257, www.scubagamma.net)
- **Scuba Life Cozumel** (Marina Fonatur, tel. 987/118-8226, www.scubalifecozumel.com)
- **Scuba Tony** (no storefront, tel. 987/876-1171, U.S. tel. 405/698-2318, www.scubatony.com)
- **Studio Blue Cozumel** (Calle Rosado Salas

Keep your eye out for spotted morays at Palancar and elsewhere.

Dive Insurance

Although diving and snorkeling accidents are relatively rare on Cozumel, especially among beginning divers, you might consider purchasing secondary accident and/or trip insurance through the **Divers Alert Network** (DAN, toll-free U.S. tel. 800/446-2671, 24-hour emergency Mex. tel. 919/684-9111, accepts collect calls, www.diversalertnetwork.org), a highly regarded international nonprofit medical organization dedicated to the health and safety of snorkelers and recreational divers. Dive accident plans cost just US$30-75 per year, including medical and decompression coverage and limited trip and lost equipment coverage. More complete travel insurance—not a bad idea in hurricane country—and life and disability coverage are also available. To be eligible for insurance, you must be a member of DAN (US$35 per year).

between Avs. 5 and 10 Sur, tel. 987/872-4330, www.studioblue.com.mx)

SNORKELING

Snorkelers have plenty of options in Cozumel, from cheap-and-easy snorkeling tours to renting gear and exploring on your own, right from shore.

Most dive shops offer snorkeling as well as diving trips, usually visiting 2-3 sites for a half hour each (US$55-65 pp). Snorkelers often go out with a group of divers and either snorkel in the same general location or go to a nearby site while the divers are underwater. This can mean some extra downtime as divers get in and out of the water, but the advantage is that you typically go to better and less crowded sites.

For a quick and easy snorkeling tour, stop by one of the booths that flank the ferry pier. These trips are somewhat less expensive (though with larger groups) and can be booked right as you disembark from the ferry. Most offer two tours daily at around 11am and 2pm; some use a glass-bottom boat for extra pizzazz. The standard trip (US$50, including

equipment) lasts 2-3 hours, visiting two or three sites, spending 30-45 minutes snorkeling at each one.

There are several terrific snorkeling spots near town and just offshore where you don't need a boat or a guide at all. Cozumel's boat drivers are careful about steering clear of snorkelers, but even so, do not swim too far from shore, look up and around frequently, and stay out of obvious boat lanes. If you plan to do a lot of snorkeling, especially outside of established snorkeling areas, consider bringing or buying an inflatable personal buoy. Designed for snorkelers, they are brightly colored and have a string you attach to your ankle or to a small anchor weight, alerting boat drivers of your presence. Also be aware of the current, which typically runs south to north and can be quite strong.

KITEBOARDING

Kiteboarding has quickly and thoroughly morphed from a novelty act to one of the most popular beach sports worldwide. Cozumel is no exception, with a dedicated cadre of kiteboarders and a growing number of options for travelers who want to learn or practice the sport.

De Lille Sports (Playa Casitas, Av. Rafael Melgar s/n, tel. 987/103-6711, www.delillesports.com) is operated by Cozumel native Raul de Lille, a former Olympic-level windsurfer and now one of Mexico's top kiters and instructors. Raul doesn't come cheap, but he's an outstanding instructor, not least for his calm demeanor and excellent English. Private lessons are US$125 per hour or US$500 per day. An intensive three-day introductory kiteboarding course includes 15 hours of instruction and costs US$900 per student (maximum 2 students per instructor); it also can be broken into modules depending on your time and previous experience. Kiteboarding rentals are US$150 per day for a full kit. For experienced kiters, de Lille offers clinics on kite control, tricks, and other specialties, plus adventuresome tours like downwinding the entire island.

Look for the De Lille stand under the Shaka Snack Bar.

Another locally run option is **Cozumel Kiteboarding** (no storefront, tel. 987/876-1558, www.cozumelkiteboarding.com). The shop offers kiting excursions around the island (4 hours, US$250-350 for 1-2 people), including to the little-visited northern lagoons: Río de Plata, Monte Cristo, and Blind Bary. Kiteboarding instruction for beginners and more experienced students also is offered.

STAND-UP PADDLING

Stand-up paddling (or SUPing) is the sport du jour in Cozumel and around the world, and for good reason: It's fun and easy to learn yet challenging to master; it's also a unique way to experience Cozumel's rich coastline and extraordinarily clear waters. The glassy waters on Cozumel's western shore are perfect for the sport, which involves standing upright on an oversized surfboard-like board and using a long paddle to cruise around. Fitness buffs appreciate the full-core workout SUPing provides, while the elevated perspective allows you to see surprisingly well into the surrounding water—significantly better than in a kayak, in fact. It's not uncommon to see fish, rays, even sea turtles and dolphins swimming below and around you. Numerous resorts have SUP boards available for guests, and a handful of agencies offer instruction, rentals, and tours.

De Lille Sports (Playa Casitas, Av. Rafael Melgar s/n, tel. 987/103-6711, www.delillesports.com) is operated by windsurfing and kiteboarding legend (and Cozumel native) Raul de Lille, but he's big on SUPing too, even designing his own line of boards. The sports complement each other well: If there's not enough wind for kiting, it's probably perfect for SUPing, and vice versa. The agency offers private and group lessons, plus tours in remote areas of the island. SUP instruction runs US$60 per student (2-3 hours, maximum 8 students), while high-quality SUP rentals are US$25 per hour or US$85 per day.

Based out of Mr. Sancho's beach club, **Ha-Haak Paddleboarding Cozumel** (Carr. Costera Sur Km 15, cell tel. 987/800-3022, www.supcozumel.com, 8am-4pm daily) offers friendly one-on-one instruction (US$35/hour) as well as paddleboard rentals (US$35/hour or US$60/day). It also has a variety of tours that depart from different parts of the island, depending on the weather (US$60, 1.5 hours). All guides are bilingual.

Isla Cozumel is one of the best places for kiteboarding.

SURFING

Owned and operated by professional surfer Nacho Gutierrez, **Cozumel Surfing** (no storefront, tel. 987/111-9290, www.cozumel-surfing.com, price varies) provides beginner surf lessons to adults and children of all ages. Instruction is given on the east side of the island in either a private or group setting. Classes typically begin with a 30-60-minute lesson on land to learn and practice the basics of surfing. Then it's straight to the water for two separate 75-minute sessions alongside Nacho and his team. Snacks and drinks are provided, and rentals are available.

KAYAKING

Cozumel's calm, clear waters make it a nice place to kayak. Most **all-inclusive resorts** and some **beach clubs** have a handful of kayaks available for guests to use (free to US$12/hour). If you plan to swim or snorkel along the way—a great way to enjoy little-visited spots on the reef—be sure the kayak has a small anchor to prevent it from floating away.

SPORTFISHING AND SPEARFISHING

Cozumel boasts good deep-sea fishing year-round. It's one of few places anglers can go for the grand slam of billfishing: hooking into a blue marlin, a white marlin, a sailfish, and a swordfish all in a single day. It also has plentiful tuna, barracuda, dorado, wahoo, grouper, and shark. For an extra challenge, jump out of the boat and give spearfishing a try.

Albatros Charters (tel. 987/872-7904, toll-free U.S. tel. 888/333-4643, www.albatros-charters.com, US$500 for 4 hours, US$600 for 6 hours, US$700 for 8 hours) has a variety of boats, each able to carry at least six anglers. Trips include hotel pickup and drop-off, beer and soda, snacks, bait, and gear. Other recommended outfits include **Aquarius Fishing** (tel. 987/869-1096, toll-free U.S. tel. 800/371-2924, www.cozumelflatsfishing.com) and **Tres Hermanos Fishing Charters** (tel. 987/107-2030, www.cozumelfishing.com).

Spearfishing Today (Puerto de Abrigo, Carr. Costera Norte Km 1.5, tel. 987/876-0862, www.spearfishingtoday.com, US$250-850 for 2-6 people) gets rave reviews for its excellent service and wide variety of spearfishing excursions, from mellow first-timer and family tours to private "deep blue" outings for intermediate and advanced hunters. Half-day trips include gear, instruction, refreshments, and complimentary fish cleaning at the end of the tour. Although Cozumel is known for its currents, most trips head to the calmer protected waters at the island's north end (and outside the marine park, of course).

ECOPARKS AND WATER PARKS

TOP EXPERIENCE

★ Parque Punta Sur

Parque Punta Sur (Carr. Costera Sur Km 27, tel. 987/872-0914, www.cozumelparks.com, 9am-4pm Mon.-Sat., US$14 adult, US$8 child under 12) is a massive natural reserve on the southern tip of Cozumel. The park spans thousands of acres of coastal dunes, beaches, mangroves, and wetlands, and extends well out into the ocean, including large areas of coral reef. Its home to a vast array of land and sea creatures, including 30 types of seabirds and some huge crocodiles that live in the park's large inland lagoons. There's a small Maya ruin known as El Caracol, which dates to AD 1200 and is believed to have been used for navigation, plus the park's famous lighthouse (which you can climb for great views) and a small but rewarding maritime museum. At the park's long, lovely beach—about a kilometer past the lighthouse—there are beach chairs, restrooms, a small eatery, and a shop to rent snorkel gear and kayaks. The snorkeling here is outstanding, including sea fan "forests" that wave gently in the current.

Most visitors visit on package tours, but it's perfectly easy to visit independently; there's even a separate area away from the volleyball nets and buffet lines for people arriving on their own. You'll need a car or to hire a cab (US$15 from downtown) and be sure to arrive no later than 1pm in order to take full advantage of all the park has to offer.

Chankanaab

Some nine kilometers (5.6 miles) south of town, **Chankanaab** (Carr. Costera Sur Km 9, tel. 987/872-0914, www.cozumelparks.com, 8am-4pm daily, US$21 adult, US$14 child under 12) is a national park that operates mainly as a beach club and water park; that is to say, more Xcaret than Punta Sur. A visit here includes sunbathing by the pool, snorkeling in the ocean, relaxing in a hammock, and watching the sea lion shows (included in the ticket price); there is also a zip line course, a crocodile sanctuary, replicas of various Maya ruins, and a small tequila "museum" (i.e., a bar with a hacienda feel, old photos, and a small agave patch). **Dolphin Discovery** (toll-free Mex. tel. 800/727-5391, toll-free U.S. tel. 866/393-5158, www.dolphindiscovery.com) has a facility within the park, with various interactive programs with dolphins, manatees, and sea lions, for an additional fee. Reserve in advance or right upon arrival, as they fill up fast. Chankanaab also has a fully equipped dive shop on-site, plus two thatch-roofed restaurants, a handful of gift shops, lockers, and restrooms. Chankanaab may be a bit commercialized for independent travelers—consider Punta Sur instead—but it's a great option for families looking for an easy all-day option.

GOLF

Jack Nicklaus designed the par-72 championship course at **Cozumel Country Club** (Carr. Costera Norte Km 6.5, tel. 987/872-9570, www.cozumelcountryclub.com.mx, 6:30am-6pm daily), located at the far end of the northern hotel zone. Greens fees are US$99 before 8am (and all day Sunday), US$125 until 1:30pm, and US$89 afterwards. Carts are required and included in the rate. In addition to the slightly rolling, moderately challenging course, the club has a driving range, putting and chipping areas, overnight bag storage, a retail shop, and lessons from PGA golf pros. Book online for a discount.

SPAS

Spa del Sol (Calle 5 between Avs. 5 and Rafael Melgar, tel. 987/872-6474, www.spadelsolcozumel.com, 9am-7pm Mon.-Sat., 10am-2pm Sun.) provides a variety of traditional and holistic treatments in its quaint downtown location. Almost a dozen types of massages are offered, including Swedish,

The road into Parque Punta Sur, a large natural reserve with excellent beaches and snorkeling.

Parque Punta Sur

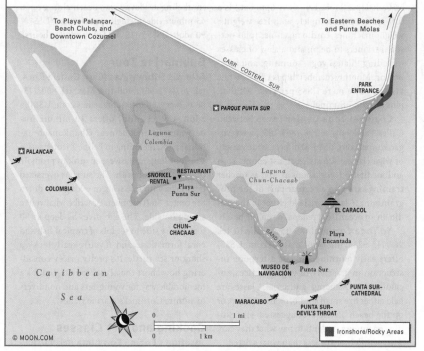

To Playa Palancar, Beach Clubs, and Downtown Cozumel

To Eastern Beaches and Punta Molas

CARR COSTERA SUR

PARK ENTRANCE

★ PARQUE PUNTA SUR

Laguna Colombia

★ PALANCAR

Laguna Chun-Chacaab

SNORKEL RENTAL RESTAURANT
Playa Punta Sur

COLOMBIA

EL CARACOL

CHUN-CHACAAB

SAND RD

Playa Encantada

MUSEO DE NAVIGACIÓN ★ Punta Sur

Caribbean

Sea

PUNTA SUR-CATHEDRAL

MARACAIBO

PUNTA SUR-DEVIL'S THROAT

0   1 mi
0   1 km

© MOON.COM

Ironshore/Rocky Areas

Thai, and Aquasana (a treatment performed in open water). Acupuncture, Reiki, and ear candling, among other alternative treatments, also are performed regularly. One-hour treatments run US$60-80. Walk-ins are very welcome, and shorter and longer sessions are available, too.

Barefoot in Cozumel (Calle 3 between Avs. 25 and 30, tel. 987/878-4662, www.barefootincozumel.com, 9am-7pm daily by appointment only, US$60/85 per 60/90 minutes) is the one-woman business of U.S. certified massage therapist Sally Hurwitch. She offers a popular Ashiatsu massage, which is administered using her feet to help clients who suffer from chronic back pain. Swedish massages as well as energy treatments, like Reiki, are also offered.

Temazcal Cozumel (Xcan-Ha Reserve,

tel. 987/876-3565, experiencia.cozumel@gmail.com, US$80) provides a traditional Maya steam lodge experience. It's a favorite practice of health- and spiritual-minded folks of all stripes, and especially popular in the region. Temazcal Cozumel has an especially lovely spot to experience this unique treatment, a leafy retreat well inland from Cozumel's busy western shore. A session here begins by addressing the cardinal directions before entering the low, circular brick hut, where a guide leads guests through additional exercises and visualizations, related to ancient Maya beliefs as well as one's own experiences, all intended to further the cleansing and mind-opening process. Afterward, you can take a dip in a nearby freshwater cenote and relax in hammocks with a fresh-made juice.

FITNESS

EGO (Calle 11 at Av. 5, tel. 987/872-4897, 5:30am-11pm Mon.-Fri., 6am-6pm Sat.) is a full-service gym complete with free weights, weight machines, cardio machines (plus personal trainers to help), and a slew of classes including Pilates, yoga, spinning, and kickboxing. Monthly membership is US$35, while visitors pay a mere US$5 per visit. All that, plus air-conditioning!

Cozumel Yoga Center (Av. 5 between Calles 9 and 9 Bis, tel. 987/869-1055, www.yogacozumel.com, US$5-8) offers a wide variety of yoga classes—26 styles at last count. Yoga and meditation workshops as well as teacher trainings are also a regular part of the programming. Classes are held either in the studio, in an oceanfront *palapa,* or on the beach.

Yo Yoga Cozumel (Av. 15 at Calle 10, tel. 987/113-5283, info@yoCozumel.com, US$5) offers early morning and late afternoon instruction in a variety of yoga practices, including flow, Ashtanga, and aerial. Classes are held either in a small studio, on the rooftop, or on the beach. Prices are suggested—the studio encourages students to pay what they can, whether it's more or less than what's listed.

TOURS AND CLASSES
Horseback Riding

Located on the inland side of the highway across from Nachi-Cocom beach club, **Rancho Palmitas** (Carr. Costera Sur Km 16, cell tel. 987/118-3032, palmitas_ernesto@hotmail.com, 8am-4pm daily) offers two horseback tours. A 2.5-3-hour tour (US$40 pp) includes stops at a cavern with a cenote, the archaeological site of El Cedral, and a few unexcavated Maya ruins. A shorter 1.5-hour tour (US$35 pp) leads to the cavern only. Call to set up a tour or just drop in—the last excursion leaves at 3pm.

ATV Excursions

Though catering to cruise ship passengers, **Wild Tours** (Av. 95 at Calle 11, tel. 987/872-5876, toll-free U.S./Can. tel. 888/497-4283, www.wild-tours.com) offers ATV excursions to everyone. Tours include off-roading through the jungle, visiting a cenote and inland cave, exploring isolated Maya ruins, relaxing and snorkeling at Playa Uva's beach club, even a 45-minute ride in a high-speed jet boat (US$70-90 adult, US$95-115 child with adult, 4 hours).

Submarine Tour

Atlantis Submarines (Carr. Costera Km 4, tel. 987/872-5671, toll-free Mex. tel. 800/715-0804, www.atlantissubmarines.com, US$105 adult, US$65 child) offers 40-minute underwater excursions near Chankanaab national park, including to Felipe Xicotencatl, a 154-foot-long minesweeper sunk to promote the coral reef's health. The sub has oversized portholes with low seats in a long row down the center. Staff members describe what you're seeing outside. The sub dives as deep as 80 feet; you're sure to see lots of tropical fish and coral formations, and, if you're really lucky, a shark or sea turtle. It's pretty pricey considering how short the actual tour is, but it's a memorable way for youngsters and nondivers to admire Cozumel's marine riches.

Cooking and Art Classes

Josefina's Cocina Con Alma (tel. 987/105-5300, www.cozumelchef.com, US$80 adult, US$70 teen 13-17, US$30 child 6-12, by appointment only) is a small cooking school offering private bilingual instruction in Yucatecan and classic Mexican dishes. Classes begin with a field trip to the market to select fresh ingredients, and then it's straight to the kitchen to learn to create a preselected meal. Dishes offered range from *cochinita pibil* (pork marinated in orange juice, achiote, and other spices and baked in banana leaves) and *sopa de lima* (a citrus-based soup with shredded turkey and fried tortilla strips) to *chiles en nogada* (poblano peppers stuffed with meat or cheese and topped with a walnut-based cream sauce and pomegranate seeds) and tamales (seasoned meat, cheese, or vegetables stuffed in a cornmeal dough and wrapped in corn husks). Afterward, students enjoy their creations at a sit-down meal. Chef Josefina gets rave reviews for her expertise and warm manner.

Food

Cozumel's food scene is steadily improving, with an ever-increasing variety and quality of restaurants. Like most islands, it has terrific seafood, always served fresh, from gourmet restaurants to simple eateries. (You may be surprised to learn, though, that much of the catch actually comes from around Isla Mujeres because the waters around Cozumel are protected.) The island's popularity with Americans, especially hungry divers, means you'll never want for steak, pizza, or big breakfasts either.

MEXICAN AND YUCATECAN

★ **Otates Tacos** (Av. 15 between Calles Rosado Salas and 3, tel. 987/120-1076, noon-4am Sun.-Thurs., noon-5am Fri.-Sat., US$2-6) is a bustling taco joint serving authentic Mexican grub at nearly street-cart prices. Tacos are just the beginning, served piping hot on tiny corn tortillas; the quesadillas, *tortas* (Mexican-style sandwiches), and *pozole* (pork and hominy soup) are all terrific, and the guacamole is rave-worthy. Service is

fast and friendly, with menus in Spanish and English.

Kinta (Av. 5 between Calles 2 and 4 Norte, tel. 987/869-0544, www.kintarestaurante. com, 5pm-11pm daily, US$8-17) is a chic bistro serving gourmet Mexican dishes and knockout cocktails. Seating is indoors in a modern, welcoming space or outdoors in a leafy tropical garden. The menu is seasonal but often includes specialties like *chile relleno*, a poblano chile stuffed with ratatouille and Chihuahua cheese, and *peskado,* catch of the day baked in a pumpkin-sesame seed crust and smothered in a spicy *mole verde* sauce. Be sure to try the margarindo—an unforgettable tamarind-based margarita. Reservations are recommended.

Kondesa (Av. 5 between Calles 5 and 7, tel. 987/869-1086, www.kondesacozumel. com, 5pm-11pm daily, US$8-18) may well be Cozumel's classiest restaurant, with its sister restaurant, Kinta, its closest competition. Seating is in a lush garden with tables under a high *palapa,* on a central wooden platform, or right under the stars. The menu has some

a plate of huevos rancheros, a classic Mexican breakfast—perfect before a morning dive

classic Mexican and Mediterranean dishes, but is mostly contemporary fusion. The guacamole trio and lionfish cakes are popular appetizers and go well with the restaurant's creative cocktails, including mojitos and sangria. The catch of the day is always flavorful and inventive, while homemade churros and coffee make a perfect dessert.

Crazy King Burrito (Av. 5 at Calle 4, tel. 987/102-6638, 11am-7pm Mon.-Sat., US$2.50-9.50) is a tiny family-run eatery serving up massive burritos, stuffed with classics like chicken, meat, and beans. If you're looking for something different, try one of the shrimp combos or brave the California, which features chicken strips, french fries, beans, cheese, and lettuce, all smothered in ranch dressing. Take your meal to go or grab a seat at one of the street-front tables.

The breezy *palapa*-roofed **La Candela** (Av. 5 at Calle 6 Norte, tel. 987/878-4471, 8am-11pm Mon.-Sat., US$4-9) offers an extensive lineup of Mexican and traditional Yucatecan dishes in a cafeteria-style setting. Check out what's steaming behind the glass window cases, find a seat, and then place your order with your waitperson. Lunch specials typically include soup or pasta, a main dish, and a drink (US$5-6).

Opened in 1962, **La Cozumeleña** (Av. 10 Sur at Calle 3, tel. 987/872-0189, 7am-3pm daily, US$3-7) is a longtime favorite with local families and professionals, serving classic dishes in a quiet air-conditioned dining area. For breakfast, try *chilaquiles* (fried tortilla strips, scrambled eggs, and chicken doused in green or red salsa) or eggs with *chaya*. Lunch specials include a main dish, like fish tacos or baked chicken, and a drink. There's a bakery next door for dessert-on-the-go afterward.

SEAFOOD

Mariscos Camilo's (Av. 5 between Calles 2 and 4, tel. 987/872-6161, 11am-9pm Mon.-Sat., 11am-8pm Sun., US$8-16) is a small place offering an abundance of fresh seafood: ceviche, shrimp cocktail, lobster tail, fried fish, grilled

fish, soups, tacos, salads, and even seafood sandwiches—you name it, they've probably got it. Popular with locals and expats.

Lobster Shack (Calle 3 near Av. Rafael Melgar, tel. 987/869-0812, 11am-10pm Mon.-Sat., US$7-18) is exactly what it sounds like: a hole-in-the-wall serving lobster goodness. Think po'boys, burritos, and bowls all featuring lobster purchased directly from the fishermen. Steak and shrimp are also offered, just in case. Can't decide? Try the Cozumel Box (US$15), which features three half po'boys of lobster, steak, and shrimp with a side of chips and coleslaw and a drink.

Spacious **La Conchita del Caribe** (Av. 65 between Calles 13 and 15, tel. 987/872-5888, 11am-8pm daily, US$6-13) is another locals' favorite and a great off-the-beaten-path option. Whole fish served grilled or fried is the house specialty—choose your own out of a cooler by the counter and pay according to size. Beyond fresh fish, the menu is rife with shrimp, octopus, squid, and conch, almost all swimming earlier in the day. Takeout is also available.

OTHER SPECIALTIES

Sal de Mar (Calle 3 between Avs. 5 and 10, tel. 987/872-2708, www.saldemarczm.com, 1pm-11pm Mon.-Sat., 4pm-10pm Sun, US$11-17) serves creative Mediterranean fusion dishes with Asian, Mexican, and American twists. Think lobster mac n' cheese or thin-crust pizza with chorizo, miso, and chipotle toppings. The setting is "welcoming hipster," with a mid-century modern design and trees growing through the middle of the restaurant. Service is excellent.

La Cocay (Calle 8 between Avs. 10 and 15, tel. 987/872-5533, www.lacocay.com, 5:30pm-11pm daily, US$15-22) offers Mediterranean cuisine with flair. The menu changes seasonally, but expect to see dishes like fish of the day with Cajun spice and mango sauce and blue-cheese-filled phyllo dough rolls with black cherry sauce. Seating is in a candlelit dining room or on the breezy garden patio—perfect for a special night out.

★ **Le Chef** (5 Av. near Calle 5, tel. 987/878-4391, noon-11pm Mon.-Sat., US$7-15) is a cozy bistro serving gourmet baguettes, pasta dishes, and salads. The most popular item is the lobster bacon sandwich, a hefty and flavorful dish packed with fresh lobster meat; order a salad and it's plenty for two. Seating is in a whimsical dining room or in a breezy back patio.

Founded in 1978, **Guido's** (Av. Rafael Melgar between Calles 6 and 8, tel. 987/872-0946, www.guidoscozumel.com, 11am-11pm Mon.-Sat., 3pm-9:30pm Sun., US$13-25) is a bit pricey but worth every peso, serving unique Italian dishes like brick-oven-baked lasagna, homemade pastas, memorable seafood dishes (like prosciutto-wrapped sea scallops served with risotto and citrus beurre blanc sauce), and excellent desserts. The leafy courtyard setting makes a meal here all the more worthwhile.

New Especias (Calle 3 between Avs. 5 and 10, tel. 987/869-7947, 6pm-11pm Thurs.-Tues., US$15-28) is a longtime go-to restaurant that serves up excellent Italian dishes along with friendly service. Favorites include smoked salmon with asparagus fettucine and filet mignon with peppercorn sauce. A plate of complimentary bruschetta comes with every meal. Seating is either in a dimly lit dining room or on a breezy balcony with street views.

LIGHT FARE

Tiny, bright, and welcoming, ★ **Cali Café** (Av. Rosado Salas between Avs. 10 and 15, tel. 987/872-6275, 8am-8pm Tues.-Fri., 9am-8pm Sat.-Sun., US$3-6) serves up a tasty menu of vegetarian and vegan dishes. Plant-based tacos, burgers, scrambles, and bowls form the basis of the offerings; ask about the protein of the day. A remarkable menu of fresh-squeezed juices and smoothies make this a good place for a midday stop as well.

Corazón Contento (Av. 10 at Calle 2, tel. 987/872-0838, 7am-2pm Mon.-Sat., US$3-6) has a peaceful and welcoming ambience befitting its name (Contented Heart). A home converted into a restaurant, service is friendly, with great bottomless coffee and simple breakfast and lunch specials. Watch out: The bread basket is charged per item, and the chocolate-filled croissants are almost impossible to resist!

Nacho Crazy Boy (Av. 20 Sur between Av. Benito Juárez and Calle 1, 8am-11pm Mon.-Sat., 10am-2pm Sun., US$2-3) serves

Cozumel's colorful municipal market

outstanding juices and smoothies right from the patio of the owner's modest house. Fruits fresh from the market are squeezed and blended on the spot by Nacho Crazy Boy himself, an earnest and interesting guy who makes time for conversation with customers.

SWEETS

A display case of beautiful French pastries greets you at **Sucré y Sale** (Calle 2 between Avs. 5 and 10, tel. 987/115-5968, 8am-10pm daily, US$3-5), a cozy café just a block from the sea. Everything is freshly made, from the tarts and chocolate gateau to the baguette sandwiches and quiche. It's a perfect place for a cappuccino, a light meal, or an indulgent hour.

Rave reviews keep the small **Chocolateria Isla Bella** (Av. 5 between Calles 2 and 4, tel. 987/111-8462, noon-8pm Mon.- Sat., US$2 per chocolate) hopping. A mother-daughter team creates exquisite handmade chocolates in a variety of flavors, including vanilla bean, TLC (tequila, lime, and coconut), and a luscious triple dark chocolate. New creations and holiday specials are announced on the restaurant's Facebook page, as well as special events such as truffle-making classes.

At **Zermatt** (Av. 5 Norte at Calle 4, tel. 987/872-1384, 7am-9pm Mon.-Sat., US$1-2.50) you may have to jostle with locals for a crack at the island's best traditional Mexican baked goods. Be sure to grab a tray and tongs to make your selections—and maybe consider getting a little something extra for the stray pooch that is often hanging around out front.

La Flor de Michoacán (Calle 1 near Av. 10, 9am-11pm daily, US$1-2) serves cool treats, including *aguas* (fruit drinks), *helados* (ice cream), and *paletas* (Popsicles).

GROCERIES

Whatever groceries you need, you'll find them and more at **MEGA** (Av. Rafael Melgar at Calle 11, tel. 987/872-3658, 7am-11pm daily), the island's largest supermarket.

For a traditional market experience, Cozumel's **Mercado Municipal** (Av. 25 between Calles 1 and Rosado Salas, 7am-3pm daily) has stalls brimming with colorful produce, freshly butchered chickens, eggs, cheeses, spices, and more, all at reasonable prices.

Accommodations

DOWNTOWN COZUMEL
Under US$50

One block from the central plaza, **Hostelito** (Av. 10 between Av. Benito Juárez and Calle 2 Norte, tel. 987/869-8157, www.hostelcozumel.com, US$15 dorm, US$18-20 dorm with a/c, US$40 s/d with a/c, US$50-60 suite with a/c and kitchenette) is a stylish hostel with a large coed dorm packed with 20 bunks, lockers, and fans. Groups of four or more should ask about the air-conditioned dorm with private bathroom—at US$18-20 per head, it's a steal. Private doubles have air-conditioning and TVs. There also are a couple of spacious suites with kitchenettes and lots of natural light. A fully equipped rooftop kitchen is available for all to use, as is a great lounge, solarium, and even a pool.

A brilliant idea, **2Tank Dive Hostel Cozumel** (Av. Juárez between Avs. 5 and 10, tel. 987/872-6601, www.divehostel.com, US$11-15 dorm with a/c, US$30-34 s/d with a/c) is a modern place aimed at budget travelers who are more interested in diving than partying. Dorms and private rooms are sparse and windowless but beds are comfortable enough and the air-conditioning is turned on, full blast, at night. There's a clean common kitchen, a comfortable lounge, and most importantly, a full-service dive shop with knowledgeable staffers. Fun dives and lots of PADI courses are offered. Best of all, guests receive a US$10 discount on their room rate per day if they dive with the shop.

Though a long way from downtown, **Amigos Hostel Cozumel** (Calle 7 between Avs. 25 and 30, tel. 987/872-3868, www.cozumelhostel.com, US$12 dorm, US$45 s/d/t) is a great option for budget travelers looking for a peaceful place to stay. The hostel sits on a sprawling property complete with a well-tended pool, a fully equipped communal kitchen, an open-air game room (with a pool table), and lots of hammocks and lounge chairs. There are two mixed dorms with four bunks apiece and en suite bathrooms. There's also one private room with a kitchenette that sleeps three comfortably. All units have air-conditioning, but it's only turned on May-October (10pm-8am).

Hotel Caribe (Calle 2 Norte between Avs. 15 and 20, tel. 987/872-0325, US$45-50 s/d with a/c) has a small, appealing pool in a leafy central garden—a rare and welcome feature in the ranks of budget hotels. Rooms are plain but clean, with one, two, or three beds, decent bathrooms, and old-school air conditioners. Service can be ambivalent, but you can't argue with the value.

Located a half block from the central plaza, **Hotel El Pirata** (Av. 5 near Calle 1, tel. 987/872-0051, US$45-55 s/d with a/c) is a solid budget option. Rooms are modern in decor and have thick beds, flat-screen TVs, and mini-split air conditioners. More expensive rooms have partial views of the park. Wi-Fi is available in the lobby. The only bummer is that guests must climb a steep set of stairs to access rooms—a challenge for some.

US$50-100

★ **Mi Casa en Cozumel** (Av. 5 between Calles 7 and 9, tel. 987/111-9512, www.micasaencozumel.com, US$55 s/d, US$70 s/d with a/c, US$85 suite with a/c and kitchenette, US$165 penthouse) is a terrific boutique hotel and architectural gem—the curves of the spiral staircase and interior walls are counterbalanced by triangular patios and angled nooks

occupied by whirlpool tubs. All nine units have contemporary Mexican decor, private balconies or patios, mini fridges, and TVs; one has a kitchenette. All but one unit has air-conditioning, though all were designed for natural ventilation and are quite comfortable with fans only. The split-level penthouse is stunning, with full kitchen, outdoor hot tub, front and rear patios, and great views. The hotel's lofty structure is equally impressive, but could be difficult for guests who have trouble climbing stairs. Breakfast is included and is served in a cozy ground-floor dining area. Weekly rates are available.

Updated in 2017, **Tamarindo Bed and Breakfast** (Calle 4 between Avs. 20 and 25 Norte, tel. 987/120-9995, www.tamarindobedandbreakfast.com, US$20 pp dorm, US$60-70 s/d with a/c, US$85-95 suite with a/c and kitchenette) is a beautiful B&B owned by a friendly U.S.-Mexican couple who live on-site. The hotel has seven units bordering a large, leafy garden, including an artful eight-bed dorm with en suite bathroom and *palapa* roof. Each private room is slightly different from the other, from two boxy hotel-type rooms to whitewashed suites with lots of windows and tasteful murals. All integrate traditional Mexican textiles into the décor. Full breakfast is included in the rate and is served on a rooftop patio. There's also a small but well-equipped communal kitchen.

Amaranto Bungalows & Suites (Calle 5 between Avs. 15 and 20 Sur, cell tel. 987/106-6220, www.amarantobedandbreakfast.com, US$65 s/d bungalow with a/c, US$65 s/d suite, US$75 s/d suite with a/c) offers seclusion and privacy, while still within easy walking distance from downtown. The shining stars are the suites, in a three-story tower, each with a sitting area and 360-degree views; the lower unit has air-conditioning, high ceilings, and a modern feel, while the upper one has a *palapa* roof that offers a bird's-eye view. There also are three thatch-roofed bungalows with modern bathrooms and beachy decor. Each room has either a king-size or two queen-size beds, mini fridge, microwave, cable TV, and security box. There's a plunge pool and Wi-Fi runs throughout the entire place. Amaranto doesn't have a full-time attendant, so it's best to reserve in advance.

Hotel Flamingo (Calle 6 between Avs. Rafael Melgar and 5 Norte, tel. 987/872-1264, toll-free U.S. tel. 800/806-1601, www.hotelflamingo.com, US$87-105 s/d with a/c, US$230 penthouse) offers classy, well-priced rooms with modern furnishings, mosaic tile bathrooms, and colorful Guatemalan decor, all in a quiet north-of-center location. Rooms have mini-split air conditioners, electronic safes, and cable TV. Three common areas provide lots of extra outdoor space for guests— a rooftop solarium with lounge chairs and whirlpool tub, a shady midlevel area with hammocks, and a garden courtyard with tables and chairs. Families might consider the penthouse, a two-bedroom apartment with full-size kitchen, private whirlpool tub, and even a rooftop grill.

Located in the heart of San Miguel, **Villa Escondida** (Av. 10 Sur between Calles 3 Sur and Rosado Salas, tel. 987/120-1225, www.villaescondidacozumel.com, US$90 s/d with a/c) is an adults-only B&B with just four guest rooms. Each is modern—if a bit sparse—in style, with comfortable beds and spacious bathrooms. All look onto a well-tended garden with an inviting swimming pool, lounge chairs, hammocks, and Wi-Fi. A full breakfast, from pancakes to *chilaquiles,* is served on the hotel terrace. Complimentary bicycles and snorkeling gear also are available to guests.

Over US$100

★ **Villa Las Anclas** (Av. 5 Sur between Calles 3 and 5, tel. 987/872-5476, www.hotel-villalasanclas.com, US$110 1-bedroom apartment) is a great option for those who want a little home away from home. Seven pleasantly decorated apartments open onto a leafy, private garden, each with a fully equipped kitchenette, living room, and loft master bedroom accessed by spiral stairs. Using the sofas as beds, the apartments can accommodate up

to four people while still not feeling overcrowded. All units also have air-conditioning and Wi-Fi. There's also a mosaic tile pool plus an outdoor area for grilling and hanging out.

Guido's Boutique Hotel (Av. Rafael Melgar between Calles 6 and 8 Norte, tel. 987/872-0946, www.guidosboutiquehotel.com, US$110-130 1-bedroom apartment) is less a hotel and more do-it-yourself apartments, but the location, amenities, and price make Guido's an outstanding option. Masters have king beds, while juniors have queens; all are spacious, with full-size kitchens, stylish decor, and satellite TV and Wi-Fi. Each has a small balcony overlooking the street and ocean—traffic can get noisy but the views are priceless. The hotel is located just north of the center, above Guido's Restaurant, one of the island's best. There's no formal reception, so reserve ahead.

Casa Mexicana (Av. Rafael Melgar between Calles 5 and 7, tel. 987/872-9080, toll-free U.S. tel. 877/228-6747, www.casamexicanacozumel.com, US$160-167 s/d with a/c) is a modern beauty with a soaring interior courtyard and gorgeous views of the Caribbean from the oceanside rooms, including cruise ships gliding in and out of port. Rooms are spacious and bright, with good beds and quiet air-conditioning, though less inspired than the building itself. There's a small infinity pool overlooking the water on one end of the lobby (though, admittedly, it's a little strange to take a dip so close to the front desk). Rates include buffet breakfast.

A long walk from town but worth every step, **Casa Colonial** (Av. 35 between Calles 8 and 10, U.S. tel. 954/525-1539, www.casacolonial-cozumel.com, US$1,075/week with a/c) has four fully equipped Mexican-style villas. All are two stories with two bedrooms, 2.5 bathrooms, a living room, a dining room, a modern kitchen, cable TV, Wi-Fi, and even a washer and dryer. And unlike many longer-term rentals, you still get daily maid service and complimentary concierge service. All villas face a lush courtyard with a large pool and hot tub. Dive rinse tanks are available, too.

NORTHWESTERN COZUMEL
Under US$200

Maya stelae decorate the facade of **Condumel** (Zona Hotelera Norte Km 1.5, tel. 987/872-0892, www.condumel.com, US$142 1-bedroom apt), an old-school but very agreeable oceanfront condo complex a 15-minute walk from downtown. Ten spacious one-bedroom apartments have king-size beds, Wi-Fi, fully equipped kitchens, and daily maid service. Oversized sliding-glass doors offer awesome views of the Caribbean and incoming airplanes. The coast here is ironshore, so there's just a small patch of sand; steps and a ladder make swimming and snorkeling easy.

Miramar Condominiums (Zona Hotelera Norte Km 3.4, toll-free U.S. tel. 866/564-4427, www.cozumelvillas.com/miramar, US$170-250 1-bedroom condo, US$240-250 2-bedroom condo) is a well-maintained complex with units varying in style, though all are updated and very comfortable. There's a fabulous infinity pool overlooking the Caribbean and entry points to the ocean that make snorkeling easy. The staff does a good job of making guests feel welcome—from fresh flowers upon arrival to concierge services like booking rental cars. There's no on-site beach, which is a drawback, but if you enjoy exploring the island, this is a great place to stay. It's especially suitable for families and those traveling in small groups.

Over US$200

Hotel Playa Azul (Zona Hotelera Norte Km 4, tel. 987/869-5160, www.playa-azul.com, US$202 s/d with a/c, US$255-310 suite with a/c) caters mostly to golfers—guests pay no greens fees at Cozumel Country Club—but has packages for divers and honeymooners as well. Medium-size rooms and spacious suites all have fairly modern furnishings, large bathrooms, and excellent ocean views from balconies and terraces; master suites have private outdoor whirlpool tubs, too. Full breakfast is included in the rates. The pool is clean and attractive, but the beach (already small) can get crowded with day-trippers visiting the hotel's beach club.

Oozing cool, **Hotel B Cozumel** (Zona Hotelera Norte Km 2.5, tel. 987/872-0300, www.hotelbcozumel.com, US$279-336 s/d with a/c, US$423-538 suite with a/c) is a boutique hotel that combines mid-century aesthetic with traditional Mexican decor.

the pool at Hotel B Cozumel

Rooms have clean lines and lots of natural light, and feature gorgeous Mexican folk art. All have a balcony or patio and the amenities you'd expect—silent air-conditioning, cable TV, and Wi-Fi. Most have ocean views, too. Outdoors, there's a breezy restaurant, a great half-moon pool, a whirlpool tub, plus lots of sandy areas with hammocks and beach chairs. The main thing missing is a beach; the waterfront is mostly ironshore, so the hotel has done its best to create plenty of entry points to the water. Customer service can be hit or miss.

SOUTHWESTERN COZUMEL
Under US$200

A laid-back dive resort, **Blue Angel Resort** (Carr. Sur Km 2.2, tel. 987/872-0819, www.blueangelresort.com, US$706-976 s/d with a/c for four nights plus daily diving) provides all the amenities a diver could want: a reputable dive shop, reliable boats, an on-site dock, and drying racks and lockers for gear. The rooms themselves are modern but basic; all have great ocean views and private balconies. There's also an open-air restaurant, a well-tended pool, and plenty of shady places to sit back and relax. The only thing really missing is a beach. If you can live with that, this a perfect place to stay awhile. There's a four-night minimum.

Scuba Club Cozumel (Carr. Sur Km 1.5, tel. 987/872-0853, toll-free U.S. tel. 844/792-6976, www.scubaclubcozumel.com, US$140 pp all-inclusive) is an old-school dive hotel with great packages, an on-site dock, and drying racks for your gear. Rooms are basic—clean and bare bones (good beds and a balcony yes, cable TV and updated amenities no). There's a small pool and a sandy area on the water. Meals are typically included in the rate and are served in a bustling dining room with plastic tables and chairs. It's not exactly a tropical getaway, but it's perfect if you'll be underwater most of the time anyway.

Over US$200

★ **Presidente InterContinental Cozumel Resort Spa** (Carr. Sur Km 6.5, tel. 987/872-9500, toll-free U.S. tel. 800/593-5447, www.intercontinental.com, US$223-440 s/d with a/c, US$520-1,357 suite with a/c) may well be the best resort in Cozumel, with sleek mid-century modern rooms with high-end amenities, views, and niceties like twice-daily maid service and turndown service. While balconies face either the tropical gardens or turquoise ocean, all roads lead to a mellow and welcoming pool scene and a great beach—despite the ironshore—with plenty of access points for snorkelers and shore divers. A well-regarded dive shop, three restaurants, and a full-service spa round out this elegant hotel.

The Explorean Cozumel (Carr. Sur Km 7.5, tel. 443/310-8137, www.explorean.com, US$264-366 pp all-inclusive) is a small hotel nestled in the low forest behind its sister resort, the Fiesta Americana. Guests enjoy the amenities of both—pools, restaurants, spas, oceanfront relaxation—with the added benefit of newer facilities and more personalized service. The biggest plus is that the Explorean integrates daily excursions into the rate: snorkeling and paddleboarding, catamaran trips, tours of San Gervasio ruins and Parque Sur. Guides are knowledgeable and professionally trained, bringing a different (and welcome) adventure each day.

The Landmark of Cozumel (Carr. Sur Km 6.5, tel. 987/869-5130, www.thelandmarkresortofcozumel.com, US$503 1-brdm condo, US$503-608 2-bedroom condo, US$755-818 3-bedroom condo) is a condo-hotel with spacious 1-, 2-, and 3-bedroom "residences." All are modern in style and amenities (think granite countertops and washer/dryers) and have balconies with sweeping ocean views. Daily maid service is included. There's a well-tended pool and guests enjoy access to the VIP area of the Money Bar Beach Club, with a small sandy section, hammocks, lounges, and direct access to the Dzul-Há, one of the best DIY snorkel sites on the island.

SOUTHEASTERN COZUMEL

The only hotel on the east side of the island, **Ventanas al Mar** (south end of Playa Tortugas, tel. 984/267-2237, www.ventana-salmar.com.mx, US$145 s/d with kitchenette and a/c, US$228 s/d suite with kitchenette and a/c) is run almost entirely on wind and solar power. It has 14 large rooms and two suites, all with high ceilings and private patios or decks, all with marvelous ocean views. The décor is a bit dated but suits the hotel's isolated feel. There's also a heart-shaped pool, which is a huge plus because the ocean is often too rough for swimming. There's a popular restaurant and beach club next door but not much else (including no ATM or grocery stores). Some guest rent cars for easy access to the rest of the island while many embrace the isolation, spending a week or more without going to town at all. Rates include full breakfast; Wi-Fi is in the lobby only. Children 12 and over only.

Information and Services

TOURIST INFORMATION

The **city tourist office** (Plaza del Sol, Av. 5 Norte between Av. Benito Juárez and Calle 1, tel. 987/869-0212, 8am-3pm Mon.-Fri.) is located on the central plaza. It also has **information booths** with interactive displays in the central plaza (8am-2pm and 4pm-9pm Mon.-Sat., 9am-2pm Sun.), the international pier (8am-3pm daily), and at the Puerta Maya pier (8am-3pm daily). English is spoken at all locations.

There are numerous websites with news, tips, maps, special deals, discussion groups, and other information about Cozumel, including www.thisiscozumel.com, www.cozumelinsider.com, www.cozumelmycozumel.com, www.cozumeltoday.com, and even www.cruiseportinsider.com.

EMERGENCY SERVICES

Costa Med (Calle 1A Sur at Av. 50, tel. 987/872-9400, toll-free Mex. tel. 800/900-1133, toll-free U.S. tel. 855/301-4111, www.costamed.com.mx, 24 hours daily) accepts many foreign insurance plans, though the prices tend to be high.

Cozumel International Hospital (Calle 5 between Avs. Rafael Melgar and 5 Sur, tel. 987/872-1430, www.sssnetwork.com, 24 hours daily) specializes in diver-related medical treatment, though nondiving ailments also are regularly treated.

For meds, try **Farmacia Similares** (Calle 1 Sur at Av. 15 Norte, tel. 987/869-2440, 9am-10pm Mon.-Sat., 9am-2pm Sun.). Mexico now requires a prescription for many antibiotics; this pharmacy has an on-site *consultorio* (doctor's office), open roughly the same hours.

The **tourist police** (Calle 11 Sur near Av. Rafael Melgar, 8am-11pm daily) are stationed in a kiosk near Punta Langosta, though officers often can be found patrolling the central plaza.

The **police station** (Palacio Municipal, Calle 13 between Avs. 5 and Rafael Melgar, tel. 987/872-0092, 24 hours) can be reached toll-free at 066.

MONEY

Accessing your money is not difficult in Cozumel, especially near the central plaza. **HSBC** (Av. 5 Sur at Calle 1, 9am-5pm Mon.-Fri.), **Bancomer** (Av. 5 Sur between Av. Juárez and Calle 1, 8:30am-4pm Mon.-Fri.), and **Banorte** (Av. 5 Norte between Av. Juárez and Calle 2, 9am-5pm Mon.-Fri.) all have ATMs and exchange foreign cash.

MEDIA AND COMMUNICATIONS

Cozumel's **post office** (Av. Rafael Melgar at Calle 7, no phone, 9am-4pm Mon.-Fri., 9am-1pm Sat.) is next to Punta Langosta shopping center.

There are a handful of Internet cafés where you can get online and make international phone calls. **Phonet** (Calle Rosado Salas near Av. 10, no phone, 9am-9pm daily) is a quiet, reliable place charging US$1 per hour for Internet use and US$0.35 per minute for calls to the United States, Canada, and Europe. Another option is **Speedl@nd** (Calle 5 near Av. 5, tel. 987/878-4390, 9am-midnight Mon.-Sat., 10am-11pm Sun.), which charges US$0.50 per hour for Internet, US$.020 per minute for calls to the United States and Canada, and US$0.20-.040 for calls to Europe.

LAUNDRY AND STORAGE

Lavandería Margarita (Av. 20 between Calle 3 and Av. Rosado Salas, cell tel. 987/112-5740, 7am-9pm Mon.-Sat., 8am-4pm Sun.) charges US$7.75 per load to wash and dry up to eight kilos (17.5 pounds). There also are self-service machines (US$1.75/washer, US$1.25/dryer per 10 min.); detergent, fabric softener, and dryer sheets are sold separately.

Getting There and Around

GETTING THERE
Air
Cozumel International Airport (CZM, tel. 987/872-2081, www.asur.com.mx) is approximately three kilometers (1.9 miles) from downtown. The airport has an ATM in the departures area, currency exchange at arrivals, and a few magazine stands and duty-free shops. The **airport taxi cooperative** (tel. 987/872-1323) provides private and shared transport to the center and to resorts along the western coast. Prices vary by destination. Private taxis are US$7-25 per person, while shared transport costs US$5-7 per person and utilizes 10-person shuttles or Suburbans; departures are every 5-20 minutes. A taxi stand near the exit sells tickets and has prices prominently displayed.

Airlines servicing Cozumel International Airport include:

- **Air Canada** (toll-free Mex. tel. 800/719-2827, toll-free U.S./Can. tel. 888/247-2262, www.aircanada.com)
- **American Airlines** (toll-free Mex. tel. 800/904-6000, toll-free U.S./Can. tel. 800/433-7300, www.aa.com)
- **Delta** (toll-free Mex. tel. 800/266-0046, toll-free U.S. tel. 800/241-4141, www.delta.com)
- **InterJet** (toll-free Mex. tel. 800/011-2345, toll-free U.S. tel. 866/285-9525, www.interjet.com.mx)
- **MAYAir** (airport tel. 998/881-9413, toll-free Mex. tel. 800/962-9247, toll-free U.S./Can. tel. 844/622-0800, www.mayair.com.mx)
- **United Airlines** (toll-free Mex. tel. 800/900-5000, toll-free U.S./Can. tel. 800/864-8331, www.united.com)
- **Volaris** (tel. 551/102-8000, toll-free U.S. tel. 855/865-2747, www.volaris.com)

Bus
Ticket Bus (Calle 2 at Av. 10 Sur, tel. 987/869-2553, 8am-9pm Mon.-Sat., 9:30am-7pm Sun.) sells tickets for ADO buses leaving from Playa del Carmen at no extra charge, a handy service for when you're ready to move on.

Ferry
Passenger ferries to Playa del Carmen (30 minutes) leave from the passenger ferry pier across from the central plaza. **UltraMar** (tel. 998/293-9092, www.ultramarferry.com, US$13), **Mexico Water Jets** (tel.

987/872-1588, www.mexicowaterjets.com, US$13), and **Barcos Caribe** (tel. 987/869-2079, www.barcoscaribe.com, US$7) compete for customers during the day (although there are a few time slots when only one boat leaves, making it an easy choice). The boats are equally fast, though UltraMar's tend to be newer. The ferry ticket booths are opposite each other partway down the pier, with the time of the next departure displayed prominently. The ticket seller may try to sell you a round-trip ticket, but there's no savings in doing so; better to buy a *sencilla* (one-way ticket) and wait to see which company's ferry is departing when you're ready to leave. Between the three companies, there are ferries every 45-60 minutes 5:45am-10pm daily.

Car ferries operated by **Transcaribe** (tel. 987/872-7683, www.transcaribe.net) depart the international pier in Cozumel for the Calica dock south of Playa del Carmen at 6am, 11am, 4pm, and 8:30pm Monday-Saturday and at 9am, 5pm, and 9pm on Sunday. Returning ferries leave Calica at 4am, 8am, 1:30pm, and 6pm Monday-Saturday and at 7am, 11:30am, and 7pm on Sunday. The trip takes about 1.25 hours and costs US$25 for a passenger car including driver, and US$3.50 per additional passenger. Reservations are available online, by phone, or at the pier, and are strongly recommended.

GETTING AROUND

In town, you can walk just about anywhere or else grab a public van, or *combi,* circulating on various routes between the city center and outskirts (US$0.75, every 10-25 minutes 6am-8pm, less frequently on Sunday). However, the powerful taxi union has succeeded in quashing any and all efforts to start public bus service out of town and around the island. It is a shame, really, because it would be so easy and convenient to have a fleet of buses making loops around the island, or even just up and down the western shore. Until that changes (don't hold your breath), you'll need a car, moped, or bike to explore the rest of the island on your own.

Bicycle

A bike can be handy for getting to beach clubs and snorkel sites outside of town. Traffic on Avenida Rafael Melgar can be heavy south of town, but once clear of that, the roadway is relatively unhurried.

A highly recommended biking outfit is **Rent A Bike Cozumel** (no storefront, tel. 987/113-1082, www.rentabikecozumel.com,

ISLA COZUMEL
GETTING THERE AND AROUND

Mopeds are convenient for getting around town.

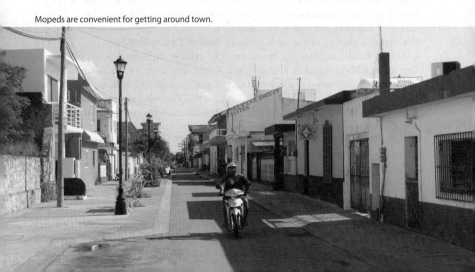

US$20-50/day), which has a wide variety of bicycles—from beach cruisers and mountain bikes to hybrids and road bikes. All rentals include a helmet and lock; road bikes also include an emergency repair kit. Extras like lights and saddlebags also can be rented. Bikes are brought to your hotel or location of choice; rates go down the longer you rent. Reserve in advance, especially during the high season.

If you want a last-minute rental, consider renting a bicycle from **Best Bikes Cozumel** (Av. 10 between Av. Juárez and Calle 2, tel. 987/126-0503, www.bestbikescozumel.com, 9am-6pm daily, US$8.50-18/day), which offers a variety of bikes, including helmet and lock. Snorkel gear is also rented.

Taxi

Taxis are everywhere—you can easily flag one down on Avenida Rafael Melgar, near the main passenger pier, and around the plaza. If you want to be picked up at a specific place and time, call the **taxi union office** (Calle 2 between Avs. 5 and 10, tel. 987/872-0041, 24 hours daily). Cabs typically charge US$3 around town and US$5 from the center to the airport, for up to four people. For hotels and beach clubs on the western shore south of town, you'll pay US$12-25, depending on the distance. Fares to the east side are a bit more, US$13.50-35, while San Gervasio costs US$50-60, including wait time. A trip around the island, including stops, runs around US$130 for four hours. Most taxi stands have the current fares prominently displayed; always agree on a price before getting into a taxi.

Car and Moped Rental

Renting a car is a nice way to get out of downtown and see the rest of the island. It is virtually impossible to get lost, and you can visit all the main spots in a day or two.

If you do decide to rent some wheels, go to the agency yourself—don't let one of the friendly guys at the pier lead you there. They are *comisionistas,* freelancers who earn hefty commissions for bringing tourists to particular shops, which then pass the cost on to you.

Shop owners go along begrudgingly; if they decline the "service," the same freelancers will actively steer future tourists away from the shop, saying it's closed, burned down, fresh out of cars—you get the idea.

Excluding commissions, rental cars in Cozumel start at around US$45-65 for a compact car, including insurance and taxes. Mopeds rent for around US$25-35 per day. Be aware that scooters account for the majority of accidents here, as speed bumps, potholes, and windy conditions can upend even experienced drivers; having a second person on the back is even more dangerous. Also remember that unpaved roads are not covered by most rental car insurance plans.

Rentadora Isis (Av. 5 Norte between Calles 2 and 4, tel. 987/872-3367, www.rentadoraisis.com.mx, 8am-6:30pm daily) consistently has the island's best rates, and friendly service to boot; their Internet specials often are good, too. Another good local option is **Sol y Mar Rentals** (Calle 2 near Av. 5 Norte, tel. 987/869-0545, 7am-8pm daily).

International companies have newer fleets, and sometimes have better rates if you book online. Try **Avis** (airport, tel. 987/872-0219, www.avis.com), **Hertz** (airport tel. 987/869-8184, www.hertz.com), or **Thrifty** (Av. Juárez at Av. 10 Norte, tel. 987/869-8090, airport tel. 987/869-2957, www.thrifty.com).

Motorcycle Rental

To explore the island in style, head to **Eaglerider** (Palmar Plaza, Carr. Costera Sur Km 3.8, tel. 987/857-0106, toll-free U.S. tel. 888/900-9901, www.eaglerider.com, US$169/day), which rents several types of Harley-Davidson motorcycles, from Sportsters to Road Kings and Electra Glides.

Highways and Road Conditions

The distance around the island—on paved roads, and including the northwestern arm that dead-ends after Cozumel Country Club—is approximately 93 kilometers (58 miles). Driving without stopping, it takes a little under two hours to circumnavigate the island. If doing this, consider going counterclockwise so there's nothing between your vehicle and the ocean, especially on the east side. Biking around the island is possible but challenging, given the strong crosswinds.

Cozumel has three **PEMEX gas stations** (7am-midnight daily). Two are in town on Avenida Benito Juárez (at Avs. Pedro Joaquin Coldwell and 75), and the third is four kilometers (2.5 miles) south of town on the Carretera Costera Sur, across from Puerta Maya, the main cruise ship pier.

Note: Most streets are one-way in town; if you're driving, be aware that *avenidas* (avenues) run north-south and have the right-of-way over *calles* (streets), which run east-west. Once you leave town, there is a single road that circles the entire island.

The Riviera Maya

Cancún may be the name everyone recognizes, but for many people—especially repeat visitors—the best of Mexico's Caribbean coast is the Riviera Maya.

Stretching more than 130 kilometers (81 miles) south from Cancún to Tulum, the Riviera Maya is home to fast-growing cities like Playa del Carmen, low-key towns like Puerto Morelos, and tiny beachfront settlements like Tankah Tres. It boasts megaresorts and tiny bed-and-breakfasts, and is flanked by the world's longest underground river on one side and the world's second-longest coral reef on the other. And, of course, the Riviera Maya has the same spectacular beaches Cancún is famous for.

There's plenty to see and do, much of it do-it-yourself: Go snorkeling in freshwater cenotes and lagoons, help release newly hatched sea turtles into the sea, explore little-visited Maya ruins, or spend the day at a family-friendly ecopark. For party hounds, Cancún still has a lock on over-the-top nightspots, though Playa del Carmen has several of its own, and there are plenty of lounge bars, beach clubs, and resort nightclubs where visitors can kick back or cut loose.

PLANNING YOUR TIME

You'll probably want to pick a home base (or two) for your time here and make day trips from there. Playa del Carmen is the area's only big city, with all the expected urban amenities, including nightlife. (It's also the gateway to Isla Cozumel.) Puerto Morelos and Akumal are smaller but still have a decent selection of hotels and restaurants. If isolation is more important than convenience, the Riviera Maya has some secret getaways, like Xpu-Há and Tankah Tres. If you've got a week or more, consider spending half your time in the northern section—around Playa del Carmen, for example—and then move farther south, to enjoy Akumal, Tankah Tres, and even Tulum.

A rental car isn't absolutely necessary but will certainly make exploring the Riviera Maya a lot easier. Cheap public shuttles zip up and down the coast, but they only stop along the highway, which in most places is about a kilometer (0.6 mile) from the ocean. That leaves you to make the hot, dusty walk up and

---

Previous: Playa del Carmen's beachfront; fishing boats on Puerto Morelos' main beach.
Above: a performance at Xcaret.

Look for ★ to find recommended
sights, activities, dining, and lodging.

Highlights

★ **Snorkeling Puerto Morelos's Coral Reef:** Go snorkeling where the reef is still healthy, the water uncrowded, and the price unbeatable (page 160).

★ **Playa del Carmen's Quinta Avenida:** Ever growing yet still walkable, Playa's 5th Avenue has block after block of tempting restaurants, hipster boutiques, and lively bars (page 168).

★ **Xcaret:** Xcaret is the most ambitious eco-park—a safe, active, family friendly place, with tubing and snorkeling, an aquarium, and an end-of-the-day extravaganza (page 172).

★ **Laguna Yal-Ku:** A long elbow of water fed by freshwater cenotes and flowing into the sea, this lagoon is a snorkeler favorite for its colorful fish and jumble of underwater rocks (page 196).

★ **Playa X'cacel:** Just off the highway down an easy-to-miss sand road, this glorious stretch of white-sand beach is home to a sea turtle nesting area protected from development (page 203).

The Riviera Maya

EL MECO

Cancún
180

EL REY
307

180D

*Caribbean
Sea*

To Valladolid
and Chichén Itzá

Siete
Bocas   CROCO
Boca   RUTA DE   CUN ZOO
del Puma LOS CENOTES
                    SNORKELING
                    CORAL REEF
                    Puerto Morelos
                    JARDÍN BOTÁNICO
Verde   LOS COLIBRIS   "DR. ALFREDO
Lucero MAYAN JUNGLE SPA BARRERA MARÍN"

To Selvática,
Cenotes Zapote Ecoparque,
and Leona Vicario

Punta Maroma
307
                    Isla
Punta Bete/   Cozumel
Playa Xcalacoco

Passenger
Ferry
                    San Miguel
QUINTA AVENIDA   de Cozumel
XPLOR Playa del Carmen
DELPHINUS   XCARET
RIVIERA MAYA
            Car Ferry
CALICA PIER
Paamul

Cenote   Puerto Aventuras
Cristalino
Jardín del Edén
Cenote Azul   Xpu-Há

            LAGUNA YAL-KU
Aktun
Chen   Half Moon Bay
    Akumal
        Aventuras Akumal

To Cobá and   PLAYA X'CACEL
Valladolid
        307
Dos Ojos   XEL-HÁ
        Soliman Bay   0   5 mi
Gran El Pit Cenote Manatí
Cenote Yax Kin Tankah Tres   0   5 km
Calavera
Tulum   TULUM
To the Costa Maya To Punta Allen and Sian
and Chetumal   Ka'an Biosphere Reserve
                    © MOON.COM

down the access roads, especially in more un-populated areas where taxis are uncommon.

Puerto Morelos

Puerto Morelos has largely escaped the mega-development that has swept up and down the Riviera Maya, despite being squeezed between the booming cities of Cancún and Playa del Carmen. It remains, for the most part, a quiet seaside town. Yes, the town fills up with tourists in the high season—and more and more condos and resorts are cropping up—but it is still a place where a substantial part of the local population lives by fishing, where life revolves around the central plaza, and where kids and dogs romp in the streets.

The beach in Puerto Morelos has improved significantly in the last few years, and more and more travelers are spending lazy afternoons in the sun and sand. But Puerto Morelos is best known for the reef system just offshore. Local residents fought tirelessly (and successfully) to have a large section in front of town designated a national reserve, and as a result, the snorkeling and diving are superb. A town cooperative and several local dive shops offer tours of various sorts, most highly recommended and quite affordable. Puerto Morelos also is gaining popularity as a destination for yoga and meditation groups—no surprise given its serene atmosphere—and a growing number of hotels and resorts cater to that market.

Be aware that the low season here is *very* low, and many businesses close in May, September, and/or October.

SIGHTS AND BEACHES
Playa Principal

Over the years, Puerto Morelos has improved its beachfront area considerably, with leafy arbors and palm-shaded benches. The beach itself, however, lacks the creamy white sand found elsewhere in the Riviera Maya, and the same regulations that protect the town's

Puerto Morelos

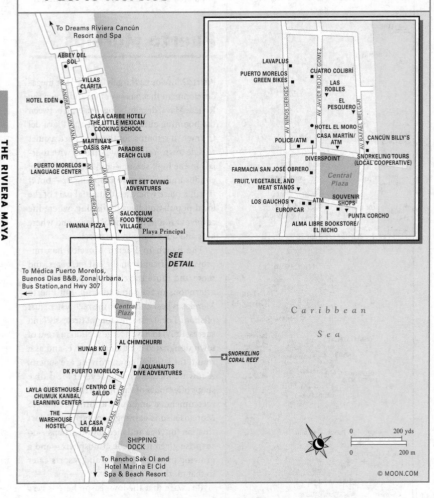

To Dreams Riviera Cancún
Resort and Spa

ABBEY DEL
SOL
VILLAS
CLARITA
HOTEL EDÉN
CASA CARIBE HOTEL/
THE LITTLE MEXICAN
COOKING SCHOOL
MARTINA'S
OASIS SPA
PARADISE
BEACH CLUB
PUERTO MORELOS
LANGUAGE CENTER
WET SET DIVING
ADVENTURES
SALCICCIUM
FOOD TRUCK
VILLAGE
I WANNA PIZZA
Playa Principal

AV ANDRES QUINTANA ROO
AV JAVIER ROJO GOMEZ
AV NIÑOS HEROES

SEE
DETAIL

To Médica Puerto Morelos,
Buenos Dias B&B, Zona Urbana,
Bus Station, and Hwy 307

Central
Plaza

Caribbean

Sea

AL CHIMICHURRI
HUNAB KÚ
DK PUERTO MORELOS
AQUANAUTS
DIVE ADVENTURES
LAYLA GUESTHOUSE/
CHUMUK KANBAL
LEARNING CENTER
CENTRO DE
SALUD
THE
WAREHOUSE
HOSTEL
LA CASA
DEL MAR

AV RAFAEL MELGAR

SNORKELING
CORAL REEF

SHIPPING
DOCK

To Rancho Sak Ol and
Hotel Marina El Cid
Spa & Beach Resort

0   200 yds
0   200 m

© MOON.COM

Detail:

LAVAPLUS
PUERTO MORELOS
GREEN BIKES
CUATRO COLIBRÍ
LAS
ROBLES
EL
PESQUERO
HOTEL EL MORO
CASA MARTÍN/
ATM
CANCÚN BILLY'S
POLICE/ATM
DIVERSPOINT
SNORKELING TOURS
(LOCAL COOPERATIVE)
FARMACIA SAN JOSÉ OBRERO
Central
Plaza
FRUIT, VEGETABLE, AND
MEAT STANDS
LOS GAUCHOS
EUROPCAR
ATM
SOUVENIR
SHOPS
PUNTA CORCHO
ALMA LIBRE BOOKSTORE/
EL NICHO

AV NIÑOS HEROES
AV JAVIER ROJO GOMEZ
AV RAFAEL MELGAR

---

famous coral reef also prevent the removal of seagrass in the shallow areas. Fishing boats also moor on the beach, though there's still plenty of room to lay out a towel, especially toward the northern and southern ends. A popular beach option is **Paradise Beach Club** (end of Calle Plutarco Elías, tel. 998/206-9354, www.myparadise.com.mx, 10am-7pm daily), which rents lounge chairs and umbrellas and offers tasty beach food and well-priced drinks.

The Central Plaza

Puerto Morelos's peaceful central plaza is a highlight of the town, with shaded benches, a basketball court, and a well-maintained play structure for kids, making it a great place to while away the early evening hours, especially for families. Many of Puerto Morelos's best restaurants face the plaza or are just a block away, so you're sure to pass by more than once.

Ruta de los Cenotes

Marked by an enormous mustard-yellow arch on Highway 307, the "Cenote Route" is one of the newest developments along the Riviera Maya, and a sign, for better or worse, that the megaresorts are finally starting to appreciate cenotes. The route is simply a paved road, which begins just south of Puerto Morelos and extends nearly 20 kilometers (12.4 miles) into the scrub forest, passing several cenotes along the way. The most popular stops, at least for tour groups, are cenotes like **Boca del Puma** and **Selvática,** which also have ATV tours, zip lines, roller coasters—you get the picture. But the route also has some true gems: gorgeous and remote cenotes, undeveloped and all but overlooked by the package tours, and well worth the drive to reach them.

Independent travelers will particularly enjoy **Siete Bocas** (Carr. Pto. Morelos-Vallarta Km 15.5, tel. 998/208-9199, 8am-4pm daily, US$15), so named for its seven openings (or "mouths"). Three openings have steep wooden stairways leading straight into the cool, clear water; another is a jumping-screaming-cannonball-entry spot for the more adventurous (apparently, the cenote is 492 feet deep); the other three allow sunlight into the underground chamber, lighting up the water dramatically, especially around midday. Inside, you can swim or float through the cave, with its spectacular stalagmites and stalactites, often with no one else around (BYO snorkel gear and underwater flashlight; life vests provided).

Just down the road from Siete Bocas is **Verde Lucero** (Carr. Pto. Morelos-Vallarta Km 18, cell tel. 998/224-3731, 8am-5pm daily, US$7.50), an open-air cenote surrounded by huge tropical trees. Completely different from its neighbor but no less dramatic, Verde Lucero is like an enormous swimming hole with clear turquoise water and seemingly no bottom. There's a zip line as well as a thick safety line stretching across the cenote. Look for the freshwater turtles that make their home here. It's popular with locals, especially on weekends.

A good option for those who prefer organized tours is **Cenotes Zapote Ecoparque** (Carr. Pto. Morelos-Vallarta Km 19, tel. 998/100-2406, www.cenoteszapote.com, 8am-5pm, US$35-79). The park consists of three cenotes in a lush and minimally commercialized setting: Zapote, an open cenote with a 14-meter platform for jumping (in diving circles, this cenote is known as "Hells Bells" for the remarkable bell-shaped formations found at 120 feet); Palmas, another open cenote with a 30-meter-long zip line running over it (snorkelers enjoy this cenote for its fish and turtles); and El Abuelo Che Che, an otherworldly domed cenote with crystal-clear water that is surrounded by stalagmites and stalactites. Visitors have the option of tagging on a 500-meter zip line ride over the jungle, a bike tour, as well as lunch. Regardless of the package, admission includes guides who lead visitors through the park, lockers, hammocks, and well-maintained bathrooms and showers. Transportation to and from hotels is available.

Croco Cun Zoo

A small tropical petting zoo, **Croco Cun Zoo** (Hwy. 307, tel. 998/850-3719, www.crococun-zoo.com, 9am-5pm daily, US$32 adult, US$22 child 6-12, free 5 and under) is located five kilometers (3.1 miles) north of the Puerto Morelos turnoff. Seventy-five-minute guided tours, offered in English or Spanish, bring visitors up close and personal to all sorts of local creatures. You can feed spider monkeys and white-tailed deer, walk through a crocodile enclosure, be "kissed" by macaws, and hold boas and baby crocs. Though pricey, it's well managed and, for many, a highlight of a trip.

Jardín Botánico "Dr. Alfredo Barrera Marín"

Just south of the Puerto Morelos turnoff is the peaceful **Jardín Botánico "Dr. Alfredo Barrera Marín"** (aka Ya'ax Ché Jardín Botánico, Hwy. 307 Km 320, tel. 998/206-9233,

Cenotes: Then and Now

divers exploring the otherworldly depths of the Riviera Maya's cenotes

Cenotes are intriguing features of the Yucatán Peninsula. These freshwater sinkholes, sometimes hundreds of meters deep, are filled with crystalline fresh water that is fed by underground rivers. Cenotes owe their formation to the massive meteorite that hit the Yucatán Peninsula 65 million years ago. The impact shattered the peninsula's thick limestone cap like a stone hitting a car windshield, and in the millions of years that followed, rainwater seeped into the cracks, carving huge underground caverns and hundreds of kilometers of channels out of the highly soluble limestone. Cenotes are former caverns whose roofs collapsed—cave-ins are extremely rare today, however—and together the channels form the world's longest underground river system.

Cenotes were sacred to Maya, who relied on them for water and viewed them as apertures to the underworld. (The name is derived from the Yucatec Maya word *dz'onot,* meaning "well.") Sacrificial victims were sometimes thrown into their eerie depths, along with finely worked stone and clay items, and archaeologists have learned a great deal about early Maya rituals by dredging cenotes near archaeological sites, most notably Chichén Itzá. Indeed, the name Chichén Itzá means Well of the Itzá, undoubtedly a reference to the ancient city's dramatic cenote.

Today the peninsula's cenotes attract worshippers of a different sort: snorkelers and scuba divers. The unbelievably clear water—100-meter (328-foot) visibility in places—is complemented by what other inland and underground diving environments (like lakes and flooded mines) lack: stunning stalactites and stalagmites. During early ice ages, water drained from the cenotes, giving time for the slow-growing features to form. When the climate warmed, the cenotes filled with water once again, their depths now forested with dramatic stone spires, pillars, and columns.

Divers with open-water certification can dive in the cenotes. Though "full-cave" diving requires advanced training, most cenote tours are actually "cavern" dives, meaning you are always within 40 meters (130 feet) of an air pocket. It's a good idea to take some open-water dives before your first cenote tour—buoyancy control is especially important in cenotes, and you'll be contending with different weights and finning techniques.

8am-4pm daily Nov.-Apr., 9am-5pm daily May-Oct., US$6 adult, US$2.50 child), which has four kilometers (2.4 miles) of trails winding through diverse habitat, from tropical forest to mangrove swamp. In addition to hundreds of marked plants, there's a scenic lookout tower, a 130-foot suspension bridge, the remains of a small Maya ruin, and recreations of a modern Maya home and *chicle* camp. Monkeys can be sometimes spotted in the afternoon. Wear long sleeves, pants, and plenty of bug repellent.

SHOPPING

Mayan Jungle Market (Calle 2 near Calle Vallarta, Zona Urbana, tel. 998/180-5424, www.mayaecho.com, 10am-1pm Sun., Dec.-April only) is held at Casa Cacahuate B&B in the residential part of Puerto Morelos, on the other side of the highway. This cheerful, family-friendly event is facilitated by the nonprofit founded by the bed-and-breakfast's owners. The market features a variety of handicrafts produced by local women, as well as tasty food and drink. A traditional Maya dance is held at 11:30am.

Cuatro Colibrí (Av. Javier Rojo Gómez s/n, cell tel. 998/198-1235, 10am-1pm and 4pm-9pm Mon.-Sat.) specializes in high-end *artesanía* and jewelry from around the country. You'll find everything from *corazónes de latón* (tin hearts) to Huichol-inspired T-shirts. Prices are somewhat higher here, but the quality is tough to beat.

The artisan's market of **Hunab Kú** (Av. Javier Rojo Gómez s/n, 9am-8pm daily) may be your best bet for finding local handicrafts in Puerto Morelos. There are a bunch of stands with colorful blankets, ceramics, hammocks, masks, jipi hats, and shell art. A **string of souvenir shops** (8am-8pm daily) on the central plaza sell similar items, in case you don't find what you're looking for at the market.

One of the best bookstores on the peninsula, **Alma Libre Bookstore** (central plaza, tel. 998/251-1206, www.almalibrebooks.com, 10am-6pm daily) has a whopping 20,000 titles, new and used, ranging from "beach trash to Plato," in the words of the friendly Canadian owners. There's Maya culture, Mexican cooking, ecology, mysteries, guidebooks, maps, and more—not just in English, but Spanish, French, German, Dutch, Italian, and others. The store's website is an outstanding resource for everything Puerto Morelos, too.

shopping in Puerto Morelos

SPORTS AND RECREATION

★ Snorkeling

Puerto Morelos's top attraction is snorkeling on the coral reef. Directly in front of the village, around 500 meters (0.3 mile) offshore, the reef here takes on gargantuan dimensions—up to 30 meters (99 feet) wide. Winding passages and large caverns alive with fish and sea flora make for great exploring. And because it's a marine reserve, and fishing and motor traffic are limited, the reef is more pristine here than almost any place along the Riviera. A **local cooperative** (central plaza, Av. Rafael Melgar s/n, cell tel. 998/121-1524, 9am-3pm Mon.-Sat., US$25 pp for 2 hours) offers guided tours of the reef, with boats leaving every 30 minutes—or sooner, if there are four snorkelers—from the municipal pier. The tour includes visits to two snorkeling sites, gear, and a certified guide. The **dive shops** in town also offer snorkeling tours to the town reef and beyond, for slightly higher prices.

Caution: *Do not swim to the reef* from anywhere along the beach. Although it's close enough for strong swimmers to reach, boats use the channel between the reef and the shore, and tourists have been struck and killed in the past.

Scuba Diving

Puerto Morelos has over two dozen dive sites within a 15-minute boat ride, virtually all in protected marine reserve waters. Add to that the nearby cenotes, plus night and wreck diving, and even diving with bull sharks, and folks have plenty to keep them happy and interested. The dive shops in town tend to have small groups and offer a full range of fun dives and certification courses. Prices range US$60-85 for one tank, US$100-120 for two tanks, and US$425-440 for open-water certification. Be sure to ask about any extra fees, like equipment, taxes, and the marine park fee. Shop hours are generally 8am-5pm Monday to Saturday, and reservations are strongly recommended.

Wet Set Diving Adventures (Hotel Ojo de Agua, Av. Javier Rojo Gómez s/n, tel. 998/206-9204, www.wetset.com) is one of the longest-running dive shops around, offering top-to-bottom service and extensive area expertise.

Aquanauts Dive Adventures (Hotel Hacienda Morelos, Av. Rafael Melgar 5, cell

Coral reefs occupy just 1% of the sea floor, but are home to 25% of the ocean's sealife.

tel. 984/126-7966, www.aquanautsdiveadventures.com) is another long-operating dive shop offering personalized service.

Diverspoint (Av. Javier Rojo Gómez s/n, tel. 998/206-9051, www.diverspoint.com) is a small shop run by a friendly Dutch couple. English, Spanish, Dutch, French, and German are spoken.

Sportfishing

The dive shops in Puerto Morelos also offer fishing trips, whether trolling for barracuda or marlin, or dropping a line for "dinner fish" like grouper or snapper. **Wet Set Water Adventures** (Hotel Ojo de Agua, Av. Javier Rojo Gómez s/n, tel. 998/871-0198, www.wetset.com) has been taking visitors fishing for many years; the **local cooperative** (central plaza, Av. Rafael Melgar s/n, no phone, 9am-3pm Mon.-Sat.) does the same. Both charge around US$65-150 per hour, depending on the size of the boat.

Another popular—though pricier—option is the fishing fleet at **Marina El Cid** (Hotel Marina El Cid Spa & Beach Resort, Blvd. El Cid Unidad 15, tel. 998/871-0185, toll-free U.S. tel. 888/870-3010, www.elcidmarinas.com). Trips run US$550-1,100 for 4-8 hours, but the boats tend to be newer and faster. The cost includes captain, crew, fishing license, tackle, ice, and insurance; food and beverages are optional. Taxidermy, filleting, and cooking are offered, too.

Golf

You'll find two Jack Nicklaus courses at **Moon Palace Cancún** (Hwy. 307 Km 36.5, tel. 998/881-6100, www.moonpalacecancun.com, US$303 for 18 holes, US$187 for 9 holes), just 10 minutes north of town. It has three nine-hole courses spanning nearly 11,000 yards. Greens fees include a shared golf cart, snacks, drinks, and round-trip transportation to select hotels; from 2:30pm until closing at 6pm, greens fees are US$187 for as many holes as you can play. There's also a driving range, a green-side bunker, and putting and chipping greens.

Tours

ECAB Explorer (cell tel. 998/123-5062, www.ecabexplorer.com) is a small but reliable tour operator run by a longtime Puerto Morelos resident. Tours include not only the main destinations—Chichén Itzá, Cobá, Ek' Balam, Sian Ka'an—but also whale shark snorkeling tours and interesting add-ons like bird-watching and visits with a local family. Groups are small and rates reasonable considering the tours' length and depth: around US$85-135 adult, with discounts for children and groups. Check the website for scheduled outings or to arrange a private tour.

Chumuk Kanbal Learning Center (Layla Guesthouse, Av. Rafael Melgar s/n, cell tel. 998/104-9831, www.laylaguesthouse.com, US$100) offers a popular cenote tour to a little-visited site about 90 minutes from Puerto Morelos. The trip includes a guided nature walk, a visit to a dry cave, a swim in a gorgeous cenote, and a traditional lunch at a local Maya home. Tours run 8:30am-5:30pm and must be booked in advance.

Over 50 visual artists live in the Zona Urbana of Puerto Morelos, located on the west side of the highway. Get an inside look at some of these artists' studios through the **Art Tour of Puerto Morelos** (tel. 998/322-5672, nadjabvd@gmail.com, US$35 for up to 3 people), a three-hour tour of 4-5 workshops led by bilingual guide Nadja Billard. Tours include meeting the artists and learning about their processes. Discounts are available if you provide your own transportation. Tours are held on Thursdays only.

Spas

Ixchel Jungle Spa (Casa Cacahuate B&B, Calle 2 near Calle Vallarta, Zona Urbana, tel. 998/180-5424, www.mayaecho.com, 10am-4pm Tues.-Sat., Sun. by appointment only) is one of several community projects undertaken by Maya Echo, a local nonprofit founded by a longtime expat. Local women provide professional massage and traditional Maya treatments for far less than at ordinary spas. Treat yourself to one of various available treatments, from a four-handed full-body massage (US$80, 1 hour) to a chocolate body wrap and massage (US$60, 1 hour). Group massage or *temascal* (traditional Maya sweat lodge) also can be arranged with advance notice. A cab ride from Puerto Morelos's central plaza runs about US$3.

Martina's Oasis Spa (Av. Andres Quintana Roo at Av. Plutarco Elias, tel. 998/213-4595, www.martinasoasis.com, by appointment only) draws on the considerable skills of its owner, Martina, a licensed massage therapist with an uncanny ability to zero in on the precise source of discomfort and know just how to alleviate it. Prices are reasonable: US$40-85 for facials, manipedis, and so forth; US$65-165 for one- and two-hour massages, including Swedish, Thai, deep tissue, and hot stone; and US$65-125 for Reiki energy treatments. Treatments are also offered off-site.

Set on a jungle plot along the Ruta de los Cenotes, **Los Colibris Mayan Jungle Spa** (Ruta de los Cenotes Km 15, cell tel. 998/105-2016, www.loscolibries.mx, 9am-5pm daily) offers Maya massages, *temascal* sessions, and outdoor bath treatments. Prices range US$50-90 for 1-2.5 hours. A nice way to end a day of cenote-hopping.

Cooking Classes

The Little Mexican Cooking School (Casa Caribe, Calle Rojo Gómez 768, tel. 998/251-8060, www.thelittlemexicancookingschool. com, 10am-3:30pm Tues.-Fri., US$128 pp, including complimentary recipe book and apron) offers a fun and unique introduction to Mexican cuisine. Class begins with pastries and coffee, followed by an hour-long discussion of regional food and ingredients, and moves to demonstrations and hands-on practice of 7-8 Mexican recipes and drinks. Class ends with a luncheon from the dishes you helped create. Note that the class size is maxed at 18 people, which may be too big for some.

FOOD

Who knows how it happened, but modest little Puerto Morelos is home to an amazing array of restaurants and eateries, from cheerful holes-in-the-wall to international cuisine that draws diners all the way from Cancún and Playa del Carmen.

Mexican and Seafood

Overlooking the central plaza, ★ **Punta Corcho** (Av. Rafael Melgar at Calle Tulum, tel. 998/206-9105, 1pm-11pm daily, US$12-20)

Fish tacos are a Riviera Maya staple: simple, classic, delicious.

is a shabby-chic restaurant serving gorgeous seafood creations, most of them made in a wood-fired oven. Expect dishes liked grilled octopus in adobo sauce, seafood risotto, and lobster ceviche wrapped in banana leaves. The cocktails, many of them made with mezcal, are equally creative—and strong. Reservations are recommended on weekends.

DK Puerto Morelos (Av. Rafael Melgar at Calle Isla Mujeres, cell tel. 998/192-4307, www.dk-puertomorelos.com, 1pm-10:30pm Tues.-Sun., US$4-7) is a hipster eatery with a kitchen set in a converted shipping container (complete with spray-painted murals) and handmade tables spread out on a gravel lot. The menu is decidedly Mexican-Asian fusion with a focus on seafood—think octopus tostadas, shrimp tacos, and spicy lionfish with coconut rice. Cocktails change with the season, but count on drinks with a kick that use premium mezcal. It's a popular spot, especially after the sun sets.

A *palapa*-roofed eatery with sand floors and plastic tables, **El Pesquero** (Av. Rafael Melgar 4, tel. 998/206-9129, 12:30pm-8pm daily, US$6-14) specializes in fresh seafood—everything from *chipachole* soup (a seafood medley of shrimp, fish, octopus, and squid) and ceviche to whole fish and lobster tail. Portions are generous and often include sides like coleslaw, rice, beans, and cucumber salad.

Cancún Billy's (Av. Rafael Melgar s/n, tel. 987/871-0913, 9am-11pm daily, US$5-16) is one of the only beachfront restaurant-bars in town, making it a go-to simply for the views. The food varies from excellent barbecue platters to solid seafood dishes like ceviche, fish tacos, and whole fried fish. Best of all is the atmosphere: It's laid ,back and friendly, with live music Thursday-Sunday and karaoke on Wednesday. There's two-for-one draft beer every day.

Other Specialties

★ **Al Chimichurri** (Av. Javier Rojo Gómez s/n, tel. 998/252-4666, 5pm-11pm Tues.-Sun., US$7-21) serves up Uruguayan specialties, with the shining stars being the grilled meats, chicken, and homemade sausage (don't be afraid to ask for extra chimichurri sauce for dipping). Food is served at candlelit tables in an open-air dining room and along the sidewalk, perfect for people-watching. If you have room, finish off your meal with the flambéed apple crepe topped with vanilla ice cream.

Salciccium Food Truck Village (Av. Javier Rojo Gómez s/n, tel. 998/871-0943, www.salciccium.com, 1:30pm-11:30pm Wed.-Mon., US$8-13) is a sit-down restaurant that accesses the kitchens of a handful of food trucks, all surrounding an open-air dining area with picnic tables. Offerings range from lobster po'boys and crepes to gyros and steaks. Take-out is also available—a great option for a sunset picnic on the beach.

On the central plaza, **El Nicho** (Av. Javier Rojo Gómez at Av. Tulum, tel. 998/201-0992, www.elnicho.com.mx, 8am-2pm daily, US$3-7) is a buzzing café serving up all manner of egg dishes, creative salads, and fresh panini. Many items are organic and most have healthy twists. Think plates of papaya with bee pollen, chia, and hemp seeds and scrambled eggs with spinach, feta, and pumpkin seeds. Fresh-squeezed juices and to-die-for cappuccinos are a must.

Draped in art, **Las Robles** (Av. Javier Rojo Gómez s/n, tel. 998/380-0568, 7:30am-10pm Mon.-Sat., 7:30am-2pm Sun., US$4-7) is a cute little café featuring a full menu of vegan and vegetarian dishes, much of it organic. Think fruit plates and omelets, big salads and sandwiches…even veggie hot dogs. Come here for a light meal or for a midafternoon break—the smoothies alone are worth a stop.

Considered one of the best pizza joints in town, **I Wanna Pizza** (Av. Javier Rojo Gómez s/n, tel. 984/281-3036, 4pm-11pm Tues.-Sun, US$8-10) lives up to the hype. Pizzas are made in a brick oven, with a soft-on-the-inside-crisp-on-the-outside crust and a range of toppings varying from pepperoni to red onion reduction with prosciutto, mushrooms, and feta cheese. Plastic tables are set up on an outdoor patio with soft lighting and inch-thick tree rounds for plates. Bring bug repellent—the restaurant backs into the mangrove, which can be buggy, especially in the rainy season.

There's great homemade pasta at **Los Gauchos** (Calle Tulum s/n, cell tel. 998/206-9243, 1pm-11pm Wed.-Mon., US$5-15), but don't leave without trying the empanadas: a classic Argentinean snack made of puffy, crispy fried dough stuffed with cheese, olives, or other goodies. At just US$1.50-2.50 apiece, a plate of five or six and a couple of sodas make a great cheap meal for two. Live tango is presented most Friday or Saturday nights starting around 8pm (with plenty of room to join, if you're inclined to dance).

Groceries

Casa Martín (central plaza, 6:30am-10pm daily) has a fairly large selection of canned foods, pastas, snacks, and drinks; there's also a small produce section near the back.

Every Wednesday, **fruit, vegetable, and meat stands** (Calle Tulum near Av. Javier Rojo Gómez, 7am-2pm) set up a half block from the central plaza. Prices are by the kilo.

For a bigger shopping run, head to **Super Chedraui** (Hwy. 307, 7am-11pm daily), located in front of the highway underpass. It's a traditional supermarket with a big produce section, an in-house bakery, and even beach supplies.

ACCOMMODATIONS
Under US$100

Located on the quiet end of the main drag, **The Warehouse Hostel** (Av. Javier Rojo Gómez s/n, U.S. tel. 763/398-9966, thewarehousepuerto@gmail.com, US$12/20 s/d tent, US$16 pp dorm) is a small hostel with a simple eight-bed dorm (think *palapa* roof, wood-plank bunks, and fans) and a lawn for tents (BYO gear). It's not fancy, but hot showers, lockers and linens, Wi-Fi, and a full breakfast make it a deal. Add a pool and an outdoor hangout area and it's a score for budget travelers.

★ **Buenos Dias B&B** (Calle Ciricote at Calle Che Chen, Zona Urbana, tel. 998/255-6950, www.buenosdiaspuertomorelos.com, US$52 s/d with a/c, US$67 studio with a/c) is a family-run hotel in Puerto Morelos's residential area, on the inland side of the highway. Units are modern and spic-and-span with thick beds, Wi-Fi, and powerful air-conditioning. Studios have fully equipped kitchenettes. Common areas include an outdoor kitchen, a shaded terrace, and a well-tended pool. Continental breakfast and bikes are included in the rate. This is an excellent place to experience the non-touristed side of the Riviera Maya.

A 10-minute walk from the central plaza, **Hotel Edén** (Av. Andrés Quintana Roo near Calle Lázaro Cardenas, tel. 998/871-0450, www.puertomoreloseden.com, US$70 1-bedroom apartment with a/c and kitchenette) is rather more austere than its name suggests, but is a fine budget option all the same. Decent-sized one-bedroom apartments have cable TV, Wi-Fi, clean hot-water bathrooms, and small but well-equipped kitchenettes. Air-conditioning is in the bedrooms only. Weekly and monthly rates are also available.

Hotel El Moro (Av. Javier Rojo Gómez near the central plaza, tel. 998/871-0159, www.hotelelmoro.mx, US$72 s/d with a/c, US$90-102 suite with a/c and kitchenette) is a homey hotel with spacious units, most with polished cement floors, brightly painted walls, and lots of natural light. There's Wi-Fi throughout most of the hotel, plus a pleasant little pool surrounded by hammocks and lounge chairs toward the back. Continental breakfast is included. Late-night music from nearby restaurants can be a bummer during the winter months; ask for a room facing the interior courtyard for a quiet stay.

Rancho Sak Ol (1 kilometer/0.6 mile south of the central plaza, tel. 998/292-1896, www.ranchosakol.com, US$78-87 s/d, US$87-100 s/d with a/c, US$133 suite, 2-night minimum) is a relaxing *palapa* hideaway located a 15-minute walk south of town. Rooms have hanging beds and private patios with hammocks. A buffet breakfast is included in the rate, and guests can use the well-stocked community kitchen. The beach here is just okay—very clean, with good snorkeling offshore, but boxed in by the cargo ferry on one side and a condo complex on the other. Still, there's enough breathing room so as not to spoil Rancho Sak Ol's quiet, isolated feel. The resort is for adults and teens only, except during the school holidays, when children over the age of three are welcome.

US$100-200

★ **Layla Guesthouse** (Av. Rafael Melgar s/n, cell tel. 998/104-9831, www.laylaguesthouse.com, US$130 studio with a/c) has four modern studios with aesthetic flair and homey comforts. Each integrates the outdoors through skylights, a patio or balcony, and even an airy shower. All have a well-equipped kitchenette, plush king-size bed, foldout sofa, flat-screen TV, and details like coffee-table books, fine art, soaking showerheads, and tropical wood details. There's a leafy garden plus a 3rd-floor plunge pool overlooking the ocean. The welcoming owners, Robin and Steve, are a wealth of information on the region.

Just down the street, **La Casa del Mar** (Av. Rafael Melgar s/n, cell tel. 998/130-0968, US$130 studio with a/c, US$260 penthouse, 2-night minimum) has eight studios with a modern, airy feel—think white walls, clean lines, and splashes of color here and there. Each unit has a kitchenette and includes use of beach chairs and beach umbrellas. There's also a gorgeous two-bedroom penthouse with full kitchen and ocean views. A small, well-tended pool with teak lounge chairs makes for a great place to unwind.

Occupying a converted hacienda-style house, **Casa Caribe Hotel** (Av. Javier Rojo Gómez near Calle Lázaro Cardenas, tel. 998/251-8060, U.S. tel. 512/410-8146, www.casacaribepuertomorelos.com, US$155 s/d with a/c) has four 2nd-floor rooms with whitewashed walls, colorful paintings, and large glass doors opening onto private ocean-view terraces. (A fifth room, on the ground floor, has no views.) A relaxing place, the rate includes a delicious full breakfast, served in the hotel's interior patio-garden. Hotel/cooking class packages also can be arranged with the on-site Little Mexican Cooking School.

Abbey del Sol (Av. Niños Héroes 806, tel. 998/871-0127, U.S. tel. 651/690-3937, www.abbeydelsol.com, US$90 s/d with a/c, US$125-135 1-bedroom apartment with a/c) offers nicely appointed units with king-size beds, balconies or private patios, and fully equipped kitchens (in all except one). There's a small pool in the leafy garden and a rooftop patio with *palapa*-shaded hammocks. Complimentary use of bicycles is included. If Abbey del Sol is booked, check its website for availability in its other properties around town.

Villas Clarita (Av. Niños Héroes near Calle Benito Juárez, tel. 984/217-2896, www.villasclaritamexico.com, US$120-175 with a/c) has eight comfortable one- and two-bedroom apartments that open onto two courtyards: One courtyard has a large pool with lots of lounge chairs and tables, the other has an open-air yoga studio and shady garden. Most of the apartments have a hacienda-like feel and feature heavy wood furnishings. (The best units open onto the garden courtyard, though families may like having an apartment right next to the pool.) All units have full kitchens, cable TV, Wi-Fi, purified water, and daily maid service.

Over US$200

Dreams Riviera Cancún Resort and Spa (Hwy. 307 Km 324, tel. 998/872-9200, toll-free U.S. tel. 866/237-3267, www.dreamsresorts. com, US$218-240 s with a/c, US$332-397 d with a/c, US$472-998 suite) is a bustling all-inclusive resort north of downtown Puerto Morelos. Aesthetically, it has a South Pacific feel with airy rooms that feature tropical woods and bamboo accents. The amenities are high-end and luxurious, some with their own plunge pool. Outside there are lots of infinity pools and a long, wide beach with plenty of places to relax (no need to get up at 6am to save a spot!). Nine restaurants (six à la carte) and a wide variety of activities provide enough options to keep most people happy during their stay.

Located south of town, **Hotel Marina El Cid Spa & Beach Resort** (Blvd. El Cid Unidad 15, tel. 998/872-8999, toll-free U.S. tel. 888/733-7308, www.elcid.com, US$282 s with a/c, US$301 d with a/c, US$306-381 suite, US$388 1-bedroom apartment) is Puerto Morelos's first all-inclusive resort—a milestone that didn't please everyone in this tight-knit town. The resort gets high marks from families though, with a kids club, waterslide, and manageable size, though the beach is smallish. There is a full-service spa on-site—including beachfront massage tables—as well as a great gym with floor-to-ceiling windows facing the Caribbean. Rooms have modern, tasteful decor and lots of natural light; ask for one in building 21, 22, or 23, which have ocean views over a gorgeous infinity pool.

INFORMATION AND SERVICES

Although this town sees a good number of tourists, the information services remain somewhat sparse. Check out **www.InPuertoMorelos.com** and **www.puertomorelos.com** for up-to-date information on restaurants, bars, and things to do around town.

Emergency Services

Médica Puerto Morelos (Calle Ignacio López Rayón, Col. Pescadores, tel. 998/255-3092 or 998/201-2456, 9:30am-2pm and 4pm-8pm Mon.-Sat.) is the small but well-equipped medical office of Dr. Víctor Ballestros, a Mexico City-trained surgeon and general practitioner. Look for signs leading to his office along the access road, near the highway. English is spoken.

Centro de Salud (no phone, 8am-2pm daily) is a basic medical clinic. It's located just south of the central plaza, on an unmarked connector street between Avenidas Javier Rojo Gómez and Rafaél Melgar.

Farmacia San José Obrero (central plaza, Av. Javier Rojo Gómez, tel. 998/871-0053, 8am-2pm and 4pm-10pm daily) is a mom-and-pop pharmacy selling basic meds and toiletries.

The **police station** (central plaza, Av. Javier Rojo Gómez) can be reached toll-free at 066.

Money

There is no bank in Puerto Morelos, but there are three **ATMs** in town—an HSBC one in front of Casa Martín, a Santander ATM in front of the police station, and a Banco Norte ATM inside the OXXO mini-mart on the west corner of the central plaza. The most reliable one (with the lowest transactions fees), however, is in front of the Super Chedraui supermarket, just off the highway.

Media and Communications

There's **free Wi-Fi** (24 hours) in the central plaza. Most hotels and many cafes also offer Wi-Fi to guests.

Laundry

The bustling **LavaPlus** (Av. Niños Héroes s/n, cell tel. 998/198-4850, 8am-8pm daily) charges US$1.15 per kilo (2.2 pounds). For service in five hours, the rate jumps to US$1.40 per kilo. Coin-operated machines are also available.

GETTING THERE AND AROUND

Puerto Morelos is almost exactly halfway between Cancún (36 kilometers/22 miles, 40 minutes driving) and Playa del Carmen (35 kilometers/21 miles, 35 minutes). The Cancún airport is closer, just 18 kilometers (11 miles, 20 minutes) north of Puerto Morelos. A rental car isn't really necessary around town, but makes exploring the Riviera Maya beyond Puerto Morelos significantly easier.

Europcar (Calle Tulum near Av. Javier Rojo Gómez, tel. 998/206-9372, www.europcar.com.mx, 8am-5pm daily) has a small office just off the main plaza, making it the most convenient option for renting a car.

Otherwise, Cancún's airport has a large number of agencies, and you can often find excellent deals online.

Bus

ADO buses pass the Puerto Morelos turnoff on Highway 307 but do not enter town. The northbound stop is right at the turnoff, while the southbound bus stop is across the highway and a block south. Headed north to Cancún (US$1.75, 45 minutes) or south to Playa del Carmen (US$1.65, 45 minutes), second-class buses and *combis* (shared vans) pass every 10-15 minutes 5:30am-10pm daily, and less frequently throughout the night. A handful continue to Tulum, but it may be quicker to go to Playa and transfer. Buses to the Cancún airport (US$5.50, 25 minutes) pass roughly every 30-90 minutes 3:45am-9:15pm daily. Buy your ticket a day in advance, as buses often fill in Playa del Carmen.

Colectivo

Colectivos (shared minivans) make rounds to and from Puerto Morelos Pueblo, across the highway (US$0.50, 10 minutes), every 5-10 minutes 6:30am-10pm daily. Flag one down on the main drag or wait for one to pass the central plaza. *Colectivos* also are a convenient and cheap way to get to the highway, where you can catch a bus or *combi* (shared van) to destinations along the Riviera Maya.

Taxi

Taxis (tel. 998/871-0090) line up day and night at the taxi stand on the northwest corner of the central plaza. Prices are fixed and prominently displayed on a signboard at the taxi stand. A ride around town or to the highway/ADO bus stop costs US$1.50.

Bicycle

Puerto Morelos Green Bikes (Av. Niños Héroes s/n, tel. 998/734-8132, ride@green-bikesrentals.com, US $10 per 24 hours) rents comfortable bikes—even adult trikes—that include a basket, a lock, a rear rack, blinking lights, and a bell.

Another good option is the dive shop **Diverspoint** (Av. Javier Rojo Gómez s/n, tel. 998/206-9051, www.diverspoint.com), which rents bicycles for US$2 per hour, US$9 per 24 hours, and US$35 per week.

PUNTA BETE AND PLAYA XCALACOCO

It used to be that the only way to find Punta Bete and its main beach, Playa Xcalacoco, was to look for the big Cristal water plant. That's still the best landmark, but a flurry of construction, and renovation of existing locations, has prompted hoteliers to finally add signs along the highway. The beach here is decent—the sand is clean but coarse, and the shoreline rocky in places—but the snorkeling is good, and the isolation has always been a big plus. It's still a quiet place, but all the new development—including a huge condo complex—may mark a new chapter for this long-overlooked stretch of beach.

Food

Coco's Cabañas (Hwy. 307 Km 296, tel. 998/874-7056, www.cocoscabanas.com, 8:30am-8pm daily, US$6-18) has a small outdoor bar and restaurant that specializes in wood-oven pizzas, though there are lots of seafood dishes as well. It's a bit pricey for the location, but then again you don't often see lobster pizza with hefty portions of prosciutto, arugula, and brie.

Accommodations

★ **Hotel Petit Lafitte** (Hwy. 307 Km 296, tel. 984/877-4000, www.petitlafitte.com, US$204-293 s/d with a/c, US$246-336 s/d bungalow with a/c) offers the comfort of a full-scale hotel on this isolated stretch of beach, including a large pool, plenty of lounge space, and a well-maintained beach area with *palapas* and hammocks. Accommodations are either in the main building, where all the rooms have at least partial ocean views, or in spacious beachfront bungalows. All accommodations have one or two beds, cable TV, air-conditioning, a minibar, and Wi-Fi.

Owned by a Mexican-Swiss couple, **Coco's Cabañas** (Hwy. 307 Km 296, tel. 998/874-7056, www.cocoscabanas.com, US$68-85 s/d with a/c, US$95-106 suite with a/c) has a handful of charming *palapa*-roofed bungalows on a small garden plot. The *cabañas* are comfortable and attractive, with large paintings and artful stonework, plus patios with hammocks. There's a heart-shaped pool next to the open-air restaurant and bar, and the beach is just 30 meters (100 feet) away. Continental breakfast and bicycles are included.

Getting There and Around

From the highway, follow the access road two kilometers (1.2 miles) until it forks at the Viceroy Riviera Maya resort. Bear left to reach the listed hotels and beach.

There is no taxi stand in this tiny community; when guests need one, hotels call cabs from Playa del Carmen or Puerto Morelos. A ride to the airport costs around US$50, to Playa del Carmen US$20.

Playa del Carmen

Playa del Carmen (or Playa for short) has long been a favorite among travelers looking for an alternative to Cancún, a place where boutique hotels and lounge bars outnumber glitzy high-rises and all-night clubs. There also are more opportunities for tourists and locals to interact in Playa, and it's easier to find "authentic" Mexican outlets, especially compared to Cancún's Zona Hotelera. And while Cancún is an American playground, Playa attracts many more Europeans.

But Playa is no longer the small seaside town some remember. Its population has exploded in recent years, with tourist and residential development stretching farther and farther up the coast every year. The main tourist strip, Quinta Avenida (5th Avenue), is still mostly pedestrian, but walking from end to end is no longer the casual jaunt it once was; a bike path along 10 Avenida is a smart and welcome addition. And while lounge bars and beach clubs are still the mainstay of Playa's nightlife, nightclubs like Coco Bongo Playa and Palazzo, both offshoots of famous Cancún clubs, have fanned the fears of the "Cancúnification" of Playa del Carmen.

Playa still has plenty of small hotels and hipster bars, and remains a genuine alternative to Cancún. It has pretty beaches, and the atmosphere remains decidedly mellow,

even with all the changes. Playa's location also makes it a convenient base from which to explore the rest of the Riviera Maya and Yucatán Peninsula, whether snorkeling in cenotes, diving on Isla Cozumel, or visiting inland Maya ruins.

SIGHTS AND BEACHES
★ Quinta Avenida

Playa's main pedestrian and commercial drag is Quinta Avenida, or 5th Avenue, which stretches more than 20 blocks from the ferry dock northward. Pronounced KEEN-ta av-en-EE-da, you may see it written as 5 Avenida or 5a Avenida, which is akin to "5th" in English. The southern section, especially near the ferry dock, is packed with typical tourist traps: souvenir shops, chain restaurants, and so forth. North of Avenida Constituyentes, the atmosphere is somewhat more sophisticated, with more bistros, cool bars, and high-end boutiques. The north-south division is less stark than it used to be, with some nice spots opening in the former and plenty of kitsch in the latter. You'll probably walk the length of Quinta Avenida once or twice, and everyone seems to find his or her favorite part.

Museo Frida Kahlo (5 Av. at Calle 8, tel. 984/980-0595, wwwmuseofridakahloriviera-maya.org, 9am-11pm daily, US$12) provides a fascinating look at one of Mexico's most famous painters. The museum contains no original paintings but it outlines, in detail, the defining moments of Kahlo's life: her early life, her debilitating accident, the surgeries, and, of course, her tumultuous relationship with fellow painter Diego Rivera. Copies of her paintings, letters, and photographs are displayed throughout. Knowledgeable guides lead 45-minute tours in English and Spanish; afterward, visitors are welcome to linger and revisit exhibits.

El Acuario de Playa (Plaza Calle Corazón, 5 Av. between Calles 12 and 14, tel. 984/879-4462, www.elacuariodeplaya.com, 11am-7pm daily, US$13.50) is a small-ish aquarium showcasing over 200 types of sea creatures, all found regionally. Bilingual guides lead visitors through the exhibits, answering questions along the way; tours last about 30-minutes (there also are educational placards in Spanish and English). There are some touch tanks and an eerily beautiful jellyfish room with row upon row of 360-degree tanks lit up in purple. Best of all is a glass tunnel that runs through the largest tank, allowing visitors to be surrounded by tropical fish. Look for the entrance on the 2nd floor of the Calle Corazón shopping mall.

Beaches and Beach Clubs

A series of storms and shifting currents have changed the landscape of Playa del Carmen's beaches. Once uniformly gorgeous, they are now thin and rocky in the central section (Calle 4 to Av. Constituyentes) and wide with soft white sand on the bookends (near the ferry terminal and north of Av. Constituyentes). Fortunately, Playa is blessed with clear aquamarine water and mild surf along its entire shore. The state of the beaches, though, is ever changing—it is nature, after all. Online forums are a good way to get the latest info.

All along Playa's coast are numerous beach clubs where, for a small fee or for simply ordering something from the menu, you can make use of the lounge chairs, umbrellas, restrooms, and even swimming pools and changing rooms. If beach clubs aren't your thing, there are several convenient beaches on which to lay out your own towel and umbrella.

BEACH CLUBS

Playa Tukán (end of Calle 28) has two popular beach clubs, both with waiter service, pools, changing areas, lockers, and Wi-Fi; admission includes credit toward food and drinks. **Mamita's Beach Club**

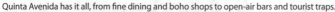

Quinta Avenida has it all, from fine dining and boho shops to open-air bars and tourist traps.

Playa del Carmen

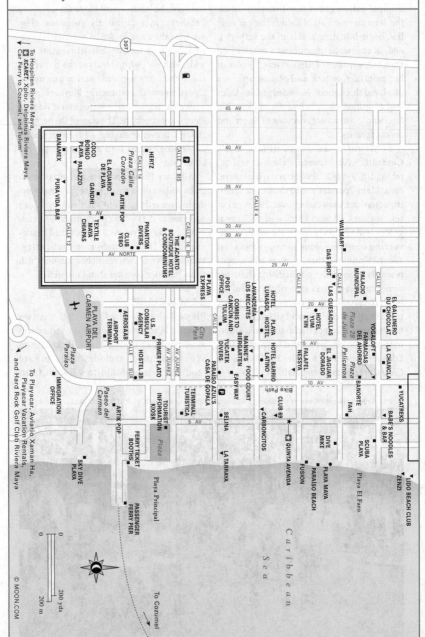

To Hospiten Riviera Maya,
XCARET, Xplor, Delphinus Riviera Maya,
Car Ferry to Cozumel, and Tulum

307

45 AV

40 AV

CALLE 14 BIS

35 AV

CALLE 4

30 AV

WALMART

CALLE 14

HERTZ

BANAMEX

COCO BONGO PLAYA PALAZZO

Plaza Calle Corazón

EL ACUARIO DE PLAYA

PURA VIDA BAR

GANDHI

ARTIK POP

5 AV

CALLE 16 BIS

PHANTOM DIVERS

TEXTILE MAYA CHIAPAS

CALLE 12

CLUB YEBO

THE ACANTO BOUTIQUE HOTEL & CONDOMINIUMS

1 AV NORTE

30 AV

25 AV

DAS BROT

CALLE 6

LAS QUESADILLAS

CALLE 8

PALACIO MUNICIPAL

CALLE 10

EL GALLINERO DU CHOCOLAT

YOGALOFT

FARMACIAS DEL AHORRO

Plaza 28 de Julio

LA CHANCLA

PLAYA EXPRESS

POST OFFICE

LAVANDERIA LOS MECATES

COMBIS TO CANCUN AND TULUM

HOTEL LUNAS

PLAYA HOSTEL

20 AV

HOTEL YUM K'IIN

Pelicanos

Plaza

BANORTE

FAH

City Park

CALLE 2

BIERGARTEN

MANNE'S FOOD COURT

YUCATEK DIVERS

15 AV

HOTEL BARRIO LATINO

EL JAGUAR DORADO

FALAFEL NESSIA

YUCATREKS

BABE'S NOODLES & BAR

PLAYA DEL CARMEN AIRPORT

Plaza Paraíso

AEROSAAB AIRPORT TERMINAL

U.S. CONSULAR AGENCY

PRIMER PLATO

AV JUAREZ

PARAISO AZUL'S CASA DE GOPALA

EASYWAY

10 AV

Bike Path

ZENZI

LIDO BEACH CLUB

HOSTEL 3B

CALLE 1 SUR

TERMINAL TURISTICA

SELINA

CLUB 69

DIVE MIKE

SCUBA PLAYA

Paseo del Carmen

ARTIK POP

TOURIST INFORMATION KIOSK

5 AV

CARBONCITOS

QUINTA AVENIDA

PLAYA MAYA

Playa El Faro

IMMIGRATION OFFICE

Plaza

LA TARRAYA

FUSION

PARAISO BEACH

To Playacar, Aviario Xaman Ha,
Playacar Vacation Rentals,
and Hard Rock Golf Club Riviera Maya

FERRY TICKET BOOTHS

Playa Principal

SKY DIVE PLAYA

PASSENGER FERRY PIER

Caribbean Sea

To Cozumel

0   200 yds
0   200 m

© MOON.COM

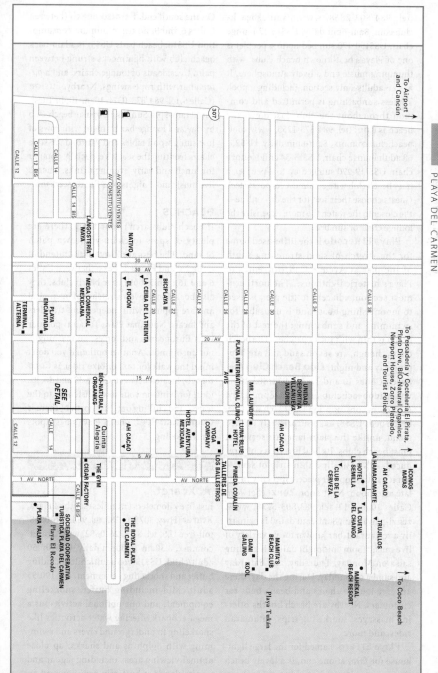

(tel. 984/803-2868, www.mamitasbeach-club.com, 8am-6pm daily, US$15-17 lounge chair, US$150-170 sun bed up to 4 people) is one of Playa's best-known beach clubs, with thumping music and a lively atmosphere. It has an adults-only section, including a pool. Topless sunbathing is permitted and common throughout the club. Just down the beach is **Kool** (tel. 984/873-1255, www.kool-beachclub.com.mx, 8am-6pm daily, US$25-68 adult lounge chair, US$13-34 child lounge chair, US$119-270 sun bed up to 4 people), a busy beach club with an almost corporate feel. Guests choose their seat for the day online—the closer to the water, the more expensive the lounge chair or sun bed.

Playa El Recodo is the little-used name for the stretch of sand stretching south of the pier at Avenue Constituyentes to Playa's historic lighthouse. The northernmost section, adjacent to the pier, is used to moor fishing boats and is unusable for swimming and sunbathing; the rest of the beach is thin with rocky patches. The beach clubs, though, are set on sand and are hopping day and night. **Lido Beach Club** (between Calles 10 and 12, tel. 984/803-1090, www.lidobeachclub.mx, 8am-8pm daily, minimum consumption US$12, chairs free, beach beds US$8) has a surprisingly refined menu, unlike the plain-Jane fair served at most beach clubs. Its beachfront is quite reduced—it's basically a thin strip of sand—but it's still a popular place, especially in the late afternoon. Next door, **Zenzi** (between Calles 10 and 12, tel. 983/803-5738, www.zenzi-playa.com, 8am-2am daily) is primarily a restaurant-bar known for its variety of live music (5pm-midnight daily), including salsa on Monday, Thursday, and Saturday and samba on Sunday. During the day, there are free lounge chairs and beach beds for customers. Nearby are beach booths offering massages, snorkeling trips, catamaran rides, and more.

Playa El Faro, named for the large lighthouse (or *faro*) at one end, is a lovely beach that's convenient to just about everywhere.

On the south end, **Paraíso Beach** (between Calles 6 and 8, no tel., minimum consumption US$10, beach beds US$5) is a laid-back beach club with hammocks strung between palm trees, loads of lounge chairs, and a *palapa* bar with rope swings. Nearby, **Fusion** (Calle 6, tel. 984/873-0374, 10am-10pm Tues.-Sat., 11am-9pm Sun.) is a popular beach club by day and lounge bar by night with rows of low-slung wood tables and Adirondack-style chairs fronting the sea. It's especially popular for lunch and early-evening drinks. There's live music most nights plus fire dancers too.

BEACHES

If beach clubs aren't your thing, there are plenty of spots to claim your own patch of sand. The best are **Playa Tukán** (end of Calle 28) and **Playa El Faro** (between Calles 6 and 16); while both have beach clubs, they also boast long, lovely stretches of open sand and are popular with independent travelers and locals. Note that Playa Tukán is popular with Europeans, and topless sunbathing is not uncommon. Another option, if you don't mind the walk (or taxi or bike ride), is **Coco Beach;** located between Calles 38 and 46, it's ideal for lying on your towel, listening to the waves, and chilling out. Just north of there is **Chunzubul Reef,** one of Playa's best spots for snorkeling.

TOP EXPERIENCE

★ Xcaret

Just five kilometers (3.1 miles) south of Playa, **Xcaret** (Hwy. 307 Km 282, tel. 984/206-0038, toll-free U.S. tel. 855/326-0682, www.xcaret.com.mx, 8:30am-10:30pm daily, US$100/50 adult/child, US$130/65 adult/child including buffet and snorkeling equipment, US$190/95 adult/child including buffet, snorkeling equipment, and one optional activity) is a mega-ecopark offering water activities like snorkeling in underground rivers and swimming with dolphins and sharks; up-close animal viewing areas including jaguar and puma islands, a butterfly pavilion, and an aquarium; a phenomenal folk art museum that's brimming with *artesanía* from around Mexico; and spectacular shows, like a Maya ball game, regional dances, and music performances. Xcaret is thoroughly touristy and prepackaged, yes, but also surprisingly well done and a worthwhile day trip, especially for families. There are numerous packages and prices, including combo visits with sister parks **Xplor** and **Xel-Há;** be sure you know what you're getting (and not getting) when you book. Discounts are available for booking online.

Xplor

Xplor (Hwy. 307 Km 282, tel. 984/206-0038, toll-free U.S. tel. 855/326-06852, www.xplor. travel, 9am-5pm Mon.-Sat., US$140/70 adult/child) is adjacent to the mother ship and focused on adventure activities. The park has two zip line circuits with seven segments each, including tandem lines and a splashdown in the mouth of a cavern. Other activities include swimming and rafting through caverns bristling with stalactites, and driving amphibious ATVs through the forest and underground passages. Admission includes lockers, showers, buffet lunch, and fresh-made smoothies, water, and snacks. Xplor also offers

evening-only admission (5:30pm-11:30pm daily, US$100/50 adult/child), with colored lights and torches lighting up the park and its activities, adding an additional rush.

Aviario Xaman Ha

A short distance inside the Playacar entrance off 10 Avenida, the small bird sanctuary **Aviario Xaman Ha** (Paseo Xaman Ha s/n, tel. 984/873-0593, 9am-5pm daily, US$20 adult, children under 12 free) is home, or a stopover, for more than 60 species of tropical birds, including toucans, flamingos, cormorants, and parrots. Some birds are in enclosures, but many are not, and a stone path meanders through the leafy grounds. It's a pleasant place to spend an hour, though the admission price is ridiculously inflated. If you do go, be sure to bring bug repellent.

ENTERTAINMENT

Playa del Carmen's nightlife has long been dominated by bars and lounges, as if deliberately leaving the raucous clubs and discotheques to Cancún. While that's still mostly the case, Playa is definitely getting rowdier, with several major nightclubs and the increasingly boisterous cluster of club-like bars at the corner of 1 Avenida and Calle 12.

Mexican folk dancing is part of the end-of-day extravaganza at Xcaret.

Lounges and Bars

A hipster little hole-in-the-wall right on Quinta Avenida, **Club de la Cerveza** (5 Av. near Calle 38, tel. 984/147-0635, www.club-delacerveza.mx, 4pm-2am daily) has a laid-back vibe, knowledgeable bartenders, and the area's best selection of craft beers. Over half the brews are from Mexico, including a few locals like Akumal IPA and Mundo Maya's citrusy ale "The Warrior." There's also tasty bar food and prices that won't kill your buzz.

Fah (5 Av. between Calles 8 and 10, tel. 984/803-1166, www.siestafiestahotelplaya. com, 8am-midnight) is an open-air restaurant-bar with seating on the pedestrian walkway and even more near a small stage inside. There's live music most nights; some of the bands are quite good, while others…well, at least they're giving it a go. But there's always a crowd and a fun time to be had, and the food and cocktails are outstanding.

Manne's Biergarten (Calle 4 between Avs. 10 and 15, tel. 984/876-5363, 4pm-1am) is owned by the namesake German transplant who handles much of the customer service himself at this popular bar-restaurant. The bar, the walls, and even the ceiling are crammed with German memorabilia. Come here for tall glasses of German brew and to sample authentic dishes from the homeland: sauerkraut, brats, spätzle, and a great Sunday prime rib special.

La Chancla (Calle 10 at 10 Av., tel. 984/158-1948, 4pm-4am daily) is a locals' favorite, and just hard enough to find to keep it that way. Beer is sold here by the bottle or by the *litro* (liter), and there's good bar food, all at very reasonable prices. There's live rock music occasionally, and always a fun, relaxed atmosphere.

Nightclubs

Coco Bongo Playa (Calle 12 at Av. 10, tel. 984/803-5939, toll-free U.S. tel. 800/841-4636, www.cocobongo.com, 10:30pm-3:30am Mon.-Sat., US$70 including open bar) is an offshoot of the famous nightclub in Cancún. Like the original, Coco Bongo Playa features a slew of celebrity impersonations, from Beetlejuice to Rihanna, plus acrobats, light shows, and multiple DJs to keep everyone dancing. The space here is fairly small, but the crowds can be huge and boisterous—tons of fun, assuming you're not claustrophobic. Check with your hotel concierge about VIP tickets and party-hopper tours; shows begin at 11:30pm.

There are two more clubs nearby, which either benefit from or are overshadowed by the crowds amassing outside Coco Bongo. Directly next door to Coco Bongo is another Cancún offshoot, **Palazzo** (Calle 12 near Av. 10, tel. 984/803-0730, www.palazzodisco. com, 10pm-3am Thurs.-Sat., US$60), a sister club to the City and Palazzo Cancún in the Zona Hotelera. It offers a somewhat more traditional techno nightclub scene, while aiming to inject old-school glamour through its décor and image. **Pura Vida Bar** (Calle 12 between 5 and 10 Avs., no tel., 8pm-3am daily, no cover) is a laid-back bar with a dance floor that gets packed by midnight. Guest DJs and live bands, playing everything from cumbia to funk, keep people spinning. Tuesday and Wednesday are Ladies Nights (free drinks!).

One of Playa's only gay clubs, **Club 69** (off 5 Av. between Calles 4 and 6, tel. 984/876-9466, 9pm-5am Tues.-Sun., US$5) doesn't get interesting until after 1am, and sometimes later. There are regular drag shows and exotic dancers, and, of course, music and dancing. Drinks are so-so and the place could use a good scrub, but it's not bad considering Playa's slim pickings for gay travelers. The entrance is easy to miss—look for the 7-Eleven mini-mart on the west side of Quinta Avenida, then follow the rainbow sign down an alley.

SHOPPING

Playa del Carmen offers some of the best shopping on the Riviera Maya, and Quinta Avenida is (mostly) where it's at. Here you'll find numerous souvenir shops, from small to gargantuan, open all day every day. For something more unique, try the following stores.

Artesanía

A hidden gem, **El Jaguar Dorado** (Calle 8 between Avs. 10 and 15, cell tel. 984/147-2705, 10am-8pm Mon.-Sat.) sells whimsical and unique art and textiles. Many of the objects are made on-site; others have been created by cooperatives of artists from the Yucatán and Chiapas. You'll find embroidered masks, handmade dolls, lithographs, T-shirts, bags, and more.

Pineda Covalín (5 Av. between Calles 26 and 28, tel. 984/803-2285, www.pinedacovalin.com, 10am-11pm daily) has gorgeous high-end accessories, including purses, scarves, and wallets, made from silk and other luxurious fabrics printed with traditional Mexican and indigenous images. This is the largest Pineda Covalín store in the Riviera Maya, with smaller shops in the Cancún and Cozumel airports.

Textile Maya Chiapas (5 Av. near Calle 14, no phone, 9am-2am daily) is a huge open-air shop bursting with colorful handicrafts from Chiapas. Piles of handwoven blankets and runners, baskets of handmade wool toys, shelves upon shelves of embroidered clothing, countless traditional garments hanging from the rafters—the abundance and the quality are breathtaking. Prices are fair (and fixed).

A small, colorful shop, **La Hamacamarte** (Calle 38 near 5 Av., tel. 984/873-1338, 9am-9pm Mon-Sat., 9am-6pm Sun.) specializes in high-end hammocks and hammock spinoffs like hanging chairs and knit bags, all made in the Yucatán. There's also a small selection of handwoven linens and hats.

Specialty Items

Prison Art (5 Av. Benito Juárez and Calle 1, no tel., www.prisonart.com.mx, 9am-10pm daily) sells handmade leather goods that are inspired by tattoo art and created by men and women serving time in Mexican prisons. The shop is an arm of Fundación Proarca, a non-profit organization that works to support and rehabilitate prisoners as well as to help reintegrate them into society.

Iconos Mayas (5 Av. between Calles 38 and 40, tel. 984/873-3111, www.iconosmayas.com, 9am-10pm daily) sells gorgeous hand-crafted jewelry integrating Maya glyphs, mostly in silver. Customers provide the date or name that they'd like represented (e.g., a birth date, their child's name) and choose the jewelry type (e.g., bracelet, necklace), including any semiprecious stones. By the end of the day, a one-of-a-kind piece is ready to wear. All items come with an explanation of each glyph.

Textiles make a memorable souvenir—and are easy to get home!

Talleres de los Ballestros (5 Av. at Calle 24, tel. 984/803-1923, www.ballesteros. net, 9am-11pm daily) is a well-respected silver shop selling gorgeous items from Taxco, Mexico's silver capital. Jewelry and home décor figure prominently. For more options, check out the like-named **sister shop,** located in the Paseo del Carmen mall (tel. 984/803-3939, 9am-11pm daily). Light haggling is welcome at both stores.

Gandhi (Plaza Calle Corazón, 5 Av. between Calles 12 and 14, toll-free Mex. tel. 800/426-3440, www.gandhi.com.mx, 11am-11pm daily) is an excellent bookshop located on the first floor of Calle Corazón shopping center. Come here if you're hankering for a good read that won't run out of battery. Novels, guidebooks, and more are sold in several languages.

With workers rolling cigars at the front of the store, it's tough to walk by **Cigar Factory** (5 Av. at Calle 16, no phone, 10am-11pm daily) without taking a second look. Inside you'll find a good variety of Cuban and Mexican *puros* sold individually (US$7-17) or by the box (US$60-450).

Shopping Centers and Markets

Caminarte (5 Av. between Calles 24 and 34) is an outdoor market held along Quinta Avenida featuring works by local artists; paintings, prints, pottery, and jewelry are among the items you'll find. It's held every Thursday 6pm-11pm.

At the southern end of Quinta Avenida, **Paseo del Carmen** (5 Av. at Calle 1, no phone, www.paseodelcarmen.com, 10am-10pm daily) is a leafy outdoor shopping center with high-end clothing boutiques, jewelry stores, art galleries, and restaurants. Its series of modern fountains make it an especially pleasant place to window-shop or enjoy a nice lunch after a morning at the beach.

What was once a quiet cobblestone street is now **Plaza Calle Corazón** (5 Av. between Calles 12 and 14, no phone, www.callecorazon.com, 10am-10pm), a swanky two-level shopping center with several outdoor lounges.

You'll find international boutique shops, gourmet restaurants, even an aquarium.

At Avenida Constituyentes, **Quinta Alegria** (5 Av. s/n, tel. 984/803-2358, www. quintaalegria.com.mx, 10am-11pm daily) is an airy and verdant three-story shopping center with big-name shops like Nike, Levi's, Victoria's Secret, Forever 21, and, of course, Starbucks. Not exactly a slice of Mexico but a pretty place to shop.

SPORTS AND RECREATION
Scuba Diving

Playa del Carmen has decent offshore diving—virtually all drift dives, thanks to prevailing currents—and relatively easy access to Cozumel and inland cenotes. It's a logical base if you want a taste of all three, plus the convenience of being in a major town. However, if diving is the main reason you came, consider basing yourself on Cozumel itself, or closer to the cenotes, such as at Akumal or Tulum. This will save you the time, money, and effort of going back and forth.

Diving prices in Playa del Carmen are reasonable, and fairly uniform from shop to shop. Two-tank reef dives cost US$70-85, Cozumel trips run US$95-165, cenote trips are around US$120-175, and open-water certification courses run US$395-430. Gear is included in the courses but may be charged separately for fun dives (US$15-20/day). Most shops do not include the price of taking the ferry to Cozumel, and additional fees, like marine park and cenote admissions, may also apply.

Dive Mike (Calle 8 between 5 Av. and the beach, tel. 984/803-1228, www.divemike.com, 7am-7:45pm daily) is a friendly, professional, and reasonably priced shop.

Phantom Divers (Av. 1 Norte at Calle 14, tel. 984/879-3988, www.phantomdivers.com, 8am-8pm daily) is one of a handful of locally owned dive shops offering lower-than-average prices.

Pluto Dive (Calle 40 between 5 and 10 Avs., cell tel. 984/151-9046, www.plutodive.

com, 9am-7pm Mon.-Sat.) is an Italian-run shop that keeps its trips limited to five divers.

Scuba Playa (Calle 10 between 1 and 5 Avs., tel. 984/803-3123, www.scubaplaya. com, 7:30am-9pm daily) specializes in small groups and offers a six-dive package that includes two tanks apiece in Cozumel, the cenotes, and the reef.

Yucatek Divers (15 Av. between Calles 2 and 4, tel. 984/803-2836, www.yucatek-divers. com, 8am-5pm daily) is a longtime shop with instruction available in several languages. Notably, all fun dives are led by instructors.

Snorkeling

In Playa itself it's best to go snorkeling with a boat tour, since the snorkeling off the beach isn't too rewarding. There are also numerous nearby cenotes that make for unique snorkeling, most of which you can visit on your own.

Most of Playa's dive shops offer guided snorkeling tours to excellent sites. Ocean trips cost US$40-50, while cenote trips are US$70-80, all gear included. Be sure to clarify how many reefs or cenotes you'll be visiting and for how long. A wetsuit is strongly recommended, even if it means paying extra to rent one. Cenotes can be quite cold, while sunburn is a serious concern in the open ocean; wetsuits

protect against both, as well as against accidental scrapes and cuts.

Dani Sailing (Calle 28 near the beach, cell tel. 984/136-3363, 9am-6pm daily) offers catamaran trips (US$65) with an hour spent sailing and another hour snorkeling. Or rent snorkel gear (US$12/hour) and a kayak or stand-up paddleboard (US$25/hour) and find a spot of your own. Look for the small shop where Calle 28 hits the beach.

Sociedad Cooperativa Turística Playa del Carmen (Playa El Recodo, end of Calle 14, no phone, 9am-6pm daily) is a local fisherman's cooperative offering snorkeling tours from a kiosk on the beach (US$35/45 pp for one/two sites). Trips typically are to **Moc Che**, a shallow snorkel site on the north end of Playa, and **Inah**, a reef known for its huge coral heads and sea turtle sightings, located about 10 kilometers (6 mi) south of Playa.

Wind Sports

Kiteboarding, sailboarding, and sailing have grown in popularity along the Caribbean, a trickle-down effect from the world-famous wind belt on the Gulf coast. You can catch at least some breeze almost any time of the year, but the strongest, most consistent winds blow November-March.

catamaran sailing off Playa del Carmen

Dani Sailing (Calle 28 near the beach, cell tel. 984/136-3363, 9am-6pm daily) offers catamaran rentals and tours, with or without snorkeling, as well as kiteboarding rentals and instruction. Prices vary.

Arguably a wind sport, Sociedad Cooperativa Turística Playa del Carmen (Playa El Recodo, end of Calle 14, no phone, 9am-6pm daily) offers parasailing—either single or double seated. Rides last 12-15 minutes (US$65 pp).

Stand-Up Paddling and Kayaking

Stand Up Paddle Playa del Carmen (tel. 512/822-3692, www.suppdc.com) is a one-man operation offering hour-long lessons for US$65 (US$50 pp for 2 people) at the beach nearest you, with an hour's free rental afterward to practice your skills. There's no fixed storefront, so reservations are recommended; otherwise, look for SUP gear near the pier at Avenida Constituyentes or near Fusion beach bar (end of Calle 6). Rental gear is available (US$30/hour, US$80/half day).

Do-it-all beach sports outfit Dani Sailing (Calle 28 near the beach, cell tel. 984/136-3363, 9am-6pm daily) rents kayaks (US$18/hour single, US$23/hour double) and stand-up paddleboards (US$23/hour). Hour-long instructional courses (US$30) are available for anyone new to "SUPing."

Sociedad Cooperativa Turística Playa del Carmen (Playa El Recodo, end of Calle 14, no phone, 9am-6pm daily) also rents stand-up paddleboards for US$25 per hour.

Swimming with Dolphins

With swimming pens set up in the ocean, Delphinus Riviera Maya (Hwy. 307 Km 282, toll-free Mex. tel. 800/335-3461, toll-free U.S./Can. tel. 888/526-2230, www.delphinusworld.com, US$99-499) is about as good as it gets for performing dolphins. There are various packages, from 30-minute group interactions to 45-minute one-on-one encounters. Book online to access discounts. Transportation is available for a fee.

There's a stand-up paddleboard waiting for you in the Riviera Maya.

Sportfishing

Playa de Carmen has excellent sportfishing and bottom fishing, with plentiful wahoo, dorado, mackerel, snapper, barracuda, and—especially April-June—sailfish and marlin. Trips depend mostly on the size and power of the boat that's used, but a 4-5-hour trip for 1-4 people usually costs US$230-260, including tackle and drinks. Many dive shops offer tours, as does Sociedad Cooperativa Turística Playa del Carmen (Playa El Recodo, end of Calle 14, no phone, 7am-6pm daily).

Golf

Hard Rock Golf Club Riviera Maya (Paseo Xaman-Há s/n, tel. 984/873-4990, toursinfo@allinclusivecollection.com, 7am-sundown daily) is a challenging 7,144-yard championship course designed by Robert Van Hagge and located in Playacar, the upscale hotel and residential development south of Playa del Carmen proper. Greens fees are US$180 per person, US$96 after 3pm, including cart and all-inclusive food and drinks from the beverage carts that travel the course and at the on-site restaurant; hotel pickup is available for a fee. Reserve at least a day in advance November-January.

Skydiving

Gleaming white beaches and brilliant turquoise seas make the Riviera Maya a spectacular place for skydiving. If you're up for it, **Sky Dive Playa** (Plaza Marina, just south of the ferry dock, tel. 984/873-0192, www.skydive.com.mx, 9am-4pm Mon.-Sat.) has been throwing travelers out of planes at 10,000 feet since 1996. You freefall for 4,500 feet—about 45 seconds—and then the chute opens for a 7-8-minute ride down to a soft landing on the beach. Tandem dives (you and an instructor, US$269) are scheduled every hour; walk-ups are accepted, but reservations are highly recommended. For an additional US$99, a cameraman also can be booked to **freefall** alongside you to record your jump either in an eight-minute video or 50-60 digital photographs.

Tours

YucaTreks (Av. 10 between Calles 10 and 12, tel. 984/803-1265, www.yucatreks.com, 9:30am-2pm Mon.-Fri., 10am-1pm Sat.) offers highly recommended tours to a variety of sites in the region: archaeological zones like Cobá and Chichén Itzá, snorkeling (cenote or reef), whale shark tours, and sailboat excursions. Trips are limited to small groups and are led by knowledgeable and enthusiastic—and punctual—people. Private tours also can be arranged.

Alltournative (Hwy. 307 Km 287, tel. 984/803-9999, toll-free U.S. tel. 877/437-4990, www.alltournative.com, 9am-7pm daily) offers a variety of conservation-minded full-day tours, including a combination of activities like canoeing, zip lines, ATV riding, and snorkeling, plus visits to the Tulum or Cobá archaeological zone—even to a small Maya village.

AeroSaab (Playa Del Carmen Airport, 20 Av. Sur near Calle 1, tel. 998/865-4225, www.aerosaab.com, 7am-7:30pm daily) offers stunning panoramic flights of the Riviera Maya (US$195-1,064, 4-6 passengers, 15 minutes-2 hours), as well as scenic full-day tours to places like Isla Holbox (US$696-754, 5-6 passengers) and Mérida/Uxmal (US$1,305-1,515, 5-6 passengers). Trips are in 5- and 6-seat Cessna airplanes and typically require a minimum of 2-4 people.

Spas and Gyms

The Gym (Av. 1 near Calle 16 Bis, tel. 984/873-2098, www.thegymplaya.com, 6am-midnight Mon.-Fri., 7am-7pm Sat., 8am-5pm Sun.) is a modern facility offering state-of-the-art equipment and a host of classes, including yoga, Pilates, spinning, and jiujitsu. There are personal trainers on-site, too. Day passes are US$15; multiday and monthly passes also are available.

Yoga Company (Calle 26 between 5 and 10 Avs., tel. 984/803-3295, hours vary Mon.-Sat., US$10/class) is a popular 2nd-floor studio just steps from Quinta Avenida. Instruction focuses on vinyasa yoga, with classes for all levels of students. If you prefer a bigger studio, check out **Yogaloft** (Plaza Pelícanos, Calle 10 between 10 and 15 Avs., tel. 984/803-0352, www.yogaloftplaya.com, hours vary Mon.-Sun., US$13/class), which has two airy and modern studios and a wider variety of classes. Private instruction is available at both studios.

You can get a **massage on the beach** at various locations—look for the white tents and massage tables—for about US$60 per hour.

The recently renovated **Unidad Deportiva Villanueva Madrid** (Av. 10 near Calle 30, no phone, 6am-10pm daily) is Playa del Carmen's public sporting facility, with a gym, tennis and basketball courts, track, and soccer field. All have night lighting and are open to the public free of charge, but you need to bring your own gear.

FOOD

Playa del Carmen has restaurants and eateries for all tastes and budgets. Those on Quinta Avenida are pricier, of course—many for good reason, others less so. Cheaper eats tend to be off the main drag.

Mexican

A popular taco place, ★ **El Fogón** (Av. Constituyentes between 25 and 30 Avs., tel. 984/803-0885, 1pm-6am daily, US$3-12) serves up mean plates of grilled food—everything from tacos and fajitas to brochettes and T-bone steaks. There are some options for vegetarians—cheese-based dishes like quesadillas and fondue, mostly. Drinks are cheap and strong, and lines can be long but move fast. Get here early to beat the crowds or head to its second location at Avenida 30 at Calle 6 Bis (same hours).

La Cueva del Chango (Calle 38 near 5 Av., cell tel. 984/147-0271, www.lacuevadelchango.com, 8am-11pm Mon.-Sat., 8am-2pm Sun., US$5-11) means The Cave of the Monkey, but there's nothing dim or primitive about it: The covered dining area has light-hearted décor (and a back patio ensconced in leafy vegetation), while the menu features crepes, empanadas, and innovative items like eggs with *chaya*, cactus, and Oaxacan cheese. It's often packed with Playa's upper crust, though the prices make it accessible to all.

Las Quesadillas (Calle 8 near Av. 20, no tel., 8am-midnight, US$1.50-4) is a friendly, low-key eatery serving simple but tasty sopes and quesadillas at red plastic tables, accompanied by *aguas de sabor* (fresh fruity drinks). The tortillas are made by hand and grilled fresh, and fillings are hearty and flavorful. It's a favorite among locals and tourists for an authentic Mexican meal at a very affordable price.

Carboncitos (Calle 4 between 5 and 10 Avs., tel. 984/873-1382, 7:30am-11pm daily, US$7-30) is a traveler favorite in Playa, serving terrific Mexican food and some things you may be missing from home, like fresh salads. Prices are a bit inflated but the restaurant gets the little things right, like tasty guacamole and homemade salsas.

Seafood

★ **Pescadería y Coctelería El Pirata** (Calle 40 between 5 and 10 Avs., no phone, 11am-8pm daily, US$10-52 per kg) serves up freshly caught fish, shrimp, octopus, and lobster—all sold by weight—and prepared to your liking. Sides are à la carte and include rice, beans, and tortillas. Seating is in the casual dining room or on the sidewalk under big umbrellas. It's a bustling place, especially on weekends; live music is often featured streetside.

A classic beachfront restaurant, **La Tarraya** (Calle 2 at the beach, no phone, noon-9pm daily, US$3-11.50) serves up tasty fish and seafood dishes that are easy on the wallet: think ceviche, shrimp cocktail, and fish tacos for under 10 bucks. The downer? Service can be painfully slow. Prepare to spend a few hours for a simple meal.

Unassuming and off the beaten track, **Langostería Maya** (Av. 30 near Av. Constituyentes, tel. 984/873-1037, www.langosteriamaya.com, 11am-midnight daily, US$5-16) specializes in super-fresh seafood, including hefty fish and shrimp plates, tasty ceviche, choose-you-own lobster, and great fish tacos. It's a bit of a hike from the center and has a view of a supermarket parking lot, but it is a tasty way to get off Quinta Avenida.

Vegetarian

BÍO-Natural Organics (Av. 10 between Av. Constituyentes and Calle 16, cell tel. 984/267-2208, 8am-11pm daily, US$4-8) specializes in vegan and vegetarian dishes, all organic, with lots of gluten-free options. The menu includes items like quinoa bowls, hummus and baba ghanoush plates, vegetarian paella, and lots of fresh fruits, veggies, and nuts. Look for it behind the Quinta Alegria mall. A **second location** (same hours, same menu) is on Quinta Avenida between Calles 40 and 42.

It's all about wood-fire grilling and roasting at ★ **Zorro Plateado** (5 Av. at Av. CTM, tel. 984/859-0298, 8am-midnight daily, US$5-12). There's steak and seafood, of course, but the inventive menu veers towards vegetables: grilled purple cabbage with bay leaf and orange, baked yucca with quail eggs, grilled cucumber and fish ceviche. Cocktails are equally interesting and pack a punch. All menu items are organic and locally sourced. Service is tops.

La Ceiba de la Treinta (Av. 30 at Av. 20, tel. 984/873-1255, 7am-10pm Mon. and Wed., 9am-8pm Tues., 8am-8pm Thurs., 9am-7pm Fri., 8am-4pm Sat., 7am-2pm Sun., US$4-10) is a bustling café serving up all manner of salads, wraps, and sandwiches—almost all vegetarian. Drinks focus heavily on freshly squeezed juices: liter-sized combos integrating seasonal fruit and veggies like beets, spinach, and cactus. Come early or late to guarantee a seat. It's located next to a small health food market.

Nativo (Calle 30 near Av. Constituyentes, tel. 984/873-0758, 7am-1am daily, US$4-10) serves up gigantic plates of Mexican classics and fruit-based meals. The fruit plate is remarkable—a heaping bowl of cut fruit (six types) with granola, yogurt, and honey; one bowl is enough for two. The freshly squeezed juices and smoothies aren't a joke either. Served in one-liter cups, combos include the Alma Grande (*chaya*, pineapple, guava, and orange juice) and Indio Mora (spinach, kiwi, strawberry, and OJ). The restaurant sits in a two-story *palapa*-roofed building, with an airy 2nd floor decked out in dramatic murals. If this place is full, try its sister restaurant a few doors south.

Other Specialties

★ **Falafel Nessya** (Calle 6 between Avs. 10 and 15, cell tel. 984/182-0643, noon-11pm daily, US$4-7) is a hole-in-the-wall serving up some of the best falafel on the coast. The menu is centered on falafel, of course: in a light and fluffy pita with hummus, as a sandwich with fried eggplant, a boiled egg and hummus, as a "plato completo" with hummus, fresh salad, and homemade potato chips. Be sure to load up at the fixins' bar before grabbing a seat at one of a handful of tables.

The name **Primer Plato** (Av. 15 between Av. Juárez and Calle 1, tel. 984/804-3196, 9am-6:30pm Mon.-Sat., US$3-5) is a reference to the Italian custom of starting a meal with pasta. So it's no surprise that pasta is the specialty here, and it could hardly be more fresh—the dough is cut and boiled right before your eyes, from spaghetti to ravioli. The location is out of the way, and there's only

La Tarraya

limited counter space, but if you love home-made pasta (and who doesn't?), Primer Plato is the real deal, and well worth the trip.

Dubbed by some the "Jungle Restaurant," **Trujillos** (Calle 38 near Av. 1, tel. 984/688-8207, 6pm-1:30am daily, US$9-16) is nestled in a grove of trees along the main drag, a pleasant pocket of nature where signs of greenery are fast disappearing. The menu ranges from organic chicken to baked octopus, plus cocktails like cucumber mezcal.

Although occasionally missing the mark, old-timer **Babe's Noodles and Bar** (Calle 10 between 5 and 10 Avs., tel. 984/879-3569, www.babesnoodlesandbar.com, 5pm-midnight Tues.-Sun., US$8-18) still serves up delicious Thai-fusion meals in a retro-hip bistro setting. Dishes come in half and full orders. Don't miss a chance at ordering the *limonmenta*, an awesome lime-mint slushie. It's not a huge place, so you may have to wait for a table during high season.

A set of repurposed shipping containers serve as Playa's most hipster **food court** (Calle 4 at Av. 10, no tel., 7am-10pm daily, US$2-6). Offerings range from a cool-cat coffee shop and a rooftop bar to a Jamaican eatery and a vegetarian cafe. Come after 4pm—the metal containers can get pretty hot during the day, plus the evening is when locals show.

Sweets

A puff of pink, **El Gallinero du Chocolat** (Av. 20 at Calle 10, cell tel. 984/120-3250, www.elgalleroduchocolat.com, 9am-11pm daily, US$2-7) is a dreamy place for anyone with a sweet tooth. Specializing in all that is sugar, you'll find artisanal chocolates, homemade ice cream, freshly made baked goods, plus a mouthwatering number of crepes and waffles.

Playa has lots of great bakeries but German-style **Das Brot** (Av. 20 at Calle 8, tel. 984/801-9391, 8am-1pm and 3:30pm-7pm Mon.-Fri., 8am-2pm Sat., US$1.50-4) is a real standout (the name means "the bread" in German). The cinnamon buns are to die for, especially fresh

from the oven in the morning. There are also loafs, tarts, and, of course, hot coffee.

Mexicans make great *paletas* (Popsicles) and Italians make great gelatos, so why not combine the two? **Artik Pop** (Paseo del Carmen and Paseo Corazón malls, tel. 984/167-1942, www.artikpop.com, 10am-10pm daily, US$3-4) does just that. The bars at this bright and welcoming mall kiosk are little works of art, with colorful exteriors and creamy fillings. The hard part is picking a flavor, which range from biscotti to pistachio nut and everything in between.

Chocolate lovers will melt over **Ah Cacao** (5 Av. at Av. Constituyentes, tel. 984/803-5748, www.ahcacao.com, 7:15am-11:30pm daily, US$3-6), a chocolate café where every item on the menu—from coffees to cakes—is homemade from the finest of beans. **Two sister shops** are located nearby, with the same operating hours (Calle 30 near 5 Av., and 5 Av. between Calles 38 and 40).

Groceries

MEGA Comercial Mexicana (Av. 30 at Av. Constituyentes, tel. 984/876-2236, www.comercialmexicana.com, 7am-11pm daily) is a huge supermarket that sells everything from clothes, shoes, and snorkel gear to groceries, prepared food, and booze. If you don't find what you're looking for, head three blocks north to **Walmart** (Calle 8 between Avs. 20 and 25, toll-free Mex. tel. 800/710-6352, www.walmart.com.mx, 7am-midnight daily).

At the far end of Quinta Alegria shopping center, **La Europea** (5 Av. at Av. Constituyentes, 10am-9pm Mon.-Sat., 10am-5pm Sun.) has an excellent selection of wines, beer, and liquors. It also has a high-end deli and a small baked goods section, with freshly made pastries and baguettes.

ACCOMMODATIONS

Playa del Carmen has a huge selection and variety of accommodations, from youth hostels to swanky resorts to condos and long-term rentals. There are a couple of all-inclusives in town, though most are located in Playacar, just south of Playa.

Under US$50

A hostel with hipster style, **Hostel 3B** (Av. 10 at Calle 1, tel. 984/803-2901, www.hostel3B.com, US$15-17 dorm with a/c, US$40-45 s/d with a/c) offers clean and comfortable dorms—mixed and female-only—on the southern end of town. Each has custom-designed bunk beds with matching lockers, individual bed lamps, air-conditioning, and muted décor. Two of the private rooms open onto the spacious rooftop lounge with a pool and popular bar—a party zone really, complete with guest DJs on Sundays (don't expect to go to bed early). There's a small but well-equipped galley kitchen and lots of indoor common areas for chilling out. The name "3B" is a reference to the Mexican saying *Bueno, Bonito, Barato* (Good, Pretty, Cheap)—an accurate description for this place, we'd say.

Opened in 2018, ★ **Selina** (Calle 2 between 5 and 10 Avs., tel. 984/873-2799, www.selina.com, US$9-14 pp dorm with a/c, US$40 s/d with shared bath and a/c, US$53-61 s/d with a/c, US$82 suite) feels more like an upscale resort than a budget hotel. The 389-bed behemoth has a mid-century modern style with Mexican flair—think clean lines with traditional tiles, tropical wood furnishings, and gorgeous murals. Rooms themselves are spacious and airy, with excellent beds, air-conditioning, and strong Wi-Fi. Common areas are just as comfortable and include a huge outdoor lounge with a bar, a well-tended pool, a library, a movie screening room, a yoga deck, a fully equipped modern kitchen, even a co-working space. All in all, it's an excellent place to land.

Enjoy Playa Hostel (Calle 4 between Avs. 15 and 20, cell tel. 984/132-2953, US$10-13 dorm with a/c, US$30 s/d with shared bath and a/c, US$50 s/d with a/c) is a small hostel decked out in murals and colorful furnishings. Dorms vary from four to ten beds, all tidy, with big lockers and air-conditioning

that runs from 9pm to 9am only. There's a tiny common kitchen as well as a breezy rooftop lounge and bar where most of the socializing happens (it shuts down at 11pm to let folks sleep). Continental breakfast is included, as is a free tequila shot every evening at 9pm.

Hotel Yum K'iin (Av. 20 between Calles 6 and 8, tel. 984/873-0173, www.hotelyumkiin.com, US$40 s/d with a/c) is a clean, well-located budget alternative. Rooms won't win any awards for charm but are well maintained and perfectly comfortable, all with flat-screen TVs and mini-split air-conditioning. All open onto a long, leafy courtyard. The Wi-Fi is hit or miss—head to the reception area for the best connection.

US$50-100

Hotel Barrio Latino (Calle 4 between Avs. 10 and 15, tel. 984/873-2384, www.hotelbarriolatino.com, US$50-78 with a/c) has charming rooms with mosaic-tile bathrooms, stone-inlaid floors, and private balconies with hammocks. A complimentary continental breakfast is served in a leafy courtyard with a *palapa*-roofed lounge that's a good place to play cards or check email. Be sure to confirm online reservations—the system experiences occasional glitches (which may mean no reservation). Adults only.

Hotel LunaSol (Calle 4 between Avs. 15 and 20, tel. 984/873-3933, www.lunasolhotel.com, US$80-90 s/d with a/c) offers 16 comfortable rooms, all with private balconies or terraces, on spacious, leafy grounds. The rooms are a bit sparse but have nice tile bathrooms, mini fridges, and flat-screen TVs; 2nd-floor rooms have higher ceilings and better light. Though well located for eating out, the hotel has a fully equipped outdoor kitchen if you'd rather stay in. There's a nice swimming pool and whirlpool tub too.

Wabi Hotel (35 Av. between Calles 4 and 6, tel. 984/147-4898, www.wabihotel.com, US$50-55 s/d with a/c, US$61 suite) is a small hotel offering clean and comfortable rooms that range from modern to shabby-chic in style. Two breezy terraces and an interior garden make good places to relax or to meet other guests. Service is friendly and helpful.

An old-school hotel, **Paraíso Azul's Casa de Gopala** (Calle 2 between Avs. 10 and 15, tel. 984/873-0054, www.casadegopala.com, US$75 s/d with a/c, US$85-140 s/d with a/c and kitchenette) has 19 spacious units, with rustic Mexican furnishings and colorful fabrics, that open onto shared leafy terraces. The comfortable but unremarkable rooms all have air-conditioning, mini fridges, and TVs. Head upstairs for the rooftop solarium with a small, well-kept pool and an enviable view of Playa del Carmen, the Caribbean, and, on a clear day, Cozumel.

US$100-150

A crate full of fresh fruit, eggs, bread, and jam greets you upon arrival at **Newport House** (Av. 10 at Calle 44, tel. 984/859-1557, www.newporthouseplaya.com, US$97-147 1-bedroom apt), a small apart-hotel with stylish one-bedroom apartments. All have king-size beds and fully equipped kitchenettes; the more expensive ones are bigger and have washer-dryers and two balconies. A major plus is the rooftop, with a well-maintained lap pool, cozy lounge chairs, and city views. Located on the far north end of 5a Avenida, the hotel is in a quiet part of town—you'll feel like a local—but close enough to the restaurants, bars, and beach that you'll still feel a part of the action.

The adults-only ★ **Luna Blue Hotel** (Calle 26 between 5 and 10 Avs., tel. 984/873-0990, www.lunabluehotel.com, US$89-115 s/d with a/c, US$125-135 suite) is a leafy oasis, and an excellent value, just off busy Quinta Avenida. Units are tidy and cool, some with pithy travel-related quotes stenciled on the wall, and range from standard hotel rooms to suites with balconies and kitchens. A pleasant garden has colorful Adirondack chairs and a sunken pool, all beneath a canopy of tropical trees. Wi-Fi, beach club passes, purified water, and morning coffee and baked goods are included in the rate.

Tucked into a leafy courtyard, **Club Yebo**

(Av. 1 at Calle 14, tel. 984/803-3966, toll-free Mex. tel. 800/681-9510, toll-free U.S./Can. tel. 888/676-4431, www.clubyebo.com, US$65 s/d with a/c, US$85-105 studio with a/c, US$120 1-bedroom apartment with a/c) is a small hotel offering tasteful studios and apartments with modern furnishings and fully equipped kitchens (plus a couple of basic hotel rooms). All have quiet air-conditioning, cable TV, Wi-Fi, and daily maid service. Common areas include a small pool and two *palapa* lounges with hammocks. Each room also comes with a "beach kit," which includes beach chairs, towels, and a cooler—perfect for a DIY beach day.

Hotel Aventura Mexicana (Calle 24 between 5 and 10 Avs., tel. 984/873-1876, www.aventuramexicana.com, US$115-125 s/d with a/c, US$125-143 suite with a/c) has two sections: The adults-only area has deluxe rooms with muted colors, elegant furnishings, and a nicely manicured garden and pool. The original section has colorful rooms with traditional heavy wood furnishings and has a long, thin pool squeezed in the center of the courtyard; it's slightly cheaper and open to families. Guests give both areas top marks, though, making it a versatile option. À la carte breakfast is included in the rate, plus there's a yoga studio on-site with daily all-level classes. An all-inclusive food and drink option available is in both sections; typically, children 12 and under enjoy the upgrade for free with a paying adult.

US$150-250

The boutique ★ **Hotel La Semilla** (38 Av. between. 1 and 5 Avs., tel. 984/147-3234, www.hotellasemilla.com, US$195-225 s/d with a/c, US$245 suite with a/c) sits on a lush lot, a tropical oasis just steps from Quinta Avenida. Trees and greenery are everywhere—the gorgeous garden patio, windowsills, the rooftop lounge—creating a sense of tranquility. The nine rooms are equally soothing with shabby-chic décor, fine linens, and modern amenities. A full gourmet breakfast and wine hour are included in the rate, both good times to chat with the affable owners and meet other guests. Use of bicycles is complimentary.

Playa Palms (Av. 1 Bis near Calle 14, tel. 984/803-3966, toll-free Mex. tel. 800/681-9510, toll-free U.S./Can. tel. 888/676-4431, www.playapalms.com, US$200-290 s/d with kitchenette and a/c, US$250 1-bedroom suite with kitchenette and a/c) is a classy beachfront hotel, with airy and colorful rooms, kitchenettes, and fine ocean views. A thin pool winds through the hotel's leafy interior courtyard; it's picturesque and refreshing, though not practical for actual swimming. Likewise, the beach area is comfortable, but fishing boats typically moor there, making it hard to enjoy the water. Still, the location and amenities made this a popular option.

Playa Maya (on the beach between Calles 6 and 8, tel. 984/803-2022, toll-free U.S./Can. tel. 888/866-2988, www.playa-maya.com, US$180-200 s/d with a/c) is one of the few small hotels in Playa with direct beach access. All 20 rooms are modern and comfortable, many with balconies and ocean views. There's a tiny pool, whirlpool tub, and sundeck, located somewhat awkwardly at the entrance. Steps away, though, is the beach with plenty of lounge chairs, umbrella shade, and waiter service. There's a 4-5-night minimum, varying with the season (shorter stays are possible, depending on the occupancy). Breakfast is included in the rate. Note: The entrance faces the beach, so you may need a porter to help carry bags across the sand.

On a shady street just a block from the beach, **The Acanto Boutique Hotel & Condominiums** (Calle 16 Bis between Avs. 1 and 3, tel. 984/873-1252, toll-free U.S. tel. 888/331-2177, www.acantohotels.com, US$128 s/d with a/c, US$150 studio, US$150-180 1-bedroom condo, US$207-248 2-bedroom condo, US$270-325 3-bedroom condo) is a peaceful place with 21 units, most with modern kitchens, spacious living-dining rooms, and balconies. Each is decked out in dark woods, marble floors, luxurious fabrics, and fine art. A small swimming pool sits in the lush central courtyard, where complimentary continental breakfast is served each morning. There's also a rooftop lounge with several grills and a whirlpool tub—a fine place for a sunset dinner.

Over US$250

Mahékal Beach Resort (Calle 38 near 5 Av., tel. 984/873-0611, toll-free Mex. tel. 800/836-8942, toll-free U.S. tel. 877/235-4452, www.mahekalplaya.com, US$289-399 s/d with a/c) is a huge yet tranquil resort on the northern end of town. All units are in thatch-roofed one- and two-story bungalows, each with a modern beachy feel. Each features a private terrace with hammocks; there's Wi-Fi and phone but no TV. The resort has four pools and a gorgeous beach. Breakfast and dinner plans are available.

Smack-dab in the middle of Playa del Carmen, the all-inclusive **The Royal Playa del Carmen** (Av. Constituyentes at Av. 1, toll-free U.S./Can. tel. 800/627-5328, www.realresorts.com, US$294-1,230 s, US$184-769 d all-inclusive) is an adults-only Mediterranean-style resort. A winding pool (one of many) runs through the center of its manicured gardens, leading to a beautiful beach. All of the units are suites, which means ocean views, private terraces, and luxurious amenities, with extras like a minibar stocked with top-shelf liquors, soft bathrobes, even umbrellas; some units even open up to a semiprivate pool. There are a dozen buffet and à la carte restaurants as well as a spa, tennis courts, and lounges. Almost best of all, Playa is right outside your door.

Rental Properties

Playacar has scores of houses for rent, of all sizes and styles. Prices vary considerably, but expect to pay a premium for ocean views and during peak seasons. A number of property-management companies rent houses, including **Playacar Vacation Rentals** (Bahía del Espiritu Santo s/n, tel. 984/873-0418, toll-free U.S. tel. 866/862-7164, www.playacarvacationrentals.com), one of the oldest agencies in the Riviera Maya. Good online alternatives include **AirBnB** (www.airbnb.com) and **Vacation Rentals by Owner** (www.vrbo.com).

INFORMATION AND SERVICES
Tourist Information

There is no tourist information office in Playa, but there's a **tourist information kiosk** on the plaza (5 Av. at Av. Juárez, 8am-8pm Mon.-Sat.) that is stocked with brochures and maps and often is manned by a reasonably knowledgeable staffer.

Other good sources of information include *The Playa Times* (www.theplayatimes.com), a bimonthly newspaper that covers, among other topics, art and culture, area sites, and upcoming events, and www.everythingplayadelcarmen.com, a good place to get a pulse on local trends and hot spots.

Emergency Services

Hospiten Riviera Maya (Hwy. 307 at Paseo Tulum, tel. 984/159-2200, www.hospiten.com, 24 hours daily) is a private hospital offering modern, high-quality medical service at reasonable rates. Many of the doctors have U.S. training and speak English, and are accustomed to treating foreign visitors. It is located along the east side of the highway, near the entrance to Playacar.

Playa International Clinic (10 Av. at Calle 28, tel. 984/873-1755, 24-hr emergency tel. 984/873-1365, www.sssnetwork.com, 9am-8pm daily) offers specialized medical care for recreational and commercial scuba divers. It has a hyperbaric chamber and lab on-site.

Prescriptions are required for many antibiotics now, unlike years past. **Farmacias del Ahorro** (10 Av. at Calle 10, toll-free Mex. tel. 800/711-2222, 24 hrs daily) has a full pharmacy on the 1st floor and a **free walk-in clinic** (9am-3pm and 5pm-10pm Mon.-Fri.) on the 2nd floor, where a doctor can write prescriptions after a short interview or exam.

The **tourist police** (Av. 1 at Calle CTM,

tel. 984/877-3340, or 060 from any pay phone) have an office on the north side of town.

Money

Banamex (Calle 12 at 10 Av., 9am-4pm Mon.-Fri.) and **Banorte** (Plaza Pelícanos, 10 Av. between Calles 8 and 10, 8am-4pm Mon.-Fri., 9am-2pm Sat.) are full-service banks with ATMs and foreign exchange. There also are several freestanding **ATMs** around town; use ones that are affiliated with recognizable banks to avoid exorbitant service charges.

Media and Communications

The **post office** (Calle 2 at 20 Av., 8am-4pm Mon.-Fri., 9am-1pm Sat.) is easy to miss—look for the pink-striped building near the *combi* terminal.

Internet cafés have gone from ubiquitous to nearly obsolete. Today, most hotels have free Wi-Fi for guests, as do many restaurants and coffee shops.

Laundry and Storage

At the north end of town, **Mr. Laundry** (10 Av. between Calles 28 and 30, 7am-10pm Mon.-Sat., 8am-5pm Sun.) charges US$1 per kilo with a two-kilo (4.4-pound) minimum. **Lavandería Los Mecates** (Calle 4 near 20 Av., 8am-9pm Mon.-Sat.) charges US$0.70 per kilo and has a three-kilo (6.6-pound) minimum. At both places, rates are for next-day service; same-day service is available for an additional fee.

Luggage storage is available at both bus stations. **Guarda Plus** (6am-10pm daily) charges US$0.30-1 per hour depending on the size of the bag, or US$5 per day.

GETTING THERE
Air

Playa del Carmen has a small airport a few blocks from the ferry pier, but it's used for private and charter flights only. Commercial service is available at Cancún International Airport.

*Schedules are subject to change.

Playa del Carmen Bus Schedules

Terminal Turística (5 Av. and Av. Juárez, tel. 984/873-0109, ext. 2501, toll-free Mex. tel. 800/702-8000) is located near the ferry dock and has frequent service along the Caribbean coast and throughout the Yucatán Peninsula. Long-distance buses to other parts of the country use the **Terminal Alterna** (Calle 20 between Calles 12 and 12 Bis, tel. 984/803-0944, toll-free Mex. tel. 800/702-8000).

Most Tulum-bound buses stop at the turnoffs for destinations along the way, including **Paamul** (US$1.25, 15 minutes), **Puerto Aventuras** (US$1.75, 20 minutes), **Xpu-Há** (US$2.25, 25 minutes), **Akumal** (US$2.75, 30 minutes), **Xel-Há** (US$2.85, 45 minutes), and **Dos Ojos** (US$3.25-5.25, 40 minutes).

Most Chetumal-bound buses stop in **Bacalar** (US$10.50-17, 4 hours).

Most Cancún-bound buses stop at **Puerto Morelos** (US$1.75, 35 minutes), but *not* the airport or Cancún's Zona Hotelera.

Destination	Price	Duration	Schedule*
Cancún	US$2-4	1 hr	every 15-30 mins 12:15am-11:40pm
Cancún Int'l Airport	US$9.50	1.25 hrs	every 30-60 mins 3am-10:20pm
Chiquilá (Isla Holbox)	US$13	2.5 hrs	9:25am and 10:15am
Chetumal	US$9-23	4.5 hrs	every 60-90 mins 1:50am-11:58pm
Chichén Itzá	US$11	4 hrs	8am
Chiquilá (Isla Holbox)	US$13	3.5 hrs	9:25am, 10:15am, 10:25am
Cobá	US$5.50-8	2 hrs	9am and 10:30am
Mérida	US$15-30	4.5-5.5 hrs	every 60-90 mins 1:30am-11:59pm
Puerto Morelos	US$1.75	35 min	every 15-30 mins 12:15am-11:40pm
Tulum	US$1.75-5.50	1 hr	every 15-30 mins 1:30am-11:40pm
Valladolid	US$5.75-11	2.5 hrs	every 15-90 mins 1:30am-9:30pm
Xcaret (main entrance)	US$3.50-4	20 mins	8:30am, 9:40am, 9:50am

Bus

Playa del Carmen has two bus stations: **Terminal Turística** (aka Terminal Riviera, 5 Av. and Av. Juárez) is in the center of town and has frequent second-class service to destinations along the coast, including Cancún, Tulum, and everything in between; **Terminal Alterna** (Calle 20 between Calles 12 and 12 Bis) has first-class and deluxe service to interior destinations such as Mérida, Campeche, and beyond. There is some overlap, and you can buy tickets for any destination at either station, so always double-check from which station your bus departs.

Combi

Combis (shuttle vans) are an easy way to get up and down the Riviera Maya. In Playa, northbound *combis* line up on Calle 2 near 20 Avenida, with service 24 hours a day (every 10-15 minutes, US$2, 1 hour). For slightly more, **Playa Express** has larger, air-conditioned shuttles, departing from a lot on Calle 2 between 20 and 25 Avenidas (every 10-15 minutes, 24 hrs daily, US$2.25). The final destination of both services is Cancún's main bus terminal (50 minutes), but you can be dropped off anywhere along the highway, including Puerto Morelos (US$1.25, 30 minutes). *Combis* do not enter Cancún's Zona Hotelera, but you can catch a bus there from outside the terminal.

South from Playa del Carmen, ordinary *combis* leave from the same corner around the clock, going as far as the Carrillo Puerto bus station (US$4.50, 2 hours), passing the turnoffs for Puerto Aventuras (US$1.50, 10 minutes), Xpu-Há (US$1.75, 20 minutes), Akumal (US$2, 25 minutes), Tankah Tres (US$2.75, 45 minutes), Tulum Ruins (US$2.25, 50 minutes), and Tulum (US$2.75, 1 hour). To return, flag down a *combi* anywhere along the highway.

Car

If you are driving to Playa del Carmen, look for the two main access roads to the beach—Avenida Constituyentes on the north end of town and Avenida Benito Juárez on the south. Playacar has its own entrance from the highway but can also be reached by turning south on Calle 10 off Avenida Juárez.

Ferry

There are three passenger ferries to Cozumel (hourly, 7am-11pm daily, 30 minutes), all leaving from the pier at the end of Calle 1 Sur: **UltraMar** (www.ultramarferry.com, US$9.50 adult, US$6.75 child), **Mexico Water Jets** (tel. www.mexicowaterjets.com.mx, US$9.50 adult, US$5.25 child), and **Barcos Caribe** (www.barcoscaribe.com, US$8 adult, US$4 child). They have almost identical schedules, though UltraMar tends to have newer boats and Cozumel Express tends to be a bit cheaper. The ferry ticket booths are side by side at the foot of the pier, with the time of the next departure displayed prominently. The ticket seller will try to sell you a round-trip ticket, but there's no disadvantage to buying a *sencilla* (one-way ticket) and avoiding the risk of losing your return ticket.

Car ferries operated by **Transcaribe** (tel. 987/872-7688, www.transcaribe.net) depart from the Calica dock south of Playa at 4am, 8am, 1:30pm, and 6pm Monday; 8am, 1:30pm, and 6pm Tuesday-Saturday; and 7am, 11am, and 7:30pm on Sunday. Returning from Cozumel, the ferry leaves from the international pier at 6am, 11am, 4pm, and 8:30pm Monday-Saturday; and 9am, 5pm, and 9pm on Sunday. The trip takes about 1.25 hours and costs US$25 for a car including passengers. Reservations are strongly recommended.

GETTING AROUND

Playa del Carmen is a walking town, although the steady northward expansion is challenging that description. The commercial part of Quinta Avenida now stretches over 44 blocks and keeps getting longer. Bicycles are a great way to get around town—head to Calle 10, which has a bike lane. Cabs also are a good option, especially if you have luggage.

Bicycle

BiciPlaya II (30 Av. at Calle 20, tel. 984/147-0317, biciplaya2 @gmail.com, 9am-9pm Mon.-Sat., 10am-4pm Sun.) rents decent bikes by the day (US$5). Another good option is **Playa Encantada** (Calle 12 Bis at 20 Av., tel. 984/803-5602, 7am-9:30pm daily), which rents bicycles for US$10 per day, including lock. A US$25 deposit, or an ID, is required to rent at the latter.

Taxi

Taxis around town cost US$5-8, or a bit more if you use a taxi stand or have your hotel summon one. All taxi drivers carry a *tarifário*—an official fare schedule—which you can request to see if you think you're getting taken for a ride (no pun intended). Prices do change every year or two, so ask at your hotel what the current rate is, and always be sure to agree on the fare with the driver before setting off.

Car Rental

Playa has myriad car rental agencies, with prices starting around US$32 per day, including insurance. Local chain **Easy Way** (Av. 10 btwn Calles 2 and 4, toll-free Mex. tel. 800/327-9929, toll-free U.S./Can. tel. 877/640-3279, www.easywayrentacar.com) offers well-maintained cars and no-hassle service. Major international agencies like **Avis** (Fiesta Inn, 10 Av. between Calles 26 and 28, tel. 984/688-8154, www.avis.com) and **Hertz** (10 Av. at Calle 14, toll-free Mex. tel. 800/709-5000, www.hertz.com) also are reliable options and often have online specials.

Parking in Playa in the high season can be a challenge, especially south of Avenida Constituyentes. Many hotels have secure parking; there are also parking lots around town, including on Calle 2 at 10 Avenida (8am-10pm daily) and at Calle 14 Bis and 10 Avenida (8am-10pm daily), charging around US$1 per hour or US$12.50 per day.

PAAMUL

What started out as an unassuming trailer park on a beautiful stretch of beach has now become a seaside community all its own. Located about 20 kilometers (12.4 miles) south of Playa del Carmen, Paamul has everything from RVs with elaborate wood and *palapa* structures over them to hotel rooms, a restaurant, and even a dive shop.

Beach

Paamul stretches over a wide, curving beach. It's classically pretty with white sand and turquoise water, perfect for swimming and exploring. Watch your step on the south end of the beach, as its waters harbor prickly sea urchin—consider wearing water shoes.

Snorkeling and Scuba Diving

Scuba-Mex Dive Center (Hwy. 307 Km 85, tel. 984/807-7866, toll-free U.S. tel. 888/871-6255, www.scubamex.com, 8am-5pm daily) is a full-service shop offering fun dives, dive packages, and dive courses at good prices; cenote dives require reservations. If you're just interested in snorkeling off the beach, the shop also rents snorkel gear.

THE RIVIERA MAYA
PLAYA DEL CARMEN

Paamul's beach

Food

The only eatery in Paamul, **Reefs of Paamul Restaurant and Bar** (Hwy. 307 Km 85, tel. 984/875-1050, 8am-8pm daily, US$6-18) is open-air, modern, and has great views of the Caribbean. It serves up classic Mexican dishes along with a variety of international meals—there's something for everyone. It's a solid option (despite being the only option!).

For groceries, the very mini **Mini Super Paamul** (7am-8pm Mon.-Sat., 7am-2pm Sun.) sells basic foodstuffs. It's located at the highway turnoff to Paamul.

Accommodations

Sitting on a gorgeous bay all its own is **Paamul Hotel & Cabañas** (Hwy. 307 Km 85, tel. 984/875-1050, U.S. tel. 612/597-0888, www.paamul.com, US$12 pp camping, US$50 s/d RVs, US$195 s/d with a/c). From classy hotel rooms to well-kempt campsites, it appeals to travelers of all budgets. The hotel rooms are simple and elegant with features like mini fridges and microwaves, quiet air-conditioning, Wi-Fi, and ocean views from private terraces. The tent and trailer spaces are just steps from the Caribbean, have electricity and running water, and share clean hot-water bathrooms. A true find and a perfect getaway, especially considering the on-site restaurant and dive shop.

Information and Services

There are no health, banking, postal, or laundry services in Paamul. The closest town for a full range of services is Playa del Carmen, 20 kilometers (12.4 miles) north.

Puerto Aventuras

Puerto Aventuras is an odd conglomeration of condos, summer homes, and hotels with a marina that's home to a swim-with-dolphins program as well as several restaurants and bars. It's more than a resort but not really a town. Whatever you call it, Puerto Aventuras's huge signs and gated entrance are impossible to miss, located a few minutes north of Akumal on Highway 307.

SPORTS AND RECREATION

Swimming with Dolphins

Dolphin Discovery (Marina, tel. 984/873-5078, toll-free U.S. tel. 866/393-5158, www.dolphindiscovery.com, 9am-5pm daily) offers several dolphin encounter activities; prices vary according to the duration and degree of interaction (US$99-169 adult, US$89 child). The center also has a manatee program (US$59 adult/child) that can be combined with dolphin activities. Programs start at 9am, 11am, 1pm, and 3pm daily; round-trip shuttle service is available to/from area hotels for US$10 per person.

Snorkeling and Scuba Diving

Some 25 dive sites lie within a 10-minute boat ride from town, each boasting rich coral, abundant sealife, and interesting features such as pillars and swimthroughs.

Aquanauts (Bldg. A, tel. 984/873-5041, toll-free U.S./Can. tel. 877/623-2491, www.aquanautsdiveshop.com, 8am-5pm Mon.-Sat.) is a full-service shop that enjoys lots of repeat guests. The shop offers the full range of dives and courses, including reef dives (US$71/one tank, US$132/two tanks) and cenote dives (US$100/one tank, US$140/two tanks); equipment rental, other than tanks and weights, not included. The shop also offers snorkel tours, including one with a stop at the Tulum ruins (US$60-100).

Another great option is **Planet Scuba** (Calle Bahía Xcacel s/n, cell tel. 984/182-0227, www.planetscubamexico.com, 8am-6pm daily), which offers specialized cavern (US$150-250/two tanks), cave (US$250/two tanks), and tech (300/two tanks) dives. Reef dives (including with bull sharks) and a full line of certification courses are also offered.

Sportfishing

Captain Rick's Sportfishing Center (past Omni Puerto Aventuras Beach Resort, tel. 984/873-5195, toll-free U.S. tel. 888/449-3562, www.fishyucatan.com, office 8am-6pm daily) offers customized trips—trolling, drift fishing, and fly-fishing—utilizing a fleet of a dozen boats, including a 48-foot yacht with room for up to 12 people. You can also arrange time for visiting a deserted beach or Maya ruin, snorkeling on the reef, or just cruising by upscale homes and hotels. Rates are for half day (US$450-695), three-quarter day (US$580-850), and full day (US$690-1,050).

Sailing

Fat Cat (Bldg. E, cell tel. 984/116-3040, www.fatcatsail.com, 8:30am-5pm Mon.-Sat.) offers a spacious, custom-designed catamaran used for half-day excursions (US$110 adult, US$78 child 3-11) that include sailing north toward Bahia Ihna or south toward Xpu-Há—both with good snorkeling in shallow and protected waters. Daily trips leave at 9:30am and 2pm; all include a box lunch.

Golf

Puerto Aventuras Club de Golf (across from Bldg. B, tel. 984/873-5109, 7am-dusk daily, US$62 for 18 holes, US$54-57 for 9 holes) offers a nine-hole, par-36 golf course right in town. The course, designed in 1991 by Tom Lehman, is flat but has two par 5s over a total 2,961 yards (3,255 championship).

FOOD

Buzzing with expats, **Paparazzi** (Bldg. F, tel. 984/873-5651, 8am-5pm daily, US$5-11) is a small Italian restaurant with a whopping menu of pastas, salads, and panini. The main attraction, though, is the thin-crust pizza, made in a brick oven, and topped with all manner of yummy goodness—everything from mussels to Nutella. Come early for a seat or take your pie to go.

Café Olé in Puerto Aventuras (Bldg. A, tel. 984/873-5125, 8am-10pm daily, US$7-22) has an extensive international menu with something for just about everyone. It's best known, though, for its filet mignon and homemade desserts like coconut cream pie and dulce de leche cheesecake. A welcoming place, there's karaoke on Tuesday and Thursday nights and live music (by professionals) every night starting at 7pm.

★ **Taquería El Arbolito** (Hwy 307 Km 270, no tel., 5:30am-3pm daily, US$2-4) is a popular roadside eatery selling mouthwatering tacos stuffed with your choice of over 35 different takes on eggs, chicken, beef, pork, vegetables, and seafood. Order your meal cafeteria-style, make a pit stop at the fixins' bar, and join other diners at plastic communal tables. Look for it on the west side of the highway (or just follow your nose).

If you're cooking for yourself or just want some fresh fruit, check out the outdoor **fruit and vegetable market** (8am-5pm), which is held every Wednesday and Saturday next to the town's kiosk.

Located across from the Omni hotel, **OXXO** (9am-9pm Mon.-Sat., 9am-1pm Sun.) is a convenience store with basic foodstuffs. For serious shopping—and better prices—head to the mega-store **Chedraui** (tel. 984/802-8773, 7am-10pm daily), located directly across Highway 307 from the Puerto Aventuras entrance.

ACCOMMODATIONS

The road into town bumps right into **Omni Puerto Aventuras Beach Resort** (tel. 984/875-1950, toll-free U.S. tel. 888/444-6664, www.omnihotels.com, US$180-270 s/d with a/c), a small resort with the marina on one side and a fine, palm-shaded beach on the other. There are just 30 rooms, all spacious with colorful regional décor, private patios, and hot

CEDAM and the Riviera Maya

Maya artifacts have been found in cenotes, probably thrown in as offerings to the gods.

In 1948, a small group of Mexican divers—active frogmen during World War II—created a nonprofit organization called Club de Exploración y Deporte Acuáticos de México (Exploration and Aquatic Sports Club of Mexico, or CEDAM). Their mission was to promote ocean conservation and educate others about the sea's treasures and resources.

In 1958, the group set about salvaging the *Mantanceros*, a Spanish galleon that foundered offshore in 1741. It set up camp in present-day Akumal, then just an uninhabited beach owned by a man named Argimiro Arguelles. Arguelles leased CEDAM an old work boat for their project, the SS *Cozumel*, and worked as its captain.

It was this relationship that sealed Akumal's—and arguably, the Riviera Maya's—destiny. Sitting around the campfire one night, Arguelles sold Pablo Bush Romero, one of CEDAM's founders, the bay of Akumal and thousands of acres of coconut palms north and south of it. For the next 12 years, CEDAM continued its work in the rustic and beautiful place—replacing its tents with sturdy *palapa* huts, and using the creaky SS *Cozumel* to carry divers to work sites along the coast.

It wasn't long before the idea of promoting tourism on Mexico's forgotten Caribbean coast arose. In 1968, the group—which had changed the words behind its initials to Conservation, Ecology, Diving, Archaeology, and Museums—donated 5,000 acres of land to the government, including the Cove of Xel-Há, to create a national park. The aim was to open the isolated area to tourists and, in so doing, create jobs for local residents. CEDAM also provided housing, food, electricity, running water, a school for the children, and a first-aid station with a trained nurse.

Based in Akumal for many years, CEDAM grew into an important scientific and conservation organization. It played an active role in the archaeological exploration of the region's cenotes and ocean. The group is no longer in existence, but a small museum in Puerto Aventuras—**Museo Sub-Acuático CEDAM** (Bldg F, no tel.)—showcases CEDAM's work and findings. It was temporarily closed when we passed through, but hopefully, will reopen soon.

tubs; ocean-view rooms are particularly nice. The resort's small size and low-key atmosphere make it easy to meet other guests, and night-time typically finds everyone around the main hot tub/beach bar overlooking the ocean.

Casa del Agua (Punta Matzoma 21, tel. 984/873-5184, www.casadelagua.com, US$262-750 pp) is a beacon of class and charm amid the cookie-cutter commercialism of Puerto Aventuras. What looks like a private home is actually a boutique hotel with a handful of spacious suites. Each has elegant decor, a king-size bed, and luxurious bathrooms and amenities. There is a small sunny pool and private beach as well as complimentary kayaks and snorkeling gear. Daily maid service and a private chef are included in the rate. The per night rate is based on private use of the entire villa (maximum 8 guests). There's a seven-night minimum during Thanksgiving, Christmas/New Year's, and Easter, and a three-night minimum most of the rest of the year.

INFORMATION AND SERVICES

Tourist Information

On the main drag, **Puerto Aventuras Activity Center** (Bahía Xcacel s/n, tel. 984/802-9047, puertoaventurasactivitycenter@gmail.com, 9am-3pm and 5pm-7pm Mon.-Sat., 9am-1pm Sun.) offers tourist information on area sites; most staffers speak English. The lounge has free Wi-Fi.

The town website—www.puertoaventuras.com—also is a good source of information.

Emergency Services

There is one pharmacy in town: **Emergency** **911 Pharmacy** (Bldg. A, tel. 984/873-5305, 8am-10pm daily, or by telephone 24 hours). Delivery is available.

Money

Puerto Aventuras doesn't have a bank, but there's a **Banamex ATM** in the Omni hotel.

Media and Communications

The **post office** (11am-2:30am Mon.-Thurs.) is in a large kiosk a short distance from the golf club entrance.

The tourist information office, **Puerto Aventuras Activity Center** (Bahía Xcacel s/n, tel. 984/802-9047, puertoaventurasactivitycenter@gmail.com, 9am-3pm and 5pm-7pm Mon.-Sat., 9am-1pm Sun.), has free Wi-Fi in its lounge. Most hotels and condos also offer Wi-Fi to guests.

GETTING THERE AND AROUND

Arriving by public transportation, you can take a *combi* from Cancún, Playa del Carmen, or Tulum. Let the driver know where you're going, and he'll drop you off on the side of the highway. From there, it's 500 meters (0.3 mile) into town. Arriving by car, you'll pass through a large control gate, but no one who looks like a tourist is stopped.

You can walk to virtually all restaurants and shops in Puerto Aventuras because they're centered on the main marina. To explore the complex and its beaches a bit more, **Puerto Aventuras Activity Center** (Bahía Xcacel s/n, tel. 984/802-9047, puertoaventurasactivitycenter@gmail.com, 9am-3pm and 5pm-7pm Mon.-Sat., 9am-1pm Sun.) rents golf carts (US$10/hr, US$40/day).

Xpu-Há

This long, picturesque beach has clusters of development on either end and a couple of small hotels and beach clubs in between. It seems only a matter of time before the owners of this enviable stretch of sand give their blessing to a megaresort, but for now it's a gorgeous and peaceful spot where you could easily while away the whole day, or several.

SPORTS AND RECREATION
Beach Clubs

La Playa Xpu-Há (Hwy. 307 Km 264, tel. 984/133-6701, www.laplayaxpuha.com, 10am-7pm Mon.-Wed., 10am-10pm Thurs.-Sun.) is a bustling club with a few rows of lounge chairs and *palapa* shade. There's a full-service restaurant and bar (stick to finger food and beer). On weekends and holidays, there's a US$5 per person "toll" at the entrance, charged by the landowner for upkeep of the access road. You get it back, though, as a credit on restaurant bills over US$10. There's live music on weekends.

Just down the beach, **KSM Beach Club** (Hwy. 307 Km 264, tel. 984/140-2339, 9am-8pm Sun.-Thurs., 9am-2am Fri.-Sat.) has a hipper vibe with more areas to chill out, away from the scene. There's also a hut renting snorkeling gear, kayaks, and paddleboards, and it offers kiteboarding and windsurfing instruction too. A *palapa*-roofed restaurant is a good option for eats and drinks. There's also plenty of parking—though, like La Playa Xpu-Há, there's a US$5 "toll" at the entrance. To get here, look for a narrow dirt road with a small sign, just south of the Catalonia Royal Tulum resort.

Scuba Diving

Bahía Divers (Hwy. 307 Km 265, cell tel. 984/156-9898, www.bahiadivers.com, 8am-4pm Mon.-Sat.) operates out of a collection of huts a short distance down the beach from La Playa Xpu-Há beach club. It offers the full gamut of ocean and cenote dives, plus certification courses, all with the advantage of small groups (6 divers maximum) and personalized service. They also provide transport to and from your hotel, which is very handy. Ocean dives cost US$90 for two tanks, while cenote diving runs US$120 for two tanks, all including gear.

Snorkeling

In addition to the ocean reef, there's great snorkeling in the numerous cenotes along the inland side of Highway 307, including a cluster just north of Xpu-Há. They vary in size, but most are like large ponds, some with high or overhanging limestone walls, and all filled with cool crystalline water—heaven on a hot day. The cenote floor is often a jumble of stone slabs and in places quite deep—some even have gaping underwater caves that descend out of sight. The cenotes near Xpu-Há are not, however, the huge stalactite-laden caverns you may have seen in photos; for those, head south to Dos Ojos cenote parks, near Tulum.

Half-moon-shaped **Cenote Cristalino** (Hwy. 307, 2 kilometers/1.2 miles north of Xpu-Há, 8am-6pm daily, US$4 adult, US$2.50 child, no rental gear available), much of which is shallow and covered in algae, has a unique section that extends under a deep, overhanging rock ceiling.

Jardín del Edén (formerly Ponderosa Cenote, Hwy. 307, 1.75 kilometers/1 mile north of Xpu-Há, 9am-6pm daily, US$6 adult, US$3.50 child, US$4 mask and snorkel, US$4 life vest) is much larger than most cenotes—almost like a small lake—with a craggy floor that makes for fun snorkeling. At one end, the floor falls away into a deep underwater cave, where you can see divers emerging—or disappearing—into the abyss, their halogen lights piercing the shadows. A six-meter (19.7-foot) cliff is fun to jump off; just be alert for divers who may be coming up. Between cave-diving classes, snorkeling groups, and independent travelers, Jardín del Edén can get busy but is generally big enough to make a stop here worthwhile.

Cenote Azul (Hwy. 307, 1.5 kilometers/0.9 mile north of Xpu-Há, 8:30am-5:30pm daily, US$5 adult, US$2.50 child) is made up of three refreshing pools with teal waters: two small ones toward the front that are teeming with tiny fish and surrounded by thin leafy trees, and one large pool with a section of overhanging rock (great for jumping off of) and walkways along the edges for exploring or easing into or out of the cenote. Snorkel gear rentals also are available (US$2.50 mask and snorkel, US$2.50 life vest).

Kiteboarding and Stand-Up Paddling

A small hut on the beach, **KSM Kiteboarding & Paddle Surfing Center** (Hwy. 307 Km 264, tel. 984/140-2339, 9am-5pm daily) offers kitesurfing instruction to all levels of students (US$80-500, 1-9 hours). Classes include KSM Beach Club entrance fee, and all equipment. The shop also rents stand-up paddleboards (US$25 per hour), kayaks (US$20-25 per hour), and snorkel gear (US$15 per hour).

FOOD AND ACCOMMODATIONS

Hotel Esencia (Hwy. 307 Km 265, tel. 984/873-48350, www.hotelesencia.com, US$700 s/d with a/c, US$777-1,544 suite, US$2,395 2-bedroom villa with pool) is a luxurious private estate turned resort. It boasts 38 gorgeous units, including classy garden-view rooms (some with private plunge pools), larger ocean-view suites, and a stunning split-level villa with a private swimming pool. The beach is just steps away and stretches, virtually untouched, for over a mile. Meal plans are available at the hotel's three gourmet restaurants and beach bar, plus there's a full-service spa and health club on-site. Service, as expected, is impeccable.

Set on a tropical plot near the beach, **Serenity Eco-Luxury Camp** (Hwy. 307 Km 264, tel. 984/803-3980, toll-free U.S./Mex. tel. 800/960-7019, https://en.serenitycamp.com, US$205-255 s/d with a/c) is all about glamping: spacious and sturdy tents with wood floors, real beds, nice linens, electricity, air-conditioning, and private bathrooms (yes, even running water); some even have patios with whirlpool tubs. All to say, these are nice hotel rooms with soft walls. The "camp" itself has a u-shaped pool with a Buddha facade, a cozy fire pit, a restaurant, and a path leading to its beach club, about a five-minute walk away. Check the website for discounts and bring bug repellent.

KSM Beach Club (Hwy. 307 Km 264, tel. 984/140-2339, 9am-8pm Sun.-Thurs., 9am-2am Fri.-Sat., US$5-14) has a relaxed restaurant-bar with a high *palapa* roof, sand floor, tree trunks for chairs, and a bar with swing-style seats. The food is solid—mostly tacos, empanadas, seafood, salads, and nibblers like nachos and fries. The bar, as expected, is fully loaded, though at US$3, the *chelas* (a combo of beer, lime juice, and hot spices) are tough to pass up.

INFORMATION AND SERVICES

There are no services in Xpu-Há, save what's available to guests at the hotels. For laundry, an ATM, and other services, head to Akumal or Puerto Aventuras.

GETTING THERE AND AROUND

Each of the listings for Xpu-Há has its own access road, marked with large or small signs, and located at or near Kilometer 265 on the main coastal highway (Hwy. 307). Catalonia Royal Tulum resort is the largest and most obvious landmark; the other access roads are within a few hundred yards. La Playa and KSM Beach Clubs, at the southern end of the beach, are the best access points if you're only staying the day, and are located 25 kilometers (15.5 miles) south of Playa.

Akumal

Unreachable by land until the 1960s, Akumal (Yucatec Maya for Place of the Turtle) is a quiet destination community that has developed on two bays, known as Akumal Bay and Half Moon Bay. It's a very agreeable midrange place with dozens of condominiums and rental homes. The beach in town is quite nice, if you don't mind the boats parked on the sand and paying a small fee to access it; the beach at Half Moon Bay is long and curving with soft white sand, though it's narrow in places. Just offshore, a spectacular portion of barrier reef makes for great diving and snorkeling, and protects Akumal's bays from heavy surf.

A short distance south of Akumal proper is **Aventuras Akumal,** another small bayside development. It doesn't have the town-like feel or activity that Akumal does, but a good condo-hotel and a truly gorgeous beach make this a tempting alternative. Aventuras Akumal has a separate access road from the highway, and walking there along the beach takes about 45 minutes.

SIGHTS AND BEACHES
Beaches
Akumal Bay—the one right in front of town—has a slow-curving shoreline, with soft sand shaded by palm trees. It's a beautiful beach and a turtle habitat, both for feeding and nesting. In 2016, the bay was declared a marine conservation area in order to protect the turtles from the growing number of visitors. The results have been mixed. Once an easily accessible beach and great place for snorkeling, public access now costs US$5—the only way around this is staying at one of the beachfront hotels or cutting through a dive shop. Beachgoers are only allowed to snorkel as part of a guided tour (you can, however, walk south a bit and snorkel on your own). Needless to say, the chain-link fences, throngs of guides pushing snorkeling tours, and guards watching over the water has dampened a day at this beach. It hard to argue with all of these changes, though, since it's about protecting and saving sea turtles.

Down the road, **Half Moon Bay** is a much more relaxed and typical beachgoing experience. It's a long and wide bay that's nice for swimming and snorkeling with a white-sand beach to match. Turtles are spotted swimming here too (and snorkeling is unrestricted!). It can be rocky underfoot in some places, though—water shoes come in handy.

★ Laguna Yal-Ku
At the mouth of an elbow-shaped lagoon at the north end of Akumal, an endless upwelling of underground river water collides with the tireless flow of seawater. The result is a great place to snorkel, teeming with fish and plants adapted to this unique hybrid environment. Once a secret snorkelers' getaway, **Laguna Yal-Ku** (tel. 984/875-9065, 9am-5pm daily, US$14 adult, US$10 child 4-12, free 3 and under, US$5 apiece for mask, fins, and life vest, US$3 locker) now has a spot in every guidebook and tour group itinerary—come before 10am or anytime on Sunday for the least traffic. That, and a shot at snagging a private picnic area (US$20), complete with *palapa* shade, a table, and chairs. Use a T-shirt or wetsuit instead of sunscreen, as even the biodegradable kind can collect on plants and coral. The lagoon is dotted with 34 intriguing bronze sculptures by Mexican artist Alejandro Echeverría.

Centro Ecológico Akumal
Facing the town basketball court, **Centro Ecológico Akumal** (CEA, Plaza Ukana, tel. 984/875-9095, www.ceakumal.org, 9am-1pm and 2pm-6pm Mon.-Fri.) is a nonprofit founded in 1993 to monitor the health of Akumal's ecosystems, particularly those related to coral and sea turtles. May through October, CEA operates monthlong

volunteer projects on reef monitoring, sea turtle monitoring, and environmental education. Volunteers stay in the center's dorms, with kitchen and Internet access; the minimum age is 21, and some fees are required. See the website for details.

Aktun Chen

Yucatec Maya for "Cave with an Underground River," **Aktun Chen** (Hwy. 307 Km 107, tel. 984/806-4962, toll-free Mex. tel. 800/099-0875, www.aktun-chen.com, 9:30am-5:30pm daily, last tour 1 hour before closing, US$29-106 adult, US$23-85 child) is certainly that, plus a cenote for swimming and snorkeling, and a canopy/zip line route. You can do all three activities, or just the ones that interest you. The cave tour is a walk of about 0.6 kilometer (0.3 mile) amid a breathtaking array of stalactites and stalagmites; at the end is a 12-meter-deep (39-foot) cenote filled with crystalline water. Lighting and a pathway make it accessible to all. You can't swim in that cenote, but there's another nearby, with stairs and platforms for getting in and out. Lastly, the canopy tour is made up of 10 zip lines and two wobbly suspension bridges, covering a full kilometer (0.6 mile). Between activities, check out the park's small "zoo," with spider monkeys, toucans, and more.

Tours are offered in English and Spanish and last about 90 minutes. Look for the turn-off just across from Aventuras Akumal, and continue three kilometers (1.9 miles) to the entrance. Mosquito repellent and a bottle of water are recommended. You'll encounter the least crowding before 11am and on weekends.

SHOPPING

MexicArte (tel. 984/875-9115, www.mexicarte.shop, 8am-9pm daily) is the small, bright pink shop just inside the arch on your right. The owner hand-selects the best folk art from around the region and country. Prices are high, but so is the quality and artisanship.

Galería Lamanai (tel. 984/875-9055, 8am-9pm daily) offers similar wares, both in quality and price. The shop is located on the beach near Snack Bar Lol Ha.

There is an open-air *artesanía* market (8am-6pm daily) behind Plaza Ukana, facing the town basketball court. The items are standard Mexican handicrafts, such as colorful ceramics from Puebla and textiles from Chiapas.

Laguna Yal-Ku is a snorkeling favorite.

Akumal

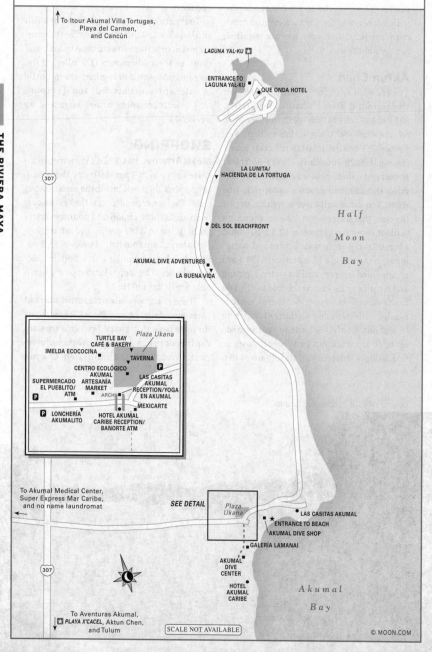

To Itour Akumal Villa Tortugas,
Playa del Carmen,
and Cancún

LAGUNA YAL-KU

ENTRANCE TO
LAGUNA YAL-KU

QUE ONDA HOTEL

LA LUNITA/
HACIENDA DE LA TORTUGA

DEL SOL BEACHFRONT

Half
Moon
Bay

AKUMAL DIVE ADVENTURES

LA BUENA VIDA

307

Plaza Ukana

TURTLE BAY
CAFÉ & BAKERY

IMELDA ECOCOCINA

TAVERNA

CENTRO ECOLÓGICO
AKUMAL

LAS CASITAS
AKUMAL
RECEPTION/YOGA
EN AKUMAL

SUPERMERCADO
EL PUEBLITO/
ATM

AKUMAL ARTESANÍA
MARKET

ARCH

MEXICARTE

LONCHERÍA
AKUMALITO

HOTEL AKUMAL
CARIBE RECEPTION/
BANORTE ATM

To Akumal Medical Center,
Super Express Mar Caribe,
and no name laundromat

SEE DETAIL

Plaza
Ukana

LAS CASITAS AKUMAL

ENTRANCE TO BEACH

AKUMAL DIVE SHOP

GALERÍA LAMANAI

AKUMAL
DIVE
CENTER

HOTEL
AKUMAL
CARIBE

Akumal
Bay

307

To Aventuras Akumal,
PLAYA X'CACEL, Aktun Chen,
and Tulum

SCALE NOT AVAILABLE

© MOON.COM

SPORTS AND RECREATION
Scuba Diving

Some of the Riviera Maya's first scuba divers waded into the waves right here at Akumal Bay, and the area has been special to the sport ever since. Akumal's diving is easy and fun, with a mellow current and moderate depths; few profiles go below 20 meters (66 feet). The reef here is predominantly boulder coral, which isn't as picturesque as other types, but it still teems with tropical fish and plant life.

Founded more than 30 years ago, **Akumal Dive Shop** (Akumal Bay, tel. 984/875-9032, toll-free Mex. tel. 800/462-1212, www.akumaldiveshop.com, 8am-5pm daily) was one of the first dive shops in the Riviera Maya. Still located on the beach, the shop offers fun dives and various certification courses in both open-water and cave/cavern diving. Divers can take one- or two-tank reef dives (US$53/100) or cavern dives (US$75-120), or buy dive packages. Note: Fun dives don't include equipment rental. Just down the beach, **Akumal Dive Center** (tel. 984/875-9025, www.akumaldivecenter.com, 8am-5pm) offers the same dives and courses for slightly less.

On Half Moon Bay, **Akumal Dive Adventures** (next to La Buena Vida restaurant, tel. 984/875-9157, www.akumaldiveadventures.com, 8am-5pm daily) offers somewhat lower prices than the other shops (US$40/70 one tank/two tanks) as well as dive and accommodation packages at Del Sol Beachfront hotel next door.

Snorkeling

Snorkeling in **Akumal Bay** offers a great opportunity to see turtles in their natural habitat. The increased number of visitors to this beach, however, led to the adoption of new regulations to protect these creatures, including requiring that all snorkelers be part of an organized tour. Trips are limited to 45 minutes, following a loop outlined by buoys that start from shore. The cost is US$25-50, depending on the outfit (i.e., independent guide vs. tour operator); all include snorkel gear and life vests. Independent guides typically stand near the entrance to the beach but also walk the shores, hawking their services. Note: Snorkeling is prohibited in February and September, which mark the beginning of the turtle nesting and hatching seasons, respectively.

Laguna Yal-Ku (tel. 984/875-9156, caleta_yalku@hotmail.com, 9am-5pm daily, US$14 adult, US$5 child 4-12, free 3 and under, US$5 apiece for mask, fins, and life vest, US$3 locker) is a favorite among many snorkelers for its large area, calm water, and unique mix of fresh- and saltwater ecosystems.

The dive shops also offer **snorkel tours** in the area, which typically last 60-90 minutes. Those along the reef run US$40-50 per person while cenote tours start at US$70 per person.

You also can **rent snorkel gear** at any of Akumal's dive shops for US$14 per day and head out on your own in Half Moon Bay, which has plentiful fish and a decent chance of seeing sea turtles. If you've rented a car, cenote-hopping is another good way to spend the day.

Sailing

Akumal Dive Shop (Akumal Bay, tel. 984/875-9032, toll-free Mex. tel. 800/462-1212, www.akumaldiveshop.com, 8am-5pm daily) offers a popular "Robinson Crusoe" cruise: a five-hour excursion on a catamaran sailboat, with stops for fishing and snorkeling (US$111 adult, US$52 child including lunch and gear). Or try the two-hour Sunset Cruise, which doesn't include snorkeling or fishing, but offers beautiful evening views of the bay (US$53 pp).

Sportfishing

Akumal's dive shops also offer fishing tours year-round. The price, duration, and group size vary considerably based on the season, type of fishing, and boat. That said, expect to pay US$250-300 for a three-hour tour with 2-6 anglers; gear, bait, and license are included. Fishing is excellent year-round, but

April-August are when sailfish and marlin are most prevalent.

Yoga

Yoga en Akumal (town arch, 2nd Fl., tel. 984/876-2652, www.facebook.com/pg/YogaEnAkumal) offers a variety of hatha classes for all experience levels in a breezy studio inside the arch at the entrance to town. Sessions are led by certified instructors; they cost US$15 per class, US$45 for four classes, or US$100 for an unlimited month pass; check Facebook for the monthly schedule.

FOOD
In Town

★ **Taverna** (Plaza Ukana, tel. 984/875-9009, www.tavernabylombardi.com, noon-10pm daily, US$7-15) is a high-end Italian restaurant set in a two-story *palapa* with tables inside and out. The menu features a full line of homemade pasta dishes, wood-fired pizza, and fresh seafood. Start with an order of avocado fries—slices of fresh avocado, breaded and fried, that's an unexpected treat. Craft beers and top-shelf cocktails are also on offer (happy hour is 3pm-5pm daily). There's live music most nights starting at 7pm.

Turtle Bay Café & Bakery (Plaza Ukana, tel. 984/875-9138, www.turtlebaycafe.com, 7am-10pm daily, US$6-19) offers creative comfort food like crab cakes, seafood-stuffed chiles rellenos, and "Black and Bleu" salad. For breakfast, try the famous sticky buns and eggs Benedict. Enjoy your meal surrounded by palm trees, either in the outdoor *palapa*-roofed dining room or on the porch of the main building. Free Wi-Fi is available.

Just outside of the town arch, ★ **Lonchería Akumalito** (no tel., 7am-9pm daily, US$3-5) is a no-frills Mexican eatery serving everything from pancakes and eggs to hamburgers and enchiladas. Order a fresh *agua* (fruit drink) or smoothie to go with your meal. Seating is at a few outdoor tables with a view of the road. Service is blazing fast. Cash only.

For a fresh, healthy meal, try **Imelda Ecococina** (no phone, 8am-5pm Mon.-Sat., US$4-7). Breakfast options include eggs, omelets, pancakes, and French toast. For lunch, the *comida corrida* (lunch special) comes with a choice of main plate and a side dish or two. Look for it near the town basketball court.

For groceries, the best prices are across from the Akumal turnoff on Highway 307 in **Super Express Mar Caribe** (Av. Gonzalo Guerrero, 7am-11pm daily); look for the store about 100 meters (328 feet) west of the highway. Otherwise, just outside the arch, **Supermercado El Pueblito** (7am-9pm daily) is a pricey market selling basic foodstuffs plus sunscreen and bug repellent. Both markets sell fresh fruit and veggies too, but you may find a better selection at the **farmers market** held Wednesday and Saturday in Plaza Ukana.

Half Moon Bay

A skeleton of a flying serpent greets diners at **La Buena Vida** (beachfront, tel. 984/875-9061, http://labuenavidarestaurant.com, 8am-11pm daily, US$5-15), where clients enjoy the varied menu—from French toast to shrimp ceviche—under *palapa*-shaded tables on the beach. If you've already had a meal, stop in for a drink at the swing-lined bar; happy hour runs 5pm-6pm.

★ **La Lunita Restaurant** (Hacienda de la Tortuga, tel. 984/875-9070, lalunita@prodigy.net.mx, 1:30pm-11pm daily, US$14-26) is an intimate bistro serving gourmet Mexican and international dishes, both small plates or full entrées. Seafood is king here, though there are plenty of options for vegetarians and serious meat eaters. With only a handful of tables, some overlooking the Caribbean, La Lunita is a perfect place for a romantic dinner—just be sure to make reservations.

Aventuras Akumal

★ **Beached Bikini Bar and Grill** (beachfront, tel. 998/845-4528, www.beachedbikini.com, 11am-last person leaves, US$6-14) is a classic chilled-out beach joint with swing seats at the bar, plastic tables on the beach, and palm tree shade. It's a friendly, jocular place where everyone is treated like a regular. Stick to the basics—nachos, burgers, and ceviche—and you won't be disappointed. Order a mango jalapeño margarita to wash it all down.

ACCOMMODATIONS

Akumal draws many long-term visitors and has a large number of fully equipped condos and villas, in addition to ordinary hotels.

In Town

Hotel Akumal Caribe (reception in the arch at the entrance to town, tel. 984/875-9012, www.hotelakumalcaribe.com, US$189 s/d bungalow, US$215 s/d with a/c, US$230 s/d with a/c and kitchenette) is the oldest hotel in town, and the bungalows show it in their bamboo furnishings and floral prints. Hotel rooms, however, have been updated and feature amenities like sleek espresso furnishings, stainless steel mini fridges, and mini-split air conditioners. They also have balconies with ocean views. The property fronts the town's gorgeous palm tree-laden main beach, plus there's a great pool with a small waterfall. Continental breakfast is included in the rate.

On the eastern end of town, ★ **Las Casitas Akumal** (tel. 984/875-9071, toll-free U.S./Can. tel. 800/525-8625, www.lascasitasakumal.com, US$351-398 2-bedroom condo with a/c) has 18 airy condominiums, each with two bedrooms, two baths, a living room, fully equipped kitchen, and private patio. Some have two floors and space for six people, and most feature bright, colorful Mexican artwork. All have ocean views and direct access to a semiprivate section of the beach. There's a five-night minimum in the high season.

Half Moon Bay

Del Sol Beachfront (tel. 984/875-9060, toll-free U.S. tel. 888/425-8625, www.akumalinfo.com, US$101-118 s/d with a/c, US$160-252 studio to 3-bedroom condo with a/c) has 16 spacious condos plus 15 smallish hotel rooms, all overlooking a lovely stretch of beach. Condos are decorated in colorful Mexican décor and have long balconies or porches, fully equipped kitchens, separate living and dining rooms, and master bedrooms with king-size beds. Some have whirlpool tubs too. Hotel rooms are comfortable but may feel a bit cramped for longer stays. All units have daily maid service and share a well-tended beach with lounge chairs and *palapa* shades. All that, plus a beachfront pool.

★ **Hacienda de la Tortuga** (tel. 984/875-9068, www.haciendatortuga.com, US$178 1-bedroom condo, US$238 2-bedroom condo) has just 16 units and cultivates a quiet, relaxed atmosphere geared toward couples. Roomy one-bedroom and two-bedroom condos all have huge ocean-view windows, plus a living room, kitchen, king-size bed(s), and air-conditioning in the bedrooms. Each is uniquely decorated, many with fine Mexican artwork and homey touches like a well-stocked bookcase. There's a small pool just steps from the beach, and a well-regarded Mexican restaurant, La Lunita, on-site.

Just a block from Laguna Yal-Ku, **Que Onda Hotel** (tel. 984/875-9101, maribel.ondarte@gmail.com, US$90-105 s/d with a/c, US$180-220 suite) has seven rooms, each lovingly decorated with beautiful fabrics and unique works of art. Two suites are similar in style, can accommodate up to six guests, and include terrific upper-floor views of the Caribbean and Yal-Ku. All face a verdant garden with a pool. The on-site restaurant can get a bit busy, but fortunately it stops receiving guests at 10pm. Use of snorkel gear is included in the rate.

Aventuras Akumal

Villa Las Brisas (tel. 984/875-9263, www.aventuras-akumal.com, US$100 s/d, US$75 studio with A/C, US$150 1-bedroom condo, US$200 2-bedroom condo) has just three units, two of which can be combined to make a two-bedroom condo. All are spacious, spotless, and meticulously furnished, down to a stocked spice rack in the kitchen. The condos have large terraces with hammocks and stunning views; the smaller units have balconies that overlook a tidy garden. With comfortable beds, modern Mexican-style furnishings, and space to stretch out, it's easy to feel at home here. Snorkel gear and kayaks are included in the rate. There's a simple minimart at the entrance (8am-4pm Mon.-Sat.), but you'll have to go to Akumal for additional shopping and services. There is free Wi-Fi throughout but only the studio has air-conditioning.

A small all-inclusive resort, **Akumal Bay Beach & Wellness Resort** (Hwy 307 Km 254, www.akumalbayresort.com, US$274-327 pp all-inclusive) sits on a gorgeous stretch of beach, within easy walking distance of Akumal proper. The restaurant options include an international buffet and à la carte restaurants serving Japanese, Brazilian, and Mexican fare. Rooms are a bit stark in décor but are modern and comfortable and have with stocked mini fridges; daily turndown service is a nice touch. Best of all are the activities: yoga, meditation, core energetics, snorkeling tours, and free use of standup paddleboards, kayaks, bikes, and tennis courts. There's also an on-site spa and a gorgeous oceanfront pool, surrounded by lounge chairs and beach beds.

Outside of Town

Located on the inland side of Highway 307, **Itour Akumal Villa Tortugas** (Hwy. 307 Km 256, cell tel. 984/146-3669, US$42-46 s/d with a/c) is a great little place offering six studios amid a leafy jungle setting. Each unit is a colorful casita with a kitchenette, one or two firm beds, a private patio, air-conditioning, and Wi-Fi; they are spic-and-span, with daily maid service. The grounds include a mosaic-tiled pool and an outdoor lounge area, both surrounded by a well-tended garden. Located 3 kilometers (1.8 miles) north of Akumal, it's a peaceful place to base yourself, especially if you have a car and don't mind being a few miles from the beach.

Rental Properties

The majority of rooms for rent in Akumal are in privately owned homes and condos, especially along Half Moon Bay. Most are managed and rented by one of various property management companies. Some reliable agencies include **Caribbean Fantasy** (toll-free U.S. tel. 800/523-6618, www.caribbfan.com), **Akumal Villas** (toll-free U.S. tel. 866/535-1324, www.akumalvillas.com,), and **Akumal Rentals** (U.S. tel. 815/642-4580, www.akumal-rentals.com). Reliable online sources for rentals include **Loco Gringo** (www.locogringo.com), **AirBnB** (www.airbnb.com), and **Vacation Rentals by Owner** (www.vrbo.com).

INFORMATION AND SERVICES

Tourist Information

Akumal doesn't have an official tourist office, but it's a small town, and you can probably find what you're looking for by asking the first person you see. If that fails, the folks at **Centro Ecológico Akumal** (CEA, Plaza Ukana, tel. 984/875-9095, www.ceakumal.org, 9am-1pm and 2pm-6pm Mon.-Fri.) are friendly and well informed, and most speak English.

Emergency Services

In a residential neighborhood across the highway form the main town entrance, **Akumal Medical Center** (Av. Gonzalo Guerrero s/n, tel. 984/875-9090, cell tel. 984/806-4616, www.akumaldoctoroncall.com, 24 hours daily) is the medical office of longtime Akumal provider Dr. Néstor Mendoza Gutiérrez.

The **police** can be reached by calling 060.

Money

There is no bank in town, but there is a **Banorte ATM** inside the arch at the entrance. **Supermercado El Pueblito** (7am-9pm daily) also has an ATM.

Media and Communications

Most hotels and condos offer free Wi-Fi to

guests, as does **Turtle Bay Café & Bakery** (tel. 984/875-9138, www.turtlebaycafe.com, 7am-10pm daily) in Plaza Ukana.

Laundry

There's an **unnamed laundry** (Av. Gonzalo Guerrero s/n, no tel., 8am-5pm Mon.-Sat.) on the west side of the highway, along the main street. Next-day service costs US$0.50 per kg (2.2 lbs).

GETTING THERE AND AROUND

The turnoff to Akumal is between kilometers 254 and 255 on the main highway. For Aventuras Akumal, the access road is just south of the main Akumal entrance; look for the sign to Hotel Villas DeRosa, as the community itself isn't well signed.

Bus and *Combi*

Combis and second-class buses stop at the Akumal turnoff, but it's a kilometer (0.6 mile) walk into town. Likewise, you can manage the center area by foot, but walking to and from Half Moon Bay can be long, hot, and dusty. Consider hiring a cab, which are often parked just outside the town arch.

Combis and second-class buses also stop at the Aventuras Akumal entrance; it's only about 500 meters (0.3 mile) into the community from there.

Car

If you drive into town, there is a small **town parking lot** (7am-4pm daily, US$1/hour) in front of Plaza Ukana. Some shops and restaurants can validate your parking—be sure to bring your receipt. There also are a handful of **public parking lots** just outside the town arch charging US$2.50 per day.

Taxi

Taxis gather near the entrance of Akumal, just outside of the arch. A ride from town to Laguna Yal-Ku costs US$5.

★ PLAYA X'CACEL

For all the breakneck construction along the Riviera Maya, much of the coastline remains virtually untouched, including some gorgeous stretches of white-sand beach. **Playa X'cacel** (Hwy. 307 Km 247.5, 9am-5pm daily, US$1) is one of those, a gently curving band of thick white sand, with only a small parking lot, restrooms, and changing area, and popular with local residents. X'cacel's pristine state is thanks in part to the fact that sea turtles nest

The Riviera Maya still has long stretches of untouched beach, including gorgeous Playa X'cacel.

here, and development is restricted by federal law. Along the inland edge of the beach are scores of wood blades with dates on them, marking where and when sea turtles laid eggs; needless to say, do not move the markers or disturb the nests! A small freshwater cenote is located down a slippery path, about 350 meters (0.2 mile) south of the main entrance; due to its popularity, visitors are admitted in waves of 30 people, with swim time limited to just 20 minutes. The turnoff to Playa X'cacel is easy to miss, but it's located 11 kilometers (7 miles) north of Tulum, just south of Chemuyil community.

Tankah Tres and Soliman Bay

Tucked innocuously between Akumal and Tulum, Tankah Tres and Soliman Bay see only a fraction of the tourist traffic that their better-known neighbors do. But that's just the way visitors to this little stretch of coastline prefer it, enjoying excellent snorkeling, diving, and pretty beaches, with a sense of isolation that's hard to find in these parts. The area has three small bays. The scattered hotels, villas, and private homes along their shores were once connected by a U-shaped access road, but development cut the U in half; the southern entrance is still marked Tankah Tres, while the northern entrance has a sign for Soliman Bay.

SIGHTS AND BEACHES
Playa Tankah

The handful of hotels here have nice beachfronts along three sandy bays. If you aren't staying here, consider having a meal at the hotel restaurants of **Blue Sky Tulum** and **Casa Cenote,** which allow nonguests to enjoy the facilities and beach if they order something.

Cenote Manatí
(aka Casa Cenote)

Across from Casa Cenote (and sometimes called by the same name), **Cenote Manatí** (Tankah Tres, 1.5 kilometers/0.9 mile from the southern turnoff, no phone, sunrise-sunset, US$6) is a series of interconnected cenotes and lagoons extending from the road well inland. (An underground channel drains into the ocean.) The crystal-clear water, winding channels, and tangle of rocks, trees, and freshwater plants along the edges and bottom all make for terrific snorkeling. Look for schools of tiny fish near the surface and some bigger ones farther down. Admission includes a life jacket; snorkel gear rental is available for US$6.

Yax Kin Cenote

Located just north of the Soliman Bay access road, **Yax Kin Cenote** (Hwy. 307 Km 242, cell tel. 998/244-0612, 10am-6pm daily, US$4 adult, US$2.50 child under 10) is a pool of shimmering teal water with a limestone shelf that makes entering the cool water easy (and less stressful for parents of small children). Snorkeling equipment can be rented (US$4) to get a better view of the small fish darting about. Camping (US$10 pp, BYO gear) is permitted in two-story towers located about 50 meters (164 feet) from the cenote.

SPORTS AND RECREATION
Scuba Diving and Snorkeling

There are excellent dive and snorkel sites in and near Tankah Tres and Soliman Bay. Located inside the Tankah Inn, **Tankah Divers Tulum** (Tankah Tres, tel. 984/128-2000, www.tankahdivers.com, hours vary) is a full-service shop offering guided trips (US$50/85 one-tank reef/cenote, US$80/130 two-tank reef/cenote) and all levels of PADI dive instruction. The shop also offers snorkeling excursions (US$40/60 reef/cenote).

FOOD

The restaurant at **Blue Sky Tulum** (Tankah Tres, 1.7 kilometers/1 mile from the southern turnoff, cell tel. 984/202-2185, www.blueskytulum.com.mx, 7:30am-9pm daily, US$10-24) specializes in Italian food, prepared to order, with simple but beautiful presentation. The pizza is famously good, handmade with fresh ingredients and baked in a custom brick oven. Appetizers like ceviche and mains like grilled calamari with vegetables are also worth sampling.

Set in a large palm grove along the curving Soliman Bay, ★ **Chamico's** (Soliman Bay, end of road, cell tel. 984/115-0260, 11am-5pm daily, US$6-15) is a family-run restaurant serving up unbelievably fresh seafood and fish dishes. "Restaurant" is a bit of a stretch, though; it's more like a handful of plastic tables and chairs set under swaying palms, and a Maya-style hut with a couple of open-fire grills and rickety wood tables serves as the kitchen. Meals range from whole grilled fish and lobster tail to fish ceviche and seafood stews.

The restaurant at **Casa Cenote** (Tankah Tres, 1.5 kilometers/0.9 mile from the southern turnoff, tel. 984/115-6996, www.casacenote.com, 8am-9pm daily, US$6-16) has a breezy *palapa*-roofed dining area just steps from the ocean. Stick to beach food like quesadillas or guacamole, or, better yet, come on Sunday afternoon when the hotel hosts a Texas-style barbecue (US$11) that's popular with expats. There's live music on weekends.

ACCOMMODATIONS

Tankah Inn (Tankah Tres, 1.1 kilometers/0.6 mile from the southern turnoff, tel. 984/100-0703, www.tankah.com, US$140 s/d with a/c) has five spacious rooms with murals of Maya temples. Each room has a private terrace and ocean views; all feature minifridges, drinking water, and remote-controlled air-conditioning. A breezy common room has sweeping views of the Caribbean—comfy chairs and tables, lots of board games, and an honor bar make this a popular place to hang out. The beach, with its lounge chairs and hammocks, is a tempting alternative. À la carte breakfast is included, as is use of kayaks and Wi-Fi.

Blue Sky Tulum (Tankah Tres, 1.7 kilometers/1 mile from the southern turnoff, cell tel. 984/202-2185, www.blueskytulum.com.mx, US$289-329 s/d with a/c, US$409-519 suite with a/c) is not in Tulum, regardless of its name. But, it is an excellent small hotel in Tankah, offering 10 breezy rooms with views

the view from Chamico's in Soliman Bay

of the Caribbean or the jungle. Units are simple but elegant with large private terraces and amenities like luxurious linens, high-pressure showers, and, in some, a plunge pool. Turndown service is provided each night; breakfast is provided each morning. There's also a refreshing pool facing the beach and lots of lounge chairs and hammocks for relaxing and kayaks, snorkel gear, and paddleboards for playing.

A gorgeous boutique hotel, ★ **Jashita** (Soliman Bay, 1.2 kilometers/0.7 mile from the northern turnoff, tel. 984/875-4158, www.jashitahotel.com, US$250 s/d with a/c, US$630-1,750 suite) sits on the curving Soliman Bay. It's an intimate place with elegant rooms that have marble floors, fine hardwoods, basin sinks, and rainfall showerheads—some even have private plunge pools. The common areas are just as sophisticated without losing a sense of hominess; fine art and beautiful furnishings make you feel like you're staying at your most stylish friend's home. There are also three great pools, a yoga studio and spa, a gourmet restaurant, and a breathtaking beach. Use of kayaks, stand-up paddleboards, and snorkel gear is included in the rate, as is breakfast. There's a minimum three-night stay; it's a seven-night minimum December 20-January 10.

If you have camping gear, make a beeline to **Chamico's** (Soliman Bay, end of road, cell tel. 984/115-0260, US$10 pp camping). A basic restaurant is located in a gorgeous palm grove,

and tents can be set up at the far end of the beach. Rustic bathrooms are the only bummer, but it seems a small price to pay considering the location—swaying palms, gentle ocean waves, and, on a clear night, an endless array of stars. All to say, a slice of heaven.

INFORMATION AND SERVICES

There are no formal services here, because it's not really a formal town. Head to Tulum for ATMs, medical services, Internet, groceries, and more.

GETTING THERE AND AROUND

The turnoff to the southern portion of Tankah Tres is between kilometers 237 and 238 on the main highway, and marked with a large road sign. Driving south from Cancún, you'll have to overshoot the entrance a short distance until a break in the median (at Dreams Tulum Resort and Spa) allows you to make a U-turn and return to the turnoff; this access road makes a beeline for the shore and then turns abruptly to the left, hugging the beach and passing the listed hotels and sights. The access road to the northern section is a bit farther and is marked with a large sign for Oscar & Lalo's Restaurant, which is actually on the west side of the highway. If you don't have a car, you can ask a *combi* to drop you at either turnoff, but it will not enter Tankah Tres or Soliman Bay itself.

Tulum and the Costa Maya

Look for ★ to find recommended
sights, activities, dining, and lodging.

Highlights

★ **Tulum's Southern Beaches:** Mile after mile of powdery white sand, tranquil turquoise water, cozy bungalows peeking out from behind softly bending palm trees . . . these are the beaches you've been dreaming of (page 217).

★ **Cenotes near Tulum:** Don't miss these eerie and unforgettable limestone caverns, bristling with stalagmites and stalactites, and filled with the crystalline water of the world's longest underground river system (page 218).

★ **Cobá Archaeological Zone:** Just an hour from Tulum are the terrific jungle-cloaked ruins of Cobá, where you can climb the Yucatán's second-highest pyramid (page 235).

★ **Cenotes near Cobá:** A visit to Cobá is made even better with a stop at three impressive cenotes a short distance from the ruins (page 240).

★ **Bahía de la Ascensión:** A huge protected expanse of calm ocean flats and tangled mangrove forests make this a world-class destination for bird-watchers and anglers (page 243).

★ **Banco Chinchorro:** A punishing two-hour boat ride across the open sea is rewarded with spectacular diving on one of the world's largest coral atolls (page 250).

★ **Canal de los Piratas:** Tours of Laguna Bacalar (available by pontoon, kayak, even SUP) inevitably stop at this lovely natural waterway, a great place for swimming, mud baths, and basking in the sun (page 263).

Tulum has long been favored by travelers who cringe at the splashy resorts and package tourism found in Cancún (and increasingly the Riviera Maya).

In that sense, Tulum is a fitting bridge between Quintana Roo's booming northern section and its far-less-traveled south. Tulum has so far managed to avoid the impulse to fill the coast with ever-bigger resorts; prices have certainly gone up, but there are still no megadevelopments here, or even power lines for that matter. Its beaches and *cabañas* remain as idyllic as ever.

If Tulum is the anti-Cancún, you might call southern Quintana Roo, or the "Costa Maya," the non-Cancún. Though fairly close in distance, it's worlds apart by any other measure. Immediately south of Tulum is the massive Sian Ka'an Biosphere Reserve, one of the Yucatán's largest and richest preserves, whose bays, lagoons, mangrove stands, and inland forests support a vast array of plants and animals, from dolphins to jaguars; there's even a large Maya ruin and several smaller temples. Beyond Sian Ka'an is the Costa Maya, the sparsely populated stretch of coast reaching down to the Belize border; the largest towns are Mahahual and Xcalak, with numerous

small bed-and-breakfasts and seaside hotels in both (and a highly incongruous cruise ship port in Mahahual). Most of the beaches aren't postcard perfect like Tulum's, but the isolation—not to mention the far-less-expensive lodging—is hard to match. Inland and farther south is the multicolored Laguna Bacalar and several significant but all-but-forgotten Maya ruins. Chetumal, the state capital, isn't much of a destination itself but has some unexpectedly appealing areas nearby, and it is the gateway to Belize.

Less than an hour from Tulum—and a great alternative to the overcrowded ruins there—is the ancient city of Cobá (42 kilometers/26 miles from Tulum), home of the second-tallest known Maya pyramid. Unlike many other ruins, Cobá is ensconced in a thick tropical forest that teems with birdlife, including parrots and toucans.

PLANNING YOUR TIME

Tulum is the first stop, of course, and for many people their main destination. From Tulum

---

Previous: scenic Maya ruins; diving in one of the region's many cenotes. **Above:** Tulum's gorgeous southern beaches.

Tulum and the Costa Maya

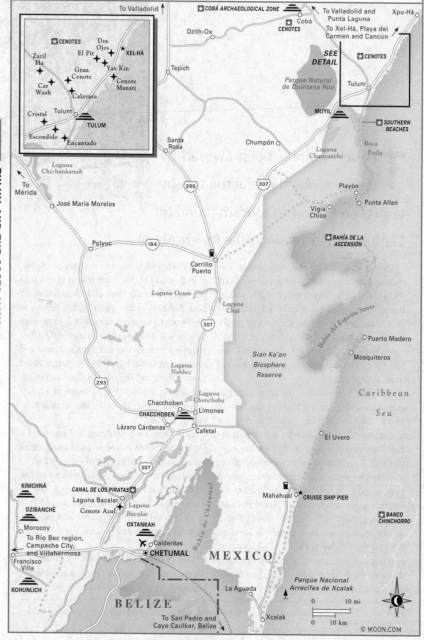

Tulum detail map (inset):

- To Valladolid
- ★ CENOTES
- Zazil Ha
- El Pit
- Dos Ojos
- ★ XEL-HÁ
- Gran Cenote
- Yax Kin
- Car Wash
- Calavara
- Cenote Manatí
- Cristal
- Tulum
- Escondido
- Encantado
- ▲ TULUM

Main map:

- To Valladolid
- ★ COBÁ ARCHAEOLOGICAL ZONE
- To Valladolid and Punta Laguna
- Xpu-Há
- Cobá
- ★ CENOTES
- To Xel-Há, Playa del Carmen and Cancún
- Dzith-Ox
- ★ CENOTES
- SEE DETAIL
- Tepich
- Parque Natural de Quintana Roo
- Tulum
- ▲ MUYIL
- ★ SOUTHERN BEACHES
- To Mérida
- Laguna Chichankanah
- Santa Rosa
- Chumpón
- Laguna Chunyaxché
- Boca Paila
- José María Morelos
- Playón
- Punta Allen
- Vigía Chico
- Polyuc
- 184
- 295
- 307
- Carrillo Puerto
- ★ BAHÍA DE LA ASCENSIÓN
- Laguna Ocum
- Laguna Chaic
- Puerto Madero
- Mosquiteros
- Laguna Nohbec
- Sian Ka'an Biosphere Reserve
- Bahía del Espíritu Santo
- Caribbean Sea
- 293
- Chacchoben
- Laguna Chonchoba
- ▲ CHACCHOBEN
- Limones
- Lázaro Cárdenas
- Cafetal
- El Uvero
- 307
- KINICHNÁ
- CANAL DE LOS PIRATAS
- Mahahual
- ★ CRUISE SHIP PIER
- Laguna Bacalar
- ▲ DZIBANCHÉ
- Cenote Azul
- Laguna Bacalar
- ★ BANCO CHINCHORRO
- Morocoy
- ▲ OXTANKAH
- To Río Bec region, Campeche City, and Villahermosa
- Calderitas
- Francisco Villa
- ⊙ CHETUMAL
- MEXICO
- Bahía de Chetumal
- KOHUNLICH
- La Aguada
- Parque Nacional Arrecifes de Xcalak
- BELIZE
- Xcalak
- To San Pedro and Caye Caulker, Belize
- 0   10 mi
- 0   10 km
- © MOON.COM

you can take day trips or short overnighters to the Sian Ka'an reserve and Cobá archaeological site, both fascinating. To venture any farther south you'll probably want a rental car, as bus service grows infrequent. Mahahual and Xcalak are certainly worth savoring; despite their isolation, there's plenty to do in both, including snorkeling, diving, kayaking, fishing, and, of course, just relaxing. Laguna Bacalar is worth a day or possibly two, to take a boat trip on the Caribbean-like water, swim in Cenote Azul, and visit the surprisingly good history museum in town. Chetumal is a logical stopover for those headed west toward the Río Bec region or crossing into Belize, and it has an interesting Maya museum.

Tulum

Tulum is the subject of a thousand postcards, and justly so. It's hard to know if the name is more closely associated with the ancient Maya ruins—perched dramatically on a cliff overlooking the Caribbean—or the idyllic beaches and oceanfront *cabañas* that have long been the jewel of the Riviera Maya. What's certain is that Tulum manages to capture both the ancient mystery and modern allure of Mexico's Riviera Maya.

Tulum has definitely grown and changed, with more changes on the way. The beach used to be a haven for backpackers and bohemians, with simple *cabañas* facing beautiful untouched beaches. The beaches are still beautiful, but the prices have long since gone through the *palapa* roof, catering more to urban escapists and upscale yoga groups. It's still a lovely place to stay, no matter who you are, it's just not as cheap as it used to be.

One consequence of the spike in prices on the beach is that the inland village of Tulum (aka Tulum Pueblo) has perked up significantly. Long a dumpy roadside town, it now has a growing number of hotels, B&Bs, and recommendable restaurants catering to independent travelers who have been priced out of the beachfront hotels. To be sure, a beachside *cabaña* will always be the most appealing place to stay in Tulum—and there are a handful of bargains still to be had—but staying in town is no longer the huge step down that it once was.

ORIENTATION

The name Tulum is used for three separate areas, which can be confusing. The first is Tulum archaeological zone, the scenic and popular Maya ruins. This is the first part of Tulum you encounter as you drive south from Cancún. A kilometer and a half (1 mile) farther south (and well inland) is the town of Tulum, known as Tulum Pueblo, where you'll find the bus terminal, supermarket, and numerous restaurants, hotels, tour guides, and shops. The third area is Tulum's beachfront hotel zone, or Zona Hotelera. Located due east of Tulum Pueblo, the Zona Hotelera extends for almost 10 kilometers (6 miles) from the Maya ruins to the entrance of the Sian Ka'an Biosphere Reserve, with fantastic beaches and bungalow-style hotels virtually the entire way. There's a walking path, but no road, connecting the Tulum ruins to the upper end of Tulum's Zona Hotelera.

TULUM ARCHAEOLOGICAL ZONE

The Maya ruins of **Tulum** (8am-5pm daily, US$3.50) are one of Mexico's most scenic archaeological sites, built atop a 12-meter (40-foot) cliff rising abruptly from turquoise Caribbean waters. The structures don't compare in grandeur to those of Cobá, Uxmal, or elsewhere, but are interesting and significant nevertheless.

Tulum is the single most frequently visited Maya ruin in the Yucatán Peninsula,

Tulum Archaeological Zone

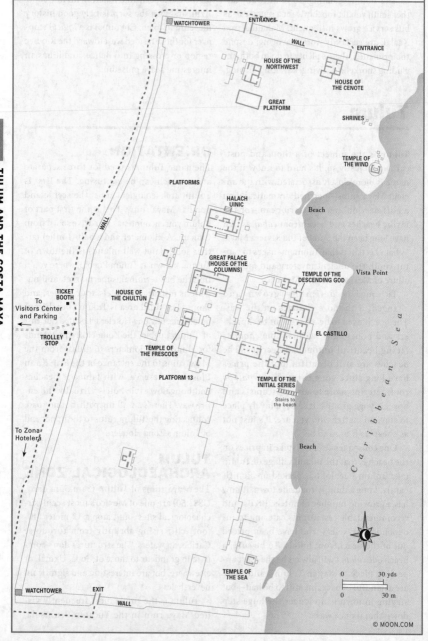

WATCHTOWER

ENTRANCE

WALL

ENTRANCE

HOUSE OF THE NORTHWEST

HOUSE OF THE CENOTE

GREAT PLATFORM

SHRINES

TEMPLE OF THE WIND

PLATFORMS

Beach

HALACH UINIC

Vista Point

GREAT PALACE (HOUSE OF THE COLUMNS)

TEMPLE OF THE DESCENDING GOD

HOUSE OF THE CHULTÚN

Caribbean Sea

To Visitors Center and Parking

TICKET BOOTH

EL CASTILLO

TROLLEY STOP

TEMPLE OF THE FRESCOES

TEMPLE OF THE INITIAL SERIES

PLATFORM 13

Stairs to the beach

To Zona Hotelera

Beach

TEMPLE OF THE SEA

WATCHTOWER

EXIT

WALL

0   30 yds

0   30 m

© MOON.COM

receiving thousands of visitors every day, most on package tours from nearby resorts. (In fact, it's second only to Teotihuacán, near Mexico City, as the country's most visited archaeological site.) For that reason, the first and most important piece of advice for independent travelers regarding Tulum is to **arrive early.** It used to be that the tour bus madness didn't begin until 11am, but it creeps earlier and earlier every year. Still, if you're there right at 8am, you'll have the ruins mostly to yourself for an hour or so—which is about all you need for this small site—before the hordes descend. Guides can be hired at the entrance for around US$40 for 1-4 people. Bring your swimsuit if you fancy a morning swim: This is the only Maya ruin with a great little beach right inside the archaeological zone.

History

Tulum was part of a series of Maya forts and trading outposts established along the Caribbean coast from the Gulf of Mexico as far south as present-day Honduras. Its original name was Zamá-Xamanzamá or simply Zamá (derived from *zamal,* or dawn) but was later called Tulum, Yucatec Maya for fortification or city wall, in reference to the thick stone barrier that encloses the city's main structures. Measuring 380 by 165 meters (1,250 by 540 feet), it's the largest fortified Maya site on the Quintana Roo coast (though small compared to most inland ruins).

Tulum's enviable patch of seashore was settled as early as 300 BC, but it remained little more than a village for most of its existence, overshadowed by the Maya city of Tankah a few kilometers to the north. Tulum gained prominence between the 12th and 16th centuries (the Late Postclassic era), when mostly non-Maya immigrants repopulated the Yucatán Peninsula following the general Maya collapse several centuries prior. Tulum's strategic location and convenient beach landing made it a natural hub for traders, who plied the coast in massive canoes measuring up to 16 meters (52 feet) long, laden with honey, salt, wax, animal skins, vanilla, obsidian, amber, and other products.

It was during this Postclassic boom period that most of Tulum's main structures were built. Although influenced by Mayapán (the reigning power at the time) and Central Mexican city-states, from which many of Tulum's new residents had emigrated, Tulum's structures mostly exemplify "east

House of the Cenote

Rediscovering the Maya

The Maya ruins of the Yucatán Peninsula were all but unknown in the United States and Europe until well into the 19th century. Although Spanish explorers and colonizers had occupied the peninsula for more than two centuries, conflicts with local Maya and Catholic antipathy for all things pagan probably account for the Spaniards' lack of research or even apparent interest. To be fair, the immensity of the task was surely daunting—by the time the Spanish reached the Yucatán in the early 1500s, the majority of sites had been abandoned for at least 300 years, and in some cases double or triple that. Many were piles of rubble, and those still standing were mostly covered in vegetation. Just getting to the sites was a task in itself.

And so it was an American and an Englishman—diplomat **John Lloyd Stephens** and artist-architect **Frederick Catherwood**—who brought global attention to the Maya world. Between 1839 and 1841, they conducted two major explorations of the Maya region, including present-day Yucatán, Chiapas, and Central America, visiting a total of 44 ruins. Stephens kept a detailed account of their travels, making many observations on the nature of Maya civilization that proved remarkably prescient. He correctly surmised that Maya writing contained detailed dynastic and historical accounts, and rejected the prevailing notion that Mesoamerican civilizations were descended from Egyptian or other Old World societies, declaring the mysterious ruins "a spectacle of a people skilled in architecture, sculpture, and possessing the culture and refinement attendant upon those, not derived from the Old World, but originating and growing here without models or masters like the plants and fruits of the soil, indigenous." Meanwhile, Catherwood made incredibly precise drawings of numerous structures, monuments, hieroglyphs, and scenes of peasant life. (Though they've been widely reprinted, you can see a rare collection of original Catherwood prints in Mérida, at the highly recommended museum-gallery Casa Catherwood.)

Stephens and Catherwood published their work in two volumes, both of which were instant sensations in the United States and Europe, awakening immense interest in ancient Maya civilization. Their books now are condensed into a single, very readable volume, *Incidents of Travel in Yucatán* (Hard Press, 2007), available in English and in many bookstores in the Yucatán. It is a fascinating read, not only for the historical value but also as a backdrop for your own travels throughout the region.

coast architecture," defined by austere designs with relatively little ornamentation and a predominantly horizontal orientation (compared to high-reaching pyramids elsewhere). Ironically, construction in these later eras tended to be rather shoddy, thanks in part to improvements in stucco coverings that meant the quality of underlying masonry was not as precise. Today, with the stucco eroded away, Tulum's temples appear more decayed than structures at other sites, even those built hundreds of years prior.

The Spanish got their first view of Tulum, and of mainland indigenous society, on May 7, 1518, when Juan de Grijalva's expedition along the Quintana Roo coast sailed past the then brightly colored fortress. The chaplain of the fleet famously described the city as "a village so large that Seville would not have appeared larger or better." Tulum remained an important city and port until the mid-1500s, when European-borne diseases decimated its population. The once-grand city was effectively abandoned and, for the next three centuries, slowly consumed by coastal vegetation. In 1840, Spanish explorers referred to an ancient walled city known as Tulum, the first recorded use of its current name; two years later John Lloyd Stephens and Frederick Catherwood visited Tulum, giving the world its first detailed description and illustrations of the dramatic seaside site. During the Caste War, Tulum was occupied by members of the Talking Cross cult, including the followers of a Maya priestess known as the Queen of Tulum.

Temple of the Wind

House of the Cenote

The path from the ticket booth follows Tulum's wall around the northwest corner to two low corbel arch entryways. Using the second entrance (closest to the ocean), you'll first see the Casa del Cenote. The two-room structure, with a third chamber added later, is less impressive than the gaping maw of its namesake cenote. The water is not drinkable, thanks to saltwater intrusion, but that may not have been the case a half millennium ago; it's unlikely Tulum could have grown to its size and prominence without a major water source, not only for its own residents but passing traders as well. Cenotes were also considered apertures to Xibalba, or the underworld, and an elaborate tomb discovered in the floor of the House of the Cenote suggests it may have had a ceremonial function as well.

Temple of the Wind

Following the path, the next major structure is the Temple of the Wind, perched regally atop a rocky outcrop overlooking a picturesque sandy cove. If it looks familiar, that's because it appears on innumerable postcards, magazine photos, and tourist brochures. (The view is even better from a vista point behind El Castillo and from the ocean.) The name derives from the unique circular base upon which the structure is built: In Central Mexican cosmology, the circle is associated with the god of the wind, and its presence here (and at other ruins, like San Gervasio on Isla Cozumel) is evidence of the strong influence that Central Mexican migrants/invaders had on Postclassic Maya societies.

Temple of the Descending God

One of Tulum's more curious structures is the Temple of the Descending God, named for the upside-down winged figure above its doorway. Exactly who or what the figure represents is disputed among archaeologists—theories include Venus, the setting sun, the god of rain, even the god of bees (as honey was one of the coastal Maya's most widely traded products). Whatever the answer, it was clearly a deeply revered (or feared) deity, as the same image appears on several of Tulum's buildings, including the upper temple of Tulum's main pyramid. The Temple of the Descending God also is notable for its cartoonish off-kilter position, most likely the result of poor construction.

El Castillo

Tulum's largest and most imposing structure is The Castle, a 12-meter-high (40-foot) pyramid constructed on a rocky bluff of roughly the same height. Like many Maya structures, El Castillo was built in multiple phases. The first iteration was a low, broad platform, still visible today, topped by a long palace fronted by a phalanx of stout columns. The second phase consisted of simply filling in the center portion of the original palace to create a base for a new and loftier temple on top. In the process, the builders created a vaulted passageway and inner chamber, in which a series of intriguing frescoes were housed; unfortunately, you're not allowed to climb onto the platform to see them. The upper temple (also off-limits) displays Central Mexican influence, including snakelike columns similar to those found at Chichén Itzá and grimacing Toltec masks on the corners. Above the center door is an image of the Descending God. Archaeologists believe a stone block at the top of the stairs may have been used for sacrifices.

Temple of the Frescoes

Though quite small, the Temple of the Frescoes is considered one of Tulum's most archaeologically significant structures. The name owes to the fading but remarkably detailed paintings on the structure's inner walls. In shades of blue, gray, and black, they depict various deities, including Chaac (the god of rain) and Ixchel (the goddess of the moon and fertility), and a profusion of symbolic imagery, including corn and flowers. On the temple's two facades are carved figures with elaborate headdresses and yet another image of the Descending God. The large grim-faced masks on the temple's corners are believed to represent Izamná, the Maya creator god.

Halach Uinic and the Great Palace

In front of El Castillo are the remains of two palatial structures: the House of the Halach Uinic and the Great Palace (also known as the House of the Columns). Halach Uinic is a Yucatec Maya term for king or ruler, and this structure seems to have been an elaborate shrine dedicated to Tulum's enigmatic Descending God. The building is severely deteriorated, but what remains suggests its facade was highly ornamented, perhaps even painted blue and red. Next door is the Great Palace, which likely served as residential quarters for Tulum's royal court.

Practicalities

Tulum's massive parking lot and strip-mall-like visitors complex ought to clue you in to the number of tourists that pass through here every day. (Did we mention to get here early?) You'll find a small museum and bookshop amid innumerable souvenir shops and fast-food restaurants. (If this is your first visit to a Maya ruin, don't be turned off by all the hub-bub. Tulum is unique for its excessive and obnoxious commercialization; most sites have just a ticket booth and restrooms.)

The actual entrance and ticket booth are about one kilometer (0.6 mile) from the visitors center; it's a flat, mild walk, but there are also **trolleys** that ferry guests back and forth for US$2 per person round-trip (kids under 10 ride free).

Getting There

The Tulum archaeological zone is a kilometer (0.6 mile) north of Tulum Pueblo on Highway 307. There are two entrances off the highway; the one farther south is newer and better, leading directly to the main parking lot (parking US$6). Arriving by bus or *combi*, be sure to ask the driver to let you off at *las ruínas* (the ruins) as opposed to the town. To return, flag down a bus or *combi* on the highway.

The ruins also can be accessed by foot from Tulum's beach road—from the northernmost spot in the Zona Hotelera, it's about a 500-meter (0.3 miles) walk to the entrance.

BEACHES AND CENOTES
Northern Beaches

The road from Tulum Pueblo hits the coast near the upper end of the Zona Hotelera, which stretches from the archaeological zone down to the entrance of the Sian Ka'an reserve, almost exactly 10 kilometers (6 miles). The area north of the Tulum/Zona Hotelera junction has two easy-to-reach beach areas that are ideal for people staying in town. There is plenty of open space to lay out your own towel as well as a handful of beach clubs if you're looking for lounge chairs and food services.

Playa El Paraíso (Carr. Tulum-Punta Allen, 2 kilometers/1.2 miles north of junction, cell tel. 984/113-7089, www.elparaiso-hoteltulum.com, 10am-6pm daily) is the most popular beach club on the north end of Tulum. Once little more than a bar and some hammocks, it has morphed into a bustling expanse of lounge chairs, beach beds, and umbrellas (US$10-20/day), with waiters weaving between them and the full restaurant and beach bar. It's busy but still scenic and relaxing.

Directly north of Playa El Paraíso is **Playa Mar Caribe** (Carr. Tulum-Punta Allen, 2.3 kilometers/1.4 miles north of junction), named after the rustic bungalows that have long fronted this portion of beach. Broad and unspoiled, this is a great place to lay out your towel on the soft white sand, which you share with a picturesque array of moored fishing boats. There are few services here—mostly beachfront kiosks—so be sure to bring snacks and plenty of water.

South of Playa El Paraíso, **Pocna Beach Club** (Carr. Tulum-Punta Allen, 1.6 kilometers/1 miles north of junction, cell tel. 984/154-1825, 8am-11pm daily) fronts a quiet stretch of beach with lots of beach beds for lounging (US$25 per four people). Get here early to stake out a spot and to enjoy the all-you-can eat breakfast buffet (US$8 pp) with loads of fresh fruit, breads, freshly squeezed OJ, and, almost best of all, bottomless coffee. There's free parking for clients.

★ Southern Beaches

Tulum's very best beaches—thick white sand, turquoise-blue water, gently bending palm trees—are toward the southern end of the Zona Hotelera. Not surprisingly, Tulum's finest hotels are in the same area, and there are no official public access points. That said, hotels rarely raise an eyebrow at the occasional nonguest cutting through to reach the beach. You can also grab breakfast or lunch at one of the hotel restaurants and cut down to the beach afterward; in some cases, you can even use the lounge chairs.

Aimed at an older crowd, **Ana y José Beach Club** (Carr. Tulum-Punta Allen, 2.4 kilometers/1.5 miles south of junction, cell tel. 998/112-5229, 8am-6pm daily, free) is located about a kilometer (0.6 mile) north of the resort of the same name and is open to guests

and nonguests alike. An airy, sand-floored dining area serves mostly seafood, including ceviche, shrimp cocktail, and grilled fish, at decent prices (US$8-14), and there is a full bar (US$3-10). Chaise lounges and four-poster beach beds (US$10-20/day) are arranged a bit too close together, but they are comfy and relaxing nonetheless.

Ziggy Beach (Carr. Tulum-Punta Allen, 3.5 kilometers/2.1 miles south of junction, cell tel. 984/871-1145, 9am-5pm daily, free) is a mellow beach club with rows of thick queen-size beach beds and lounge chairs plus hammocks strung from palm trees. They're free to use if you buy something from the restaurant-bar. (Drinks often come with a complimentary round of chips and salsa, too). The beach, as expected, is gorgeous. Service is personable and efficient.

A popular spot for weddings, **Ak'iin Beach Club** (Carr. Tulum-Punta Allen, 4 kilometers/2.4 miles south of junction, cell tel. 984/113-7293, www.akiintulum.com, 9am-5pm daily, free) is truly a beautiful place. A wood-plank walkway snakes through the leafy property before arriving at the white-sand beach. Along the way, guests pass the restaurant, a spacious high-roofed *palapa* structure with a solid menu of Mexican and international dishes (US$7-12). There's also a two-for-one happy hour 5pm-7pm most days. Like neighboring beach clubs, use of the comfy beach couches, beds, and chairs are complimentary with the purchase of pretty much anything on the menu.

Maxa Camp Beach Club (Carr. Tulum-Punta Allen, 3 kilometers/1.8 miles south of junction, tel. 984/180-7151, www.maxacamp.com, 8am-11pm daily, free) is a bohemian-chic beach club that's a part of the Venado Azul glamping site (the huge tents are on the north side of the property). Beach beds and huge cushions are set up on the sand, with gourmet Mayan-inspired meals served in a rustic oceanfront restaurant. Driftwood art, flowing bolts of cloth, and dream catchers abound. Admission is free with purchase of food or drink.

★ Cenotes

Dos Ojos (Hwy. 307 Km 244, tel. 984/108-3312, www.parquedosojos.com, 8am-5pm daily), or Two Eyes, is a reference to twin caverns that are the largest openings—but far from the only ones—into the labyrinthine river system that runs beneath the ground here. You can snorkel on your own (US$18 pp, US$6 pp snorkel gear), but you'll see a lot more on a guided snorkeling tour (US$30 pp, no reservations required). There is no limit to the amount of time guests can stay; many bring food and drinks and make a day of it (there are hammocks, lockers, and a restaurant on-site too). Visitors also can dive at Dos Ojos ($29) but must bring their own equipment and guide; the two primary dive "lines" are technically cavern dives, ideal for those new to overhead environments. There are various other cenotes in the Dos Ojos system for much more challenging diving, including **The Pit** (US$29 pp), at 40 meters the deepest dive site and with a spectacular halocline. (Each cenote has a separate entrance fee, from US$29 to $50, which you should confirm with your dive shop.) A rental car will make visiting Dos Ojos more rewarding; the primary visitor area is 4 kilometers (2.5 miles) from the main highway down a dirt road, passing various cenotes along the way, while others lie beyond. Cash only.

One of the only cenotes in the Zona Hotelera that's open to the public, **Cenote Encantado** (aka Cenote Yax Chen, Carr. Tulum-Punta Allen Km 10.5, 8am-sunset) is a winding channel of cool clear water with freshwater plants along the edges. Measuring about 300 meters (984 feet) in length, it's part of an intricate network of about 100 cenotes on the jungle side of Tulum. Three small hotels—Cabañas y Cenote Yaxchen, Cenote Encantado, and Hotel Maya Cabañas & Cenote—provide easy access (US$2.50 pp) and rent kayaks (US$5-9) and snorkel gear (US$5) to better explore it. Look for schools of tiny fish (and some say baby crocs) in the water as well as herons in the low-hanging trees.

Other favorite cenotes include **Zazil Ha, Car Wash, Gran Cenote,** and **Calavera Cenote** (all west of Tulum on the road to Cobá); **Cristal** and **Escondido** (Hwy. 307 just south of Tulum); **Casa Cenote** (at

The Yucatán Peninsula has hundreds of cenotes, like this one outside Cobá.

Tankah Tres); and **Cenote Cristalino, Jardín del Edén,** and **Cenote Azul** (Hwy. 307 just north of Xpu-Há). All can be visited on a tour or by yourself, and most have snorkel gear for rent (US$4-7). Most are on private or *ejido* (collective) land and charge admission fees, usually US$5-10. If you take a tour, ask if admission fees are included in the rate. Most cenotes are open 8am-5pm daily.

TOURS

Mexico Kan Tours (Av. Tulum between Orion and Centauro, tel. 984/688-5864, www.mexicokantours.com, 7am-10pm Mon.-Sat., 3pm-10pm Sun.) offers excellent excursions throughout the Riviera Maya—kayaking in Sian Ka'an Biosphere Reserve, snorkeling in cenotes, bird-watching and monkey tours, even inland trips to Chichén Itzá and Valladolid. Groups are small—often no more than three or four people—and focus on sustainable travel like offering reusable canteens instead of disposable water bottles and encouraging the use of biodegradable sunblock. Guides are enthusiastic, knowledgeable, and fluent in English and Spanish. Private and custom tours are also offered.

Community Tours Sian Ka'an (Calle Osiris Sur near Calle Sol Ote, tel. 984/871-2202, www.siankaantours.org, 7am-7pm daily) is co-op offering a variety of tours (US$75-109, 3-7 hours) to the Sian Ka'an Biosphere, a 1.3-million-acre reserve of coastal and mangrove forests and wetlands. Among the most popular outings are the "Muyil" route, which begins with a visit to the Muyil archaeological zone, followed by a boat tour of Muyil and Chunyaxche lagoons, including a chance to jump in and float down a long mangrove-edged canal; "Mayaking" in Sian Ka'an, a bird- and animal-spotting tour by kayak through the lagoons and mangroves; and a "Chicle" tour, where you learn about the practice of tapping *chicle* (gum) trees, from Maya times to today, followed by a swim in the lagoon.

ENTERTAINMENT AND SHOPPING
Entertainment
ZONA HOTELERA

Papaya Playa Project (Carr. Tulum-Punta Allen, 1.5 kilometers/1 mile south of junction, cell tel. 984/116-3774, www.papayaplayaproject.com, hours vary) has a regular lineup of live musical acts, plus full-moon parties, bongo drum sessions, and an overall counterculture vibe. Saturday is the main night, but look for schedules online for upcoming events. Papaya Playa is actually a rustic-chic resort, hence all the *cabañas*, but is better known (and better liked, really) as a place to party. Most shows begin around 10pm; cover is US$5-15.

Capturing the essence of boho hipster, **Maxa Camp Beach Club** (Carr. Tulum-Punta Allen, 6.5 kilometers/4 miles south of junction, tel. 984/180-7151, www.maxacamp.com, 8am-11pm daily, free) is an earthy place with colorful cushions and hammocks, dream catchers, and huge driftwood sculptures. A beach club by day, Maxa transforms into a lounge by evening: movie nights, chilled-out barbecues, DJ dance parties, and general revelry rule.

The lounge bar at **La Zebra** (Carr. Tulum-Punta Allen, 4.8 kilometers/3 miles south of junction, cell tel. 984/124-0337, www.lazebratulum.com, 8am-10pm daily) serves up shots and mixed drinks, including its signature Zebra negroni, made with tequila and homemade orange and cinnamon bitters. Most afternoons, a DJ spins acoustic tunes, keeping things chill.

The oceanfront bar at its namesake boutique resort, **Mezzanine** (Carr. Tulum-Punta Allen, 1.3 kilometers/0.8 mile north of junction, tel. 984/131-1596, www.mezzaninetulum.com) is a go-to spot on Friday nights, with cocktails prepped by a master mixologist and a hipster vibe to match.

Gitano (Carr. Tulum-Punta Allen, 3 kilometers/1.8 mile south of junction, tel. 984/745-9068, www.gitanotulum.mx, 6pm-midnight Mon.-Thurs., 6pm-3am Fri.,

6pm-1am Sat.-Sun.) is a jungle restaurant-bar known for its mixologists, DJs, and dance floor. It's definitely a scene—down to the beautiful people inside and the velvet ropes keeping out the riffraff. That said, if you like mescal, can clean up nicely, and want to run with the "it" crowd, this is a great option. There's live music on Sunday, Wednesday, and Thursday.

IN TOWN

Just off the main drag, **El Batey** (Calle Centauro Sur between Av. Tulum and Calle Andromeda, tel. 984/745-4571, 8am-2am Mon.-Sat., 5pm-1am Sun.) is a welcoming and often packed bar featuring live jazz, blues, acoustic, and Mexican *bohemia* groups most nights starting at 7:30pm. There's a leafy courtyard in the back where bands set up, an artsy bar in front, and a VW Bug converted into a mojito bar (with drinks made with real sugarcane!).

Encanto Cantina (Av. Tulum between Calles Alfa and Jupiter, tel. 984/871-2019, 5pm-1am daily) is equal parts bar and restaurant, with great Mexican *lotería*-themed flourishes throughout. Snag a spot in the long front area, where the bar is located and the atmosphere is lively. (For meals, the rear garden

is sublime—just be sure to bring bug spray.) Music varies from cool electronic jazz to classic rock and occasional live bands, and the staff are known to spontaneously break into dance. There's craft beer and a super-creative cocktail menu featuring fresh fruit and quality tequila and mescal.

The craft beer revolution has hit Tulum, and **Hermana República** (Calle Sol at Calle Centauro, tel. 999/405-1117, 1pm-11pm Mon.-Thurs., 1pm-midnight Fri.-Sat., 1pm-6pm Sun.) is ground zero. Pick from a variety of house brews, from a refreshing pilsner or German wheat to a vanilla porter or in-your-face IPA. Samplers are a good option for the indecisive, served on a wood tray cleverly formed in the shape of a hops bud, and growlers are available if you can't get enough. Hip industrial-chic décor and tasty cantina-plus eats round out the experience.

Boheme Tulum (Calle Sol between Calles Alfa and Jupiter, U.S. tel. 617/669-8799, bohemetulum@gmail.com, 2pm-midnight Thurs.-Sat.) is an artsy multipurpose compound, housing a cool café-bar, artist workshops, a boutique hotel, and the studios of Radio Tulum. Evenings bring indie films, live music broadcasts with well-known DJs (aka

painted *calaveras*, a kind of *artesanía*

great dance parties), and art show openings. Look online for upcoming events.

Shopping

Tulum's main drag is peppered with *artesanía* and knickknack shops. You'll find everything from T-shirts and magnets to high-end Maya replicas and custom-made jewelry. Consider window-shopping a bit—it won't take long to peruse most of the shops. A couple of standouts include:

Mexik (Av. Tulum between Calles Alfa and Jupiter, tel. 984/871-2136, 9am-9pm Mon.-Sat., 9am-7pm Sun.) has a large selection of quality folk art, from green copper suns to carved wooden angels and masks. Cool T-shirts, jewelry, cards, and more also are sold. There's a sister shop of the same name in the Zona Hotelera (Punta Piedra, Carr. Tulum-Punta Allen, 1 kilometer/0.6 mile south of junction, same hours).

Cabrón (Av. Tulum near Calle Acuario, cell tel. 984/144-4203, www.karaniart.com. mx, 10:30am-9:30pm daily) sells artful T-shirts that celebrate Mexican culture in tongue-in-cheek ways: a storm trooper mask decorated with Maya glyphs, a Batman logo with an ancient bat design, a Day of the Dead skull made from a flurry of flowers. T-shirts aren't cheap (US$18-25) but they're unique, making a great memento or gift.

SPORTS AND RECREATION
Scuba Diving

The reef here is superb, but Tulum's diving claim to fame is the huge and easily accessible network of freshwater cenotes, caverns, and caves, offering truly one-of-a-kind dive environments. Divers with open-water certification can dive in cenotes (little or no overhead) and caverns (no more than 30 feet deep or 130 feet from an air pocket) without additional training. Full-cave diving requires advanced certification, which is available at many of Tulum's shops. If you haven't dived in a while, definitely warm up with some open-water dives before doing a cenote or cavern

trip. Buoyancy control is especially important in such environments because of the roof above and the sediment below, diving is complicated by the fact that it's fresh water instead of salt water, and it entails gear you may not be accustomed to, namely thick wetsuits and a flashlight.

Prices for cenotes and caverns are fairly uniform from shop to shop: around US$90-160 for one tank or US$150-190 for two. Be sure to ask whether gear and admission to the cenotes are included. Shops also offer multi-dive packages, cave and cavern certification courses, and hotel packages. As always, choose a shop and guide you feel comfortable with, not necessarily the least expensive one.

If you plan on cave and cavern diving (or want to learn to do either), **Xibalba Dive Center** (Calle Andrómeda between Calles Libra and Geminis, tel. 984/871-2953, www.xibalbadivecenter.com, 9am-7pm daily) has an excellent record for safety and professionalism. It also has an on-site hotel with comfortable rooms, a small swimming pool, and space to dry, store, and repair gear. Good packages are available. Xibalba also fills its own tanks and offers free Nitrox to experienced clients. The shop's name, aptly enough, comes from the Yucatec Maya word for the underworld.

Koox Dive Center (Av. Tulum between Calles Beta and Osiris, tel. 984/141-5502, www.kooxdiving.com, 7:30am-9pm daily) is another reliable option for diving and snorkeling, on the reef and in cenotes.

La Calypso Dive Center (Calle Sagitario at Calle Osiris, cell tel. 984/106-8002, www.lacalypsodive.com, 8:30am-1pm daily) offers highly professional service with a deep nod to customer service.

In the Zona Hotelera, **Mexi-Divers** (Punta Piedra, Carr. Tulum-Punta Allen, 1.5 kilometers/0.9 mile south of junction, tel. 984/807-8805, www.mexidivers.com, 8am-7pm daily) is located opposite Zamas Hotel in the Punta Piedra area and has regularly scheduled snorkeling and diving trips, in the ocean and nearby cenotes.

Snorkeling

Like divers, snorkelers have an embarrassment of riches in Tulum, with great reef snorkeling and easy access to the eerie beauty of the area's many cenotes. **Dive shops in Tulum** offer snorkel trips of both sorts; prices vary considerably, so be sure to ask which and how many reefs or cenotes you'll visit, for how long, and what's included (gear, entrance fees, transport, snacks, etc.). Reef trips cost US$25-45 and visit 1-3 different spots, while cenote trips run US$75-99; snorkel gear can also be rented.

Kiteboarding

Mexican Caribbean Kitesurf (Ahau Tulum, Carr. Tulum-Punta Allen Km 4.4, tel. 984/168-1023, www.mexicancaribbeankitesurf.com, 9am-5:30pm daily) is a friendly shop with IKO-certified instructors and top-of-the-line equipment. Private and group (two people max) instruction is offered by the hour (US$40-50/hour group, US$60-80/hour private). Radio helmets also are provided so students and instructors can easily communicate on the water.

Morph Kiteboarding (Coco Limited Tulum, Carr. Tulum-Punta Allen Km 8, cell tel. 984/114-9524, www.morphkiteboarding.

com, 9am-sunset daily) also offers classes to all levels of kiteboarders. Rates are for private classes, though group lessons can be arranged as well: US$240, US$390, and US$468 for three-, five-, and six-hour courses, respectively.

Stand-Up Paddling

Stand-up paddling, or "SUPing," is especially well-suited to the calm, clear waters found in much of the Riviera Maya. You can see a surprising amount of sealife doing SUP instead of kayaking, thanks simply to the vantage point.

Pro Kite Tulum (Villa Las Estrellas, Carr. Tulum-Punta Allen Km 8, cell tel. 984/100-5878, www.prokitetulum.com, 9am-5pm daily) offers SUP tours to the Tulum ruins (US$65), a nearby lagoon (US$90), and the reef, including snorkeling (US$95). Instruction is also offered, starting with safety and theory on the beach, graduating to kneeling paddling, and then standing. Private classes are US$60 per hour, while groups of two or three start at US$45 per person per hour. Gear and refreshments are included. Rentals (US$20/hr, US$80/day) also are available. **Mexican Caribbean Kitesurf** (Ahau Tulum, Carr. Tulum-Punta Allen Km 4.4, tel. 984/168-1023,

For some, stand-up paddling is a family affair.

www.mexicancaribbeankitesurf.com, 9am-5:30pm daily) has similar offerings and price points.

A dreamy experience, **SUP Yoga Tulum** (cell tel. 984/134-9721, www.supyogatulum.com, 9am-3:30pm, US$100) offers yoga instruction while floating on paddleboards. The 1.5-hour class is held on a private lagoon or cenote, both in the Sian Ka'an Biosphere Reserve. Afterward, students are welcome to explore and paddle at their leisure. Transportation, post-class paddling, gear, and a light snack included. No prior paddleboarding experience required (but expect to get wet!).

Ecoparks

Built around a huge natural inlet, **Xel-Há** (Hwy. 307, 9 kilometers/5.6 miles north of Tulum, tel. 998/883-0524, toll-free U.S./Can. tel. 855/326-2696, www.xel-ha.com, 8:30am-6pm daily, US$90 adult all-inclusive, US$45 child under 12, child under 5 free) is all about water—being in and around it. Activities include snorkeling, tubing, aquatic zip lines, and for an additional fee, interactive programs with dolphins, manatees, and stingrays. Although it doesn't compare to snorkeling on the reef, there's a fair number of fish darting about, and it makes for a fun, easy intro for children and beginners. Several buffet restaurants are available for breakfast and lunch. An open bar is included. Check the website for online deals and combo packages with sister parks Xcaret and Xplor.

Spas and Gyms

On the jungle side of the road, the luxurious **Yaan Wellness Energy Spa** (Carr. Tulum-Punta Allen Km 10, tel. 984/179-1530, www.yaanwellness.com, 9:30am-9pm daily) offers a wide range of spa services. Massages, body treatments, facials, soaking baths—even energy healing and traditional *temascal* (pre-Hispanic sweat lodge) ceremonies. All treatments begin with a "Healing Water Circuit," which integrates purified cenote waters and includes leisurely stops in the sauna,

steam room, and hot and cold massage pools. Most services run around US$175 per hour—pricey for sure, but totally worthwhile.

Mayan Clay Spa (Carr. Tulum-Punta Allen Km 8.5, tel. 984/807-9376, www.mayanclayspa.com, 9am-6pm daily) offers a memorable and immensely relaxing spa experience that's especially popular with couples and groups. The 1-2-hour clay massages include a full body massage with silky-smooth clay, followed by a hot shower (or a dip in the ocean) and a classic oil massage. The bathhouse treatment lasts a full three hours, and includes a variety of skin-soothing treatments at its jungle location. The leafy open-air setting is lovely, but privacy is not absolute (very Tulum-esque); full nudity is not required but definitely adds to the experience if you're comfortable with it. Leave valuables in your car or hotel, as there's no good place to stow them.

Tulum Jungle Gym (Carr. Tulum-Punta Allen Km 7.5, cell tel. 998/243-4533, www.tulumjunglegym.com, 8am-5pm daily) is certainly one of the more unique gyms you're likely to encounter. Not only is it right on a gorgeous beach, but the equipment is fashioned from local products, like tree log bench presses and a rope-pull full of rocks. Hourlong classes include the "Jungle Gym Circuit," "Beach Body Bootcamp," and "Booty Bootcamp." All levels are welcome, and no reservations are needed.

Yoga

Yoga Shala Tulum (Carr. Tulum-Punta Allen Km 7.4, cell tel. 984/141-8116, www.yogashalatulum.com, 8:30am-6:30pm Mon.-Sat., 11am-6:30pm Sun.) offers a wide range of yoga instruction in its gorgeous open-air studio. Classes cost US$20 each or US$70 per week for unlimited classes. Look for it on the jungle side of the Zona Hotelera road, alongside its namesake hotel.

Tree Top Yoga Shala (Carr. Tulum-Punta Allen Km 10, tel. 984/179-1530, www.yaanwellness.com, US$20) offers drop-in yoga classes—vinyasa and hatha, mostly—in an open-air studio at the upscale **Yaan Wellness**

Energy Spa. Classes are at 10am and 5pm every day; guided meditation also is offered at 9:15am on Tuesday, Thursday, and Saturday (45 min., US$15).

On the road between the beach and town, **Tribal Yoga** (Av. Cobá s/n, www.tribaltulum.com, tel. 984/871-2508, 8:30am-7:30pm Mon.-Sat., 10am-11:15am Sun.) is a welcoming studio with huge picture windows overlooking the jungle. Classes are led by a well-trained cadre of instructors and vary from yin to flow. The drop-in rate is US$15; 5- and 12-packs are available at a discount.

FOOD
Zona Hotelera

Health food aficionados will need no convincing, but even skeptics may be converted at ★ **Raw Love Café** (Ahau Hotel, Carr. Tulum-Punta Allen, 7.5 kilometers/4.5 miles south of junction, cell tel. 984/130-2013, www.rawlovekitchen.com, 9am-6pm daily, US$4-9), a raw, vegan, organic, gluten-free, sugar-free restaurant. Steps from the beach, there's a great vibe here and a long menu: favorites include the living pizza, maki rolls, fruit smoothies and bowls, and coffee with coconut milk (made daily from fresh coconuts). Cash only.

Kitchen Table (Carr. Tulum-Punta Allen, 1.5 kilometers/0.9 miles north of junction, cell tel. 984/188-4924, www.kitchentabletulum.com, 6pm-10pm daily, US$14-31) is fine dining at its most deconstructed: meals are made from mostly local ingredients and are prepped at a long kitchen table in plain view. Pan-fired octopus and the grilled deviled avocado appetizer are perennial favorites, as are cocktails like the tamarind margarita. You'll be ushered from the bar, to your table, to a separate dessert nook; the whole experience is impressive, albeit a bit precious, even for Tulum—come here for a sophisticated meal, not a family gathering or après-beach chill out.

Mexican and Japanese foods may not seem fusible, but the wizards at **Ukami** (Carr. Tulum-Punta Allen, 6.7 kilometers/4 miles south of junction, tel. 984/205-0709, www.ukamitulum.com, 4pm-midnight Wed.-Mon., US$12-20) make it work with items like tuna sashimi tostadas and miso tortilla soup. There's also a lot of straight-up great sushi and sashimi, plus noodle dishes, rice bowls, and more; most people find their way here because they're craving a break from traditional Mexican food. The presentation is a bit over-wrought—like nigiri connect-the-dots—but the flavors, service, and overall experience are superb.

Thai is the specialty at **Mezzanine** (Carr. Tulum-Punta Allen, 1.3 kilometers/0.8 mile north of junction, cell tel. 984/124-0888, www.mezzaninetulum.com, 7:30am-10pm daily, US$8-26), one of Tulum's chicest hotel restaurants. Curries—red, green, sweet potato, pineapple—and house specialties like crispy-style whole fish and lemongrass soup are among the dishes served in a sleek dining area or on a shaded outdoor patio, both with fine sea views. A full bar—martinis are the thing to order here—and DJ spinning cool tunes make this a place to linger.

La Zebra (Carr. Tulum-Punta Allen, 4.8 kilometers/3 miles south of junction, cell tel. 984/124-0337, www.lazebratulum.com, 8am-10pm daily, US$10-23) serves up classic Mexican dishes like cochinita pibil, chicken in mole sauce, and tamales. For lighter fare, check out the ceviche bar, with everything from fish and shrimp to octopus and tuna (there's even a vegan option). Tables are set up on a lovely beachfront patio and in a *palapa*-roofed dining area; at night, the long entry path is lit by lanterns. Every Tuesday and Friday, the "Chef's Table" tasting menu is offered to just eight diners, served in an intimate dining room set just off the kitchen.

In Town

★ **El Asadero** (Av. Satélite near Calle Sagitario, tel. 984/157-8998, 4:30pm-11pm Mon.-Sat., US$6-18) is the go-to steak house for locals and expats looking for a spectacular meal without breaking the bank. Meat, chicken, and yes, even veggies, are grilled in the open kitchen, the flavorful smells wafting

Everyone loves tortas: toasted bread rolls stuffed with meat and fresh veggies.

chicken options are available. Complete your order—and fill your belly—with an order of *papas rústicas* (hand-cut fries) and a freshly squeezed juice.

One of the best breakfast places in town, **Azafrán** (Av. Satélite near Calle Polar, cell tel. 984/129-6130, www.azafrantulum.com, 8am-2pm daily, US$5-11) serves up superb morning meals made with gourmet products: homemade bagels with prosciutto and brie, crepes stuffed with an assortment of fresh fruits, *chaya* omelets, and pâté platters with freshly baked bread. Organic coffee is a must, as is the fresh-squeezed orange juice. The only bummer is that this place gets crowded fast— come early to beat the morning rush.

Taquería El Carboncito (Av. Tulum between Calles Acuario and Jupiter; 6pm-2am Wed.-Mon., US$2-5) serves up sizzling tacos at plastic tables in the driveway of an auto shop that closes in the evening. It's a great place for a cheap tasty meal, and popular with local families. If there aren't any free tables, cross the street to **Antojitos La Chiapenca** (Av. Tulum at Jupiter, tel. 984/112-3249, 5:30pm-1am, US$2-5), a no-frills taco joint known for its tacos al pastor (pork tacos).

★ **Sabor de Mar** (Calle Jupiter at Av. Tulum, tel. 984/116 3187, 11am-9:30pm, US$5-10) is a classic Mexican street-side eatery with six or eight tables with vinyl tablecloths and bad lighting. But the seafood here is outstanding, and it's not uncommon to have to wait for a table (it's worth it). Lots of menu items come in towers—literally, food stacked like a Greek column—with fish, shrimp, avocado, and cucumbers providing most of building material. It's a nice change from the hipster eateries on the beach, and incredibly cheap too.

La Barracuda (Av. Tulum near Calle Luna Norte, tel. 984/160-0325, noon-8pm daily, US$6-13) is another popular, no-frills seafood eatery with plastic tables and chairs. Ceviche and fish soup are the specialty, but the shrimp cocktail and made-to-order fish dishes are tough to resist. Come hungry—portions are generous.

For homestyle Mexican cooking, head

throughout the dining room and out to the streetside tables. Try the hearty taco plate with your choice of fillings, cooked to order. All meals come with crispy tortilla chips and a trio of homemade salsas.

An unexpected budget eatery, **Uno: Japanese Noodles** (Calle Jupiter near Av. Tulum, tel. 984/234-4394, 2pm-11pm Thurs.-Tues., US$4-6) is a hole-in-the-wall ramen noodle place with just a handful of tables, inside and out. Big bowls of steaming noodle soup come topped a hardboiled egg, seaweed, and fresh seafood like shrimp, octopus, or fish; veggie, chicken, and pork options are also available. If it's too hot outside for soup, opt for one of the many sushi rolls or dumplings with a plate of lightly salted edamame.

Roraima Burgers Tulum (Calle Jupiter near Av. Tulum, cell tel. 984/142-8980, noon-11pm daily, US$5-7) is an appealing open-air eatery serving up a huge variety of burgers and *tortas* (Mexican sandwiches). All are made to order, and come with toppings like bacon, avocado, eggplant, and gouda or brie. Vegan and to **Don Cafeto** (Av. Tulum between Calles Centauro and Orion, tel. 984/871-2207, 7am-11pm daily, US$5-16), serving Mexican staples like mole and enchiladas, plus ceviche plates that are meals unto themselves. On a hot day, try a tall, cold *chayagra,* an uplifting blend of pineapple juice, lime juice, cucumber, and *chaya* (similar to spinach).

Sweets and Groceries

A classic Mexican bakery, **Pan del Carmen** (Av. Tulum near Calle Osiris, 6am-11pm daily, US$0.50-1.50) is a bustling shop offering everything from fresh rolls to chocolate-filled *cuernos* (croissants). Be sure to grab a metal tray and tongs to carry your selections.

La Reyna de Michoacan (Calle Alfa Sur at Calle Sol Ote, no phone, 7:30am-11pm, US$1.50-3) specializes in *paletas* (frozen ice pops), *helado* (ice cream), *aguas* (juices), and *licuados* (smoothies), all made with fresh fruits. There's a huge variety of flavors—from coconut and strawberry to guava and pineapple with chili. It's a perfect stop while strolling about town.

For a supermarket with the basics and then some, head to the **Chedraui** (Av. Cobá s/n, 7am-10pm daily), located between Tulum town and the Zona Hotelera; beyond fresh, dry, and canned food, you'll find a bakery, a beachwear and shoe section, and even home appliances.

On Sunday, check out the **Tianguis Orgánico y Natural** (central plaza, 10am-3pm), a farmers market featuring organic produce, artisanal products, and homeopathic medicines.

ACCOMMODATIONS

Chances are you've come to Tulum to stay in one of the famous beachside bungalow-type hotels. There are many to choose from, each slightly different but most sharing a laid-back atmosphere and terrific beaches. However, some travelers are surprised by just how rustic some accommodations are, even those charging hundreds of dollars per night. The root of the matter is that there are no power lines or freshwater wells serving the beach. Virtually all accommodations have salty water in the showers and sinks. Most (but not all) have fans, and electricity may be limited to nighttime hours only. Air-conditioning is available in only a handful of places. At the same time, some hotels use generators to power their restaurants and reception, so it's worth asking for a room away from the generator; nothing is a bigger killjoy than a diesel motor pounding outside your window when the point of coming here was to enjoy the peace and quiet.

If staying on the beach is out of your budget (join the club!), staying in town is a perfectly good alternative. The options have improved significantly, with a crop of new bed-and-breakfasts and boutique hotels to go along with a burgeoning number of hostels and budget digs. The beach is just a short drive or bike ride away, and prices for food, drinks, and laundry are much lower.

Zona Hotelera
UNDER US$100

Fronting a winding cenote, ★ **Cenote Encantado** (Carr. Tulum-Punta Allen Km 10.5, cell tel. 984/142-5930, www.cenoteencantado.com, US$25 pp tent) is, in some ways, a throwback to Tulum's beginnings: a haven for backpackers with boho spirit. The hotel is more like a camping village, with 17 tents set up around the leafy property. Each is set on a platform and has a bed with sheets, a bedside table, lamp, fan (there's electricity 7:30pm-midnight), Wi-Fi (10am-midnight), even a rug. There's also a clean communal kitchen and a cozy wood-floor lounge for meditating, yoga classes (price varies), and just hanging out; both structures are breezy but enclosed with strong mosquito netting. Open-air showers and dry toilets round out the camping-plus experience. Admission to the cenote also is included; kayaks, paddleboards, and snorkeling equipment are available for rent.

Cabañas y Cenote Yaxchen (Carr. Tulum-Punta Allen Km 10.5, cell tel. 984/209-9837, US$50-70 s/d with shared bathroom) has eight simple *palapa*-roofed cabins on a palm-laden property. Each has a decent bed with mosquito netting, big screened windows, and electricity (5:30pm-2am only). There's also an open-air kitchen with a gas-operated fridge to keep your perishables kicking, as well as a comfortable lounge with Wi-Fi. Admission to Cenote Encantado (in the backyard) is included in the rate, as is use of kayaks.

Santa Fe (Carr. Tulum-Punta Allen, 2.5 kilometers/1.5 miles north of junction, tel. 984/136-5248, US$13 pp tent) is a beachfront restaurant (8am-6pm daily) that welcomes campers on its property. The facilities are very basic—wear your flip-flops in the shower—and there's no electricity after 10pm. (All the better to enjoy the night sky!)

US$100-200

One of the best deals in the hotel zone, **Las Palmas Maya** (Carr. Tulum-Punta Allen Km 8.5, tel. 984/213-1515, www.laspalmasmaya. com, US$130-155 s/d) has large, comfortable rooms and awesome showers (the heat and water pressure can't be beat!). The catch is that it doesn't have air-conditioning and it's on the jungle side of the road. That's a small price to pay, as fans keep the rooms perfectly cool and the beach is literally just steps away. There's also free coffee and a communal kitchen, and wonderful personalized service.

Ahau Tulum (Carr. Tulum-Punta Allen Km 4.4, tel. 984/231-1081, www.ahautulum. com, US$112 hut, US$246-308 s/d with a/c, US$490-504 suite with a/c) is by no means a budget place—it has stunning rooms, some going for over US$500—but its stick-built "Bali Huts" are among the cheapest digs on the beach. Though very comfortable, they're small and set back near the administrative buildings; they also have gaps in the walls (natural ventilation!) and have fans only. It's the price you pay to be on the sand for this cheap—a bargain for boho beach hounds.

Although sharing a bathroom for almost US$150 a night doesn't seem quite right, **Coco Tulum** (Carr. Tulum-Punta Allen

Km 8, cell tel. 984/157-4830, www.cocotulum.com, US$108-145 s/d with shared bath, US$218-267 s/d with a/c, US$267-305 suite with a/c) does the basics with style. Tidy *palapa*-roofed bungalows have cement floors, comfy beds, hanging bookshelves, fans, and sleek black exteriors with private patios. The shared bathrooms are actually quite nice, with modern basin sinks, rainfall shower-heads, hot water, and thrice-daily cleaning. And if sharing a bathroom really is beyond the pale, there's a handful of cabañas as well as deluxe rooms, each with private bathroom, air-conditioning (7pm-7am only), and stellar views. Wind- and solar-powered electricity is available 24 hours.

Tita Tulum (Carr. Tulum-Punta Allen Km 8, tel. 984/877-8513, www.titatulum. com, US$185-205 s/d) has a lovely beachfront and low-key atmosphere—a great option for families and travelers who prefer modest comforts and a lower rate (especially off-season) over boutique eco-chic embellishments. Ten guest rooms form a semicircle around a sandy, palm-fringed lot; they're a bit worn around the edges but have polished cement floors, clean bathrooms, and indoor and outdoor sitting areas, plus fans, Wi-Fi, and 24-hour electricity. Tita is a charming and attentive proprietor, and prepares authentic Mexican dishes in the hotel's small restaurant.

Posada Lamar (Carr. Tulum-Punta Allen Km 6, cell tel. 984/106-3682, www. posadalamar.com, US$156-219 s/d) has eight comfortable and artful bungalows, with salvaged-wood detailing and rich colors and fabrics. There is no air-conditioning, and electricity (wind and solar powered) is available only at night; fortunately, the sea breezes and one fan keep the units cool (and the bugs at bay) most nights. The bungalows are a bit too close together, diminishing privacy, especially since you often need the windows and doors open, but the beach here is clean and beautiful, with plenty of chairs, beds, and *palapas*. Continental breakfast is included, served every morning on your private terrace.

Tulum Town and Zona Hotelera

To Cenote Cristal Escondido, Muyil Archaeological Zone, Mahahual, and Chetumal

307

HOTEL DON DIEGO DE LA SELVA

JARDIN DE FRIDA

CHAN-CHEN

ZAZIL-HA

KUKULCAN

AVENIDA TULUM

PRIV. NORTE

LUNA NORTE

TAURO PTE.

LA BARRACUDA

SECRET GARDEN

AQUARIO NORTE

PRIV. NORTE

LUNA NORTE

SATURNO SUR

MERCURIO OTE

ROBALMA BURGERS TULUM

POSADA LUNA DEL SUR

HOSPITAL DE TULUM

BUS STATION

AQUARIO SUR

MEXIK

LA REYNA DE MICHOACAN

FARMACIA SIMILARES

TAQUERIA EL CARBONCITO

CABRON

ENCANTO CANTINA

UNO. TULUM

SABOR

DE MAR.

BOHEME

JAPANESE NOODLES

CENTRO DE SALUD TULUM

OMEGA

PLUTON SUR

NEPTUNO OTE

PRIV. ALFA SUR

AYA SUR

Central Plaza

SATURNO OTE

ARIES SUR

LEO SUR

JUPITER SUR

MERCURIO OTE

AEROCITO

OSIRIS SUR

BETA SUR

0   300 yds

0   300 m

To Sian Ka'an, El Ultimo Maya, Sol Caribe, Mukan Resort, and Punta Allen

Cenote Encantado

YAANWELLNESS ENERGY SPA/ TREE TOP YOGA SHALA

CENOTE ENCANTADO

CABAÑAS Y CENOTE YAXCHEN

DOS CEIBAS

SUEÑOS TULUM

MAYAN CLAY SPA

LAS PALMAS MAYA

LA ZEBRA

HOTEL NUEVA VIDA DE RAMIRO

TITA TULUM

IKIIN BEACH CLUB

TULUM JUNGLE GYM

RAW LOVE CAFÉ/ AHAU TULUM/ MEXICAN CARIBBEAN KITESURF

YOGA SHALA TULUM

YOKTE TULUM

PRO KITE TULUM

ZIGGY BEACH

GITANO

CABAÑAS LA LUNA

MORPH KITEBOARDING

MAYA CAMP BEACH CLUB

COCO TULUM

POSADA LAMAR

UKAMI

ULTRAMAR SHUTTLE

Z O N A

Caribbean Sea

TULUM'S SOUTHERN BEACHES

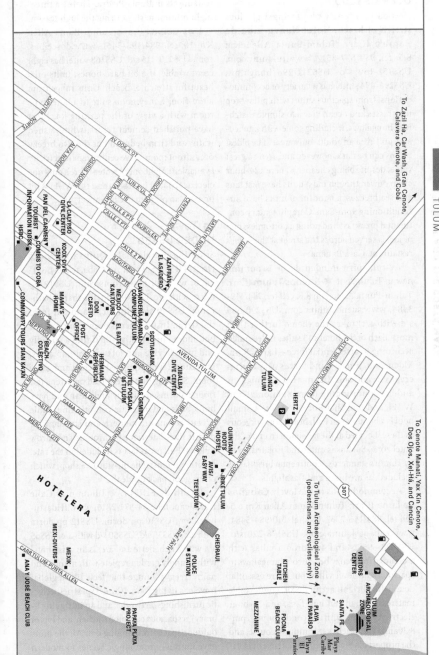

OVER US$200

Nestled in a jungly plot facing a glorious stretch of beach, **Hotel Nueva Vida de Ramiro** (Carr. Tulum-Punta Allen Km 8.5, tel. 984/877-8512, www.tulumnv.com, US$151-160 s/d, US$211-296 bungalow, US$296-494 suite) has a variety of accommodations, from spacious suites with pillow-top mattresses and ocean views to simple thatch-roof bungalows, including some with kitchenette, and even an adults-only area. (The oldest rooms can be dark, however, and aren't a great value, despite being cheaper.) There's 24-hour clean power, though most units have just fans and sea breezes; a handful of units have air-conditioning 9pm-8am. Complimentary continental breakfast, including a bottomless cup of joe, is served across the street at the hotel's restaurant, Casa Banana.

Artful, spirit-minded decor is nothing new in Tulum, but ★ **Sueños Tulum** (Carr. Tulum-Punta Allen Km 8.5, cell tel. 984/119-3484, www.suenostulum.com, US$290-585 s/d with a/c) takes the theme further than most. Each of the hotel's 13 suites is decorated according to an essential force—Earth, Rain, Moon, Sun, Jungle—and there's Maya imagery inside and out. All units have ceiling fans and air-conditioning (8am-8pm only) and Wi-Fi, and most have ocean views. A small pool is a bonus, even with beaches as gorgeous as these. Located at the far southern end of the hotel zone, Sueños is quiet and isolated, even by Tulum's standards. Continental breakfast is included, as are bikes and flashlights.

Accommodations at the lovely **Cabañas La Luna** (Carr. Tulum-Punta Allen Km 6.5, cell tel. 984/146-7737, U.S. tel. 310/984-5484, www.cabanaslaluna.com, US$178-220 s/d, US$328-595 2- and 4-bedroom villas with a/c) range from cozy beachfront bungalows to spacious split-level villas, but share essential details like bright, artful décor, comfortable mattresses, high ceilings, fans, and 24-hour electricity (some with air-conditioning 7pm-8:30am). The beach is stunning, of course, and the property is big enough for a sense of isolation, yet within walking distance of shops and restaurants in Punta Piedra. There's a three-night minimum stay during the high season.

Dos Ceibas (Carr. Tulum-Punta Allen Km 10, tel. 984/198-5461, www.dosceibas.com, US$210-315 s/d, US$368 suite) has eight comfortable, if a bit bare-bones, units on a beautiful stretch of beach. Units range from a top-floor honeymoon suite to a hotel-type room with a view of the parking lot. Most have polished cement floors, whitewashed walls, and firm beds; all but the two breezy oceanfront rooms have ceiling fans (electricity available at night only). Note: There's only one electrical outlet per room and the Wi-Fi is hit or miss, so prepare to disconnect.

In Town
UNDER US$50

Stunning murals make **Quintana Roots Hostel** (Calle Sol near Av. Cobá, tel. 984/871-2426, www.quintanaroots.com, US$12 pp dorm with a/c, US$30 s/d with shared bathroom, US$40 s/d with a/c) stand out from the street. Inside, there's even more wall art but, more importantly, you'll find a friendly and mellow vibe and lots of common areas, including a well-equipped kitchen and game room. Sleeping units are spread out over a few floors: Dorms are sunny and clean and have bunk beds and quiet air-conditioning, while private rooms are modern and stylish, with details like slate-floor bathrooms and throw pillows. Full breakfast is included in the rate. Another bonus? The on-site dive shop, which offers good package deals.

Jardín de Frida (Av. Tulum near Calle Kukulcán, tel. 984/871-2816, www.fridastulum.com, US$10 pp dorm, US$12 pp dorm with a/c, US$35 s/d, US$50 s/d with a/c, US$65 s/d with kitchenette and a/c) is an artsy hotel with a jungly garden replete with mango and palm trees, a lounge that feels like a global traveler's living room (think tapestries, eclectic furnishings, artworks, and an intriguing library), a spacious common kitchen, and lots of outdoor spaces for hanging out. All the units have murals—from jungle scenes to modern art. Dorms have twin beds (no bunks here) and en suite bathrooms. Private rooms are different in style and size but are comfortable and homey. Continental breakfast and Wi-Fi are included in the rate.

Known for its elaborate daily breakfasts, **Mama's Home** (Calle Orion Sur between Calles Venus and Sol Ote., cell tel. 984/137-1393, US$16 pp dorm, US$19 pp dorm with a/c, US$67-80 s/d with a/c) is a popular spot for budget travelers. Two mixed dorms and eight private rooms—all with thick mattresses—open onto a colorful courtyard with Maya-inspired murals, hammocks, and long tables. There's a small communal kitchen plus a living room with a couple of computers for Internet access (there's also Wi-Fi). Weekly themed events like Mojito Demo, Flamenco Night, and Karaoke Night make it easy to meet other travelers.

US$50-100

Tucked into a quiet residential street, ★ **Secret Garden** (Calle Sagitario near Calle Acuario, tel. 984/157-8001, www.secretgardentulum.com, US$50-68 s/d with a/c, US$68 s/d with a/c and kitchenette) offers stylish, comfortable rooms at affordable rates (guests over age 16 only). Units vary in size and layout—some with kitchenettes, some with lofts—but all have artful décor and high-end amenities. Rooms open onto a long, leafy central garden with hammocks and low couches, perfect for relaxing day or night. Service is outstanding, and purified water, fruit, and baked goods are offered daily.

Mango Tulum (Calle Polar Pte. near Av. Cobá, tel. 984/169-9097, www.mangotulum.com, US$55-70 s/d with a/c, US$100 studio with a/c) is a pleasantly sparse hotel with whitewashed walls, polished cement floors, and a spacious garden with mature trees and a pool. Rooms are bright and airy and open onto the garden; some have king-size beds. The studio penthouse is especially spacious and has a fully equipped kitchen and TV. Fresh fruit, coffee, and tea are available in the morning. Mango is located behind the OXXO convenience store on Avenida Cobá.

Hotel Don Diego de la Selva (Av. Tulum s/n, cell tel. 984/114-9744, www.dondiegodelaselva.com, US$70 s/d, US$85-130 s/d with a/c) offers spacious rooms and bungalows with classy understated decor, comfortable beds, and large glass doors opening onto a shady garden. There's a large pool, and the hotel restaurant serves good French-Mexican cuisine; half-board options are available. The only catch is the location, about a kilometer (0.6 mile) south of the plaza. The hotel rents bikes, but most guests find a rental car indispensable. Wi-Fi and continental breakfast are included.

Wearing many hats, **Boheme Tulum** (Calle Sol between Calles Alfa and Jupiter, U.S. tel. 617/669-8799, bohemetulum@gmail.com, US$62-120 s/d with a/c) is a hipster cultural center and home to Radio Tulum. It's also a boutique hotel with four gorgeous and well-equipped rooms. Each varies in size and décor but has a shabby-chic feel that integrates polished cement, antiques, modern art, and details like a hanging desk and a live tree in the shower. (Really.) There's also a pool and gourmet café on site. Before booking be sure to ask about the events schedule; some can go until the wee hours of the night.

OVER US$100

Posada Luna del Sur (Calle Luna Sur near Av. Tulum, tel. 984/182-9696, www.posadalunadelsur.com, US$110 s/d with a/c) has compact but pleasant rooms, with whitewashed walls, comfortable beds (king or two twins), and small terraces overlooking a leafy garden. A full à la carte breakfast is included in the rate; it's served in a pleasant rooftop lounge that's a great evening hangout, with plenty of tables and chairs. Service is friendly and accommodating.

On the road to the beach, **Teetotum** (Av. Cobá Sur s/n, cell tel. 984/143-8956, www.hotelteetotum.com, US$135 s/d with a/c) has a handful of minimalist rooms—ceramic basin sinks, low bed stands—and artful decor throughout, including playful oversized murals in the dining room. All rooms have air-conditioning and Wi-Fi but no TV or telephone. Guests enjoy free continental breakfast and bike rentals, as well as a lovely plunge pool and rooftop sun beds. The on-site restaurant serves a little of everything, from hummus plates to bacon cheeseburgers, with an equally varied (and enticing) drink menu.

A long, thin pool winds its way through **Hotel Posada 06 Tulum** (Calle Andromeda near Calle Geminis, tel. 984/160-0428, www.posada06tulum.com, US$100-130 s/d with a/c), a small hotel in the quiet part of town. Rooms feel fresh and airy, with adobe walls, muted colors, and simple décor; all have small private balconies or patios. The grounds and common areas are equally welcoming and well maintained. Full breakfast is included in the rate and is served at its street-front café. Adults only.

★ **Villas Geminis** (Calle Andrómeda at Calle Gemini, tel. 984/140-4501, www.villas-geminis.com, US$155 s/d with a/c, US$195 studio with a/c, US$185 1-bedroom condo with a/c, US$225 2-bedroom condo with a/c) has spacious rooms, penthouse studios, and one- and two-bedroom condos with modern kitchens and private terraces. All are simple but elegant in décor; some have luxurious outdoor soaking tubs. There's 24-hour security and daily maid service, and the owners and staff are friendly and attentive, making you feel at home and very taken care of. The interior courtyard has a nice swimming pool surrounded by a lush garden. Complimentary bicycles are available for guests.

INFORMATION AND SERVICES
Tourist Information

A **tourist information kiosk** (no phone, 9am-4pm Mon.-Fri., 10am-3pm Sat.-Sun.) is located on the central plaza, across from the HSBC bank. The chief attendant is quite knowledgeable, her teenage disciples less so. You often can glean useful information from the stacks of brochures here. The website **www.todotulum.com** also offers good information on current goings-on and offerings in Tulum.

Emergency Services

Hospital de Tulum (Av. Tulum between Calles Luna and Acuario Norte, tel. 984/871-2271, www.hospitaldetulum.com, 24 hours daily) is a small private hospital offering emergency and preventative services and has a bilingual staff. For minor medical issues, Tulum's local clinic, **Centro de Salud Tulum** (Calle Andrómeda between Calles Jupiter and Alfa, tel. 984/871-2050, 24 hours), is a decent option. For serious health problems, head to Cancún.

Farmacia Similares (Av. Tulum at Calle Jupiter Sur, tel. 984/871-2736) is open 9am-11pm Monday-Saturday and 9am-9pm Sunday; it also has a doctor on staff for simple consultations 9am-9pm Monday-Saturday and 9am-3pm Sunday.

The **police** (toll-free tel. 066, 24 hours) share a large station with the fire department, about two kilometers (1.2 miles) from Tulum Pueblo on the road to the Zona Hotelera.

Money

HSBC (Av. Tulum at Calle Alfa, 9am-5pm Mon.-Fri.) has reliable ATMs and will change foreign cash and AmEx travelers checks. If there's a line, **ScotiaBank** (Av. Tulum at Calle Satélite, 8:30am-4pm Mon.-Fri.) is another good option.

Media and Communications

Tulum's **post office** (Calle Orion Sur at Calle Andrómeda Sur) is open 8am-4pm Monday-Friday and 9am-1pm Saturday.

Most hotels offer free Wi-Fi for guests; in the Zona Hotelera, many only offer Wi-Fi in the reception or restaurant areas. In town, **Compunet Tulum** (Av. Tulum near Av. Satélite, 8:30am-7:30pm Sun.-Fri., 8am-2pm Sat., US$1/hour) has flat-screen computers and killer air-conditioning.

Laundry and Storage

Tucked into an alley just off the main drag,

Tulum Bus Schedule

Departures from the **bus terminal** (Av. Tulum between Calles Alfa and Jupiter, tel. 984/871-2122) include:

Destination	Price	Duration	Schedule*
Cancún	US$4.50-11	2.5 hrs	every 15-60 mins 3:45am-10pm
Cancún International Airport	US$12.50	2 hrs	Five departures 7:10am-3pm
Chetumal	US$8-19	3.5-4 hrs	every 60-90 mins 8:30am-11:50pm
Chichén Itzá	US$7.50	3 hrs	9am and 2:45pm
Cobá	US$3-4.50	45-60 mins	10:10am and 11:35am
Mahahual	US$7.50-10	3 hrs	8:55am and 6:50pm
Mérida	US$8.50-17	4 hrs	9 departures 2:30am-9:40pm
Playa del Carmen	US$2-5.50	1 hr	every 15-90 mins 12:20am-9:55pm
Valladolid	US$5-7	1.5-2hrs	every 30-90 mins 2:30am-10:20pm

Lavandería Mandala (Av. Tulum near Av. Satélite, 8am-9pm daily) charges US$1.25 per kilo (2.2 pounds) with a three-kilo (6.6-pound) minimum. Next-day service only.

The **bus terminal** (Av. Tulum between Calles Alfa and Jupiter, tel. 984/871-2122, 24 hours) has luggage storage for US$0.50-1.25 per hour or US$5 per 8-24 hours, depending on the size of the bag.

GETTING THERE
Bus

Tulum's **bus terminal** (Av. Tulum between Calles Alfa and Jupiter, tel. 984/871-2122) is at the south end of town, a block from the main plaza.

*Schedules are subject to change.

Combi

Combis are white collective vans that zip between Tulum and Playa del Carmen all day, every day (US$2.25, 1 hour, every 10 minutes 5am-10pm). They leave more frequently than buses and are handier for intermediate stops, such as Dos Ojos, Akumal, and Xpu-Há. Flag them down anywhere on Avenida Tulum or Highway 307.

Combis also go to Cobá (US$3.50, 1 hour), stopping at cenotes along the way. They leave hourly 8am-6pm Monday-Saturday and every two hours on Sunday. Look for the stop on Avenida Tulum at Calle Osiris Norte. You can also catch them at the intersection of Highway 307 and the Cobá/Zona Hotelera road.

Ferry Shuttle

Ultramar (Carr. Tulum-Punta Allen Km 6.7, tel. 998/881-5898, www.ultramarferry.com) offers shuttle service to its ferry terminal in Playa del Carmen for boats headed to Cozumel (US$42 pp), and to the Gran Puerto ferry terminal in Cancún for ferries headed to Isla Mujeres (US$62). Shuttles leave at 7:45am, 9:30am, and 6pm daily. The fare includes round-trip shuttle service as well as the round-trip ferry ticket.

Car

Highway 307 passes right through the middle of Tulum Pueblo, where it is referred to as Avenida Tulum. Coming south from Cancún or Playa del Carmen, you'll first pass the entrance to Tulum archaeological site, on your left. A kilometer and a half later (1 mile) you'll reach a large intersection, where you can turn left (east) toward the beach and Zona Hotelera, or right (west) toward Cobá. Continuing straight ahead takes you into Tulum Pueblo, then onward to the Costa Maya.

GETTING AROUND
Bicycle

A bike can be very handy, especially for getting to or from the beach, or anywhere along the now-paved road through the Zona Hotelera.

In the Zona Hotelera, check out **Yokte Bikes** (Carr. Tulum-Punta Allen Km 7.5, cell tel. 984/145-4061, 9am-6pm daily), which rents beach cruisers for US$10 per 24 hours, including helmet, lock, and safety vest. Drop-off and pickup at your hotel is included.

In town, **iBike Tulum** (Av. Cobá Sur at Calle Sol, tel. 984/802-5518, www.ibiketulum. com, 8am-5:30pm Mon.-Sat.) rents a variety of bikes and trikes, including beach cruisers and mountain bikes (US$10-13 per 24 hours), most in top condition. All come with helmet, lock, lights, and roadside assistance. Accident insurance is included.

Beach Shuttle

There is a local *colectivo* (US$0.75) labeled "Cabañas" that goes from Tulum town to the arch at the southern end of the Zona Hotelera and back again, every 20-30 minutes 6am-8pm. Another *colectivo* (US$1), labeled "Ruínas," goes from town to the northern end of the Zona Hotelera at 8am, 8:30am, 5:30pm, and 6pm. Both routes start at the corner of a little playground at Calle Sol Ote and Orion Sur. You also can catch both *colectivos* along Avenida Tulum and on the road to and along the beach. Schedules often change, so be sure to confirm the departure and return times.

Car

A car can be very useful in Tulum, especially in the Zona Hotelera, even if you don't plan on using it every day. Renting a car from the airport in Cancún is the easiest and most affordable option for most travelers, especially if you book online and in advance. In Tulum, agencies include **Easy Way** (Av. Cobá near Calle Sol, toll-free Mex. tel. 800/327-9929, toll-free U.S./Can. tel. 877/640-3279, www. easywayrentacar.com), **Avis** (Av. Cobá Sur at Calle Sol Ote, cell tel. 984/871-2937, www.avis. com), and **Hertz** (Hwy. 307 at Av. Cobá, toll-free Mex. tel. 800/709-5000, www.hertz.com).

Taxi

Taxis are plentiful, and fares run about US$3 in town and US$8-12 to get to the Zona Hotelera. In the Zona Hotelera, there's an unofficial taxi stand in Punta Piedra and across from the Mezzanine hotel; rates are roughly the same within the Zona Hotelera or back into Tulum Pueblo. From either area, a ride to Tulum ruins costs about US$5.

Cobá

The Maya ruins of Cobá make an excellent complement—or even alternative—to the memorable but vastly overcrowded ruins at Tulum. Cobá doesn't have Tulum's stunning Caribbean view and beach, but its structures are much larger and more ornate—in fact, Cobá's main pyramid is the second tallest in the Yucatán Peninsula, and it's one of few you are still allowed to climb. The ruins are surrounded by lakes and thick forest, making it a great place to see birds, butterflies, and tropical flora.

★ COBÁ ARCHAEOLOGICAL ZONE

Cobá (8am-5pm daily, US$3.50) is especially notable for the complex system of *sacbeob,* or raised stone causeways that connected it to other Maya cities, near and far. (The term *sacbeob*—whose singular form is *sacbé*—means white roads.) Dozens of such roads crisscross the Yucatán Peninsula, but Cobá has more than any other ancient city, underscoring its status as a commercial, political, and military hub. One road extends in an almost perfectly straight line from the base of Cobá's principal pyramid to the town of Yaxuna, more than 100 kilometers (62 miles) away—no small feat considering a typical *sacbé* was 1-2 meters (3.3-6.6 feet) high and about 4.5 meters (15 feet) wide, and covered in white mortar. In Cobá, some roads were even bigger—10 meters (32.8 feet) across. In fact, archaeologists have uncovered a massive stone cylinder believed to have been used to flatten the broad roadbeds.

History

Cobá was settled as early as 100 BC around a collection of small lagoons; it's a logical and privileged location, as the Yucatán Peninsula is virtually devoid of rivers, lakes, or any other aboveground water. Cobá developed into an important trading hub, and in its early existence had a particularly close connection with the Petén region of present-day Guatemala. That relationship would later fade as Cobá grew more intertwined with coastal cities like Tulum, but Petén influence is obvious in Cobá's high, steep structures, which are reminiscent of those in Tikal. At its peak, around AD 600-800, Cobá was the largest urban center in the northern lowlands, with some 40,000 residents and over 6,000 structures spread over 50 square kilometers (31 square miles). The city controlled most of the northeastern portion of the Yucatán Peninsula during the same period before being toppled by the Itzás of Chichén Itzá following a protracted war in the mid-800s. Following a widespread Maya collapse—of which the fall of Cobá was not the cause, though perhaps an early warning sign—the great city was all but abandoned, save as a pilgrimage and ceremonial site for the ascendant Itzás. It was briefly reinhabited in the 12th century, when a few new structures were added, but had been abandoned again, and covered in a blanket of vegetation, by the time of the Spanish conquest.

Cobá Group

Passing through the entry gate, the first group of ruins you encounter is the Cobá Group, a collection of over 50 structures and the oldest part of the ancient city. Many of Cobá's *sacbeob* initiate here. The primary structure, **La Iglesia** (The Church), rises 22.5 meters (74 feet) from a low platform, making it Cobá's second-highest pyramid. The structure consists of nine platforms stacked atop one another and notable for their round corners. Built in numerous phases beginning in the Early Classic era, La Iglesia is far more reminiscent of Tikal and other Petén-area

Cobá Archaeological Zone

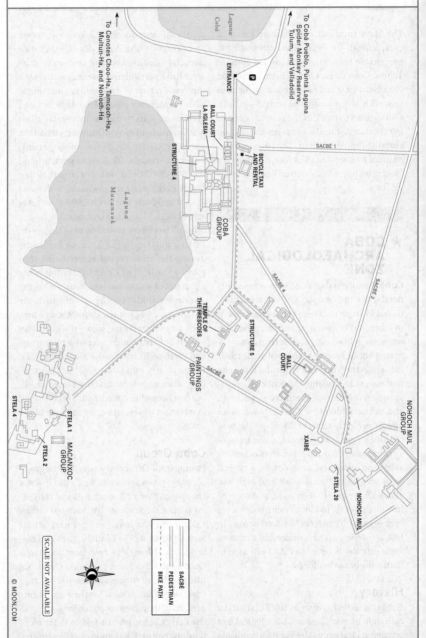

To Cobá Pueblo, Punta Laguna
Spider Monkey Reserve,
Tulum, and Valladolid

To Cenotes Choo-Ha, Tamcach-Ha,
Multun-Ha, and Nohoch-Ha

Laguna Cobá

ENTRANCE

P

Laguna Macanxoc

BALL COURT

LA IGLESIA

STRUCTURE 4

COBÁ GROUP

BICYCLE TAXI AND RENTAL

SACBÉ 1

SACBÉ 4

SACBÉ 2

TEMPLE OF THE FRESCOES

STRUCTURE 5

PAINTINGS GROUP

SACBÉ 8

BALL COURT

XAIBÉ

STELA 20

NOHOCH MUL GROUP

NOHOCH MUL

STELA 4

STELA 1

MACANXOC GROUP

STELA 2

SCALE NOT AVAILABLE

© MOON.COM

SACBÉ
PEDESTRIAN
BIKE PATH

Cobá is home to the Yucatán Peninsula's second tallest Maya pyramid.

Nohoch Mul Group

From the Cobá Group, the path winds nearly two kilometers (1.2 miles) through dense forest to Cobá's other main group, Nohoch Mul. The name is Yucatec Maya for Big Mound—the group's namesake pyramid rises an impressive 42 meters (138 feet) above the forest floor, the equivalent of 12 stories. (It was long believed to be the Yucatán Peninsula's tallest structure until the main pyramid at Calakmul in Campeche was determined to be some 10 meters higher.) Like La Iglesia in the Cobá Group, Nohoch Mul is composed of several platforms with rounded corners. A long central staircase climbs steeply from the forest floor to the pyramid's lofty peak. A small temple at the top bears a fairly well-preserved carving of the Descending God, an upside-down figure that figures prominently at Tulum but whose identity and significance is still unclear. (Theories vary widely, from Venus to the god of bees.)

Nohoch Mul is one of few Maya pyramids that visitors are still allowed to climb, and the view from the top is impressive—a flat green forest spreading almost uninterrupted in every direction. A rope running down the stairs makes going up and down easier.

Where the path hits Nohoch Mul is **Stela 20,** positioned on the steps of a minor structure, beneath a protective *palapa* roof. It is one of Cobá's best-preserved stelae, depicting a figure in an elaborate costume and headdress, holding a large ornate scepter in his arms—both signifying that he is an *ahau,* or high lord or ruler. The figure, as yet unidentified, is standing on the backs of two slaves or captives, with another two bound and kneeling at his feet. Stela 20 is also notable for the date inscribed on it—November 30, 780—the latest Long Count date yet found in Cobá.

Xaibé and the Ball Court

Between the Cobá and Nohoch Mul Groups are several smaller but still significant structures. Closest to Nohoch Mul is a curiously conical structure that archaeologists have

structures than it is of the long palaces and elaborate facades typical of Puuc and Chenes sites. Visitors are no longer allowed to climb the Iglesia pyramid due to the poor state of its stairs, but it is crowned with a small temple where archaeologists discovered a cache of jade figurines, ceramic vases, pearls, and conch shells.

The Cobá Group also includes one of the city's two **ball courts,** and a large acropolis-like complex with wide stairs leading to raised patios. At one time these patios were connected, forming a long gallery of rooms that likely served as an administrative center. The best-preserved structure in this complex, **Structure 4,** has a long, vaulted passageway beneath its main staircase; the precise purpose of this passageway is unclear, but it's a common feature in Cobá and affords a close look at how a so-called Maya arch is constructed.

The Cobá Group is directly opposite the stand where you can rent bicycles or hire bike taxis. Many travelers leave it for the end of their visit, after they've turned in their bikes.

dubbed **Xaibé,** a Yucatec Maya word for crossroads. The name owes to the fact that it's near the intersection of four major *sacbeob,* and for the same reason, archaeologists believe it may have served as a watchtower. That said, its unique design and imposing size suggest a grander purpose. Round structures are fairly rare in Maya architecture, and most are thought to be astronomical observatories; there's no evidence Xaibé served that function, however, particularly since it lacks any sort of upper platform or temple. Be aware that the walking path does not pass Xaibé—you have to take the longer bike path to reach it.

A short distance from Xaibé is the second of Cobá's **ball courts.** Both courts have imagery of death and sacrifice, though they are more pronounced here: a skull inscribed on a stone in the center of the court, a decapitated jaguar on a disc at the end, and symbols of Venus (which represented death and war) inscribed on the two scoring rings. This ball court also had a huge plaque implanted on one of its slopes, with over 70 glyphs and dated AD 465; the plaque in place today is a replica, but the original is under a *palapa* covering at one end of the court, allowing visitors to examine it more closely.

Paintings Group

The Paintings Group is a collection of five platforms encircling a large plaza. The temples here were among the last to be constructed in Cobá and pertain to the latest period of occupation, roughly AD 1100-1450. The group's name comes from paintings that once lined the walls, though very little color is visible now, unfortunately. Traces of blue and red can be seen in the upper room of the **Temple of the Frescoes,** the group's largest structure, but you aren't allowed to climb up to get a closer look.

Although centrally located, the Paintings Group is easy to miss on your way between the more outlying pyramids and groups. Look for a sign for **Structure 5,** where you can leave your bike (if you have one) and walk into the group's main area.

Macanxoc Group

From the Paintings Group, the path continues southeasterly for about a kilometer (0.6 mile) to the Macanxoc Group. Numerous stelae have been found here, indicating it was a place of great ceremonial significance. The most famous of these monuments is **Stela 1,** aka the Macanxoc Stela. It depicts a scene from the Maya creation myth—"the

Touring Cobá on two wheels is a popular option.

Deciphering the Glyphs

For years, scholars could not agree whether the fantastic inscriptions found on Maya stelae, codices, and temple walls were anything more than complex records of numbers and dates.

Mayanist and scholar Michael D. Coe's *Breaking the Maya Code* (Thames and Hudson, 2012) is a fascinating account of the decipherment of Maya hieroglyphics. Coe describes how, in 1952, reclusive Russian scholar Yuri Valentinovich Knorosov made a crucial breakthrough by showing that Maya writing did in fact convey spoken words. Using a rough alphabet recorded by Fray Diego de Landa (the 16th-century bishop who, ironically, is best known for having destroyed numerous Maya texts), Knorosov showed that ancient texts contain common Yucatec Maya words such as *cutz* (turkey) and *tzul* (dog).

But Knorosov's findings were met with staunch resistance by some of the field's most influential scholars, which delayed progress for decades. By the mid-1980s, however, decipherment picked up speed; one of many standouts from that era is David Stuart, the son of Maya experts, who went to Cobá with his parents at age eight and passed the time copying glyphs and learning Yucatec Maya words from local playmates. As a high school student he served as chief epigrapher on a groundbreaking exploration in Belize, and at age 18 he received a US$128,000 MacArthur Fellowship (aka "Genius Award") to, as he told Michael Coe, "play around with the glyphs" full-time.

Researchers now know that Maya writing is like most other hieroglyphic systems. What appears at first to be a single glyph can have up to four parts, and the same word can be expressed in pictorial, phonetic, or hybrid form. Depending on context, one symbol can have either a pictorial or phonetic role; likewise, a particular sound can be represented in more than one way. One of David Stuart's great insights was that for all its complexity, much of Maya glyphic writing is "just repetitive."

But how do scholars know what the symbols are meant to sound like in the first place? Some come from the Landa alphabet, others are suggested by the pictures that accompany many texts, still others from patterns derived by linguistic analyses of contemporary Maya languages. In some cases, it is simply a hunch that turns out to be right. If this seems like somewhat shaky scientific ground, it is—but not without a means of being proved.

Hundreds of glyphs have been deciphered, and most of the known Maya texts can be reliably translated. Some archaeologists lament, not unreasonably, that high-profile glyphic studies divert attention from research into the lives of everyday ancient Maya, who far outnumbered the nobility but are not at all represented in the inscriptions. That said, the effort has lent invaluable insight into Maya civilization, especially dynastic successions and religious beliefs.

hearth stone appears"—along with a Long Count date referring to a cycle ending the equivalent of 41.9 billion, billion, billion years in the future. It is the most distant Long Count date known to have been conceived and recorded by the ancient Maya. Stela 1 also has reference to December 21, 2012, when the Maya Long Count completed its first Great Cycle, equivalent to 5,125 years. Despite widespread reports to the contrary, there is no known evidence, at Cobá or anywhere, that the Maya believed (much less predicted) that the world would end on that date.

Flora and Fauna

The name Cobá ("Water Stirred by the Wind" in Maya) is surely a reference to the group of shallow lagoons here (Cobá, Macanxoc, Xkanha, and Sacakal). The archaeological site and the surrounding wetlands and forest are rich with birdlife—herons, egrets, motmot, parrots, and the occasional toucan are not uncommon. Arrive early to see the most birds—at the very least you'll get an earful of their varied songs and cries. Later, as the temperature climbs, you'll start to see colorful butterflies, including the large, deep-blue morphidae and the bright yellow-orange barred sulphur.

If you look on the ground, you'll almost certainly see long lines of leaf-cutter ants. One column carries freshly cut leaves to the burrow, and the other marches in the opposite direction, empty-jawed, returning for more. The vegetation decays in their nests, and the fungus that grows on the compost is an important staple of the ants' diet—a few scientists even claim that this makes leaf-cutter ants the world's second species of agriculturists. Only particular types of leaves will do, and the columns can be up to a kilometer (0.6 mile) long.

Practicalities

Cobá's main groups are quite spread apart, and visiting all of them adds up to several kilometers. Fortunately, you can rent a bicycle (US$2.50) or hire a *triciclo* (US$6 for 1 hour, US$10 for 2 hours) at a large stand a short distance past the entryway, opposite the Cobá Group. Whether you walk or ride, don't forget a water bottle, comfortable shoes, bug repellent, sunscreen, and a hat. Watch for signs and stay on the designated trails. Guide service is available—prices are not fixed but average US$40 per group (1.5 hours, up to 6 people). Parking at Cobá is US$2.50.

Cobá is not nearly as crowded as Tulum (and is much larger), but it's still a good idea to arrive as early as possible to beat the ever-growing crowds.

COBÁ PUEBLO

It's fair to say that the town of Cobá, a rather desultory little roadside community, has never regained the population or stature that it had as a Maya capital more than 1,000 years ago. Most travelers visit Cobá as a day trip from Tulum or Valladolid, or on a package tour from resorts on the coast. There are two decent hotels in town, used mostly by those who want to appreciate Cobá's rich birdlife, which means being at the gate right when the site opens at 8am; if you're lucky, the gatekeeper may even let you in early.

Sights

Cobá Pueblo itself doesn't have much in the way of sights—besides the ruins, of course—but a number of small eco-attractions have cropped up, all a short distance from town.

RESERVA DE MONOS ARAÑAS PUNTA LAGUNA

The **Punta Laguna Spider Monkey Reserve** (Otoch Ma'ax Yetel Kooh, cell tel. 985/107-9182, puntalagunamexico@gmail.com, 7:30am-5:30pm daily, US$10) is a nationally protected forest that's home to various families of boisterous spider monkeys, as well as smaller groups of howler monkeys—it's estimated that there are up to 800 individual monkeys living in the reserve. There are also numerous bird species as well as coati, white-tailed deer, and even pumas. A short path winds through the reserve, passing a small unexcavated Maya ruin and a large lagoon with a lookout tower and pier where you can rent canoes (US$8.50). There's also a zip line and a place to rappel into a cenote (and climb out on a rope ladder), but it's typically reserved for large groups. Your best chance of spotting monkeys is by going in late afternoon, and by hiring one of the guides near the entrance (US$20, 2-4 people). The reserve (whose official name is Otoch Ma'ax Yetel Kooh, Yucatec Maya for House of the Spider Monkey and Puma) is operated by a local cooperative, whose members live in the nearby village and serve as guides; most speak at least some English. Be sure to wear good walking shoes and bring plenty of bug repellent. The reserve is located 18 kilometers (11 miles) north of Cobá, on the road toward Nuevo X'can.

TOP EXPERIENCE

★ CENOTES

If you've got a car, a cluster of three well-maintained and well-run cenotes (no phone, 8am-5pm daily) are a great addition to a day spent at Cobá. **Choo-Ha, Tamcach-Ha,** and **Multun-Ha** are southwest of Cobá and are operated jointly (US$5/7/10 for 1/2/3 cenotes); a fourth cenote called **Nohoch-Ha** is a bit farther and requires a separate entrance fee (US$4). Each is slightly different—one has a high roof and platform for jumping, another is wide and low—but all are impressive enclosed chambers bristling with stalactites, filled with cool crystalline water that's heaven on a hot day. Cement or wooden stairways lead down to pools; showers and changing areas are available at Choo-Ha. To get there, continue past the Cobá ruins on the road to Tepich and follow the signs.

Food

Approaching town, **El Cocodrilo** (facing Laguna Cobá, tel. 984/137-5711, 8am-7pm daily, US$3-7) is a bustling restaurant with plastic tables and chairs on a small leafy plot facing the lagoon. Dishes are classic Mexican with some Yucatecan faves—*poc chuc, panuchos, salbutes*—with a handful of sandwiches and tasty vegan options too. The freshly squeezed juices and smoothies alone are worth a stop.

With a large raised patio overlooking the lagoon, **La Pirámide** (Calle Principal at Laguna Cobá, tel. 984/206-7018, 8am-5pm daily, US$6-15) is a nice place for breakfast or lunch après-ruins. The restaurant receives a number of tour groups, and it often has a buffet set up (US$12); otherwise, the menu has grilled fish, chicken, and meat dishes as well as typical Mexican fare.

Accommodations

The simple **Hotel Sac Be** (Calle Principal, tel. 984/144-3006, www.hotelsacbe.com, US$28-33 s/d with a/c) has friendly service and spotless rooms with one or two beds, televisions, Wi-Fi, and a small desk. All have gleaming tile floors and colorful bedspreads. Guests get 10 percent off at the hotel's open-air restaurant; nab a seat on the 2nd floor for the best breeze.

Hacienda Cobá (Calle Principal s/n, tel. 55/5351-3798, www.haciendacoba.com, US$85-95 s/d with a/c) is a small and very pleasant colonial-style hotel, with just six rooms and a relaxing hands-off atmosphere. Rooms are large and airy, with either a king

or two queen beds, and tidy bathrooms with basin sinks and walk-in showers. (Hot water is a bit spotty, however.) Located near the traffic circle at the northeast entrance to town, you can be first at the ruins in the morning. Light continental breakfast is included.

Information and Services

Cobá has neither an official tourist office nor a health clinic. There also are no banks or ATMs—the nearest banking and medical services are in Tulum and Valladolid.

Facing the lagoon, **Farmacia El Porvenir** (Calle Principal s/n, no phone, 9am-1pm and 2pm-9pm Mon.-Sat.) is a small shop selling basic medicines and toiletries.

The **police station** (toll-free tel. 066) is halfway down the main drag, before you hit the lagoon.

Getting There and Around

Except for Hacienda Cobá, you can easily walk to any of the listed businesses in town; the archaeological site is a five-minute walk down the main road, alongside the lagoon.

BUS

A tiny bus station operates out of El Bocadito restaurant (Calle Principal). For the coast, the lone first-class bus departs Cobá at 3:10pm, with stops in Tulum (US$4.50, 1 hour) and Playa del Carmen (US$7.75, 2.5 hours). Second-class buses to the same destinations cost a bit less but take longer; there are five departures from 9:30am to 6pm.

CAR

Getting to Cobá is easiest by car. No matter what direction you're coming from, the roads are smooth and scenic, cutting through pretty farmland and small towns. Keep your speed down, however, as there are innumerable *topes* (speed bumps) and occasional people and animals along the shoulder. Buses ply the same routes, but somewhat infrequently.

Three different roads lead to Cobá; none are named or marked, so they are known by the towns on either end. There are no formal services along any of the roads, save a gas station in the town of Chemax.

The Cobá-Tulum road (45 kilometers/28 miles) is the busiest, cutting southeast to Tulum and the coastal highway (Hwy. 307). The other two roads connect to Highway 180, the main highway between Cancún and Chichén Itzá. The Cobá-Nuevo X'Can road (47 kilometers/29 miles) angles northeast, connecting with Highway 180 about 80 kilometers (50 miles) outside Cancún and passing places like the Punta Laguna monkey reserve along the way. The Cobá-Chemax road (30 kilometers/19 miles) angles northwest to the town of Chemax; from there it's another 20 kilometers (12.4 miles) to Valladolid and Highway 180, connecting to the highway about 40 kilometers (25 miles) from Chichén Itzá.

All three roads, plus the short access road to Cobá, intersect at a large roundabout just north of Cobá village. Pay close attention to which road you want to avoid a long detour.

Sian Ka'an Biosphere Reserve

Sian Ka'an is Yucatec Maya for "where the sky is born," and it's not hard to see how the original inhabitants arrived at such a poetic name. The unkempt beaches, blue-green sea, bird-filled wetlands and islets, and humble accommodations are manna for bird-watchers, artists, snorkelers, and kayakers. But most visitors come here for the fishing. Sian Ka'an is one of the best fly-fishing spots in the world, with all three "grand slam" catches: bonefish, tarpon, and permit.

The reserve was created in 1986, designated a UNESCO World Heritage Site in 1987, and expanded in 1994. It now encompasses around 1.3 million acres of coastal and mangrove forests and wetlands, and some 113 kilometers (70 miles) of pristine coral reefs just offshore.

A huge variety of wildlife thrive in the reserve, including about 300 species of birds, including toucans, parrots, frigate birds, herons, and egrets. Monkeys, foxes, crocodiles, and boa constrictors also populate the reserve and are spotted by locals and visitors with some regularity. Manatees and jaguars are the reserve's largest animals but also the most reclusive: You need sharp eyes and a great deal of luck to spot either one. More than 20 Maya ruins have been found in the reserve, though most are unexcavated.

Spending a few days in Sian Ka'an is the best way to really appreciate its beauty and pace. Hotels and tour operators there can arrange fishing, bird-watching, and other tours, all with experienced local guides. But if time is short, a number of tour operators in Tulum offer day trips into the reserve as well.

SIGHTS
Muyil Archaeological Zone
The most accessible Maya site within the Sian Ka'an reserve is Muyil (Hwy. 307, 25 kilometers/15.5 miles south of Tulum, 8am-5pm daily, US$2.50), on the western edge of the park. Also known as Chunyaxché, it is one of the oldest archaeological sites in the Maya world, dating back to 300 BC and occupied continuously through the conquest. It's believed to have been primarily a seaport, perched on a limestone shelf near the edge of Laguna Muyil; it is connected to the Caribbean via a canal system that was constructed by ancient Maya traders and still exists today.

Only a small portion of the city has been excavated, so it makes for a relatively quick visit. There are six main structures ranging from two-meter-high (6.6-foot) platforms to the impressive Castillo. At 17 meters (56 feet), it is one of the tallest structures on the peninsula's Caribbean coast. The Castillo is topped with a unique solid round masonry turret from which the waters of the Caribbean Sea can be seen. Climbing to the top is prohibited.

Once a sacbé (raised stone road), a

Muyil Archaeological Zone

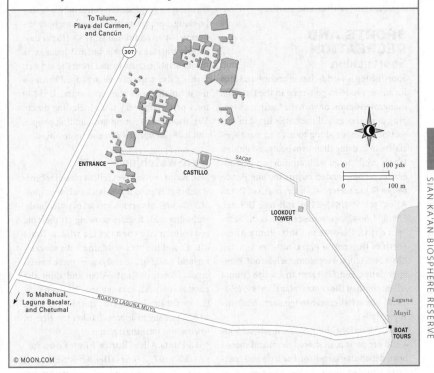

To Tulum, Playa del Carmen, and Cancún

307

ENTRANCE

CASTILLO

SACBÉ

LOOKOUT TOWER

To Mahahual, Laguna Bacalar, and Chetumal

ROAD TO LAGUNA MUYIL

Laguna Muyil

BOAT TOURS

0   100 yds
0   100 m

© MOON.COM

boardwalk-like path now runs through a low swampy forest for about a half kilometer (0.3 mile) from the center of the archaeological site to the edge of the **Laguna Muyil**. Part of this *sacbé* is on ejido property, however, so if you want to access the lagoon from the ruins—you also can get to it by car—there is an additional charge of US$2.50 per person. Along the way, there is a teetering lookout tower with views over Sian Ka'an to the Caribbean.

Once you arrive at the water's edge, it's possible to take a **boat tour** (8am-4pm daily, US$35 pp) that crosses both Muyil and Chunyaxché Lagoons, which are connected by a canal that was carved by the ancient Maya in order to reach the ocean; visitors typically get off the boats and float down the canal with life vests (wear a swimsuit!). It's a pleasant way to enjoy the water, and you'll also get a view of

several otherwise inaccessible ruins along the lagoons' edges and through the mangroves, with the final stop being **Xlapak ruins,** a small site thought to have been a trading post. If arriving by car, look for signs to Muyil Lagoon on Highway 307, just south of the similarly named archaeological site. More thorough tours of this part of Sian Ka'an can be booked in Tulum.

★ Bahía de la Ascensión

Ascension Bay covers about 20 square kilometers (12.4 square miles), and its shallow flats and tangled mangrove islands teem with bonefish, tarpon, and huge permit—some of the biggest ever caught, in fact. It is a fly fisher's dream come true, and it has been attracting anglers from around the world since the mid-1980s. Don't fly-fish? No worries: The spin fishing is also fantastic, while the offshore reef yields plenty of grouper, barracuda, dorado, tuna, sailfish, and marlin.

SPORTS AND RECREATION
Sportfishing

Sportfishing is world-class in and around Sian Ka'an—it's hard to go wrong in the flats and mangrove islands, or with the Caribbean lapping at its shores. All the hotels listed in this section arrange fishing tours, and most specialize in it, using their own boats and guides. If you prefer to go with an independent operator, recommended outfits include **Pesca Maya** (7 kilometers/4.3 miles north of Punta Allen, tel. 998/848-2496, toll-free U.S. tel. 888/894-5642, www.pescamaya.com, 8am-7pm daily); **Palometa Club** (Punta Allen, north of the central plaza, toll-free U.S. tel. 888/824-5420, www.palometaclub.com, 8am-6pm daily); and **Fisherman Lodge** (Punta Allen, south of the central plaza, tel. 999/351-5328, www.fishermanlodge.com, 6:30am-10pm daily).

Weeklong fly-fishing trips range US$3,900-4,300 per person, in shared room and shared boat, depending largely on the style and comforts afforded by the lodge. Most packages

include airport transfer, daily guided fishing, meals, and admission to the reserve, but it's always a good idea to confirm this before booking. For private room or private boat, expect to pay an additional US$150-215 per day; shorter trips are available, but may incur extra transportation costs to and from the airport. Fishing day trips can be arranged through most hotels; rates start at around US$480 for a private full-day tour, including lunch. Variations like renting gear, adding people, and half-day options can also be arranged.

Bird-Watching

Sian Ka'an is also an excellent place for bird-watching. Trips to Bird Island and other spots afford a look at various species of water birds, including male frigates showing off their big red balloon-like chests in the winter. Tours often combine bird-watching with snorkeling and walking around one or more bay islands. Hotels in Punta Allen and along the coastal road can arrange tours, as can outfits in Tulum. Prices are typically per boat, so don't be shy to approach other travelers in town about forming a group.

In Punta Allen, **Punta Allen Coop** (tel. 984/807-1073, toursallen@hotmail.com, 6:30am-2pm daily) is a local cooperative that

dolphin spotting in the Sian Ka'an Biosphere Reserve

Sport and Game Fishing

Cozumel and the Riviera Maya are well known for trolling and deep-sea fishing, while Ascension Bay and the Costa Maya have terrific fly-fishing. Although you can hook into just about any fish at any time of the year, below is information on the peak and extended seasons for a number of top target species. Those fish not listed—tuna, barracuda, yellowtail, snapper, grouper, and bonefish—are prevalent year-round.

SPORTFISHING

Fish	Peak Season	Extended Season	Description
Sailfish	Mar.-June	Jan.-Sept.	Top target species, with a dramatic dorsal fin and a high-flying fighting style.
Blue Marlin	Apr.-Aug.	Mar.-Sept.	Largest Atlantic billfish, up to 500 pounds locally, but much larger elsewhere.
White Marlin	May-July	Mar.-Aug.	Smaller than the blue marlin, but still challenging.
Wahoo	Nov.-Jan.	June-Feb.	Lightning fast, with torpedo-like shape and distinctive blue stripes.
Dorado	May-July	Feb.-Aug.	Hard fighter with shimmery green, gold, and blue coloration; aka dolphin or mahimahi.

FLAT-WATER FISHING

Fish	Peak Season	Extended Season	Description
Tarpon	Mar.-Aug.	Feb.-Oct.	Big hungry tarpon migrate along the coast in summer months.
Snook	July-Aug.	June-Dec.	Popular trophy fish, grows locally up to 30 pounds.
Permit	Mar.-Sept.	year-round	March and April see schools of permit, with some 20-pound individuals.

offers bird-watching tours (US$120-145, 2-3 hours, up to 6 people); look for their two-story wooden shack along the main road near the entrance to town. Other operators to consider include **Community Tours Sian Ka'an** (Calle Osiris Sur near Calle Sol Ote, tel. 984/871-2202, www.siankaantours.org, 7am-7pm daily); and, if your budget permits, **Visit Sian Ka'an** (Sian Ka'an Biosphere Reserve, Carr. Tulum-Punta Allen Km 15.8, cell tel. 984/141-4245, www.visitsiankaan.com), which offers customized private tours.

Kayaking

The tangled mangrove forests, interconnected lagoons, and scenic bays make Sian Ka'an ideal for kayaking. **Community Tours Sian Ka'an** (Calle Osiris Sur near Calle Sol Ote, tel. 984/871-2202, www.siankaantours.org, 7am-7pm daily) offers several kayak excursions, with tours starting at US$75 per person.

FOOD

Punta Allen isn't a foodie's village, but it does have a handful of eateries, all specializing in fresh seafood. A few mini-marts and a tortilleria round things out a bit, especially if you're planning on staying more than a couple of days.

With a gorgeous view of the Caribbean, **Muelle Viejo** (just south of the central plaza, no phone, 11am-9pm Tues.-Sun., US$6-13) serves up fresh seafood dishes and cold beers—perfect for a long, lazy lunch.

Next to the elementary school, **Las Palapas de Juan y Martha** (north of the central plaza, tel. 998/171-9953, 6pm-10pm daily, US$5-12) is a popular dinner spot with an outdoor dining room. Fresh seafood, of course, is served but tacos are the specialty. There's no set menu; instead, the affable owners visit with guests and share what's on offer for the evening.

There are three **mini-marts** in town: on the north end (near the road to the lagoonside dock), south end (two blocks west of Cuzan Guesthouse), and near the central plaza (one block west). Each sells basic foodstuffs and snacks, though you may have to visit all three to find what you're looking for. If you plan to cook a lot, stock up on supplies in Tulum.

ACCOMMODATIONS

Punta Allen is the only town on the peninsula and has the most options for lodging, food, tours, and other services. Along the long unpaved road leading there is a smattering of lodges and private homes, amid miles and miles of deserted coastline. **Note:** The town of Punta Allen often switches off the electricity grid at midnight—and hotels outside of town are entirely off the grid—so air-conditioning and TV are not functional unless the establishment has a generator. (Fans work as long as the hotel has solar or wind power.) If you're staying in a room with kitchen facilities, keep the fridge shut as much as possible to conserve the cold.

Toward Punta Allen

El Ultimo Maya (cell tel. 984/181-8691, www.elultimomaya.com, US$12.50-40 pp tent) is a low-key beach club (US$5 pp) and campsite. There's a simple thatch-roof restaurant serving fresh seafood and beach snacks (US$6-16)

A handful of beachfront hotels dot the road between Tulum and Punta Allen.

and a long beach that's kept clean of seaweed and trash. Campers set up in the sandy parking lot; the cheaper rates are BYO tent and gear, more expensive ones include a tent, a real bed with linens, plus breakfast. The bathrooms are clean enough and there's security in the evenings. Best of all is the isolated beach getaway feel…and the stars! It's located two kilometers (1.5 miles) south of the Sian Ka'an arch. Cash only.

Eight kilometers (5 miles) north of Punta Allen, **Sol Caribe** (cell tel. 984/139-3839, www.solcaribe-mexico.com, US$175 s/d, US$195-250 cabaña, US$100/40 extra per adult/child all-inclusive) offers modern rooms and cabañas set on a breezy, palm-laden beach. All feature tropical wood furnishings, terraces with hammocks, 24-hour electricity (fan only), and gorgeous views of the ocean—a true hidden getaway of the Riviera Maya. There's a full-service restaurant on-site.

★ **Mukan Resort** (tel. 998/800-3914, www.mukan.com, US$420-600 s/d all-inclusive) embodies tropical chic with hardwood floors, thatch roofs, sleek furnishings, and fine art. The luxuriousness is only highlighted by staff that anticipate guest needs, such as appearing with cold drinks at the beach or setting up a table for lunch in the shade of a palm tree. Beyond the beach, there's a spacious lounge, a small pool, a rooftop whirlpool tub, and even a cigar bar. The restaurant has a seasonal menu that integrates fresh seafood and local ingredients. Note that except for a daily cocktail hour, the rate does not include alcoholic beverages; those can be added à la carte or as a separate package. It's located ten kilometers (6 miles) north of Punta Allen.

Punta Allen

Facing the central plaza, **Posada Sirena** (cell tel. 984/139-1241, www.casasirena.com, US$38-75 s/d) offers simple Robinson Crusoe-style rooms. Most are quite spacious, sleeping 6-8 people, and all have private bathrooms, fully equipped kitchens, and plenty of screened windows to let in the ocean breeze. Area excursions, including fly-fishing,

snorkeling, and bird-watching, can be arranged on-site.

The accommodations at **Serenidad Shardon** (road to the lighthouse, cell tel. 984/107-4155, www.shardon.com, US$150 s/d, US$350 cabaña for up to 5 guests, US$500 beach house for up to 8 guests) vary from oceanfront *cabañas* to a large beach house; all have basic furnishings but are clean and well equipped. You also can camp using your own gear, or rent deluxe tents with real beds, electric lighting, and fans; access to hot showers and a full kitchen is included.

A dedicated fishing lodge, **The Palometa Club** (Punta Allen, north of the central plaza, toll-free U.S. tel. 888/824-5420, www.palometaclub.com) has just six rooms in a two-story structure facing the beach. Each has two double beds, air-conditioning, and a private bathroom. Meals are served family-style, with cocktails and snacks available at the club's outdoor bar, après fishing. The Palometa is designed for serious anglers, with a fly-tying study, one-to-one guiding, and an emphasis on landing permits (*palometa* in Spanish). The all-inclusive seven-night/six-day rate is US$4,250 per person (non-anglers US$2,000/person) in a shared room and boat.

INFORMATION AND SERVICES

Don't expect much in the way of services in Sian Ka'an—if there is something you can't do without, definitely bring it with you. There are **no banking services,** and few establishments accept credit cards. **Wi-Fi** is available at most hotels, though often in the common areas only. Cell phones typically don't work in Sian Ka'an, but there are **public telephones** in town. Punta Allen also has a modest **medical clinic**—look for it on the main road as you enter town. There is **no laundry,** but most hotels will provide the service.

GETTING THERE

Many hotels include airport pickup/drop-off, which is convenient and helps you avoid paying for a week's car rental when you plan on fishing all day. That said, a car is useful if you'd like to do some exploring on your own.

Public Transportation

Public transport to and from Punta Allen is unpredictable at best—build some flexibility into your plans in case of missed (or missing) connections.

A privately run **Tulum-Sian Ka'an shuttle** leaves the iTour Mexico Hotel (Av. Tulum at Av. Cobá, cell tel. 984/115-3875, US$10pp, 1 hour) at 2pm most days. The shuttle drops passengers off at the Sian Ka'an visitors center dock about nine kilometers (5.5 miles) south of the reserve's entrance. There, tour boats that double as **water taxis** (45 min., US$10) are typically waiting to take passengers to Punta Allen. A taxi from Tulum to the visitors center costs around US$30. Return boats leave Punta Allen starting at 5am. The shuttle back to Tulum typically leaves around 7:30am.

If arriving from the Costa Maya, you also can get to Punta Allen from Carrillo Puerto. From there, state-run *combis* (US$10, 10am and 3pm daily) leave from the market in Carrillo Puerto (a block from the main traffic circle) for a bone-jarring four-hour trip down a private road to the small settlement of Playón. There, **water taxis** (US$2.50 pp, 15 minutes) wait to ferry passengers across the lagoon to Punta Allen. The *combi* back to Carrillo Puerto leaves Playón at 6am.

Car

To get to Punta Allen by car, head south along the coast through (and past) Tulum's Zona Hotelera. About eight kilometers (5 miles) from the Tulum/Zona Hotelera junction is *el arco* (the arch), marking the reserve boundary where you register and pay a US$2 per person per day park fee. From there it's 56 kilometers (35 miles) by dirt road to Punta Allen. The road is much improved from years past, and an ordinary car can make it in 2-3 hours. It can be much more difficult after a heavy rain, however. Be sure to fill the tank in Tulum—there is no gas station along the way or in Punta Allen, though some locals sell gas from their homes.

The Costa Maya

The coastline south of Tulum loops and weaves like the tangled branches of the mangrove trees that blanket much of it. It is a mosaic of savannas, marshes, lagoons, scattered islands, and three huge bays: Bahía de la Ascensión, Bahía del Espiritu Santo, and Bahía de Chetumal. Where it's not covered by mangroves, the shore has sandy beaches and dunes, and just below the turquoise sea is one of the least-impacted sections of the great Mesoamerican Reef. Dozens of Maya archaeological sites have been discovered here, but few excavated, and much remains unknown about pre-Hispanic life here. During the conquest, the snarled coastal forest proved an effective sanctuary for indigenous rebels and refugees fleeing Spanish control, not to mention a haven for pirates, British logwood cutters, and Belizean anglers.

In the 1990s, Quintana Roo officials launched an effort to develop the state's southern coast, which was still extremely isolated despite the breakneck development taking place in and around Cancún. (It has always been a famous fly-fishing area, however.) The first order of business was to construct a huge cruise ship port, which they did in the tiny fishing village of Mahahual. They also needed a catchy name, and came up with the "Costa Maya." The moniker generally applies to the coastal areas south of Tulum, particularly the Sian Ka'an Biosphere Reserve; the towns of Mahahual and Xcalak; Laguna Bacalar; and

The Caste War

On July 18, 1847, a military commander in Valladolid learned of an armed plot to overthrow the government that was being planned by two indigenous men—Miguel Antonio Ay and Cecilio Chí. Ay was arrested and executed. Chí managed to escape punishment and on July 30, 1847, led a small band of armed men into the town of Tepich. Several officials and Euro-Mexican families were killed. The military responded with overwhelming force, burning villages, poisoning wells, and killing scores of people, including many women, children, and elderly. The massacre—and the long-standing oppression of indigenous people at its root—sparked spontaneous uprisings across the peninsula, which quickly developed into a massive, coordinated indigenous rebellion known as the Caste War.

Indigenous troops tore through colonial cities, killing and capturing scores of non-Maya. In some cases, the Maya turned the tables on their former masters, forcing them into slave labor, including building the church in present-day Carrillo Puerto's central plaza. Valladolid was evacuated in 1848 and left abandoned for nearly a year, and by 1849, the peninsula's indigenous people were close to expelling the colonial elite. However, as they were preparing their final assaults on Mérida and Campeche City, the rainy season came early, presenting the Maya soldiers with a bitter choice between victory and (were they to miss the planting season) likely famine. The men turned their backs on a hard-fought and near-certain victory to return to their fields to plant corn.

Mexican troops immediately took advantage of the lull, and the Maya never regained the upper hand. For the next 13 years, captured indigenous soldiers (and increasingly *any* indigenous person) were sold to slave brokers and shipped to Cuba. Many Maya eventually fled into the forests and jungles of southern Quintana Roo. The fighting was rekindled when a wooden cross in the town of Chan Santa Cruz (today, Carrillo Puerto) was said to be channeling the voice of God, urging the Maya to keep fighting. The war ended, however, when troops took control of Chan Santa Cruz in 1901. An official surrender was signed in 1936.

Chetumal, the state capital and by far the largest city in the area.

It's hard not to be a little cynical about cruise liners coming to such a remote area, whose entire population could fit comfortably on a single ship. The town of Mahahual, nearest the port, is utterly transformed when cruise ships arrive, their passengers moseying about Mahahual, beer bottles in hand, the beaches packed with sun worshippers serenaded by the sound of Jet Skis. Then again, it's doubtful the area would have paved roads, power lines, or telephone service if not for the income and demand generated by cruise ships. Driving down the old rutted coastal road to Xcalak (an even smaller town south of Mahahual) used to take a half day or more; today, a two-lane paved road has cut the trip to under an hour. The state government has vowed to control development by limiting hotel size and density, monitoring construction methods, and protecting the mangroves and coral reef. Small, ecofriendly bed-and-breakfasts have thrived, not surprisingly, and more and more independent travelers are drawn to the Costa Maya for its quiet isolation and pristine natural beauty.

Highway 307 from Tulum to Chetumal passes through Carrillo Puerto, the gateway to the Costa Maya. It's a small city that holds little of interest to most travelers except an opportunity to fill up on gas.

MAHAHUAL

Mahahual is a place of two faces: cruise ship days, when the town's one road is packed with day-trippers looking to buy T-shirts and throw back a few beers; and non-cruise ship days, when Mahahual is sleepy and laid back, and the narrow white-sand beaches are free to walk for miles. Whether you stay here a night or a week, you're likely to see both, which is a

Mahahual

MAYA LOST MAYAN KINGDOM
CALLE ISAAC
SHOPPING CENTER
MAIN STREET
LAS CASITAS
CRUISE SHIP PIER
AV PASEO DEL PUERTO
CHICLE
ZAPOTE
CACAO
MATI
AV DEL MANGLAR
RIO HONDO
OXTANKAH
CALDERITAS
CHETUMAL
LAVANDA
KOHUNLICH
MINISUPER BERE
BACALAR
COSTA MAYA YOGA
THE NATIVE CHOICE
CHACCHOBEN
CHINCHORRO
MOBIUS INTERNET
MAHAHUAL ECOTOURS
CARRETERA CAFETAL MAHAHUAL
PRIVATE ROAD TRANSIT CHECK USE

← To gas station, Xcalak, Mayan Beach Garden Inn, and Hwy 307

CARRETERA CAFETAL MAHAHUAL

AV MALECÓN MAHAHUAL
HUACHINANGO
Caribbean Sea
PARGO
SARDINA
RUBIA
LAVANDERÍA 4 HERMANOS
PHARMACY MÉRIDA
CAFÉ COLONIAL
HOSTAL JARDÍN MAHAHUAL
SIERRA
ÑAM ÑAM
BUS TERMINAL
CHERNA
MARTILLO
POLICE
POSADA PACHAMAMA
UNDERTOE MÉXICO
CENTRO DE SALUD
CORONADO
HOTEL CABALLO BLANCO/DOCTOR DIVE
DIVINO DELICIA ITALIANA
NACIONAL BEACH CLUB AND BUNGALOWS
BARRACUDA
AMIGOS DEL MAR
ROBALO
MERO
MOJARRA
LIZA
CAZÓN
ATÚN
NOHOCH KAY
PESCADERÍA SAURI
CENTRO DE ACOPIO DE LANGOSTA
SULUMAR
ALMEJA

0 _____ 500 yds
0 _____ 500 m

LAS CABAÑAS DEL DOCTOR
To Maya Luna,
Balamku Inn on the Beach,
Travel In', and Almaplena Eco
Resort and Beach Club ↓

© MOON.COM

good thing. You can be in a major party zone one day, and the next be the only snorkeler in town—all without changing hotels. If you seek long, quiet days every day, though, definitely stay outside of town.

Whether or not there is a cruise ship in town, Mahahual is pretty easy to manage. Most of its hotels and services are located on, or just off, Avenida Mahahual (aka El Malecón), the three-kilometer (1.9-mile) pedestrian walkway that runs through town until it meets up with the coastal road heading south, the Carretera Antigua (literally, Old Highway). Just northwest of town, the tiny residential community of Las Casitas has additional services like an Internet café and a laundry.

Sights

★ BANCO CHINCHORRO

Chinchorro Bank is by some measurements the largest coral atoll in the Northern Hemisphere and a paradise for divers and snorkelers alike. About 44 kilometers (27 miles) east of Mahahual and 65.4 kilometers (40 miles) northeast of Xcalak, Chinchorro is a marine reserve known for its spectacular coral formations, massive sponges, and abundant sealife...even the largest known population of American crocodiles. Scores of ships have foundered on the shallow reefs through the years, but (contrary to innumerable misreports) the wrecks cannot be dived. Not only are they protected as historical sites, but most are on the eastern side of the atoll, where the surf and currents are too strong for recreational diving. The famous **40 Cannons wreck,** in about three meters (10 feet) of water on the atoll's northwest side, is good for snorkeling but not diving, and thanks to looters there are far fewer than 40 cannons there. There are small government and fishermen's huts on Cayo Centro, one of the three cays; tourists are permitted to stay overnight, which means spectacular multiday diving and snorkeling opportunities. Reaching Chinchorro requires a 1.5- to 2-hour boat ride, which can be pretty

Sea fans are a type of soft coral that can bend and sway in the currents.

punishing depending on conditions. Groups typically set out around 7am and return to port around 5pm. Dive shops usually require at least five divers or six snorkelers (or a combination of the two) and may not go for days at a time if the weather is bad (summer months are best).

Sports and Recreation

SCUBA DIVING

Mahahual has terrific diving on the coral reef just offshore, with dozens of sites a short boat ride away. It's also one of two jumping-off points for trips to Chinchorro Bank, the largest coral atoll in the Northern Hemisphere. The other departure point is Xcalak, south of Mahahual.

Amigos del Mar (Av. Mahahual at Coronado, cell tel. 983/151-6758, www.amigosdelmar.net, 8am-6pm daily) is a friendly shop offering a wide array of dives to local sites (US$70 one tank, US$110 two tanks). It also offers fantastic overnight trips to Banco Chinchorro (US$399pp, 1 night) that include

five dives, meals (including a lobster dinner), drinks, and basic lodging in a stilt house on the water's edge. Snorkelers are welcome, too (US$200 pp). Longer trips to Chinchorro also can be arranged.

Doctor Dive (Yaya Beach Club, Malécon at Calle Coronado, cell tel. 983/834-5619, www.doctordive.com, 8am-6pm daily) offers personalized service for independent travelers; fun dives are US$65 for one tank, US$95 for two; gear is an extra US$25 per day. Specialty trips, including lionfish hunting and diving unexplored locations, also can be arranged.

SNORKELING

You can rent snorkel gear for around US$10-12 a day from the dive shops or from the kiosks that pop up on cruise ship days. Swim or kayak out to the reef for a do-it-yourself experience, or join a guided tour, where you'll likely see more sealife, plus have extra safety and convenience. Mahahual's dive shops all offer guided snorkel trips for US$40-50 per person, including gear and about 90 minutes in the water.

STAND-UP PADDLING

UnderToe Mexico (Ibiza Sunset Beach Club, Malécon near Calle Coronado, cell tel. 983/154-2293, www.undertoemexico.com, hours vary) offers paddleboarding lessons (US$38.50, 90 minutes) from certified bilingual instructors. Afterwards, students enjoy full access to the Ibiza Sunset Beach Club, including two drinks and a snack. SUP yoga—a floating yoga class—also is offered (US$55, 90 minutes).

YOGA

Located in a spacious and bright studio in Las Casitas neighborhood, **Costa Maya Yoga** (Av. Caribe between Calles Bacalar and Kohunlich, cell tel. 983/105-8040, www.costamaya-yoga.com, hours vary) offers mostly vinyasa, hatha, and restorative yoga classes. Classes run US$15 per person; check the website for the current schedule.

Lionfish

lionfish mural in Puerto Morelos

The lionfish is a spectacular striped fish with a "mane" of fins and poisonous spines that is changing the underwater landscape of the entire Caribbean. Historically found only in the warm regions of the Pacific and Indian Oceans, lionfish were first sighted in Atlantic waters in 1992 in Biscayne Bay, Florida; it's believed they were released into the wild after a private aquarium was swept into the ocean by Hurricane Andrew. Since then, lionfish have been documented in the Florida Keys, the Bahamas, Cuba, and elsewhere; the first lionfish sighting in the region was in Cozumel in January 2009. Voracious hunters with no natural predators, lionfish can grow to 20 inches long and devour everything from small reef fish to commercial fish like snapper and juvenile grouper. They thrive at depths of just a few feet to over 500 feet, and their coloring makes them especially well suited for coral environments. Government agencies have taken proactive efforts to help curb the growth of this invasive fish, garnering widespread community support. There now are fishing tournaments targeting lionfish, and spear-fishing training for local sport divers; experts are even trying, with some success, to "train" wild sharks and mature grouper to prey on lionfish by introducing them into known hunting grounds. Restaurants are doing their part by creating innovative and tasty dishes from lionfish meat.

TOURS

The Native Choice (Las Casitas, Av. Paseo del Puerto at Calle Chinchorro, tel. 998/869-4000, www.thenativechoice.com) offers a range of area tours, all led by guides who are extremely knowledgeable about Maya history, culture, and belief systems. Tours include visiting the archaeological sites of Chacchoben, Kohunlich, or Dzibanché (US$55-100 adult, US$45-85 child), a "Mayan Experience Tour," which includes touring Chacchoben ruins and a visit to a home in Chacchoben village

(US$75 adult, US$65 child), plus a kayaking and hiking trip on and around Laguna Bacalar (US$55 adult, US$40 child). The tours are geared toward the cruise ship crowd, but hotel owners warmly recommend the outfit to independent travelers as well.

Mahahual Ecotours (Las Casitas, Calle Caribe s/n, www.mahahualecotours.simdif.com, tel. 983/136-2827) is a tour operator that just gets it. The team of certified guides has a profound knowledge of the area, and a passion for sharing its history and hidden riches, that make for a fascinating outing every time. There's a standard menu of tours, including kayaking, bird-watching, and ruin-hopping, but the operation really specializes in mixing and matching to make custom excursions. The team is out to blow your mind, and there isn't much that can't be arranged.

AMUSEMENT PARKS

For the record, appropriating the Maya pyramids to create a water park for foreign tourists is pretty obnoxious. But in terms of giving families something fun to do, the creators of **Mayá Lost Mayan Kingdom** (Las Casitas, end of Calle Isaac, www.maya-park.com, 8am-5pm Mon.-Sat., US$99/89 adult/child) nailed it. The park includes zip lines, a lazy river, and numerous waterslides (named after Maya gods, of course) ranging from exciting to heart-stopping.

Food
IN TOWN

An open-air eatery and beach club, ★ **Nohoch Kay** (aka Big Fish, Malecón between Calles Liza and Cazón, tel. 983/834-5981, 8am-7pm Mon.-Tues., 8am-10pm Wed.-Sun., US$7-16) serves up some of the best fish tacos in town. Thick pieces of fish—fried or grilled—are served with small tortillas, onion, cilantro, and plenty of lime. On cruise ship days, it gets overrun with clients, but otherwise it's a laid-back place to get a beachfront meal.

A breezy restaurant with hanging shell lamps and a *palapa* roof, **Divino Delicia Italiana** (Calle Huachinango at Calle Coronado, tel. 983/700-2995, 5pm-11pm Tues.-Sun., US$7-14) serves up freshly made pastas, seafood salads, and wooden tablets loaded with gourmet cheeses and meats. Thin-crust pizzas also are baked in the wood-burning stove, visible from the dining room. An extensive wine list combined with friendly service round out a meal nicely.

★ **Ñam** (Calle Cherna between Malecón and Huachinango, cell tel. 983/131-4417, 3pm-11pm Wed.-Mon., US$3-5) is a hole-in-the-wall eatery serving legit hamburgers as well as tasty empanadas from the owners' native Uruguay. Burgers range from traditional to the "Oink Oink" (half beef, half pork, with caramelized pineapple and barbecue sauce), all served with fries. The empanadas are crispy and flavorful, and all dishes are served on paper-lined baskets at a handful of tables on the sidewalk.

Sulumar (Malecón near Calle Atún, tel.

Mahahual

983/119-2920, 10am-5pm daily, US$4-8) is a great little beachfront restaurant specializing in (what else?) seafood and beach grub. It's best known for its ceviche, and rightly so. Local fisherman come ashore a short distance from here with their daily catch, and Sulumar chefs reportedly get first pick. It's not exactly a locals' place, but certainly far enough south that the clientele is a mix of cruise-shippers and indie travelers. Service is friendly but can be slow.

Café Colonial (Calle Sierra near Malécon, tel. 983/137-3705, 7am-5pm Tues.-Sat., US$3-6) is a good place to grab breakfast. Package deals include a hearty plate of eggs with bread, coffee, and juice for US$6. À la carte items like fruit plates and breakfast sandwiches also are offered. Tables are in a small wood house or on the pedestrian walkway in front.

If you're cooking for yourself, stop by the local fisherman's co-op, **Pescardería Sauri: Centro de Acopio de Langosta** (Calle Huachinango near Calle Almeja, no phone, 7am-7pm daily). At this roadside shack, you can take your pick of lobsters and buy shrimp and fish fillets, all by the kilo.

OUTSIDE OF TOWN

Travel In' (Carr. Antigua Km 5.8, cell tel. 983/110-9496, www.travel-in.com.mx, 5:30pm-9pm Tues.-Sat., US$5-20) is a great little restaurant a few kilometers down the coastal road. Homemade pita bread is baked fresh every day—order it as an appetizer with an assortment of homemade dips. Daily seafood specials vary according to the day's catch. It's open on Mondays from Christmas to Easter.

For basic groceries, try **Minisuper Bere** (Las Casitas, Av. Paseo del Puerto near Calle Kohunlich, 8am-11pm daily).

Accommodations

Many of Mahahual's lodgings, especially the ones with beachfront, are outside of the village itself, along the Carretera Antigua that hugs the coast south of town. The rest are in town, either on the Malecón or a stone's throw away.

IN TOWN

Under US$50: Hostal Jardín Mahahual (Calle Sardina near Calle Sierra, tel. 983/834-5722, www.mahahualjardin.co, US$15 pp dorm with a/c, US$64 s/d with a/c) is an appealing hostel with a small interior garden and a friendly staff. The eight-bed dorm has overhead fans, sturdy bunks, thick mattresses, and spotless single-sex bathrooms. Four private rooms are located on the other side of the garden, with whitewashed walls, polished cement floors, and details like throw pillows and original art. Added pluses include a clean common kitchen and complimentary use of bikes.

Set on a grassy lot, **Las Cabañas del Doctor** (Av. Mahahual Km 2, tel. 983/832-2102, www.lascabanasdeldoctor.com, US$5 pp camping, US$45 s/d cabaña, US$50 s/d, US$60 s/d with a/c) has a decent range of accommodations—but camping is the reason to stay here. Campers must bring their own gear, but the rate includes an oceanfront tent site, access to cold-water bathrooms, and Wi-Fi.

US$50-100: ★ Nacional Beach Club and Bungalows (Malécon near Calle Coronado, tel. 983/834-5719, www.nacionalbeachclub.com, US$65-85 s/d bungalows, US$85-125 s/d with a/c) is a tasteful beachfront hotel with spectacular ocean views and excellent service. Units vary from thatched-roof bungalows with private terraces to spacious hotel rooms with high ceilings and Mexican tile bathrooms. There's a small pool right on the Malecón and a good restaurant on-site. Guests are welcome to use the hotel beach club and its amenities.

Posada Pachamama (Calle Huachinango between Calles Martillo and Coronado, tel. 983/834-5762, www.posadapachamama.com, US$53-67 s/d with a/c) is a small hotel a block from the beach. Rooms are small and sparsely decorated but have updated furnishings and stone-inlaid floors; all have air-conditioning, Wi-Fi, and satellite TV. The higher-priced rooms have small balconies, some with partial beach views. A pleasant patio café is a good place for breakfast.

Over US$100: With direct access to the beach and a rooftop bar, **Hotel Caballo Blanco** (Malecón between Calles Martillo and Coronado, tel. 983/834-5830, www.hotelelcaballoblanco.com, US$110-140 suite with a/c) is a great place to land. If you can turn a blind eye to the old-world village murals and polyester curtains, rooms are quite modern in style. More importantly, they are immensely comfortable with air-conditioning, flat-screen TVs, mini fridges, coffee makers, and Wi-Fi. Most have private balconies too, the more expensive ones overlooking the Caribbean.

OUTSIDE OF TOWN
Under US$100: Owned and operated by friendly Canadian expats, ★ **Balamku Inn on the Beach** (Carr. Antigua Km 5.7, tel. 983/732-1004, www.balamku.com, US$85 s, US$95 d) offers artfully decorated rooms in a handful of *palapa*-roofed buildings. All run on solar power, wind turbines, and a nonpolluting wastewater system. Full breakfast is included, as is use of the hotel's kayaks and a library. Wi-Fi is available in every room.

Maya Luna (Carr. Antigua Km 5.6, tel. 983/836-0905, www.hotelmayaluna.com, US$85 s/d) has four modern bungalows with 24-hour solar/wind power, rainwater showers, and *palapa*-shaded porches. Each has a private rooftop terrace with views of the Caribbean in front and the jungle in back; all have Maya- or ocean-themed murals, too. A hearty and healthy breakfast is included in the rate. Pets are welcome (and will join a cadre of friendly cats and a dog who live on-site).

About 21 kilometers (13 miles) north of Mahahual, **Mayan Beach Garden Inn** (cell tel. 983/130-8658, www.mayanbeachgarden.com, US$75-85 s/d, US$85 s/d with kitchenette, US$25 extra for a/c at night) is a quiet hotel with several rooms and one *cabaña*, all with whitewashed walls and Mexican-style decor, most with ocean views. A hearty breakfast is included in the rate, as are Wi-Fi and the use of kayaks. All-inclusive meal packages are also available. In the high season, there's a three-night minimum.

Over US$100: About 20 minutes south of town, **Almaplena Eco Resort and Beach Club** (Carr. Antigua Km 12.5, cell tel. 983/137-5070, www.almaplenabeachresort.com, US$127-161 s/d) is a small boutique resort with just eight rooms facing a gorgeous isolated stretch of beach. All have king-size beds, ceiling fans (no air-conditioning), cool stone floors, and tasteful decor. Suites are on the top floor and have private terraces, while standards share a wooden patio with direct access to the beach. All have Wi-Fi, too. Continental breakfast is included, and the on-site restaurant serves fine Mediterranean and Mexican meals.

Information and Services
Cruise ships have brought considerable modernization to this once-isolated fishing village, but services are still somewhat limited.

EMERGENCY SERVICES
The **Centro de Salud** (Calle Coronado between Calles Huachinango and Sardina, no phone, 8am-2:30pm daily, after 2:30pm emergencies only) offers basic health services. For serious health matters, head to Chetumal.

For meds, try **Pharmacy Mérida** (Calle Sardina between Calles Rubia and Sierra, cell tel. 983/132-1845, 7am-11pm Mon.-Fri., 9am-11pm Sat.-Sun.), the best-stocked pharmacy in town.

The **police department** (Calle Huachinango near Calle Martillo, toll-free Mex. tel. 066) is open 24 hours.

MONEY
There is no bank in town, but there are a handful of **ATMs,** all along El Malecón. At the time of research, however, none were affiliated with local banks, so withdrawal charges were hefty. Another option is to go to the gas station outside of town, where there's an **HSBC ATM** (though it often runs out of cash); alternatively, consider bringing enough money to get you through your stay.

MEDIA AND COMMUNICATIONS

The only Internet café is in Las Casitas, where **Mobius Internet** (Calle Chinchorro near Av. Paseo del Puerto, 9am-10pm Mon.-Fri., 9am-2pm and 5pm-10pm Sat.) charges US$1 per hour and offers international telephone service, too (US$0.35-0.45/minute calls to the United States and Europe). Most hotels and some restaurants offer Wi-Fi as well.

LAUNDRY

Lavandería 4 Hermanos (Calle Huachinango near Calle Rubia, 7am-8pm daily) offers same-day laundry service for US$1.50 per kilo (2.2 pounds).

In Las Casitas, try **Lavanda** (Av. Paseo del Puerto at Calle Chetumal, 9am-6pm Mon.-Sat.), which charges US$1.25 per kilo (2.2 pounds).

Getting There and Around

Just south of the grubby roadside town of Limones, a good paved road with signs to Mahahual breaks off Highway 307 and cuts through 58 kilometers (36 miles) of coastal forest and wetlands tangled with mangroves. It's a scenic stretch, whether in a car or on a bus, along which you can occasionally see egrets, herons, and other water birds.

Mahahual proper is very walkable—in fact, the main road that runs through town, El Malecón, is a three-kilometer (1.9-mile) pedestrian walkway. If you're staying outside of town, a car certainly comes in handy, but plenty of people manage without; dive shops and tour operators typically offer hotel pickup, and there are cabs and a local bus.

BUS

Mahahual's bus terminal is a modest affair on Calle Huachinango near Calle Sierra toward the north end of town. Buses to Cancún (US$14, 5 hours) leave at 10:30am and 5:30pm daily, stopping at Carrillo Puerto (US$3.50-8, 2 hours), Tulum (US$8.25, 3 hours), and Playa del Carmen (US$13-19, 4 hours) along the way. To Chetumal (US$6, 2.5 hours) and Bacalar (US$4.50, 1.5 hours), buses depart at 2:30pm and 7:30pm daily. All long-distance buses stop in Limones (US$3, 1 hour). For Xcalak, a second-class bus leaves at 6:30am daily (US$3, 1 hour).

Note: Buses entering Mahahual stop in Las Casitas before arriving at the bus terminal; be sure you get off at the latter if you're headed to the beach or any of the hotels.

CAR AND TAXI

There is a PEMEX gas station (24 hours) on the main road to Mahahual, just east of the turnoff to Xcalak. It occasionally runs out of gas, so definitely fill your tank in Carrillo Puerto or Chetumal on your way here.

Note: There's often a military checkpoint set up just west of the turnoff to Xcalak, where officials conduct searches for illicit drugs and other contraband. As long as you or your passengers don't have anything illegal in the car, the longest you should be delayed is a couple of minutes.

Cabs abound in this town, especially on cruise ship days. Rates are set by zone; in general, rates run around US$1 per kilometer (0.6 mile). If in doubt, ask to see the *tarifario* (official rate chart).

AIRPORT

Mahahual has a small airport just outside of town. Well, it's more like a well-maintained airstrip with a nice shelter. At the time of research, it was only used by private or chartered planes.

XCALAK

The tiny fishing village of Xcalak lies just a short distance from the channel that marks the Mexico-Belize border, and a blessed long way from anything else. The town started out as a military outpost and didn't get its first real hotel until 1988. Villagers had to wait another decade to get a paved road; before that, the only way in or out of town was by boat or via 55 kilometers (34 miles) of rutted beach tracks. Electrical lines were installed in 2004 but only in the village proper, so many outlying areas (including most of the better hotels) still rely on solar and wind power, as well as generators. The town has no bank, no public phones, and no gas station. That is to say: perfect!

The area doesn't have much beach but makes up for it with world-class fly-fishing, great snorkeling and diving, and a healthy coral reef and lagoon. A small contingent of expats, mostly American and Canadian, have built homes here, some for personal use, others for rent, others as small hotels. Large-scale tourism may be inevitable but still seems a long way off, and Xcalak remains a small and wonderfully laid-back place, perfect for those looking for some honest-to-goodness isolation.

Sights
PARQUE NACIONAL ARRECIFES DE XCALAK
Xcalak Reef National Park was established at the end of 2003, affording protection to the coastal ecosystem as well as Xcalak's nascent tourist economy. The park spans nearly 18,000 hectares (44,479 acres), from the Belize border to well north of town, and includes the reef—and everything else down to 100 meters (328 feet)—as well as the shoreline and numerous inland lagoons.

The main coral reef lies just 90-180 meters (100-200 yards) from shore, and the water is less than 1.5 meters (5 feet) deep almost the whole way out. Many snorkelers prefer the coral heads even closer to shore, which have plenty to see and less swell than the main reef. The shallow waters keep boat traffic to a minimum, and anglers are good about steering clear of snorkelers (you should still stay alert at all times, however).

Divers and snorkelers also can explore the reef at 20 or so official sites and many more unofficial ones. Most are a short distance from town, and shops typically return to port between tanks. **La Poza** is one of the more distinctive dives, drifting through a trench where hundreds, sometimes thousands, of tarpon congregate, varying in size from one-meter (3-foot) "juveniles" to two-meter (7-foot) behemoths. If you have an underwater camera, be sure to bring it.

A fee of US$3.25 per day technically applies to all divers and snorkelers (and kayakers and anglers) in the Parque Nacional Arrecifes de Xcalak; dive shops typically add it to their rates, while most hotels have a stack of wristband permits to sell to guests who want to snorkel right from shore.

Sports and Recreation
SCUBA DIVING AND SNORKELING
XTC Dive Center (north end of town, across bridge, no phone, www.xtcdivecenter.com, 8am-6pm daily) is a highly recommended full-service dive shop offering dives to dozens of sites within Xcalak Reef National Marine Park (US$80 for one tank, US$125 for two tanks). It also specializes in trips to Chinchorro Bank (US$275 for two tanks, US$185 per snorkeler), including lunch, drinks, and a hike on Cayo Centro, the main cay; overnight trips are also offered. Full gear rental costs US$35 extra. A variety of dive classes also are available; a nice three-meter-deep (9-foot) pool is used for the open-water certification course.

A variety of snorkeling tours are offered by a handful of local tour operators. They cost US$45-75 per person depending on how long and far you go; five-hour trips include jaunts into Chetumal Bay and Bird Island, which can be fascinating, especially in January and February when the birds are most plentiful. Recommended guides include **XTC Dive Center** (north end of town, across bridge, no phone, www.xtcdivecenter.com, 8am-6pm daily) and **Osprey Tours** (no storefront, no phone, www.xcalak-flyfishing.com).

KAYAKING AND STAND-UP PADDLING
XTC Dive Center (north end of town, across bridge, no phone, www.xtcdivecenter.com, 8am-6pm daily, US$35-70 pp) offers 2-5-hour kayaking tours in Xcalak's coastal habitats, including the reef, mangroves, river, and lagoon. If DIY is more your thing, kayak rentals, including an hour of instruction, are available

for US$40/60 half/full day. Paddleboards rentals are offered at the same rates.

SPORTFISHING

Xcalak boasts world-class sportfishing, with huge saltwater and brackish flats where hooking into the grand slam of fly-fishing—tarpon, bonefish, and permit—is by no means impossible. Add a snook, and you've got a super slam. Oceanside, tarpon and barracuda abound, in addition to grouper, snapper, and others.

Costa de Cocos (3 kilometers/1.9 miles north of town, no phone, www.costadecocos.com) is the area's oldest fishing resort, with highly experienced guides and numerous magazine write-ups. Two- to seven-night packages (US$2,130-4,405 s, US$1,720-3,395 d) include transportation to and from the Cancún or Chetumal airport, lodging, meals, open bar, fishing license, marine park wristband, and, of course, nonstop fly-fishing. The resort also offers half- and full-day fishing trips (US$175-350), in case you want to fish while in Xcalak without making it a full-on fishing vacation.

Hotel Tierra Maya (2.1 kilometers/1.3 miles north of town, tel. 983/839-8012, www.tierramaya.net) also offers fly-fishing packages for 6-7 nights (US$3,496-4,237 s, US$2,243-2,760 d), though they don't include all the perks—like airport transportation, open bar, and fishing license fees—that the Costa de Cocos packages do.

With several experienced guides, **Osprey Tours** (no storefront, no phone, www.xcalak-flyfishing.com) is a good option for longtime and beginner fly-fishers. It offers half- and full-day fly-fishing excursions in nearby Chetumal Bay (US$200-300) that include drinks, snacks or lunch, and a guide. Gear is available for rent.

Food

★ **Leaky Palapa** (2 blocks north of the lighthouse, cell tel. 983/165-3223, www.leakypalaparestaurant.com, 5pm-10pm Fri.-Sat. Nov.-May, US$12-27) is an upscale restaurant with boho flair and a menu that reflects the day's catch and market offerings. It is invariably delicious, with such dishes as homemade ravioli with huitlacoche, lobster, and squash flower cream as well as fresh fish fillet served on a bed of squid ink risotto. Reservations are required and payment is cash or PayPal only.

Restaurant Toby (center of town, across from volleyball court, cell tel. 983/107-5426, 11am-9pm Mon.-Sat., US$7-14) is a popular seafood restaurant serving up, among other tasty dishes, heaping plates of ceviche, coconut shrimp, and fish soup. It's a friendly, low-key place perfect for a beer and a good meal after a day of diving or relaxing on the beach. Wi-Fi is available.

The Maya Grill (Hotel Tierra Maya, 2.1 kilometers/1.3 miles north of town, tel. 983/839-8012, www.tierramaya.net, 6:30am-9pm daily, US$6-14) is a hotel beachfront restaurant with spectacular floor-to-ceiling windows with views of the Caribbean. The menu is solidly Mexican—tacos, quesadillas, enchiladas—with a fair share of seafood, too. Ingredients are fresh and portions are hearty.

The restaurant at Costa de Cocos, **The Reel Inn** (3 kilometers/1.9 miles north of town, no phone, www.costadecocos.com, 7am-8:30pm daily, US$5-26) serves up breakfast classics, burgers, steak, pizza, and all manner of tall tales—though with fishing as good as it is, many just happen to be true. The service is seriously lacking, but the schedule, reservations policy (none required), and full bar make it a reliable option.

If you are cooking for yourself, a **grocery truck** passes through town and down the coastal road several times per week—ask at your hotel for the current schedule. It comes stocked with eggs, yogurt, grains, basic produce, fresh meats, and canned food. You also can buy a broom or two. In town, there are a handful of small **mini-marts** selling basic canned and dried foods. Most are open 9am-9pm daily.

Accommodations

Xcalak's most appealing accommodations are

on the beach road heading north out of town. Few places accept credit cards on-site, but many have payment systems on their websites.

UNDER US$100

Facing the town beach, **Xcalak Caribe Lodge** (center of town, near volleyball court, www.xcalakcaribe.com, cell tel. 983/130-5580, US$35 s, US$60-70 d) is a small hotel with five simple, modern rooms. Three have floor-to-ceiling windows and glass doors for better views of the ocean; these open onto a public sidewalk, however, making them less than private. A breezy rooftop *palapa* serves as the hotel's common space. Snorkeling and fly-fishing tours are offered.

Hotel Tierra Maya (2.1 kilometers/1.3 miles north of town, tel. 983/839-8012, toll-free U.S. tel. 800/216-1902, www.tierramaya.net, US$90-100 s/d, US$150 apartment) is a pleasant hotel with ample rooms decorated with simple furnishings and colorful Mexican rugs. All have private terraces or balconies with views of the Caribbean. Continental breakfast is included in the rate and served in the hotel's excellent beachfront restaurant. Single and double kayaks are available for guests' use. Fly-fishing packages are also offered.

US$100-150

It's hard not to feel at home at ★ **Sin Duda** (8 kilometers/5 miles north of town, Can. tel. 306/500-3240, www.sindudavillas.com, US$110 s/d, US$125 studio, US$145 apartment), a gem of a hotel with beautifully decorated rooms and apartments featuring Mexican folk art and breathtaking views. Evening often brings cocktail hour, when guests can join the friendly Canadian hosts for margaritas in the cozy lounge that doubles as a common kitchen and library. Kayaks are available for guests, as are a rooftop solarium and hammocks on the beach. A healthy continental breakfast is included.

Cheerful units with fully equipped kitchenettes make **Casa Paraíso** (2.5 kilometers/1.6 miles north of town, U.S. tel. 404/502-9845, www.casaparaisoxcalak.com, US$130 studios) a great choice for indie travelers. Add ocean views from private balconies and a wide beach with palm trees, and it's a classic beach vacation. Full breakfast is included in the rate and is served in a pleasant *palapa*-roofed dining area. Kayaks, paddleboards, snorkel gear, and bicycles are available to guests free of charge. Snorkeling and fishing trips also can be arranged, with pickup at the hotel's private dock.

OVER US$150

Playa Sonrisa (6.9 kilometers/4.3 miles north of town, no phone, www.playasonrisa.com, US$160-180 s/d, US$180-250 suite) is a clothing-optional resort on a palm-tree-laden stretch of beach. Units are clean and comfortable, though they lack the charm that you'd expect for the rate. What you mostly pay for is the freedom to enjoy the Caribbean in the buff. A continental breakfast is included in the rate, as is Wi-Fi. Geared at naturist couples, the hotel welcomes naturist families from May to October only.

Affiliated with XTC Dive Center, **Flying Cloud** (north end of town, across bridge, no phone, www.xtcdivecenter.com/flyingcloud, US$115-155 s/d, US$145 1-bedroom apt, US$165 suite, US$250 2-bedroom apt) is a five-unit hotel with whitewashed walls, polished cement floors, and spectacular ocean views. Mattresses are thick and bathrooms are spotless. While each unit has different amenities—some have king-size beds, others have kitchenettes—all are comfortable. The top-floor suite has sweeping 360-degree views from its private balcony. Guests enjoy use of the dive shop's pool and sea kayaks.

Information and Services

Xcalak has **no bank, ATM, or currency-exchange office,** and only a few places take credit cards—plan accordingly!

There's a basic **health clinic** (no phone, 8am-noon and 2pm-6pm Mon.-Fri.) two blocks from the soccer field, near the entrance to town.

Chacchoben Archaeological Zone

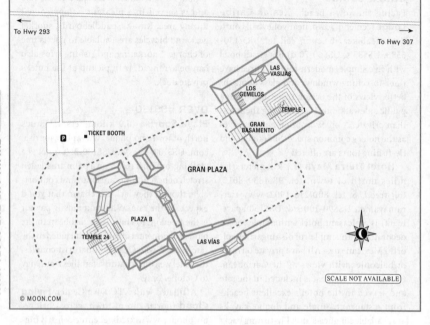

←
To Hwy 293

→
To Hwy 307

LAS VASIJAS

LOS GEMELOS

TEMPLE 1

GRAN BASAMENTO

P TICKET BOOTH

GRAN PLAZA

PLAZA B

TEMPLE 24

LAS VÍAS

SCALE NOT AVAILABLE

© MOON.COM

TULUM AND THE COSTA MAYA
THE COSTA MAYA

The **police station** (toll-free Mex. tel. 066) is located behind the lighthouse.

Most hotels have Wi-Fi; in a pinch many hotel owners will let you use their computers to send a quick email. To make an international or domestic call, head to **Telecomm/Telégrafos** (2 blocks north of the lighthouse, 9am-3pm Mon.-Fri.).

Getting There and Around

Bus service is somewhat erratic in Xcalak. Theoretically, buses bound for Chetumal (US$7, 4-5 hours) with stops in Mahahual (US$3, 1 hour) and Limones (US$5, 2.5 hours) leave twice daily, typically around 5am and 2pm, but it's not unusual for one or both departures to be delayed or canceled. Upon arrival to Xcalak, your hotel may send a car to pick you up; otherwise, a taxi from town is about US$10. A cab from Mahahual runs around US$40.

Most travelers come in a rental car, which certainly simplifies life here. The closest gas station is on the main road to Mahahual, near the turnoff for Xcalak. However, it occasionally runs out of gas, so you should fill up on Highway 307 as well—Carrillo Puerto is a good spot. In a pinch, a few Xcalak families sell gas from barrels in their front yards; ask your hotel owner for help locating them.

If your budget permits, there also is a well-maintained airstrip approximately 2 kilometers (1.2 miles) west of town. Despite rumors that commercial flights will begin using it regularly, at the time of research, it was only used sporadically by private or chartered planes.

CHACCHOBEN ARCHAEOLOGICAL ZONE

Chacchoben (8am-5pm daily, US$2.50) got its name from archaeologists who, after uncovering no inscription indicating what the city's original residents called it, named it after the Maya village to which the land pertained. The meaning of that name is also lost, even to local villagers, though the accepted translation is Place of Red Corn. The area may have been settled as early as 1000 BC, and most of the building activity probably took place AD 200-700, the Classic period.

Visiting the Ruins

Entering the site, a short path leads first to **Temple 24,** a squat pyramid that is the primary structure of a small enclosed area called **Plaza B.** Across that plaza—and the larger Gran Plaza beyond it—is a massive raised platform, the **Gran Basamento,** with the site's largest pyramid, **Temple 1,** atop it; this pyramid is believed to have served astronomical and religious purposes. Also on the platform, two smaller structures, dubbed **Las Vasijas** and **Los Gemelos,** were likely used for ceremonial functions. The site has some well-preserved stucco and paint, and for that reason none of the pyramids can be climbed. Though it can get crowded when there's a cruise ship at Mahahual, Chacchoben has an appealingly remote feel, nestled in the forest with towering mahogany and banyan trees, its paths dotted with bromeliads.

Practicalities

Chacchoben is located about 70 kilometers (43 miles) north of Mahahual and 4 kilometers (2.5 miles) west of Limones. By **car,** take Highway 307 and turn west at the sign to Chacchoben ruins and like-named town, about 3 kilometers (1.9 miles) down a well-paved road. Alternatively, take a **bus** to Limones and then a **cab** (US$5) to the ruins.

Chacchoben's Temple 24 has unusual, rounded corners.

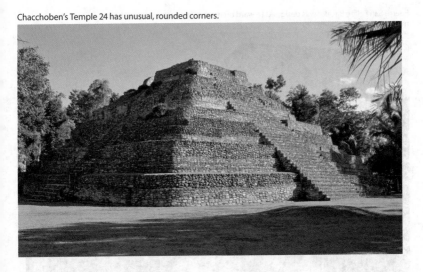

Laguna Bacalar

Almost 50 kilometers (31 miles) long, Laguna Bacalar is the second-largest lake in Mexico and certainly among the most beautiful. Well, it's not technically a lake: A series of waterways lead to the ocean, making Bacalar a lagoon, but it is fed by natural springs, making the water on the western shore, where the hotels and town are, 100 percent *agua dulce* (fresh water).

The Maya name for the lagoon translates as Lake of Seven Colors. It is an apt description, as you will see on any sunny day. The lagoon's sandy bottom and crystalline water turn shallow areas a brilliant turquoise, which fades to deep blue in the center. If you didn't know better, you'd think it was the Caribbean.

The hub of the Laguna Bacalar region is the town of Bacalar. Located on the west side of the lake, it is evolving into an indie traveler hot spot with a growing number of hotels, eateries, and opportunities to enjoy the gorgeous waters.

SIGHTS AND EVENTS
Fuerte San Felipe Bacalar

The mid-18th-century **Fuerte San Felipe Bacalar** (central plaza, no phone, Av. 3 at Calle 20, 9am-7pm Tues.-Sun., US$5) was built by the Spanish for protection against English pirates and Maya that regularly raided the area. The fort was captured in 1858 by Maya during the Caste War. It was not returned to Mexican officials until 1901. Today, the star-shaped stone edifice has been restored to its former glory—drawbridge, cannons, moat, and all. The fort also houses the excellent **Museo del Fuerte de San Felipe Bacalar,** a modern museum with exhibits on the history of the area, including details on the pirates who regularly attacked these shores.

Cenote Azul

As good or better than Laguna Bacalar for swimming, **Cenote Azul** (Hwy. 307 Km 15, tel. 983/157-6932, 10am-5:30pm, US$1.50) is two kilometers (1.2 miles) south of town. It's

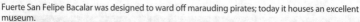
Fuerte San Felipe Bacalar was designed to ward off marauding pirates; today it houses an excellent museum.

Laguna Bacalar

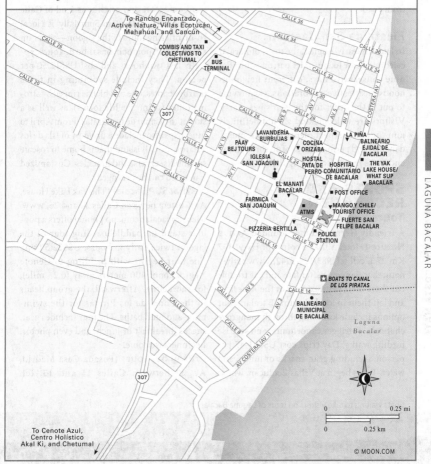

the widest cenote in Mexico, some 600 meters (1,969 feet) across at its widest, and 150 meters (492 feet) deep, with crystalline blue water. A rope stretches clear across, so even less-conditioned swimmers can make it to the far side. A large, breezy **restaurant** (tel. 983/834-2038, 9:30am-6pm daily, US$6-16) has the only entrance to the cenote, and charges the admission fee only if you don't order something.

★ Canal de los Piratas

A waterway directly across from the Fuerte San Felipe de Bacalar, the **Canal de los Piratas** is a shallow canal connecting Laguna Bacalar to Laguna Mariscal. Said to have been used by pirates to approach—and attack—the town of Bacalar during the colonial era, the waters are calm and turquoise blue and there are several sandy areas where boats moor while visitors swim, play in the water, and cover themselves in exfoliating mud. Tour operators do a brisk business shuttling people between Bacalar and the canal, charging US$30 per round-trip (up to six people); typically, they sell rides from a kiosk on the main plaza or along the waterfront road.

Fiesta de San Joaquín

In late July/early August, the town of Bacalar celebrates San Joaquín, its patron saint. For nine consecutive days, different neighborhoods host festive celebrations, each trying to outdo the other for the year's best party. Visitors are welcome and should definitely join the fun—expect plenty of food, music, dancing, and performances of all sorts. Kayak and horse races also are popular.

SPORTS AND RECREATION
Tours

A friendly German couple founded **Active Nature** (Hotel Villas Ecotucán, Hwy. 307 Km 27.3, cell tel. 983/120-5742, www.active-naturebacalar.com) after fate and car trouble cut short their planned tour of the Americas and left them in lovely Laguna Bacalar. Tour options include kayaking through mangrove channels, outrigger canoe tours, and sunrise birding walks. Day trips cost US$13-47 per person, including gear, snacks or lunch, and water. Tours begin at Villas Ecotucán, whose

guests get a 10 percent discount. Overnight tours can also be arranged.

Asociación de Lancheros (end of Calle 14, tel. 983/835-5505, 8am-5pm daily) is a local co-op offering tours of the lagoon—either on a catamaran, pontoon, or sailboat. Tours typically last two hours and cost US$12.50 per person. They include swimming in three nearby cenotes, one of which is ringed by stromatolites (primitive life forms), as well as a stop at the Canal de los Piratas. From April to June, trips also include a drive-by of Isla de los Pajaros, a small island that is home to roseate spoonbills, egrets, and grackles. Customized tours also can be arranged.

What SUP Bacalar (The Yak Lake House, Av. Costera between Calles 24 and 26, www.whatsupbacalar.com, no phone) offers a popular stand-up paddleboarding tour of the lagoon twice daily (3 hours, US$22.50 pp). The tour begins with paddling to Cenote Negro, about 400 meters away (0.25 mile), for snorkeling. Afterward, the group heads to the Canal de los Piratas for the swimming and mud baths. The tour includes gear, snacks, breakfast or lunch, and even photos. Beginners welcome.

Páay bej Tours (Posada Casa Madrid, Av. 22 between Calles 11 and 13, tel.

boats waiting to take visitors on tours of Laguna Bacalar

983/154-7580, www.bacalar-tours-paaybej. com) offers guided tours of Maya ruins like Kohunlich, Dzibanché, and Chaccoben (US$45-80 pp, including transport, entrance fees, and boxed lunch), led by a friendly multilingual guide. You can also rent bikes here (US$1/hour, US$8/day).

Swimming

Balneario Ejidal de Bacalar (Av. Costera near Calle 26, no phone, 8am-7pm, US$0.50) is a public swimming area complete with *palapas* for rent (US$3/day), bathrooms, and a restaurant (9am-7pm, US$3-10). There are also kayaks for rent (US$7.50 per hour). Located just 250 meters (0.2 mile) from the central plaza, it's a convenient and inexpensive place to enjoy the water.

Basic but still nice, **Balneario Municipal de Bacalar** (Av. Costera at Calle 14, no phone, 9am-6pm, free) has a large, well-kept grassy area right on the lagoon, a long dock with a ladder for easy entry into the water, and a big *palapa* for shade and snacks (sodas and chips, mostly.) Use of bathrooms is US$0.25.

FOOD

★ **El Manatí Bacalar** (Calle 22 between Avs. 5 and 7, tel. 983/834-2021, 8am-9pm Wed.-Mon., US$4-9) is cavernous café with a gorgeous outdoor patio surrounded by tropical trees and flowering plants. Farm-to-table Mexican dishes are the mainstays—think enchiladas, *pozole*, fruit and yogurt dishes, and tortas. A modern art gallery and handicraft shop, both showcasing local artists, entice diners to linger and shop. Live acoustic music is a breakfast treat during the high season.

Next to the fort, ★ **Mango y Chile** (Av. 3 near Calle 22, tel. 983/688-2000, 1pm-9pm Wed.-Mon., US$5-7) serves an entirely vegan menu of burgers, tacos, and salads. Portions are huge and integrate foods like hemp, falafel, and pumpkin seeds. A good variety of coffee drinks, freshly squeezed juices, smoothies, and kombucha round out the menu. Order at the counter and vie for a seat on the patio, which has enviable views over the lagoon.

La Piña (Av. 3 between Calles 26 and 28, no phone, 8am-9pm Thurs.-Tues., US$3-6) is a mom-and-pop restaurant with boho flair. Set in long, narrow garden with tall trees and a small *palapa*, the menu is classically Mexican with extras like hummus platters and pizza. Good drinks specials—both alcohol- and fruit-based—make this a good place to while away an afternoon.

Cocina Orizaba (Av. 7 between Calles

Find utter peace and tranquility at little-visited Laguna Bacalar.

24 and 26, tel. 983/834-2069, 8am-3:45pm daily, US$3-10) serves a variety of traditional Mexican dishes in a thatch-roof restaurant a few blocks from the central plaza. The daily *comida corrida* (lunch special) includes an entrée, main dish, and drink.

On the main plaza, the Italian-owned and operated **Pizzeria Bertilla** (Av. 5 between Calles 18 and 20, cell tel. 983/136-8525, 4:30pm-10:30pm Thurs.-Tues., US$6-15) specializes in homemade pasta and pizza, made with top-of-the-line ingredients and toppings. Service can be a bit grumpy, but think of it as part of the experience.

Food stands (US$1.50-3) set up on the central plaza every evening starting at 5pm. You'll find favorites like hot dogs and tacos as well as *marquesitas* (crispy, crepe-like pancakes stuffed with savory or sweet fillings) and *elote* (corn on the cob, served with mayo, chile, and lime). It's a good place for cheap, tasty eats, with the best people-watching in town.

ACCOMMODATIONS
In Town
Backpackers love **The Yak Lake House** (Av. Costera between Calles 24 and 26, tel. 983/834-3175, yakbacalar@gmail.com, US$18-22 pp dorm with a/c, US$85 s/d with a/c), a modern and stylish hostel right on the lake with a hipster vibe and great views. Dorms and private rooms are available, with nighttime air-conditioning and continental breakfast; dorms have individual lockers and reading lights. A long terrace overlooking the lake is perfect for hanging out, and the hostel organizes various free tours and activities; many guests end up extending their stay more than once. Desk service can be oddly surly, however.

★ **Hostal Pata de Perro** (central plaza, Calle 22 between Calles 3 and 5, tel. 983/834-2062, www.patadeperrobacalar.com, US$33 s/d with shared bath and a/c, US$60 suite with kitchen and a/c) is a pleasant surprise, tucked behind a bustling restaurant. A hybrid hotel-hostel, it has five private rooms in the main

building that are simple and appealing, with thick mattresses, tropical wood bed frames, and colorful bedding. All share updated bathrooms and a spacious common kitchen, where complimentary coffee and pastries are laid out every morning. For those traveling with kids or in a group, ask about the suites—small apartments, really—which are similar in style to the rooms but have private kitchens.

Hotel Azul 36 (Av. 3 between Calles 26 and 28, tel. 983/834-3165, www.azul36.com. mx, US$65 s/d with a/c) is a small inn that integrates natural building materials—exposed tree trunks, thatch roofs, bamboo fences—with modern furnishings and flair. Rooms have polished cement floors, thick beds on cement frames, and signature blue walls; bathrooms are simple and sleek with washbasin sinks. Units on the 2nd floor have small balconies. Grassy areas run throughout the property and lead to a well-tended pool, complete with wood-frame loungers and handcrafted tables.

Outside of Town
Villas Ecotucán (Hwy. 307 Km 27.3, cell tel. 983/120-5743, www.villasecotucan.com, US$68 s/d) has 11 solar-powered, *palapa*-roofed *cabañas,* each spacious and simply decorated and with a veranda to enjoy the view of the lake and surrounding tropical forest. The verdant grounds have hammocks strung throughout, a main building that serves as a restaurant and communal space, and a peaceful dock. A full breakfast and use of kayaks is included. The hotel specializes in guided nature excursions by kayak and on foot.

Rancho Encantado (Hwy. 307 Km 24, tel. 998/884-2071, www.encantado.com, US$106-180 s/d with a/c) has spacious *palapa*-roofed casitas and modern suites, both featuring Mexican tile floors, good beds, and views of either the lush garden or the lagoon; all but one have air-conditioning. The prettiest spot here, however, is a pier that leads to a shady dock strung with hammocks—it's perfect for swimming and relaxing. Guests can receive

Bacalar Bus Schedule

Departures from the **bus terminal** (Hwy. 307 near Calle 30, no phone) are almost all *de paso* (mid-route service), which means there's often a limited availability of seats. Destinations include:

Destination	Price	Duration	Schedule*
Cancún	US$18-21.50	5-6 hours	every 30-60 minutes 12:15am-10:50pm
Chetumal	US$2.50-3.50	50 minutes	every 30-90 minutes 1:20am-11:50pm
Chetumal International Airport	US$7.50	45 minutes	3:50pm
Mahahual	US$5	2 hours	9:45am
Playa del Carmen	US$15-17	4-4.5 hours	take Cancún bus
Tulum	US$11-12	3 hours	take Cancún bus
Xcalak	US$4.50	2.5-3 hours	6:30am and 5:20pm

massages and body treatments in a small kiosk built over the lake; a hot tub is nearby. Breakfast is included.

Set on the shores of Laguna Bacalar, ★ **Centro Holístico Akal Ki** (Hwy 307, Km 12.5, tel. 983/106-1751, www.akalki.com, US$280-US$406 s/d) is a whole-body experience—from the yoga classes and holistic body treatments to organic meals and breathtaking views. Eleven *cabañas* and suites are simple and elegant, with whitewashed walls, tropical wood floors, thick mattresses, and luxurious linens (plus no Wi-Fi or TVs in any of them, so guests can disconnect). Best of all, most units are built over the water—guests fall asleep to the gentle lapping of the lagoon (or jump in, from their private sundeck, first thing in the morning). Guided hikes in the tropical forest as well as tours of the owners' organic farm are offered too. Breakfast and complimentary use of kayaks and bicycles are included.

INFORMATION AND SERVICES
Tourist Information

Bacalar's **tourist office** (Av. 3 between Calles 22 and 24, turismobacalar@hotmail.com, 8am-4pm Mon.-Fri., tel. 983/834-2886) is located across from the hospital; it has loads of brochures and knowledgeable staff members. Also, **www.bacalarmosaico.com** is a bilingual website with useful information on the area's sights, activities, and businesses.

Emergency Services

Hospital Comunitario de Bacalar (Av. 3 between Calles 22 and 24, tel. 983/834-2969, 24 hours) offers emergency services as well non-urgent medical care; for serious matters, head to Chetumal. For meds, try **Farmacia San Joaquín** (Av. 7 between Calles 20 and 22, no phone, 8am-3pm and 6pm-9pm daily). The **police station** (Calle 20 near Av. 3, toll-free Mex. tel. 066, 24 hours) is located across from the Fuerte San Felipe Bacalar.

Money

There is no bank in town, but there are several ATMs on the west side of the central plaza, including **Banorte and Santander.** If you need other money services, the closest bank is in Chetumal.

Media and Communications

The **post office** (Av. 3 near Calle 24, 8am-4pm Mon.-Fri., 9am-1pm Sat.) is just east of the Fuerte San Felipe Bacalar. For Internet access, most hotels offer complimentary Wi-Fi to guests. The central plaza also has free Wi-Fi.

Laundry

Lavandería Burbujas (Av. 7 between Calles 24 and 26, tel. 983/183-8965, 8am-8pm Mon.-Sat., 9am-1pm Sun.) offers next-day service for US$0.75 per kilo (2.2 pounds).

GETTING THERE AND AROUND

You can easily walk to all the sites of interest in Bacalar, with the exception of Cenote Azul. A taxi there from town costs around US$3; cabs typically wait for passengers around the central plaza and on Avenida 7 in front of Iglesia San Joaquín.

Bus

Bacalar's modest **bus terminal** (Hwy. 307 near Calle 30, tel. 983/833-3163) is on the highway, about a 20-minute walk from the central plaza or a US$1 cab ride. The buses are almost exclusively *de paso* (mid-route) service, which means there's often limited availability (i.e., as soon as you know your schedule, buy your ticket).

*Schedules are subject to change.

Combi

Combis and *taxi colectivos* (US$2.50, every 30 minutes, 5am-11pm) run between Bacalar and Chetumal daily. You can catch either in front of the bus terminal (Hwy. 307 near Calle 30).

Chetumal

Chetumal is the capital of Quintana Roo and the gateway to Central America. It's not the prettiest of towns, and most travelers just pass through on their way to or from Belize or southern Campeche. However, Chetumal's modern Maya museum is one of the best you'll find in the region (albeit with few original pieces) and is well worth a visit. And if you're dying to see the Guatemalan ruins of Tikal, a shuttle from Chetumal can get you there in eight hours (cutting through Belize) and back again just as fast; a 90-minute boat ride also will take you to San Pedro, Belize, for a quick overnighter. The area around Chetumal is worth exploring, too, whether the bayside town of Calderitas or the intriguing and little-visited Maya ruins of Kohunlich, Dzibanché, Kinichná, and Oxtankah.

SIGHTS

Museo de la Cultura Maya

One of the best museums in the region, the **Maya Culture Museum** (Av. de los Héroes at Calle Cristóbal Colón, tel. 983/832-6838, 9am-7pm Tues.-Sun., US$2.50 adult, US$1 child) extends over three levels—the upper represents the world of gods, the middle the world of humans, and the lower Xibalba, the underworld. Each floor has impressive, well-designed exhibits describing Maya spiritual beliefs, agricultural practices, astronomy, and more, all in English and Spanish. In fact, the only thing lacking is original artifacts. (The replicas, however, are quite good.) The exhibition area past the ticket booth usually has good temporary art shows, plus a cinema that hosts free screenings of independent films.

Monumento al Mestizo

Across from the Museo de la Cultura Maya is the **Monumento al Mestizo** (Av. de los Héroes s/n), a striking sculpture symbolizing the creation of a new race—the mestizo—through the union of the shipwrecked Spanish sailor Gonzalo Guerrero and Zazil Há, a Maya woman. Hernán Cortés offered to take Guerrero back to Spain, but Guerrero chose to stay in the Americas, wedding Zazil

Há in a Maya marriage ritual. Note that the Maya symbol for the number zero as well as the cycle of life, the snail shell, provides the framework for the entire work of art.

Museo de la Ciudad

The **City Museum** (Calle Héroes de Chapultepec between Avs. Juárez and de los Héroes, tel. 983/832-1350, 9am-5pm Tues.-Sat., 9am-3pm Sun., US$2.50 adult, US$1 child, free Sundays) is small and well organized, and describes the political, economic, and cultural history of Chetumal, spanning the period from its founding in 1898 to the present day. Signage is in Spanish only.

El Malecón

Running six kilometers (3.7 miles) on the Boulevard Bahía, this breezy promenade makes for a fine bayfront stroll. Along it you'll find monuments, plazas, a lighthouse, government buildings, and, hopefully, a cooling breeze. Of particular note are two impressive **murals** found within the **Palacio Legislativo** (end of Av. Reforma, 9am-10pm Mon.-Fri.), a shell-shaped building that houses the state congress. Created by local artist Elio Carmichael, one mural outlines the state's history—from the creation of man to the devastating effects of Hurricane Janet in 1955—while the other depicts the law of the cosmos. Both are located in the reception area and are open to the public.

Maqueta Payo Obispo

Maqueta Payo Obispo (Calle 22 de Enero near Av. Reforma, 9am-2pm Mon.-Fri., free) is a scale model of Chetumal as it looked in the 1930s, with brightly colored clapboard houses, grassy lots, and plenty of palm trees. It's a reproduction of a model made by longtime resident Luis Reinhardt McLiberty. Look for it in a glass-enclosed building across the street from the Palacio Legislativo; glare on sunny days can make it hard to see the exhibit. A small history museum of the city also is on-site; signage is in Spanish only.

ENTERTAINMENT AND SHOPPING

Sunday on El Malecón

Every Sunday after 6pm, locals gather at the **Esplanada de la Bandera** (southern end of Av. de los Héroes) to enjoy city-sponsored events, typically performances by the municipal band or local musicians and singers. The events are free and family friendly, with vendors selling drinks and munchies.

The Museo de la Cultura Maya has fascinating displays on Maya sculpture, writing, mathematics, astronomy, and more.

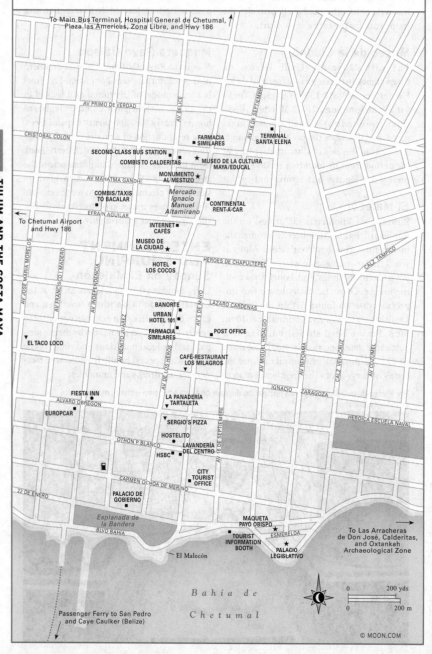

Chetumal

To Main Bus Terminal, Hospital General de Chetumal, Plaza las Americas, Zona Libre, and Hwy 186

AV PRIMO DE VERDAD

AV BELICE

AV 16 DE SEPTIEMBRE

CRISTOBAL COLON

FARMACIA SIMILARES

TERMINAL SANTA ELENA

SECOND-CLASS BUS STATION

COMBIS TO CALDERITAS

★ MUSEO DE LA CULTURA MAYA/EDUCAL

AV MAHATMA GANDHI

MONUMENTO AL MESTIZO ★

COMBIS/TAXIS TO BACALAR

Mercado Ignacio Manuel Altamirano

CONTINENTAL RENT-A-CAR

EFRAIN AGUILAR

← To Chetumal Airport and Hwy 186

INTERNET CAFÉS

MUSEO DE LA CIUDAD ★

AV JOSE MARIA MORELOS

AV FRANCISCO MADERO

AV INDEPENDENCIA

HOTEL LOS COCOS

HEROES DE CHAPULTEPEC

CALZ TÁMPICO

BANORTE

URBAN HOTEL 101

AV DE LOS HEROS

AV 5 DE MAYO

LAZARO CARDENAS

FARMACIA SIMILARES

POST OFFICE

AV BENITO JUÁREZ

AV MIGUEL HIDALGO

AV REFORMA

CALZ VERACRUZ

AV COZUMEL

▼ EL TACO LOCO

CAFÉ-RESTAURANT LOS MILAGROS ▼

FIESTA INN

ALVARO OBREGON

LA PANADERÍA TARTALETA

IGNACIO ZARAGOZA

EUROPCAR

SERGIO'S PIZZA

HOSTELITO

AV 16 DE SEPTIEMBRE

HEROICA ESCUELA NAVAL

OTHON P BLANCO

LAVANDERÍA DEL CENTRO

HSBC

CITY TOURIST OFFICE

CARMEN OCHOA DE MERINO

22 DE ENERO

PALACIO DE GOBIERNO

Esplanada de la Bandera

BLVD BAHIA

MAQUETA PAYO OBISPO

★ ESMERELDA

To Las Arracheras de Don José, Calderitas, and Oxtankah Archaeological Zone

TOURIST INFORMATION BOOTH

PALACIO LEGISLATIVO ★

El Malecón

Bahia de Chetumal

0   200 yds
0   200 m

Passenger Ferry to San Pedro and Caye Caulker (Belize)

© MOON.COM

Cinema

If you're hankering to watch the latest Hollywood film, head to **Cinépolis** (Plaza Las Ámericas, Av. Insurgentes s/n, tel. 983/837-6044, www.cinepolis.com, US$3.50-5), an 11-screen theater where most films are in English with Spanish subtitles.

Shopping

Educal (Av. de los Héroes at Calle Cristóbal Colón, tel. 983/129-2832, www.educal.com.mx, 9am-7pm Tues.-Sat., 9am-2pm Sun.) is a good bookstore located inside the Museo de la Cultura Maya.

Mercado Ignacio Manuel Altamirano (Efraín Aguilar between Avs. Belice and de los Héroes, 8am-8pm Mon.-Sat., 8am-3pm Sun.) is a two-story building mostly selling everyday items, from clothing to kitchenware. For travelers, it's a good place to buy a pair of flip-flops, a travel clock, or kitschy souvenirs.

Plaza Las Ámericas (Av. Insurgentes s/n, 9am-10pm daily) is a classic shopping mall with clothing and shoe boutiques, a megaplex movie theater, and even a Walmart. You'll also find all the typical amenities like ATMs, a food court, and public bathrooms.

The **Zona Libre** (Corozal Duty Free Zone, 9am-7pm daily) is an area just across the Belize border that's jam-packed with stores selling products from around the world, including shoes, clothing, alcohol, and household items. Bring your passport along, but guard it carefully.

FOOD

A locals' favorite, ★ **El Taco Loco** (Av. Morelos near Av. Zaragoza, tel. 983/129-2090, www.tacoloco.mx, 8am-6pm daily, US$6-8) serves excellent seafood at very accessible prices. It's hard to pick just one item, but you can't really go wrong with dishes like Caribbean ceviche, shrimp cocktail, or octopus tacos. Service is sometimes spotty, and the dining room is decidedly no-frills, but it's all part of the experience.

La Panadería Tartaleta (Av. de los Héroes at Av. Obregón, no phone, 7am-10pm daily, US$2.50-4) is a bustling little bakery, serving a sophisticated menu of panini—think smoked salmon, roasted vegetables with goat cheese, and Granny Smith apples with brie. There are also coffee drinks, smoothies, and, of course, beautiful desserts. (Be sure to leave room for the chocolate croissants!)

Sergio's Pizza (Av. 5 de Mayo at Av. Alvaro Obregón, tel. 983/108-1438, 7am-midnight daily, US$5-14) serves much more

TULUM AND THE COSTA MAYA
CHETUMAL

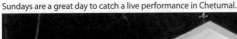
Sundays are a great day to catch a live performance in Chetumal.

than pizza in its dimly lit dining room. The extensive menu covers the gamut of Italian and Mexican dishes—from meat lasagna to *molletes rancheros*. Meals are hearty, making it popular with families.

Located on the Malecón, **Las Arracheras de Don José** (Blvd. Bahía at Calle Josefa Ortiz de Dominguez, tel. 983/832-8895, 5pm-3am daily, US$4-10) serves some of the best tacos in town. Try the *tacos de arrachera* (broiled skirt steak marinated in lemon and spices), which are only improved when paired with a beer.

Café-Restaurant Los Milagros (Calle Ignacio Zaragoza near Av. 5 de Mayo, tel. 983/832-4433, 7am-3pm Mon.-Sat., 7am-1pm Sun., US$3-7) serves up strong coffee drinks and especially good breakfasts. The best seating is outdoors—snag a table where you can, as it can get crowded fast.

ACCOMMODATIONS

Chetumal's status as the state capital and its location on the Belize border make it a busy town, and reservations are recommended, especially on weekdays.

Under US$50

Draped in murals, **Hostelito** (Av. Othón Blanco near Av. de los Héroes, tel. 983/833-3419, US$10 pp dorm with a/c, US$28 s/d with a/c, US$75 suite with kitchen) is an excellent option for budget travelers. The private rooms are where it's at—spacious, clean, and modern—all opening onto a multilevel courtyard with a well-maintained pool, common outdoor kitchen, and hammock lounge. There's one dorm, which is dark and a bit cramped, but the bunks have good mattresses, individual lights, and outlets; air-conditioning is turned on at night. Continental breakfast is included.

Located up a steep set of stairs, **Urban Hotel 101** (Av. de los Héroes near Calle Lázaro Cárdenas, cell tel. 983/752-0735, www.hotelurban101.com, US$35 s/d with a/c) is worth the climb. This new hotel mixes boho charm with clean modern lines, creating a welcoming feel. Rooms have polished cement floors, sleek furnishings, rainfall showerheads, and splashes of color in side chairs and wall art. A nice touch is the windows—long and thin, they let in the sun but keep out the city noise. Continental breakfast is offered daily in a small, quirky lounge.

Over US$50

★ **Fiesta Inn** (Av. Obregón at Av. Independencia, www.fiestainn.com, tel. 983/267-3200, US$88 s/d with a/c, US$115-264 suite) oozes cool with mid-century modern flair. Rooms have gleaming floors and big picture windows with comfortable beds and high-end amenities. There's a spectacular rooftop pool and fitness center with views of the bay; a sushi and sake lounge opens onto it in the evenings. Mornings bring a popular buffet in the main restaurant (US$11/5.50 adult/child), complete with made-to-order omelets and a full line of freshly squeezed juices. Best of all is the service—attentive, personalized, and making you wish you could stay longer.

Hotel Los Cocos (Av. de los Héroes at Calle Héroes de Chapultepec, tel. 983/835-0430, toll-free Mex. tel. 800/719-5840, www.hotelloscocos.com.mx, US$45-55 s/d with a/c) has three categories of rooms, all pleasant and with updated furnishings and modern amenities. The more expensive ones have flat-screen TVs, quiet air-conditioning, and more stylish decor. They all open onto a lush garden, which has a small, inviting pool area. The on-site restaurant, with a spacious outdoor dining area, is great for breakfast and people-watching.

Outside of Chetumal

On the road to the like-named ruins, ★ **Explorean Kohunlich** (off Hwy 186, tel. 443/310-8137, www.theexplorean.com, US$329-438 s/d all-inclusive) is a luxurious all-inclusive resort with 40 deluxe bungalows set on 30 hectares (74 acres) of tropical forest. Each has gleaming stone floors, high *palapa* ceilings, elegant furnishings, and privacy walls for sunbathing. Larger cabaña suites also have plunge pools. The main building houses a fine restaurant, a full-service spa, and a lap pool that overlooks the jungle (you can see the ruins at Kohunlich from here). The rate includes daily excursions with experienced guides, including rappelling in the jungle, kayaking through a crocodile reserve, or trekking through forgotten forests to little-visited ruins.

INFORMATION AND SERVICES
Tourist Information

Near the waterfront, the **city tourist office** (Av. 5 de Mayo at Carmen Ochoa de Merino, tel. 983/835-0860, 8am-4pm Mon.-Fri.) has a decent selection of brochures and maps. There also are **tourist information booths** in the main bus terminal (Av. Insurgentes at Av. Palermo, 10am-8pm daily) and on El Malecón (near the Palacio Legislativo, Av. Reforma, 8am-3pm Mon.-Fri.).

For online information, check out **www.tuchetumal.com**, an online directory to Chetumal and area sights.

Emergency Services

About two kilometers (1.2 miles) from the center of town, **Hospital General de Chetumal** (Av. Chapultepec between Calles Isla Cancún and Juan José Siordia, tel. 983/835-1920, 24 hours) is the city's main hospital.

For meds, try **Farmacia Similares** (Av. de los Héroes near Calle Plutarco Elias, tel. 983/833-2232, 8am-10pm Mon.-Sat., 9am-9pm Sun.) or its **sister store** (Calle Cristóbal Colón between Avs. Belice and de los Héroes, tel. 983/833-2331, 24 hours Thurs.-Tues.).

The **police** can be reached by dialing toll-free 066.

Money

HSBC (Av. Othon Blanco between Av. 5 de Mayo and Av. de los Héroes, 9am-4pm Mon.-Fri., 9am-3pm Sat.) is conveniently located downtown. There also is an ATM at the **main bus station** (Av. Insurgentes at Av. Palermo, tel. 983/832-5110).

Media and Communications

The **post office** (Av. Plutarco Elias Calles between Avs. 5 de Mayo and 16 de Septiembre, 8am-4pm Mon.-Fri., 9am-1pm Sat.) is just a block from the main drag. For Internet access, there is a string of **Internet cafés** across from the Mercado Ignacio Manuel Altamirano (Efraín Aguilar between Avs. Belice and de los Héroes); most charge US$0.75 per hour and are open 7:30am-midnight Mon.-Fri., 8am-10pm Sat.-Sun.

Laundry

Lavandería del Centro (Av. Othón Blanco near Av. 5 de Mayo, tel. 983/832-1149, 8am-8pm Mon.-Fri., 9am-2:30pm Sat.) provides next-day laundry service for US$0.75 per kilo (2.2 pounds).

GETTING THERE AND AROUND

Chetumal is a relatively large city, but the parts most travelers are interested in are all within easy walking distance of each other—mostly along Avenida de los Héroes and El Malecón. The exception is the main bus terminal, which is four kilometers (2.5 mi) from the center of town.

Air

The **Chetumal International Airport** (CTM, tel. 983/832-6625) receives only a few flights each day. Airlines serving it include **Interjet** (toll-free Mex. tel. 800/011-2345, toll-free U.S. tel. 866/285-9525, www.interjet.com.mx), **MAYAir** (toll-free Mex. tel. 800/962-9247, toll-free U.S./Can. tel. 844/622-0800, www.mayair.com.mx), and **Volaris** (Mex. tel. 551/102-8000, toll-free U.S. tel. 855/865-2747, www.volaris.com).

Bus

All first-class buses leave from the **main bus terminal** (Av. Insurgentes at Av. Palermo, tel. 983/832-5110), though most second-class buses also stop here on the way in or out of town.

The **second-class bus station** (Avs.

Chetumal Bus Schedule

Departures from Chetumal's **main bus terminal** (Av. Insurgentes at Av. Palermo, tel. 983/832-5110) are for first-class service, though some second-class buses stop here as well; tickets for either service can be purchased downtown, in the **second-class bus terminal** (Av. Belice at Av. Cristóbal Colón, no phone). Unless otherwise noted, the schedule is from the main bus terminal:

Destination	Price	Duration	Schedule*
Bacalar	US$2-3.50	50 minutes	every 30-90 minutes 12:30am-11:50pm
Belize City (Belize)	US$10	5 hours	every 60 minutes 11am-5pm (second-class bus terminal only)
Cancún	US$11.50-28	5.5-6 hours	every 30-90 minutes 12:30am-11:59pm
Corozal (Belize)	US$3	1 hour	7am
Flores (Guatemala)	US$35	8-9 hours	8am and 9:30am
Mahahual	US$6-12	2-2.5 hours	8:30am, 8:40am, and 10:30am or take Xcalak bus
Mérida	US$17-22	5.5-6 hours	Five departures from 12:30am to 11:30pm
Playa del Carmen	US$10.50-23.50	4.5-5 hours	take any Cancún bus
Tulum	US$8.50-19	3.5-4 hours	take any Cancún bus
Xcalak	US$6.50	3.5-4 hours	5:40am and 4:10pm (second-class bus terminal only)

Buses to the **Zona Libre** (US$1.75, 30 minutes) leave the **Terminal Santa Elena** (Av. Primo de Verdad near Av. Miguel Hidalgo, tel. 983/832-0639) every 20 minutes 6:30am-9pm Mon.-Sat., 7:30am-8:30pm Sun.

Belice and Cristóbal Colón, tel. 983/832-0639) is located just west of the Museo de la Cultura Maya; tickets for first-class buses also can be purchased here if you want to buy your tickets in advance but don't want to make the trek to the main terminal.

Terminal Santa Elena (Av. Primo de Verdad near Av. Miguel Hidalgo, tel. 983/832-0639) has daily bus service to the Zona Libre.

*Schedules are subject to change.

Combi

Combis and taxis colectivos (US$2.50, every 30 minutes, 4am-10pm) run between Chetumal and Bacalar daily. You can catch either on Avenida Independencia near Calle Efraín Aguilar. Vehicles leave every 30 minutes or as soon as there are four passengers.

Car

The highways in this area are all paved and well maintained. Car rental agencies in town include **Continental Rent-a-Car** (Av. de los Héroes near Av. Mahatma Gandhi, tel. 983/832-2411, www.continentalcar.com.mx, 8am-8pm daily) and **Europcar** (Av. Obregón at Av. Independencia, tel. 983/833-9959, www.europcar.com, 9am-6pm daily).

Taxi

Taxis can be flagged down easily in downtown Chetumal. Few are metered, so be sure to agree on a price before you set off toward your destination. A cab around downtown and along El Malecón costs around US$2-3.

Water Taxi

Water Jets International (El Muelle Fiscal, Blvd. Bahía s/n, tel. 983/833-3201, Belize tel. 501/226-2194 www.sanpedrowatertaxi.com) provides daily ferry service to San Pedro (US$55, 1.5 hours) and Caye Caulker (US$60, 3 hours) in Belize. Boats leave at 3pm and pass through immigration in San Pedro before continuing onto Caye Caulker. The return

ferry to Chetumal leaves Caye Caulker at 7am and San Pedro at 8am.

San Pedro Belize Express (El Muelle Fiscal, Blvd. Bahía s/n, Belize tel. 501/223-2225, www.belizewatertaxi.com) offers similar ferry service to Belize (same prices, same destinations as Water Jets), leaving Chetumal at 3:30pm every other day, alternating monthly (i.e., in January, March, May, July, September, and November the ferry operates on even days—the 2nd, 4th, 6th, etc. In February, April, June, August, October, and December, the ferry operates on odd days—the 3rd, 5th, 7th, etc.). The ferry returns from Caye Caulker at 7am and San Pedro at 8:30am.

Around Chetumal

The area around Chetumal has a number of worthwhile attractions, all the better because so few travelers linger here.

CALDERITAS

Located just seven kilometers (4 miles) north of Chetumal, Calderitas is a bayside town known for its **seafood restaurants** (8am-6pm daily, US$4-10)—most along the waterfront across from the main plaza—and its **public beaches.** During the week it's a mellow scene, but on weekends locals descend upon the town for a day of R&R and some revelry, too.

Boat rides can be arranged at many of the bayside establishments to explore **Chetumal Bay** (US$150, up to 8 people) in search of manatees, which were once abundant in these waters, or to visit **Isla Tamalcab** (US$40, up to 8 people), an uninhabited island with white-sand beaches and good snorkeling. It's home to spider monkeys and *tepescuintles* (pacas in English).

If you want to stay overnight, **Yax Há Resort & Explorer** (Av. Yucatán 415, tel. 983/834-4127, US$7.50 pp camping, US$7.50-18 per RV, US$45 s/d with a/c, US$60 s/d with

a/c and kitchenette) offers everything from camp- and RV sites to bungalows, right on the water. The bungalows, while dated in décor, are quite comfortable. They range from one-room units with air-conditioning, TV, and mini fridges to two-bedroom units with fully equipped kitchens; all have porches overlooking the bay. There's also a pool on-site.

Getting There

Calderitas is a quick bus ride from downtown Chetumal. *Combis* leave from Avenida Cristóbal Colón, behind the Museo de la Cultura Maya, roughly every 30 minutes 6am-9pm daily (US$0.25, 25 minutes). If you have a car, head east out of Chetumal on Boulevard Bahía, which becomes the main drag in Calderitas. Alternatively (though less scenic), take Avenida Insurgentes east until you get to the turnoff, and follow the signs from there.

OXTANKAH ARCHAEOLOGICAL ZONE

Oxtankah (8am-5pm daily, US$2.50) is a small archaeological site whose name means Between Branches, so called by early archaeologists after the many trees growing amid,

Oxtankah Archaeological Zone

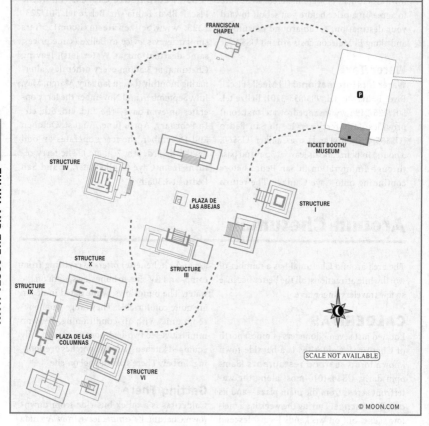

FRANCISCAN CHAPEL

TICKET BOOTH/MUSEUM

STRUCTURE IV

PLAZA DE LAS ABEJAS

STRUCTURE I

STRUCTURE X

STRUCTURE III

STRUCTURE IX

PLAZA DE LAS COLUMNAS

STRUCTURE VI

SCALE NOT AVAILABLE

© MOON.COM

and on top of, the structures. Relatively little is known about Oxtankah—including its true name—but it probably arose during the Classic era, between AD 300 and 600, and was dedicated primarily to trade and salt production. At its height, the city extended to the shores of Chetumal Bay and included the island of Tamalcab.

Oxtankah's principal structures were constructed in this period, suggesting it was a fairly robust city, but it was apparently abandoned around AD 600, for unknown reasons. The city was reoccupied by Maya settlers almost a thousand years later, in the 14th or 15th century, during which time a number of structures were expanded or enhanced. It was still occupied, mostly by modest earthen homes, when the first Spanish explorers arrived.

Some researchers have suggested the infamous Spaniard castaway Gonzalo Guerrero lived here; Guerrero was shipwrecked in this area in 1511 and adopted Maya ways, even marrying a chieftain's daughter. Their children are considered the New World's first mestizos, or mixed-race people.

In 1531, conquistador Alonso de Avila attempted to found a colonial city on the site,

Calderitas costs US$3.50 each way; one from Chetumal will run about US$18 round-trip, including wait time.

KOHUNLICH ARCHAEOLOGICAL ZONE

Swallowed by the jungle over the centuries, **Kohunlich** (8am-5pm daily, US$3.25) was rediscovered in 1912 by American explorer Raymond Merwin, but it was not until the 1960s that excavation of the site began in earnest. Today, the ruins are in harmony with the surrounding vegetation: The site has more than 200 structures, stelae, and uncovered mounds that have trees growing out of them and moss spreading over their stones—a beautiful sight. Most date to the Late Preclassic (AD 100-200) through the Classic (AD 600-900) periods.

Kohunlich's most famous and compelling structure is the **Temple of the Masks.** Constructed in AD 500, it features six two-meter-tall (6.6-foot) stucco masks, believed to be representations of the Maya sun god, with star-incised eyes, mustaches, and nose plugs. Intriguingly, each is slightly different, leading some to speculate that they also represent successive members of the ruling dynasty; it would not have been unusual for the city's elite to draw an overt connection between themselves and a high god.

Southwest of the Temple of the Masks is **27 Escalones,** the largest and most impressive residential area in Kohunlich. Built on a cliff with a spectacular bird's-eye view of the jungle, it is one of the largest palaces in the Maya world, reached by climbing its namesake 27 steps. As you walk through the site, keep an eye out for *aguadas* (cisterns) that once were part of a complex system of Kohunlich's reservoirs.

The famous red-painted masks at Kohunlich are believed to represent the Maya sun god.

but he was driven out after two years of bitter conflict with local residents. He did manage to have a Franciscan chapel built, the skeleton of which remains, including an impressive eight-meter (26-foot) arch.

Today, most of the excavated structures in Oxtankah surround two plazas: **Abejas** (Bees), the city's main ceremonial and elite residential center, and the somewhat smaller **Columnas** (Columns), whose large palace probably served an administrative function. Architecturally, the structures are more closely related to those of the Petén region (present-day Guatemala) than to Yucatecan ones, suggesting a close relationship with that area. There's a small **museum** on-site; signage is in Spanish only.

Getting There

Oxtankah is located seven kilometers (4 miles) north of Calderitas, about one kilometer (0.6 mile) off the bayside road. There's no public transportation to the site; a **cab** from

Getting There

Kohunlich is located about 60 kilometers (37 miles) west of Chetumal. By **car,** take Highway 186 west and turn south (left) at the sign to Kohunlich. An 8.5-kilometer

Kohunlich Archaeological Zone

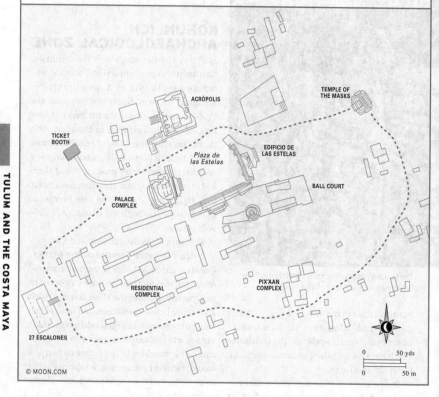

© MOON.COM

(5.3-mile) paved road leads straight to the site. There is no public transportation to the site.

DZIBANCHÉ AND KINICHNÁ ARCHAEOLOGICAL ZONES

If the crowds at Chichén Itzá and Tulum get you down, these picturesque twin ruins may be the antidote. Dzibanché and its smaller neighbor, Kinichná, see very few visitors—it's not uncommon to have them to yourself, in fact—and feature modest-size temples in varying states of restoration. (A great many structures aren't excavated at all, but even they—abrupt tree-covered mounds—hold a certain mystery and appeal.)

Dzibanché

The larger of the two sites, Dzibanché is Yucatec Maya for Etched in Wood, a name created by archaeologists in reference to a wood lintel inscribed with hieroglyphics that was found in one of the primary temples. A date on the lintel reads AD 618, and the site seems to have flourished between AD 300 and 800. Archaeologists believe this area was occupied by a sprawling, widely dispersed city that covered some 40 square kilometers (25 square miles).

The site has three main plazas, each higher than the next. Dzibanché's namesake lintel is still in the temple atop **Structure VI**, also called the Building of the Lintels, facing one of the plazas. Climbing Structure VI is no longer allowed, but it's just one of several large pyramids here, the rest of which you can clamber up. The largest is **Structure II**, with an ornate temple at its summit where archaeologists found a tomb of a high-ranking leader (judging from the rich offering found with his remains). The steep stairways and lofty upper temples here are reminiscent of Tikal and other temples in the Petén area of present-day Guatemala, suggesting a strong connection between the two regions.

Kinichná

Kinichná (House of the Sun) has just one structure, but it's a biggie: a massive pyramid whose summit affords a great view of the surrounding countryside. The structure has three distinct levels, each built in a different era over the course of around 400 years. As you climb, it's fascinating to observe how the craftsmanship and artistry changed—generally for the better—over the centuries. At the top is a stucco image of the sun god, hence the site's name. As in Structure II in Dzibanché, archaeologists uncovered a tomb here, this one containing the remains of two people and a cache of fine jade jewelry and figurines.

Practicalities

Dzibanché and Kinichná are open 8am-5pm daily; admission is US$2.75 and valid for both archaeological zones. There is no public transportation to or from the area, and precious little local traffic, so a **car** (or tour van) is essential. To get here, take the turnoff 50 kilometers (31 miles) west of Chetumal on Highway 186, before reaching the town of Francisco Villa; from there it's about 25 kilometers (15 miles) north to the ruins. Along the way, you'll hit the small town of Morocoy; about three kilometers past the town, take a right onto a bumpy road that leads to Dzibanché first, then Kinichná (there's a sign).

Chichén Itzá

I f you can drag yourself away from the beaches, a short trip inland will bring you to two of the Yucatán Peninsula's most intriguing ancient ruins—Chichén Itzá and Ek' Balam.

Each is quite different from the other, and together they form an excellent introduction to Maya archaeology and architecture. Venturing inland will also give you an opportunity to sneak a peek at how ordinary Yucatecans, including modern-day Maya, live today.

For many, Chichén Itzá is the Eiffel Tower of the Yucatán Peninsula—you can't possibly go home without visiting it. And for good reason: Chichén Itzá was selected as one of the "New Seven Wonders of the World" and boasts some of Mexico's most recognizable ancient structures, including its four-sided main pyramid and the Maya world's largest ball court. Plus it's only 200 kilometers (124 miles) from Cancún and 150 kilometers (90 miles) from Tulum.

Even closer to the coast, but far less visited, is the small ruin of Ek' Balam (175 km/109 mi from Cancún; 125 km/75 mi from Tulum), boasting an exquisitely preserved stucco frieze partway up a massive pyramid. The frieze features winged priests and a gaping monster mouth that are so well preserved they look like they could be modern-day plaster art. A kilometer (0.6 mile) away, a cenote provides a welcome respite from the heat.

Lastly, Valladolid is a lovely but oft-overlooked colonial town, with beautiful churches, nearby cenotes (even one in town), and plenty of options for lodging and eating—definitely consider basing yourself there. Throughout the area, look for cenotes to explore and admire, or even to take a refreshing dip.

PLANNING YOUR TIME

Chichén Itzá and Ek' Balam can each be reached as a day trip from Cancún or Tulum. You can visit both in one or two days, staying overnight at hotels near the sites or in Valladolid.

All destinations can be reached by bus or

Previous: Iglesia y Ex-Convento San Bernardino de Siena; El Castillo. **Above:** Iglesia de San Gervasio.

Look for ★ to find recommended
sights, activities, dining, and lodging.

Highlights

★ **Chichén Itzá Archaeological Zone:**
Voted one of the New Seven Wonders of the
World, the Yucatán's most famous ruin is all
about hyperbole: the iconic star-aligned pyramid, the gigantic Maya ball court, even the
crush of bikini-clad day-trippers from Cancún
(page 284).

★ **Iglesia y Ex-Convento San
Bernardino de Siena:** Located in a quiet
corner of Valladolid, this elegant church has
a spacious esplanade and beautiful interior, a
small museum, plus a natural cenote inside the
convent walls (page 295).

★ **Ek' Balam Archaeological Zone:** A
stunning stucco frieze with angel-like figures and
a huge "monster mouth" is the highlight of this
serene site near Valladolid (page 304).

★ **Cenotes Agua Dulce:** A visit to this set of
four cenotes makes for an eerily beautiful afternoon of underground swimming and exploring
(page 307).

Chichén Itzá

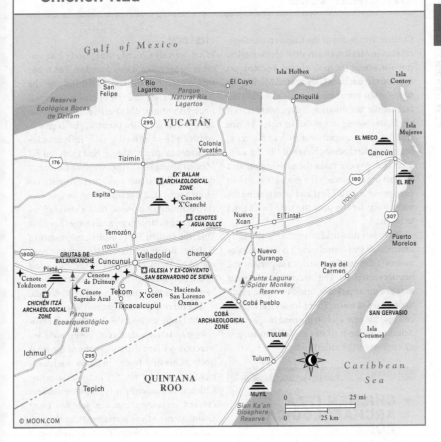

taxi, but if you plan on visiting more than one a rental car may make your trip easier and more rewarding. You won't be tied to a bus schedule, and you'll be able to beat the crowds by getting to the archaeological sites bright and early. There also are numerous organized tours to Chichén Itzá from Cancún (though fewer to Ek' Balam). While certainly convenient, many travelers find the large groups off-putting.

Chichén Itzá

Chichén Itzá is one of the finest archaeological sites in Mexico, and in all of Mesoamerica. It is also one of the most visited. Located just two hours from both Cancún and Mérida, the site is often inundated by tour groups. That fact should not dissuade independent travelers from visiting—crowded or not, Chichén Itzá is a truly magnificent ruin and a must-see on any archaeology tour of the Yucatán. That said, you can make the most of your visit by arriving right when the gates open, so you can see the big stuff first and be exploring the outer areas by the time the tour buses start to roll in.

Pisté is a one-road town that is strangely underdeveloped considering it is just two kilometers (1.2 miles) from such an important and heavily visited site. The hotels and restaurants here are unremarkable, and there's not much to do or see in town. There are several higher-end options near and on the road to the ruins. Another option is to stay in **Valladolid,** just 42 kilometers (25 miles) away.

TOP EXPERIENCE

★ CHICHÉN ITZÁ ARCHAEOLOGICAL ZONE

Chichén Itzá (8am-5pm daily, US$12, US$11-25 sound and light show only) is a monumental archaeological site, remarkable for both its size and scope. The ruins include impressive palaces, temples, and altars, as well as the largest-known ball court in the Maya world. One of the most widely recognized (and heavily visited) ruins in the world, it was declared a World Heritage site by UNESCO in 1988 and one of the New Seven Wonders of the World in 2007. In 2012, INAH (Instituto Nacional de Antropología e Historia) partnered with Google to photograph—by bicycle—the site for Google Street View maps.

History

What we call Chichén Itzá surely had another name when it was founded. The name means Mouth of the Well of the Itzá, but the Itzá, an illiterate and semi-nomadic group of uncertain origin, didn't arrive here until the 12th century. Before the Itzá, the area was controlled—or at least greatly influenced—by Toltec migrants who arrived from central Mexico around AD 1000. Most of Chichén's most notable structures, including its famous four-sided pyramid, and images like the reclining *chac-mool*, bear a striking resemblance to structures and images found at Tula, the ancient Toltec capital, in the state of Hidalgo. Before the Toltecs, the area was populated by Maya, evidenced by the Puuc- and Chenes-style design of the earliest structures here, such as the Nunnery and Casa Colorada.

The three major influences—Maya, Toltec, and Itzá—are indisputable, but the exact chronology and circumstances of those groups' interaction (or lack thereof) is one of the most hotly contested issues in Maya archaeology. Part of the difficulty in understanding Chichén Itzá more fully is that its occupants created very few stelae and left few Long Count dates on their monuments. In this way Chichén Itzá is different from virtually every other ancient city in the Yucatán. It's ironic, actually, that Chichén Itzá is the most widely recognized "Maya" ruin considering it was so deeply influenced by non-Maya cultures, and its history and architecture are so atypical of the region.

Chichén Itzá's influence ebbed and flowed over its many centuries of existence and occupation. It first peaked in the mid-9th century, or Late Classic period, when it eclipsed Cobá as the dominant power in the northern Yucatán region. The effects of a widespread collapse of Maya cities to the south (like Calakmul, Tikal, and Palenque) reached

Chichén Itzá Archaeological Zone

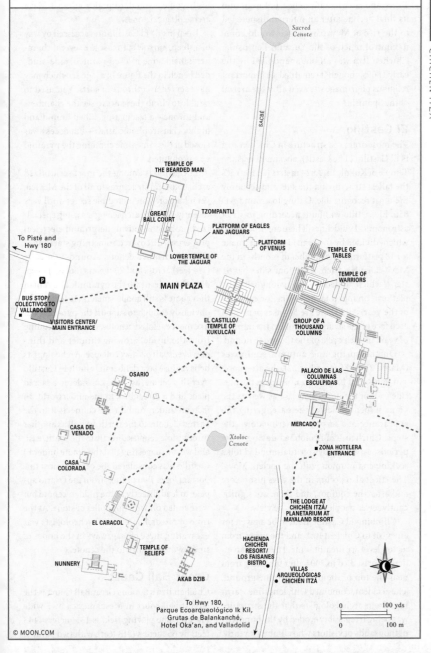

Sacred Cenote

SACBÉ

TEMPLE OF
THE BEARDED MAN

TZOMPANTLI

GREAT
BALL COURT

PLATFORM OF EAGLES
AND JAGUARS

PLATFORM
OF VENUS

TEMPLE OF
TABLES

To Pisté and
Hwy 180

LOWER TEMPLE OF
THE JAGUAR

TEMPLE OF
WARRIORS

P

MAIN PLAZA

BUS STOP
COLECTIVOS TO
VALLADOLID

GROUP OF A
THOUSAND
COLUMNS

VISITORS CENTER/
MAIN ENTRANCE

EL CASTILLO/
TEMPLE OF
KUKULCÁN

OSARIO

PALACIO DE LAS
COLUMNAS
ESCULPIDAS

CASA DEL
VENADO

MERCADO

CASA
COLORADA

Xtoloc
Cenote

ZONA HOTELERA
ENTRANCE

EL CARACOL

THE LODGE AT
CHICHÉN ITZÁ/
PLANETARIUM AT
MAYALAND RESORT

TEMPLE OF
RELIEFS

HACIENDA
CHICHÉN
RESORT/
LOS FAISANES
BISTRO

NUNNERY

AKAB DZIB

VILLAS
ARQUEOLÓGICAS
CHICHÉN ITZÁ

To Hwy 180,
Parque Ecoarqueológico Ik Kil,
Grutas de Balankanché,
Hotel Oka'an, and Valladolid

0   100 yds

0   100 m

© MOON.COM

Chichén Itzá in the late 900s, and it too collapsed abruptly. The city rose again under Toltec and later Itzá influence, but went into its final decline after an internal dispute led to the rise of Mayapán, which would come to control much of the Yucatán Peninsula. Chichén Itzá was all but abandoned by the early 1200s, though it remained an important religious pilgrimage site even after the arrival of the Spanish.

El Castillo

The most dramatic structure in Chichén Itzá is El Castillo (The Castle), also known as the Temple of Kukulcán. At 24 meters (79 feet), it's the tallest structure on the site, and certainly the most recognizable. Dating to around AD 850, El Castillo was built according to strict astronomical guidelines. There are nine levels, which, divided by the central staircase, make for 18 platforms, the number of months in the Maya calendar. Each of the four sides has 91 steps, which, added together along with the platform on top, total 365—one for each day of the year. And there are 52 inset panels on each face of the structure, equal to the number of years in each cycle of the Calendar Round.

On the spring and autumn equinoxes (March 21 and September 22), the afternoon sun lights up a bright zigzag strip on the outside wall of the north staircase as well as the giant serpent heads at the base, giving the appearance of a serpent slithering down the steps. Chichén Itzá is mobbed during those periods, especially by spiritual-minded folks seeking communion with the ancient Maya. The effect also occurs in the days just before and after the equinox, and there are significantly fewer people blocking the view.

Climbing El Castillo used to be a given for any visit to Chichén Itzá, and the views from its top level are breathtaking. However, an elderly tourist died in 2005 after tumbling from near the top of the pyramid to the ground. The accident, combined with longtime warnings from archaeologists that the structure was being irreparably eroded by the hundreds of thousands of visitors who climbed it yearly, prompted officials to close it off. Pyramids at other sites have been restricted as well, and it's become a standard policy at most Maya archaeological zones.

Deep inside El Castillo and accessed by way of a steep, narrow staircase are several chambers; inside one is a red-painted, jade-studded bench in the figure of a jaguar, which may have served as a throne of sorts. You used to be able to climb the stairs to see the chambers and throne—a fascinating, albeit humid and highly claustrophobic affair—but access was closed at the same time climbing the pyramid was prohibited.

El Castillo is among the most scrutinized archaeological structures in all of the Mexico, yet it harbored an incredible secret until very recently. In 2015, archaeologists using specialized probes to study underground electrical properties, discovered something startling—there's a massive cenote, around 35 meters (114 feet) across and 20 meters (66 feet) deep, directly underneath the pyramid. The roof of the cenote is still about 5 meters (16 feet) thick, obviously enough to support the pyramid, but like most enclosed cenotes, the roof is eroding from the inside, growing thinner and thinner; eventually it may collapse. Archeologists believe the Maya deliberately built El Castillo over this cenote, as it was considered a sacred place and a direct link to the underworld. In fact, an underground river connects it to the Sacred Cenote, to the north, as well as another three visible cenotes directly to the south, east, and west—suggesting that the cenote under El Castillo was considered the central, most important, one. Two tunnels from the Osario appear to lead directly to the hidden cenote but were sealed off with huge piles of stone. At the time of research, a team of archeologists was excavating these passageways in the hopes of finding an entrance to the cenote.

Great Ball Court

Chichén Itzá's famous Great Ball Court is the largest ball court in Mesoamerica by a wide margin. The playing field is 135 meters (443 feet) by 65 meters (213 feet), with two parallel

The Maya Collapse

Something went terribly wrong for the Maya between the years AD 800 and 900. Hundreds of Classic Maya cities were abandoned, monarchies disappeared, and the population fell by millions, mainly due to death and plummeting birthrates. The collapse was widespread, but was most dramatic in the Southern Lowlands, a swath of tropical forest stretching from the Gulf of Mexico to Honduras and including once-glorious cities such as Palenque, Tikal, and Copán. (Archaeologists first suspected a collapse after noticing a sudden drop-off in inscriptions; it has been confirmed through excavations of peasant dwellings from before and after that period.)

sculpture at Museo Maya de Cancún

There are many theories for the collapse, varying from climate change and epidemic diseases to foreign invasion and peasant revolt. In his carefully argued book *The Fall of the Ancient Maya* (Thames and Hudson, 2002), archaeologist and professor of anthropology at Pennsylvania State University David Webster suggests it was a series of conditions, rather than a single event, that led to the collapse.

To a certain degree, it was the very success of Maya cities during the Classic era that set the stage for their demise. Webster points to a population boom just before the collapse, which would have left agricultural lands dangerously depleted just as demand spiked. Classic-era farming techniques were ill-suited to meet the challenge; in particular, the lack of draft animals kept productivity low, meaning Maya farmers could not generate large surpluses of corn and other food. (Even if they could, storage was difficult given the hot, humid climate.) The lack of animals also limited how far away farmers could cultivate land and still be able to transport their crops to the city center; as a result, available land was overused. As Webster puts it, "Too many farmers [growing] too many crops on too much of the landscape left the Classic Maya world acutely vulnerable to an environmental catastrophe, such as drought or crop disease."

Certain kingdoms reached their tipping point before others (prompting some to launch 11th-hour military campaigns against weakened rivals), but few escaped the wave of malnutrition, disease, lower birthrates, and outright starvation that seems to have swept across the Maya world in the 9th century. Kings and nobility would have faced increasing unrest and insurrection—after all, their legitimacy was based on their ability to induce the gods to bestow rain, fertility, and prosperity—further destabilizing the social structure and food supply.

The collapse was not universal, of course, and the fall of lowland powers gave other city-states an opportunity to expand and gain influence. But the Maya world was dramatically and permanently changed by it; the grand cities built by the Classic Maya were abandoned to the jungle, most never to be reoccupied, and, as Webster notes, "Cortés and his little army almost starved in 1525 while crossing a wilderness that had supported millions of people seven centuries earlier."

walls 8 meters high (26 feet) and scoring rings in impossibly high perches in the center. The players would've had to hit a 12-pound rubber ball through the rings using only their elbows, wrists, and hips (they wore heavy padding). The game likely lasted for hours; at the game's end, the captain of one team—or even the whole team—was apparently sacrificed, possibly by decapitation. There's disagreement about *which* team got the axe, however. Some say it was the losers—otherwise the game's best players would constantly be wiped out. Some argue that it was the winners, and that being sacrificed would have been the ultimate honor. Of course, it's likely the game varied from city to city and evolved over the many centuries it was played. Along the walls, reliefs depict the ball game and sacrifices.

On the outside of the ball court, the **Lower Temple of the Jaguar** has incredibly fine relief carvings depicting the Maya creation myth. An upper temple, off-limits to visitors, is decorated with a variety of carvings and remnants of what were likely colorful murals.

The Platforms

As you make your way from the ball court to the Temple of Warriors, you'll pass the gruesome **Tzompantli** (Wall of Skulls). A low T-shaped platform, it is decorated on all sides with row upon row of carved skulls, most with eyes staring out of the large sockets. Among the skulls are images of warriors holding the heads of decapitated victims, skeletons intertwined with snakes, and eagles eating human hearts (a common image in Toltec design, further evidence of their presence here). It is presumed that ceremonies performed on this platform culminated in a sacrificial death for the victim, the head then left on display, perhaps with others already in place. It's estimated that the platform was built AD 1050-1200. Nearby, the **Platform of Venus** and **Platform of Eagles and Jaguars** are smaller square structures, each with low stairways on all four sides, which were likely used for ritualistic music and dancing.

Sacred Cenote

This natural well is 300 meters (984 feet) north of the main structures, along the remains of a *sacbé* (raised stone road) constructed during the Classic period. Almost 60 meters (197 feet) in diameter and 30 meters (98.4 feet) down to the surface of the water, it was a place for sacrifices, mostly to Chaac, the god of rain, who was believed to live in its depths. The cenote has been dredged and scoured by divers numerous times, beginning as early as 1900, and the remains of scores of victims, mostly children and young adults, have been recovered,

as well as innumerable jade and stone artifacts. (Most are now displayed at the Museo Nacional de Antropología in Mexico City.) On the edge of the cenote is a ruined sweat bath, probably used for purification rituals before sacrificial ceremonies. The name Chichén Itzá (Mouth of the Well of the Itzá) is surely derived from this deeply sacred cenote, and it remained an important Maya pilgrimage site well into the Spanish conquest.

Temple of Warriors and Group of a Thousand Columns

The Temple of Warriors is where some of the distinctive reclining *chac-mool* figures are found. However, its name comes from the rectangular monoliths in front, which are carved on all sides with images of warriors. (Some are also prisoners, their hands tied behind their backs.) This temple is also closed to entry, and it can be hard to appreciate the fading images from the rope perimeter. You may be able to get a closer look from the temple's south side, where you can easily make out the figures' expressions and dress (though access is sometimes blocked there as well). The south side is impressive for its facade, too, where a series of well-preserved human and animal figures adorn the lower portion, while above, human faces emerge from serpents' mouths, framed by eagle profiles, with masks of Chaac, the hook-nosed god of rain, on the corners.

The aptly named Group of a Thousand Columns is adjacent to the Temple of Warriors. Its perfectly aligned cylindrical columns likely held up a grand roof structure.

Across the plaza, the **Palacio de las Columnas Esculpidas** (Palace of Sculptured Columns) also has cylindrical columns, but with intricate carvings, suggesting this was the ceremonial center of this portion of the complex. Continuing through the trees, you'll reach the **Mercado** (market). The name is purely speculative, though it's easy to imagine a breezy, bustling market here, protected from the sun under a wood and *palapa* roof built atop the structure's remarkably high columns.

Osario, El Caracol, and the Nunnery

From the market, bear left (away from El Castillo, just visible through the trees) until you meet the path leading to the site's southern entrance. You'll pass the **Osario** (ossuary), also known as the Tomb of the High Priest. Like a miniature version of El Castillo, the pyramid at one time had four stairways on each side and a temple at the crest. From the top platform, a vertical passageway leads into a chamber where seven tombs were discovered, along with numerous copper and jade artifacts indicating the deceased were of special importance (and hence the temple's name). Continuing on, you'll pass two more large structures, **Casa del Venado** (House of the Deer) and **Casa Colorada** (Red House).

The highlight of this portion of Chichén Itzá is **El Caracol** (The Snail Shell), also known as the Observatory, and perhaps the most graceful structure at Chichén Itzá. A two-tiered circular structure is set atop a broad rectangular platform, with window slits facing south and west, and another aligned according to the path of the moon during the spring equinox. Ancient astronomers used structures like this one to track celestial events and patterns—the orbits of the moon and Venus, and the coming of solar and lunar eclipses, for example—with uncanny accuracy.

Beyond El Caracol is the **Nunnery**, so-named by Spanish explorers who thought it looked like convents back home. Judging from its size, location, and many rooms, the Nunnery was probably an administrative palace. Its exuberant facades show strong Chenes influence, another example of the blending of styles in Chichén Itzá.

Sound and Light Show

There's a nightly high-tech **sound and light show** (www.nochesdekukulkan.com, US$25 Mon.-Sat., US$11 Sun.), telling a broad-stroke history of the Maya, that's projected onto the ruins at 7pm in the winter (Oct.-Mar.) and at 8pm in the summer (Apr.-Sept.). The show itself only lasts about 25 minutes but is preceded by a 45-minute self-guided evening tour of Chichén Itzá's most prominent structures, which are lit up for visitors—a special experience in of itself.

Admission to the show is separate from the general daytime admission to the ruins; tickets must be purchased online. During peak season, be sure to buy tickets in advance because it can sell out. The sound and light show

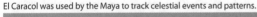

El Caracol was used by the Maya to track celestial events and patterns.

is presented in Spanish, but for a small fee, you can rent headphones with a recorded English-language translation of the program.

Practicalities

The ruins are open 8am-5pm daily. Admission is US$12 per adult, free for children under 13; you'll receive a wristband as well as a ticket (respectively, they represent the state and federal fees). Be sure to keep both handy because you'll be asked to show them at the entrance. Note that the admission fee does not include entrance to the sound and light show (www.nochesdekukulkan.com, US$25 Mon.-Sat., US$11 Sun.), which must be purchased online. Additionally, visitors must pay US$2.25 to enter with a video camera; parking is US$2.50.

Guides can be hired at the entrance according to fixed and clearly marked prices: US$40 for a two-hour tour in Spanish, US$45 in English, French, Italian, or German. Prices are per group, which can include up to eight people. Tips are customary and not included in the price. The visitors center has restrooms, an ATM, free luggage storage, a café, a bookstore, a gift shop, and an information center.

MAYALAND PLANETARIUM

The **Planetarium at Mayaland Resort** (Zona Hotelera, Carr. Mérida-Valladolid Km 120, tel. 998/887-2495, www.mayaland.com, US$9) offers half-hour shows about Maya astronomy and scientific advances. Built in 2013, the planetarium replicates the shape of Chichén Itzá's famous Caracol structure, just steps away, and itself believed to be an observatory. Typically part of pricey all-day Chichén Itzá package tours from Cancún or Mérida, the show can be seen by independent travelers too; stop by the concierge desk for the schedule and to buy tickets.

GRUTAS DE BALANKANCHÉ

Six kilometers (3.7 miles) east of Chichén Itzá are the **Balankanché Caves** (9am-4pm daily, US$6.25). Excavated in 1959 by National Geographic Society archaeologist Dr. E. Wyllys Andrews, the artifacts and ceremonial sites found here gave researchers a better understanding of ancient Maya cosmology, especially as related to the notion of *Xibalba* (the underworld). Nowadays, the caves are just a step above a tourist trap—a wide path meandering 500 meters (0.3 mile) down a tunnel with urns and other artifacts supposedly set up in their original locations. Wires and colored lights illuminate the path, but the recorded narration does nothing of the sort—it's so garbled you can hardly understand it, no matter what language it's in.

Entry times are fixed according to language: English at 11am, 1pm, and 3pm; Spanish at 9am, noon, 2pm, and 4pm; and French at 10am. A minimum of six visitors are needed for the 45-minute tour to depart (the maximum number is 30). It's worth a visit if you're traveling with kids. Be sure to wear walking shoes—the path can be slippery in places.

PARQUE ECOARQUEOLÓGICO IK KIL

Three kilometers (1.9 miles) east of Pisté is the **Parque Ecoarqueológico Ik Kil** (Carr. Mérida-Cancún Km 122, tel. 985/851-0002, www.hotelikkil.com, 9am-5pm daily, US$4.75/2.35 adult/child). The site of the Red Bull Cliff Diving World Series (three times), it's home to the immense, perfectly round **Cenote Sagrado Azul.** Although the cenote is real, the alterations to its natural state—supported walls, a set of stairs, a waterfall—make it feel artificial. Still, it's a good and pretty option if you're traveling with small children and need a spot to cool off. The cenote and on-site restaurant (breakfast US$6, lunch buffet US$8) get packed with tour groups 11:30am-2:30pm; try visiting outside those times for a mellower experience. Better yet, stay at one of the comfortable on-site bungalows (US$54 s/d with a/c, US$129 2-bedroom with a/c).

FOOD

Eating options are pretty limited in Pisté but improve somewhat if you have a car and can get to and from the large hotels.

Restaurante Las Mestizas (Calle 15 s/n, tel. 985/851-0069, 9am-10pm daily, US$4-9) is the best sit-down place to eat in Pisté, with an airy, colonial-style interior and tasty, good-sized portions. Expect a bustling dining room; if there's a wait list, it typically moves fast. The food is classic Yucatecan fare, from *panuchos* to *pollo pibil.*

Popular with locals, ★ **La Gran Chaya** (Calle 15 s/n, tel. 985/115-2589, 7am-10:30pm daily, US$2.50-5) is a hole-in-the-wall eatery across from the town church with bright plastic tables and chairs set up in front. Meals range from egg plates to piping hot *salbutes.* Be sure to order an *agua* or a *licuado*—frothy cold drinks made with a variety of fresh fruits—to wash it all down.

Set in a 16th-century hacienda-turned-hotel, **Los Faisanes Bistro** (Hacienda Chichén Resort, Zona Hotelera, Carr. Mérida-Valladolid Km 120, tel. 999/920-8407, 7am-10pm daily, US$12-25) is a soothing place to eat after a long day at the ruins. The menu is varied—Yucatecan specialties, pastas, sandwiches—and on the occasional evening, a trio plays regional music. Much of the produce used is grown in the hotel's extensive organic gardens.

For groceries, **Abarrotes Willy's** (Calle 15 s/n, 7am-10pm daily) has the best selection of foodstuffs in town.

ACCOMMODATIONS

A handful of upscale hotels make up the small Zona Hotelera on the east side of Chichén Itzá, complete with its own entrance to the ruins. Nearby, in the town of Pisté, there are also a few budget and midrange options. Be sure to reserve early during the spring and fall equinoxes. All the options below (except Ik Kil) have Wi-Fi available, though often in the reception area only. Book rooms online for the lowest rates.

Under US$50

Pirámide Inn (Calle 15 at Calle 20, tel. 985/851-0115, www.chichen.com, US$30 s/d with a/c, US$5 pp camping or in hammock) is a low, sprawling hotel with large rooms that have a distinctly 1970s den look, some sporting bubblegum paint jobs and lacquered brick walls. The air conditioners appear to be from the same era, and while effective, can be loud. There's also a big, clean pool—a popular

Many Maya today live in homes not much different than those built by their ancestors, more than a millennium ago.

Pisté

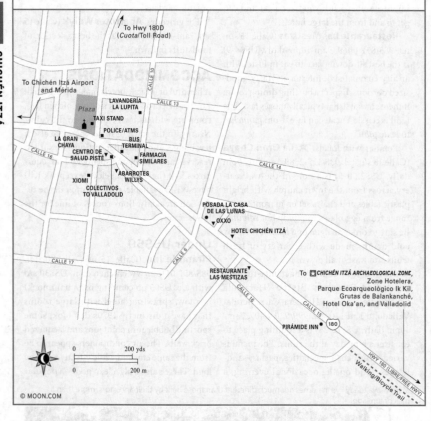

To Hwy 180D
(*Cuota*/Toll Road)

CALLE 10

To Chichén Itzá Airport
and Mérida

Plaza

LAVANDERÍA
LA LUPITA

CALLE 13

TAXI STAND

POLICE/ATMS

LA GRAN
CHAYA

BUS
TERMINAL

CENTRO DE
SALUD PISTÉ

CALLE 16

FARMACIA
SIMILARES

CALLE 14

ABARROTES
WILLYS

XIOMI

COLECTIVOS
TO VALLADOLID

POSADA LA CASA
DE LAS LUNAS

OXXO

HOTEL CHICHÉN ITZÁ

CALLE 6

CALLE 17

To ★ CHICHÉN ITZÁ ARCHAEOLOGICAL ZONE,
Zone Hotelera,
Parque Ecoarqueológico Ik Kil,
Grutas de Balankanché,
Hotel Oka'an, and Valladolid

RESTAURANTE
LAS MESTIZAS

CALLE 18

CALLE 15

PIRÁMIDE INN   180

HWY 180 (LIBRE/FREE HWY)

Walking/Bicycle Trail

0   200 yds

0   200 m

© MOON.COM

post-ruins spot—and lots of green areas with fruit trees. Budget travelers can camp or set up hammocks here but must bring their own gear.

The best deal in town, ★ **Posada La Casa de las Lunas** (Calle 15 s/n, tel. 985/851-0289, posada.laslunas@gmail.com, US$30-45 s/d with a/c) has spic-and-span modern rooms with thick beds, tile bathrooms, TVs, and silent air-conditioning. All share a covered porch that faces a tidy courtyard with a pool. There's off-street parking too. The different rates reflect bed number and size—the cheapest room has one full-size bed, the most expensive has two queens. Look for the entrance just west of the OXXO convenience store.

US$50-100

Hotel Chichén Itzá (Calle 15 s/n, tel. 985/851-0022, www.mayaland.com, US$54-69 s/d with a/c) is the one of the nicest hotels in downtown Pisté, featuring rooms with one king or two queen beds, comfortable furnishings, large modern bathrooms, and simple Mexican decor. The less-expensive rooms face the street and can be noisy, while the top-floor ones are larger and overlook the hotel's attractive garden and pool area. There's a cavernous restaurant (7am-10pm daily) that's often packed with tour groups.

Villas Arqueológicas Chichén Itzá (Zona Hotelera, Carr. Mérida-Valladolid Km

120, tel. 985/851-0187, www.villasarqueologicas.com.mx, US$58 s/d with a/c, US$101 suite with a/c) is a pleasant two-story hotel with a mellow ambience. Boxy but nice rooms are set around a lush courtyard with an inviting L-shaped pool. There's a library/TV room with comfy couches and a variety of reading material—from romance novels to archaeology books—and there's a decent restaurant on-site. Very tall folks should note that alcove walls bracket the ends of the beds.

Set in a lush forest, **Hotel Ik Kil** (Parque Ecoarqueológico Ik Kil, Carr. Mérida-Cancún Km 122, tel. 999/437-0148, www.hotelikkil.com, US$54 s/d with a/c, US$129 2-bedroom suite with a/c) offers 14 modern and ultracomfortable bungalows. All are spacious and have whirlpool tubs and comfortable beds. One unit is a two-bedroom suite that's perfect for families. Silent air-conditioning and private porches make them all the better. Guests get unlimited use of the on-site cenote, including after hours.

A holistic retreat center, **Hotel Oka'an** (Carr. Mérida-Cancún Km 122, tel. 985/851-0281, www.hotelokaan.com, US$50-59 s/d with a/c, US$85-96 suite with a/c) beckons with a full spa, mind and body workshops, and the occasional spiritual ceremony. Ample rooms are bright and tasteful in a pastel sort of way, with modern bathrooms and private balconies. There's a pleasant open-air restaurant and, for post-ruin lounging, an infinity pool. Don't miss the view from the *mirador* terrace—Chichén Itzá's El Castillo pops up over the (arduously manicured) treeline. Look for the billboards just west of the **Parque Ecoarqueológico Ik Kil** and continue 1.5 kilometers (0.9 mile) on an unpaved road.

Over US$100

Once the headquarters for the Carnegie Institute's Chichén Itzá expedition, the ★ **Hacienda Chichén Resort** (Zona Hotelera, Carr. Mérida-Valladolid Km 120, tel. 985/851-0045, toll-free U.S. tel. 877/631-4005, www.haciendachichen.com, US$179-199 s/d with a/c, US$215-299 suite with a/c) is now a tranquil hotel set on lush tropical grounds. Newer units are quite charming, with exposed beams, tropical wood furnishings, and folk art. Many of the older units occupy the original cottages used by the first archaeologists to study Chichén Itzá—enticing in theory, though the cinderblock walls and pervasive mustiness diminish the charm. Still, these are usually booked solid. Be sure to wander the grounds with an eye for the past—such as stone blocks from the ruins incorporated into the main building and narrow-gauge railroad tracks that were used to transport artifacts. There's also a gorgeous pool, full-service spa, a fine-dining room, even a private garden entrance to the ruins.

The Lodge at Chichén Itzá (Zona Hotelera, Carr. Mérida-Valladolid Km 120, tel. 998/887-2495, toll-free Mex. tel. 800/719-5465, toll-free U.S. tel. 877/240-5864, www.mayaland.com, US$195-214 s/d with a/c, US$256-434 suite with a/c) is set on the larger Mayaland resort's grounds: 100 acres of tamed tropical jungle featuring walking and horseback riding trails, a full-service spa, three restaurants, and three pools. The lodge's *palapa*-roofed bungalows are pleasant, with stained glass windows, hardwood furniture, and terraces with rocking chairs. Lodge accommodations are typically reserved for independent travelers, and their location—including a separate access road and parking lot—is fairly removed from Mayaland proper, where groups are handled. Still, you're bound to encounter various flocks of guests during your stay, especially in the restaurants, diminishing the charm for some.

INFORMATION AND SERVICES

There is no tourist office in Pisté; hotel receptionists are sometimes helpful, as are other travelers. Pisté also doesn't have a bank, but there are three local ATMs: one inside the OXXO market, another inside the Palacio

Municipal (across from the church), and the last in Chichén Itzá's visitors center.

Emergency Services

The **police** have an office (tel. 985/851-0365) in the Palacio Municipal, facing the town church. An officer is on duty 24 hours a day, and there's usually one waving through traffic near the plaza. **Centro de Salud Pisté** (Calle 15 s/n, no phone, 7am-1pm and 5pm-7pm Mon.-Fri., 8am-8pm Sat.-Sun.) is one of two clinics in town. For anything serious, you're better off going to Mérida or Cancún. **Farmacia Similares** (Calle 15 s/n, no phone, 7am-10pm Mon.-Sat., 9am-9pm Sun.) is just east of the main plaza.

Media and Communications

Most hotels offer free Wi-Fi to guests. If you don't have a tablet or computer, **Xiomi** (Calle 16 s/n, 10am-10pm daily, US$0.75/hour) is a reliable Internet café located behind Abarrotes Willy's supermarket.

Laundry

Lavandería La Lupita (Calle 10 near Calle 13, 8am-8pm Mon.-Sat.) charges US$1.75 per kilo (2.2 pounds) to wash and dry clothes; same-day service is available if you drop off your clothes first thing in the morning.

GETTING THERE AND AROUND
Bus

Pisté's small **bus terminal** (Calle 15 s/n, 8:30am-5:30pm daily, cash only) is just southeast of the Palacio Municipal, and about 2.5 kilometers (1.5 miles) from the entrance to Chichén Itzá; it is mostly used by second-class buses, which also pick up and drop off passengers at **Parque Ecoarqueológico** Ik Kil and the **Balankanché Caves**. For first-class buses, head to the **ticket office** in the Chichén Itzá gift shop (tel. 985/851-0377, 9am-5pm daily). (The visitors center at Chichén Itzá also has **free luggage storage,** which makes it easy to catch a bus right after visiting the ruins.)

All first-class departures leave from Chichén Itzá only. Second-class departure times listed here are for the terminal in Pisté. Second-class buses coming and going between 8am and 5:30pm stop at both the terminal and the parking lot at the ruins. If you are planning to catch a second-class bus at the ruins, keep in mind that buses headed toward Cancún stop at the ruins slightly after the listed times, while those bound for Mérida pass by slightly earlier. Most bus service to and from Pisté and Chichén Itzá is on Oriente, ADO's second-class line, but the few first-class buses are worth the extra cost. Note that the schedule listed below is subject to change.

- **Cancún:** One first-class bus (US$16, 3.5 hours) at 4:30pm; second-class buses (US$7.50, 4-4.5 hours) every 30-60 minutes 12:30am-9:30pm.

- **Cobá:** For the town and archaeological site, one first-class bus (US$3.50, 2.5 hours) at 7:30am. Alternatively, take a second-class bus to Tulum; the first-class buses don't stop there.

- **Mérida:** One first-class bus (US$9, 2 hours) at 5:35pm; second-class buses (US$4.50, 2.5 hours) every 30-60 minutes 6am-11:30pm.

- **Playa del Carmen:** One first-class bus (US$16.75, 3.5 hours) at 4:30pm; second-class buses (US$7.75, 4 hours) at 12:25am, 7:35am, and 1:05pm.

- **Tulum:** First-class buses (US$11.65, 2.5 hours) at 8:35am and 4:30pm; second-class departures (US$5.25, 3.5 hours) at 12:25am, 7:30am, and 1pm.

- **Valladolid:** First-class buses (US$4.50-5.50, 50 minutes) at 8:25am, 10:10am, 11:10am, and 4:30pm; second-class service (US$1.50, 1 hour) every 30-60 minutes 12:25am-10:30pm.

Colectivos (US$1.75, 1 hour) leave for Valladolid every 30 minutes 7am-6pm from in front of the bus terminal as well as the Chichén Itzá parking lot.

Taxi

There's a **taxi stand** on Piste's central plaza, towards the west end of town. The fare from there to the ruins is US$2-3; to Parque Ecoarqueológico Ik Kil it's US$4-5; and to the Balankanché Caves expect to pay US$9-10. Taxis aren't metered, so be sure to agree on the fare before you get into the cab.

Car

Chichén Itzá lies adjacent to Highway 180, 40 kilometers (25 miles) west of Valladolid, 120 kilometers (75 miles) east of Mérida, and 200 kilometers (124 miles) west of Cancún. For drivers, the quickest way to get there is via the *cuota,* a large, modern freeway extending from Cancún most of the way to Mérida, with a well-marked exit for Chichén Itzá and Pisté. There's a price for speed and convenience, though: The toll from Mérida is US$5, and a whopping US$17 from Cancún. You can also take the old *carretera libre* (free highway) all or part of the way; it's in reasonably good condition but takes much longer, mainly because you pass through numerous small villages and seemingly innumerable *topes* (speed bumps).

Air

Aeropuerto Internacional Chichén Itzá is 16 kilometers (9.9 miles) east of Pisté, near the town of Kaua. Inaugurated in April 2000, it is one of the most modern airports in the country, with an 1,800-meter (5,900-foot) runway capable of receiving 747 jets. Although it initially received dozens of regular and charter flights, its license was suspended in 2001. Today it stands virtually empty, receiving only a trickle of small charter flights, mostly from Cancún, Cozumel, and Chetumal.

Valladolid

Valladolid draws tourists because of its mellow colonial atmosphere and its central location: 30 minutes from the archaeological zones of Chichén Itzá and Ek' Balam, an hour from the ruins at Cobá, and two hours from Mérida, Cancún, and Tulum. It's an easy bus or car ride to any of these destinations, restaurants and hotels are reasonably priced, and you have the advantage of staying in a colonial Mexican town. If you're en route to one of the regional sites or simply want to have a small-city experience, consider spending a night here—you're sure to be happily surprised.

HISTORY

The site of several Maya revolts against the Spanish, Valladolid was conquered in 1543 by Francisco de Montejo, cousin of the like-named Spaniard who founded Mérida. It was once the Maya city of Zací. Montejo brutalized its inhabitants and crushed their temples, building large churches and homes in their place. It is perhaps not surprising, then, that the Caste War started in Valladolid, and that the city played an important role in the beginning of the Mexican Revolution. Today, Valladolid is a charming colonial town with a rich history and strong Maya presence.

ORIENTATION

Valladolid is easy to get around. It's laid out in a grid pattern with even-numbered streets running north-south, odd-numbered streets running east-west. The central plaza is bordered by Calles 39, 40, 41, and 42.

SIGHTS
★ Iglesia y Ex-Convento San Bernardino de Siena

Located at the end of the Calzada de los Frailes, the **Iglesia y Ex-Convento San Bernardino de Siena** (Calle 41-A, tel. 985/856-2160, 8am-noon and 5pm-8pm daily) is one of Valladolid's most attractive structures. Built by Franciscan missionaries between 1552 and 1560, the church is entered

Valladolid

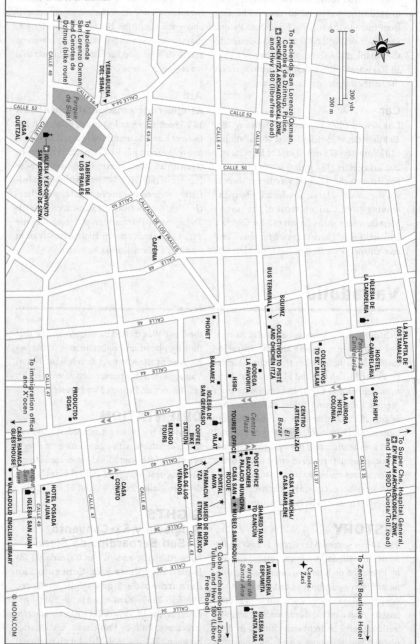

0   200 yds
0   200 m

To Hacienda San Lorenzo Oxman,
Cenotes de Dzitnup, Police,
CHICHÉN ITZÁ ARCHAEOLOGICAL ZONE,
and Hwy 180 (libre/free road)

To Hacienda
San Lorenzo Oxman
and Cenotes de
Dzitnup (bike route)

CALLE 49

YERBABUENA
DEL SISAL

CALLE 54-A

CALLE 52

CALLE 51-A

CALLE 62

CASA
QUETZAL

CALLE 51

Parque
de Sisal

IGLESIA Y EX-CONVENTO
SAN BERNARDINO DE SIENA

CALLE 50

CALLE 43-A

CALLE 41

CALLE 39

TABERNA DE
LOS FRAILES

CALZADA DE LOS FRAILES

CALLE 50

CALLE 52

CALLE 50

CAFEINA

CALLE 48

IGLESIA DE
LA CANDELARIA

LA PILAPITA DE
LOS TAMALES

BUS TERMINAL

SQUIMZ

CALLE 46

PHONET

COLECTIVOS TO PISTÉ
AND CHICHÉN ITZÁ

COLECTIVOS
TO EK' BALAM

Parque la
Candelaria

HOSTEL
CANDELARIA

CASA HIPIL

To Super Che, Hospital General,
EK' BALAM ARCHAEOLOGICAL ZONE,
and Hwy 180D (cuota/Toll road)

BANAMEX

BODEGA
LA FAVORITA

CALLE 44

HSBC

IGLESIA DE
SAN GERVASIO

CENTRO
ARTESANAL ZACI

LA AURORA
HOTEL
COLONIAL

CALLE 47

PRODUCTOS
SOSA

CALLE 42

COFFEE
STATION
BIKE

YALAT

El
Bazar

Central
Plaza

TOURIST OFFICE

CASA TÍA MICHA/
CASA MARLENE

CALLE 37

CALLE 35

To immigration office
and X'ocen

MEXICO
TOURS

CALLE 40

CASA DE LOS
VENADOS

PORTAL
MAYA

POST OFFICE
BANCOMER
PALACIO MUNICIPAL
CASA SAN
ROQUE

SHARED TAXIS
TO CANCÚN

Parque San
San Juan

CASA HAMACA Juan
GUESTHOUSE

HOTEL POSADA
SAN JUAN

IGLESIA SAN JUAN

CALLE 49

CASA
CONATO

CALLE 45

CALLE 38

FARMACIA
YZA

MUSEO DE ROPA
ETNICA DE MEXICO

CALLE 43

MUSEO SAN ROQUE

To Cobá Archaeological Zone,
Tulum, and Hwy 180 (Libre/
Free Road)

LAVANDERIA
ESPUMITA

Cenote
Zaci

CALLE 36

Parque de
Santa Ana

IGLESIA DE
SANTA ANA

CALLE 34

To Zentik Boutique Hotel

VALLADOLID ENGLISH LIBRARY

© MOON.COM

through a series of arches, and the facade, covered in a checkerboard-like stucco pattern, rises into a squat tower with turrets. Inside, there are original 16th-century frescoes, catacombs, and crypts. Mass is held at 7am and 7pm Monday-Friday; 7am, 8:30am, and 7pm Saturday; and eight times from 7am to 8:30pm on Sunday. An impressive **sound and light show,** depicting the history of Valladolid, is projected onto its façade during winter at 8pm in Spanish and 8:30pm in English and an hour later, respectively, during the summer months.

Annexed to the church is the **former convent** (9am-7pm daily, US$1.50; free on Sundays). Its rooms radiate from a center courtyard that features a cenote. Called Sis-Há (Cold Water), the cenote helped the monks be self-reliant. In 2004, an INAH-funded exploration of the cenote resulted in the discovery of 164 muskets, bayonets, spears, and one cannon. The arms were thrown into the cenote between 1847 and 1848; they are believed to have been sent by the British via Jamaica. The arms were used when the monastery served as a fortress during the Caste War. A small exhibit room displays some of these weapons as well as photos and descriptions of the INAH exploration.

Casa de los Venados

If you have even a passing interest in Mexican folk art—or an infatuation with colonial buildings—visit **Casa de los Venados** (House of the Deer, Calle 40 between Calles 41 and 43, 985/856-2289, www.casadelosvenados.com, 10am tour daily, US$5 donation requested). After an award-winning remodel of this 17th-century house, the American owners, John and Dorianne Venator, had so many visitors that they began offering tours of their home and their impressive 3,000-piece Mexican folk art collection—the largest collection not owned by a museum. The pieces span the Venators' lifelong search and commission of *catrinas*, clay sculptures, wood carvings, paintings, and other decorative objects created by Mexico's most talented

artisans. All donations benefit a local volunteer-run medical clinic and the Lions Club. Tours are offered in Spanish and English.

Iglesia de San Gervasio

Overlooking the central plaza, the **San Gervasio Church** (Calle 41 at Calle 42, tel. 985/856-3116) has a sober Franciscan style. It was originally built in 1545 but in 1705 was deemed profane and ordered demolished by the local bishop as the result of a political rivalry that involved the storming of the church, the desanctification of its altar, and the death of four politicians. (The incident is now known as *El Crimen de los Alcaldes,* or The Mayors' Crime.) The church was rebuilt a year later, but its orientation changed so that the new altar would not be in the same position as the prior—indeed, the Iglesia de San Gervasio is one of the only colonial-era churches in the Yucatán whose facade faces north instead of west.

Museo San Roque

A long, high-ceilinged room—this used to be a church—the **San Roque Museum** (Calle 41 between Calles 38 and 40, no phone, 8am-7pm daily, free) needs a serious updating but is still a worthwhile stop, with historical exhibits on Valladolid, many focusing on the Caste War and the beginning of the Mexican Revolution. Try not to get freaked out by the mannequins. Signage is in Spanish only.

Museo de Ropa Etnica de México

On the verge of its inauguration when we passed through, the **Museum of Traditional Clothing of Mexico** (Calle 41 between Calles 38 and 40, no phone, 10am-6pm daily, free) is a small museum dedicated to Mexico's impressive range of traditional clothing, much of which is handcrafted and still worn in some indigenous communities. Exhibits will rotate every three months.

Palacio Municipal

The 2nd floor of the **city hall** (8am-8pm

daily, free) has a large balcony featuring four paintings by local artist Manuel Lizama. The works depict events in the region's history: pre-Hispanic communities, Valladolid's founding, the Caste War, and the Mexican Revolution. It's not spectacular, but still interesting (plus, there's a nice view of the central plaza from here).

Cenote Zaci

In the middle of town, **Cenote Zaci** (Calle 36 between Calles 37 and 39, no phone, 8:30am-5:30pm daily, US$1.50 adult, US$0.75 child) is a dark natural pool at the bottom of a huge cavern, with a bank of trees on one side and a path looping down from the entrance above. It's often pooh-poohed as inferior to cenotes at Dzitnup, but it's a perfectly peaceful and attractive spot, and a lot quicker and easier to get to. You may find leaves and pollen floating on the water's surface, but it's still great for swimming. To have the cenote to yourself, go midweek, or better yet right after closing time, entering through the restaurant (you can use their bathroom to change) instead of the main gates.

Hacienda San Lorenzo Oxman

About three kilometers (1.8 miles) southwest of town, **Hacienda San Lorenzo Oxman** (off Calle 54, no phone, 9am-6pm daily, US$3.50 cenote, US$5 cenote and pool) was once a henequen plantation but is now best known for its spectacular cenote. The cenote is around 20 meters (66 feet) from the rim to the water, with tree roots dangling down the sheer walls into the cool turquoise water. There's a stairway to the water's edge, and several spots, including a fun rope swing, where you can leap right in. The hacienda also has a regular pool and restaurant; late afternoon can get busy with tour groups.

Cenotes de Dzitnup

Four kilometers (2.5 miles) west of Valladolid on Highway 180 is the small community of Dzitnup, home to two appealing cenotes. Both make for a unique and refreshing

Cenote Samula is a short bike—or cab—ride from Valladolid's central plaza.

swim—though on warm days you may find them somewhat crowded. The cenotes share a ticket kiosk and a large parking lot; there's a small discount if you buy tickets for both. Many small *artesanía* stands sit at the entrance, and you'll be aggressively pursued by children offering to watch your car. Many people also ride bikes here, following a paved path that runs parallel to the highway. A cab to the cenotes costs about US$4.

Although the two are across the street from each other, **Cenote Xkeken** (no phone, 8:30am-5:30pm daily, US$3) is better known; many postcards and travel guides call it "Cenote Dzitnup." After a reasonably easy descent (in a few places you'll have to bend over because of a low ceiling; there's a hanging rope to help), you'll come to a circular pond of clear, cool water. It's a pretty, albeit damp, place, with a high dome ceiling that has one small opening at the top letting in a ray of sun and dangling green vines. Often an errant bird can be seen swooping low over the water before heading to the sun and sky through the tiny opening. Stalactites and one large stalagmite adorn the ceiling and cenote floor.

At **Cenote Samula** (no phone, 8:30am-5:30pm daily, US$3), tree roots dangle from the cavern roof all the way down to the water. You enter through a narrow tunnel, which opens onto a set of stairs that zigzag down. Fearless kids jump from the stairs into the clear turquoise water below.

Tours

MexiGo Tours (Calle 43 between Calles 40 and 42, tel. 985/856-0777, www.mexigo-tours.com, 8:30am-7pm daily) is highly recommended for **tours** to local and regional attractions. Popular trips include visits to archaeological sites, cenotes, and caves, and outings to spot wildlife like flamingoes, howler monkeys, and even bat-eating snakes. Tours range from US$35 to US$109, depending on the distance and length of each; they often include breakfast, lunch, and transportation, but not site entrance fees. A minimum of three people is required for excursions.

Based in the nearby community of X'ocen, **Yucatán Jay Expeditions and Tours** (cell. tel. 985/103-4918, www.yucatanjay.com, 8:30am-8pm daily) is a co-op specializing in bird-watching tours. (There are 543 species of birds registered in the entire peninsula—a true hot spot for birders.) Tours are led by experienced guides with a passion for their work. Many tours also combine stops in traditional Maya villages and cenotes.

ENTERTAINMENT AND EVENTS

Sundays feature a year-round cultural event called **Domingo Vallisoletano.** From 10am to 10pm, the city closes the streets around the central plaza for artisan expositions, *trova* balladeers, folkloric dancing, and programs for kids. In the evening, locals come to dance to live music, mostly cumbia and danzón.

In late January-early February, Valladolid celebrates its patron saint, La Vírgen de la Candelaria, in the **Expo-Feria Valladolid.** It's a blowout outdoor festival, where you'll see bullfights, rodeos, musical entertainment, and lots of food stands selling local delicacies and heart-stopping goodies. Venues vary; ask at the tourist office or your hotel for details.

SHOPPING

Calzada de los Frailes, the charming colonial street that connects the Iglesia San Bernardino de Siena with central Valladolid, is dotted with boutique shops selling mostly

Artisan stands, like this one of *jipi* hats, are set up for Valladolid's weekly Domingo Vallisoletano.

high-end goods—window-shopping at its best! You'll find traditional *jipi* hat makers, folk art shops, custom leather wear, and even an artisanal chocolate shop. Most stores are open 10am-8pm daily.

A tranquil courtyard of workshops and shops, the **Centro Artesanal Zaci** (Calle 39 between Calles 40 and 42, no phone, 7am-10pm daily) showcases the work of Maya women from Valladolid and nearby villages who make and sell their *huipiles* and hand-stitched blouses on-site.

If you're interested in high-end Mexican handicrafts and art, **Yalat** (Calle 41 between Calles 40 and 42, tel. 985/856-1969, 9am-8pm daily) is worth a stop. It also sells artisanal products like chocolate, coffee, and honey in its back garden.

A family-owned distillery still chugging away after more than 100 years, **Productos Sosa** (Calle 42 between Calles 47 and 49, tel. 985/856-2142, 8:30am-1:30pm and 4pm-7:30pm Mon.-Fri., 8:30am-2:30pm Sat.) sells smooth sugarcane liquors infused with ingredients like mint or anise with honey.

FOOD

Yucatecan and Mexican

★ **Yerbabuena del Sisal** (Calle 54-A between Calles 41-A and 45, tel. 985/856-1406, 8am-5pm Tues.-Sun., US$3.50-5) is a whimsical place offering fresh Mexican dishes with a good variety of vegetarian options. Entrees range from tortas (Mexican-style sandwiches) and chilaquiles (a tortilla and egg dish) to veggie burgers and stuffed peppers. Seating is in a colorful patio garden.

The low lighting, open-air *palapa* dining room, and attentive service at **Taberna de los Frailes** (Calle 49 at Calle 41A, tel. 985/856-0689, www.tabernadelosfrailes.com, 1pm-11pm daily, US$8-16) set an elegant backdrop for a menu of creative Yucatecan mainstays, seafood cocktails, and a few vegetarian entrées. Its upscale bar has sofa seating and a terrace area shaded by a profuse canopy of passion fruit. Look for it across from the San Bernardino de Siena church.

Though doing a brisk business in takeout, **La Palapita de los Tamales** (Calle 42 at Calle 33, tel. 985/856-2895, 8am-10:30pm Mon.-Sat., US$1.50-4) is a great little sit-down restaurant selling Yucatecan-style tamales. The chef heats the tamales over an open-fire stove at the entrance while diners come and go. Among the most popular are the chachawa (chicken and egg tamale served in a tomato sauce), espelón (pork, beans, and egg tamale wrapped in a banana leaf), and colados (strained corn dough tamales).

El Bazar Municipal (central plaza, Calle 39 at Calle 40, 6am-10pm, US$1.50-4) is a local food court with a dozen or so inexpensive eateries selling mostly Yucatecan specialties. Hours vary, but all are open for breakfast and lunch. Order something off the menu, like *huevos rancheros* or *salbutes*, to be sure it's freshly made.

Other Specialties

Next to the bus station, ★ **Squimz** (Calle 39 near Calle 46, tel. 985/856-4156, www.squimz.com.mx, 7am-11pm daily, US$3-6) is well worth a stop even if you're not on your way out of town. Big breakfasts and sandwiches are the specialties, though the coffee drinks and to-die-for milkshakes shouldn't be overlooked. If you've got a sweet tooth, try the homemade flan.

Bohemia is alive and well at **Casa Conato** (Calle 40 between Calles 45 and 47, tel. 985/856-2586, 5pm-1am daily, US$5-9), where religious iconography, murals, and images of Frida Kahlo cover the walls of the spacious garden dining patio. Yucatecan-influenced dishes, big salads, and pasta dishes have creative flourishes, while the dessert crepes are almost too pretty to eat. Live music and late hours make this a popular place for drinks.

Cafeína (Calzada de los Frailes near Calle 48, tel. 985/856-2654, 7am-2am daily, US$4-7) is a locals' favorite serving up thin-crust pizza, pasta dishes, salads, and even chicken wings in a dimly lit pub-like setting. Try the Yuc-Mex pizza with homemade sausage, cheese, avocado, and pico de gallo (fresh tomato-based topping with cilantro, onion, and serrano chili)—it packs an unexpected punch. Drink specials, from beer to milkshakes, are often offered.

Coffee Bike Station (Calle 40 between Calles 41 and 43, tel. 985/122-2439, 8:30am-2pm Mon.-Fri., US$1.50-4) really is what it claims to be: a coffee and bike shop. Come here for great brew and to join a bike tour of the city and surroundings. There's a long menu of coffee creations, from a simple but divine espresso to cafechata (coffee and horchata—it's good), plus cakes and cookies. Burn off all that sugar on a bike tour, which visits various parts of the city and includes stops at favorite spots for drinks and a quick bite.

Groceries

Bodega La Favorita (Calle 39 between Calles 42 and 44, 7am-10pm daily) is a small grocery store with a decent selection of fresh and canned foods. If you have a car, head to the better-stocked **Super Che** (Plaza Bella, Calle 42 s/n, 7am-10pm daily), which is on northern end of town, on the road to Ek' Balam.

ACCOMMODATIONS

Valladolid offers a good selection of simple and midrange hotels. Most are convenient to the central plaza. All have free Wi-Fi and most provide parking.

Under US$50

Hostel Candelaria (Parque la Candelaria, Calle 35 between Calles 42 and 44, tel. 985/856-2267, www.hostelvalladolidyucatan.com, US$11.50-14 pp dorm, US$13.25-14 pp dorm with a/c, US$25 s/d with shared bathroom, US$51 s/d) has 10-14 beds sharing one bathroom, with a low-ceilinged women-only dorm and a roomier mixed dorm. What the dorms lack in space is more than made up for by a sprawling back garden thick with papaya trees and hibiscus, shading an al fresco kitchen and hammocks tucked into nooks with personal reading lights. Inside, you'll find free computers, lockers—including some for charging electronics—and a TV room. Socialize with other travelers over the free breakfast and then rent a bicycle to tour the local cenotes.

Just a short walk from the main plaza, ★ **Casa Hipil** (Calle 42 between Calles 33 and 35, tel. 985/856-0832, http://casahipil.wix-site.com/hotelcasahipil, US$47 s/d with a/c) is a charming little hotel and a great value. Large guest rooms have attractive stone and tile work and patios facing the interior courtyard. You can cool off in a small plunge pool or relax in a lounge chair beneath the fruit trees; guests also have access to a communal kitchen and speedy Wi-Fi. The hotel's name derives from a type of traditional embroidery, and there are some incredible examples on display.

La Aurora Hotel Colonial (Calle 42 between Calles 35 and 37, tel. 985/856-1219, www.hotellaaurora.com, US$34/42 s/d with a/c, US$49 suite) is a charming place with two floors of rooms opening onto a sunny courtyard with a pool. Units are basic but very comfortable with good beds, modern bathrooms, and flat-screen TVs. Original Talavera tile floors, loads of bromeliads, and ironwork lanterns help create a colonial ambience. For a treat, head to the roof, where two soaking pools, lounge chairs, and views of the city make it hard to leave.

US$50-100

Casa Quetzal (Calle 51 between Calles 50 and 52, tel. 985/856-4796, www.casa-quetzal.com, US$52-66 s/d with a/c, US$67-71 suite with a/c) is a charming, well-run bed-and-breakfast near the San Bernardino de Siena church. Large, attractive, high-ceilinged rooms surround a pretty garden and swimming pool, while a reading room featuring Oaxacan folk art lends a homey feel. All rooms have hammocks, air-conditioning, and cable TV. Continental breakfast is included. The hotel is somewhat removed from the central plaza, but the 10-minute walk there—along the iconic Calzada de los Frailes—is a pleasure in itself.

Casa San Roque (Calle 41 between Calles 38 and 40, tel. 985/856-2642, www.casasanroquevalladolid.com, US$70 s/d with a/c) is a six-room hotel with modern rooms that have a colonial feel. All have gleaming tile floors, heavy wood furnishings, and splashes of bright colors; the bathrooms are sleek and spotless. There's a pleasant outdoor sitting area where breakfast is served. There's a refreshing pool too—a welcome sight after a long day of sightseeing. It's located just one block from the central plaza.

Steps from the central plaza are the combined hotels of **Casa Tía Micha** and **Casa Marlene** (Calle 39 between Calles 38 and 40, 985/856-0499, www.casatiamicha.com, US$75-80 s/d with a/c, US$80-90 suite with a/c). Both are quite comfortable, but the feel is very colonial meets grandma—not bad, just unexpected. Think stately wooden doors and antique furniture alongside wall stenciling, porcelain knickknacks, and rocking chairs. There's a refreshing pool plus a full breakfast that is served in the tranquil fruit tree garden, near the old *pozo* (well).

Over US$100

★ **Hotel Posada San Juan** (Parque San Juan, Calle 40 at Calle 49, tel. 985/856-0129, www.posadasanjuan.com, US$114 s/d with a/c) is a meticulously renovated 19th-century mansion located just a few blocks south of the central plaza. The eight rooms are elegant but homey with high-end furnishings, Mexican folk art, and custom-designed Talavera tile floors. Bathrooms bring the outside in with skylights, exposed stone walls, rainfall showerheads, and tropical plants. A full breakfast is served on the wide and breezy veranda with views of the garden and pool. Service is genuinely friendly, and families are very welcome.

Casa Hamaca Guesthouse (Parque San Juan, Calle 49 at Calle 40, tel. 985/856-5287, www.casahamaca.com, US$94-150 s/d with a/c) faces a quiet church plaza about five blocks south of the main square. A lush garden and small pool add to the tranquility, while the guesthouse is spacious and bright. The eight rooms vary in size and décor though all have dramatic Maya-inspired murals. There's an open-air restaurant (7am-10pm daily) where a hearty complimentary breakfast is served. Rewarding volunteer opportunities also can be arranged.

Zentik Boutique Hotel (Calle 30 between Calles 27 and 29, tel. 985/104-8503, www.zentikhotel.com, US$110 s/d with a/c) is a fantastic (and fantastical) hotel with wow-inducing features at every turn. It has an underground saltwater pool, built into a cenote-like cavern on the property, plus an aboveground pool and a private spa. Murals, sculptures, and other artwork abound, including huge surreal paintings splashed across some guestroom walls. Rooms are spacious and comfortable, and the restaurant serves inventive and delicious meals.

INFORMATION AND SERVICES
Tourist Information

Try your best at prying some useful information from staffers at Valladolid's **tourist office** (Palacio Municipal, Calle 40 at Calle 41, tel. 985/856-2551, ext. 114, 8am-8pm Mon.-Fri., 9am-7pm Sat.-Sun.). At the very least, daily **walking tours,** led by licensed bilingual guides, leave here at 7pm; they're free, though tips are appreciated.

Valladolid English Library (Parque San Juan, Calle 49 at Calle 40, tel. 985/111-7688, 11am-3pm Mon.-Fri., 10am-1pm Sat.) is a lending library with over 2,500 books. Visitors will find everything from children's books and beach fiction to Mesoamerican history books and "how-to" reads. The library hosts an interesting speaker series on topics as varied as public safety, Reiki, and Maya medicine—check online for an updated schedule.

Emergency Services

If you need medical assistance, the modern

Valladolid Bus Schedule

Departures from Valladolid's bus station (Calle 39 at Calle 46, tel. 985/856-3448) include:

Destination	Price	Duration	Schedule*
Cancún	US$7.50-12	2.25 hrs	12 departures 12:25am-9:55pm
Chichén Itzá (Pisté)	US$4.50-5.50	50 mins	10:55am, 11am, 4:35pm
Chiquilá (Isla Holbox)	US$9.15	2.5 hrs	9:55pm
Mérida	US$9.75-11.50	2.25 hrs	32 departures 1:10am-10:30pm
Playa del Carmen	US$10.50-11.50	2.5-3.5 hrs	14 departures 12:25am-10:40pm
Tulum	US$5.50-6.75	2 hrs	9 departures 8am-10:40pm

Hospital General de Valladolid (Av. Chan Yokdzonot, tel. 985/856-2883, 24 hours) is located 4.5 kilometers (2.8 miles) south of the *cuota* highway; for meds only, **Farmacia Yza** (Calle 41 near Calle 40, tel. 985/856-4018, 7am-11pm Mon.-Sat., 8am-10pm Sun.) is just off the central plaza.

The **police** (Parque Bacalar, Calle 41 s/n, 24 hours) can be reached at 985/856-2100 or toll-free at 066.

Money

On or near the central plaza, **HSBC** (Calle 41 between Calles 42 and 44, 9am-5pm Mon.-Fri., 9am-1pm Sat.), **Banamex** (Calle 41 between Calles 42 and 44, 9am-4pm Mon.-Fri.), and **Bancomer** (Calle 40 between Calles 39 and 41, 8:30am-4pm Mon.-Fri.) all have ATMs. **Note:** Bancomer charges an exorbitant US$5 for ATM withdrawals by foreign cards.

Media and Communications

A tiny **post office** (Calle 40 between Calles 39 and 41, 8am-4:30pm Mon.-Fri., 8am-1pm Sat.) sits on the central plaza.

There's free Wi-Fi in the central plaza; the signal is strongest in front of the Palacio Municipal (look for the cadre of teens on their phones and tablets). For computers with Internet access, try **Phonet** (Calle 46 at Calle 41, 7am-midnight daily, US$0.75/hour).

Laundry

The bustling **Lavandería Espumita** (Calle 39 between Calles 34 and 36 at Calle 33, no phone, 8am-8pm Mon.-Sat., 8am-1pm Sun.) charges US$0.75 per kilo (2.2 pounds).

GETTING THERE AND AROUND

Bus

Valladolid's **bus terminal** (Calle 39 at Calle 46, tel. 985/856-3448) is an easy walk from the central plaza, or if you have a lot of bags, a cheap taxi ride.

*Schedules are subject to change.

Taxi

Taxis are relatively easy to flag down, especially around the central plaza, and typically cost US$1.50-2 around town.

Colectivos (shared vans and taxis) to Pisté and Chichén Itzá (US$1.75, 1 hour, every 30 minutes, 7am-7pm daily) depart from Calle 39 near the ADO bus terminal, and those for Mérida (US$9, 2.5 hours) leave from the terminal. Shared taxis for Cancún (US$10, 2.5 hours) congregate at Calle 38 between Calles 39 and 41 from 3am to 10pm daily.

Car

If you arrive from the toll highway (*cuota*), you'll enter town via Calle 42 (and return on Calle 40). It's a sobering US$14 toll from Cancún, US$8 from Mérida (Kantunil), and US$3 to Chichén Itzá (Pisté). In the center, eastbound Calle 41 and westbound Calle 39 access the free highway (*libre*).

The tour agency **Portal Maya** (Calle 41 between Calles 38 and 40, tel. 985/107-0073, portalmaya@hotmail.com, 9am-1:30pm and 4pm-8pm Mon.-Sat.) is your lone option for car rentals; economy cars typically run US$40-50 with insurance included. Custom tours also can be arranged.

Bicycle

For bike rentals, including tandems, head to **MexiGo Tours** (Calle 43 between Calles 40 and 42, tel. 985/856-0777, www.mexigotours.com, 8:30am-7pm daily); bikes rent for US$1-2.50 per hour or US$6-17.50 per day.

Ek' Balam

Ek' Balam, Maya for black jaguar, is a unique and fascinating archaeological site whose significance has only recently been revealed and appreciated. Serious restoration of Ek' Balam didn't begin until the mid-1990s, and it was then that an incredibly well-preserved stucco frieze was discovered, hidden under an innocuous stone facade near the top of the site's main pyramid. The discovery rocketed Ek' Balam into preeminence, first among Maya scholars and more slowly among travelers in the Yucatán, once the frieze was excavated and opened to the public. Much remains a mystery about Ek' Balam, but archaeologists believe it was founded around 300 BC and became an important commercial center, its influence peaking in AD 700-1100.

Ek' Balam sees a fraction of the tourists that visit other Maya sites, despite its proximity to Valladolid, Cancún, and Mérida. The site is small enough that even an hour is enough to appreciate its treasures; even better, it's a tranquil place that doesn't get besieged by mammoth tour groups.

ORIENTATION

Ek' Balam is located 30 kilometers (19 miles) north of Valladolid, off of Highway 295. Ek' Balam **village** is two kilometers (1.2 miles) west, with only one good option for an overnight stay and one restaurant open to the general public; for more alternatives and traveler services, head to Valladolid.

★ EK' BALAM ARCHAEOLOGICAL ZONE

Entering **Ek' Balam** (8am-5pm daily, US$10.25), you'll pass through a low thick wall and an elegant corbeled arch. Walls are rare in Maya cities, and were most commonly used for defense, as in the cases of Becán and Tulum. Ek' Balam's walls would not have slowed marauding rivals, however, and so they most likely served to enforce social divisions, with some areas off-limits (but not out of view) to all but the elite. They may also have been decorative—the city possessed great aesthetic flair, as the entry arch and the famous stucco frieze demonstrate.

Acrópolis and El Trono

The highlight of Ek' Balam is an artful and remarkably pristine stucco frieze known as **El Trono** (The Throne), located under a protective *palapa* roof two-thirds of the way up Ek' Balam's main pyramid, the **Acrópolis.** A steep stairway leads up the center of the pyramid, and a platform to the left of the stairs provides visitors a close-up view of El Trono.

Ek' Balam Archaeological Zone

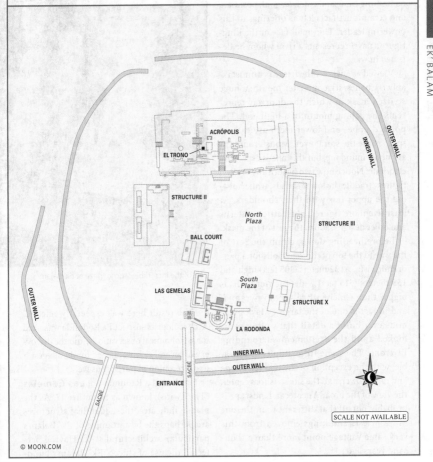

ACRÓPOLIS

EL TRONO

STRUCTURE II

North Plaza

STRUCTURE III

BALL COURT

South Plaza

LAS GEMELAS

STRUCTURE X

LA RODONDA

INNER WALL

OUTER WALL

ENTRANCE

SACBÉ

OUTER WALL

INNER WALL

OUTER WALL

SACBÉ

SCALE NOT AVAILABLE

© MOON.COM

About 85 percent of El Trono is the original stucco. Often structures like this would have been painted blue or red, but not so here. In fact, shortly after it was built, El Trono was sealed behind a stone wall 50-60 centimeters (19-24 inches) thick. It remained there untouched until the 1990s, when restoration workers accidentally—and fortuitously—dislodged one of the protective stones, revealing the hidden chamber beneath.

The tall, winged figures immediately catch your eye, as they appear so much like angels.

In fact, they are high priests. Notice that one is deformed—his left arm is longer than the right and has only four fingers. The Maya considered birth defects to be a sign of divinity, and the priest depicted here may have risen to his position precisely because of his deformation.

Directly over the door is a seated figure (unfortunately, the head is missing). This represents Ukit Kan Le'k Tok', one of Ek' Balam's former rulers, described in inscriptions as the "king of kings," and the person for whom

El Trono was built and dedicated. A tomb was discovered in the chamber behind the frieze, containing thousands of jade, gold, obsidian, and ceramic artifacts left as offerings to this powerful leader. The small face at the king-figure's navel represents a rival whom he defeated in war.

Viewed as a whole, the frieze is unmistakably a Chenes-style monster mouth: a huge stylized mask in which the doorway represents the gaping mouth of a high god. The pointed upper and lower teeth are easy to spot, as are the spiral eyes. Monster mouths are never mundane, but this one is especially elaborate: Notice how two beautifully crafted figures straddle the lower eyelids, while hoisting the upper lids with their shoulders. At least five more figures, plus lattice patterns and other designs, adorn the rest of the mask.

Before heading down, climb the rest of the way to the top of the Acrópolis for a panoramic vista. At 32 meters (105 feet) high and 158 meters (515 feet) wide, the Acrópolis is bigger than Chichén Itzá's main pyramid, and in fact is one of the largest Maya pyramids ever built, a detail that's often overlooked amid the excitement surrounding El Trono. The scene from atop is memorable; with the exception of the odd telephone and radio tower, and the site's visitors center, the view of the broad Yucatecan landscape is probably not all that different than the one Maya priests and kings enjoyed from this very same vantage point more than a thousand years ago.

part of the incredible stucco frieze at Ek' Balam

South Plaza

Descending the pyramid, you can see that Ek' Balam is a fairly small site, with two midsize plazas (north and south), a ball court in the middle, and its main structures crowded together.

On the south side of the south plaza stands **La Rodonda,** or the Oval Palace. A squat midsize structure, La Rodonda has an eclectic array of overlapping lines and curves, stairs, and terraces. It underwent numerous iterations, as did virtually all Maya temples, but the result here was especially eclectic. Archaeologists suspect La Rodonda was used for astronomical observations, and the discovery of several richly adorned tombs suggest it had a ceremonial purpose as well.

Flanking La Redonda are **Las Gemelas** (The Twins), known as Structure 17. As the plaque indicates, these identical structures are perhaps the best example of Ek' Balam's particular architectural style. Having perfected the use of stucco, Ek' Balam's builders did not concern themselves with precise masonry, as the stones would be covered in a thick stucco cap. However, stucco proved much less resilient to erosion, and centuries later the structures here appear shabbier than even much older ones, such as those in Campeche's Río Bec region, where stucco was less common and stone blocks were more carefully cut and fitted. Recent excavations have focused on these two buildings, where intriguing freehand marks and paintings—perhaps akin to graffiti today—have been discovered.

Practicalities

Guides can be hired at the entrance to the ruins (US$30, 1-1.5 hours, available in Spanish or English). French- and Italian-speaking guides are sometimes available. Additionally, there's a US$2.25 fee to enter with a video camera; parking is free.

CENOTE X'CANCHÉ

Cenote X'Canché (cell tel. 985/100-9815, www.ekbalam.com.mx, 9am-5pm daily, US$2.50) is an excellent community-run ecotourism project, and a great add-on to a visit to Ek' Balam. From the ruins' parking lot, follow the signs to a wide path that winds 1.5 kilometers (0.9 mile) through low dense forest to the cenote, which is 14 meters (46 feet) deep and nearly circular, with sheer walls and tree roots descending picturesquely to cool, clean water. A wooden staircase leads to the water's edge, great for swimming. For an adrenaline rush, consider rappelling from the cenote edge or zip-lining across it instead (US$5-25).

The path from the parking lot to the cenote is a pleasant shaded walk, though many visitors rent bikes (US$3.50 per 3 hours) or take advantage of the tricycle taxis (US$6 pp round-trip). Facilities include restrooms, shower and changing areas, a restaurant, and *palapa*-shaded hammocks. For those wanting to stay overnight, there are simple **cabins** (US$30 s/d) and **campsites** (US$6 pp, BYO gear).

CENOTE SAK' AWA

Cenote Sak' Awa (no phone, 11am-sunset daily, US$3) is a rewarding post-ruins visit if you have a car. Located 15 kilometers (9 miles) east of Ek' Balam, the trip there is an adventure in of itself, undertaken via a back road from Ek' Balam to Highway 180 through the Mayan villages of Hunukú and Dzalbay; remarkably large signage marks the way. You'll pass men on bikes loaded down with wood or crops, women balancing jugs of water on their heads, and skinny dogs running after your car. Once at the cenote, a 350-meter (0.2 miles) trail leads to the entrance—a hole in the

ground with a rickety staircase. As your eyes adjust, you'll see an island in a perfectly round cavern—a doughnut hole, of sorts—surrounded by crystal-clear teal water. Openings in the cavern roof let in light and long tree roots. The water itself is refreshing and cool, and you'll see small catfish and turtles and an occasional swallow swooping down from above to skim the surface of the water. It's an eerily gorgeous site with few visitors, so you're likely to have it to yourself. Facilities include changing rooms and a questionable toilet.

★ CENOTES AGUA DULCE

The stunning **Cenotes Agua Dulce** (tel. 985/856-2200, 8:30am-5pm daily, US$2.50-4.50 à la carte cenotes, US$13.25 all cenotes) comprises four separate cenotes: **Agua Dulce, Palomitas, Las Cavernas,** and **El Oasis.** The first two are classic cenotes—deep underground pools of crystalline turquoise water surrounded by stalagmites and stalactites. They're reached by long staircases leading down into the earth several dozen meters. The second two are for exploring—one is dry (making it a cavern, not a cenote), the other is too shallow to swim in. They're worth a visit if you can avoid the tour groups, which typically stop here on Mondays and Fridays. There's a restaurant on-site serving buffet lunch (US$7), and there are changing areas and bathrooms. Life vests are included. The site is just north of the village of Yalcobá, about 20 kilometers (12 miles) from Ek' Balam and 24 kilometers (14.5 miles) northeast of Valladolid.

FOOD AND ACCOMMODATIONS

In the Maya village near the ruins, ★ **Genesis Eco-Oasis** (cell tel. 985/101-0277, www.genesisretreat.com, US$45 s/d with shared bathroom, US$58 s/d with shared bathroom and a/c, US$65-75 s/d, US$79 s/d/t/q) has nine rooms and *cabañas* set on a leafy enclosed property, all different in style and made from recycled materials. Each faces a natural bio-filtered pool in a jungle garden.

Morning pastries and coffee are included in the rate; full breakfasts and dinners—using produce from the property's organic farm—are available to guests for an additional fee. The hardworking Canadian owner also offers tours of Ek' Balam village and local artisan workshops, and is involved in a number of educational projects around town. Be aware that a number of friendly pooches lounge about the property—fine if you like dogs, but not everyone's thing.

The **restaurant at Dolce Vacanza** (tel. 999/913-9670, vacanzadolce@gmail.com, noon-6pm Tues.-Sun., US$5-7) serves solid Italian food, including fresh handmade ravioli, fettuccini, and other pasta. Meals are served in a large, tasteful dining room overlooking a somewhat unkempt garden.

Near the ruins, **Cenote X'Canché** (cell tel. 985/100-9815, www.ekbalam.com.mx, US$6 pp tent, US$30 s/d) rents three well-built and solar-powered *palapa cabañas* near the cenote, each with queen bed and a hammock (plus mosquito nets). The windows have good screens, and there's hot water and fans. There also are campsites (US$6 pp, BYO gear). A three-course lunch or dinner at the on-site restaurant costs US$8; breakfast is US$7.

GETTING THERE AND AROUND
Car

From Valladolid, drive north on Highway 295 toward Tizimín for about 17 kilometers (10.5 miles), past the town of Temozón, to a well-marked right-hand turnoff to Ek' Balam. From there, drive another 11 kilometers (6.8 miles) to an intersection: Turn left to reach the village and accommodations, or continue straight to reach the archaeological site.

Taxi

Colectivo (shared) taxis from Valladolid to the village of Ek' Balam leave from a stop on Calle 44 between Calles 35 and 37 (US$2.50); mornings have the most frequent departures. Otherwise, a private taxi costs about US$15 for up to four people. If you're planning on visiting the ruins only, you can often negotiate with the driver to wait there for a couple of hours and bring you back for around US$25.

A set of steps leads to the eerily beautiful world of cenotes.

Background

The Landscape

The history of the Yucatán Peninsula is deeply intertwined with its unique geology and ecology. From the ancient Maya to modern-day tourism, the land and its resources have shaped the course of Yucatecan events. And the Yucatán, in turn, has helped shape the course of Mexican history, from being the stage upon which the early Spanish conquest was conducted to helping rescue a moribund Mexican economy in the 1980s. An understanding of the Yucatán Peninsula's land, ecology, culture, and politics is vital to understanding the region today.

GEOGRAPHY

The Yucatán Peninsula spans some 113,000 square kilometers (70,215 square miles) in southeastern Mexico, and is made up of three states: Yucatán, Campeche, and Quintana Roo. It has more than 1,600 kilometers (994 miles) of shoreline, with the Caribbean Sea to the east and the Gulf of Mexico to the north and west. To the southwest are the Mexican states of Tabasco and Chiapas, and directly south are the countries of Belize and Guatemala.

Geologically, the Yucatán Peninsula is a flat shelf of limestone, a porous rock that acts like a huge sponge. Rainfall is absorbed into the ground and delivered to natural stone-lined sinks and underground rivers. The result is that the Yucatán has virtually no surface water, neither rivers nor lakes. It also has very few hills. The geology changes as you move south, and the first sizable river—the Río Hondo—forms a natural boundary between Belize and Mexico.

The Coast

The northern and western coasts are bordered by the emerald waters of the Gulf of Mexico. Just inland, the land is dotted with lagoons, sandbars, and swamps. The east coast is edged by the turquoise Caribbean, and the glorious islands of Isla Cozumel, Isla Mujeres, and Isla Contoy lie just offshore. Along the coast runs the Mesoamerican Reef, the second-longest coral reef in the world.

Cenotes

Over the course of millennia, water that seeped below the Yucatán's porous limestone shelf eroded a vast network of underground rivers and caves. When a cave's ceiling wears thin, it may eventually cave in, exposing the water below. The Maya called such sinkholes *dzo'not,* which Spanish explorers recorded as *cenotes.* Most cenotes are extremely deep, and interconnected by way of underground channels. A cenote's surface may be near ground level, but more often it is much farther down, as much as 90 meters (295 feet) below ground level. In those cases, the Maya gathered water by carving stairs into the slick limestone walls or by hanging long ladders into abysmal hollows that led to underground lakes.

CLIMATE

The weather in the Yucatán falls into a rainy season (May-October) and a dry season (November-April). Travelers to the region in the dry season will experience warm days, occasional brief storms called *nortes,* and plenty of tourists. In the rainy season, expect spectacular storms and hot, muggy days. The region is infamous for its heat and humidity in May and June, which hovers around 90°F *and* 90 percent humidity.

Hurricane season runs July-November, with most activity occurring mid-August to

---

Previous: a skilled guide can bring the ancient ruins to life; the Yucatán and Riviera Maya are excellent for bird-watching.

mid-October. Cloudy conditions and scattered showers are common during this period, occasionally developing into tropical storms. Hurricanes are still relatively rare, but their effects are wide-reaching—even if a storm isn't predicted to hit the Yucatán, it may send plenty of heavy rain and surf that direction. If a hurricane *is* bearing down, don't try to tough it out; cut short your trip or head inland immediately.

ENVIRONMENTAL ISSUES

Hurricanes

Evidence that climate change may cause an increase in the number and/or intensity of Atlantic hurricanes has serious implications for the Yucatán Peninsula, already known to be within Hurricane Alley. The region has weathered countless storms, but something was different about Hurricanes Wilma (2005) and Dean (2007)—both storms broke records for intensity and caused major structural damage, but they also reshaped the shoreline in a way not seen before. Cancún's beaches were especially hard hit, the sand stripped away in many places to expose the hardened limestone beneath. Elsewhere, unusually thick deposits of sand on the coral reef and inland mangroves wiped out large portions of both important ecosystems.

Overdevelopment

Runaway construction along the Riviera Maya has a host of interconnected environmental impacts, some well-known, others poorly understood (and surely many that have yet to be identified). An obvious impact is the destruction of mangrove swamps, which extend along much of the coast a short distance inland from the beach. Well known for supporting wildlife, mangroves also help mitigate the effects of hurricane-related surge and currents and are an important source of nutrients for coral and other sealife, as water from the wetlands drains into the ocean. Although protected by federal law, mangroves have been a primary victim of massive development projects.

Mangroves are emblematic of a more general characteristic of the Riviera Maya: highly porous earth and a weblike underground watershed. Contamination is extremely difficult to clean up or even contain, as it spreads quickly in multiple directions via underground currents, including into the ocean. This is damaging not only to the environment but also to local communities—and the resorts themselves—which draw drinking water from the same system.

And those local communities are growing even faster than the resorts—by some estimates, resorts require an average of five employees for every guest room. Multiply that by the number of resorts operating and being built, and it's no surprise that the region's population is booming. In that sense, development is doubly dangerous: increasing the risk of contamination while simultaneously spurring demand for the very resource it most threatens.

Deforestation

Among the top concerns of environmentalists in Mexico is deforestation, which has accelerated with Mexico's burgeoning population. Slash-and-burn farming is still widely practiced in remote areas, with or without regulation. In an effort to protect the land, environmentalists are searching for alternative sources of income for locals. One is to train them to become guides by teaching them about the flora and fauna of the region as well as how to speak English. While not solving the problem, it does place an economic value on the forest itself and provides an incentive for preserving it.

Another focus is the plight of the palm tree. The palm is an important part of the cultural and practical lifestyle of the indigenous people of Quintana Roo. The fan-like chit palm (*thrinax radiate)* and ghostly Mexican silver palm (*coccothrinax readii)* have been used for millennia for everything from thatch roofing to constructing lobster traps. However, both palms are increasingly threatened; they grow best on coastal areas, right where development is more intense. NGOs like Amigos de Sian Ka'an and the World Wildlife Fund have worked to better understand the palms' growth patterns and to develop sustainable management plans. Other forest-friendly projects include establishing nature reserves, forming partnerships with local Maya communities, and developing ecotourism projects.

Plants and Animals

Quintana Roo's forests are home to mangroves, bamboo, and swamp cypresses. Ferns, vines, and flowers creep from tree to tree and create a dense growth. The southern part of the Yucatán Peninsula, with its classic tropical rainforest, hosts tall mahoganies, *campeche zapote,* and *kapok*—all covered with wild jungle vines. On the topmost limbs, orchids and air ferns reach for the sun.

Many animals found nowhere else in Mexico inhabit the Yucatán Peninsula's expansive flatlands and thick jungle forests. Spotting them can be difficult, though with patience and a skilled guide, not impossible.

TREES
Palms
A wide variety of palm trees and their relatives grow on the peninsula—tall, short, fruited, and even oil-producing varieties. Though similar, palms have distinct characteristics:

- Queen palms are often used for landscaping and bear a sweet fruit.
- Thatch palms are called *chit* by Maya, who use the fronds extensively for roof thatch.
- Coconut palms—the ones often seen on the beach—produce oil, food, drink, and shelter and are valued by locals as a nutritious food source and cash crop.
- Royal palms are tall with smooth trunks.
- Henequen is a cousin to the palm tree; from its fiber come twine, rope, matting, and other products. Because of its abundance, new uses for it are constantly sought.

Fruit Trees
Quintana Roo grows sweet and sour oranges, limes, and grapefruit. Avocado is abundant, and the papaya tree is practically a weed. The *mamey* tree grows full and tall (15-20 meters/49-65 feet), providing not only welcome shade but also an avocado-shaped fruit, brown on the outside with a vivid, salmon-pink flesh that tastes like a sweet yam. The *guaya* is another unusual fruit tree and a member of the lychee nut family. This rangy evergreen thrives on sea air and is commonly seen along the coast. Its small, green, leathery pods grow in clumps like grapes and contain a sweet, yellowish, jellylike flesh—tasty! The calabash tree provides gourds used for containers by Maya.

Other Trees
The ceiba (also called *kapok*) is a sacred tree for the Maya. Considered the link between the underworld, the material world, and the heavens, this huge tree is revered and left undisturbed—even if it sprouts in the middle of a fertile cornfield.

When visiting in the summer, you can't miss the beautiful *framboyanes* (royal poinciana). When in bloom, their wide-spreading branches are covered in clusters of brilliant orange-red flowers. These trees often line sidewalks and plazas, and when clustered together present a dazzling show.

FLOWERS
While wandering through jungle regions, you'll see numerous flowering plants. Here in their natural environment, these plants thrive in a way unknown to windowsills at home: Crotons exhibit wild colors, pothos grow 30-centimeter (11.8-inch) leaves, the philodendron splits every leaf in gargantuan

glory, and common morning glory creeps and climbs effortlessly over bushes and trees. You'll also be introduced to lesser-known residents of this semitropical world: the exotic white and red ginger, plumeria (sometimes called frangipani) with its wonderful fragrance and myriad colors, and hibiscus and bougainvillea, which bloom in an array of bright hues.

Orchids

Orchids can be found on the highest limbs of the tallest trees, especially in the state of Quintana Roo. Of the 71 species reported in the Yucatán Peninsula, 80 percent are epiphytic, attached to host trees and deriving moisture and nutrients from the air and rain. Orchids grow in myriad sizes and shapes: tiny buttons spanning the length of a half-meter-long (two-foot) branch, large-petaled blossoms with ruffled edges, or intense tiger-striped miniatures.

MAMMALS
Nine-Banded Armadillos

The size of a small dog and sporting a thick coat of armor, this peculiar creature gets its name from the nine bands (or external "joints") that circle its midsection and give the little tank some flexibility. The armadillo's keen sense of smell can detect insects and grubs—its primary food source—up to 15 centimeters (6 inches) underground, and its sharp claws make digging for them easy. An armadillo also digs underground burrows, into which it may carry a full bushel of grass to make its nest, where it will sleep through the hot day and emerge at night. Unlike armadillos that roll up into a tight ball when threatened, this species will race to its burrow, arch its back, and wedge in so that it cannot be pulled out. The Yucatán Peninsula is a favored habitat for its scant rainfall; too much rain floods the burrow and can drown young armadillos.

Giant Anteaters

A cousin of the armadillo, this extraordinary animal measures two meters (6.6 feet) from the tip of its tubular snout to the end of its bushy tail. Its coarse coat is colored shades of brown-gray; the hindquarters are darker in tone, while a contrasting wedge-shaped pattern of black and white decorates the throat and shoulders. Characterized by an elongated head, long tubular mouth, and extended tongue (but no teeth), it can weigh up to 39 kilograms (86 pounds). The anteater walks on the knuckles of its paws, allowing its claws to remain tucked under while it looks for food.

Giant anteaters are found in forests and swampy areas in Mexico and throughout Central and South America. It is mainly diurnal in areas where there are few people but nocturnal in densely populated places. Its razor-sharp claws allow it to rip open the leathery mud walls of termite and ant nests, the contents of which are a main food source. After opening the nest, the anteater rapidly flicks its viscous tongue in and out of its small mouth opening. Few ants escape.

Tapirs

The Central American tapir, or the Baird's tapir, is the largest land mammal in Central America and Mexico, with adults averaging two meters (6.6 feet) in length and weighing from 150kg (330lb) to a whopping 400kg (880lb). The nose and upper lip extend into a short but very mobile proboscis. Baird's tapirs are mostly black or gray, save distinctive cream-colored patches on their faces. Tapirs usually live near streams or rivers, which they use for daily bathing and as an escape from predators, especially jaguars and humans. If attacked, the tapir lowers its head and blindly crashes off through the forest; they've been known to collide with trees and knock themselves out in their chaotic attempt to flee. Tapirs are solitary and require large tracts of land for their nighttime foraging; this makes them especially vulnerable to habitat fragmentation. In Mexico, there are around a thousand wild tapirs found in only four states—Chiapas, Oaxaca, Campeche, and

Quintana Roo—down from eight states extending coast to coast.

Peccaries

Next to deer, peccaries are the most widely hunted game on the Yucatán Peninsula. Two species of peccaries are found here: the collared javelina peccary and the white-lipped peccary. The feisty collared javelina stands 50 centimeters (20 inches) at the shoulder and can be one meter (3.3 feet) long, weighing as much as 30 kilograms (66 pounds). It is black and white with a narrow, semicircular collar of white hair on the shoulders. The name javelina (which means spear in Spanish) comes from the two tusks that protrude from its mouth. A related species, the white-lipped peccary, is reddish brown to black and has an area of white around its mouth. Larger than the javelina, it can grow to 105 centimeters (41 inches) long and is found deep in tropical rainforests living in herds of 100 or more. Peccaries often are compared to the wild pigs found in Europe, but in fact they belong to entirely different families.

Felines

Seven species of cats are found in North America, four in the tropics. One of them—the jaguar—is heavy chested with sturdy, muscled forelegs. It has small, rounded ears and its tail is relatively short. Its color varies from tan and white to pure black. The male can weigh 65-115 kilograms (143-254 pounds), females 45-85 kilograms (99-187 pounds). The largest of the cats on the peninsula, the jaguar is about the same size as a leopard. Other cats found here are the ocelot and puma. In tropical forests of the past, the large cats were the only predators capable of controlling the populations of hoofed game such as deer, peccaries, and tapirs. If hunting is poor and times are tough, the jaguar will go into rivers and scoop up fish with its large paws. The river is also one of the jaguar's favorite spots for hunting tapirs, when the latter come to drink.

Monkeys

The jungles of Mexico are home to three species of monkeys: spider, howler, and black howler. Intelligent and endearing, these creatures are prime targets for the pet trade. They have been so hunted, in fact, that today all three are in danger of extinction. Experts estimate that for every monkey sold, three die during transportation and distribution. In an effort to protect these creatures, the Mexican government has prohibited their capture or trade. Tropical monkeys are most active at sunrise and sundown. If you go to Muyil, Cobá, or Punta Laguna Spider Monkey Reserve, keep your ears perked and your eyes peeled. You may see—or at least hear—a few monkeys. If possible, consider waking early or staying late to increase your chances of spotting a few.

SEALIFE
Coral Reefs

The spectacular coral reefs that grace the peninsula's east coast are made up of millions of tiny carnivorous organisms called polyps. Individual polyps can be less than a centimeter (0.4 inch) long or up to 15 centimeters (6 inches) in diameter. Related to the jellyfish and sea anemone, coral polyps capture prey with tiny tentacles that deliver a deadly sting.

Reef-building polyps have limestone exoskeletons, which they create by extracting calcium from the seawater. Reefs are formed as generation after generation of polyps attach themselves to each other. Different species attach in different ways, resulting in the many shapes and sizes of ocean reefs: delicate lace, trees with reaching branches, pleated mushrooms, stovepipes, petaled flowers, fans, domes, heads of cabbage, and stalks of broccoli. Though made up of individual polyps, coral structures function like a single organism, sharing nutrients through a central gastro-vascular system. Even in ideal conditions, most coral grows no more than five centimeters (two inches) per year.

Reefs are divided into three types: barrier, atoll, and fringing. A barrier reef runs parallel to the coast, with long stretches separated by narrow channels. The Mesoamerican Reef extends 250 kilometers (155 miles) from the tip of Isla Mujeres to Sapodilla Cay in the Gulf of Honduras—only the Great Barrier Reef in Australia is longer. An atoll typically forms around the crater of a submerged volcano. The polyps begin building their colonies along the lip of the crater, forming a circular coral island with a lagoon in the center. The Chinchorro Bank, off the southern coast of Quintana Roo, is the largest coral atoll in the Northern Hemisphere, measuring 48 kilometers long and 14 kilometers wide (30 miles by 9 miles). A fringing reef is coral living on a shallow shelf that extends outward from shore into the sea.

Fish

The Yucatán's barrier reef is home to myriad fish species, including parrot fish, candy bass, moray eels, spotted scorpion fish, turquoise angelfish, fairy basslets, flame fish, and gargantuan manta rays. Several species of shark also thrive in the waters off Quintana Roo, though they're not considered a serious threat to swimmers and divers. Sport fish—sailfish, marlin, and bluefin tuna—also inhabit the outer Caribbean waters.

Inland, anglers will find hard-fighting bonefish and pompano in the area's lagoons, and snorkelers and divers will find several species of blind fish in the crystal-clear waters of cenotes. These fish live out their existence in dark underground rivers and lakes and have no use for eyes.

Sea Turtles

Tens of thousands of sea turtles of various species once nested on the coastal beaches of Quintana Roo. As the coast became populated, turtles were severely overhunted for their eggs, meat, and shell, and their numbers began to fall. Hotel and resort developments have hastened the decline, as there are fewer and fewer patches of untrammeled sand in which turtles can dig nests and lay their eggs. The Mexican government and various ecological organizations are trying hard to save the dwindling turtle population. Turtle eggs are dug up and reburied in sand on safe beaches; or, when the hatchlings break through their shells, they are brought to a beach and allowed to rush toward the sea in hopes of imprinting a sense of belonging there so that they will later return to the spot. In some cases the hatchlings are scooped up and placed in tanks to grow larger before being released into the

sea turtle

open sea. The government is also enforcing tough penalties for people who take turtle eggs or capture, kill, or sell these creatures once they hatch.

Manatees

The manatee—sometimes called the sea cow—is a gentle, inquisitive giant. They are closely related to dugongs, and more distantly to elephants, aardvarks, and hyraxes. Newborns weigh 30-35 kilograms (66-77 pounds), while adults can weigh nearly 1,600 kilograms (3,500 pounds) and measure four meters (13 feet) in length. Shaped like an Idaho potato, manatees have coarse pinkish-gray skin, tiny sunken eyes, a flattened tail and flipper-like forelimbs (including toenails), and prehensile lips covered in sensitive whiskers. The manatee is the only aquatic mammal that's completely vegetarian, eating an astounding 10 percent of its body weight every day in aquatic grass and vegetation; it's unique among all mammals for constantly growing new teeth to replace those worn down by its voracious feeding.

Large numbers of them once roamed the shallow inlets, bays, and estuaries of the Caribbean; their images are frequently seen in the art of the ancient Maya, who hunted them for food. Today, though posing no threat to humans or other animals, and ecologically important for their ability to clear waterways of oxygen-choking vegetation, manatees are endangered in the Yucatán and elsewhere. The population has been reduced by the encroachment of people in their habitats along the riverways and shorelines. Ever-growing numbers of motorboats also inflict deadly gashes on these surface-feeding creatures. Nowadays it is very rare to spot one; the most sightings are reported in Punta Allen and Bahía de la Ascensión.

BIRDS

Since a major part of the Yucatán Peninsula is still undeveloped and covered with trees and brush, it isn't surprising to find exotic, rarely seen birds across the landscape. The Mexican government is beginning to realize the great value in this and is making efforts to protect nesting grounds. In addition to the growing number of nature reserves, some of the best bird-watching locales are the archaeological zones. At dawn and dusk, when most of the visitors are absent, the trees that surround the ancient structures come alive with birdsong. Of all the ruins, Cobá—with its marsh-rimmed lakes, nearby cornfields, and relatively tall, humid forest—is a particularly good site for bird-watching. One of the more impressive birds to look for here is the keel-billed toucan, often seen perched high on a bare limb in the early hours of the morning. Others include *chachalacas* (held in reverence by the Maya), screeching parrots, and, occasionally, the ocellated turkey.

Flamingos

The wetlands along the Yucatán's northern coast are shallow and murky and bordered in many places by thick mangrove forests. The water content is unusually high in salt and other minerals—the ancient Maya gathered salt here, and several salt factories still operate. A formidable habitat for most creatures, it's ideal for *phoenicopterus ruber ruber*—the American flamingo, the largest and pinkest of the world's five flamingo species. Nearly 30,000 of the peculiar birds nest here, feeding on algae and other tiny organisms that thrive in the salty water. Flamingos are actually born white, but they turn pink from the carotene in the algae they eat.

For years, flamingos only nested around Río Lagartos, near the peninsula's northeastern tip. But in 1988, Hurricane Gilbert destroyed their nesting grounds—not to mention the town of Río Lagartos—and forced the birds to relocate. They are now found all along the north coast, including at three major feeding and reproduction grounds: Río Lagartos, Celestún, and Uaymitún. Though in smaller numbers, they also can be found on Isla Holbox.

The best way to observe flamingos is on a boat tour at sunrise, when the birds are most active, turning their heads upside down and dragging their beaks along the bottom of the shallow water to suck in the mud that contains their food. (In the morning, you should see dozens of other birds too, such as storks, herons, and kingfishers.) If you go in the spring, you may see the male flamingos performing their strange mating dance—craning their necks, clucking loudly, and generally strutting their stuff.

Although flamingos live in the region year-round, you'll see the highest numbers at Río Lagartos in the spring and summer and at Celestún in the winter. Uaymitún has a pretty steady population but has no boat tours—instead you observe the birds through binoculars from a raised platform. No matter when you go, make as little noise as possible and ask your guide to keep his distance. Flamingos are nervous and easily spooked into flying away en masse. While the exodus is no doubt an impressive sight, it may cause the birds to abandon the site altogether.

Quetzals

Though the ancient Maya made abundant use of the dazzling quetzal feathers for ceremonial costumes and headdresses, they hunted other fowl for food. The quetzal is the only known bird remaining from the pre-Columbian era and is now almost extinct. Today, quetzals are still found (though rarely) in the high cloud forests of Chiapas and Central America, where they thrive on the constant moisture.

Estuaries

The Yucatán's countless estuaries, or *rías,* play host to hundreds of bird species; a boat ride into one of them will give you an opportunity to see American flamingos, a variety of wintering ducks from North America, blue-winged teals, northern shovelers, and lesser scaups. You'll also see a variety of wading birds feeding in the shallow waters, including numerous types of heron, snowy egrets, and, in the summer, white ibis. There are 14 species of birds endemic to the Yucatán Peninsula, including the ocellated turkey, Yucatán whip-poorwill, Yucatán flycatcher, orange oriole, black catbird, and the yellow-lored parrot. Río Lagartos and Celestún are the best-known and most-visited estuaries, but those in Sian Ka'an Biosphere Reserve, Isla Holbox, and Xcalak are also vibrant and accessible.

REPTILES

Although reptiles thrive in Yucatán's warm, sunny environment, humans are their worst

caymans

enemy. In the past, some species were greatly reduced in number—hunted for their unusual skin. Although hunting them is now illegal, black marketers still take their toll on the species.

Caymans

The cayman is a member of the crocodilian order. Its habits and appearance are similar to those of crocodiles, with the main difference being in its underskin: The cayman's skin is reinforced with bony plates on the belly, making it useless for the leather market. (Alligators and crocodiles, with smooth belly skin and sides, have been hunted almost to extinction in some parts of the world because of the value of their skin.)

Several species of cayman frequent the brackish inlet waters near the estuaries of Río Lagartos (literally, River of Lizards); though seen less frequently, they also inhabit mangroves on the Caribbean coast. A large cayman can be 2.5 meters (8.2 feet) long and very dark gray-green and broad-snouted with eyelids that look swollen and wrinkled. Some cayman species have eyelids that look like a pair of blunt horns. They are quicker than alligators and have longer, sharper teeth. Skilled hunters, caymans are quick in water and on land, and will attack a person if cornered. The best advice is to give caymans a wide berth if spotted.

Iguanas

This group of American lizards—Iguanidae family—includes various large plant-eaters seen frequently in Quintana Roo. Iguanas grow to be one meter (3.3 feet) long and have a blunt head and long flat tail. Bands of black and gray circle its body, and a serrated column reaches down the middle of its back almost to the tail. The young iguana is bright emerald green and often supplements its diet by eating insects and larvae.

The lizard's forelimbs hold the front half of its body up off the ground while its two back limbs are kept relaxed and splayed alongside its hindquarters. When the iguana is frightened, however, its hind legs do everything they're supposed to, and the iguana crashes quickly (though clumsily) into the brush searching for its burrow and safety. This reptile is not aggressive—it mostly enjoys basking in the bright sunshine along the Caribbean—but if cornered it will bite and use its tail in self-defense.

From centuries past, recorded references attest to the iguana's medicinal value, which partly explains the active trade of live iguanas in the marketplaces. Iguana stew is believed to cure or relieve various human ailments.

Other Lizards

You'll see a great variety of other lizards on the peninsula; some are brightly striped in various shades of green and yellow, while others are earth-toned and blend in with the gray and beige limestone that dots the landscape. Skinny as wisps of thread running on hind legs, or chunky and waddling with armor-like skin, the range is endless and fascinating.

Be sure to look for the black anole, which changes colors to match its environment, either when danger is imminent or as subterfuge to fool the insects on which it feeds. At mating time, the male anole puffs out its bright red throat fan so that female lizards will see it.

Coral Snakes

Two species of coral snakes, which are related to the cobra, are found in the southern part of the Yucatán Peninsula. They have prominent rings around their bodies in the same sequence of red, black, yellow, or white and grow to 1-1.5 meters (3.3-4.9 feet). Their bodies are slender, with no pronounced distinction between the head and neck.

Coral snakes spend the day in mossy clumps under rocks or logs, emerging only at night. Though the bite of a coral snake can kill within 24 hours, the chances of the average tourist being bitten by a coral (or any other) snake are slim.

Tropical Rattlesnakes

The tropical rattlesnake (*cascabel* in Spanish) is the deadliest and most treacherous species of rattler. It differs slightly from other species by having vividly contrasting neckbands. It grows 2-2.5 meters (6.6-8.2 feet) long and is found mainly in the higher and drier areas of the tropics. Contrary to popular myth, this serpent doesn't always rattle a warning of its impending strike.

INSECTS AND ARACHNIDS

Air-breathing invertebrates are unavoidable in any tropical locale. Some are annoying (gnats and no-see-ums), some are dangerous (black widows, bird spiders, and scorpions), and others can cause pain when they bite (red ants); but many are beautiful (butterflies and moths), and *all* are fascinating.

Butterflies and Moths

The Yucatán has an incredible abundance of beautiful moths and butterflies, some 40,000 species in all. Hikers might see the magnificent blue morpho, orange-barred sulphur, copperhead, cloudless sulphur, malachite, admiral, calico, ruddy dagger-wing, tropical buckeye, and emperor. The famous monarch is also a visitor during its annual migration from the northeastern United States. It usually makes a stopover on Quintana Roo's east coast on its way south to the Central American mountains where it spends the winter. The huge black witch moth—males can have a wingspan of seven inches and are sometimes mistaken for bats—is called *mariposa de la muerte* ("butterfly of death" in Spanish) or *ma ha na* (Yucatec Maya for "enter the home"), stemming from a common belief that if the moth enters the home of a sick person, that person will soon die.

Spiders and Scorpions

The Yucatán has some scary-looking spiders and scorpions (*arañas* and *alacranes*), but none is particularly dangerous. The Yucatán rust rump tarantula is surely the most striking, a hairy medium-size tarantula with long legs and a distinctive orange or rust-colored rear. Like most tarantulas, they are nocturnal and fairly timid, with females spending much of their time in burrows in the ground, and males roaming around incessantly looking for them. Its bite is harmless, but that doesn't mean you should handle one: When threatened, tarantulas can shake off a cloud of tiny hairs, which are highly irritating if inhaled.

The Yucatán is home to a wide variety of butterflies and moths.

The Yucatán's long black scorpions—up to 10 centimeters (4 inches)—have a painful sting that can cause swelling, and for some people shortness of breath, but is not deadly. Like tarantulas, scorpions avoid humans and are therefore rare to see; that said, it's always a good idea to shake out shoes and beach towels before using them, just in case.

Bees

The Yucatán's most famous bee—of numerous species found here—is the aptly named Yucatán bee, also known as the Maya bee. The small stingless insect produces a particularly sweet honey that was prized by the ancient Maya, and was one of the most widely traded commodities in the Maya world. (Some researchers say the Descending God figure at Tulum and other archaeological sites is the god of bees.) The ancient Maya were expert beekeepers, a tradition that lives on today, albeit much reduced thanks in part to the availability of cheap standard honey. Yucatán honey (harvested using more modern methods) is still sold in Mexico and abroad, mostly online and in organic and specialty stores.

History

ACROSS THE BERING LAND BRIDGE

People and animals from Asia crossed the Bering land bridge into North America in the Pleistocene epoch about 50,000 years ago, when sea levels were much lower. As early as 10,000 BC, ice age humans hunted woolly mammoth and other large animals roaming the cool, moist landscape of central Mexico. The earliest traces of humans in the Yucatán Peninsula are obsidian spear points and stone tools dating to 9,000 BC. The Loltún caves in the state of Yucatán contained a cache of mammoth bones, which are thought to have been dragged there by a roving band of hunters. As the region dried out and large game disappeared in the next millennia, tools of a more settled way of life appeared, such as grinding stones for preparing seeds and plant fibers.

ANCIENT CIVILIZATION

Between 7,000 and 2,000 BC, society evolved from hunting and gathering to farming; corn, squash, and beans were independently cultivated in widely separated areas in Mexico. Archaeologists believe that the earliest people who we can call Maya, or proto-Maya, inhabited the Pacific coast of Chiapas and Guatemala. These tribes lived in villages that held more than 1,000 inhabitants apiece; beautiful painted and incised ceramic jars for food storage have been found from this region and time period. After 1,000 BC this way of life spread south to the highlands site of Kaminaljuyú (now part of Guatemala City) and, through the next millennium, to the rest of the Maya world. Meanwhile, in what are now the Mexican states of Veracruz and Tabasco, another culture, the Olmecs, was developing what is now considered Mesoamerica's first civilization. Its influence was felt throughout Mexico and Central America. Archaeologists believe that before the Olmecs disappeared around 300 BC, they contributed two crucial cultural advances to the Maya: the Long Count calendar and the hieroglyphic writing system.

LATE PRECLASSIC PERIOD

During the Late Preclassic era (300 BC -AD 250), the Pacific coastal plain saw the rise of a Maya culture in Izapa near Tapachula, Chiapas. The Izapans worshipped gods that were precursors of the Classic Maya pantheon and commemorated religious and historical events in bas-relief carvings that emphasized costume and finery.

The great efflorescence of the southern Maya world stopped at the end of the Early Classic period (AD 250-600). Kaminaljuyú and other cities were abandoned; researchers believe that the area was invaded by Teotihuacano warriors extending the reach of their Valley of Mexico-based empire. On the Yucatán Peninsula, there is evidence of Teotihuacano occupation at the Río Bec site of Becán and at Acanceh near Mérida. You can see Teotihuacano-style costumes and gods in carvings at the great Petén city of Tikal and at Copán in Honduras. By AD 600, the Teotihuacano empire had collapsed, and the stage was set for the Classic Maya eras.

LATE CLASSIC PERIOD

The Maya heartland of the Late Classic period (AD 600-900) extended from Copán in Honduras through Tikal in Guatemala and ended at Palenque in Chiapas. The development of these city-states, which also included Yaxchilán and Bonampak, almost always followed the same pattern. Early in this era, a new and vigorous breed of rulers founded a series of dynasties bent on deifying themselves and their ancestors. All the arts and sciences of the Maya world, from architecture to astronomy, were focused on this goal. The Long Count calendar and the hieroglyphic writing system were the most crucial tools in this effort, as the rulers needed to recount the stories of their dynasties and of their own glorious careers.

During the Late Classic era, painting, sculpture, and carving reached their climax; objects such as Lord Pakal's sarcophagus lid from Palenque are now recognized as among the finest pieces of world art. Royal monuments stood at the center of large and bustling cities. In 2017, researchers used airborne lasers to reveal tens of thousands of previously unknown structures at Tikal and other northern Guatemalan sites; most are stone platforms for small dwellings, suggesting a much larger and denser population throughout the Maya world than previously

intricately decorated pottery at the Museo Maya de Cancún

During the same period, the northern Guatemalan highlands were booming with construction; this was the heyday of Kaminaljuyú, which grew to enormous size, with more than 120 temple-mounds and numerous stelae. The earliest calendar inscription that researchers are able to read comes from a monument found at El Baúl to the southwest of Kaminaljuyú; it has been translated as AD 36.

In the Petén jungle region just north of the highlands, the dominant culture was the Chicanel, whose hallmarks are elaborate temple-pyramids lined with enormous stucco god-masks (as in Kohunlich). The Petén sites of Nakbé and El Mirador are the most spectacular Chicanel cities yet found. El Mirador contains a 70-meter-tall (230-foot) temple-pyramid complex that is the tallest ancient structure in Mesoamerica. Despite the obvious prosperity of this region, there is almost no evidence of Long Count dates or writing systems in either the Petén jungle or the Yucatán Peninsula just to the north.

thought—perhaps as high as 15 million people, three times higher than long-held estimates. The study also revealed huge raised causeways, most likely a sign of vigorous intercity trade. Each Classic city-state reached its apogee at a different time; the southern cities peaked first, with the northern Puuc region cities following close behind.

By AD 925, nearly all of the city-states had collapsed and were left in a state of near-abandonment. The Classic Maya decline is one of the great enigmas of Mesoamerican archaeology. There are myriad theories—disease, invasion, peasant revolt—but many researchers now believe the collapse was caused by a combination of factors, including overpopulation, environmental degradation, and a series of devastating droughts. With the abandonment of the cities, the cultural advances disappeared as well. The last Long Count date was recorded in AD 909, and many religious customs and beliefs were never seen again.

EARLY POSTCLASSIC PERIOD

After the Puuc region was abandoned—almost certainly because of a foreign invasion—the center of Maya power moved east to Chichén. During this Early Postclassic era (AD 925-1200), the Toltec influence took hold, marking the end of the most artistic era and the birth of a new militaristic society built around a blend of ceremonialism, civic and social organization, and conquest. Chichén was the great power of northern Yucatán. Competing city-states either submitted to its warriors or, like the Puuc cities and Cobá, were destroyed.

LATE POSTCLASSIC PERIOD

After Chichén's fall in AD 1224—probably due to an invasion—a heretofore lowly tribe calling themselves the Itzá became the Late Postclassic (AD 1200-1530) masters of Yucatecan power politics. Kukulcán II of Chichén founded Mayapán in AD 1263-1283. After his death and the abandonment

---

Early Civilizations and Maya Timeline

- **Paleoindian:** before 7000 BC
- **Archaic:** 7000-2500 BC
- **Early Preclassic:** 2500-1000 BC
- **Middle Preclassic:** 1000-400 BC
- **Late Preclassic:** 400 BC-AD 250
- **Early Classic:** AD 250-600
- **Late Classic:** AD 600-800
- **Terminal Classic:** AD 800-1000
- **Early Postclassic:** AD 1000-1250
- **Late Postclassic:** AD 1250-1519

---

of Chichén, an aggressive Itzá lineage named the Cocom seized power and used Mayapán as a base to take over northern Yucatán. They succeeded through wars using Tabascan mercenaries and intermarrying with other powerful lineages. Foreign lineage heads were forced to live in Mayapán where they could easily be controlled. At its height, the city covered 6.5 square kilometers (4 square miles) within a defensive wall that contained more than 15,000 inhabitants. Architecturally, Mayapán leaves much to be desired; the city plan was haphazard, and its greatest monument was a sloppy, smaller copy of Chichén's Pyramid of Kukulcán.

The Cocom ruled for 250 years until AD 1441-1461, when an upstart Uxmal-based lineage named the Xiu rebelled and slaughtered the Cocom. Mayapán was abandoned and Yucatán's city-states were weakened in a series of bloody intramural wars that left them hopelessly divided when the conquistadors arrived. By the time of that conquest, culture was once again being imported from outside the Maya world. Putún Maya, seafaring traders, brought new styles of art and religious beliefs back from their trips to central Mexico. Their influence can be seen in the Mixtec-style frescoes at Tulum on the Quintana Roo coast.

SPANISH ARRIVAL AND CONQUEST

After Columbus's arrival in the New World, other adventurers traveling the same seas soon found the Yucatán Peninsula. In 1519, 34-year-old Hernán Cortés set out from Cuba—against the wishes of the Spanish governor—with 11 ships, 120 sailors, and 550 soldiers to search for slaves, a lucrative business. His search began on the Yucatán coast but eventually encompassed most of present-day Mexico. However, it took many decades and many lives for Spanish conquistadors to quell the Maya's resistance and cunning, despite a major advantage in military technology, including horses, gunpowder, and metal swords and armor. Francisco de Montejo, who took part in Cortés's earlier expedition into central Mexico, spent 1528-1535 trying to conquer the Yucatán, first from the east at Tulum and later from the west near Campeche and Tabasco, but was driven out each time. Montejo's son, also named Francisco de Montejo "El Mozo" (The Younger), took up the effort and eventually founded the city of Mérida in 1542 and Campeche in 1546. From those strongholds, the Spanish conquest slowly spread across the peninsula.

Economic and religious oppression were central to the conquest. The Xiu indigenous group proved an important ally to the Spanish after its leader converted to Christianity. And in 1562, a friar named Diego de Landa, upon learning his converts still practiced certain Maya ceremonies, became enraged and ordered the torture and imprisonment of numerous Maya spiritual leaders. He also gathered all the religious artifacts and Maya texts—which he said contained "superstitions and the devil's lies"—and had them burned. It was a staggering loss—at least 27 codices—and one that Landa later seemed to regret and attempted to reconcile by writing a detailed record of Maya customs, mathematics, and writing.

The Caste War

By the 1840s, the brutalized and subjugated Maya organized a revolt against Euro-Mexican colonizers. Called the Caste War, this savage war saw Maya taking revenge on every white man, woman, and child by means of murder and rape. European survivors made their way to the last Spanish strongholds of Mérida and Campeche. The governments of the two cities appealed for help to Spain, France, and the United States. No one answered the call. It was soon apparent that the remaining two cities would be wiped out.

But just as Mérida's leaders were preparing to evacuate the city, the Maya abruptly picked up their weapons and left. The reason was an unusually early appearance of flying ants, a sign of coming rain and to the Maya an all-important signal to begin planting corn. Despite the suffering visited upon them over three centuries of Spanish conquest, the Maya warriors, who were also farmers, simply could not risk missing the planting season. They turned their backs on certain victory and returned to their villages to tend their fields.

The unexpected reprieve allowed time for thousands of troops to arrive from Cuba, Mexico City, and the United States, and the vengeance was merciless. Maya were killed indiscriminately. Some were taken prisoner and sold to Cuba as slaves; others left their villages and hid in the jungles—in some cases, for decades. Between 1846 and 1850, the population of the Yucatán Peninsula was reduced from 500,000 to 300,000. Quintana Roo along the Caribbean coast was considered a dangerous no-man's-land for almost another 100 years.

Growing Maya Power

Many Maya Indians escaped slaughter during the Caste War by fleeing to the isolated coastal forests of present-day Quintana Roo. A large number regrouped under the cult of the "Talking Cross"—an actual wooden cross that, with the help of a priest and a ventriloquist, spoke to the beleaguered indigenous fighters, urging them to continue fighting. Followers called themselves *Cruzob* (People of

Friar Diego de Landa and the Maya Alphabet

Just north of Oxkutzcab, the town of Maní has a quiet, peaceful atmosphere that belies a wrenching history. It was here, in 1562, that Friar Diego de Landa conducted a now-infamous *auto de fé*, in which he burned at least two dozen irreplaceable Maya codices and thousands of painted vases and other items, because he deemed them works of the devil. He accused numerous Maya religious leaders and laypeople of idolatry, and ordered them tortured, publicly humiliated, and imprisoned. The act was outrageous, even by Spanish colonial standards, and Landa was shipped back to Spain to face the Council of the Indies, the colonial authority, for conducting an illegal inquisition. He was eventually absolved—a panel of inspectors found he had broken no laws—but not before Landa came to regret his act, at least somewhat. Confined to a convent awaiting judgment, he set about writing down all he could remember about the Maya.

It was no minor undertaking: Landa spoke Yucatec Maya fluently, and had lived, traveled, and preached throughout the Yucatán for 13 years before his expulsion. In all, Landa spent close to a decade completing *An Account of the Things of Yucatán*. He returned to Mérida in 1571 as the newly appointed bishop of Yucatán, and died there in 1579. Landa's manuscript was largely forgotten until being rediscovered in 1863. Among other things, the manuscript contains a crude alphabet (or more precisely, a syllabary), which has proved invaluable to the modern-day decoding of the Maya hieroglyphics. Ironically, the very man who destroyed so much of the Maya's written history also provided the key for future researchers to unlock what remained.

the Cross) and made a stronghold in the town of Chan Santa Cruz, today Carrillo Puerto. Research (and common sense) suggests the Maya knew full well that a human voice was responsible for the "talking," but that many believed it was inspired by God.

Close to the border with British Honduras (now Belize), the leaders of Chan Santa Cruz began selling timber to the British and were given weapons in return. Simultaneously (roughly 1855-1857), internal strife weakened the relations between Campeche and Mérida, and their mutual defense as well. Maya leaders took advantage of the conflict and attacked Fort Bacalar, eventually gaining control of the entire southern Caribbean coast.

Up until that time, indigenous soldiers simply killed the people they captured, but starting in 1858 they took lessons from the colonials and began to keep whites for slave labor. Women were put to work doing household chores and some became concubines, while men were forced to work the fields and build new constructions. (The main church in Carrillo Puerto was built largely by white slaves.)

For the next 40 years, the Maya people and soldiers based in and around Chan Santa Cruz kept the east coast of the Yucatán for themselves, and a shaky truce with the Mexican government endured. The native people were economically independent, self-governing, and, with no roads in or out of the region, almost totally isolated. They were not at war as long as everyone left them alone.

The Last Stand

Only when President Porfirio Díaz took power in 1877 did the Mexican federal government begin to think seriously about the Yucatán Peninsula. Through the years, Quintana Roo's isolation and the strength of the Maya in their treacherous jungle had foiled repeated efforts by Mexican soldiers to capture the region. The army's expeditions were infrequent, but it rankled Díaz that a relatively small and modestly armed Maya force had been able to keep the Mexican army at bay for so long. An assault in 1901, under the command of General Ignacio Bravo, broke the government's losing streak. The general captured a village, laid railroad tracks, and built a walled fort. Supplies arriving by rail kept the fort stocked, but the indigenous defenders responded by holding the fort under siege for an entire year. Reinforcements finally came from the capital and the Maya were forced to retreat, first from the fort and then from many of their villages and strongholds. A period of brutal Mexican occupation followed, lasting until 1915, yet Maya partisans still didn't give up. They conducted guerrilla raids from the tangled coastal forest until the Mexican army, frustrated and demoralized, pulled out and returned Quintana Roo to the Maya.

Beginning in 1917 and lasting to 1920, however, influenza and smallpox swept through the Maya-held territories, killing hundreds of thousands of Maya. In 1920, with the last of their army severely diminished and foreign gum-tappers creeping into former Maya territories, indigenous leaders entered into a negotiated settlement with the Mexican federal government. The final treaties were signed in 1936, erasing the last vestiges of Maya national sovereignty in the region.

LAND REFORMS

Beginning in 1875, international demand for twine and rope made from henequen, a type of agave cactus that thrives in northern Yucatán, brought prosperity to Mérida, the state capital. Beautiful mansions were built by entrepreneurs who lived the good life, sending their children to school in Europe and cruising with their wives to New Orleans in search of new luxuries and entertainment. Port towns were developed on the Gulf coast, and a two-kilometer (1.2-mile) wharf in Progreso was built to accommodate the large ships that came for sisal (hemp from the henequen plant).

The only thing that didn't change was the lifestyle of indigenous people, who provided most of the labor on colonial haciendas. Henequen plants have incredibly hard, sharp spines and at certain times emit a horrendous stench. Maya workers labored long, hard hours, living in constant debt to the hacienda store.

Prosperity helped bring the Yucatán to the attention of the world. But in 1908, an American journalist named John Kenneth Turner stirred things up when he documented the difficult lives of the indigenous plantation workers and the accompanying opulence enjoyed by the owners. The report set a series of reforms into motion. Carrillo Puerto, the first socialist governor of Mérida, helped native workers set up a labor union,

The banner on this mural reads "The Maya region is not an ethnographic museum; it is a people on the move."

educational center, and political club that served to organize and focus resistance to the powerful hacienda system. Carrillo made numerous agrarian reforms, including decreeing that abandoned haciendas could be appropriated by the government. With his power and popularity growing, conservatives saw only one way to stop him: In 1923, Carrillo Puerto was assassinated.

By then, though, the Mexican Revolution had been won and reforms were being made throughout the country, including redistribution of land and mandatory education. Mexico entered its golden years, a 40-year period of sustained and substantial growth dubbed the Mexican Miracle, all the more miraculous because it took place in defiance of the worldwide Great Depression. In the late 1930s, President Lázaro Cárdenas undertook a massive nationalization program, claiming the major electricity, oil, and other companies for the state, and created state-run companies like PEMEX, the oil conglomerate still in existence today. In the Yucatán, Cárdenas usurped large parts of hacienda lands—as much as half of the Yucatán's total arable land, by some accounts, most dedicated to the growing of henequen—and redistributed it to poor farmers.

THE PRI YEARS

The economic prosperity allowed the ruling Institutional Revolutionary Party (PRI) to consolidate power, and before long it held every major office in the federal government, and most state governments as well. The Mexican Miracle had not ameliorated all social inequalities—and in fact had exacerbated some—but the PRI grew increasingly intolerant of dissent. Deeply corrupt, the party—and by extension the state—resorted to brutal and increasingly blatant repression to silence detractors. The most notorious example was the gunning down of scores of student demonstrators—some say up to 250—by security forces in 1968 in Mexico City's Tlatelolco Plaza. The massacre took place at night; by morning the plaza was cleared of bodies and scrubbed of blood, and the government simply denied that it ever happened.

The oil crisis that struck the United States in the early 1970s was at first a boon for Mexico, whose coffers were filled with money from pricey oil exports. But a failure to diversify the economy left Mexico vulnerable; as oil prices stabilized, the peso began to devalue. It had fallen as much as 500 percent by 1982, prompting then-president López Portillo to nationalize Mexico's banks.

henequen, a type of agave cactus that thrives in northern Yucatán

Foreign investment quickly dried up, and the 1980s were dubbed La Década Perdida (The Lost Decade) for Mexico and much of Latin America, a time of severe economic stagnation and crisis. In September 1985, a magnitude-8.1 earthquake struck Mexico City, killing 9,000 people and leaving 100,000 more homeless. It seemed Mexico had hit its nadir.

Yet it was during this same period that Cancún began to take off as a major vacation destination, drawing tourism and much-needed foreign dollars into the Mexican economy. The crises were not over—the implementation of the North American Free Trade Agreement (NAFTA) in 1994 was met simultaneously by a massive devaluation of the peso and an armed uprising by a peasant army called the Zapatistas in the state of Chiapas—but Mexico's economy regained some of its footing. A series of electoral reforms implemented in the late 1980s and through the 1990s paved the way for the historic 2000 presidential election, in which an opposition candidate—former Coca-Cola executive Vicente Fox of the right-of-center Partido de Acción Nacional (PAN)—defeated the PRI, ending the latter's 70-year reign of power. Fox was succeeded in 2006 by another PAN member, Felipe Calderón Hinojosa, in an election in which the PRI finished a distant third.

President Calderón campaigned on a promise to expand Mexico's job market and encourage foreign investment, including for new tourism projects in the Yucatán and elsewhere. But it was another pledge—to break up the drug trade and the cartels that controlled it—that consumed his entire presidency and plunged parts of Mexico into a spasm of violence unlike any since the revolution.

THE DRUG WAR

"The Drug War," as it is generally called, has its roots in the insatiable demand for drugs in the United States. Mexican drug cartels gained strength as operations in Colombia and the Caribbean were choked off in the 1990s; drug production in Mexico itself has also grown, especially methamphetamines. Mexican cartels traditionally operated within strictly defined territories—such as the Gulf cartel, the Sinaloa cartel, the Juárez cartel—and did so largely with impunity, thanks to corruption in the police and PRI-controlled local governments. The arrangement, though illicit, kept violence to a minimum as cartels kept to themselves and politicians and police turned a blind eye.

In 2006, encouraged by the United States, President Calderón dispatched the Mexican military to various northern cities to break up the cartels and their distribution networks. They achieved some initial success, but the broader effect was to disrupt the longtime balance of power. As control of routes and territories wavered, violence between rival cartels erupted with shocking speed and ferocity, with frequent shoot-outs and a gruesome cycle of attacks and reprisals. The official death toll is a staggering 60,000 people, though some estimates put it at double that. The vast majority of victims were gang-affiliated, though at least 2,000 police, soldiers, journalists, politicians, and even children were killed; 27,000 people are still classified as "missing." It's notable that virtually all the weapons used in the Drug War were smuggled into Mexico from the United States.

Drug violence fell in 2012 with the election of PRI presidential candidate Enrique Peña Nieto, who scaled back the aggressive military-guided approach used by his predecessor. Violence continued falling for five years, and cities like Ciudad Juarez and Chihuahua seemed to reawaken. At the same time, Mexican and U.S. agents scored several high-profile arrests and extradition of top drug cartel figures, including Joaquin "El Chapo" Guzmán Loera in Mazatlán. (A year later, El Chapo escaped his maximum-security prison via a sophisticated mile-long tunnel, adding to his fame and embarrassing Mexican authorities; he was recaptured in January 2016 and eventually extradited to the United States.) The arrests were cheered, but they also sparked succession conflicts within the cartels; violence surged again in 2017, mostly among cartel members, but spilled into previously tranquil places like Playa del Carmen.

MEXICO TODAY

In 2012, Mexico's national soccer team won its first Olympic gold medal, defeating heavily favored Brazil at the London games. It was a small blessing perhaps, but one that lifted the country's collective spirit. The lull in drug violence helped tourism bounce back stronger than ever, with record numbers of visitors, especially to Cancún and the Riviera Maya. The region is in the midst of a US$1 billion infrastructure overhaul, including new roads, bridges, and bus and ferry terminals. Such progress could be undermined, however, if the recent uptick of violence proves more than a temporary flare-up. In the meantime, U.S. president Donald Trump has helped to unite Mexicans, if only in opposition to his insults and obsessions over crime, immigration, and building a border wall. Former president Vicente Fox has emerged as an unlikely online sensation, trolling Trump with wry Tweets and video posts.

Government and Economy

GOVERNMENT

Mexico enjoys a constitutional democracy modeled after that of the United States, including a president (who serves one six-year term), a two-house legislature, and a judiciary branch. For 66 years (until the year 2000), Mexico was controlled by one party, the so-called moderate Partido Revolucionario Institucional (PRI). A few cities and states elected candidates from the main opposition parties—the conservative Partido de Acción Nacional (PAN) and leftist Partido de la Revolución Democrática (PRD)—but the presidency and most of the important government positions were passed from one hand-picked PRI candidate to the next, amid rampant electoral fraud.

Indeed, fraud and corruption have been ugly mainstays of Mexican government for generations. In the 1988 presidential election, PRI candidate Carlos Salinas Gortari officially garnered 51 percent of the vote, a dubious result judging from polls leading up to the election, and rendered laughable after a mysterious "breakdown" in the election tallying system delayed the results for several days.

Salinas Gortari ended his term under the same heavy clouds of corruption and fraud that ushered him in, accused of having stolen millions of dollars from the federal government during his term. That said, Salinas pushed through changes such as increasing the number of Senate seats and reorganizing the federal electoral commission that helped usher in freer and fairer elections. He also oversaw the adoption of NAFTA in 1993, which has sped up Mexico's manufacturing industry but seriously damaged other sectors, especially small farmers, many of whom are indigenous.

The 1994 presidential election was marred by the assassination in Tijuana of the PRI candidate Luis Donaldo Colosio, the country's first major political assassination since 1928. Colosio's campaign manager, technocrat Ernesto Zedillo, was nominated to fill the candidacy and eventually elected. Zedillo continued with reforms, and in 2000, for the first time in almost seven decades, the opposition candidate officially won. PAN candidate Vicente Fox, a businessman and former Coca-Cola executive from Guanajuato, took the reins, promising continued electoral reforms, a stronger private sector, and closer relations with the United States. He knew U.S. president-elect George W. Bush personally, having worked with him on border issues during Bush's term as governor of Texas. Progress was being made until the terrorist attacks of September 11, 2001, pushed Mexico far down on the U.S. administration's priority list. With Mexico serving a term on the U.N. Security Council, Fox came under intense pressure from the United States to support an invasion of Iraq. He ultimately refused—Mexican people were overwhelmingly opposed to the idea—but it cost Fox dearly in his relationship with Bush. The reforms he once seemed so ideally poised to achieve were largely incomplete by the time Fox's term ended.

The presidential elections of 2006 were bitterly contested and created—or exposed—a deep schism in the country. The eventual winner was PAN candidate Felipe Calderón Hinojosa, a former secretary of energy under Fox. His main opponent, Andrés Manuel López Obrador, was a former mayor of Mexico City and member of the left-leaning PRD. Though fraught with accusations and low blows, the campaign also was a classic clash of ideals, with Calderón advocating increased foreign investment and free trade, and López Obrador assailing the neoliberal model and calling for government action to reduce poverty and strengthen social services. Both men claimed victory after Election Day; when Calderón was declared the winner, López Obrador alleged widespread fraud and called for a total recount. His supporters blocked major thoroughfares throughout the country for weeks. The Mexican Electoral Commission did a selective recount and affirmed a Calderón victory; the official figures set the margin at under 244,000 votes out of 41 million cast, a difference of just 0.5 percent. Calderón's inauguration was further marred by legislators fist-fighting in the chamber and the new president shouting his oath over jeers and general ruckus.

Calderón was confronted with a number of thorny problems upon inauguration, including a protest in Oaxaca that had turned violent, and spiraling corn prices that in turn drove up the cost of tortillas, the most basic of Mexican foods. While addressing those and other issues, he pressed forward with promised law-and-order reforms, raising police officers' wages and dispatching the Mexican military to stanch rampant gang- and drug-related crime in cities like Tijuana and Juárez. The latter sparked an all-out war between cartels, police, and the military.

In 2012, Mexicans elected Enrique Peña Nieto, the PRI candidate, as president. The results may be less a sign that Mexicans have forgiven the PRI its misdeeds of the not-so-distant past, and more that they're simply exhausted by the violence that's taken place under the PAN (whose candidate finished a distant third). Peña Nieto has focused on addressing drug abuse, unemployment, and corruption on a local level, rather than the drug war, though he is widely seen as ineffectual and his approval ratings have never been high. He was roundly criticized for a too-tepid response to the kidnapping and murder of 43 student-teachers in the state of Guerrero in September 2014; a local mayor, the mayor's wife, and over 40 police officers were eventually arrested in connection with the killings. Peña Nieto earned praise for rejecting U.S. president Trump's border wall proposal and standing firm in negotiations over the North American Free Trade Agreement, or NAFTA. The 2018 presidential election resulted in a victory for Lopez Obrador, who will take office in December.

ECONOMY
Oil

Oil is a leading industry on the Yucatán Peninsula and throughout the Gulf coast, from Campeche to the Texas border. Mexico has long been one of the largest oil producers in the Western Hemisphere and the world, and for years it was a net exporter of crude oil and natural gas to the United States and elsewhere. However, declining crude oil production in the Gulf of Mexico, a lack of refining capacity in Mexico, and the rapid expansion of U.S. natural gas production (and high Mexican demand for natural gas) has turned the relationship on its head. Mexico still exports crude oil to the United States, but is one of the main importers of American refined products such as gasoline. Mexico also imports natural gas and liquified natural gas from the United States, spurring plans for cross-border pipelines. Cities in the Yucatán Peninsula have long benefitted from Mexico's strong energy sector, but the effects of the worldwide decline in oil prices, coupled with a shifting relationship with the United States, may spell changes in the future.

Fishing

Yucatecan fisheries are abundant along the Gulf coast. At one time fishing was not much more than a family business, but today fleets of large purse seiners with their adjacent processing plants can be seen on the Gulf of Mexico. With the renewed interest in preserving fishing grounds for the future, the industry could continue to thrive for many years.

Tourism

Until the 1970s, Quintana Roo's economy amounted to very little. For a few years the chicle boom brought a flurry of activity up and down the state, with the gum being shipped from the harbor of Isla Cozumel. Native and hardwood trees have always been in demand; coconuts and fishing were the only other natural resources that added to the economy, but neither on a large scale.

With the development of an offshore sandbar—Cancún—into a multimillion-dollar resort town, tourism became the region's number one moneymaker. The development of the Riviera Maya (extending from Cancún to Tulum)—and now, the Costa Maya (south of Sian Ka'an to the border of Belize)—only guaranteed the continued success of the economy. New roads now give access to previously unknown beaches and Maya structures. Extra attention is going to archaeological zones ignored for hundreds of years; all but the smallest now have restrooms, ticket offices, and gift shops.

Fishing remains a major source of income for locals.

Regional Holidays and Celebrations

- Jan. 1: **New Year's Day**
- Jan. 6: **Día de los Reyes Magos:** Three Kings Day—Christmas gifts exchanged
- Feb. 2: **Virgen de la Candelaria:** Religious candlelight processions light up several towns
- Feb./Mar.: **Carnaval:** Seven-day celebration before Ash Wednesday; celebrated big on Isla Cozumel
- Mar. 21: **Birthday of Benito Juárez:** President of Mexico for five terms; born in 1806
- Mar. 21: **Vernal Equinox in Chichén Itzá:** A phenomenon of light and shadow displays a serpent slithering down the steps of El Castillo
- Apr. 19: **Festival de San Telmo:** Culmination of a two-week festival honoring the patron saint of fishermen; celebrated on Isla Holbox
- May 1: **Día del Trabajador:** Labor Day
- May 3: **Day of the Holy Cross:** Dance of the Pigs' Head performed in the town of El Cedral on Isla Cozumel
- May 5: **Cinco de Mayo:** Commemoration of the Mexican army's 1862 defeat of the French at the Battle of Puebla
- Sept. 16: **Independence Day:** Celebrated on the night of the 15th
- Sept. 29: **Fiesta de San Miguel Arcángel:** Celebration of Isla Cozumel's patron saint
- Oct. 12: **Día de la Raza:** Indigenous Peoples Day; celebrated instead of Columbus Day
- Nov. 1-2: **All Souls' Day and Day of the Dead:** Church ceremonies and graveside celebrations in honor of the deceased
- Nov. 20: **Día de la Revolución:** Celebration of the beginning of the Mexican Revolution in 1910
- Dec. 12: **Virgen de Guadalupe:** Religious celebration in honor of Mexico's patron saint
- Dec. 25: **Christmas:** Celebrated on the night of the 24th

People and Culture

DEMOGRAPHICS

Today, 75-80 percent of the Mexican population is estimated to be mestizo (a combination of the indigenous and Spanish-Caucasian races). Only 10-15 percent are considered to be indigenous peoples. For comparison, as recently as 1870, the indigenous made up more than 50 percent of the population. While there are important native communities throughout Mexico, the majority of the country's indigenous peoples live in the Yucatán Peninsula, Oaxaca, and Chiapas.

RELIGION

The vast majority of Mexicans are Roman Catholic, especially in the generally conservative Yucatán Peninsula. However, a vigorous evangelical movement gains more and more converts every year.

Papel Picado

Mexicans are famous for their celebrations—whether it's to honor a patron saint or to celebrate a neighbor's birthday, partying is part of the culture. Typically, fiestas feature live music, lots of food, fireworks, and brightly colored decorations, often including *papel picado* (literally, diced paper).

Papel picado is tissue paper cut or stamped with a design that reflects the occasion in some way: a manger scene at Christmas, church bells for a wedding, skeletons in swooping hats for Day of the Dead. Once cut, row upon row of *papel picado* is strung across city streets, in front of churches, or in people's backyards. It typically stays up until wind or rain leaves just a thin cord and a few bits of torn paper as a reminder of the celebration that was.

LANGUAGE

The farther away you are from a city in the Yucatán—and in Mexico in general—the less Spanish you'll hear and the more dialects of indigenous languages you'll encounter. The government estimates that of the 10 million indigenous people in the country, about 25 percent do not speak Spanish. Of the original 125 native languages, 70 are still spoken, 20 of which are classified as Maya languages, including Tzeltal, Tzotzil, Chol, and Yucatec.

Although education was made compulsory for children in 1917, this law was not enforced in the Yucatán Peninsula until recently. Today, schools throughout the peninsula use Spanish-language books, even though many children do not speak the language. In some of the rural schools, bilingual teachers are recruited to help children make the transition.

ART

Mexico has an incredibly rich colonial and folk-art tradition. While not considered art to the people who make and use it, traditional indigenous clothing is beautiful, and travelers and collectors are increasingly able to buy it in local shops and markets. Prices for these items can be high, for the simple fact that they are hand-woven and can literally take months to complete. Valladolid is an especially good place to purchase pottery, carving, and textiles from around the Yucatán and beyond.

HOLIDAYS AND FESTIVALS

Mexicans take celebrations and holidays seriously—of their country, their saints, and their families. You'll be hard-pressed to find a two-week period when something or someone isn't being celebrated. On major holidays—Christmas, New Year's Eve, and Easter—be prepared for crowds at the beaches and ruins. Be sure to book your hotel and buy your airline and bus tickets well in advance; during holidays, the travel industry is saturated with Mexican travelers.

In addition to officially recognized holidays, villages and cities hold numerous festivals and celebrations: for patron saints, birthdays of officials, a good crop, a birth of a child. You name it, it's probably celebrated. Festivals typically take place in and around the central plaza of a town with dancing, live music, colorful decorations, and fireworks. Food booths are set up around the plaza and typically sell tamales (both sweet and savory), *buñuelos* (sweet rolls), tacos, *churros* (fried dough dusted with sugar), *carne asada* (grilled meat), and plenty of regional drinks.

Essentials

Transportation

GETTING THERE

For centuries, getting to the Yucatán Peninsula required a major sea voyage to one of the few ports on the Gulf of Mexico, only to be followed by harrowing and uncertain land treks limited to mule trains and narrow paths through the tangled jungle. Today, the peninsula is easily accessible. Visitors from around the world arrive every day via modern airports, a network of good highways, excellent bus service, or cruise ship.

Air

The main international airports on the Yucatán Peninsula are in Cancún and Mérida. The **Cancún** airport is by far the busiest, with dozens of daily domestic and international flights. There are smaller airports in **Cozumel** and **Chetumal**, and another reportedly being built in **Tulum**, though it remains far from completion. There also is an airport near **Chichén Itzá**, but at the time of research it was not receiving any flights. In addition, there are small airports in **Playa del Carmen, Mahahual,** and **Isla Holbox** for private planes and air taxis.

Most travelers use the Cancún airport—it's well located for those vacationing in the Caribbean as well as for those traveling inland. Fares typically are cheaper to Cancún than to any other airport in the region.

Travelers who are planning to spend their entire time inland often choose to fly to Mérida instead—the city itself is an important destination, and it's close to many of the area's key sights and archaeological ruins.

Similarly, many travelers who only will be visiting Isla Cozumel fly directly there—it's often more expensive than landing in Cancún but avoids the time and hassle of traveling from the mainland to the island (more time to dive and to enjoy the island!).

There also is an airport in Chetumal, which is typically used for domestic travel. However, for travelers planning to spend most of their time in the Costa Maya, this may be more convenient.

DEPARTURE TAX

There is a departure tax to fly out of any Mexican airport—the cost varies depending on the location (US$48 at the Cancún International Airport, US$18 at the Cozumel International Airport). Most airlines incorporate the tax into their tickets, but it's worth setting aside some cash just in case.

Bus

The Yucatán's main interstate bus hubs are Mérida and Cancún, with service to and from Mexico City, Veracruz, Oaxaca, and other major destinations in the country. There also are buses between Chetumal and cities in Belize and Guatemala.

Car

Foreigners driving into Mexico are required to show a valid driver's license, title, registration, and proof of insurance for their vehicle. Mexican authorities do not recognize foreign-issued insurance; Mexican vehicle insurance is available at most border towns 24 hours a day, and several companies also sell policies over the Internet. Do not cross the border with your car until you have obtained the proper papers.

Cruise Ship

Increasing numbers of cruise ships stop along Mexico's Caribbean coast every year, some

---

Previous: ferries run between islands; public transportation often consists of small vans like these, known as *combis*.

Navigating the Cancún Airport

Some travelers find Cancún's airport somewhat daunting to navigate. The key is to not get drawn into any of the many sales pitches you'll encounter. Leaving the plane, simply follow the crowd, queueing first for immigration, then retrieving your luggage, then queueing again for customs, where you're asked to press a button: Green means go, red means stop and have your bags searched. Once through customs, you'll enter a large, busy foyer packed with vendor booths, salespeople, and tourist office folks ranging from peppy to pushy, virtually all of whom you can ignore or politely rebuff with a *"no, gracias."* If you're renting a car, look for the booth of the company you've reserved with and let the attendant know you've arrived; he or she will direct you to a shuttle to take you to the rental center. If you need a taxi, look for one of three "Yellow Transfers" booths, the official airport taxi service. To catch a bus, walk out of the terminal—ignoring the hagglers and taxi drivers clustered in front—and look for the large ADO buses parked a few steps to your right; you can buy your ticket at the mobile desk set up there. If your resort has arranged transport for you, look for a driver outside the terminal with your name or the name of the resort on a sign. None of the options requires much walking so you don't really need a porter; if you do use one, a couple dollars per bag is the customary tip.

carrying as many as 5,000 people. Many sail out of Miami and Fort Lauderdale, stopping at Key West before continuing to Punta Venado (Riviera Maya), Isla Cozumel, and Mahahual.

Prices are competitive, and ships vary in services, amenities, activities, and entertainment. Pools, restaurants, nightclubs, and cinemas are commonplace. Fitness centers and shops also make ship life convenient. To hone in on the type of cruise you'd like to go on, research options on the Internet, in the travel

section of your local newspaper, and by contacting your travel agent.

If your budget is tight, consider traveling standby. Ships want to sail full and are willing to cut their prices—sometimes up to 50 percent—to do so. Airfare usually is not included. **Note:** Once you're on the standby list, you likely will have no choice of cabin location or size.

Neighboring Countries

Cancún is an important international hub, not only for tourists from North America and Europe but also for regional flights to Central America and the Caribbean. In southern Quintana Roo, Chetumal is the gateway to Belize, and there's a direct bus to Flores, Guatemala (the town neighboring the Tikal Archaeological Zone). Most travel to Guatemala, however, is through Chiapas, from the towns of Palenque and San Cristóbal de las Casas. Most travelers do not need prearranged visas to enter either country, but they may have to pay an entrance fee at the airport or border.

Cancún has long been a major gateway to Cuba, especially for Americans circumventing U.S. travel restrictions to the island. In 2014, the Obama administration made it much easier for Americans to travel to Cuba legally and directly, but many of those changes were rescinded by President Trump just three years later. For many Americans, Cancún remains a convenient and necessary portal to Cuba.

GETTING AROUND
Air

Although budget airlines like Interjet are starting to appear on the Mexican airline scene, flying domestically is still relatively expensive, and the Yucatán is no exception. Once you factor in the check-in process, security, and baggage claim, there are very few flights within the region that make sense travel-wise, unless your time is incredibly tight. And if that is the case, you may as well see what you can do by car or bus and start planning a return trip.

Bus

Mexico's bus and public transportation system is one of the best in Latin America, if not the Western Hemisphere. In the Yucatán Peninsula, ADO and its affiliate bus lines practically have a monopoly, but that has not made bus travel any less efficient or less affordable. Dozens of buses cover every major route many times per day, and even smaller towns have frequent and reliable service.

Buses come in three main categories:

First Class: Known as *primera clase* or sometimes *ejecutivo,* first class is the most common and the one travelers use most often. Buses have reclining seats and TVs where movies are played on long trips. First-class buses make some intermediate stops but only in large towns. The main first-class line in the Yucatán is ADO.

Deluxe Class: Usually called *lujo* (luxury), deluxe class is a step up; it often is slightly faster since it's typically nonstop. The main deluxe line is ADO-GL, which costs 10-25 percent more than regular ADO. ADO-GL buses have nicer seats and better televisions (and even more recent movies). Sometimes

there are even free bottles of water in a cooler at the back. Even nicer are ADO-Platino buses, which often charge twice as much as regular ADO. Platino offers cushy, extra-wide seats (only three across instead of four), headphones, and sometimes a light meal like a sandwich and soda.

Second Class: *Segunda clase,* or second class, is significantly slower and less comfortable than first class, and not all that much cheaper. Whenever possible, pay the dollar or two extra for first class. Second-class buses are handy in that you can flag them down anywhere on the roadside, but that is also precisely the reason they're so slow. In smaller towns, second class may be the only service available, and it's fine for shorter trips. The main second-class lines in the Yucatán are Mayab, Oriente, Noreste, and ATS.

For overnight trips, definitely take first class or deluxe. Not only will you be much more comfortable, second-class buses are sometimes targeted by roadside thieves because they drive on secondary roads and stop frequently.

Wherever bus service is thin, you can count on there being frequent *colectivos* or *combis*—vans or minibuses—that cover local routes. They can be flagged down anywhere along the road.

First-class buses have air-conditioning, reclining seats, and even movies.

Driving Distances in Kilometers

Ferry

Ferries are used to get to and from the region's most visited islands, including Isla Mujeres (reached from Cancún), Isla Cozumel (reached from Playa del Carmen), and Isla Holbox (reached from Chiquilá). Service is safe, reliable, frequent, and affordable.

Car

As great as Mexico's bus system is, a car is the best way to tour the Yucatán Peninsula. Most of the sights—ruins, deserted beaches, haciendas, caves, cenotes, wildlife—are well outside of the region's cities, down long access roads, or on the way from one town to

the next. Having a car also saves you the time and effort of walking or the cost of cabbing to all those "missing links"; it also allows you to enjoy the sights for as much or as little time as you choose.

If you're here for a short time—a week or less—and want to sightsee, definitely get a car for the simple reason that you'll have the option of seeing and doing twice as much. If renting for your entire vacation isn't feasible moneywise, consider getting a car for just a couple of days to explore a bit: Chichén Itzá and other nearby archaeological zones, DIY cenotes, and the less-accessible parts of Quintana Roo like the Sian Ka'an Biosphere

Driving in the Yucatán

Having a car can make exploring the Yucatán Peninsula quicker and easier, and there are many places you can only reach with your own wheels. Here are some tips to make your driving experience a bit smoother:

Off the highways, the biggest hazard are *topes* (speed bumps). They are common on all roads and highways, save the toll roads. They vary in size, but many are big and burly, and hitting them at even a slow speed can do a number on you, your passengers, and your car. As soon as you see a sign announcing an upcoming town or village, be ready to slow down.

Narrow one-way streets are common in many cities in the Yucatán. Fortunately, the **stop signs** in those areas usually have smaller plaques (beneath the big red one) indicating direction and right of way. A **black rectangle** means you have the right of way, a **red one** means you don't.

If you break down or run out of gas on a main road during daylight hours, stay with your car. **Los Ángeles Verdes** (The Green Angels, toll-free Mex. tel. 078 or 800/903-9200), a government-sponsored tow-truck and repair service, cruise many of these roads on the lookout for drivers in trouble 8am-6pm daily. They carry a CB radio, gas, and small parts, and are prepared to fix tires. If you have a cell phone—or happen to be near a pay phone—call your car rental agency first; the Ángeles Verdes are a great backup.

Reserve and the Costa Maya. You also may want a car for a day in Cozumel to check out the island. Cars aren't necessary to visit Cancún, Isla Mujeres, or Playa del Carmen.

CAR RENTAL

The best rates (and best vehicles) are typically found online with the major international rental chains like Hertz, Thrifty, Budget, and Avis. That said, there are many local agencies in cities like Cancún, and they occasionally have good deals.

- It's best to book on the car rental company's own website rather than a travel website. The prices are virtually the same, and if there are any problems, the rental office can't blame it on the other website.

- Ask your credit card company if your card provides free collision (liability) insurance on rental cars abroad. (Most do.) Unlike ordinary insurance, if you have an accident, you'll have to pay for repairs upfront and then file for reimbursement. The coverage is usually better, though, with zero deductible and coverage even on dirt roads. Remember you have to actually use the card to pay for the rental in order to get the benefit!

- Car rental agencies make most of their money off the insurance, not the vehicle. That's why they push so hard for you to buy coverage. They'll warn you that with credit card insurance you'll have to pay 100 percent of any damages upfront; this is true, but it will be reimbursed when you file a claim back home. They may require you to authorize a larger "hold" on your card, as much as US$5,000, for potential damages. This is no big deal—it's not an actual charge—but that amount will be unavailable for other purchases. Consider bringing two or more credit cards, especially if your credit limit is low.

- Third-party insurance is required by law, and rental agencies are technically required to provide it. However, rental agencies typically say third-party coverage is free for anyone who also purchases collision insurance. But if you decline their collision insurance (because you get it through your credit card), there's a charge for third-party coverage. Credit cards typically do not offer third-party coverage, so you end up having to pay it. It's less expensive than collision insurance, but still a bummer to pay.

Before driving off, the attendant will review

Taxi Scam

Beware of any taxi driver who tries to convince you that the hotel you're going to is closed, roach infested, flooded, burned down, has no running water, or was destroyed by a hurricane (add your disaster of choice). As sincere as the driver might seem, he is more often than not retaliating against hotels that refuse to pay a finder's fee. Taxi drivers in Cancún and throughout the Riviera Maya earn significant commissions—as much as US$10 per person *per night*—for bringing guests to certain establishments. Some hotels refuse to pay the fee, and taxi drivers, in turn, try to take their clients to "cooperative" hotels instead. Don't fall for it. You may have to be firm, but insist that your driver take you to the hotel of your choice. Your best option is to call ahead for a room reservation, which also serves to confirm that the hotel actually is open and operational.

the car for existing damage—be an active part of it and don't be shy about pointing out every nick, scratch, ding, and crack. If the care has hubcaps, be sure all the tires have them. Other things to confirm before driving off include:

- There is a spare tire (preferably a full-size, not temporary, one) and a working jack and tire iron.

- All doors lock and unlock, including the trunk.

- The headlights, brake lights, and turn signals work.

- All the windows roll up and down properly.

- The proper—and current—car registration is in the car. In some cases, your car rental contract serves as the registration.

- The amount of gas in the tank—you'll have to return it with the same amount.

- There is a 24-hour telephone number for the rental agency in case of an emergency.

HIGHWAYS AND ROAD CONDITIONS

Driving in the Yucatán isn't as nerve-racking as you might think. The highways are in excellent condition, and even secondary roads are well maintained. There are a few dirt and sand roads, mostly along the Costa Maya and in the Sian Ka'an Biosphere Reserve. If anything, frequent—and sometimes unexpected—*topes* (speed bumps) in small towns are the biggest driving hazard.

The main highways in the region are Highway 307, which runs the length of Mexico's Caribbean coast; Highway 180, the thoroughfare that links Cancún, Mérida, and Campeche City; and Highway 186, which crosses the southern portion of the Yucatán Peninsula and leads travelers to Campeche's Río Bec region and Comalcalco in Tabasco.

In the entire region, there are only two toll roads, both sections of Highway 180: between Mérida and Cancún (a whopping US$22—US$14 from Cancún to Valladolid, US$3 from Valladolid to Pisté, and US$5 from Pisté to Mérida) and between Campeche City and the town of Champotón (US$3.50). Although far from cheap, these toll roads can save you a significant amount of driving time, and are safer for driving at night. Secondary roads are free and pass through picturesque countryside and indigenous villages; they are slower and have more obstacles like pedestrians, bicycles, and speed bumps, but can be a rewarding way to go.

DRIVING SCAMS

Most travelers have heard horror stories about Mexican police and worry about being taken for all their money or trundled off to jail without reason. While it is true that there is corruption among the police, they don't target tourists; foreigners are, after all, the economic lifeblood of the region—the police don't want to scare them away.

As long as you are a careful and defensive driver, it is very unlikely you'll have any interaction with the police. Most travelers who are pulled over actually have done something wrong—speeding, running a stop sign, turning on red. In those situations, remain calm and polite. If you have an explanation, definitely give it; it is not uncommon to discuss a given situation with an officer. Who knows, you may even convince him you're right—it's happened to us!

Of greater concern are gas station attendants. Full service is the norm here—you pull up, tell the person how much you want, and the attendant does the rest. A common scam is for one attendant to distract you with questions about wiper fluid or gas additives while another starts the pump at 50 or 100 pesos. Before you answer any questions, be sure the attendant resets, or "zeroes," the pump before starting to pump.

Hitchhiking

Hitchhiking is not recommended for either men or women. That said, it sometimes can be hard to know what is a private vehicle and what is a *colectivo* (shared van). If there's no bus terminal nearby, your best bet is to look for locals who are waiting for public transportation and see which vans they take. If you have no choice but to hitch a ride, opt for a pickup truck, where you can sit in the back.

Tours

Local tour operators offer a vast range of organized trips. You pay extra, of course, but all arrangements and reservations are made for you, from guides and transportation to hotels and meals. Special-interest trips also are common—archaeological tours, hacienda and convent routes, bird-watching and dive trips. Ask around and surf the Internet—you'll find a world of organized adventure.

Visas and Officialdom

PASSPORTS

Gone are the days you could zip down to Mexico with just your driver's license and birth certificate. All nationalities must have a valid passport to enter Mexico by air, land, or sea.

VISAS AND TOURIST CARDS

Citizens of most countries, including the United States, Canada, and members of the EU, do not need to obtain a visa to enter Mexico. All foreigners, however, are issued a white tourist card when they enter, with the number of days that they are permitted to stay in the country written at the bottom, typically 30-60 days. If you plan to stay for more than a month, politely ask the official to give you the amount of time you need; the maximum stay is 180 days.

Hold onto your tourist card! It must be returned to immigration officials when you leave Mexico. If you lose it, you'll be fined and may not be permitted to leave the country (much less the immigration office) until you pay.

To extend your stay up to 180 days, head to the nearest immigration office a week *before* your tourist card expires. Be sure to bring it along with your passport. There, you'll fill out several forms, go to a bank to pay the processing fee (US$25 approximately), make photocopies of all the paperwork (including your passport, entry stamp, tourist card, and credit card), and then return to the office to get the extension. For every extra 30 days requested, foreigners must prove that they have US$1,000 available, either in cash or by showing a current credit card. The process can take anywhere from a couple of hours to a week, depending on the office.

Immigration Offices

- **Cancún:** Av. Nader at Av. Uxmal, tel. 998/881-3560, 9am-1pm Mon.-Fri.
- **Chetumal:** Av. México s/n, tel. 983/834-5046, 9am-1pm Mon.-Fri.

- **Cozumel:** Av. 15 at Calle 5 Sur, tel. 987/872-0071, 9am-1pm Mon.-Fri. There are also immigration agents at the airport (7am-9pm daily).
- **Isla Mujeres:** Av. Rueda Medina near Av. Morelos, tel. 998/877-0189, 9am-4pm daily
- **Playa del Carmen:** Plaza Antigua, Av. 10 s/n, 2nd Fl., tel. 984/873-1884, 9am-1pm Mon.-Fri.

CUSTOMS

Plants and fresh foods are not allowed into Mexico, and there are special limits on alcohol, tobacco, and electronic products. Archaeological artifacts, certain antiques, and colonial art cannot be exported from Mexico without special permission.

Above all, do not attempt to bring marijuana or any other narcotic into or out of Mexico. Jail is one place your trusty guidebook won't come in handy.

Returning home, you will be required to declare all items you bought in Mexico. Citizens of the United States are allowed to reenter with US$800 worth of purchases duty-free; the figure for other travelers varies by country.

CONSULATES

The consulates in Cancún handle passport issues (replacing a lost one, adding pages, etc.) and can help their citizens if they are in a serious or emergency situation, including hospitalization, assault, arrest, lawsuits, or death. They usually do not help resolve common disputes—with tour operators or hotels, for example.

In Cancún, the Casa Consular (Blvd. Kukulcán Km 13, tel. 998/840-6082, www.casaconsular.org, 9am-3pm Mon.-Fri.) helps international travelers connect with their consular representatives. The office also offers advice to those travelers needing to contact Mexican authorities with everything from immigration issues to theft. English is spoken.

Foreign consulates and consular agencies in the region include:

AUSTRALIA
Cancún: Av. Nader 28, 3rd Fl., tel. 998/898-1900, ext. 213, asis.consul.australia@gmail.com, by appointment only

CANADA
Cancún: Centro Empresarial, Blvd. Kukulcán Km 12, tel. 998/883-3360, www.canada.org.mx, 9am-1pm Mon.-Fri.
Playa del Carmen: Plaza Paraíso Caribe, Av. 10 between Calles 3 y 5, tel. 984/803-2411, www.canada.org.mx, 9am-1pm Mon.-Fri.

CUBA
Cancún: Pecari 17, tel. 998/884-3423, www.consuladocuba.com, 9am-1:30pm Mon.-Fri.

UNITED KINGDOM
Cancún: Torre La Europea, Blvd. Kukulcán Km 13, 24-hr tel. 551/670-3200, www.ukinmexico.fco.gov.uk, 8am-1pm Mon.-Fri.

UNITED STATES
Cancún: Torre La Europea, Blvd. Kukulcán Km 13, tel. 998/883-0272, https://mx.usembassy.gov/embassy-consulates/merida/consular-agencies, 8:30am-1pm Mon.-Fri., appointment required for some services
Cozumel (emergencies only): tel. 999/942-5700, conagentcozumel@state.gov, by appointment only
Mérida: Calle 60 between Calles 29 and 31, tel. 999/942-5700, https://mx.usembassy.gov/embassy-consulates/merida, 7:30am-4:30pm Mon.-Fri., appointment required for some services
Playa del Carmen: Plaza Progreso, Carretera Puerto Juarez-Chetumal between Calles 27 and 29, tel. 984/873-0303, https://mx.usembassy.gov/embassy-consulates/merida/consular-agencies, 9am-1pm Mon.-Fri.

UNDERAGE TRAVELERS

In the United States, anyone under 18 traveling internationally without *both* parents or legal guardians must present a signed, notarized letter from the parent(s) or guardian(s) granting the minor permission to leave the country. This requirement is aimed at preventing international abductions, but it causes frequent and major disruptions for vacationers.

Food and Accommodations

FOOD

Considered among the most distinct cuisines of the country, Yucatecan food reflects the influences of its Maya, European, and Caribbean heritage. Some of the most popular menu items include:

- *Cochinita Pibil:* pork marinated in achiote, orange juice, and other spices and then wrapped in banana leaves and baked.
- *Panucho:* small thick tortillas stuffed with refried beans and covered with shredded turkey, pickled onion, and avocado.
- *Poc-Chuc:* slices of pork marinated in orange juice and coated with a tangy sauce.
- *Salbute:* small handmade tortillas topped with shredded turkey, pickled onion, and slices of avocado.
- *Sopa de Lima:* turkey stock soup with shredded turkey, fried tortilla strips, and *lima* juice.

ACCOMMODATIONS

Lodging in the Yucatán Peninsula truly runs the gamut: campgrounds, hostels, small hotels, bed-and-breakfasts, boutique hotels, large modern hotels, and all-inclusive resorts. There also are fishing lodges in places like the Sian Ka'an Biosphere Reserve and the Costa Maya.

Taxes on your hotel bill, referred to generally as IVA (value-added tax; pronounced *EE-va* in Spanish), are usually 12 percent but can be as high as 17-22 percent. Be sure to ask if the rate you're quoted includes taxes (*¿Incluye impuestos?*); in many cases, especially at smaller hotels, the taxes are charged only if you pay by credit card.

You may be required to make a deposit in order to reserve a room, especially in popular areas during high season. However, in Mexico credit cards cannot be charged without a physical signature, so occasionally, smaller hotels won't accept them for deposits. Many hotels utilize PayPal or a similar service; those that do not will give you the name of their bank and account number, and you must transfer the money or stop by a branch and make the deposit in person. In either case, be sure to get a receipt, and notify the hotel after making the deposit.

Cancellation policies tend to be rather unforgiving, especially during high season; you may be required to give a month or more advance notice to receive even a partial refund. Trip insurance is a good idea if your plans are less than concrete.

Conduct and Customs

CLOTHING

Perhaps the single most abused social custom in Mexico is the use of shorts. Mexicans rarely wear them outside the home or off the beach, while many foreign travelers seem to have packed nothing but shorts. There is a bit more flexibility in beach areas, but it's worth getting in the habit of wearing long pants or skirts whenever going to dinner, attending performances, and especially when entering churches and government offices, where shorts and tank tops are considered inappropriate (and, in some cases, disrespectful).

Topless and nude sunbathing are not customary on Mexican beaches, and are rarely practiced in Cancún and other areas frequented by Americans and Canadians. However, on beaches popular with Europeans, especially Playa del Carmen and Tulum, it is more commonplace. Wherever you are, take a look around to help decide whether baring some or all is appropriate.

PHOTOGRAPHING LOCALS

No one enjoys having a stranger take his or her picture for no good reason, and Mexicans—indigenous or otherwise—are no different. The best policy is simply not to take these photographs unless you've first asked the person's permission and he or she has agreed. **Tip:** If the potential subject of your photo is a vendor, buy something and *then* ask if you can take a photo—you're more likely to get a positive response.

GREETINGS

Even a small amount of Spanish can go a long way in showing respect and consideration for people you encounter. Make a point of learning basic greetings like *buenos días* (good morning) and *buenas tardes* (good afternoon) and using them in passing, or as preface to a conversation; it is considered somewhat impolite to launch into a discussion without greeting the other person first.

Travel Tips

WHAT TO TAKE

Essentials for the Yucatán include sunscreen, sunglasses, and a billed hat. If you wear contacts or glasses, bring a replacement set. A good pair of shoes—or at least Teva-style sandals—is vital for exploring Maya ruins safely, and insect repellent definitely can come in handy. If you lose or forget something, Cancún, Cozumel, Playa del Carmen, Tulum, and Chetumal all have huge supermarkets, including Walmart.

ACCESS FOR TRAVELERS WITH DISABILITIES

Mexico has made many improvements for the blind and people in wheelchairs—many large stores and tourist centers have ramps or elevators. A growing number of hotels also have rooms designed for guests with disabilities, and museums occasionally create exhibits with, for example, replicas of Maya artifacts or folk art that visually impaired travelers can hold and touch. That said, Mexico is still a hard place to navigate if you have a disability. Smaller towns are the most problematic, as their sidewalks can be narrow, and even some main streets are not paved. Definitely ask for help—for what Mexico lacks in infrastructure, its people often make up for in graciousness.

TRAVELING WITH CHILDREN

The Yucatán Peninsula is a great place to take kids, whether youngsters or teenagers. The variety of activities and relative ease of transportation help keep everyone happy and engaged. Cancún and the Riviera Maya are especially family friendly, with several different ecoparks and water parks, miles of beaches, and (if all else fails) plenty of malls with movie theaters, arcades, bowling, mini-golf, aquariums, and more. Perhaps best of all, Mexico is a country where family is paramount, so kids—even fussy ones—are welcome just about everywhere.

WOMEN TRAVELING ALONE

Solo women should expect a certain amount of unwanted attention, mostly in the form of whistles and catcalls. It typically happens as they walk down the street and sometimes comes from the most unlikely sources—we saw a man dressed as a clown turn mid-balloon animal to whistle at a woman walking by. Two or more women walking together attract much less unwanted attention, and a woman and man walking together will get none at all (at least of this sort—street vendors are a different story). While annoying and often unnerving, this sort of attention is almost always completely benign, and ignoring it is definitely the best response. Making eye contact or snapping a smart retort only will inspire more attention. Occasionally men will hustle alongside a woman and try to strike up a conversation—if you don't want to engage, a brief "*no, gracias*" should make that clear. To minimize unwanted attention, avoid revealing clothing, such as tight jeans, low-cut shirts, or bikini tops, as street wear.

Have child, will travel.

Carrying a notebook—or creating the appearance of working—also helps.

SENIOR TRAVELERS

Seniors should feel very welcome and safe visiting the Yucatán. Mexico is a country that affords great respect to *personas de la tercera edad* (literally, "people of the third age"), and especially in the tradition-minded Yucatán Peninsula. But as anywhere, older travelers should take certain precautions. The Yucatán, particularly inland areas, is known to be extremely hot and humid, especially May-July. Seniors should take extra care to stay cool and hydrated. Exploring the Maya ruins also can be hot, not to mention exhausting. Bring water and snacks, especially to smaller sites where they may not be commonly sold. Travelers with balance or mobility concerns should think twice about climbing any of the pyramids or other structures. They can be deceptively treacherous, with steps that are steep, uneven, and slick.

Cancún and Playa del Carmen have state-of-the-art hospitals, staffed by skilled doctors, nurses, and technicians, many of whom speak English. Most prescription medications are available in Mexico, often at discount prices. However, pharmacists are woefully under-trained, and you should always double-check the active ingredients and dosage of any pills you buy here.

GAY AND LESBIAN TRAVELERS

While openly gay women are still rare in Mexico, gay men are increasingly visible in large cities and certain tourist areas. Cancún and Playa del Carmen both have a visible gay presence and a number of gay-friendly venues. Nevertheless, many locals—even in large cities—are not accustomed to open displays of homosexuality and may react openly and negatively. Many hotel attendants also simply don't understand that two travel companions of the same gender may prefer one bed—in some cases they will outright refuse to grant the request. Some couples find it easier to book a room with two queen-size beds and just sleep in one.

TRAVELING WITH IMPORTANT DOCUMENTS

Scan and/or make copies of your passport and tourist card. Whether you're traveling solo or with others, leave a copy of each with someone you trust at home. Store another copy online (i.e., your email account or on the cloud) and if you have a travel companion, give a copy to him or her. Be sure to carry a *copy* of your passport and tourist card in your purse or wallet and leave the originals in the hotel safe or locked in your bag; they're a lot more likely to be lost or stolen on the street than taken by hotel staff. When you move from place to place, carry your passport and important documents in a travel pouch, always under your clothing. Write down your credit card and ATM numbers and the 24-hour service numbers and keep those in a safe place.

Health and Safety

SUNBURN

Common sense is the most important factor in avoiding sunburn. Use waterproof and sweatproof sunscreen with a high SPF. Reapply regularly—even the most heavy-duty waterproof sunscreen washes off faster than it claims to on the bottle (or gets rubbed off when you use your towel to dry off). Be extra careful to protect parts of your body that aren't normally exposed to the sun—a good way to cover every inch is to apply sunscreen *before* you get dressed—and give your skin a break from direct sun every few hours. Remember that redness from a sunburn takes several hours to appear—that is, you can be sunburned long before you *look* sunburned.

If you get sunburned, treat it like any other burn by running cool water over it for as long and as often as you can. Do not expose your skin to more sun. Re-burning the skin can result in painful blisters that can easily become infected. There are a number of products designed to relieve sunburns, most with aloe extracts. Finally, be sure to drink plenty of water to keep your skin hydrated.

HEAT EXHAUSTION AND HEAT STROKE

The symptoms of heat exhaustion are cool moist skin, profuse sweating, headache, fatigue, and drowsiness. It is associated with dehydration and commonly happens during or after a strenuous day in the sun, such as while visiting ruins. You should get out of the sun, remove any tight or restrictive clothing, and sip a sports drink such as Gatorade.

Cool compresses and raising your feet and legs help too.

Heat exhaustion is not the same as heat stroke, and is distinguished by a high body temperature, a rapid pulse, and sometimes delirium or even unconsciousness. It is an extremely serious, potentially fatal condition, and victims should be taken to the hospital immediately. In the meantime, wrap the victim in wet sheets, massage the arms and legs to increase circulation, and do not administer large amounts of liquids. Never give liquids if the victim is unconscious.

DIARRHEA

Diarrhea is not an illness in itself, but your body's attempt to get rid of something bad in a hurry; that something can be any one of a number of strains of bacteria, parasites, or amoebae that are often passed from contaminated water. No fun, it is usually accompanied by cramping, dehydration, fever, and, of course, frequent trips to the bathroom.

If you get diarrhea, it should pass in a day or two. Anti-diarrheals such as Lomotil and Imodium A-D will plug you up but don't cure you—use them only if you can't be near a bathroom. The malaise you feel from diarrhea typically is from dehydration, not the actual infection, so be sure to drink plenty of fluids—a sports drink such as Gatorade is best. If it's especially bad, ask at your hotel for the nearest *laboratorio* (laboratory or clinic), where a stool sample can be analyzed for around US$5 to determine if you have a parasitic infection or a virus. If it's a common infection, the lab technician will tell you what medicine to take. Be aware that medicines for stomach infection are seriously potent, killing not only the bad stuff but the good stuff as well; they'll cure you but leave you vulnerable to another infection. Avoid alcohol and spicy foods for several days afterward.

A few tips for avoiding diarrhea include:

- Only drink bottled water. Avoid using tap water even for brushing your teeth.

- Avoid raw fruits or vegetables that you haven't disinfected and cut yourself. Lettuce is particularly dangerous since water is easily trapped in the leaves. Also, as tasty as they look, avoid the bags of sliced fruit sold from street carts.

- Order your meat dishes well done, even if it's an upscale restaurant. If you've been to a market, you'll see that meat is handled very differently here.

INSECTS

Insects are not of particular concern in the Yucatán, certainly not as they are in other parts of the tropics. Mosquitoes are common, but are not known to carry malaria. Dengue fever, also transmitted by mosquitoes, is present but still rare. Some remote beaches, like Isla Holbox and the Costa Maya, may have sand flies or horseflies, but they have been all but eliminated in the more touristed areas. Certain destinations are more likely to be buggy, like forested archaeological zones and coastal bird-watching areas, and travelers should bring and use insect repellent there, if only for extra comfort.

VACCINATIONS

Vaccines are recommended for anyone traveling to Cancun, Cozumel, and the surrounding areas. Be aware that some vaccines require several months to be effective, so plan ahead. The Centers for Disease Control (CDC) recommend all travelers be vaccinated against flu, typhoid, and hepatitis A, the latter being spread through contaminated food and water. A hepatitis B vaccine is recommended for anyone at risk of exposure to bodily fluids, such as sexual contact, tattooing, or needle sharing. (Combination hepatitis A and B vaccines are widely available.) Likewise, a rabies vaccine is recommended for travelers whose plans put them at high risk of animal bites, such as hiking or caving in remote areas. Malaria, dengue, and Zika, all spread by mosquitos, are also present but transmission is not common in most tourist areas. Some medications can help prevent malaria infection, but there is no vaccine for these diseases. The best prevention is to be vigilant against mosquito bites, including slathering on insect repellant (except children under 2 months) and using long sleeves and pants. Mosquitos bite day and night, but especially around sunrise and sunset. The CDC recommends pregnant women not travel to this region due to the risk of Zika.

CRIME

The Yucatán Peninsula is generally quite safe, and few travelers report problems with crime of any kind. There has been an uptick of violent crime in Cancun and Playa del Carmen since 2017, and the U.S. State Department issued an advisory to travelers to "exercise increased caution." However, the incidents are almost certainly related to drug cartel rivalries, with particular people targeted, as opposed to random muggings and assaults. While certainly shocking, this sort of violence rarely impacts tourists, assuming you steer well clear of drug activity. Drug possession has always been prosecuted vigorously

here, especially involving foreigners, and the cartel-related violence is another reason to avoid drugs while in Mexico. (Your country's embassy can do very little to help in these situations, by the way.)

Sexual assault and rape have been reported by women at nightclubs, sometimes after having been slipped a "date rape" drug. While the clubs are raucous and sexually charged by definition, women should be especially alert to the people around them and wary of accepting drinks from strangers.

In all areas, commonsense precautions are always recommended, such as taking a taxi at night instead of walking (especially if you've been drinking) and avoiding flashing your money and valuables, or leaving them unattended on the beach or elsewhere. Utilize the safety deposit box in your hotel room, if one is available; if not, consider locking your valuables in your luggage. If you rent a car, get one with a trunk so your bags will not be visible through the window.

Information and Services

MONEY
Currency and Exchange Rates
Mexico's official currency is the peso, divided into 100 centavos. It is typically designated with the symbol $, but you may also see MN$ (*moneda nacional,* or national currency). We've listed virtually all prices in their U.S. dollar equivalent, but occasionally use M$ to indicate the price is in Mexican pesos.

U.S. dollars and EU euros are accepted in a few highly touristed locations such as the Zona Hotelera in Cancún and the shopping districts of Cozumel and Playa del Carmen. However, you'll want and need pesos everywhere else, as most shopkeepers appreciate visitors paying in the local currency. **Note:** Foreign bills only are accepted because coins can't be changed to pesos.

At the time of research, US$1 was equal

to M$20; one Canadian dollars was approximately M$16; and one euro was M$23.

ATMs
Almost every town in the Yucatán Peninsula has an ATM, and they are without question the easiest, fastest, and best way to manage your money. Be aware that you may be charged a transaction fee by the ATM (US$2-3 typically) as well as your home bank (as much as US$10). It's worth asking your bank if it partners with a Mexican bank, and whether transaction fees are lower if you use that bank's cash machines. Also, be sure to use ATMs that are affiliated with a recognizable bank, to avoid exorbitant service charges.

Travelers Checks
With the spread of ATMs, travelers checks have stopped being convenient for most

travel, especially in a country as developed as Mexico. If you do bring them, you will have to exchange them at a bank or a *casa de cambio* (exchange booth).

Credit Cards

Visa and MasterCard are accepted at all large hotels and many medium and small ones, upscale restaurants, main bus terminals, travel agencies, and many shops throughout Mexico. American Express is accepted much less frequently. Some merchants tack on a 3-10 percent surcharge for any credit card purchase—ask before you pay. And many credit card companies, but not all, charge a foreign transaction fee; it pays to check in advance which of your cards has the lowest fees.

Cash

It's a good idea to bring a small amount of U.S. cash, on the off chance that your ATM or credit cards suddenly stop working; a US$200 reserve should be more than enough for a two-week visit. Stow it away with your other important documents, to be used only if necessary. Credit cards are widely accepted; the only exceptions are Isla Holbox and Tulum, especially along the beach road, where many restaurants accept cash only.

Tax

A 12 percent value-added tax (*IVA* in Spanish) applies to hotel rates, restaurant and bar tabs, and gift purchases. When checking in or making reservations at a hotel, ask if tax has already been added. In some cases, the tax is 17 percent.

Bargaining

Bargaining is common and expected in street and artisans' markets, but try not to be too aggressive. Some tourists derive immense and almost irrational pride from haggling over every last cent, and then turn around and spend several times that amount on beer or snacks. The fact is, most bargaining comes down to the difference of a few dollars or even less, and earning those extra dollars is a much bigger deal for most artisans than spending them is to most tourists.

Tipping

While tipping is always a choice, it is a key supplement to many workers' paychecks. In fact, for some—like baggers at the grocery store—the tip is the *only* pay they receive. And while dollars and euros are appreciated, pesos are preferred. **Note:** Foreign coins can't be changed to pesos, and thus are useless to

A little haggling is okay, but avoid going overboard.

Useful Telephone Numbers

TRAVELER ASSISTANCE

- Emergencies: 060 or 066

- Ángeles Verdes (Green Angels): 078 or 800/903-9200

- Directory Assistance: 044

LONG-DISTANCE DIRECT DIALING

- Domestic long-distance: 01 + area code + number

- International long-distance (United States only): 001 + area code + number

- International long-distance (rest of the world): 00 + country code + area code + number

LONG-DISTANCE COLLECT CALLS

- Domestic long-distance operator: 02

- International long-distance operator (English-speaking): 09

ESSENTIALS
INFORMATION AND SERVICES

workers. Average gratuities in the region include:

- Archaeological zone guides: 10-15 percent if you're satisfied with the service; for informal guides (typically boys who show you around the site), US$2-3 is customary.

- Gas station attendants: around US$0.50-1 if your windshield has been cleaned, tires have been filled, or the oil and water have been checked; no tip is expected for simply pumping gas.

- Grocery store baggers: US$0.25-0.50.

- Housekeepers: US$2-3 per day; either left daily or as a lump sum at the end of your stay.

- Porters: about US$2 per bag.

- Taxi drivers: Tipping is not customary.

- Tour guides: 10-15 percent; don't forget the driver—US$1-2 is typical.

- Waitstaff: 10-15 percent; make sure the gratuity is not already included in the bill.

COMMUNICATIONS AND MEDIA
Postal Service

Mailing letters and postcards from Mexico is neither cheap nor necessarily reliable. Delivery times vary greatly, and letters get "lost" somewhat more than postcards. Letters (under 20 grams) and postcards cost around US$0.60 to the United States and Canada, US$0.70 to Europe and South America, and US$0.75 to the rest of the world. Visit the **Correos de México** website (www.correos-demexico.gob.mx) for pricing on larger packages and other services.

Telephone

It is very likely you can continue to use your personal cell phone in Mexico for calls, text, and Internet, though the cost ranges from zero to outrageous. Most smartphones are functional in Mexico, and most carriers offer international roaming of some sort, whether standard or as an add-on. Just be sure to check the price for your particular plan. (And, of course, many phones allow for Wi-Fi calling.) If you have an unlocked GSM cell phone,

Cell Phone Calls

MEXICAN LANDLINE TO MEXICAN CELL PHONE:

· Within the same area code: 044 + 3-digit area code + 7-digit phone number

· Different area code: 045 + 3-digit area code + 7-digit phone number

MEXICAN CELL PHONE TO MEXICAN CELL PHONE:

· Within the same area code: 7-digit number only

· Different area code: 3-digit area code + 7-digit number

INTERNATIONAL LANDLINE/CELL PHONE TO A MEXICAN CELL PHONE:

· From U.S. or Canada: 011 + 52 + 1 + 3-digit area code + 7-digit number

· From other countries: international access code + 52 + 1 + 3-digit area code + 7-digit number

you can also purchase a local SIM card for around US$10, including US$5 credit, for use during your trip. Calls can be expensive, but text messaging is relatively cheap, including internationally.

Public telephones are becoming increasingly obsolete in Mexico. If you find one that's working, you'll need a *tarjeta Ladatel*—a plastic phone card, the size and stiffness of a credit card, bearing a chip—to get phone service. The cards are sold at mini-marts and supermarkets in 50-, 100-, and 200-peso denominations. Insert the card into any public pay phone, and the amount on the card will be displayed on the screen. Rates and dialing instructions (in Spanish and English) are inside the phone cabin. At the time of research, rates were roughly US$0.15 per call to a local landline, US$0.08 per minute to a local cell phone, and US$0.30 per minute for calls to the United States and Canada.

Internet cafés typically offer inexpensive **Web-based phone service.** Rates tend to be significantly lower than those of public telephones, and you don't have to worry about your card running out.

Beware of phones offering "free" collect or credit card calls; far from being free, their rates are outrageous.

Internet Access

Wireless Internet (Wi-Fi) is widely available, usually for free, at hotels, restaurants, coffee shops, and even in the central plazas of many towns and cities. Some first-class buses often offer Wi-Fi as well, though the connection can be spotty.

Internet cafés are sprinkled throughout the region. Most charge around US$1 per hour, though prices can be much higher in heavily touristed areas.

Newspapers

The most popular daily newspapers in the Riviera Maya are *Milenio Novedades* (https://sipse.com/milenio/), *Novedades Quintana Roo* (www.sipse.com/novedades), MILED (http://miledqroo.com.mx/), *¡Por Esto!* (www.poresto.net), and *El Diario de Yucatán* (www.yucatan.com.mx). The main national newspapers are also readily available, including *Reforma* (www.reforma.com), *La Prensa* (www.la-prensa.com.mx), and *La Jornada* (www.jornada.unam.mx). For news in English, check out The Yucatan Times (http://www.theyucatantimes.com); you'll find the *Miami Herald Cancún Edition* in Cancún and occasionally in Playa del Carmen and Isla Cozumel.

Radio and Television

Most large hotels and a number of midsize and small ones have cable or satellite TV, which usually includes CNN (though sometimes in Spanish only), MTV, and other U.S. channels. AM and FM radio options are surprisingly bland—you're more likely to find a good *rock en español* station in California than you are in the Yucatán.

MAPS AND TOURIST INFORMATION
Maps

A husband-and-wife team creates **MapChick maps** (www.cancunmap.com), exhaustively detailed maps of Cancún, Playa del Carmen, the Riviera Maya, Isla Cozumel, Isla Mujeres, and inland archaeological zones. They're as much guidebooks as maps, with virtually every building and business identified, many with short personal reviews, plus useful information like taxi rates, driving distances, ferry schedules, and more. Maps cost around US$15 and often come with a couple of smaller secondary maps; they're sold on the MapChick website as well as on Amazon.com.

Most local tourist offices distribute maps to tourists free of charge, though quality varies considerably. Car rental agencies often have maps, and many hotels create maps for their guests of nearby restaurants and sights.

Tourist Offices

Most cities in the region have a tourist information office or kiosk. Some are staffed with friendly and knowledgeable people and have a good sense of what tourists are looking for. At others, you'll seriously wonder how the people there were hired. It is certainly worth stopping in if you have a question—you may well get it answered, but don't be surprised if you don't.

Photography and Video

Digital cameras are as ubiquitous in Mexico as they are everywhere else, but memory cards can be prohibitively expensive; bring a spare one in case your primary memory card gets lost or damaged. If your card's capacity is relatively small, plan on uploading your photos to your tablet or the cloud.

Video is another great way to capture the color and movement of the region. Be aware that archaeological sites charge an additional fee to bring in a video camera; tripods often are prohibited.

WEIGHTS AND MEASURES
Measurements

Mexico uses the metric system, so distances are in kilometers, weights are in kilograms, gasoline is sold by the liter, and temperatures are given in Celsius. See the chart at the back of this book for conversions from the imperial system.

Time Zone

The entire Yucatán Peninsula used to be on Central Standard Time (along with Mexico City and much of central Mexico), with a region-wide shift in fall and spring for daylight saving. However, beginning in 2015, the state of Quintana Roo (which includes the entire Riviera Maya and Costa Maya) shifted to Eastern Standard Time for October-April only. Put another way, while the rest of the Yucatán and Central Time Zone "fall back" in October, Quintana Roo stays on daylight saving time, making it one hour ahead of its neighbors (and thus the same as the Eastern Time Zone). In April, the Central Time Zone "catches up" and the entire region is on the same hour again. The change is meant to give the Riviera Maya a longer-feeling day during the winter months and make travel from the U.S. East Coast easier. It can makes travel to and from the Yucatecan interior a bit confusing, however; be sure to double-check your flight and bus times to avoid missed connections.

Electricity

Mexico uses the 60-cycle, 110-volt AC current common in the United States. Bring a surge protector if you plan to plug in a laptop.

Resources

Spanish Glossary

The form of Spanish spoken in the Yucatán Peninsula is quite clear and understandable, and far less clipped or colloquial than in other countries. That's good news for anyone new to the language, and hoping to use their trip to learn more.

abarrotería: small grocery store

alcalde: mayor or municipal judge

alfarería: pottery

alfarero, alfarera: potter

amigo, amiga: friend

andador: walkway or strolling path

antojitos: Mexican snacks, such as huaraches, flautas, and quesadillas

artesanías: handicrafts, as distinguished from *artesano, artesana,* the person who makes handicrafts

audiencia: one of the royal executive-judicial panels sent to rule areas of Latin America during the 16th century

ayuntamiento: either the town council or the building where it meets

bienes raíces: literally "good roots," but popularly, real estate

boleto: ticket, boarding pass

bucear, buzo: to scuba dive, scuba diver

caballero: gentleman

cabecera: head town of a municipal district, or headquarters in general

cabrón: a bastard; sometimes used affectionately

cacique: chief or boss

calesa: early 1800s-style horse-drawn carriage; also called *calandria*

camionera central: central bus station; alternatively, *terminal camionera*

campesino: country person; farmworker

canasta: basket

cárcel: jail

casa de huéspedes: guesthouse, often operated in a family home

caudillo: dictator or political chief

charro, charra: cowboy, cowgirl

churrigueresque: Spanish baroque architectural style incorporated into many Mexican colonial churches, named after José Churriguera (1665-1725)

cofradía: Catholic fraternal service association, either male or female, mainly in charge of financing and organizing religious festivals

colectivo: a shared public taxi or minibus that picks up and drops off passengers along a designated route; alternatively, *combi*

colegio: preparatory school

colonia: city neighborhood or subdivision; similar to *fraccionamiento* or *barrio*

combi: a shared public minibus; alternatively, *colectivo*

comedor: small restaurant

correo: post office

criollo: person of all-Spanish descent born in the New World

cuadra: city block

Cuaresma: Lent

cuota: literally "toll," commonly refers to a toll highway

curandero, curandera: indigenous medicine man or woman

dama: lady

Domingo de Ramos: Palm Sunday

Don, Doña: title of respect, generally used for an older man or woman

ejido: a constitutional, government-sponsored form of community, with shared land owner-ship and cooperative decision making

encomienda: colonial award of tribute from a designated indigenous district

farmacia: pharmacy or drugstore

finca: farm

fraccionamiento: city sector or subdivision; similar to *colonia* or *barrio*

gasolinera: gasoline station

gringo: term referring to North American Cau-casians, sometimes derogatorily, sometimes not

grito: impassioned cry; *El Grito* commonly re-fers to Mexican Independence Day celebra-tions, from Hidalgo's *Grito de Dolores*

hacienda: large landed estate; also the gov-ernment treasury

impuestos, I.V.A. (pronounced EE-va): taxes, value-added tax

indígena: indigenous person; commonly, but incorrectly, an Indian (*indio*)

jardín: garden or small park

jejenes: "no-see-um" biting gnats

judiciales: the federal or state police, best known to motorists for their highway check-point inspections; alternatively, *federales*

lancha: small motorboat; alternatively, *panga*

larga distancia: long-distance telephone ser-vice, or the *caseta* (booth) where it's provided

licenciado: academic degree (abbr. Lic.) ap-proximately equivalent to a bachelor's degree

lonchería: small lunch counter, usually serv-ing juices, sandwiches, and *antojitos* (Mexican snacks)

machismo; macho: exaggerated sense of maleness; person who holds such a sense of himself

mescal: alcoholic beverage distilled from the fermented hearts of maguey (century plant)

mestizo: person of mixed European/indig-enous descent

milpa: native farm plot, usually of corn, squash, and/or beans

mordida: slang for bribe; literally, "little bite"

palapa: thatched-roof structure, often open air

panga: small motorboat; alternatively, *lancha*

parque central: town plaza or central square; alternatively, *zócalo*

PEMEX: government gasoline station, acro-nym for "Petróleos Mexicanos," Mexico's na-tional oil corporation

peninsulares: the Spanish-born ruling colo-nial elite

petate: a mat, traditionally woven of palm leaf

plan: political manifesto, usually by a leader or group consolidating or seeking power

plaza: shopping mall

policía: municipal police, alternatively *preven-tativa*

Porfiriato: the 34-year (1876-1910) ruling pe-riod of president-dictator Porfirio Díaz

pozole: popular stew of hominy in broth, usu-ally topped by shredded pork, cabbage, and diced onion

presidencia municipal: the headquarters, like a U.S. city or county hall, of a Mexican *mu-nicipio,* a county-like local governmental unit

propina: tip, as at a restaurant or hotel; alter-natively, *servicio*

pueblo: town or people

puta: whore

quinta: a villa or country house

retorno: highway turnaround

Semana Santa: literally Holy Week, the week before Easter, a popular travel period for Mexicans

temporada: season, as in *temporada alta/baja* (high/low season)

tenate: soft, pliable basket, without handle, woven of palm leaf

terminal camionera: central bus station; al-ternatively, *camionera central*

vecinidad: neighborhood, alternatively *barrio*

zócalo: town plaza or central square; alterna-tively, *parque central*

Abbreviations

Av.: *avenida* (avenue)

Blvd.: *bulevar* (boulevard)

Calz.: *calzada* (thoroughfare, main road)

Carr.: *carretera* (highway)

Col.: *colonia* (subdivision)

Nte.: *norte* (north)
Ote.: *oriente* (east)

Pte.: *poniente* (west)
s/n: *sin número* (no street number)

Yucatec Maya Glossary

The Maya language family includes 30 distinct languages, together spoken by nearly six million people in Mexico, Guatemala, and Belize. Yucatec Maya is spoken by around 800,000 people, and is the most commonly spoken Maya language in the Yucatán Peninsula (and second overall, after K'iche in Guatemala). Most ancient glyphs were written in early forms of Yucatec Maya or another Maya language, Ch'ol.

MAYA GODS AND CEREMONIES

Acanum: protective deity of hunters
Ahau Can: serpent lord and highest priest
Ahau Chamehes: deity of medicine
Ah Cantzicnal: aquatic deity
Ah Chuy Kak: god of violent death and sacrifice
Ahcit Dzamalcum: protective god of fishermen
Ah Cup Cacap: god of the underworld who denies air
Ah Itzám: the water witch
Ah kines: priests that consult the oracles and preside over ceremonies and sacrifices
Ahpua: god of fishing
Ah Puch: god of death
Ak'Al: sacred marsh where water abounds
Bacaboob: supporters of the sky and guardians of the cardinal points, who form a single god, Ah Cantzicnal Becabs
Bolontiku: the nine lords of the night
Chaac: god of rain and agriculture
Chac Bolay Can: butcher serpent living in the underworld
Chaces: priests' assistants in agricultural and other ceremonies
Cihuateteo: women who become goddesses through death in childbirth
Cit Chac Coh: god of war

Hetzmek: ceremony when the child is first carried astride the hip
Hobnil Bacab: bee god, protector of beekeepers
Holcanes: warriors charged with obtaining slaves for sacrifice
Hunab Ku: giver of life, builder of the universe, and father of Itzámna
Ik: god of the wind
Itzámna: lord of the skies, creator of the beginning, god of time
Ixchel: goddess of birth, fertility, and medicine; credited with inventing spinning
Ixtab: goddess of the cord and of suicide by hanging
Kinich: face of the sun
Kukulcán: quetzal-serpent, plumed serpent
Metnal: the underworld, place of the dead
Nacom: warrior chief
Noh Ek: Venus
Pakat: god of violent death
Zec: spirit lords of beehives

FOOD AND DRINK

alche: inebriating drink, sweetened with honey and used for ceremonies and offerings
ic: chili
itz: sweet potato
kabaxbuul: heaviest meal of the day, eaten at dusk and containing cooked black beans
kah: pinole flour
kayem: ground maize
macal: a root
muxubbak: tamale
on: avocado
op: plum
p'ac: tomatoes
put: papaya
tzamna: black bean
uah: tortillas
za: maize drink

ANIMALS

acehpek: dog used for deer hunting
ah maax cal: prattling monkey
ah maycuy: chestnut deer
ah sac dziu: white thrush
ah xixteel ul: rugged land conch
bil: hairless dog reared for food
cutz: wild turkey
cutzha: duck
hoh: crow
icim: owl
jaleb: hairless dog
keh: deer
kitam: wild boar
muan: evil bird related to death
que: parrot
thul: rabbit
tzo: domestic turkey
utiu: coyote

MUSIC AND FESTIVALS

ah paxboob: musicians
bexelac: turtle shell used as percussion instrument
chohom: dance performed in ceremonies related to fishing
chul: flute
hom: trumpet
kayab: percussion instrument fashioned from turtle shell
Oc na: festival where old idols of a temple are broken and replaced with new ones
okot uil: dance performed during the Pocan ceremony
Pacum chac: festival in honor of the war gods
tunkul: drum
zacatan: drum made from a hollowed tree trunk; one opening is covered with hide

ELEMENTS OF TIME

baktun: 144,000-day Maya calendar
chumuc akab: midnight
chumuc kin: midday
emelkin: sunset
haab: solar calendar of 360 days plus five extra days of misfortune, which complete the final month
kaz akab: dusk

kin: the sun, the day, the unity of time
potakab: time before dawn
yalhalcab: dawn

NUMBERS

hun: one
ca: two
ox: three
can: four
ho: five
uac: six
uuc: seven
uacax: eight
bolon: nine
lahun: ten
buluc: eleven
lahca: twelve
oxlahum: thirteen
canlahum: fourteen
holahun: fifteen
uaclahun: sixteen
uuclahun: seventeen
uacaclahun: eighteen
bolontahun: nineteen
hunkal: twenty

PLANTS AND TREES

ha: cacao seed
kan ak: plant that produces a yellow dye
ki: sisal
kiixpaxhkum: chayote
kikche: tree trunk that is used to make canoes
kuche: red cedar tree
k'uxub: annatto tree
piim: fiber of the cotton tree
taman: cotton plant
tauch: black zapote tree
tazon te: moss

MISCELLANEOUS WORDS

ah kay kin bak: meat-seller
chaltun: water cistern
cha te: black vegetable dye
chi te: eugenia, plant for dyeing
ch'oh: indigo
ek: dye
hadzab: wooden swords

halach uinic: leader
mayacimil: smallpox epidemic
palapa: traditional Maya structure constructed without nails or tools
pic: underskirt
ploms: rich people

suyen: square blanket
xanab: sandals
xicul: sleeveless jacket decorated with feathers
xul: stake with a pointed, fire-hardened tip
yuntun: slings

Spanish Phrasebook

Whether you speak a little or a lot, using your Spanish will surely make your vacation a lot more fun. You'll soon see that Mexicans truly appreciate your efforts and your willingness to speak their language.

Spanish commonly uses 30 letters—the familiar English 26, plus four straightforward additions: ch, ll, ñ, and rr.

PRONUNCIATION

Once you learn them, Spanish pronunciation rules—in contrast to English and other languages—generally don't change. Spanish vowels generally sound softer than in English.

Vowels

a like ah, as in "hah": *agua* AH-gooah (water), *pan* PAHN (bread), and *casa* CAH-sah (house)

e like eh, as in "hem": *mesa* MEH-sah (table), *tela* TEH-lah (cloth), and *de* DEH (of, from)

i like ee, as in "need": *diez* dee-EHZ (ten), *comida* ko-MEE-dah (meal), and *fin* FEEN (end)

o like oh, as in "go": *peso* PEH-soh (weight), *ocho* OH-choh (eight), and *poco* POH-koh (a bit)

u like oo, as in "cool": *uno* OO-noh (one), *cuarto* KOOAHR-toh (room), and *usted* oos-TEHD (you); when it follows a "q" the u is silent: *quiero* ki-EH-ro (I want); when it follows an "h" or has an umlaut, it's pronounced like "w": *huevo* WEH-vo (egg)

Consonants

b, d, f, k, l, m, n, p, q, s, t, v, w, x, y, z, and

ch pronounced almost as in English; **h** is silent

c like k, as in "keep": *cuarto* KOOAR-toh (room), *Tepic* tay-PEEK (capital of Nayarit state); when it precedes "e" or "i," pronounce **c** like s, as in "sit": *cerveza* sehr-VEH-sah (beer), *encima* ehn-SEE-mah (atop)

g like g, as in "gift" when it precedes "a," "o," "u," or a consonant: *gato* GAH-toh (cat), *hago* AH-goh (I do, make); otherwise, pronounce **g** like h, as in "hat": *giro* HEE-roh (money order), *gente* HEN-tay (people)

j like h, as in "has": *Jueves* HOOEH-vehs (Thursday), *mejor* meh-HOR (better)

ll like y, as in "yes": *toalla* toh-AH-yah (towel), *ellos* EH-yohs (they, them)

ñ like ny, as in "canyon": *año* AH-nyo (year), *señor* SEH-nyor (mister, sir)

r is lightly trilled: *pero* PEH-roh (but), *tres* TREHS (three), *cuatro* KOOAH-troh (four)

rr like a Spanish r, but with much more emphasis and trill: *burro* (donkey), *carretera* (highway), *ferrocarril* (railroad)

Note: The single exception to the above is the pronunciation of **y** when it's being used as the Spanish word for "and," as in *Eva y Leo.* In such case, pronounce it like the English ee, as in "keep": Eva "ee" Leo (Eva and Leo).

Accent

The rule for accent, the relative stress given to syllables within a given word, is straightforward. If a word ends in a vowel, an "n," or an "s," accent the next-to-last syllable; if not, accent the last syllable.

Pronounce *gracias* GRAH-seeahs (thank you),

orden OHR-dehn (order), and *carretera* kah-reh-TEH-rah (highway) with the stress on the next-to-last syllable.

Otherwise, accent the last syllable: *venir* vay-NEER (to come), *ferrocarril* feh-roh-cah-REEL (railroad), and *edad* eh-DAHD (age).

Exceptions to the accent rule are always marked with an accent sign: (á, é, í, ó, or ú), such as *teléfono* teh-LEH-foh-noh (telephone), *jabón* hah-BON (soap), and *rápido* RAH-pee-doh (rapid).

BASIC AND COURTEOUS EXPRESSIONS

Most Spanish-speakers consider formalities important. Whenever approaching anyone, try to say the appropriate salutation—good morning, good evening, and so forth. Standing alone, the greeting *hola* (hello) can sound brusque.

Hello. *Hola.*
Good morning. *Buenos días.*
Good afternoon. *Buenas tardes.*
Good evening. *Buenas noches.*
How are you? *¿Cómo está Usted?*
Very well, thank you. *Muy bien, gracias.*
Okay; good. *Bien.*
Not okay; bad. *No muy bien; mal.*
So-so. *Más o menos.*
And you? *¿Y usted?*
Thank you. *Gracias.*
Thank you very much. *Muchas gracias.*
You're very kind. *Muy amable.*
You're welcome. *De nada.*
Good-bye. *Adios.*
See you later. *Hasta luego.*
please *por favor*
yes *sí*
no *no*
I don't know. *No sé.*
Just a moment, please. *Un momento, por favor.*
Excuse me, please (when you're trying to get attention). *Disculpe* or *Con permiso.*
Excuse me (when you've made a mistake). *Lo siento.*
Pleased to meet you. *Mucho gusto.*
Do you speak English? *¿Habla Usted inglés?*

Is English spoken here? *¿Se habla inglés?*
I don't speak Spanish well. *No hablo bien el español.*
I don't understand. *No entiendo.*
How do you say ... in Spanish? *¿Cómo se dice ... en español?*
What is your name? *¿Cómo se llama Usted?*
My name is ... *Me llamo...*
Would you like ... *¿Quisiera Usted ...*
Let's go to ... *Vamos a...*

TERMS OF ADDRESS

When in doubt, use the formal *Usted* (you) as a form of address.

I *yo*
you (formal) *Usted*
you (familiar) *tu*
he/him *él*
she/her *ella*
we/us *nosotros*
you (plural) *ustedes*
they/them *ellos* (all males or mixed gender); *ellas* (all females)
mister, sir *señor*
missus, ma'am *señora*
miss, young lady *señorita*
wife *esposa*
husband *esposo*
friend *amigo* (male); *amiga* (female)
boyfriend; girlfriend *novio; novia*
son; daughter *hijo; hija*
brother; sister *hermano; hermana*
father; mother *padre; madre*
grandfather; grandmother *abuelo; abuela*

TRANSPORTATION

Where is ...? *¿Dónde está ...?*
How far is it to ...? *¿A cuánto está ...?*
from ... to ... *de...a...*
How many blocks? *¿Cuántas cuadras?*
Where (Which) is the way to ...? *¿Dónde está el camino a ...?*
the bus station *la terminal de autobuses*
the bus stop *la parada de autobuses*
Where is this bus going? *¿Adónde va este autobús?*
the taxi stand *la parada de taxis*

the train station *la estación de ferrocarril*
the boat *el barco* or *la lancha*
the airport *el aeropuerto*
I'd like a ticket to … *Quisiera un boleto a …*
first (second) class *primera (segunda) clase*
round-trip *ida y vuelta*
reservation *reservación*
baggage *equipaje*
Stop here, please. *Pare aquí, por favor.*
the entrance *la entrada*
the exit *la salida*
the ticket office *la taquilla*
(very) near; far *(muy) cerca; lejos*
to; toward *a*
by; through *por*
from *de*
the right *la derecha*
the left *la izquierda*
straight ahead *derecho; directo*
in front *en frente*
beside *al lado*
behind *atrás*
the corner *la esquina*
the stoplight *el semáforo*
a turn *una vuelta*
here *aquí*
somewhere around here *por aquí*
right there *allí*
somewhere around there *por allá*
street; boulevard *calle; bulevar*
highway *carretera*
bridge *puente*
toll *cuota*
address *dirección*
north; south *norte; sur*
east; west *oriente (este); poniente (oeste)*

ACCOMMODATIONS

hotel *hotel*
Is there a room? *¿Hay cuarto?*
May I (may we) see it? *¿Podría (podríamos) verlo?*
What is the rate? *¿Cuál es la tarifa?*
Is that your best rate? *¿Es su mejor precio?*
Is there something cheaper? *¿Hay algo más económico?*
a single room *un cuarto sencillo*
a double room *un cuarto doble*

double bed *cama matrimonial*
twin bed *cama individual*
with private bath *con baño privado*
hot water *agua caliente*
shower *ducha; regadera*
towels *toallas*
soap *jabón*
toilet paper *papel higiénico*
blanket *cobija*
sheets *sábanas*
air-conditioned *aire acondicionado*
fan *abanico; ventilador*
key *llave*
manager *gerente*

FOOD

I'm hungry. *Tengo hambre.*
I'm thirsty. *Tengo sed.*
menu *carta; menú*
order *orden*
glass *vaso*
fork *tenedor*
knife *cuchillo*
spoon *cuchara*
napkin *servilleta*
soft drink *refresco*
coffee *café*
tea *té*
drinking water *agua pura; agua potable*
carbonated water *agua mineral*
bottled uncarbonated water *agua sin gas*
beer *cerveza*
wine *vino*
milk *leche*
juice *jugo*
cream *crema*
sugar *azúcar*
cheese *queso*
snack *antojito; botana*
breakfast *desayuno*
lunch *almuerzo* or *comida*
daily lunch special *comida corrida*
dinner *cena*
the check *la cuenta*
eggs *huevos*
bread *pan*
salad *ensalada*

RESOURCES
SPANISH PHRASEBOOK

fruit *fruta*
mango *mango*
watermelon *sandía*
papaya *papaya*
banana *plátano*
apple *manzana*
orange *naranja*
lime *limón*
fish *pescado*
shellfish *mariscos*
shrimp *camarones*
meat (without) *(sin) carne*
chicken *pollo*
pork *puerco*
beef; steak *res; bistec*
bacon; ham *tocino; jamón*
fried *frito*
roasted *asado*
barbecue; barbecued *barbacoa; al carbón*
food to go *comida para llevar; para llevar*
delivery service *servicio a domicilio*

SHOPPING

money *dinero*
money-exchange bureau *casa de cambio*
I would like to exchange travelers
checks. *Quisiera cambiar cheques de
viajero.*
What is the exchange rate? *¿Cuál es el
tipo de cambio?*
How much is the commission? *¿Cuánto
cuesta la comisión?*
Do you accept credit cards? *¿Aceptan
tarjetas de crédito?*
money order *giro*
How much does it cost? *¿Cuánto cuesta?*
What is your final price? *¿Cuál es su último
precio?*
expensive *caro*
cheap *barato; económico*
more *más*
less *menos*
a little *un poco*
too much *demasiado*

HEALTH

Help me please. *Ayúdeme por favor.*
I am ill. *Estoy enfermo.*

Call a doctor. *Llame un doctor.*
Take me to ... *Lléveme a ...*
hospital *hospital; clinica medica*
drugstore *farmacia*
pain *dolor*
fever *fiebre*
headache *dolor de cabeza*
stomachache *dolor de estómago*
burn *quemadura*
cramp *calambre*
nausea *náusea*
vomiting *vomitar*
medicine *medicina*
antibiotic *antibiótico*
pill; tablet *pastilla*
aspirin *aspirina*
ointment; cream *pomada; crema*
bandage *venda*
cotton *algodón*
sanitary napkins *Kotex*
birth control pills *pastillas anticonceptivas*
contraceptive foam *espuma
anticonceptiva*
condoms *preservativos; condones*
contact lenses *pupilentes*
glasses *lentes*
dental floss *hilo dental*
dentist *dentista*
toothbrush *cepillo de dientes*
toothpaste *pasta de dientes*
toothache *dolor de dientes*
delivery service *servicio a domicilio*

POST OFFICE AND COMMUNICATIONS

long-distance telephone *teléfono de
larga distancia*
I would like to call ... *Quisiera llamar a ...*
collect *por cobrar*
person to person *persona a persona*
credit card *tarjeta de crédito*
post office *correo*
letter *carta*
stamp *estampilla, timbre*
postcard *tarjeta*
airmail *correo aereo*
registered *registrado*
money order *giro*

package; box *paquete; caja*
string; tape *cuerda; cinta*
Internet *internet*
Internet café *ciber café; ciber*
website *página web*
Web search *búsqueda*
link *enlace*
email *correo electrónico*
Skype *Skype*
Facebook *face*

AT THE BORDER

border *frontera*
customs *aduana*
immigration *migración*
tourist card *tarjeta de turista*
inspection *inspección; revisión*
passport *pasaporte*
profession *profesión*
marital status *estado civil*
single *soltero*
married; divorced *casado; divorciado*
widowed *viudado* (male); *viudada* (female)
insurance *seguro*
title *título*
driver's license *licencia de manejar*

AT THE GAS STATION

gas station *gasolinera*
gasoline *gasolina*
unleaded *sin plomo*
fill it up, please *lleno, por favor*
tire *llanta*
tire repair shop *vulcanizadora*
air *aire*
water *agua*
oil; oil change *aceite; cambio de aceite*
grease *grasa*
My … doesn't work. *Mi … no sirve.*
battery *batería*
radiator *radiador*
alternator *alternador*
generator *generador*
tow truck *grúa*
repair shop *taller mecánico*
tune-up *afinación*
auto parts store *refaccionería*

VERBS

In Spanish, verbs employ mostly predictable forms and come in three classes, which end in *ar*, *er*, and *ir*. Note that the first-person (*yo*) verb form is often irregular.

to buy *comprar*
I buy, you (he, she, it) buys *compro, compra*
we buy, you (they) buy *compramos, compran*

to eat *comer*
I eat, you (he, she, it) eats *como, come*
we eat, you (they) eat *comemos, comen*

to climb *subir*
I climb, you (he, she, it) climbs *subo, sube*
we climb, you (they) climb *subimos, suben*

Here are more (with irregularities indicated):

to do or make *hacer* (regular except for *hago*, I do or make)
to go *ir* (very irregular: *voy, va, vamos, van*)
to go (walk) *andar*
to love *amar*
to work *trabajar*
to want *desear, querer*
to need *necesitar*
to read *leer*
to write *escribir*
to repair *reparar*
to stop *parar*
to get off (the bus) *bajar*
to arrive *llegar*
to stay (remain) *quedar*
to stay (lodge) *hospedar*
to leave *salir* (regular except for *salgo*, I leave)
to look at *mirar*
to look for *buscar*
to give *dar* (regular except for *doy*, I give)
to carry *llevar*
to have *tener* (irregular but important: *tengo, tiene, tenemos, tienen*)

to come *venir* (similarly irregular: *vengo, viene, venimos, vienen*)

Spanish has two forms of "to be":

to be *estar* (regular except for *estoy,* I am)
to be *ser* (very irregular: *soy, es, somos, son*)

Use *estar* when speaking of location or a temporary state of being: "I am at home." *"Estoy en casa."* "I'm sick." *"Estoy enfermo."* Use *ser* for a permanent state of being: "I am a doctor." *"Soy doctora."*

NUMBERS

zero *cero*
one *uno*
two *dos*
three *tres*
four *cuatro*
five *cinco*
six *seis*
seven *siete*
eight *ocho*
nine *nueve*
10 *diez*
11 *once*
12 *doce*
13 *trece*
14 *catorce*
15 *quince*
16 *dieciséis*
17 *diecisiete*
18 *dieciocho*
19 *diecinueve*
20 *veinte*
21 *veintiuno*
30 *treinta*
40 *cuarenta*
50 *cincuenta*
60 *sesenta*
70 *setenta*
80 *ochenta*
90 *noventa*
100 *cien*
101 *cientiuno*
200 *doscientos*
500 *quinientos*

1,000 *mil*
10,000 *diez mil*
100,000 *cien mil*
1,000,000 *millón*
one half *medio*
one third *un tercio*
one fourth *un cuarto*

TIME

What time is it? *¿Qué hora es?*
It's one o'clock. *Es la una.*
It's three in the afternoon. *Son las tres de la tarde.*
It's 4am. *Son las cuatro de la mañana.*
six-thirty *seis y media*
a quarter till eleven *un cuarto para las once*
a quarter past five *las cinco y cuarto*
an hour *una hora*

DAYS AND MONTHS

Monday *lunes*
Tuesday *martes*
Wednesday *miércoles*
Thursday *jueves*
Friday *viernes*
Saturday *sábado*
Sunday *domingo*
today *hoy*
tomorrow *mañana*
yesterday *ayer*
January *enero*
February *febrero*
March *marzo*
April *abril*
May *mayo*
June *junio*
July *julio*
August *agosto*
September *septiembre*
October *octubre*
November *noviembre*
December *diciembre*
a week *una semana*
a month *un mes*
after *después*
before *antes*

Suggested Reading

Archaeology

Coe, Andrew. *Archaeological Mexico: A Guide to Ancient Cities and Sacred Sites.* Emeryville, CA: Avalon Travel Publishing, 2001.

Coe, Michael D. *Breaking the Maya Code.* New York: Thames and Hudson, 2012. A fascinating account of how epigraphers, linguists, and archaeologists succeeded in deciphering Maya hieroglyphics.

Coe, Michael D. *The Maya.* New York: Thames and Hudson, 2011. A well-illustrated, easy-to-read volume on the Maya people.

Ferguson, William M. *Maya Ruins of Mexico in Color.* Norman, OK: University of Oklahoma Press, 1985. Good reading before you go, but too bulky to carry along. Oversized with excellent drawings and illustrations of the archaeological structures of the Maya.

Maya: Divine Kings of the Rain Forest. Cologne: Könemann, 2006. A beautifully compiled book of essays, photographs, and sketches relating to the Maya, past and present. Too heavy to take on the road but an excellent read.

Stephens, John L. *Incidents of Travel in Central America, Chiapas, and Yucatán.* 2 vols. New York: Cosimo Classics, 2008. Good companions to refer to when traveling in the area. Stephens and illustrator Frederick Catherwood rediscovered many of the Maya ruins on their treks that took place in the mid-1800s. Easy reading.

Thompson, J. Eric. *Maya Archaeologist.* Norman, OK: University of Oklahoma Press, 1974. Thompson, a noted Maya scholar, traveled and worked at many of the Maya ruins in the 1930s.

Thompson, J. Eric. *The Rise and Fall of the Maya Civilization.* Norman, OK: University of Oklahoma Press, 1973. One man's story of the Maya. Excellent reading.

Webster, David. *The Fall of the Ancient Maya.* New York: Thames and Hudson, 2002. A careful and thorough examination of the possible causes of one of archaeology's great unsolved mysteries—the collapse of the Classic Maya in the 8th century.

Precolonial Mexico

Cortés, Hernán. *Five Letters.* New York: Gordon Press, 1991. Cortés's letters to the king of Spain, telling of his accomplishments and justifying his actions in the New World.

Davies, Nigel. *The Ancient Kingdoms of Mexico.* New York: Penguin Books, 1991. An excellent study of the preconquest of the indigenous peoples of Mexico.

De Landa, Bishop Diego. *Yucatán Before and After the Conquest.* New York: Dover Publications, 2012. This book, translated by William Gates from the original 1566 volume, has served as the basis for much of the research that has taken place in the region.

Nelson, Ralph. *Popul Vuh: The Great Mythological Book of the Ancient Maya.* Boston: Houghton Mifflin, 1974. An easy-to-read translation of myths handed down orally by the Quiche Maya, family to family, until written down after the Spanish conquest.

Mexican History and Culture

Díaz del Castillo, Bernal. *The Conquest of New Spain*. New York: Penguin Books, 1963. History straight from the adventurer's reminiscences, translated by J. M. Cohen.

Fehrenbach, T. R. *Fire and Blood: A History of Mexico*. New York: Collier Books, 1995. Over 3,000 years of Mexican history, related in a way that will keep you reading.

Franz, Carl, and Lorena Havens. *The People's Guide to Mexico*. Berkeley, CA: Avalon Travel, 2012. A humorous guide filled with witty anecdotes and helpful general information for visitors to Mexico. Don't expect any specific city information, just nuts-and-bolts hints for traveling south of the border.

Greene, Graham. *The Power and the Glory*. New York: Penguin Books, 2003. A novel that takes place in the 1920s about a priest and the antichurch movement that gripped Mexico.

Meyer, Michael, and William Sherman. *The Course of Mexican History*. New York: Oxford University Press, 2013. A concise one-volume history of Mexico.

Perry, Richard, and Rosalind Perry. *Maya Missions: Exploring Colonial Yucatán*. Santa Barbara, CA: Espadaña Press, 2002. Detailed and informative guide, including excellent hand-drawn illustrations, about numerous colonial missions and structures in the Yucatán Peninsula.

Wolf, Eric. *Sons of the Shaking Earth*. Chicago: University of Chicago Press, 1962. An anthropological study of the indigenous and mestizo people of Mexico and Guatemala.

Wright, Ronald. *Time Among the Maya*. New York: Grove Press, 2000. A narrative that takes the reader through the Maya country

of today, with historical comments that help put the puzzle together.

Natural Mexico

Beletsky, Les. *Travellers' Wildlife Guides: Southern Mexico*. Northampton, MA: Interlink Books, 2006. A perfect companion guide if you plan on bird-watching, diving/snorkeling, hiking, or canoeing your way through your vacation. Excellent illustrations.

Heffern, Richard. *Secrets of the Mind-Altering Plants of Mexico*. New York: Pyramid Books, 1974. A fascinating study of many substances, from ancient ritual hallucinogens to today's medicines that are found in Mexico.

Medical

Werner, David. *Where There Is No Doctor*. Palo Alto, CA: The Hesperian Foundation, 1992. This is an invaluable medical aid to anyone traveling not only to isolated parts of Mexico but to any place in the world where there's not a doctor (or Internet).

Fiction

McNay Brumfield, James. *A Tourist in the Yucatán*. Watsonville, CA: Tres Picos Press, 2004. A decent thriller that takes place in the Yucatán Peninsula; good for the beach or a long bus ride.

Sodi, Demetrio M. (in collaboration with Adela Fernández). *The Mayas*. Mexico City: Panama Editorial S.A., 1987. This small book presents a fictionalized account of life among the Maya before the conquest. Easy reading for anyone who enjoys fantasizing about what life *might* have been like before recorded history in the Yucatán.

Internet Resources

Cancún

www.cancunmap.com
Excellent source of detailed maps of Cancún, the Riviera Maya, and some inland archaeological zones.

www.cancuntips.com.mx
Online version of Cancún's main tourist magazine, with tons of listings, travel tips, and tourist resources.

Cozumel

www.cozumelinsider.com
Good website covering Cozumel, including current tourist information and issues important to locals.

www.cozumelmycozumel.com
Website offering a host of information to travelers and people considering a move to Isla Cozumel, moderated by longtime expats.

www.cozumeltoday.com
Website with articles geared toward travelers; affiliated with *Cozumel Today* magazine.

www.cruiseportinsider.com
A good source of information for travelers arriving to the region via cruise ship, including maps and shore excursion descriptions.

Isla Holbox

http://the.holboxeno.com
Excellent source of information for Holbox, including an updated schedule of events and goings-on, by day.

www.holboxisland.com
Website focused on Isla Holbox, with information on charter air tours and a handful of other tours and sights.

Isla Mujeres

www.islamujeres.gob.mx
Official website of the island of Isla Mujeres, including tourist information.

www.islamujeres.info
Excellent resource for the goings-on around Isla Mujeres, including activities, ferry schedules, and even a message board.

www.isla-mujeres.net
Informative website covering Isla Mujeres, with lodging, restaurants, activities, maps, FAQs, coupons, island history, even a Spanish primer.

www.souldeisla.com
Website offering detailed recommendations in Isla Mujeres, from restaurants to wedding planners.

Playa del Carmen

www.everythingplayadelcarmen.com
Website with tons of articles, photos, and other info on Playa, plus coupons and package deals.

www.playa.info
Established website with lots of travel-planning information to Playa and the Riviera Maya. It also has a popular forum for asking questions and sharing tips.

www.theplayatimes.com
A twice-monthly online newspaper that covers, among other topics, art and culture, area sites, and upcoming events.

Puerto Aventuras

www.puertoaventuras.com
Good website with updated information about Puerto Aventuras.

Puerto Morelos

www.almalibrebooks.com
Bookstore website that's packed with information about Puerto Morelos; also has listings for short- and long-term rentals.

www.InPuertoMorelos.com
Low-key website operated by the former owners of Alma Libre Bookstore, with info on lodging, activities, and more.

www.puertomorelos.com
Listings of local resorts, eateries, shops, and more, with an option to purchase vacation packages.

Riviera Maya

www.locogringo.com
Longtime tourism outfit's website includes extensive business listings for the Riviera Maya.

www.qroo.gob.mx
Official website of Quintana Roo state, including information for tourists.

www.travelyucatan.com
Detailed information and practical advice about traveling to and around the Yucatán Peninsula, with a focus on the Riviera Maya.

Tulum and the Costa Maya

www.bacalarmosaico.com
Extensive listings of hotels, restaurants, activities, and more in Laguna Bacalar.

www.todotulum.com
Great resource for Tulum—everything from nightlife to real estate.

www.tuchetumal.com
Informative online directory to Chetumal and area sights.

Yucatán

www.backyardnature.net/yucatan
Notes and observations by an experienced naturalist about the major plants and animal species in the northern Yucatán Peninsula.

www.yucatan.gob.mx
Official website of Yucatán state, including information for tourists.

www.yucatanliving.com
Award-winning website about living in Mérida and Yucatán state, with helpful travel info and up-to-date event listings.

www.yucatantoday.com
Website of the monthly tourist magazine of the same name. Based in Mérida but contains coverage of all of Yucatán state.

Index

List of Maps

Photo Credits

Acknowledgments

Our sincere thanks, first, to the hundreds of everyday residents of Cancún, Cozumel, the Riviera Maya, and the Costa Maya whose help and patience were essential to researching this book. We're also grateful for the tips and information we received from travelers and expats along the way—a big shout-out to Franziska Bruner in Playa—and from those who contacted us with suggestions and comments.

We are very fortunate to have such excellent editorial and production support from everyone at Moon. Many thanks to Nikki Ioakimedes for sending us off with all that we needed and to Kim Ehart for her sharp editing and unfailing good cheer and support. Thanks as well to Lucie Ericksen and Kat Bennett for making this book look so great, inside and out. And a special thank-you to everyone at Moon: it was an unexpectedly tough year for our family, and this team showed us such care, understanding, and flexibility—we are deeply grateful for it and for our longtime relationship with Moon.

We are also extremely grateful for the support and encouragement we enjoy from friends and family. Thank you especially to our dear friend Rukaiyah Adams—it's no small thing to use vacation days to fly across the country to pinch-hit with two free-spirited kids, much less take on carpools, music lessons, soccer practices, and even a puppy! You are a superstar. Thank you, too, to Lance Rushton and Jamie Morgan, Kari and Brian Campbell, Carrye and Nick Cost, and Wendy and Tom Thorpe for the kid pickups and play dates. And thank you to our friends at the Logan School for providing us with meals during an especially challenging week.

Thank you, always, to our parents for their love and support—even from afar, we can feel it. And, of course, our life is made immeasurably richer for having our kids, Eva and Leo, in it: Every day you two help us view the world in new ways and see the possibilities around us. You are the best gifts we've ever received.

Stunning Sights Around the World

COLOMBIA

ANDREW DIER

IRELAND

CAMILLE DEANGELIS

TRIP OF A LIFETIME

MACHU PICCHU

MOROCCO

NORWAY

DAVID NIKEL

TRIP OF A LIFETIME

PATAGONIA

WAYNE BERNHARDSON

ROME, FLORENCE & VENICE

ALEXEI J. COHEN

BELIZE

Guides for Urban Adventure

AMSTERDAM

AUDREY SYKES

CAFÉ BAR LA PERLA

BUENOS AIRES

NICHOLAS MILLER

HANOI

DANA FILEK-GIBSON

MEXICO CITY

MONTRÉAL

ANDREA BENNETT

OSLO

VANCOUVER

CAROLYN B. HELLER

WASHINGTON DC

MAP SYMBOLS

═══ Expressway	✦ Highlight	✈ Airport	⛳ Golf Course
═══ Primary Road	○ City/Town	✈ Airfield	Ⓟ Parking Area
═══ Secondary Road	◉ State Capital	▲ Mountain	⛩ Archaeological Site
┄┄ Unpaved Road	◉ National Capital	✚ Unique Natural Feature	⚲ Church
┄┄ Trail	★ Point of Interest		
⋯⋯ Ferry	● Accommodation	🐦 Waterfall	⛽ Gas Station
┉┉ Railroad	▼ Restaurant/Bar	♠ Park	🤿 Dive Site
═══ Pedestrian Walkway	■ Other Location	Ⓣ Trailhead	Mangrove
▥▥▥ Stairs	Λ Campground	Ⅰ Lighthouse	Reef
			Swamp

CONVERSION TABLES

°C = (°F - 32) / 1.8
°F = (°C x 1.8) + 32
1 inch = 2.54 centimeters (cm)
1 foot = 0.304 meters (m)
1 yard = 0.914 meters
1 mile = 1.6093 kilometers (km)
1 km = 0.6214 miles
1 fathom = 1.8288 m
1 chain = 20.168 m
1 furlong = 201.168 m
1 acre = 0.4047 hectares
1 sq km = 100 hectares
1 sq mile = 2.59 square km
1 ounce = 28.35 grams
1 pound = 0.4536 kilograms
1 short ton = 0.90718 metric ton
1 short ton = 2,000 pounds
1 long ton = 1.016 metric tons
1 long ton = 2,240 pounds
1 metric ton = 1,000 kilograms
1 quart = 0.94635 liters
1 US gallon = 3.7854 liters
1 Imperial gallon = 4.5459 liters
1 nautical mile = 1.852 km

MOON CANCÚN & COZUMEL

Avalon Travel
Hachette Book Group
1700 Fourth Street
Berkeley, CA 94710, USA
www.moon.com

Editor: Kimberly Ehart
Series Manager: Kathryn Ettinger
Copy Editor: Brett Keener
Graphics and Production Coordinator:
  Lucie Ericksen
Cover Design: Faceout Studios, Charles Brock
Interior Design: Domini Dragoone
Moon Logo: Tim McGrath
Map Editor: Kat Bennett
Cartographers: Austin Ehrhardt, Brian Shotwell,
  and Karin Dahl
Indexer: Greg Jewett

ISBN-13: 978-1-64049-259-2

Printing History
1st Edition — 1990
13th Edition — February 2019
5 4 3 2 1

Text © 2019 by Liza Prado & Gary Chandler.
Maps © 2019 by Avalon Travel.

Front cover photo: Cenote at Parque Eco-arqueológico Ik Kil © Dado Daniela/Getty Images
Back cover photo: Puerto Morelos beach in Riviera Maya © Lunamarina | Dreamstime.com

Printed in China by RR Donnelley, Shenzhen